c.1

W9-ARP-828

Table of Contents

Detailed Topo Maps 26–89
Index of Placenames and Physical Features 2–9
Legend .... Inside Front Cover

GAZETTEER

Amusements 14
Campgrounds 21
Freshwater Fishing 22–24
Hiking 20
Historic Sites 16–17
Hunting 25
Information Centers 15
Museums 15
National Lands 10–11
Saltwater Fishing 24–25
State Lands 11–13
Texas Travel Trails 14
Unique Natural Features 17
Wildlife Viewing 18–19

CITY MAPS

Abilene 90
Amarillo 90–91
Austin & Vicinity 92–93
Bay City 94
Baytown 94
Beaumont 95
Big Spring 94
Borger 94
Brownsville 95
Brownwood 97
Bryan/College Station 96
Cleburne 97
Conroe 97
Corpus Christi 98
Corsicana 97
Dallas/Ft Worth & Vicinity 100–125
Arlington, Balch Springs, Carrollton, Coppell, Duncanville, Farmers Branch, Garland, Grand Prairie, Grapevine, Irving, Mesquite, Richardson, Saginaw
Del Rio 99
Denison 99
Denton 99
Eagle Pass 99
El Paso & Vicinity 126–127
Galveston 126
Greenville 126
Harlingen 141
Hereford 141
Houston & Vicinity 128–140
Bellaire, Bunker Hill Village, Galena Park, Hedwig Village, Hilshire Village, Hunters Creek Village, Jersey Village, Pasadena, Piney Point Village, South Houston, Spring Valley, Stafford, West University Place
Huntsville 141
Kerrville 141
Killeen & Vicinity 142
Kingsville 141
Lake Jackson 142
Laredo 143
League City & Vicinity 146
Lewisville & Vicinity 145
Longview 143
Lubbock 144–145
Lufkin 147
Marshall 147
McAllen & Vicinity 148–149
McKinney 150
Midland 147
Mineral Wells 150
Mission 149
Nacogdoches 149
New Braunfels 150
Odessa 150
Orange 151
Palestine 151
Pampa 155
Paris 151
Plainview 155
Plano & Vicinity 152–153
Port Arthur & Vicinity 154
Round Rock 155
San Angelo 162
San Antonio & Vicinity 156–161
Alamo Heights, Balcones Heights, Castle Hills, Hill Country Village, Hollywood Park, Kirby, Leon Valley, Olmos Park, Shavano Park, Terrell Hills, Windcrest
San Benito 162
San Marcos 163
Seguin 162
Sherman 163
Stephenville 164
Sulphur Springs 164
Temple 164
Texarkana 163
Texas City & Vicinity 164–165
Tyler 165
Universal City 166
Uvalde 164
Victoria 166
Waco & Vicinity 167
Waxahachie 166–167
Weslaco & Vicinity 168
Wichita Falls 168

N

1 inch equals 79 miles

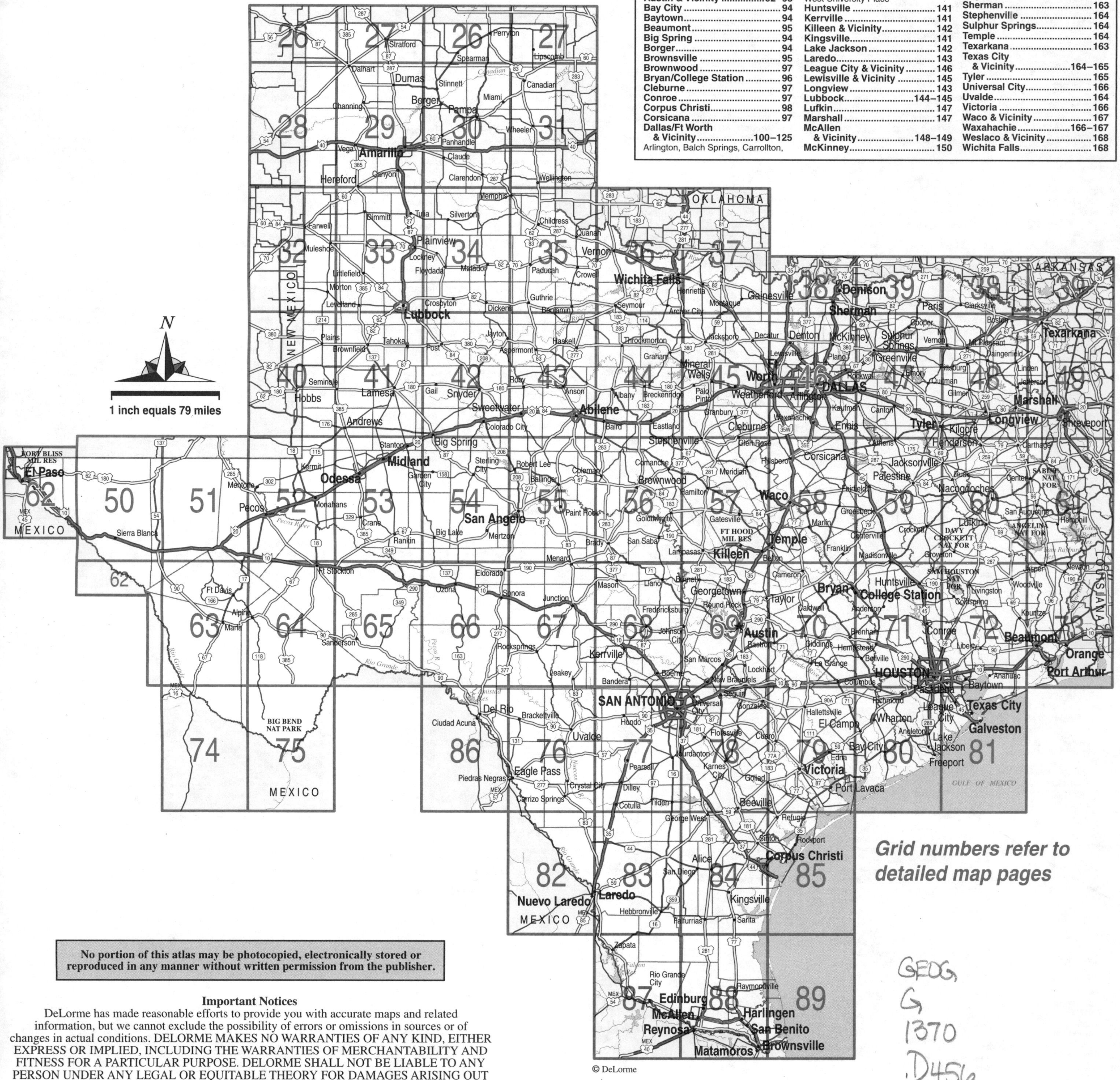

Grid numbers refer to detailed map pages

© DeLorme

No portion of this atlas may be photocopied, electronically stored or reproduced in any manner without written permission from the publisher.

GEOG
G
1370
.D456
2003

Important Notices

DeLorme has made reasonable efforts to provide you with accurate maps and related information, but we cannot exclude the possibility of errors or omissions in sources or of changes in actual conditions. DELORME MAKES NO WARRANTIES OF ANY KIND, EITHER EXPRESS OR IMPLIED, INCLUDING THE WARRANTIES OF MERCHANTABILITY AND FITNESS FOR A PARTICULAR PURPOSE. DELORME SHALL NOT BE LIABLE TO ANY PERSON UNDER ANY LEGAL OR EQUITABLE THEORY FOR DAMAGES ARISING OUT OF THE USE OF THIS PUBLICATION, INCLUDING, WITHOUT LIMITATION, FOR DIRECT, CONSEQUENTIAL OR INCIDENTAL DAMAGES.

Nothing in this publication implies the right to use private property. There may be private inholdings within the boundaries of public reservations. You should respect all landowner restrictions.

Some listings may be seasonal or may have admission fees. Please be sure to confirm this information when making plans.

Safety Information

To avoid accidents, always pay attention to actual road, traffic and weather conditions and do not attempt to read these maps while you are operating a vehicle. Please consult local authorities for the most current information on road and other travel-related conditions.

Do not use this publication for marine or aeronautical navigation, as it does not depict navigation aids, depths, obstacles, landing approaches and other information necessary to performing these functions safely.

FIFTH EDITION
Copyright © 2003 DeLorme. All rights reserved.
P.O. Box 298, Yarmouth, Maine 04096
(207) 846-7000 www.delorme.com

Index of Placenames and Physical Features

ABOUT THE INDEX

This index contains more than 9,000 features shown on the state and city maps on pages 26–168. Names are listed alphabetically with map page(s) and grid coordinates to help locate them. The grid coordinates correspond to the letters (A–K) and numbers (1–12) along the top and outside edges of all map pages.

Guidelines for using this index:

- Boldface type is used for placenames (cities, towns, crossroads), such as **Amarillo** 29 H11; 91 D10
- Italic type is used for drainage names (lakes, rivers, creeks, harbors, springs), such as *Rio Grande* 50 J2
- Roman type is used for all other features (mountains, islands, points, state and national lands, airports), such as Big Bend National Park 75 C9
- Page numbers and grid coordinates are given for each occurrence of a name, such as *Laguna Madre* 84 K6; 88 C6
- Rivers and creeks are listed by the main tributary name, followed by the fork or branch (where applicable), such as *Guadalupe River, North Fork* 67 H12
- Where necessary, airport names are supplemented with "airport," "private" or "private airfield" in parentheses, such as Bailey (private airfield) 78 D4.

A

A B Junction 76 E4
A F Siding 69 G10
A J Siding 58 K4
A L Mangham Jr. Regional (airport) 60 F4
A P Ranch (private airfield) 83 E9
Abbott 58 C2
Abell 30 F1
Abell City 52 I6
Abercrombie 69 F10; 80 F4
Aberdeen 31 J9
Aberfoyle 47 B8
Abernathy 33 I11
Abernathy Municipal (airport) 33 I12
Abilene 43 J11; 90 E4
Abilene Regional (airport) 43 J11
Abilene State Park 43 K10
Abington 35 C8
Ables Springs 47 F8
Abner 47 H7
Abram 88 H1
Academy 58 K1
Acala 62 J5
Acampo 44 G1
Ace 72 D3
Acebuche Draw 64 B4, C4
Ackerly 41 I12
Acme 35 E11
Action Aero (private airfield) 46 H2
Acton 45 J11
Acton State Historic Site 45 J11
Acuff 33 K12
Acworth 38 I2
Adair 41 E9
Adams 39 D11; 67 A8
Adams Bayou 73 G9; 151 C7
Adams Creek 36 F4
Adams Gardens 88 H4
Adamsville 57 H8
Addicks 71 I10; 128 H2
Addicks Reservoir (USACE) 71 J11; 128 F3
Addicks Reservoir 71 J11, 128 F3
Addielou 38 I1
Addington Field (private) 46 C1
Addison 46 E4; 105 A9
Addison (airport) 46 E4; 152 K5
Addran 47 B11
Adel 79 C8
Adell 45 F9
Adina 70 E2
Adinosa Creek 63 I10
Adkins 78 C2
Admiral 44 K2
Admiral Nimitz State Historic Site–National Museum of the Pacific War 68 F4
Adobe Creek 30 B3
Adobe Draw 51 J10
Adobe Walls 75 B8
Adobes 63 K8
Adrian 28 G6
Adsul 73 C9
Advance 45 E9
Ady 29 F9
Aero Country (airport) 46 C4
Aero Estates (private airfield) 46 B3; 59 B11
Aero Vista 62 F2
Aero-Bee Ranch Airstrip (private) 69 A7
Afton 34 I5
Agnes 45 E10
Agua Azul Creek 83 I9
Agua Dulce 84 E4
Agua Dulce Creek 84 D3
Agua Nueva 87 B12
Aguilares 83 H9
Agulia Creek 79 H10
Aiken 34 F1; 60 E6
Aikin Grove 38 K2
Ainsworth (private airfield) 72 F2
Air Park-Dallas (airport) 46 E4; 152 G5
Air Rice (private airfield) 71 J9
Airpark East (airport) 46 F6
Airport City 78 A1; 166 E4
Airville 58 J2
Alabama Creek 60 J2
Alamito Creek 63 F11, J11; 74 A3; 83 F9
Alamito Creek, North Fork 63 D11
Alamito Creek, South Fork 63 E10
Alamo 88 H2
Alamo Alto 62 J4
Alamo Arroyo 50 G1; 62 J5
Alamo Beach 79 J11
Alamo Creek 75 D8
Alamo Heights 77 B12; 157 J8; 159 A8
Alamo Village 76 B1
Alamocitos Creek 29 F7
Alanreed 30 H5
Alarm Creek 57 A8
Alazan Bay 84 I6
Alazan Creek 158 C6
Alba 47 G10
Albany 44 G2
Albany Municipal (airport) 44 G2
Albert 68 G6
Albion 38 I2
Alco 60 H4
Alcoa 70 D2
Alcoa Lake 70 C2
Alderbranch 59 E11
Aldine 71 I12
Aledo 45 G11
Alejandrenas 87 C9
Aleman 57 F9
Alexander 57 B8
Alexander Creek 57 E9
Alexanders Store 61 F8
Aley 47 K7
Alfalfa 62 G2
Alfred 84 E3
Algerita 56 I4
Algoa 81 C7
Alibates Flint Quarries National Monument 29 E12
Alice 84 F3
Alice Intl (airport) 84 F3
Alief 71 K11; 132 B4
Alison Air Park (private airfield) 69 J10
Allamoore 50 J5
Allen 46 D5
Allen Creek 47 H8; 60 E2; 67 F11; 70 D3
Allen Lake 96 D3
Allen Point 39 D9
Allendale 36 I6; 72 K1; 135 C8
Allenfarm 71 E7
Allenhurst 80 F3
Allens Creek 71 K8
Alley 33 H11
Alleyton 70 K6
Alligator Bayou 154 J2
Alligator Creek 47 J9; 58 D2; 59 G8, G9; 70 B1
Alligator Point 81 E7
Allison 31 E9; 45 C12, I9
Allison Ranch (private airfield) 64 E5; 67 D7
Allred 40 E5
Alma 46 K5
Almeda 80 A6; 133 J12
Almeda Plaza 133 H12
Almira 48 D5
Aloe 79 H8
Alpine 64 E1
Alpine Range (private airfield) 46 H1
Alpine-Casparis Municipal (airport) 64 E1
Alsdorf 46 J5
Alta Vista Ranch (private airfield) 63 G11
Altair 79 A12
Altita Creek 77 K8
Alto 60 E2
Alto Bonito 87 G11
Alto Colorado 84 K2
Alto Springs 58 I5
Altoga 46 C6
Alton 88 G1
Altuda 64 F2
Alum 78 D3
Alum Creek 69 H12; 70 H1
Alvarado 46 J1
Alvery Junction 55 G7; 162 B5
Alvie Cole Ranch (airport) 54 E4
Alvin 81 B7
Alvin Airpark 80 B6
Alvord 45 B11
Amaladeros Creek 60 F6
Amanda 86 C6
Amargosa Creek 84 D2
Amarillo 29 H11; 91 D10
Amarillo Intl (airport) 29 H12
Ambassador Field (private) 48 H2
Ambia 39 E10
Ambrose 38 J6
Amelia 73 H7; 95 E7
American Canal 133 K7; 80 A5
Ames 57 G10; 72 H4
Amherst 33 G8; 39 D11
Amistad National Recreation Area 86 B4
Amistad Reservoir 86 B4
Amistad Village 86 B4
Amity 56 B4
Ammannsville 70 J3
Amos Creek 55 G10
Amphion 77 F11
Anacacho 76 D2
Anacacho Mountains 76 E2
Anacacho Ranch (private airfield) 76 D2
Anadarko 60 C3
Anadarko Creek 60 C3
Anahuac 72 J4
Anahuac National Wildlife Refuge 81 A11
Anarene 44 A5
Anchor 80 D5
Anchorage 77 E11
Ander 79 G7
Anderson 71 D8
Anderson Creek 48 A3; 60 H5
Anderson Gully 73 H8
Andice 69 B10
Anding Branch 59 B9
Andrau Airpark 71 K11; 132 A4
Andrews 41 K7
Andrews County (airport) 41 K7
Angel City 78 H6
Angeles 51 C11
Angelina County (airport) 60 I3
Angelina National Forest 60 J6; 61 H1
Angelina Neches Scientific Area 61 K1
Angelina River 60 B3; 61 K7
Angelina River, East Fork 60 D3
Angler 48 H1
Angleton 80 E6
Angus 58 B6
Anhalt 68 J6
Anna 46 B5
Anna Rose 84 C2
Annandale Ranch (private airfield) 76 B5
Annaville 45 D11; 84 E5
Annetta 45 G11
Annona 38 K3
Anson 43 G10
Antelope 45 A7
Antelope Creek 30 D1; 44 F1; 56 G3, I6
Antelope Creek, East Fork 30 F1
Antelope Creek, West Fork 30 F1
Antelope Draw 50 E2; 51 J10; 64 D2
Antelope Gap 56 H6
Anthony 38 D6; 62 D1
Antioch 46 K2; 47 B10, K11; 48 C6; 56 D5; 59 J10; 60 A1; 61 D7
Antoine River 39 A11
Anton 33 I9
Anvil Park 31 B8
Apache Creek 158 D5
Apache Mountains 51 I8
Apolonia 71 D9
Appelt Hill 79 B9
Apple Springs 60 I2
Appleby 60 E4
Appurceon Creek 76 K5
Aqua De Piedra Creek 28 G6
Aqua Fria Mountain 75 B7
Aqua Negra Creek 77 E11
Aqua Poquita Creek 83 G12
Aquilla 58 D1
Aquilla Creek 58 A1, D2
Aquilla Lake (USACE) 58 C2
Aquilla Lake 58 C2
Arah 42 G3
Arania Creek 84 I4
Aransas Bay 85 C9
Aransas County (airport) 85 C8
Aransas Creek 78 K4
Aransas National Wildlife Refuge 85 A10
Aransas National Wildlife Refuge (private airfield) 85 C10
Aransas Pass 85 D8
Aransas Pass 85 E8
Aransas Pass (airport) 85 E8
Aransas River 84 A5, B6; 85 B7
Arbala 47 E10
Arbor 48 K5; 59 H12
Arbor Oaks 149 J9
Arcade 53 D8
Arcadia 60 D6; 81 C7
Archer City 36 K5
Archer City Municipal (airport) 36 K5
Arcola 80 B5
Arcola Junction 80 B5
Arden 54 G5
Ardis Heights 47 D8
Arenosa Creek 60 F6; 61 F7; 79 F9
Argenta 84 B4
Argo 48 C3
Argyle 46 D2
Arispe 50 J4
Arizona 71 B11
Arkansas City 88 D1
Arlam 60 C5
Arledge Field 43 F11
Arledge Ridge 47 A7
Arlie 35 A9
Arlington 46 G2; 111 E8
Arlington Heights 84 E5; 109 E7
Arlington Lake 110 G3
Arlington Municipal (airport) 46 H2; 111 J8
Armand Bayou 81 A7
Armstrong 70 K1
Armstrong Creek 56 A6
Armstrong Creek, Dry Fork 44 K6
Armstrong Creek, East Fork 44 K6
Armstrong Landing 48 C6
Armstrong Ranch (private airfield) 88 B4
Arneckville 79 F7
Arnett 41 A9; 57 G10
Arney 33 B10
Arno 52 E1
Arnold 46 C6
Arnold Creek 47 B7
Arp 60 A2
Arrowhead (private airfield) 84 C3
Arrowhead Park 46 D3
Arroyo Balluco 50 I2
Arroyo Baluarte 83 K11; 84 K1
Arroyo Blanco 83 K8; 87 A8
Arroyo Burro 87 A7
Arroyo Cabeza De Vaca 87 B8
Arroyo City 88 G6
Arroyo Clareno 87 C8
Arroyo Colorado 88 H5
Arroyo del Tigre Grande 87 C9
Arroyo Diablo 50 H1
Arroyo Grande 87 F9
Arroyo La Minita 87 E9
Arroyo Miguel 87 C9
Arroyo Negro 76 I6
Arroyo Nombre De Dios 84 C4
Arroyo Salado 83 K7
Arroyo Veleno 87 B8
Art 68 B3
Artesia Wells 83 A8
Artesian Creek 79 K9
Artesian Park 70 G5
Arthur City 39 B11
Arthur Creek 63 G11
Arvana 41 G11
Asa 58 G2
Ascarate Lake 127 E7
Ash 59 I10
Ash Creek 45 F11; 58 C3, D3
Asherton 76 K5
Ashland 48 H4
Ashmore 41 F9
Ashtola 30 J4
Ashwood 80 E3
Asia 58 F6
Aspermont 43 D8
Astin 70 B5
Atacosa River 78 J2
Atascosa 77 D11
Atascosa River 77 F11; 78 F1
Atco 58 G1
Ater 57 G10
Athens 59 A9
Athens Municipal (airport) 59 A9
Atkinson Island 72 K2
Atlanta 49 D7
Atlanta Municipal (airport) 49 D7
Atlanta State Park 48 C6
Atlas 39 E11
Atoy 60 D2
Atoy Creek 60 D2
Atreco 73 I8
Attoyac 60 F6
Attoyac Bayou 60 C4, E5, F6
Attwater Prairie Chicken National Wildlife Refuge 71 K7
Atwell 44 K3
Aubrey 46 B3
Auburn 46 K2
Audelia 46 F4; 106 D2
Auds Creek 39 E11
Augusta 59 F12
Augustus 42 D2
Aurora 45 D12
Austin 69 F10; 93 H8
Austin Air Ranch (airport) 69 D8
Austin Bayou 80 E6
Austin Branch 59 G12
Austin Executive Airpark 69 E11
Austin–Bergstrom International 69 G11
Austinia (private airfield) 81B8
Austonio 59 I10
Austwell 79 K10
Authon 45 F9
Avalon 58 A4
Avant Prairie 59 F7
Avenger Field 43 I7
Avenger Village 43 J7
Avery 38 K3
Avery Canyon Creek 75 C9
Avery Point 98 A2
Aviasud Airpark (private) 80 B3
Avinger 48 F5
Avoca 43 F11
Avon Park 58 F2; 167 A8
Avonak 71 H11
Avondale 45 E12; 88 H5; 141 A7
Axtell 58 E3
Ayres Bay 85 B10
Azle 45 F12; 100 E1

B

B A Steinhagen Lake 73 B7
B I Canal 72 H6
B T Averheart (private airfield) 59 C7
B A Steinhagen Lake/Town Bluff Dam (USACE) 73 A7
Babcock Place 156 F1
Baby Head 68 A5
Babyhead Creek 68 A5
Bachelor Creek 47 H7
Bachelor Prong 55 C12
Bachman Lake 105 H7
Back 30 G6
Bacliff 81 B8
Bacon 36 G6
Bader 77 C10
Badger 53 E7
Baffin Bay 84 J6
Bagby 47 A9
Bagwell 38 J1
Bahia Grande 89 I7
Bailes (airport) 80 E6
Bailey 47 A7
Bailey (private airfield) 78 D4
Bailey Branch 48 F1
Baileyboro 32 G6
Baileys Branch 57 G8
Baileys Prairie 80 E5
Baileyville 58 K4
Bainer 33 I9
Bains Private (private airfield) 68 J3
Bainville 78 H3
Baird 44 J1
Baker 35 F9; 45 H11
Baker Creek 47 A9
Bakers Crossing 66 I3
Bakersfield 65 A9
Balch Springs 46 G5; 114 E6
Balcones Creek 68 K6
Balcones Heights 77 B12; 156 K4
Bald Eagle Creek 55 E7
Bald Hill 60 I4
Bald Prairie 58 I6
Baldridge 53 K7
Baldridge Creek 70 K1
Baldwin 48 G6
Ball (private airfield) 79 G9
Ballinger 55 E10
Balm 38 D3
Balmorhea 51 K12
Balmorhea Lake 51 K12
Balmorhea State Park 51 K12
Balsora 45 D10
Bammel 71 H11
Bancroft 73 H9
Bandera 68 K3
Bandera Creek 68 J3
Bandera Falls 68 K4
Bandera Mesa 74 A6
Bangs 56 E3
Banks 58 D5 [illegible]
Banksmith 68 G4
Banks Stop 59 D7
Banquete 84 E4
Bar S Ranch (private airfield) 43 A7; 70 G3
Bar V-K Ranch (private airfield) 46 B1
Barado 71 C11
Barbarosa 69 K9
Barbers Hill Canal 72 J3, K3
Barbone Creek 84 C3
Barclay 58 J2
Barclay's Roost (private airfield) 68 I2
Bardwell 46 K4
Bardwell Lake (USACE) 46 K4
Bardwell Lake 46 K4
Barker 71 J10
Barker Reservoir (USACE) 71 J10
Barker Reservoir 71 K10; 128 J1; 132 A1
Barkman 38 K6
Barkman Creek 48 A6; 49 A7
Barksdale 67 K9
Barnes 72 A4
Barnes Creek 73 C12
Barnes Creek Reservoir 48 E4
Barnett (private airfield) 35 E12
Barnett Creek 47 B9; 72 A3
Barney M Davis Cooling Reservoir 85 G7
Barnhart 54 J3
Barnhart Creek 60 B3
Barnum 60 K4
Barrett 72 J2
Barrilla Draw 52 I2, K2; 64 A2
Barrilla Mountains 64 B1
Barroceto Creek 83 J8
Barronena Ranch (private airfield) 83 H11
Barry 58 B5
Barstow 52 G2
Bartlett 69 B12
Bartley Woods 47 A8
Barton 70 A4
Barton Corners 27 K7
Barton Creek 30 A6, I5; 45 J7; 69 F8; 92 I5
Barton Field (private) 70 E1
Barton Memorial (private airfield) 60 D5
Bartons Creek 70 I1
Bartonville 46 D2
Bartos Farm (private airfield) 41 A11
Barwise 34 G1
Bascom 48 K1
Basin Junction 75 C9
Basin Springs 38 D4
Bassett 48 B5
Bassett Creek 48 B4
Basslake (private airfield) 47 I11
Bastrop 70 H1
Bastrop Bay 81 E7
Bastrop Beach 80 E6
Bastrop State Park 70 H1
Bateman 69 I12
Bates Field (private) 53 D9
Batesville 76 F6
Bath 71 C11
Batiste Creek 72 H5
Batson 72 F4
Battle 58 F3
Battle Creek 34 A3; 44 H3, K2; 47 K11; 58 D4
Baum (private airfield) 46 I6
Bautista 29 D10
Baxter 59 A10
Bay City 80 F3; 94 G2
Bay City Municipal (airport) 80 F3
Bay Harbor 81 E8
Bay Oaks 81 A8
Bayless (private airfield) 80 C6
Baylor Lake 35 C7
Baylor Mountains 51 I7
Bayou Carrizo 60 F5
Bayou Din 73 I7
Bayou La Nana 60 E4, G4
Bayou Loco 60 E3, F3
Bayou Siepe 61 E8
Bayside 85 C7
Bayside Terrace 81 A8
Baytown 72 K2; 94 D2
Baytown (airport) 72 J2
Bayview 81 B8
Baywood Forest 149 F12
Bazette 59 A7
Beach 71 F12
Beach City 72 K3
Beach Creek 48 E6
Beach Mountains 50 J6
Beacon 58 I4
Beals Creek 42 K2; 54 A3, A4
Beaman Airpark 80 A6
Bean Creek 57 K8
Beans Creek 45 D9; 60 D1, F2
Bear Bayou 60 D5
Bear Creek 48 E5; 72 E1
Bear Creek 30 E2; 44 I6; 45 H11; 46 I4; 47 B7; 48 H5; 56 J1; 57 E8; 60 B1, K3; 61 I8; 64 H6; 67 C10; 68 H2; 69 B9; 70 J10; 72 A2; 76 A6; 103 H11; 112 A1; 128 E1
Bear Mountain 63 C9
Bear Slough 112 B4
Beard 71 K7
Beasley 80 B3
Beason Creek 71 F9
Beattie 56 B5
Beauchamp Airstrip (private) 29 C10
Beaukiss 70 E1
Beaumont 73 H7; 95 D11
Beaumont Municipal (airport) 73 H7
Beaumont Place 72 J1; 131 E10
Beauxart Gardens 73 I8
Beaver (North Canadian) River 26 A5; 27 B9
Beaver Creek 35 H11, H12; 36 H1, H3; 37 C8, I9; 59 D9, I8; 60 F2; 68 D3; 69 A7
Beaver Dam Creek 59 H9
Beaverdam 38 J4
Beaverdam Creek 38 J3
Bebe 78 B5
Becerra Creek 83 F8
Beck 33 H7
Beck Branch 57 E9
Becker 47 I7
Beckmann 77 A12; 156 B2
Beckum Creek 48 G6
Beckville 48 K5
Beckville Lookout 48 K5
Beckwith Creek 73 D11
Becton 33 I12
Bedford 46 F2; 103 H7
Bedias 71 B9
Bedias Creek 71 A8
Bee Bayou Creek 39 E12
Bee Cave 69 F9
Bee Cave Creek 57 H7
Bee Creek 57 D11; 69 C9; 70 A6; 71 C7
Bee Creek (private airfield) 46 K3
Bee House 57 H9
Bee House Creek 57 H9
Beech Creek 60 D4; 72 B6; 73 B7
Beech Grove 73 A7
Beef Canyon 65 J7
Beefmaster's Best (private airfield) 78 K2
Beeville 78 K4
Beeville Municipal (airport) 78 K4
Beggs Ranch (private airfield) 43 A7
Bel Air 48 I6
Belcherville 37 I10
Belco 58 J1
Belding 64 B4
Belen 62 G3
Belfalls 58 I2
Belgrade 73 C10
Belk 39 C10
Belknap Creek 37 J9
Bell Branch 46 K3
Bell Branch 57 A7
Bell Creek 78 H2
Bell Gin 69 C11
Bellaire 71 K11; 133 C10
Bellaire Junction 71 K12; 133 A11
Bellaire West 71 K11; 132 C4
Bellco 31 G7
Belle Plain 44 K1
Bellevue 37 J9
Bellmead 58 F2; 167 A11
Bells 38 E6
Bells Creek 72 A5
Bellshire 97 J8
Bellview 47 G10
Bellville 71 I7
Bellville Yards 71 I7
Belmena 70 A3
Belmont 78 B5
Belott 59 G12
Belton 57 J12
Belton Lake 57 I12
Belton Lake (USACE) 57 J12
Ben 47 H11
Ben Arnold 58 K3
Ben Bolt 84 G3
Ben Franklin 47 A10
Ben Hur 58 G4
Ben Wheeler 47 J10
Benavides 84 G1
Benbrook 45 H12; 108 I4
Benbrook Lake 45 H12; 108 K4
Benbrook Lake (USACE) 45 H12; 108 K5
Benchley 70 B6
Bend 56 J6
Bendetsen 72 F1
Benge Corner 53 E10
Benger Air Park (airport) 32 B6
Benjamin 35 K11
Bennett 45 G9
Bennett Creek 57 G7; 68 C4
Benoit 55 D11
Benonine 31 H10
Benson Airstrip (private) 76 D5
Benton Creek 68 J2
Bentonville 84 E3
Bentsen–Rio Grande Valley State Park 88 H1
Berclair 78 J5
Berea 48 G5; 59 H12
Berger 58 J1
Bergheim 68 J6
Bergs Mill 77 C12; 159 J9
Bergstrom ARS (private airfield) 69 G11
Bering 72 A3
Berlin 70 G6
Bernardo 70 K6
Bernecker 42 I6
Bernstein 26 I2
Berry (private airfield) 57 G10
Berry Bayou 135 D7, E8
Berry Creek 69 B10; 70 E5
Berrys Creek 45 J9
Berryville 59 B11
Bertani Ranch (private airfield) 86 B5
Bertram 69 B9
Bessie Heights 73 H8
Bessies Creek 71 K8
Bessmay 73 E8
Best 53 I12
Bethard 46 F4; 106 D3
Bethel 45 G10; 46 E3; 47 D12; 48 H3; 55 I9; 59 C9
Bethlehem 48 D5, F2
Bettie 48 G2
Bettis 39 D8
Beulah 58 G5; 60 I4
Beverly 58 F2; 167 F9
Beverly Hill 46 D6
Beverly Hills 58 G2; 167 G9
Bevil Oaks 72 G6
Bevoni-Flying B (private airfield) 38 D3
Bexar 77 D11
Beyersville 70 D1
Bi-Stone 58 E6
Biardstown 39 E11
Big Aguja Canyon 63 A12
Big Bear Creek 46 E1; 102 C5; 103 F10
Big Bend National Park 75 C9
Big Bend Ranch (private airfield) 74 B5
Big Bend Ranch State Park 63 K10; 74 B3, C5
Big Blue Creek 29 C11
Big Bluff Creek 68 B1
Big Boggy Creek 80 H3
Big Boggy National Wildlife Refuge 80 H3
Big Briary Creek 58 K3
Big Brown Creek Airstrip (private) 59 D8
Big Brushy Creek 46 G6; 79 D8
Big Caddo Creek 44 G6
Big Caney Creek 48 J2
Big Canyon 29 E11; 64 E6; 65 E9, G10
Big Cleveland Creek 45 C8
Big Cow Creek 61 K9
Big Coyote Creek 55 B10
Big Creek 30 C1; 45 B9; 47 A10, D12, E10; 58 F4, H4; 59 I11; 60 J6; 70 E2; 71 E8; 72 D2; 73 B8; 80 B4
Big Creek Reservoir 47 A10
Big Cypress Creek 48 E3; 72 C5; 73 E9
Big Elkhart Creek 59 G10, G11
Big Elm Creek 56 H1; 58 G4, J1; 70 A2
Big Fielder Draw 65 G12; 66 G1
Big Fivemile Creek 70 K2
Big Fossil Creek 46 F1; 101 G10; 102 I1
Big Gulch 131 G10
Big Hill 58 G5
Big Hill Reservoir 154 J1
Big Hollow Creek 77 H7
Big Jim Draw 54 H1
Big Joshua Creek 68 J4
Big Lake 54 I1
Big Lake 54 J1
Big Mineral Creek 38 D3
Big Onion Creek 46 K4
Big Pine Creek 38 I1; 39 C12
Big Rock 47 J9
Big Rocky Creek 79 A9
Big Rush Creek 59 A7
Big Saline Creek 67 B11
Big Sandy 48 H1
Big Sandy Creek 30 K4; 39 E11; 44 H3; 45 A9, A10, C11; 47 A11, F12; 48 H1; 58 H3, I5; 61 I9; 69 D9; 70 F1; 72 D4
Big Sandy Draw 94 I3
Big Satan Creek 66 K4
Big Silver Creek 42 K6; 54 A6
Big Skid Creek 44 C5
Big Slough 48 A3
Big Slough Wilderness 60 G1
Big Sous Creek 77 C10
Big Spring 42 K1; 94 K1
Big Spring Mc Mahon-Wrinkle (airport) 54 A1
Big Spring State Park 42 K1; 94 K1
Big Springs 60 B2
Big Square 33 D8
Big Sunday Creek 45 I8
Big Tank Ranch (private airfield) 50 G5
Big Thicket National Preserve 72 C4, D6, F5; 73 B7, D7
Big Timber Creek 31 A7
Big Walnut Run 73 A8
Big Wells 76 J6
Big Willow Creek 58 J5
Bigby Corner 53 E12
Bigfoot 77 F10
Biggers 46 D5
Biggin Hill (private airfield) 33 J10
Bighead Creek 48 K3
Billiams Creek 60 K5; 72 A5
Biloxi Creek 60 I4
Binford Park 71 F8
Binion Creek 57 J9
Birch 70 E5
Birch Creek 47 D10; 59 H7; 70 E4
Birches Creek 60 B1
Bird Creek 35 J9
Bird Dog Field (private) 46 B1
Bird's Nest (airport) 69 E11
Birdnest (private airfield) 55 A1
Birome 58 D3
Birthright 47 C11
Biry 77 D9
Bisbee 46 H2
Bishop 84 G4
Bishop Field (private) 47 F7
Bishop Municipal (airport) 84 G4
Bitter Creek 34 A5; 43 I8, I10, J8; 44 B4
Bivins 49 E7
Bivins Lake 29 J10
Bixby 88 H4
BJ McCombs Sisterdale (private airfield) 68 I4
Black 33 B7; 58 K3
Black Ankle 61 F8
Black Bass 87 B8
Black Bayou 49 C7, E7; 60 G4
Black Bear Creek 37 C11
Black Creek 45 B12; 76 D6; 73 D7; 77 E9; 83 C10
Black Cypress Creek 48 D4, E5
Black Diamond 71 F12
Black Duck Bay 94 E1
Black Flat 36 J4
Black Hill 78 F1
Black Hills Creek 74 A4
Black Jack 70 A5
Black Kettle National Grassland 31 B9, D10
Black Mark Strip (private) 46 E2
Black Mountain 63 B11; 64 I2; 76 A2
Black Mountains 50 F4
Black Oak 47 E12
Black Peak 51 K8
Blackberry 71 E9
Blackfoot 59 C9
Blackhawk Creek 60 A1
Blackjack 60 A1, B1; 61 J8
Blackland 46 F6; 58 G3
Blackwater Draw 32 E5; 33 E7, H10
Blackwell 55 B8
Blair 43 J9
Blakeney 38 I2
Blancas Creek 83 I8
Blanchard 72 B2
Blanco 69 H7
Blanco Creek 76 C6, D6; 78 I4, K6
Blanco River 68 H5; 69 H8, H9; 163 D9
Blanco State Park 69 H7
Blanconia 78 K6
Bland 57 I12; 73 H9
Bland Lake 61 F7
Blanket 56 D5
Blanket Creek 56 F5; 76 A6
Blanket Springs 56 F5
Blanton 55 D10; 58 B1
Blanton Creek 38 J1
Bleakley Ranch (private airfield) 69 G8
Bleakwood 73 C9
Bledsoe 32 K4
Bleiblerville 70 H6
Blessing 80 G1
Blevins 58 I1
Blewett 76 D3
Blind Lake 73 J7
Bliss Creek 59 G8
Blix 60 I3
Block Creek 68 H4
Block Ranch (private airfield) 46 K1
Blocker Creek 37 K12; 46 A1
Blodgett 48 D1
Blomburg 49 D7
Bloomdale 46 C5
Bloomfield 46 A3
Blooming Grove 58 B4
Bloomington 79 I9
Blossom 39 D12
Blowout 68 C6
Blox 61 K8
Blue Branch 59 B12
Blue Creek 57 G10; 75 E8; 78 B2
Blue Hills 66 H2
Blue Hole 29 G10
Blue Hole Creek 35 G10
Blue Jay Air Field (private) 46 D1
Blue Lake 151 C10
Blue Mound 101 A9
Blue Mound 46 F1; 101 H9
Blue Mound (airport) 101 G10
Blue Mountain 63 D11
Blue Mountain (private airfield) 63 D11
Blue Mountains 67 E12
Blue Ridge 46 B6; 58 I4
Blue Skies (private airfield) 45 F11
Blue Springs 61 I7
Bluebonnet Lakes 112 C3
Bluegrove 37 J8
Bluetown 88 I4
Bluett 45 D12
Bluff 38 J1; 68 J2
Bluff Creek 43 G12; 44 G1, G6; 55 A9; 56 H2; 57 F12
Bluff Dale 45 J9
Bluff Springs 69 G10
Bluff View 56 E3
Bluffton 68 A6
Blum 57 A12
Blumenthal 68 G5
Bluntzer 84 D4
Blythe Creek 48 A4
Board Creek 58 D5
Boards Ferry 48 J6
Bobville 71 F10
Bobwyn 46 H5; 115 J7
Boca Chica State Park 89 J8
Bodan Creek 60 G3
Boden 29 F10
Boe-Wrinkle (private airfield) 45 F11
Boedecker Junction 79 B12
Boening Brothers (private airfield) 78 F1
Boerne 68 J5
Boerne Stage Field 68 K5
Boeye Reservoir 148 J1
Bofecillos Canyon 74 B4
Bog Creek 60 F6
Bogan & Fontenot (private airfield) 72 H6
Bogata 48 A1
Boggy Creek 36 G2; 44 C3; 48 D3, E3; 59 I8, J9; 61 K7; 69 D12; 71 E12; 72 F6; 73 C8; 79 B8
Bois D'Arc 59 C10
Bois D'Arc Creek 46 E6
Bois D'Arc Creek 39 D8, 47 A7
Bois D'Arc Draw 54 J6
Boise 28 H5
Boldtville 78 C1
Boles Field 61 D8
Boles Home 47 E8
Bolin 27 E7
Boling 80 D3
Bolivar 46 B1
Bolivar Peninsula 81 B10
Bolton (private airfield) 60 C1
Bomarton 44 A1
Bon Ami 73 B8
Bon Wier 73 B10
Bona 38 D6
Bonanza 47 E10
Bond 48 E4
Bonham 39 E7
Bonham State Park 39 E8
Bonita 37 I11
Bonita Creek 29 G12
Bonita Junction 60 E4; 149 E10
Bonito Creek 82 B5
Bonnerville 59 D7
Bonney 80 C6
Bonnie View 85 B7
Bono 45 K12
Bonus 80 B1
Booker 27 H7
Booker (private airfield) 27 I7
Boon Slough 76 D5
Boone 33 E11
Boons Creek 45 D10; 59 F9
Boonsville 45 D10
Boonville 71 C7; 96 E5
Booth 80 B4
Boothe 34 H3
Boothe Creek 48 A4
Bootleg 28 K6
Boquillas Canyon 75 D11
Bor-ley Heights 73 G7
Borden 70 K4
Borden-Siding 70 K4
Borderland 62 E1
Bordersville 71 H12
Boregas Creek 61 G8
Borger 30 D2; 94 J6
Borrachio 63 K8
Borracho 51 J9
Borracho Peak 51 K9
Borrego Creek 78 E1
Bosque 57 D11
Bosque River 58 G1; 167 A8
Bosque River, East Branch 57 A10
Bosqueville 58 F2; 167 A7
Boss 45 I12
Bostick 48 J1; 165 A12
Boston 48 A5
Boswell Creek 71 C12
Botines 83 F7
Bouchard 46 F4; 105 D12
Bounce 53 C9
Bourland Canyon 75 A11
Bourland Field 45 H11
Bovina 32 C5
Bow Creek 44 C1
Bowers City 30 F4
Bowie 37 K10
Bowie Creek 56 I1
Bowie Municipal (airport) 37 K10
Bowles (private airfield) 76 G1
Bowles Creek 60 F1
Bowman Creek 71 B7
Bowman Ridge 57 B8
Bowman School 36 I6
Bowser 56 H4
Box Church 58 G6
Box Creek 59 F10, I12; 60 E1
Boxelder 48 A3
Boxwood 48 G3
Boyce 46 J4
Boyce Creek 46 J4
Boyd 39 D7; 45 D11
Boyds Chapel 43 G9
Boydston 30 H4
Boynton 60 I5
Boys Haven 73 H7
Boys Ranch 29 E9
Boz 46 K3
Bozar 56 G6
Brachfield 60 B4
Bracken 78 A1
Brackettville 76 C1
Brad 44 G6
Braden Branch 45 A11
Bradfield Branch 107 D7
Bradford 59 C10
Bradshaw 55 B10
Brady 56 J1; 61 E7
Brady Creek 55 J9; 56 J3
Brady Island 134 A6
Brady Mountains 55 I12
Brady Reservoir 56 J1
Bragg 72 E5
Branch 46 D5
Branchville 70 A4
Brand 42 G4
Brandon 58 B3
Brandy Branch Cooling Pond 48 J5
Branom 47 C9
Bransford 46 F2; 102 D5
Bransom Farm (private airfield) 46 I1
Branton 56 A4
Brashear 47 D10
Braunig Lake 78 D1
Brays Bayou 71 K11; 133 C12, F7; 134 B2, B5
Brazoria 80 F5
Brazoria County (airport) 80 E5
Brazoria National Wildlife Refuge 81 F7
Brazoria Reservoir 80 E5
Brazos 45 H8
Brazos Bend State Park 80 C5
Brazos Point 57 A11
Brazos River 35 K12; 36 K1; 43 A11, B10, G12; 44 A2, C4, E6; 45 G8, H9, K11; 57 A11; 58 G3, K4; 70 B5; 71 F8, K8; 80 A2, A4, D5, E5; 142 J3; 167 A10, E12
Brazos River Authority Canal 80 C6
Brazos River, Clear Fork 42 G6; 43 G8, H9; 44 E1, F3
Brazos River, Double Mountain Fork 42 E1, E5; 43 E9
Brazos River, North Fork Double Mountain Fork 42 B1; 145 H8
Brazos River, Salt Fork 42 C3; 43 A10, B8, C7
Brazos Valley 43 C8
Breakaway Park (private airfield) 69 D10
Breckenridge 44 G4
Bremond 58 J5
Brenham 70 G6
Brenham Municipal (airport) 70 G6
Breslau 79 B9
Brewington Creek 68 I1
Briar 45 E12
Briar Branch 70 C3
Briar Creek 36 K3; 44 A6, C6; 58 A5, A6, B5
Briarcliff 69 E9
Briargrove 71 K11; 129 K9
Briary 58 K3
Brice 34 A5
Brickel 27 D9
Brickhouse Gully 129 E10
Bridge City 73 H9
Bridge Creek 47 K7; 60 B1
Bridgeport 45 C10
Bridgeport Municipal (airport) 45 C10
Bridges Chapel 48 C2

Bridges Field (private) 46 A4
Brier Branch 60 A1
Brier Creek 37 K10
Briggs 69 A9
Briggs Ranch (private airfield) 82 A6
Bright Star 47 F10
Brinker 47 D11
Brinkley Creek 59 E8
Brinkman Ranch/Mt Home (private airfield) 68 G1
Briscoe 31 E8
Briscoe Canal 80 B6
Briscoes Catarina Ranch (private airfield) 82 A5
Bristol 46 I5
Brittain Creek 61 F8
Brittany Bay 146 I2
Britton 46 I2
Britton Davis 62 F2
Broaddus 60 H6
Broadview 33 J10
Broadway 34 J4
Broadway Junction 39 E11
Brock 45 H9
Brock Junction 45 G9
Bronco 40 C4
Bronco Creek 31 G8
Bronson 61 H8
Bronte 55 C8
Brook Forest 146 A2
Brooke Crossing 57 J9
Brookeen Creek 58 D3
Brookeland 61 J8
Brookesmith 56 F3
Brookhaven 57 I11; 71 K12; 134 E2
Brookhollow 149 J10
Brooks 73 H7
Brooks Air Force Base 77 C12; 159 I10
Brooks County (airport) 84 J2
Brooks Lake 132 I3
Brooks Place (private airfield) 69 I11
Brookshire 71 J9
Brookside Village 80 A6; 134 K4
Brookston 39 E10
Broome 54 D5
Brotherton 39 E8
Broussard Farm (private airfield) 72 I6
Brown 41 J12
Brown Field (private) 55 J7
Brown Hill 70 J1
Browndell 61 J8
Brownfeld Corner 50 C4
Brownfield 41 C9
Browning 48 J2
Browning Creek 47 I10
Brownlee 42 J6
Brownlee Creek 60 J1
Browns Creek 56 G5; 57 I10, J7; 59 F8
Browns Lake 167 B10
Brownsboro 47 K11; 69 J11
Brownsville 88 J6; 95 K8
Brownsville Ship Channel 89 J7
Brownsville/South Padre Island Int'l (airport) 88 J6
Brownwood 56 E3; 97 C7
Brownwood Municipal (airport) 56 D4
Bruce Field 55 E10
Bruceville 58 H1
Brumley 48 F2
Brundage 76 J5
Bruner 73 H9
Bruner (private airfield) 59 H11
Bruni 83 H10
Brunswick 60 F2
Brush Pen Hollow 78 I2
Brushie Prairie 58 B4
Brushy 45 J10; 60 B1
Brushy Creek 59 C11
Brushy Creek 38 C3; 39 E12; 44 B6, K2; 45 A11; 46 I4; 47 A12, B11, D7; 58 G3, J2; 59 B10, I7; 60 C5, G6; 61 C7; 69 D10; 70 B2, D1; 71 G9; 73 D10; 76 A6; 79 E11; 155 E10
Brushy Creek, South Fork 48 E1
Brushy Elm Creek 37 J12; 38 E1
Brushy Slough 70 C2
Bruton Creek 38 K1
Bryan 45 D12; 70 C6; 96 E4
Bryan Utilities Lake 70 B6
Bryans Mill 48 C5
Bryarly 38 J3
Bryden 29 A10
Bryson 45 D7
Buchanan Dam 69 B7
Buck Branch 57 A7
Buck Creek 31 K7; 35 B9; 43 I12; 45 I8; 46 A4; 59 I7; 60 I4; 65 H9
Buck Hill 64 J1
Buck Hollow 67 D10
Bucker Field (private) 45 H11
Buckeye 80 G2
Buckholts 70 A2
Buckhorn 71 H7; 73 B10
Buckhorn Creek 78 C5
Buckhorn Draw 54 K3; 66 B4
Buckingham 46 E4; 106 B1
Buckley Draw 66 G5
Buckner 45 H10; 46 C5
Buckners Creek 70 J2
Bucks Bayou 80 G3
Bucksnag Creek 79 B12
Bud Matthews 43 G12
Buda 69 H10
Buddy Harmel (private airfield) 33 E10
Buena Vista 53 I7; 62 F1; 89 H7
Buenos 42 B1
Buescher State Park 70 H2
Buffalo 47 K7; 56 D2, G4; 59 G8
Buffalo Bayou 72 K1; 128 I1, I5; 129 J11, K8; 130 J5; 131 K12; 134 A6; 135 A9, A12
Buffalo Chips Airpark (private) 45 I12
Buffalo Creek 27 K7; 31 G10; 42 H6; 45 K12; 55 E7; 56 F4, K4; 59 G7; 97 B11
Buffalo Gap 43 K11; 69 E9
Buffalo Lake 29 K10
Buffalo Lake National Wildlife Refuge 29 J10
Buffalo Mop 58 G4
Buffalo Springs 26 B6; 37 K8
Buffalo Springs Lake 33 K12
Bufford Creek 44 E4
Buford 42 I5; 62 G3
Bufords Field (private) 60 J5
Bug Tussle 47 A9
Bugby Creek 30 C2
Bula 33 H7
Bulah 60 E1
Bulcher 37 I12
Bull Creek 42 F1; 56 E1; 60 E1; 69 E10; 71 C8
Bull Creek, North Fork 56 H5
Bull Hide Creek 58 H2
Bull Lake 33 H8
Bull Wagon Creek 43 I10
Bullard 59 A12
Bullard Creek 39 D8; 49 I7
Bullhead Creek 67 J10; 68 C4
Bullis Gap Range 65 J7
Bullock 44 I5
Bullshead Creek 84 B5
Bulverde 68 K6
Bulverde Airpark (private) 68 K6
Buna 73 E8
Bunavista 30 D1
Buncome 60 B5
Bunger 44 E6
Bunker Hill 26 E5; 39 C10; 73 E8
Bunker Hill Village 71 J11; 129 I7
Bunyan 57 A7
Burford 48 G6
Burgess Creek 45 G10
Burk Hollow 84 A6
Burkburnett 36 G6
Burke 60 I3
Burkett 56 B2
Burkeville 61 K10
Burkhand Branch 38 K2; 48 A2
Burks Ridge 38 J3
Burleigh 71 I8
Burleson 46 I1
Burlington 58 K3
Burnell 78 I4
Burnet 69 B7
Bumet Craddock Field 69 B8
Burnett 39 E8
Burns 38 K6
Burns Canal 73 G7
Burns City 46 A2
Burnt Branch 56 B2, I6
Burr 80 C2
Burrantown 60 G1
Burress (private airfield) 39 E11
Burris 33 K12; 145 J8
Burrow 47 E7
Burton 45 K12; 70 G5
Busby 43 H7
Bush Hill 156 A3
Bush Knob Creek 44 D3
Bushland 29 H10
Bustamante 87 A9
Butler 59 E9; 70 F1
Butler Bayou 70 C6
Buzz Field (private) 34 H5
Buzzard Draw 41 J12
Byers 37 G8
Byfield Creek 60 C5
Bynum 58 C3
Byram Ranch (private airfield) 69 G7
Byrd 58 A5
Byrds 56 C3
Byrdtown 39 E12
Byrne 55 H7
Byrt (private airfield) 59 C7

C

C David Campbell Field-Corsicana Municipal (airport) 58 B6
C F C Aviation Ranch (private airfield) 69 C9
C Lazy T Ranch (private airfield) 36 K2
Caballo Creek 83 A11
Cabeza Creek 78 H6
Cabezo Creek 78 G5
Cache Creek 36 K2; 37 D7
Cactus 29 A10; 83 D7
Cactus Creek 35 F10
Caddo 78 D4
Caddo Creek 44 G5, H5; 47 E8; 48 J6; 59 B11
Caddo Lake 49 G8
Caddo Lake State Park 49 H7
Caddo Mills 47 D7
Caddo Mills Municipal (airport) 47 E7
Caddo National Grassland 39 C8, D9; 47 A8
Caddoan Mounds State Historic Site 60 F1
Cade Lakes 70 D4
Cadiz 78 K3
Caesar 78 I4
Caiman Creek 83 B8
Cain City 68 G4
Cairomiss 59 J9
Cajac Creek 67 E10
Calallen 84 E5
Calamity Creek 64 G1
Calavaras 78 D2
Calaveras Creek 78 C1
Calaveras Lake 78 C1
Calder Highlands 73 H7; 95 C9
Calder Terrace 73 H7; 95 C8
Caldwell 33 I10; 70 D4
Caldwell Municipal (airport) 70 D4
Caldwood 73 H7; 95 D8
Caldwood Acres 73 H7; 95 E8
Caledonia 60 C5
Calf Creek 38 D5; 41 K11; 55 K12
Calf Creek 56 K1
Calgary 61 F7
Calgary Woods 71 J12; 130 C5
Calhoun County (airport) 79 I10
Caliche Creek 83 G9
California Creek 43 E12, F8, F10; 44 C4
Calina 58 E4
Call 73 C8
Call Field Canal 36 H5
Call Junction 73 C8
Callaghan 83 E7
Callaghan Ranch (private airfield) 83 E7
Callahan Draw 33 G12; 34 H1
Callan 55 J11
Calliham 78 K1
Callisburg 38 D3
Calvary 47 G11
Calvert 58 K5
Calvert Creek 48 B4
Calvert Junction 58 K4
Cam 51 I9
Camden 72 A4
Camel Draw 50 J4
Cameron 70 A3
Cameron (airport) 80 E5
Cameron Creek 44 C6; 45 B7
Cameron Muni Airpark 70 A3
Camey 46 D3
Camilla 72 C2
Camino South 146 D1
Camp Branch 57 B9
Camp Bullis Military Reservation 68 K6; 156 A4
Camp Creek 27 K9; 45 K12; 48 E6; 56 G1; 58 K6; 60 F1; 71 E12
Camp Creek Lake 59 J7
Camp Lake Slough 76 F6
Camp Longhorn (private airfield) 69 B7
Camp Mabry Military Reservation 93 E7
Camp Maxey Military Reservation 39 C11
Camp Swift Military Reservation 70 F1
Camp Verde 68 I3
Camp Wood 67 K10
Camp Wood Creek 67 K10
Campbell 47 D9
Campbell Field-Corsicana Muni 58 B6
Campbells Creek 70 B6
Campbellton 78 H1
Campground Bayou 38 J2
Campground Creek 60 B2
Campo Alto 88 H2
Campo Santo Estrada 74 B3
Camps 48 I3
Campti 61 D8
Cana 47 I8
Canaan 38 E6
Canada Verde 78 D1
Canadian 31 B7
Canadian River 29 E7, F10; 30 A6, B3; 31 C9, C12
Canal Creek 35 G10
Canary 59 K7
Candelaria 63 G7
Cane Creek 39 E10; 47 A10
Cane Island Branch 71 J9
Cane Junction 80 E2
Caney 38 J3; 80 F3
Caney City 59 A8
Caney Creek 38 E6; 39 D7, J7; 47 J7; 48 F1, H5, J6; 59 E7, G11, K8; 60 A5, C5, E3, J1, K1, K4; 71 E9, E12, H7; 73 B9; 80 C1, E3
Cannon 46 A6
Cannon Aviation (private airfield) 88 G3
Cannon Field (private) 77 D12
Cannonsnap Creek 70 B3
Canoe Valley 75 B9
Canon Grande 76 F1; 86 F6
Cantau Creek 78 B4
Canton 47 I9
Canton-Hackney (airport) 47 H9
Cantonment Creek 30 F6
Cantu 88 G1
Canutillo 62 E1
Canyon 29 J11; 33 K12
Canyon City 69 J8
Canyon Creek 51 K12
Canyon Lake 69 I7
Canyon Lake 69 J8
Canyon Lake (USACE) 69 J8
Canyon Lake (private airfield) 69 I8
Canyon Springs 69 J7
Canyon Valley 42 A2
Canyon View Acres 68 K6
Cap Rock 42 A2
Capitan Reef 50 C6
Capitola 43 H7
Caplen 81 B11
Capota Creek 76 H4
Capote Peak 63 F8
Capps 29 A12
Capps Corner 37 I12
Caprock Canyons 34 C3
Caprock Canyons State Park 34 D4
Caps 43 J10
Caradan 56 F6
Carancahua 79 I12
Carancahua Bay 79 I12
Carancahua Creek 79 F12
Carancahua Lake 81 D8
Carbon 44 K4
Carbondale 48 B5
Card Aerodrome (private) 47 C8
Cardiff 71 J9
Cardiff Brothers (private airfield) 71 K9
Carey 35 C8
Cargray 30 E3
Carlisle 33 K10; 72 A1
Carlos 71 C8
Carlos Bay 85 B9
Carlsbad 54 F6
Carlson 69 E12
Carlton 57 C8
Carmine 70 G4
Carmona 60 K2
Carnes 35 D11
Caro 60 E4
Carolina 71 B12
Carpenter 78 C2
Carpenter Bayou 131 E12
Carpenters Bluff 38 C6
Carr 79 H10
Carreta Creek 84 H4
Carricitos 88 I5
Carricitos Creek 82 E5
Carrington Creek 70 D5
Carrizitos Creek 83 E8
Carrizo Creek 26 E5; 28 A6; 76 K4
Carrizo Draw 64 A1
Carrizo Springs 76 J4
Carrol 47 I11
Carroll Air Park (airport) 46 I3
Carroll Creek 47 E11
Carroll Lake-View (private airfield) 46 I2
Carrollton 46 E3; 104 A6; 152 J2
Carson 39 D8
Carta Valley 66 J6
Carter 45 F10; 46 C2; 99 K9
Carter Ranch (private airfield) 59 F10
Carters Creek 71 C7
Carters Lookout 48 F1
Carterville 48 D5, H4
Carthage 60 A6
Cartwright 47 F12, H7
Casa Blanca 84 D4
Casa Blanca Creek 79 G10
Casa de Peidras 65 J11
Casa de Piedra 75 E10
Casa Grande Peak 75 D9
Casa Navarro State Historic Site 159 D7
Casa Piedra 63 K10
Case Creek 38 E4
Cash 47 E8
Cason 48 E3
Cass 49 C7
Cassin 77 D12
Castell 68 C4
Castle 100 G2
Castle Hill Estate 45 F12; 100 G1
Castle Hill Forest 156 E5
Castle Hills 77 B12; 156 G6
Castle Mountain 64 H5
Castleman Creek 58 G2
Castolon 75 E8
Castor 56 H6
Castroville 77 C10
Castroville Municipal (airport) 77 C10
Cat Mountain 92 B6
Cat Spring 71 J7
Catarina 82 A6
Catarina Creek 82 A5
Catfish Creek 59 B9, B10
Catfish Creek 59 C9
Catfish Draw 32 B5
Cathedral Mountain 64 G1
Catlett Creek 45 C12
Cattail Creek 48 F5
Cauthorn Draw 66 E6
Cavanaugh Ranch (private airfield) 46 B4
Cavasso Creek 85 A9
Cave Creek 57 F11
Caves Spring 48 E5
Caviness 39 C11
Cavitt 57 H12
Cawthon 71 E7
Cayo de Hinoso 84 H6
Cayo del Grullo 84 I5
Cayo del Infiernillo 84 I5
Cayo del Mazon 84 H5
Cayote 57 D12
Cayuga 59 C9
Cedar Bayou 72 J2; 94 A4
Cedar Bayou 72 I2; 94 D4
Cedar Creek 69 H12; 71 G8
Cedar Creek 35 F10; 38 E5; 43 K11; 44 F5, G5; 45 J11; 47 H9, J7; 48 B3; 56 H2; 57 I12; 58 B6, K6; 59 F7, F8, F12; 60 F1, I3; 64 K2; 67 E11;69 H12; 70 C4, G2, G4, H1; 71 A7; 90 G4
Cedar Creek Reservoir 47 K8; 59 A8; 70 I4
Cedar Creek, Lacy Fork 47 J8
Cedar Creek, North Fork 60 H2
Cedar Creek, South Fork 60 I2
Cedar Grove 60 H4
Cedar Hill 34 F3; 46 H3
Cedar Hill State Park 46 H3
Cedar Lake 41 F9
Cedar Lake 80 G4
Cedar Lake Creek 80 F4
Cedar Lake Slough 59 D9
Cedar Lakes 80 G5
Cedar Lane 80 G4
Cedar Lick Branch 72 B1
Cedar Mills 38 C4
Cedar Mountain 68 D5
Cedar Park 69 D10
Cedar Point 60 E5
Cedar Springs 48 F4; 58 I3
Cedar Valley 69 G9
Cedarvale 47 I8
Cedarview 46 H3
Cedron Creek 57 C12
Cee Vee 35 E7
Cego 58 I2
Cele 69 E12
Celery Creek 55 K10
Celeste 47 B7
Celina 46 B4
Celotex 43 F9
Center 43 G7; 60 H1; 61 D7
Center City 57 G7
Center Creek 45 D11
Center Grove 48 D3
Center Line 70 E5
Center Mill 45 I10
Center Municipal (airport) 61 D7
Center Plains 33 D11
Center Point 45 E12, G11; 47 D8, D10; 48 D3, E3; 58 A3; 60 I2; 68 I3
Center Vine 48 C4
Centerpoint 69 J9
Centerview 59 I9
Centerville 46 F5; 59 I8; 60 I2; 106 F6
Centex 69 I9; 163 A9
Central 60 G3
Central Gardens 73 I8; 154 A1
Central Heights 60 E4
Centralia 60 I2
Centralia Draw 53 H11, H12; 54 G2
Century Lake 47 C10
Cereal 34 F1
Cerrito Creek 83 I8
Cestohowa 78 F3
Chacon Creek 76 H3; 77 D10; 83 F7; 143 C12, D12
Chacon Creek Ranch (private airfield) 76 I4
Chaffee Village 57 J10; 142 A1
Chalk 35 H8
Chalk Creek 67 F11
Chalk Draw 64 K3; 75 A9
Chalk Hill 48 J4
Chalk Mountain 57 A9
Chalk Mountains 75 A9
Chalmers 80 E3
Chamberlin 27 E8
Chambers County (airport) 72 J4
Chambers County-Winnie Stowell (airport) 72 J5
Chambers Creek 58 A5, A6
Chambers Creek, Middle Fork 46 K1
Chambers Creek, North Fork 46 J2
Chambersville 46 B5
Chambliss 46 B6
Chamizal National Memorial 126 B5
Champion 42 J6
Champion Creek Reservoir 42 K4
Champion Creek, North Fork 42 J5
Champion Creek, South Fork 42 K6
Chancellor 64 C4
Chances Store 70 D6
Chandler 47 K11
Chaney 44 J5
Chaney San Francisco Ranch (private airfield) 64 I5
Chaney Yard 71 J12
Channelview 72 J1
Channing 29 D8
Chaparrosa Creek 76 F3
Chaparrosa Ranch (private airfield) 76 G4
Chapel Hill 48 K1
Chapin 45 I11
Chapman 60 A4
Chapman Draw 67 A11
Chapman Ranch 84 G6
Chappel 56 J6
Chappell Branch 57 D7
Chappell Hill 71 G7
Charamusca Creek 83 C10
Charco 78 H5
Charco Creek 78 I5
Charco Marrano Creek 77 K9; 83 A9
Charles Creek 60 K2
Charles J Hughes Ranch (private airfield) 54 G1
Charles R Johnson (airport) 88 E6
Charleston 47 B11
Charlie 37 G7
Charlie Thomas Ranch (private airfield) 69 G7
Charlotte 77 G11
Charping (private airfield) 57 I12
Charquitas Creek 84 C3
Chase NAS 84 A5
Chatfield 46 K6
Chatt 58 C2
Cheapside 78 D6
Check 73 I7
Chenango 80 D5
Chenango Plantation 80 D5
Cheneyboro 58 C6
Cherokee 56 K5; 72 A5
Cherokee Bayou 48 J5
Cherokee County (airport) 60 D1
Cherokee Creek 56 K4
Cherokee Landing 59 B12
Cherry 38 J1
Cherry Creek 51 K11; 52 J1; 63 A10
Cherry Mountain 68 E4
Cherry Spring 68 D3
Cherry Spring Creek 68 D4
Chester 72 A4
Chesterville 80 A1
Cheyenne 52 C4
Chiamon Bayou 61 H7
Chicken Creek 30 C5
Chico 45 B10
Chico Creek 87 C10
Chicolete Creek 79 E9
Chicota 39 B11
Chihuahua 88 H1
Chihuahuan Desert 50 D2
Childers Creek 76 G6
Childress 35 D8
Childress Creek 57 D12, E12; 58 E1
Childress Municipal (airport) 35 D8
Chilicotal Mountain 75 D10
Chillicothe 35 E12
Chiltipin Creek 84 C6, D1; 85 C7
Chilton 58 I2
Chimney Creek 43 G12
China 72 H6
China Creek 56 I4
China Creek 43 H8; 56 I5
China Draw 51 G11
China Grove 42 I5; 78 C1; 80 C5
China Springs 58 E1
Chinati Mountains 63 I8
Chinquapin 61 H7; 80 H4
Chinquapin Landing 80 H4
Chipley 79 H8
Chireno 60 G6
Chisholm 46 F6
Chisos Mountains 75 D9
Chispa 63 B7
Chita 72 A1
Choate 78 H4
Chocolate Bay 79 J11; 81 D7
Chocolate Bayou 81 C7
Chocolate Bayou 79 I9; 80 B6; 81 D7
Chocolate Springs 81 C7
Chocolate Swale 85 B7
Choctaw Creek 38 D6
Choctaw Slough 38 D6
Choice 61 E7
Choke Canyon Lake 77 J12
Choke Canyon Reservoir 78 J1
Choke Canyon State Park—Calliham Unit 78 K1
Choke Canyon State Park—South Shore Unit 78 K2
Chriesman 70 C4
Christine 77 H12
Christmas Bay 81 F7
Christmas Creek 58 F4
Christoval 55 I7
Chub 53 B10
Chucareto Creek 83 C8
Chuckville 56 B4
Chumley 61 G8
Chunky 29 F11
Chupadera Ranch (private airfield) 82 B3
Chupaderas Creek 78 C1
Church Creek 70 K6
Cibolo 78 A2
Cibolo Creek 63 I9; 68 J4; 69 K7; 74 A3; 77 H7, I8, J9; 78 C3; 83 I12; 84 I1
Cibolo Creek Ranch (private airfield) 63 I9
Cielo Grande Ranch (private airfield) 68 G2
Cielo Vista 62 F2; 127 C8
Cienega Creek 63 D11
Cienega Mountain 64 H1
Cienega Mountains 63 J10
Cienequila Creek 26 A5
Cima 60 K5
Cinco B Ranch (private airfield) 68 J2
Cipres 88 D1
Circle 33 F9; 60 D2
Circle 'A' Ranch (private airfield) 57 A12
Circle Back 32 G6
Circle H (airport) 58 E2
Circle M Ranch (private airfield) 70 J5
Circle P Ranch (private airfield) 45 K10
Circle R Ranch (private airfield) 59 A9
Circle R Resort Ranch (private airfield) 68 J2
Circleville 69 C12
Cisco 44 J3
Cisco Municipal (airport) 44 J3
Cistern 70 J1
Cita Creek 29 K12
Citrus City 88 G1
City Of Tulia/Swisher County Municipal (airport) 33 C11
City-by-the Sea 85 D8
City-County (airport) 57 G10
Clairemont 42 C5
Clairette 57 B8
Clam Lake 73 K7
Clapps Creek 59 I9
Clardy 39 E12
Clare Creek 73 A8
Clarendon 30 J5
Clarendon Municipal (airport) 30 K5
Clareville 84 A4
Clark 72 E3
Clark (private airfield) 46 D1
Clark Creek 68 J1
Clark Field Municipal (airport) 57 A8
Clark Sky Ranch (private airfield) 71 K8
Clarks Branch 80 B1
Clarks Creek 48 J4; 79 C8, D9
Clarks Ferry 60 J3
Clarkson 58 K3
Clarksville 38 K2
Clarksville City 48 I3
Clarksville-Red River County (airport) 38 K2
Clarktown 61 I9
Clarkwood 84 E6
Claude 30 I2
Clauene 41 A8
Clawson 60 H3
Clay 70 E6
Clays Corner 32 D6
Clays Creek 70 B2
Clayton 60 B5
Claytonville 34 D1; 43 H7
Clear Branch 57 G11
Clear Creek 31 B8
Clear Creek 37 J11; 46 A1, B2; 47 K9; 48 H3; 56 A1; 57 I10, K10; 59 J7; 70 I4, K4; 71 G8; 78 E6; 80 A5; 81 A7; 133 K12; 134 J5, K1; 135 K7; 146 G1
Clear Creek Heights 146 H2
Clear Creek Village 146 G1
Clear Creek, West Fork 56 E3
Clear Fork Creek 78 D5
Clear Lake 46 D6
Clear Lake 146 D4
Clear Lake City 81 A7; 146 D2
Clear Lake Shores 81 A8; 146 D5
Clear Springs 60 G6; 69 K9
Clearview 70 H1
Clearwater 48 E1
Clearwater Cove 84 C4
Cleburne 45 J12; 97 C11
Cleburne Municipal (airport) 45 J12
Cleburne State Park 45 K12
Clegg 84 C1
Clemens Creek 78 A5
Clemons 71 J8
Clemville 80 F2
Cleo 67 C10
Cleta 29 J11
Cleveland 56 E2; 72 F2
Cleveland Municipal (airport) 72 E2
Cleveland Peak 63 H8
Click 68 D6
Cliff 77 B10
Cliffside 29 H11
Clifton 57 D11
Clifton Beach 81 B8
Clifton Municipal/Isenhower Field 57 D11
Climax 46 C6; 60 G4
Cline 76 D3
Clint 62 H3
Clinton 47 D7
Clinton Park 131 K7
CLM Ranch (private airfield) 50 C4
Clodine 71 K10
Close City 42 C1
Clover Field 81 B7
Cloverleaf 72 J1; 131 I11
Clower 47 I10
Cluck Ranch (airport) 27 E12
Clute 80 F6; 142 J6
Clute Lake 142 J6
Clutter Point 47 A8
Clyde 43 J12; 44 J1
Coady 72 J2
Coahoma 42 K2
Coal Creek 68 E5
Coalville 45 I7
Cobb 47 G8
Cobb Creek 58 C2; 59 J10
Coble 33 K7
Coburn 31 A9
Cochino Bayou 60 H1
Cochran 71 H8
Cochran County (airport) 32 J6
Cochran Mountains 64 I2
Cockrell Hill 46 G3; 112 E6
Codman 30 D5
Coesfield 38 C2
Coffee City 59 A11
Coffee Mill Creek 39 D8
Coffee Mill Lake 39 D8
Coffeeville 48 F3
Cofferville 33 G8
Coit 58 H5
Coke 47 F12
Cold Creek 68 A4
Cold Springs 57 I11
Coldspring 72 C1
Coldwater 27 B7
Coldwater Creek 26 B5, G2, I1; 27 C8, D11
Cole 46 G3; 112 G5
Coleman 56 D1
Coleman Creek 58 A2
Coleman Municipal (airport) 56 D1
Coles Creek 71 F7
Coleto Creek Reservoir 79 H8
Coletoville 79 H8
Coleyville 35 E7
Colfax 47 I10
Colita 72 A2
Collado 50 K6
College Hill 48 A4
College Mound 47 H7
College Station 70 C6; 96 H4
Collegeport 80 H1
Colley Creek 48 E6
Colleyville 46 F2; 102 F6
Collier 52 J1
Collier Creek 38 I2
Collin 46 C4
Collins 61 K8
Collins Creek 44 F1
Collins Ferry 47 G10
Collinsville 38 E3
Colmena Creek 83 D10
Colmesneil 72 A5
Cologne 79 I8
Coloma Creek 79 K11
Colonial Hills 149 F12
Colony 70 J2
Colorado 70 I2
Colorado Bend State Park 56 K6
Colorado City 42 J5
Colorado City (airport) 42 I4
Colorado River 41 H12; 42 H1, I4, K4; 54 A5; 55 D8, F11, G12; 56 G2, J6; 69 G12; 70 I2, K6; 79 A12, B12; 80 C1, G2; 93 I12, K12
Colorado River (Lake Austin) 92 E6
Colquitt 46 G6
Colton 69 G11
Columbia Heights 77 C12; 158 H5
Columbus 70 K5
Comal 69 K8; 78 A2
Comal River 150 C5
Comanche 56 C6
Comanche Caves Ranch (private airfield) 68 H1
Comanche County-City (airport) 56 C6
Comanche Creek 52 K6; 53 J7; 64 A5; 68 C2, D6; 76 I3
Comanche Peak 45 J10; 126 B3
Combes 88 H5
Combine 46 H5
Cometa 76 I4
Comfort 68 I4
Comfort Airpark (private) 68 I4
Commerce 47 C9
Commerce Municipal (airport) 47 B9
Commission Creek 31 A10
Como 47 D11; 109 F7
Comptons 75 E10
Comstock 66 K3
Comyn 56 B6
Concan 76 B5
Concepcion Creek 83 G12
Concho 55 F11
Concho River 55 G8
Concord 47 D7; 48 F3; 56 E2; 59 F8; 60 B2, C4, J6
Concordia 84 G5
Concrete 79 D7
Cone 34 I2
Cone (private airfield) 34 I2
Confederate Reunion Grounds State Historic Site 58 F5
Conlen 27 D9
Connell 73 H8
Conner Creek 60 G2
Connor 59 K9
Conoley 70 D2
Conover Lake 111 B12
Conquista Creek 78 G3
Conroe 71 F11; 97 I8
Content 58 J2
Converse 78 B1; 166 E3
Conway 30 H2
Cook 38 E2
Cook Branch 59 G12
Cooke Creek 60 D2
Cooks Point 70 C5
Cooks Slough 76 D5
Cookville 48 C3
Cool 45 G9
Coolidge 58 E5
Coon Creek 34 B2; 57 D12; 59 A9
Coon Creek Lake 59 B9
Coons Field (private) 60 I2
Cooper 47 B10
Cooper Creek 46 C2
Cooper Lake 47 B10
Cooper Lake State Park—Doctors Creek Unit 47 B10
Cooper Lake State Park—South Sulphur Unit 47 B10
Coopers Chapel 48 C3
Copano Bay 85 C8
Copano Bay State Fishing Pier 85 C9
Copano Creek 79 K8; 85 B8
Copano Village 85 C8
Copeland 48 K1
Copeville 46 D6
Coppell 46 E3; 103 A12; 104 A1
Copper Breaks State Park 35 F11
Copper Creek 42 E5
Copperas Cove 57 J10
Copperas Creek 56 B4; 67 D9; 69 K12; 70 J1
Copperas Point 145 C11
Corbet 58 B5
Corbyn 69 K8
Cordele 79 E11
Corinth 37 I12; 43 F10; 46 D2
Corlena 26 D5
Corley 48 B6
Corn Creek 56 H2
Corn Hill 69 B11
Cornett 48 D4
Cornilius Ranch (private airfield) 80 F2
Cornudas 50 D2
Cornudas Mountains 50 B2
Coronado Hills 62 F1
Corpora (private airfield) 70 B5
Corpus Christi 84 E6; 98 C4
Corpus Christi Bay 85 E7; 98 C5
Corpus Christi Intl (airport) 84 F6
Corpus Christi NAS/Truax Field (private) 85 F7
Corrigan 60 K3
Corry 33 G10
Corsicana 58 B6; 97 I11
Coryell City 57 F11
Coryell Creek 57 G11
Cossatot River 39 B7
Cost 78 B6
Cotton 71 A9
Cotton Center 33 G10; 47 A8
Cotton Creek 72 H6
Cotton Flat 53 C10
Cotton Gin 58 E6
Cotton Lake 72 J3
Cotton Patch 78 F5
Cotton Patch (private airfield) 70 E2
Cottondale 45 D11
Cottonwood 56 A2; 57 B7; 58 D2; 70 A6; 71 A8; 72 I5
Cottonwood Branch 56 I6
Cottonwood Creek 34 I5; 35 F12; 43 G11, H7; 45 B11; 46 K2; 51 G10; 56 A2; 57 H10; 58 A1, G4, J1; 59 C8; 69 F12; 70 E2; 78 B3; 94 H3
Cottonwood Shores 69 D7
Cotulla 77 K8
Cotulla-La Salle County (airport) 77 K8
Coughlin 73 G9
Coughran 78 G1
Coulter Field 70 B6
Count Draw 50 G4
Country Club Lake 96 G3
County Line 32 I6; 33 I10; 48 F3; 60 E2; 77 J7
Coupland 69 E12
Courchesne 62 F1
Courtney 53 A11; 71 F8
Coushatta Creek 70 K6
Cove 72 J3; 73 H9
Cove Harbor 85 D8
Cove Springs 59 B12
Covey Trails (private airfield) 71 K9
Covington 58 A1
Cow Bayou 58 H2; 73 F8; 146 E2
Cow Bayou, North Fork 58 H2
Cow Bayou, South Fork 58 H1
Cow Creek 56 C1; 69 C8; 70 A3; 80 D4; 83 B12; 86 A3, D6
Cow Creek, West Fork 56 H1
Cow Island Bayou 72 H4
Cow Pasture (private airfield) 46 K1; 72 C6
Cowhouse Creek 56 E6; 57 E7, G9, I11
Cowl Spur 71 F11
Cowley 46 E4; 153 H8
Cowtrap Lake 80 G5
Cox Bay 79 I11
Cox Creek 58 H6
Cox Field 39 D11
Cox Hollow 54 C4
Cox Lake 81 E7
Cox Mountain 50 H4
Coxville 69 E11
Coy City 78 H3
Coyanosa 52 I4
Coyanosa Draw 52 I4, K4; 64 A3
Coymack 58 I4
Coyote Corner 52 B6
Coyote Creek 55 D10
Coyote Lake 32 F5
Cozart 43 J10
Cozy Corner 70 J4
Crab Creek 58 B6
Crab Lake 80 I2
Crabapple 68 E4
Crabapple Creek 68 D5
Crabb 80 A4
Crabb Creek 71 B10
Crabbs Prairie 71 B10
Craft 60 C1
Craft Point 100 F4
Crafton 45 B10
Cramer Creek 28 C5
Crandall 46 H6
Crane 53 H8
Crane County (airport) 53 G8
Cranell 84 B6
Cranes Mill 69 I7
Cranfills Gap 57 D10
Crawfish Creek 34 I2
Crawford 57 F12
Crawford Creek 60 H3
Crawford Mountain 45 G7
Crazycat Mountain 126 B3
Creasy (private airfield) 81 C7
Creath 60 G1
Crecy 60 I2
Creechville 46 K5
Creedmoor 69 H11
Creek 59 J11
Cresson 45 I11
Cribb Station Creek 44 D4
Crimcrest 60 A3
Crims Chapel 48 K3
Crisp 46 J5
Crockett 59 H11
Crockett Creek 45 K9
Crockett Heights 66 B3
Cronin 59 E11
Crooked Creek 45 B8; 47 H9; 56 B1
Crosby 72 I2
Crosbyton 34 J3
Crosbyton Municipal (airport) 34 K3
Cross 71 B8; 77 I12
Cross Bayou 49 J7
Cross Creek 70 E2
Cross Cut 56 B3
Cross Plains 56 A2
Cross Road 38 J1
Cross Roads 43 G7; 48 K3; 59 B9, J8, J9
Cross Wind (private airfield) 45 F10
Crossroads 47 A10; 48 E2, J6; 53 F12; 58 K4
Crosstimber Creek 47 C12
Croton 34 J5
Croton Creek 34 K5; 42 A6; 43 B7, B9
Crow 47 H12; 87 H12
Crow Flats 50 C5
Crowell 35 H11
Crowley 46 H1
Crown 77 G11
Crows Nest Creek 55 E7
Crowther 78 J1
Crusher 50 J5
Cruz Calle 84 I1
Cryer Creek 58 A5
Crystal Beach 81 B10
Crystal City 76 I5
Crystal City Municipal (airport) 76 I5
Crystal Creek 63 J12; 71 G12
Crystal Creek, East Fork 71 E12
Crystal Creek, West Fork 71 F12
Crystal Falls 44 F4
Cuadrilla 62 H3
Cuatro Caminos 64 A1
Cuba 46 K1
Cuddihy Field (private) 84 F6
Cuero 79 E7
Cuero Creek 79 D7
Cuero Municipal (airport) 79 E7
Cuesta del Burro Mountains 63 H9
Cuevitas 87 C10, G12
Culberson County (airport) 50 J6
Culebra Creek 77 B11
Culleoka 46 D6
Culp (private airfield) 46 G4
Cumby 47 D9
Cummins Creek 46 K5; 70 G3, H4, J5
Cundiff 45 B9
Cuney 59 B12
Cunningham 47 A12
Curly Hill 158 K5
Currie 58 D6
Curry Creek 60 G6; 68 H5
Curtis 73 A7
Curtis Field 56 I1
Curtis Ranch Field (private) 56 H2
Cusenbary Draw 66 E6
Cushing 60 D3
Cusseta 48 D5
Custer City 38 D2
Custom Aire Service (airport) 80 D6
Cut 59 I11
Cut and Shoot 71 F12
Cut And Shoot (private airfield) 71 F12
Cuthand 48 A2
Cuthand Creek 38 K1; 39 E12; 48 A2
Cuthbert 42 I4
Cutoff Slough 70 A2
Cuyler 30 G2
Cyclone 58 K2
Cypress 48 E1; 71 I10
Cypress Creek 68 H3
Cypress Creek 60 J6; 61 C7; 68 H3; 69 H8; 71 H12, I9; 72 E5; 73 C8
Cypress Mill 69 E8
Cypress River (airport) 48 G6

D

D&W Ranch 58 E6
D'Hanis 77 C8
Dabney 76 E3
Dacosta 79 H9
Dacus 71 E10
Dads Corner 36 J5
Dads Creek 60 K1
Dagger Mountain 75 A10
Dagger Point 85 A10
Daingerfield 48 E4
Daingerfield State Park 48 E4
Daisetta 72 H4
Dalby Springs 48 B4
Dale 69 I11
Dalhart 29 A7
Dalhart Municipal (airport) 29 A7
Dallam 71 E7
Dallardsville 72 C4
Dallas 46 G4; 105 J11; 106 J2; 113 B10; 114 E1
Dallas Hunting and Fishing Club Lake 114 K4
Dallas Love Field 46 F4; 105 H8
Dallas NAS /Hensley Field (private) 46 G3; 112 E2
Dallas/Fort Worth International (airport) 46 F2; 103 D10; 104 D1
Dalrock 46 F5; 107 D10
Dalton 46 B2; 48 C4
Dalworthington Gardens 46 G2; 110 G6
Dalzell 56 F3
Damon 80 D4
Dan E Richards Municipal (airport) 35 G8
Danbury 80 D6
Danciger 80 E3
Danevang 80 F1
Daniels 60 B6; 71 G7
Daniels Chapel 38 K5
Danner 39 D8
Dant 71 I7
Danville 48 J3
Daphine 48 C1
Darco 48 J5
Darden 48 B4
Darilek 78 F2
Darling 76 F1
Carnell Branch 44 A6
Darrouzett 27 H8
Carrs Creek 69 A12; 70 A1
Datura 58 E5
Daugherty Lake 115 J12
Dauphin 59 A9
Davenport 38 H1
Davenport Ranch 92 D5
David Wayne Hooks Memorial (airport) 71 H11
Davidson 70 D5
Davidson Creek 70 D4, E5
Davilla 70 B1
Davis 77 H11
Davis Bayou 72 E3
Davis Creek 58 H5
Davis Hill 72 F3
Davis Mountains 63 B11
Davis Mountains State Park 63 C11
Davis Prairie 58 G5
Davisville 60 H4
Davy Crockett National Forest 60 I2
Dawn 29 K9
Dawson 58 C4
Dayton 72 H3
De Berry 49 K7
De Kalb 48 A4
De Leon Municipal (airport) 56 B6
De Long Ranch (private airfield) 76 A2
De Soto 46 H3
Dead Horse Creek 44 K3
Deadman Creek 43 H12
Deadmans Canyon 66 J2
Deadmans Creek 66 K3
Deadwood 61 A7
Deal 30 E1
Dean 37 H7
Dean (private airfield) 84 G6
Dean Ranch (private airfield) 79 B8
Deanville 70 E4
Deanwright 59 E11
Dearing Ranch (private airfield) 45 J7
Deaton Canyon 66 H4
Deaver Creek 38 D4
Deboldin Creek 48 H6
Decatur 45 C11
Decatur Municipal (airport) 45 C11
Decker 69 F11
Decker Prairie 71 G10
Deco 71 I11
Deep Creek 36 K2; 42 G4, H5; 44 A3, I2, K2; 45 D12; 56 H3; 76 B5
Deep Creek Ranch (private airfield) 56 J3
Deep Red Creek 37 E7
Deer Creek 37 J7
Deer Creek 37 J7; 46 I1; 57 K7; 58 I2
Deer Park 72 K1
Deer Pasture (private airfield) 69 A8
Del Mar 83 G7; 89 J8
Del Norte Acres 62 F2
Del Norte Heights 62 G2; 127 D9
Del Norte Mountains 64 F2
Del Rio 86 C5; 99 D8
Del Rio Intl (airport) 86 C4
Del Valle 69 G11
Del Valle (private airfield) 69 G11
Del-Tex (private airfield) 33 F10
Delaware Junction 56 D4
Delaware Mountains 51 G7
Delaware River 51 C10
Delba 46 B6
DeLeon 56 A6
DeLeon Park 164 J2
Delhi 69 J12
Delia 58 E4
Dell City 50 C4
Dell City Municipal (airport) 50 C4
Delmer 60 D1
Delmita 88 D1
Delray 60 A5
Delrose 48 G2
Delta Lake 88 F3
Delwin 35 H7
Demarco 69 C7
Democrat 56 E5

continue on next page

INDEX, cont'd

Green Acres (private airfield) 71 I9
Green Branch 83 B11
Green Creek 57 A7, B8
Green Hill 48 C2
Green Lake 79 J10
Green Lake 79 J10
Green Lake Ranch (private airfield) 79 J10
Green Pond Gully 72 H6
Green Ranch (private airfield) 44 F3
Green River 62 B6
Green Valley 46 B2
Green Valley 63 K12
Greenbelt Reservoir 30 J4
Greenbriar Creek 59 C7
Greenock 58 D1
Greens Bayou 72 J1; 131 I10
Greens Bayou 71 I11; 72 I1; 126 K2; 131 G9, J11
Greens Bluff 59 D9
Greens Lake 81 D8
Greenshores 69 F10; 92 C5
Greenview 47 E10
Greenville 47 D8; 126 I6
Greenville Reservoirs No 1 No 2 No 3 No 5 47 D8
Greenvine 70 H5
Greenwood 38 I2; 45 B12, G10; 47 D12; 53 B11; 149 F12
Greenwood Village 71 J12; 130 B4
Greer Island 100 I4
Gregg County (airport) 48 J4
Greggton 48 I3
Gregory 85 D7
Gresham 47 K12
Grey Forest 77 A11
Gribble 46 F3; 104 D5
Grice 48 G1
Grier (private airfield) 68 J5
Griffin 60 B2
Griffing Park 73 I8; 154 F5
Griffith 32 I4; 46 J2
Grigsby 60 E6
Grimes 43 J9
Grindstone Creek 45 F9
Grisham 33 E10
Grissom Creek 60 A2
Grit 68 B1
Groceville 71 F12
Groesbeck 58 F5
Groesbeck Creek 35 D12
Groom 30 H3
Grossville 68 C2
Grosvenor 56 C2
Grove Creek 46 J4
Groves 73 I8; 154 D5
Groveton 60 J1
Groveton-Trinity County (airport) 60 J1
Grow 35 I8
Grub Hill 58 B1
Grubbe 47 E11
Gruenau 78 E5
Gruene 69 K8
Gruene Siding 69 K8
Gruhlkey 28 H6
Gruver 26 J2
Gruver Municipal (airport) 26 J1
Guadalupe 79 H9
Guadalupe Bay 79 K10
Guadalupe Creek 83 A11
Guadalupe Heights 68 I3
Guadalupe Mountains 50 C6
Guadalupe Mountains National Park 50 C6
Guadalupe Mountains Wilderness 50 C6
Guadalupe Peak 50 C6
Guadalupe River 68 I3, I5; 69 J8; 78 A4; 79 B7, G8, I9; 141 K9; 150 A6, D6; 162 K5; 166 I1
Guadalupe River State Park 68 J6
Guadalupe River, North Fork 67 H12; 68 H1
Guadalupe River, South Fork 67 I12; 68 I1
Guayule Creek 64 J5
Guda 58 H2
Gude 58 E6
Guerra 87 B10
Guffey 73 H7
Guild 52 K5
Gulf 70 J6; 80 H3
Gulf Coast (private airfield) 79 K9
Gulf Hill 80 H3
Gulf of Mexico 81 G7; 85 H10; 89 D9
Gulf Park 80 F6
Gum Creek 48 G3
Gum Island (private airfield) 72 I3
Gum Slough 73 E8
Gum Springs 48 D6, J4; 60 B2
Gum Tree Branch 80 B1
Gun Barrel City 47 K8
Gunsight 44 I4
Gunter 46 A4; 47 F10
Gus 70 E4
Gustine 57 D7
Guthrie 35 K8
Guthrie Lake 41 D11
Guy 80 C4
Guys Store 59 I9

H

H & S Airfield (private) 80 C4
H H Coffield Regional (airport) 70 C3
H M Ranch (private airfield) 78 A2
Hacienda 76 D4
Hacienda Heights 62 G2
Hackberry 35 H9; 42 B1; 67 I9; 79 A9
Hackberry Creek 26 I2; 34 B4; 45 K7; 46 F6; 58 B2; 60 I3; 67 H9;104 D1
Hackberry Crossing 65 G12
Hackberry Draw 54 H4, K3
Hackberry Ranch (private airfield) 67 I10
Hadley Creek 71 B11
Haeckerville 78 A2
Hagansport 48 B1
Hager Creek 60 H1
Hagerman National Wildlife Refuge 38 D4
Hagerville 60 H2
Haggerty Creek 48 H6
Hahn 79 D12
Hahns (private airfield) 79 F11
Hail 47 A8
Hainesville 47 G12
Hairston Creek 69 C8
Hale Center 33 G11
Hale County (airport) 33 F12; 155 K8
Halesboro 47 A12
Haley Branch 45 K12
Haley Creek 59 H10
Halfway 33 F11
Hall 48 F6; 56 I3
Hall (airport) 47 I7
Hall (private airfield) 48 F4
Hall Branch 59 C9
Hallettsville 79 B9
Hallettsville Municipal (airport) 79 C9
Halls Bayou 81 C7
Halls Bluff 59 H10
Hallsburg 58 F3
Hallsville 48 I4
Halsell 37 J7
Halsted 70 I4
Haltom City 46 G1; 101 K12; 102 K1; 109 A12; 110 A1
Ham Creek 57 A12; 60 C4
Hamby 43 I12
Hamilton 57 E8
Hamilton Creek 69 C8
Hamilton Municipal (airport) 57 E8
Hamilton Ranch (private airfield) 83 G11
Hamlin 43 F9
Hamlin Municipal (airport) 43 F9
Hammond 58 J4
Hamon 79 C7
Hamrick 56 D1
Hamshire 72 J6
Hancock 41 F11
Handley 46 G1; 110 E3
Haney 29 I11
Hanger 38 D4
Hankamer 72 J4
Hannas Draw 26 K1
Hannibal 45 J7
Hanover 70 B4
Hansford 26 K2
Happy 33 A11
Happy Hill 46 I1
Happy Hollow 76 A2
Happy Union 33 G12
Happy Valley 55 A9; 60 D3
Harbican Airpark (private) 71 I9
Harbin 57 A7
Harbor Grove 46 D2
Hard Creek 78 I5
Harden Branch 55 I10
Hardin 72 G4
Hardy 37 K12
Hardy Street Yard 71 J12
Hardys Sandy Creek 79 D10
Hare 70 C1
Hargill 88 F3
Harker Heights 57 J11; 142 D6
Harkeyville 56 I5
Harlem 80 A4
Harleton 48 H4
Harley White Field (private) 57 D8
Harlingen 88 H5; 141 C8
Harmaston 72 I1
Harmon 39 E9
Harmon Creek 71 B11
Harmony 42 E6; 45 H10; 47 E12, K7; 59 D10; 61 F7; 70 E5; 71 B11; 78 F4
Harmony Field (private) 78 C1
Harmony Hills 157 G7
Harold Freeman Farm (private airfield) 71 J9
Harper 68 F2
Harpersville 44 H4
Harral Draw 65 B8
Harrells 73 C9
Harriet 55 F8
Harriet Creek 46 D1
Harrington Branch 46 C5
Harris Creek 38 D4; 48 I1; 57 G12; 58 G1
Harris Lake 147 A12
Harris Reservoir 80 D5
Harrisburg 61 K8; 71 K12; 134 B6
Harrison 58 G3
Harrison Bayou 49 I7
Harrison County (airport) 48 I6
Harrison Field Of Knox City (airport) 43 A11
Harrold 36 G3
Hart 33 D10
Hart Aerial (private airfield) 33 D10
Hart Creek 48 D2
Hart Draw 52 K1
Hart Spur 46 G2
Hartburg 73 F9
Hartex 36 I5
Hartland 88 C2
Hartlee Field (private) 46 C2
Hartley 29 B8
Hartman 49 B7
Harts Bluff 48 B2
Harts Creek 45 A12
Harvard 48 D2
Harvey 71 C7
Harvey Creek 60 H6
Harveys Creek 70 K4
Harwood 69 K12
Hasima 80 F4
Haskell 43 D11
Haskell Municipal (airport) 43 C11
Haslam 61 C8
Haslet 46 E1; 101 A9
Hasse 56 C6
Hasting Creek 42 J3
Hastings 81 B7
Hastings Siding 81 B7
Hatchel 55 D10
Hatchetville 47 C11
Hathaway 72 G5
Hatley Creek 48 J5
Havana 87 H12
Hawdon 80 B5
Hawkeye Hunting Club (private airfield) 58 D2
Hawkin's Ranch Strip (private) 45 D12
Hawkins 48 H1
Hawkins Private (private airfield) 45 H10
Hawkinsville 80 G4
Hawley 43 H11
Hawthorne 61 F8; 71 D12
Hawthorne Field 72 F6
Hawthorne Place 71 J12; 130 C2
Hay Creek 56 C1
Hayes Creek 80 C6
Haymond 64 G4
Haynesville 36 G4
Hays 69 G10
Hays City 69 H9
Hays Spring 59 G11
Haystack Canyon 43 A7
Haystack Creek 43 A7
Hayward Junction 60 F4
Hazeldell 57 C7
Headsville 58 I6
Heafer 77 C12; 158 I3
Heaker 80 A5; 133 G10
Hearne 70 A5
Hearne Municipal (airport) 70 A5
Heath 46 F6; 107 I12
Heath Canyon (private airfield) 75 B11
Heath Creek 75 C11
Heaton 30 E5
Hebbronville 83 I11
Hebert 73 I7
Hebron 46 E3; 152 G4
Heckville 33 I12
Hedley 30 K6
Hedley (private airfield) 30 K6
Hedwig Village 71 J11; 129 H7
Hedwigs Hill 68 C3
Hefner 35 K12
Hegar 71 H9
Heidelberg 88 H4
Heidenheimer 58 K1
Heights 81 C8; 165 I10
Helbig 73 G7; 95 A9
Heldnfelt 84 B4
Helena 78 F4
Helmic 60 I2
Helms 70 K6
Helotes 77 A11
Helotes Creek 77 A11
Hemming 46 A2
Hemphill 61 H9
Hemphill County (airport) 31 B7
Hempstead 71 H8
Henderson 60 A3
Henderson Creek 45 C7; 57 F8
Hendrix 47 E7
Henington (private airfield) 47 B8
Henkhaus 79 B8
Henly 69 G8
Hennessey 71 J11
Henning Creek 57 A7
Henrietta 37 I8
Henrietta (private airfield) 37 I8
Henrietta Creek 46 E1
Henrys Chapel 60 B2
Hensarling (private airfield) 59 K9
Henson Creek 57 H11
Herbert Ranch (private airfield) 69 D7
Hereford 29 K8; 141 H8
Hereford Municipal (airport) 29 K8
Heritage Creek Airstrip (private) 45 C12
Heritage Ranch (private airfield) 71 K9
Herman 45 C12
Hermits Cove 47 F9
Hermleigh 42 H5
Hermosa 52 H1
Herndon 43 I8
Herradura Lodge (private airfield) 83 B10
Herring 59 D12
Herty 60 H4
Hess (private airfield) 58 E2
Hester House 71 J12
Hewett-Knapp (private airfield) 58 C4
Hewitt 58 G2
Hext 67 A12
Heyser 79 J10
Hickey 60 B3
Hickman Creek 72 A4
Hickory Branch 73 D12
Hickory Creek 38 D2; 46 C2; 47 A11; 59 H12; 60 G1; 68 D4; 69 C8; 72 C5; 114 G6; 115 J7
Hickory Creek 46 D2; 47 B7; 145 A10
Hickory Creek Arm 145 B10
Hickory Hill 48 E2
Hickory Ridge 61 I10
Hicks 70 D3
Hicks Airfield 45 E12; 100 B6
Hicksbaugh 72 D6
Hickston 79 A7
Hico 57 C9
Hidalgo 88 I1
Hidden Acres 84 C4
Hidden Cove 158 J2
Hidden Echo 72 H1
Hidden Forest 156 D6
Hidden Hill 46 D2; 145 A9
Hidden Valley Airpark (private) 46 C2
Hide-A-Way Lake (private airfield) 47 I12
Hideaway Hill 84 B4
Higginbotham 40 F5
Higgins 27 K9; 73 H7; 95 F12
Higgins-Lipscomb County (airport) 27 K9
High 39 E10
High Hill 70 K3
High Island 81 A12
High Lonesome Draw 53 G11, G12
High Point 35 D8
High Valley 56 J6
Highbank 58 J4
Highland 46 F3; 56 A6; 57 A12; 58 F1; 104 F5
Highland Addition 45 E11
Highland Heights 71 J12; 129 B11
Highland Park 46 F4; 105 I10
Highland Village 46 D2; 145 B10
Highlands 72 J2
Highlands Reservoir 72 J2
Hilburn 33 D10
Hilda 68 C3
Hilda Siding 78 A3
Hilde-Griff Field (private) 69 B10
Hilger 39 E8
Hill City 45 K10
Hill Country State Natural Area 77 A8
Hill Country Village 77 A12; 157 D7
Hill Creek 45 H9; 57 A11; 84 A1
Hill Creek, South Fork 57 A10
Hillard 30 E2
Hillcrest 70 K5
Hillcrest Village 81 C7
Hillcrest (private airfield) 46 E1
Hillebrandt 73 I7
Hillister 72 C6
Hillje 79 E12
Hills 70 G2
Hills and Dales 156 C1
Hillsboro 58 B2
Hillsboro Municipal (airport) 58 B2
Hilltop 68 E3
Hilltop Lakes 59 J7
Hilltop Lakes (private airfield) 59 J7
Hilltop Ranch (private airfield) 69 K8
Hilshire Village 71 J11
Hilton 38 E5
Hindes 77 H11
Hindman 41 F11
Hiram 47 H8
Hirok (private airfield) 58 A3
Hitchcock 81 C8
Hitchland 26 H2
Hitex Private (private airfield) 38 C5
Hitson 43 F8
Hitson Draw 50 D3
Hitts Creek 47 I12
Hix 70 C5
Hoard 47 H12
Hoard Siding 47 H12
Hoban 52 I1
Hobbs 42 G6; 57 K12
Hobby 80 A5; 133 K9
Hobby (airport) 71 K12; 134 F6
Hobson 78 F3
Hochheim 79 C7
Hockley 71 H9
Hodges 43 H10
Hodgson 48 A4
Hoefer 80 A1
Hoen 58 D3
Hog Branch 44 H3; 56 C1
Hog Creek 38 E4; 55 G10; 56 C4; 57 E10, F12; 58 J3; 70 B2; 71 C8
Hogansville 47 F10
Hogeye 47 B7
Hogg 58 J4; 70 E4
Hogg Branch 56 H4
Hogg Island 72 K2
Hoggs Bayou 60 A6
Hogpen Creek 58 G4
Holden 58 E6
Holder 56 C3
Holiday Beach 85 B9
Holiday Lakes 80 D5
Holland 69 A12
Holland Quarters 60 A5
Holland Reservoir 83 A8
Holliday 36 I5
Holliday Creek 168 J4
Holly 59 J12
Holly Beach 89 H7
Holly Creek 38 K5; 48 H6
Holly Grove 72 D4
Holly Lake Ranch (private airfield) 48 G1
Holly Springs 47 J10; 48 F3; 60 E4; 73 A8
Hollywood Park 77 A12; 157 C7
Holman 70 J4
Holman Creek 59 F7
Holmsley Creek 56 D6
Holt 30 A3; 56 H3
Home Creek 56 F1
Home Ranch Creek 30 B6
Homer 60 I4
Homer Junction 55 J12
Hondo 77 C8
Hondo Creek 68 K1; 77 C9; 78 C1, H4; 84 D5
Hondo Municipal (airport) 77 C8
Honea 71 F11
Honey Creek 46 C5; 57 C8; 68 B2, C6
Honey Creek 68 J6
Honey Creek State Natural Area 68 J6
Honey Grove 39 E9
Honey Grove Creek 39 D9
Honey Island 72 E5
Hood 38 E1
Hooks 48 A6
Hooks Bayou 38 K5
Hoolia Creek 58 I2
Hooper Draw 51 H10
Hoot 49 B7
Hoover 30 E5; 39 E12
Hope 79 D9
Hopewell 48 D1; 59 H9, I12
Horan (private airfield)33 F12
Hords Creek 56 D2
Hords Creek Lake (USACE) 55 D12
Hords Creek Lake 55 D12
Horizon (airport) 77 D12
Horizon City 62 G3
Horn Hill 58 F5
Horn Ranch (private airfield) 86 A6
Horn-Katy Hawk Intl (private airfield) 71 J9
Hornsby 69 F11
Horse Canyon 75 B11
Horse Creek 26 K3; 28 E5; 30 B6; 44 C2; 47 C8; 48 C3; 56 H5; 60 D2
Horse Mountain 64 H4
Horse Thief Canyon 64 C1
Horsehead Draw 51 F12; 52 E1
Horsepen Creek 72 C5
Horseshoe Bay Airpark (private) 69 D7
Horseshoe Bend (airport) 45 I10
Horsleys Creek 47 J10
Hortense 72 A4
Horton 47 C9; 61 J8
Hoskins 81 E7
Hosstetter Creek 71 D11
Hostyn 70 J3
Hot Springs 75 D11
Hot Springs Creek 63 H8
Hot Wells 50 K5; 71 I10
Houmont Park 72 J1; 131 D10
House 80 B5
House Creek 57 I10
House Log 35 A8
Housen Bayou 61 H8
Housetop Mountains 64 G5
Houston 71 J12; 129 K11; 130 J2; 133 A11; 134 A2
Houston County (airport) 59 H12
Houston County Lake 59 G11
Houston Fishing Cub Lake 132 I5
Houston Gulf (airport) 81 B8
Houston Heights 71 J12; 130 G1
Houston Intercontinental (airport) 71 I12
Houston River 73 F11
Houston Ship Channel 131 K10; 135 B8
Houston-Southwest (airport) 80 B5
Hovey 64 C2
Howard 46 K4
Howard Creek 151 B12
Howard Draw 54 K2; 66 A1, C1, F1
Howards 73 B9
Howardwick 30 J4
Howe 46 A5
Howland 39 E10
Howth 71 G8
Hoxie 70 C1
Hoyte 70 B3
Huana Creek 60 D6; 61 E7
Hub 32 C6
Hub Field (private) 59 G8
Hubbard 48 A4; 58 D4
Hubbard Creek 44 F4, H2, I1
Hubbard Creek, Salt Prong 44 H1
Hubbard Creek Lake 44 F3
Huber 60 D6
Hubert 84 D5
Huckabay 45 J7
Huckleberry Creek 26 A3
Hudd 42 F6
Hudson 71 I11
Hudson Municipal (airport) 46 G5; 115 D10
Hudson Oaks 45 G10
Hudsonville 39 D8
Hueco Mountains 62 E4
Hueco Tanks 62 E4
Hueco Tanks State Historic Site 62 E4
Huff Creek 73 A8
Huff School 36 I6
Huffins 49 E7
Huffman 72 H2
Huffman Creek 72 D2
Hufsmith 71 G11
Huggins 37 I9
Hughes 79 H9
Hughes Creek 48 E5; 57 J7
Hughes Ranch (private airfield) 86 F6
Hughes Springs 48 E4
Huisache Creek 79 H11
Hulen Park 81 B8
Hull 72 G4
Hulldale 55 K7
Hulver 35 C7
Humble 47 E12; 72 I1
Hume 59 C12
Hungerford 80 C2
Hunt 68 H1
Hunt (airport) 85 E7
Hunt Ranch (private airfield) 68 H5
Hunter 69 J9
Hunter Creek 61 K9
Hunters Creek 156 E4
Hunters Creek Village 71 J11; 129 I8
Hunting Bayou 130 G5; 131 K9
Hunting Shirt Creek 44 K4
Huntington 60 I4
Huntoon 26 H6
Huntsville 71 B11; 141 G11
Huntsville Municipal (airport) 71 B11
Huntsville State Park 71 C11
Hurds Pass Draw 51 I10
Hurlwood 33 K10
Hurn (private airfield) 46 J4
Hurnville 37 H8
Huron 58 B1
Hurricane Bayou 59 H11
Hurricane Creek 59 D12; 60 I3
Hurst 46 F2; 102 J5
Hurstown 61 E8
Hutchins 46 H4; 114 J2
Hutchinson County (airport) 30 D2; 94 H5
Hutto 69 D11
Huxley 61 D8
Hyatt 72 D5
Hyatt Lookout 72 D5
Hye 68 F6
Hylton 55 A8
Hyman 54 A3
Hynds City 37 H11
Hynes Bay 79 K10

I

I. D. Fairchild State Forest 59 D12
Iago 80 D3
Iatan 42 K3
Ida 38 E6
Idalou 33 J12
Idle Airpark (private) 78 B2
Idyle Hour Acres 69 E11
Iglehart 69 F11
Ike 46 J4; 78 K2
Illinois Bend 37 H12
Illusion Lake 33 I8
Impact 43 I11; 90 B3
Imperial 52 I6
Imperial Reservoir 52 I5
Imperialist Creek 76 D1
Inadale 42 I6
Inari 79 I8
Independence 70 F6
Independence Creek 65 D8, D11
India 46 I5
Indian Camp Creek 45 K8
Indian Creek 56 G3
Indian Creek 29 E10; 30 B5; 31 H12; 34 A6, C3; 43 J10; 44 H2; 46 B6; 55 E9; 56 C1; 57 A8, D9; 59 B10; 60 D3; 61 K7; 65 I10; 67 J8; 68 H2; 69 A12; 70 G5; 76 D4; 78 J5; 152 G1
Indian Gap 57 E7
Indian Head Mountain 75 C8
Indian Hills 61 K9
Indian Hot Springs 62 A3
Indian Mesa 65 A9
Indian Mounds Wilderness 61 H9
Indian Point 85 E7
Indian Rock 48 G3
Indian Village 72 B4
Indian Wells 65 I8
Indianola 79 J12
Indio 63 K8
Indio Creek 76 K2
Industrial Canal 98 B3
Industry 70 I5
Inez 79 G10
Ingleside 85 E7
Ingleside On-the-Bay 85 E7
Ingram 68 H2
Inks Lake 69 B7
Inks Lake State Park 69 B7
Intracoastal Waterway 73 H10, K7; 79 K11; 80 H5, I2; 81 A12, E7; 84 K6; 85 H7; 88 A6; 89 G7; 154 J4
Inwood 46 E4; 105 B9
Iola 71 B8
Iona 45 H12
Ioni Creek 44 H6; 59 E12, F11
Iowa Colony 80 B6
Iowa Park 36 H5
Ira 42 H4
Iraan 65 A11
Iraan Municipal (airport) 65 A11
Irby 43 C12
Iredell 57 C10
Ireland 57 F9
Irene 58 C3
Irish Creek 79 E8
Iron Creek 59 K8
Iron Ore Creek 38 D5
Ironhead (airport) 46 B1
Irons Bayou 60 A5
Irons Creek 71 I8
Ironton 59 C12
Irving 46 F3; 104 J4; 112 A3
Irwin 27 E8
Isaac Draw 54 I2
Isbell Ranch (private airfield) 70 B1
Iser 62 J5
Isinglass Canyon 65 H8
Isla 62 I3
Isla Blanca Cabana 89 I8
Island 81 D9
Island Creek 58 A1
Islitas 82 F6
Italy 58 A3
Itasca 58 A2
Itasca Creek 58 A2
Ivan 44 F5
Ivanhoe 39 D8
Ivanhoe Creek 27 H9
Ivys Creek 71 H7
Izoro 57 H9, J10

J

J and E Junction 73 C8
J Bar WC Ranch (private airfield) 43 G10
J F Ranch (private airfield) 57 B8
J R Scherdin (private airfield) 80 E6
J-Bar Ranch (private airfield) 53 F7
Jaboncillos Creek 84 H2
Jabonoso Creek 83 C7
Jacinto City 72 J1; 131 I8
Jack Creek 60 H3
Jacks Branch 58 B2
Jacksboro 45 C8
Jacksboro Municipal (airport) 45 C8
Jackson 47 I9; 48 G4; 61 C7
Jackson Branch 106 E1
Jackson County (airport) 79 F11
Jackson Creek 48 K6; 71 F7
Jackson/Bill (private airfield) 45 D11
Jacksonville 60 C1
Jacobia 47 C8
Jacobs 35 G8
Jagoe 46 C2
Jake Creek 38 K2
James 48 H4; 61 D7
James River 68 D1, F1
Jamestown 47 H11; 73 A9
Jamoncillos Creek 83 D7
Jardin 47 B9
Jarrell 69 A11
Jarrell Creek 60 B4
Jarvis 59 E12
Jarvis Creek 80 D2
Jasper 73 A8
Jasper County-Bell Field 73 A8
Jasper Creek 45 D9
Jasper Heights 48 I6
Java 59 D12
Jay Kay Ranch (private airfield) 77 H9
Jay Ray 70 K6
Jayell 44 J1
Jayton 42 C6
Jean 44 B5
Jeanetta 71 K11
Jeddo 70 J1
Jefferson 48 G6
Jenkins 48 E4; 59 K9
Jenkins Creek 44 I1
Jennings 39 E11
Jentsch Acres 69 K8
Jericho 30 H4; 60 E6
Jermyn 45 C7
Jerrys Branch 56 H5
Jersey Lake 128 A5
Jersey Village 71 I11; 128 A5
Jewell 58 G2
Jewett 59 H8
Jiba 47 I7
Jim Bayou 48 E6; 49 F7
Jim Hogg City Historical Park 60 D1
Jim Hogg County (airport) 83 I11
Jim Ned Creek 55 B12; 56 C1
Jim Ned Creek, South Fork 55 B12
Jim Roach Field (private) 69 H10
Jim Sears (private airfield) 45 D10
Jimmys Creek 56 C5
Jinks Branch 69 C9
Joaquin 61 C7
Joe 38 C5
Joe Fleming Field (private) 78 B4
Joe Pool Lake 46 H3; 111 K12; 112 K1
Joe Pool Lake (USACE) 46 H3
Joel 29 K9
John B Connally Ranch (private airfield) 78 E1
John Fields Ranch (private airfield) 67 D7
John Henry Kirby State Forest 72 B5
John Ray Creek 29 F11
Johnfarris 34 E3
Johnnie Volk Field (private) 81 C8
Johns Creek 30 A3; 47 B10; 48 D6, E6
Johnson 41 C8; 71 G11
Johnson City 69 F7
Johnson City (private airfield) 68 F5
Johnson Creek 60 B2; 68 A4, G1; 111 E9
Johnson Creek Reservoir 48 F5
Johnson Draw 53 C12, E10; 66 C3, F3
Johnson Fork 67 D11, F12
Johnson Ranch (private airfield) 68 J1
Johnsons Station 46 H2; 111 H7
Johnston Lake 143 G11
Johnstone 86 C5
Johnsue 71 J9
Johnsville 57 A9
Johntown 48 A1
Joiner 70 I4
Joinerville 60 A3
Joliet 69 J11
Jolly 37 H7
Jollyville 69 E10
Jonah 69 C12
Jonah Creek 35 B7
Jones 47 H10
Jones Creek 45 A8, A10; 47 I7; 80 D1
Jones Creek 80 D1, F5
Jones Field 39 E7
Jones Gully 95 F9
Jones Lake 147 A8
Jones Prairie 58 K4
Jonesboro 57 F10
Jonestown 69 D9
Jonesville 49 I7; 115 F7
Joplin 45 D9
Joppa 69 A9
Jordan 70 I1
Jordan Creek 38 E3
Jordan Farms (private airfield) 71 K9
Jordan Gully 131 I10
Jordans Store 61 E8
Jordon Creek 59 C12
Joseph Ross Scherdin (private airfield) 80 E6
Josephine 47 D7
Joshua 45 I12
Josselet 43 C11
Josserand 60 K2
Jot Em Down 47 B9
Jourdanton 77 G12
Joy 37 K8
Joye Ranch (airport) 78 D5
JSI (private airfield) 46 C6
Juan Cordona Lake 53 H7
Juanita Creek 80 F1; 83 C10
Jubilee Springs 57 I12
Jud 43 B10
Judge Switch 45 I7
Judkins 53 E7
Judson 48 H3
Juilliard 29 G11
Julian 88 C3
Juliff 80 B5
Jumbo 33 A9
Junction 67 D11
Juno 66 G3
Justiceburg 42 E3
Justin 46 D1
JW (private airfield) 45 D12

K

K Ranch (private airfield) 71 B8
Kadane Corner 36 I4
Kaffie Ranch (private airfield) 83 K12
Kaffir 33 B11
Kalgary 42 A3
Kamay 36 I4
Kamey 79 I10
Kami-Kazi (private airfield) 81 B7
Kamp Koinonia 45 G9
Kanawha 38 I1
Kane 88 H1
Kardys (private airfield) 78 A2
Karen 71 F10
Karnack 49 H7
Karnes City 78 G4
Karnes County (airport) 78 H4
Karon 78 J3
Katemcy 68 A2
Katy 71 J9
Katy Lake 167 I7
Kaufman 47 H7
Kay Bee Heights 57 J10
Kay Ranch (private airfield) 48 I1
Kearny 82 A6
Keechi 59 G9
Keechi Creek 45 F8; 58 H4; 59 D10, H8, I9
Keechi Creek, East Fork 45 D8, E8
Keechi Creek, West Fork 45 D8
Keefer 72 G1
Keeler 46 I1
Keelersville 69 B12
Keenan 71 F10
Keene 46 J1
Keeter 45 E11
Keith 71 C8
Keith Lake 73 K8
Keithton 73 A8
Kelland Heights 77 C11
Keller 46 E1; 102 B1
Keller Bay 79 I12
Keller Creek 79 H12
Keller Ranch (private airfield) 68 G6
Kellerville 31 G7
Kellisons Creek 59 J11
Kellogg 47 C8
Kelly 46 B5
Kelly Air Force Base 77 C12; 158 G3
Kelly Creek 48 D4
Kellyville 48 G5
Kellyville Siding 48 G5
Kelsay 87 G11
Kelsey 48 G2
Kelsey Creek 48 G2
Kelton 31 F9
Keltys 60 H3; 147 A7
Kemah 81 A8; 146 E6
Kemp 47 J7
Kempner 57 J9
Ken Ada Ranch (private airfield) 71 G9
Kenbrook 149 E12
Kendalia 68 I6
Kendleton 80 B2
Kenedy 78 H4
Kenefick 72 H3
Kenley Ranch (private airfield) 77 K10
Kennard 60 H1
Kennedale 46 H1; 110 K3
Kennedy Creek 59 G11; 72 A3
Kenneth Copeland (private airfield) 45 E12
Kenney 71 H7
Kensing 47 A12
Kent 51 J10
Kent County (airport) 42 C6
Kent Creek 34 D4
Kentucky Town 38 E6
Kentwood Manor 77 A12; 157 C8
Kenwood 46 G3; 112 F5
Keokuk 48 I5
Kerens 59 A7
Kermit 52 D4
Kerrick 27 B9
Kerrville 68 H2; 141 J8
Kerrville Muni 68 I3
Kerrville–Schreiner State Park 68 I3
Key 41 G11
Key's Ranch (private airfield) 48 A3
Keys Creek 60 C1
Kezer Air Ranch (private airfield) 45 E11
Kicaster Creek 78 D2
Kickapoo Cavern State Park 76 A1
Kickapoo Creek 36 K4; 38 K3; 44 A4; 45 I9; 47 J9, K11; 55 I9; 60 A1, K1; 71 H9; 72 A2
Kickapoo Downtown Airpark 36 I6
Kickapoo Mountain 55 C8
Kidd-Private (private airfield) 38 C5
Kildare 48 E6
Kildare Junction 49 F7
Kilgore 48 J3; 79 H7
Kilgore (private airfield)48 J3
Killam Siding 83 H8
Killeen 57 J11; 142 B3
Killeen Municipal (airport) 57 J11; 142 E4
Killion Ranch (private airfield) 43 G9
Kimball 26 I2
Kimball Creek 72 D4
Kimble County (airport) 67 D11
Kinard Estates 73 G9
Kinchelo Creek 57 I7
Kincheonville 69 G10
King 28 B6; 57 H9
King Air (private airfield) 71 J10
King Creek 60 E3
King Mountain 53 I9
Kings Branch 83 A12
Kings Creek 44 E3, E4; 47 H7, J7
Kings Highway 59 K7
Kings Mill 30 F4
Kings Village 69 E11
Kingsbury 69 K10; 78 A4
Kingsland 68 C6
Kingsland Estates (private airfield) 68 C6
Kingston 47 C7
Kingsville 84 H4; 141 J11
Kingsville NAS 84 H4
Kingswood 46 I3
Kingwood 72 H1
Kinkler 79 A9
Kinsloe 48 J3
Kinwood 71 I12
Kiomatia 38 H1
Kiowa Creek 26 I6; 27 I7; 54 F3
Kirby 78 B1; 159 A12
Kirby Lake 43 J11
Kirbyville 73 C8
Kirbyville (airport) 73 C8
Kirk 58 F4
Kirkland 35 D9
Kirtley 70 I2
Kirvin 58 D6
Kitalou 33 J12
Kitchen Creek 48 F6; 49 G7
Kitten Farm Private (private airfield) 41 B12
Kittie Hill (airport) 69 C10
Kittyhawk (private airfield) 46 D4
Kleberg 46 H5; 114 I6
Kleberg County (airport) 84 G3
Klein 71 H11
Klein Branch 68 F2
Klondike 41 I10; 47 B10
Klump 70 G6
Klutts Field (private) 46 F6
Knickerbocker 54 I6
Knight Branch 70 E2
Knight Lake 73 K8
Knights Bluff Landing 48 C6
Knippa 76 D6
Knob Hill 45 K8
Knoblaw 28 E5
Knolle 84 D4
Knott 41 J12
Knowd 58 J1; 164 G6
Knox City 43 A11
Koerth 79 C9
Kohrville 71 H11
Kokernot 79 B7
Kokomo 44 K5
Komensky 79 A8
Koockville 68 B2
Koppe 71 D7; 96 K5
Kopperl 57 B12
Kornegay (private airfield) 88 H5
Kosciusko 78 E3
Kosmos 85 D8
Kosse 58 H5
Kossuth 59 E11
Kountze 72 E6
Kovar 70 I1
Krams Creek 78 B3
Krebsville 70 I5
Kress 33 D12
Kreutzberg 68 J5
Krum 46 C1
Kubala Store 78 E6
Kubecka Aviation (private airfield) 80 H1
Kurten 71 B7
Kuy Creek 79 I8
Kyle 69 I10
Kyle Mountain 45 F7
Kyote 77 F10

L

L Davis Ranch (private airfield) 76 B2
L P Askew Farms (private airfield) 41 E10
L W B Ranch (private airfield) 50 D3
La Bahia 70 G5
La Belle 73 J7
La Blanca 88 G3
La Casa 44 H5
La Casita 87 G11
La Cerda 60 G5
La Esperanza Ranch (private airfield) 82 C6
La Feria 88 H4
La Fonda Ranch (private airfield) 86 D6
La Fruta 84 C4
La Gloria 84 J2; 87 C12
La Grange 70 I3
La Grulla 87 G11
La Guna 62 F2
La India 84 K2
La Jarita Creek 77 I12
La Joya 87 H12
La Joya Creek 87 F12
La Joya Lake 87 G12
La Junta 45 F11; 74 A3
La Leona 88 G6
La Leona (private airfield) 75 C7
La Marque 81 C8; 165 K8
La Mota Mountain 74 B5
La Paloma 88 I5
La Para 78 K3
La Para Creek 78 K3
La Parita 77 G12
La Parita Creek 78 H1
La Parra Landing 84 J5
La Penusca 88 I6
La Porte 72 K2
La Porte Municipal (airport) 72 K2
La Pryor 76 G4
La Puerta 87 G11
La Reforma 88 D1
La Sal Vieja 88 E3
La Salle 79 H11
La Tuna 62 E1
La Vernia 78 C2
La Villa 88 G3
La Ward 79 G12
Laban 70 K6
Laborcitas Creek 83 I12; 84 I1
Laceola 59 K8
Lacey Field (private) 60 H4
Lackey Aviation (private airfield) 80 D2
Lackland AFB Training Annex 77 C11
Lackland Air Force Base 77 C11; 158 F1
Lackland City 77 C11
Lackland Heights 77 C11
Lackland Terrace 77 B11
Lacoste 77 C10
Lacy Creek 48 B3; 54 D2, D3
Lacy-Lakeview 58 F2; 167 A11
Lacyville 60 G4
Ladonia 47 A9
LaFayette 48 F3
Lafitte 71 K7
Lagarto 84 C3
Lagarto Creek 83 C12; 84 C1
Lago Vista 69 E9
Lago Vista Bar-K Airpark 69 D9
Lagrone Ranch (private airfield) 46 F6
Lagroulle Creek 60 G6
Laguna 76 B4
Laguna Atascosa 88 H6
Laguna Atascosa National Wildlife Refuge 89 H7
Laguna Heights 89 H7
Laguna Larga 84 H6; 89 I7
Laguna Madre 84 K6; 88 C6
Laguna Park 58 D1
Laguna Salada 84 J4, K2
Laguna Seca 88 E2
Laguna Vista 89 I7
Lagunillas Creek 77 G10, H11
Lahey 41 D8
Laird Hill 48 J3
Lajitas 74 D6
Lajitas (private airfield) 74 D6
Lake Abilene 43 K10
Lake Alice 84 E3
Lake Alvarado 46 J1
Lake Amon G Carter 45 A10
Lake Anahuac 72 J4
Lake Arlington 46 G2
Lake Arrowhead 37 J7
Lake Arrowhead State Park 37 I7
Lake Athens 47 K10; 59 A10
Lake Austin 69 F10; 80 H4; 92 C6
Lake Barbara 80 F6
Lake Barbara 142 J6
Lake Bastrop 70 G1
Lake Bay Gall (private airfield) 72 E1
Lake Bend 142 I5
Lake Bob Sandlin 48 D2
Lake Bob Sandlin State Park 48 D1
Lake Bonanza (private airfield) 71 F11
Lake Bonham 39 D8
Lake Brazos 167 D11
Lake Bridgeport 45 C10
Lake Brownwood 56 D3
Lake Brownwood State Park 56 D3
Lake Buchanan 69 A7
Lake Carolyn 104 G4
Lake Casa Blanca 83 G7
Lake Casa Blanca International State Park 83 H7; 143 A12
Lake Catharine 35 K11
Lake Charlotte 72 J4
Lake Cherokee 48 J4
Lake Cisco 44 J3
Lake Clyde 44 K1
Lake Coleman 55 B12; 56 B1; 164 F1
Lake Colorado City 42 J4
Lake Colorado City State Park 42 K4
Lake Como 109 E7
Lake Conroe 71 E11
Lake Corpus Christi 84 B3
Lake Corpus Christi State Park 84 C4
Lake Creek 47 A11; 58 G3
Lake Creek 36 K1; 37 I7; 43 A12, C11; 44 A1; 45 H7; 47 A11; 59 D10; 71 C9
Lake Creek Lake 58 G3
Lake Crockett 39 D9
Lake Crook 39 D11
Lake Cypress Springs 48 D1
Lake Dallas 46 D3; 145 A11
Lake Daniel 44 H4
Lake Davis 35 K11
Lake Diversion 36 I4
Lake Dunlap 69 K8
Lake Edinburg 88 F2
Lake Forest 149 J9
Lake Fork Creek 47 E9, G12
Lake Fork Reservoir 47 G11
Lake Fort Parker 58 F5
Lake Fort Phantom Hill 43 H11
Lake Georgetown (USACE) 69 C10
Lake Georgetown 69 C10
Lake Gladewater 48 I2
Lake Gonzales 78 B5
Lake Graham 44 D5
Lake Granbury 45 J11
Lake Halbert 58 B6
Lake Harlingen 141 C8
Lake Hawkins 47 H12; 48 H1
Lake Holbrook 47 H11
Lake Houston 72 I1
Lake Houston State Park 72 G1
Lake J B Thomas 42 H2
Lake Jackson 80 F6; 142 I4
Lake Jacksonville 59 C12
Lake James 148 C3
Lake June 114 D4
Lake Kemp 36 I2
Lake Kickapoo 36 J5
Lake Kiowa 38 E3

continue on next page

INDEX, cont'd

M

Mud Lake 81 A12; 146 C4
Mud Point 79 I12
Muddy Creek 46 D5; 107 C10
Mudge Draw 67 F12
Mudville 70 C5
Muehlsville 78 A3
Mueller Municipal (airport) 69 F11
Muellersville 70 H6
Muenster 38 D1
Muerto Creek 84 E2
Muhle Creek 36 K3; 44 A3
Muil 84 F2
Mukewater Creek 56 F2
Mulberry 39 D7
Mulberry Creek 30 I2, K4; 34 A4; 43 I11, J10; 54 F4; 58 I6; 68 B3; 70 K2
Mulberry Springs 48 H4
Muldoon 70 J2
Mule Creek 35 G12; 43 D11; 55 E7; 78 A6; 83 A11
Muleshoe 32 E6
Muleshoe Municipal (airport) 33 F7
Muleshoe National Wildlife Refuge 32 H6
Mulkey 33 C9
Mullin 56 F5
Mullin Creek 56 F5
Mullins Landing (private airfield) 46 D6
Mullins Prairie 70 J4
Mumford 70 B5
Muncy 34 G2
Munday 43 A12
Munday Municipal (airport) 43 A12
Munger 58 D4
Munger Branch 58 D5
Mungerville 41 G10
Munson 47 F7
Murchison 47 K10
Murchison Creek 47 K10
Murdo 29 E8
Murphee Wildlife Management Impoundments Area 73 J8
Murphy 46 E5
Murphy Creek 44 F2; 60 C5
Murray 44 D4
Murvaul Bayou 60 B5
Murvaul Bayou Creek 60 B6
Musgrove 48 E1
Musquiz Canyon 63 D12
Musquiz Creek 63 D12; 64 D2
Mussel Run Creek 58 I3
Mustang 46 B3; 58 I5
Mustang Bayou 81 D7
Mustang Beach (airport) 85 E8
Mustang Community Airfield (private) 46 B3
Mustang Creek 45 I11; 46 B3, J4; 47 A12; 55 D11; 57 F9, K11; 58 E4; 59 F8; 69 C12; 70 D1; 76 F4; 79 C8; 84 A3
Mustang Draw 41 J10; 53 A10, B11
Mustang Field 46 I3
Mustang Island 85 F8
Mustang Island State Park 85 F8
Muxworthy (private airfield) 57 E8
Mykawa 80 A6; 134 H5
Mynatt Field (private) 47 C8
Myra 38 E1
Myrtle 71 K12
Myrtle Creek 68 J3
Myrtle Springs 47 H9
Myska Field (private) 46 D2

N

Naaman 46 E5; 106 A6
Nabors Creek 56 H6
Naclina 60 H5
Nacogdoches 60 F4; 149 H11
Naconiche Creek 60 D4, E5
Nada 79 C12
Nadeau 81 C8; 165 J9
Nail Creek 60 B6
Nails Creek 70 F4
Nameless 69 D9
Nancy 60 J5
Nanny Branch 56 B4
Napier 72 D2
Naples 48 C4
Narciseno Creek 84 G2
Narcisso 35 G7
Naruna 57 K7
Nash 46 K4; 49 A7
Nash Creek 44 K5; 78 A4
Nassau Bay 81 A8; 146 E3
Nassau Bay (private airfield) 45 J11
Nat 60 E3
Natalia 77 D10
Natural Dam Lake 41 K12; 53 A12
Navarro 58 B6
Navarro Mills 58 C4
Navarro Mills Lake (USACE) 58 C4
Navarro Mills Lake 58 C4
Navasota 71 E8
Navasota Municipal (airport) 71 E8
Navasota River 58 D3, E4, F6; 59 K7; 71 A7, D7
Navidad 79 E10
Navidad River 79 A10, D10, E10
Navo 46 C3
Nazareth 33 C10
Nebletts Creek 71 D12
Necessity 44 H5
Nechanitz 70 H4
Neches 59 D11
Neches River 47 I10; 59 C12; 60 F1, K5; 73 C7, I8; 95 C11; 154 A5
Neddy Creek 78 K6
Nederland 73 I8; 154 B2
Needham House 67 G11
Needmore 32 G6; 41 B8; 47 B9; 61 J7
Needville 80 C3
Negley 38 I2
Negro Creek 59 K11
Neils Creek 57 E11
Neils Creek, Middle Fork 57 E10
Neils Creek, North Fork 57 E10
Neils Creek, South Fork 57 E10
Neinda 43 G9
Nell 78 H3
Nelleva 71 E7
Nelson 46 K3
Nelson City 68 J4
Nelson Creek 71 A11
Nelsonville 70 I6
Nelta 47 B11
Nemo 45 K11
Nena 46 K3
Neri 45 J10
Nesbit 58 J5
Nesbitt 48 H5
Neuville 61 E7
Nevada 46 E6
New Baden 58 K6
New Ballinger Lake 55 E9
New Berlin 78 B2
New Birthright 47 C11
New Blox 61 K8
New Boston 48 A5
New Braunfels 69 K8; 150 C4
New Braunfels Municipal (airport) 69 K9
New Bremen 70 I6
New Caney 72 G1
New Clarkson 58 K3
New Colony 48 D6; 58 K2
New Corn Hill 69 B11
New Davy 78 F5
New Deal 33 J11
New Fountain 77 C9
New Harmony 47 J11
New Harp 45 A11
New Home 41 B11
New Hope 43 F11; 46 C3, C5, F5; 47 H12, K11; 48 A4, E1, K3; 59 A12, C12, G7; 107 J7
New Katy 69 F12
New London 48 K2
New Lynn 41 C12
New Marlin Reservoir 58 H3
New Mesquite 46 D6
New Moore 41 E10
New Mountain 48 F3
New Prospect 60 A4
New Salem 45 H8; 60 C2
New Summerfield 60 C2
New Sweden 69 E12
New Taiton 79 C12
New Ulm 70 I6
New Waverly 71 D11
New Willard 72 B3
New Year Creek 70 F6; 71 G7
New York 59 A10
Newark 45 E12
Newark Beach 45 E12
Newburg 56 D6
Newby 59 H7
Newcastle 44 C5
Newgulf 80 D3
Newgulf (private airfield) 80 D3
Newgulf Junction 80 D3
Newlin 35 B7
Newport 45 A9; 146 H2
Newsome 48 E1
Newt 39 C9
Newton 73 A9
Newton Municipal (airport) 73 A9
Newtonville 70 K2
Neylandville 47 C8
Niblock 56 J1
Nicholas 70 B5
Nichols Creek 73 D9
Nickel 79 A7
Nickel Creek Station 51 C7
Nickleberry 48 D5
Niederwald 69 H11
Nimrod 44 K3
Nine Point Draw 75 A8, A9
Nine Point Mesa 64 K2
Ninemile Creek 55 H8
Ninemile Draw 51 J11; 52 I1
Ninemile Hill 156 H3
Nineteen Draw 64 D5; 65 C7
Ninety 50 I1
Nineveh 59 H9
Nix 57 J7
Nix Creek 163 I9
Nixon 78 D4
Noack 70 D1
Nobility 46 B6
Noble 39 E10
Nockenut 78 C3
Nocona 37 I11
Nocona (airport) 37 I10
Noelke 54 J4
Noelke Creek 53 J11
Noelke Ranch (private airfield) 54 J4
Nogalus 60 I2
Nolan 43 K8
Nolan Creek 39 C12; 57 J10
Nolan River 45 I11, J12, K12; 57 B12
Nolan River, West Fork 45 J12
Nolanville 57 J11
Nolte 78 A3
Nolton Creek 76 C6; 77 D7
Nome 72 H5
Nona 72 F6
Noodle 43 H9
Noonan 77 D10
Noonday 47 K12; 48 I4
Nopal 63 F11; 78 E5
Nordheim 78 G5
Norias 88 C4
Normandy 86 G6
Normangee 59 K8
Normanna 78 J4
Normans Crossing 69 D12
Norrick 31 H9
Norris Field (private) 43 C7
Norris Raun Ranch (private airfield) 79 D12
Norse 57 E11
North Abilene 43 I11
North Beach 84 E6; 98 A4
North Bee House Creek 57 H9
North Bennett Creek 56 F6
North Boggy Creek 44 B2
North Bosque River 57 A8, C9, C11, D12
North Bosque River, North Fork 45 K8
North Bosque River, South Fork 45 K7
North Caney Creek 47 C10
North Cita Creek 29 K12
North Concho River 54 B2, F6
North Cowden 53 B7
North Creek 45 C7; 59 H9
North Croton Creek 35 K8; 43 A9
North Elm 70 A2
North Elm Creek 31 I10; 44 C2, C3; 58 K2
North Fish Creek 38 C1
North Floodway 88 F6
North Fork Buffalo Creek Reservoir 36 G5
North Fork Creek 44 G1
North Fork Running Water Draw 33 D10, E10
North Grape Creek 68 E6
North Groesbeck 35 D11
North Groesbeck Creek 35 D9
North Hickory Creek 46 B1
North Houston 71 I11
North Lake 38 J2; 46 E3; 104 B2
North Lilly Creek 48 E1
North Llano River 67 D8, D10
North Long Dry Creek 31 H7
North Loop 77 B12; 157 H9
North McClellan Creek 30 G5
North Mesquite Creek 57 K8; 107 K7; 115 F10
North Mill Creek 38 J4
North Nolan Creek 57 J11
North Paint Creek 44 C1
North Palo Duro Creek 29 A10; 30 A1
North Paluxy River 45 J8
North Pease River 34 F4; 35 E7
North Plum Creek 29 D11
North Prairie 58 H2
North Prong Creek 46 I3
North Reese Creek 57 K10
North Richland Hills 102 H4
North Roby 43 G7
North Rocky Creek 57 K9
North Salado Creek 69 A11
North Salem 59 H8
North Shadydale 71 J12; 130 D5
North Sherman Junction 38 D5
North Shore 72 H1
North Shore Acres 69 E9
North Simms Creek 57 H7
North Sulphur River 47 A9, A11
North Tule Draw 33 B11
North Twin Creek 47 J8
North Valley Prong 67 A7
North Wichita River 34 I6; 35 I8, I12
North Willis (private airfield) 72 H5
North Zulch 71 A8
Northeast Hills 149 F12
Northfield 34 E6
Northgate 149 E11
Northrup 70 H3
Northshore 85 E7
Northside 36 E2; 109 A8
Northwest Hills 93 B7
Northwest Regional (airport) 46 D1
Norton 55 D9
Norwood 61 H7
Notrees 52 C6
Nottawa 80 A2
Nottingham Country 146 H2
Novice 39 C12; 55 C12
Novohrad 79 A8
Noxville 68 E1
Nueces 84 E6
Nueces Bay 84 E6; 98 A1
Nueces County (airport) 84 E5
Nueces River 76 A3, C4, F5, H5, K6; 77 K8; 78 K2; 83 A8, A12, C10; 84 A1, A3
Nueces River, East Prong 67 H10
Nuevo Laredo 143 D10
Nugent 43 H12
Nunnelee 39 E7
Nursery 79 G8
Nuway 62 E1
Nye 82 G6

O

O C Fisher Lake 55 G7; 162 A2
O H Ivie Reservoir 55 F11
O Neal Creek 78 C5
O S Wyatt (private airfield) 83 I12
O'Brien 43 B11
O'Brien Airpark (private) 46 I4
O'Donnell 41 E11
O'Farrell 48 D6
O'Quinn 70 J3
O. C. Fisher Lake (USACE) 162 D2
Oak Cliff 46 G4; 113 D8
Oak Creek 43 K8; 55 A8, C8
Oak Creek Reservoir 55 B8
Oak Flat 60 D3, I5
Oak Flats 60 C3
Oak Forest 78 B5
Oak Grove 38 K4; 46 H1, K5; 47 B11, F12; 49 D7; 72 E1
Oak Hill 48 K4; 69 F10; 73 B7
Oak Hills 63 G9
Oak Hollow 149 E12
Oak Island 72 K4; 77 D12
Oak Meadow 156 D5
Oak Ridge 60 F5
Oak Village 79 H8
Oakalla 57 K9
Oakbrook 146 B1
Oakdale 47 B11, C12
Oakhurst 71 B12; 109 A11
Oakland 39 D7; 45 A7; 47 I10; 60 D1; 79 A10; 80 F6
Oakland Estates 77 A12; 156 G2
Oaks 78 I3
Oaks (private airfield) 48 K2
Oakville 78 K2
Oakwood 59 F9
Oates Prairie 72 J1; 131 G8
Oatman Creek 68 C5
Oatmeal 69 C8
Oatmeal Creek 69 C8
Obar Creek 79 A8
Obregon 56 E2
Ocaw 58 F2
Ocee 58 F1
Ochoa 63 K8
Ocker 58 J2
Ocotillo Siding 63 K10
Odds 58 G4
Odell 36 D1
Odell Creek 60 H5
Odem 84 D5
Odessa 53 D8; 150 K3
Odessa Meteor Crater 53 E7
Odessa-Schlemeyer Field 53 C8
Odlaw 76 D3
Odom 47 J8
Oenaville 58 J1
Offatt Bayou 126 J1
Ogburn 48 F1
Ogden 35 G9; 44 A2; 78 A2
Ogg 29 K11
Oglesby 57 G12
Ohio 57 F8
Oil City 30 C1
Oil Springs 60 G5
Oildom 36 H6
Oilla 73 H8
Oilton 83 H9
Ojo de Angua 84 H6
Oklahoma 71 G11
Oklahoma Draw 30 K6; 31 J7
Oklahoma Flat 33 I8
Oklahoma Lane 32 D5
Oklahoma Yards 36 H6
Oklaunion 36 F2
Ola 47 I7
Olcott 81 A7; 135 J11
Old Ballinger Lake 55 D9
Old Barnum 60 K4
Old Boston 48 A5
Old Brazoria 80 F5
Old Casa Blanca Fort 84 C4
Old Davy 78 E5
Old Diana 48 G4
Old Dime Box 70 E3
Old Elwood 59 J9
Old Flatonia 70 K2
Old Fort Anahuac 72 K4
Old Fort Parker 58 F5
Old Glory 43 D9
Old Kinkler 79 A9
Old London 48 K2
Old Marlin City Lake 58 H3
Old Mobile 72 A5
Old Moulton 79 A8
Old Norway Mill 57 E11
Old Noxville 68 E1
Old Ocean 80 E4
Old Reb (private airfield) 88 H4
Old River 70 D6; 72 I3; 83 A12
Old River Cove 73 I9
Old River Lake 72 J3
Old Saint Marys 85 C8
Old Salem 48 A5
Old Santa Elena 87 C12
Old Union 48 B5, C3; 58 G6
Old Waverly 71 D12
Olden 44 J5
Oldenburg 70 I4
Oldham 46 F3; 104 F6
Oldham County (airport) 29 H8
Oletha 58 H6
Olfen 55 F10
Olin 57 C8
Oliver Creek 45 C12
Olivia 79 I12
Ollie 72 B3
Olmito 88 I6
Olmos 84 B4; 87 G11
Olmos Creek 77 A12; 78 I2; 156 E3
Olmos Park 77 B12; 157 K7; 159 A7
Olney 44 B5
Olney Municipal (airport) 44 B4
Olton 33 F9
Omaha 48 C4
Omen 60 A1
Onalaska 72 B1
Onalaska Lookout 72 A1
One Arm Creek 59 D12
One Sixty Four Place (private airfield) 45 D8
Onion Creek 58 A5
Onion Creek 36 K6; 56 I2; 58 A4; 69 G8
Opdyke 33 K9
Opelika 47 K10
Opossum Creek 69 B12
Ora 60 I5
Oran 45 E8
Orange 73 H9; 151 C8
Orange County (airport) 73 H9
Orange Grove 84 D3
Orange Harbor Island 151 D9
Orangedale 78 K4
Orangefield 73 H9
Orangeville 46 A6
Orchard 80 A3
Orchard Substation 80 A3
Ore City 48 G4
Orelia 77 I10
Orient 43 I7; 55 E8
Orla 51 D11
Orozimbo 80 D5
Orrs 48 F5
Ort 51 H9
Orton Lake 149 H11
Orvil 83 G7
Osage 57 F11
Oscar 58 K1
Osceola 58 A1
Osman 65 I12
Oso Bay 85 F7
Oso Creek 84 F6
Otey 80 D5
Otis Chalk 54 A2
Otter Creek 36 C3; 59 C10
Ottine 78 A5
Otto 58 G4
Ovalo 55 A11
Overcup Landing 48 C6
Overland 47 D10
Overton 48 K2
Ovilla 46 I3
Owens 34 K2; 56 D4
Owens Creek 58 H6
Owensville 58 J5
Owentown 48 J1
Owl Creek 57 I12
Owl Creek 57 I11; 59 C12
Owlett Green 47 I10
Ox Yoke Creek 35 J9
Oxford 68 C5
Oyster Bayou 72 K5
Oyster Creek 80 F6
Oyster Creek 80 A4, C5; 132 H1, K5; 142 I5
Oyster Lake 80 I1
Ozan Creek 39 E10
Ozona 66 B3
Ozona Municipal (airport) 66 B3

P

P-K Ranch (private airfield) 71 H7
Pacio 47 A11
Packsaddle Mountain 68 C6
Padgett 44 B4
Padre Island 85 H7; 89 B7
Padre Island National Seashore 85 H7; 89 C7
Paducah 35 G8
Pafford Crossing 66 K4
Paige 70 G2
Paint Creek 43 D11
Paint Creek 43 D12, E10; 44 D1; 56 B3; 67 G11, H11
Paint Gap Hills 75 C9
Paint Horse Draw 51 G8
Paint Rock 55 G10
Paisano 63 F12
Paisano Creek 84 J3
Paisano Ranch (private airfield) 78 K1
Pakan 31 G7
Palacios 80 I1
Palacios Municipal (airport) 80 H1
Palacios Point 80 J1
Palafox 82 E4
Palava 43 I8
Palestine 47 D9; 59 D11; 151 C11
Palestine Municipal (airport) 59 D10
Palito Blanco 84 G2
Palm Grove 88 K6
Palm Harbor 85 D8
Palma Canyon 65 I11
Palmer 46 J5
Palmer Field 46 C1
Palmetal 88 H5; 141 C10
Palmetto 80 A5
Palmetto Creek 72 B1
Palmetto Park 71 B12
Palmetto State Park 78 A5
Palmhurst 88 G1
Palo Alto 84 F4
Palo Alto Creek 68 E4; 77 E12
Palo Alto Heights 77 C12; 158 J4
Palo Blanco Creek 76 F3; 83 J12; 84 J1
Palo Duro (airport) 29 I11; 91 I10
Palo Duro Canyon 29 J12; 30 K1
Palo Duro Canyon State Park 29 J12
Palo Duro Creek 26 I3, K2; 29 J7, I9
Palo Duro Reservoir 26 I3
Palo Gaucho Bayou 61 G8
Palo Pinto 45 G7
Palo Pinto Creek 45 H7, H8
Palo Pinto Creek, North Fork 44 I6
Palo Pinto Creek, South Fork 44 J6
Palo Pinto Creek, West Fork 44 J6
Palobia Creek 84 J3
Paloduro 30 K3
Paloma 76 G1
Paluxy 45 K10
Paluxy River 45 K9
Pamela Heights 80 A5; 133 H10
Pampa 30 E4; 155 F8
Pamplin Creek 60 K6
Pancake 57 F10
Pandale 66 G1
Pandora 78 D3
Panhandle 30 G2; 48 C6
Panhandle-Carson County (airport) 30 G2
Panna Maria 78 F4
Panola 49 J7
Panola County 60 A6
Pantego 46 G2; 110 F6
Panther Bluff Waterhole 67 A8
Panther Canyon 150 B4
Panther Creek 37 I11; 46 C3; 48 K4; 55 F12; 68 D2; 78 H4
Panther Hollow 77 H8
Panther Junction 75 C9
Panther Peak 75 C9
Panther Point 85 B10
Papalote 84 B5
Papalote Creek 84 B5
Papalote de en Medio 84 I3
Papalote del Norte 88 A3
Paper Mill Creek 60 G4
Papoose Creek 35 C10
Paradise 45 D11
Paradise Creek 35 G12; 36 H1
Paris 39 D11; 151 J8
Parita Creek 78 C1
Park 70 I4
Park Place 134 C6
Park Springs 45 A10
Parkdale Lake 114 B1
Parkdale Plaza 85 F7
Parker 46 D5, K1; 70 C5
Parker County (airport) 45 G11
Parker Creek 29 F9
Parker Field 46 H6
Parker Hollow Creek 78 K5
Parkers Creek 77 C8
Parkwood Estates 71 I12
Parmerton 32 B6
Parnell 34 C6
Parrilla Creek 83 F12
Parrilla Creek South 83 G11
Parrish Airstrip (private) 57 D10
Parsley Crossing 57 F8
Partridge Creek 57 F7
Parvin 46 C3
Pasadena 72 K1; 135 D9; 146 A2
Pasche 55 I11
Paso Real 88 G6
Pass Cavallo 79 K12
Pastura 43 E10
Pat Mayse Lake (USACE) 39 C11
Pat Mayse Lake 39 C11
Patillo 45 I8
Patricia 41 I10
Patrick 46 I5
Patrick Creek 45 H10
Patroon 61 F8
Patroon Bayou 61 F8
Patterson Creek 57 I8; 67 K11
Patterson Hills 50 D6
Pattison 71 J8
Pattonville 39 E12
Paul Junction 56 J2
Pauline 47 K8
Pauls Store 61 D8
Pavlat (private airfield) 72 H2
Paw Paw Bayou 49 I7
Pawelekville 78 F3
Pawnee 78 I3
Paxton 61 C7
Payne 48 F6
Payne Springs 47 K8
Paynes 80 A5
Paynes Corner 40 G6
Payton 69 H7
Pea Patch (private airfield) 71 I8
Peace Valley Harbor 84 B4
Peach Creek 71 D7
Peach Creek 70 J1, K1; 71 D7; 72 G1; 79 B7; 80 C2
Peach Tree Village 60 K4
Peacock 43 C7
Peadenville 45 F9
Pear Valley 55 H12
Pearce Lake 146 E2
Pearl 57 G9
Pearl City 79 C7
Pearland 80 A6
Pearsall 77 G9
Pearson 77 D10
Pearson Ranch (private airfield) 79 C8
Pearsons Chapel 59 J11
Pease River 35 E9, G12; 36 F1
Peaster 45 F10
Peavy 60 H3
Pecan Bayou 38 I1, J3; 56 B1, F4; 97 A8
Pecan Bayou, North Prong 44 K1
Pecan Bayou, South Prong 43 K12; 56 A1
Pecan Creek 46 B3; 47 B9; 54 C6; 55 I7; 57 E9; 58 B3; 68 A5; 70 C1
Pecan Forest 146 G2
Pecan Gap 47 A9
Pecan Heights 48 E2
Pecan Park 71 K12; 134 B6
Pecan Plantation (private airfield) 45 J11
Pecan Springs 56 K3
Pecan Wells 57 F7
Peckerwood Hill 141 H11
Pecks Lake 53 D11
Pecos 52 G2
Pecos Municipal (airport) 52 H2
Pecos River 51 A11, E12; 52 E1, H3; 53 I7, K10; 65 A11, D12, F12; 66 G1, J2
Peden 45 E12; 100 A1
Pedernales Falls State Park 69 F8
Pedernales River 68 F2, F5; 69 F7
Pedrosa Creek 29 H9
Peel Junction 71 E10
Peeltown 46 J6
Peerless 47 C10
Pegasus Place Airstrip (private) 69 D10
Peggy 78 H2
Pelham 58 C4
Pelican Bay 100 C1
Pelican Island 79 K12; 81 C9; 100 D2
Pelon Ciz Creek 83 B7
Pemberton Draw 53 D12
Pen Branch 43 A9
Pen Creek 60 D4
Pena Colorado Creek 64 H3
Pena Creek 76 K4
Pendell 57 E12
Pendell Draw 127 G11
Pendleton 58 I1
Penelope 58 D3
Peniel 47 D8
Penitas 87 H12
Penland 38 D6
Pennington 60 I1
Pennington Branch 70 A1
Penson Creek 60 D6
Penwell 53 E7
Peoria 58 C1
Pep 33 I7
Percilla 59 F12
Perdido Creek 79 H7
Perdiz 63 I11
Perdiz Creek 63 H10
Perezville 88 H1
Perico 26 D5
Pernitas Point 84 C4
Perriman Creek 57 I9
Perrin 45 E9
Perry 58 G3
Perry Creek 58 F6, I3
Perry Foundation 84 F4
Perry Landing 80 F5
Perry Lefors Field 30 E4
Perry Ranch (private airfield) 66 C4
Perryton 26 I5
Perryton Ochiltree County (airport) 26 I5
Perryville 48 F1
Pershing 69 F11
Persimmon Creek 31 B8
Persimmon Gap 64 K4
Personville 58 G6
Pert 59 C11
Pescadito 83 H8
Peters 71 J7
Peters Creek 48 A3; 69 B7; 78 H6
Peters Prairie 38 K2
Petersburg 34 H1
Peterson Landing 81 D7
Petersville 79 C7
Petrolia 37 G8
Petronila 84 F5
Petronila Creek 84 F4
Petteway 58 I5
Pettibone 70 A2
Pettigrew 39 D8
Pettit 33 F7
Pettus 78 I4
Petty 39 E9; 41 B10
Pettytown 69 I12
Peveto 73 G9
Pew Branch 57 G12
Peyton Creek 80 G3
Pfeffer & Son Farms (private airfield) 71 I9
Pflugerville 69 E11
Phalba 47 J8
Pharr 88 H2; 148 I4
Pheasant 80 H1
Phelan 70 G1
Phelps 71 C12
Phillips 30 D2; 48 H2; 94 H6
Phillips Farm (private airfield) 46 K1
Phillips Flying Ranch (airport) 47 F7
Phillipsburg 70 H6
Philrich 30 D1
Phoenix 77 C12; 158 G5
Phoenix Lake 151 D9
Pickens 47 K9
Pickens Lake 163 D10
Pickett 58 B6
Pickton 47 E12
Picosa Creek 76 H2; 78 E2
Picosa Ranch (private airfield) 76 H3
Pidcoke 57 I10
Piedmont 71 D8
Piedra Creek 83 B10
Piedras Pintas Creek 83 F12
Pierce 80 D1
Pierce (private airfield) 37 I8
Pierce Creek 59 A10
Pierce Junction 71 K12; 134 E1
Pigeon Roost Creek 59 J7
Pike 47 B7
Pikes Peak 67 K9
Pikes Peak Draw 66 B2
Pila Blanca 83 E12
Pilgrim 78 D6
Pillar Bluff Creek 57 K8
Pilot Grove Creek 46 B6
Pilot Knob 69 G11
Pilot Knob 77 G8
Pilot Point 46 B3
Pilotgrove 46 A6
Pin Hook 39 C12
Pin Oak 70 H2
Pin Oak Creek 58 D5, I6; 70 A5, G2, J2; 79 C11
Pine 48 F2
Pine Branch 48 A1
Pine Creek 39 C12; 59 H10
Pine Crest 73 G7; 95 A10
Pine Forest 47 D12; 73 G8
Pine Grove 59 C12; 73 H9
Pine Gully 135 C7
Pine Hill 47 D12; 60 C2; 71 C11
Pine Island 72 H6
Pine Island Bayou 72 G5
Pine Island Lake 133 I9
Pine Mills 47 G12
Pine Mountain 64 I6
Pine Prairie 71 B11
Pine Ridge 72 G6
Pine Springs 38 K4; 48 J1; 50 C6
Pine Trail Estates 59 A11
Pine Valley 60 I3; 71 C11
Pinecrest 149 F12
Pinehill 60 B4
Pinehurst 71 G10; 73 H9; 151 C7
Pineland 61 I8
Pineland Municipal (airport) 61 I8
Pineview 48 F1
Pinewood 48 I4
Piney 48 C2
Piney Creek 48 C2; 60 I1, K4; 70 I1
Piney Grove 48 F1
Piney Point Gully 129 K7
Piney Point Village 71 K11; 129 J7
Pinkerton 43 C11
Pinkston Reservoir 60 E6
Pinoak (private airfield) 72 H2
Pinoak Creek 79 D12
Pintas Creek 84 F3
Pinto 86 D6
Pinto Canyon 63 I8
Pinto Creek 76 C1; 86 D6
Pioneer 56 A3
Pioneer Town 69 I8
Pipe Creek 68 K3
Pipe Creek 68 K3
Pipers Meadow 146 D1
Pippen-York Ranch (private airfield) 69 H7
Pirtle 48 K3
Pisek 70 I5
Pisgah 60 E5
Pitner Junction 48 K3
Pittsburg 48 E2
Pittsville 72 H1
Placedo 79 I10
Placedo Creek 79 H9, I10
Placid 56 H2
Plains 40 C6; 41 F12
Plains Assembly 34 H2
Plains Corral 30 K3
Plains Junction 35 C7
Plainview 33 F12; 43 E11, F10; 46 B1; 60 F4, I1; 80 E1; 155 J9
Planeport 62 F2
Plano 46 E4; 153 G10
Plantersville 71 F9
Plaska 34 B6
Plata 63 J11
Plateau 51 J8
Platt 60 G4
Pleak 80 B3
Pleasant Farms 53 E8
Pleasant Grove 46 G5; 47 A9, F12; 57 H7; 58 G5, J3; 60 B2; 114 F4
Pleasant Hill 40 E6; 44 K4; 48 D5; 69 G10; 70 D2; 71 K9
Pleasant Point 46 I2
Pleasant Ridge 59 I9; 60 B6
Pleasant Run 46 H3
Pleasant Springs 59 H9
Pleasant Valley 33 E7; 36 H6; 42 C1; 46 E5; 47 D7; 91 B10; 107 A8
Pleasanton 77 F12
Pleasanton Municipal (airport) 77 F12
Pleasure Field (private) 46 C3
Pleasure Island 154 H6
Pledger 43 G8; 80 D3
Plemons 30 C2
Plover 45 H12
Pluck 60 K4
Plum 70 I3
Plum Branch 44 H3
Plum Creek 27 K8; 29 D11; 42 I1; 57 F9, G10; 61 D7; 69 I10
Plum Creek, Clear Fork 69 I10
Plum Creek, West Fork 69 K11
Plum Grove 72 G3
Plum Hollow 35 E12; 36 E1; 56 J3
Plummers Creek 58 E6
Po-Boy 49 I7
Poblacion de Dolores 83 J7
Podo 80 E3
Poe 60 G4
Point 47 E9
Point Blank 72 B1
Point Comfort 79 I11
Point Enterprise 58 E6
Point Loma 84 C4
Point Penascal 84 J6
Point Venture 69 E9
Polecat Creek 54 B1; 58 I5; 77 C11
Pollok 60 G3
Polly Ranch (private airfield) 81 B7
Polysot Creek 60 G6
Pomeroy 30 F1
Pomona 59 B12
Pompey Creek 56 F5
Pond Creek 48 H2; 58 J2
Pond Springs 69 E10
Ponder 46 C1
Pone 60 B3
Ponton Creek 79 B8
Pontotoc 68 A3
Pony Creek 55 F10; 57 A9
Pool Lookout 71 D10
Poole 47 E10
Pooles Creek 59 K9; 71 A10
Pools Creek 72 B1
Poolville 45 E10
Poor Hollow 67 A8
Poor Joe Creek 60 E6
Poorboy Landing 48 C6
Pope City 48 H6
Porfirio 88 F5
Port Acres 73 I8
Port Alto 79 I12
Port Aransas 85 E8
Port Arthur 73 I8; 154 G5
Port Arthur Freshwater Canal 95 G10
Port Bay 85 C8
Port Bolivar 81 C9
Port Harlingen 88 H5
Port Ingleside 85 E8
Port Isabel 89 I8
Port Isabel Lighthouse State Historic Site 89 I7
Port Isabel-Cameron County (airport) 89 H7
Port Lavaca 79 I11
Port Lavaca State Fishing Pier 79 I11
Port Mansfield 88 E6
Port Mansfield Channel 89 E7
Port Neches 73 I8; 154 A3
Port O'Connor 79 K12
Port Sullivan 70 A4
Porter 72 H1
Porter Creek 61 E7
Porter Ranch (private airfield) 78 I4
Porter Springs 59 I11
Porters Creek 79 D12
Portland 85 E7
Portlock Airfield (private) 43 I12
Posey 41 A12; 47 C10
Possum Kingdom (airport) 45 F7
Possum Kingdom Lake 44 F6; 45 F7
Possum Kingdom State Park 44 F6
Post 42 C2
Post Oak 39 D8, D12; 47 B11
Post Oak Airfield 45 H10
Post Oak Bend 47 H7
Post Oak Creek 38 D5; 43 F12; 44 C4; 58 B4; 69 D9
Post Oak Point 70 I5
Post Oak Ridge 69 D9
Post-Garza County Municipal (airport) 42 C2
Postoak 45 A8
Postoak Creek 68 J5
Poteet 77 F12
Poth 78 E3
Potosi 43 K12
Potranca Creek 77 C11
Potrero Lopeno 88 A6
Potter Creek 69 I7
Potters Creek 48 J5
Pottsboro 38 C5
Pottsville 57 E7
Pounds 56 B6
Powderhorn Lake 79 J12
Powderly 39 C11
Powderly (private airfield) 39 C11
Powell 59 A7; 61 J7
Powell Point 80 B2
Poynor 59 B11
Prade Ranch (private airfield) 67 I11
Praesel 70 C2
Praha 70 K2
Prairie Aire Field (private) 80 C4
Prairie Branch 37 K9; 45 A9
Prairie Creek 47 J12; 48 J2; 59 D8; 61 D7; 114 B4, H4
Prairie Dell 69 A11
Prairie Grove 58 F6; 60 J4
Prairie Hill 58 E4; 70 F6
Prairie Lea 69 K10
Prairie Mountain 68 D4
Prairie Point 39 E8; 45 A12
Prairie Valley 58 C1; 70 I3
Prairie View 71 H8
Prairieville 47 I8
Prattville 47 A11
Preble 45 G9
Preiss Heights 69 K8
Premont 84 I2
Prescott Creek 56 H5
Presidio 74 A3
Presidio La Bahia 79 I7
Presidio Lely Intl (airport) 74 A3
Preston 38 B5
Price 47 B10; 60 A2
Price Ranch (private airfield) 76 I6
Prices 59 C12
Prickly Pear Branch 44 A6
Prickly Pear Hill 158 I5
Priddy 56 E6
Pride 41 E10
Primera 88 H4
Primrose 45 H12
Princeton 46 E5
Pringle 30 B1
Pringle Lake 85 A12
Pritchett 48 H2
Privilege Creek 68 J3
Proctor 57 C7
Proctor Lake (USACE) 56 B6
Proctor Lake 56 C6
Proctor Plaza 71 J12
Proffitt 44 C4
Progreso 88 I3
Progreso (airport) 88 I3
Progress 32 E5
Pronger Bros Ranch (airport) 27 D10
Propwash (private airfield) 46 D1
Prospect 45 A8; 48 F6
Prosper 46 C4
Providence 34 E1; 72 C3
Provident City 79 D11
Pruitt 47 I10; 48 F6
Pruitt Lake 48 E5
Pt Enterprise D&W Ranch (private airfield) 58 E6
Pueblo Nuevo 63 G7
Pueblo Vitoria 51 K12
Puenta Suelas Creek 60 G5
Puente 29 F11
Puertacitas Mountains 63 E11
Puerto Rico 88 D1
Pulliam Creek 67 J9
Pullman 29 H12
Pumphrey 55 B9
Pumpville 65 I12
Punkin Center 35 E10; 41 F10; 44 K4; 45 G11
Punta De Agua Creek 28 C6; 29 E8
Purdon 58 C5
Purdy-Nielsen Memorial Airpark (private) 80 B3
Purgatory Creek 69 J9
Purley 48 D1
Purmela 57 G9
Pursley 58 C5
Purtis Creek 47 J9
Purtis Creek State Park 47 J8
Purves 57 B7
Putnam 44 J2
Putty Ranch (private airfield) 57 C9
Putz (private airfield) 88 H1
Pyle Draw 65 F7
Pyote 52 F4
Pyramid Ranch (private airfield) 59 D7
Pyron Siding 42 H6

Q

Quail 31 K7
Quail Creek 93 A10
Quanah 35 E11
Quanah Municipal (airport) 35 E11
Quapaw Creek 48 J6
Quatro Ranch (private airfield) 76 J6
Quebec 63 D9
Queen City 49 D7
Quemado 86 F6
Quicksand Creek 73 A9
Quihi 77 C9
Quihi Creek 77 C9
Quiney 48 I5
Quinf 70 A3
Quinlan 47 F8
Quinn 73 E8
Quinta Creek 84 D3
Quintana 80 G6; 85 A8
Quintana Beach 80 G6
Quintania Creek 83 A10
Quitaque 34 D4
Quitaque Creek 34 E4
Quitman 47 G11
Quitman Canyon 50 K2
Quitman Mountains 50 J3

R

R D Williams (private airfield) 60 D5
R V Ranch (private airfield) 39 E7
R W J Airpark 72 K3
Rabb 84 E4
Rabbit Creek 48 J3
Rabbs Creek 70 H3
Raccoon Bend 71 H8
Racetrack 47 A10
Rachal 88 B2
Rachal (private airfield) 82 D4
Radicha Creek 84 I4
Radio Junction 57 J8
Radium 43 F10
Rafter J (private airfield) 46 I1
Raggedy Creek 35 G11
Ragsdale Creek 79 C10
Ragtown 39 C10; 61 E8
Ragus Lake 132 G2
Rainbow 45 K11
Rainbow Field (private) 58 C5
Rainbow International (private airfield) 58 F3
Rainey Creek 48 H5; 57 F11
Raisin 79 H8
Raleigh 58 B4
Ralls 34 J2
Rambo 49 F7
Ramirena Creek 84 B3
Ramirena Creek, Salt Branch 84 B2
Ramireno 87 A7
Ramirez 84 I1
Ramsdell 31 H7
Ramsey 70 K6
Ramsey Creek 60 C6
02 Ranch (private airfield) 64 J1
2 G Ranch (private airfield) 70 K5
4-G Ranch (private airfield) 84 I1
6666 Ranch (private airfield) 35 J8
Ranch Branch 68 A1
Ranch Creek 76 A4
Ranch-Aero (private airfield) 77 F10
Rancheros Creek 77 B7
Ranchito 65 H7; 88 I5
Rancho Blanco (private airfield) 83 I7
Rancho Buena Vista (private airfield) 89 G7
Rancho Chula Vista 76 A5
Rancho Cielo 63 E7
Rancho Corazon Nuevo 83 G8
Rancho de la Parrita 84C2
Rancho del Carmine 88 E3
Rancho Del Cielo (private airfield) 51 K10
Rancho Nuevo 88 G6
Rancho Pobre 77 G10
Rancho Viejo 88 I6
Rand 47 I7
Randado 83 K10
Randell Lake 38 C5
Randolph 47 A7
Randolph AFB 78 A1
Randolph AFB Auxiliary 78 A4
Randolph Air Force Base 166 D4
Range A Front Light 85 G7
Range A Light 85 G7
Range Creek 38 E4
Ranger 44 I5
Ranger Creek 68 J4
Ranger Municipal (airport) 44 J5
Ranger Peak 126 A3
Rangerville 88 I4
Rankin 53 I11; 58 A4
Rankin (airport) 53 I10
Rankin Draw 53 I10
Ransom Canyon 33 K12
Ratcliff 60 H1; 87 G11
Ratibor 58 J1
Ratler 56 H5
Rattan 47 A10
Rattler Creek 84 B5
Ravenna 39 D7
Raville Siding 60 H2
Rawhide Creek 77 J11
Rawlins 46 F4; 106 I1
Rawls Creek 60 K6; 68 H6
Rawls Ranch (private airfield) 63 K11
Ray Point 78 J2
Ray Roberts Lake 46 B2
Ray Roberts Lake (USACE) 46 A3
Ray Roberts Lake State Park—Isle du Bois Unit 46 B3
Ray Roberts Lake State Park—Johnson Branch Unit 46 A2
Ray Smith Farm (private airfield) 57 B9
Rayburn 72 E2
Rayford 71 G12
Rayland 36 G1
Raymond 37 H7
Raymondville 88 F4
Rayner Junction 79 A12
Raywood 72 H4
Razor 39 B10
Reagan 58 I4
Reagan Canyon 64 K6
Reagan County (airport) 54 I1
Reagan Wells 76 A5
Reagor Springs 46 K4
Real County (airport) 67 K11
Real Presidio de San Saba 67 A11
Realitos 83 H12
Reavilon 47 D8
Reb Folbre's Place (private airfield) 45 G9
Rebel Field (private) 81 C8
Record Creek 30 I4
Rector Creek 60 F5
Red Ace Ranch (private airfield) 45 C11
Red Bank Creek 55 D12, E9; 56 E1
Red Bayou 38 K6; 48 A5; 60 G3
Red Bluff 51 C11
Red Bluff Creek 66 J5; 68 K4

continue on next page

INDEX, *cont'd*

S

Storey Lake 165 F12
Stout 47 F12
Stout Creek 48 F1
Stouts Creek 47 D12
Stovall Ranch Nr 1 (private airfield) 79 D11
Stover Creek 46 B4
Stowe Creek 59 G12
Stowell 72 J6
Stowers Ranch (private airfield) 67 H12
Strain 72 G5
Stranger 58 H4
Stratford 27 C9
Stratford Field 27 C10
Stratton 79 E8
Stratton Ridge 80 F6
Strawn 44 I6
Streeter 68 B1
Streetman 59 C7
Stricklin Springs 49 J7
Striker Creek Junction 60 C2
Striker Creek 60 C2
String Prairie 70 I1
String Prairie 71 B7
Stringtown 58 K1; 60 A3; 61 I8; 73 A10
Strouds Creek 45 J10
Stubblefield 60 H1
Stubbs 47 J7
Stubbs Strip (private) 45 G12
Study Butte 75 C8
Stumptown 61 J8
Sturdivant 45 G9
Sturgeon 38 C3
Styx 47 J7
Sublett 46 H2; 111 K7
Sublime 79 B10
Sudan 33 G7
Sudan (private airfield) 33 G7
Sudduth 69 C8
Sue 77 F11
Sugar Creek 60 K6; 78 C5
Sugar Land 80 A4, A5; 132 H2
Sugar Land Muni/Hull Field 80 A4; 132 H1
Sugar Valley 80 F3
Suggs 54 J3
Sullivan City 87 G12
Sulphur 49 B7; 60 J2
Sulphur Bluff 47 B12
Sulphur Creek 57 J9; 60 D2; 78 J3
Sulphur Draw 32 K4; 40 A6; 41 B7
Sulphur River 47 B12; 48 B2; 49 B7
Sulphur Springs 47 D11; 60 C3; 164 E2
Sulphur Springs Draw 40 C6; 41 D7, F10, J11
Sulphur Springs Municipal (airport) 47 D11
Summerfield 33 A7; 48 G2
Summerville 78 B6
Summit 34 H6; 69 B8
Sumner 39 D10
Sun Valley 39 D12
Sundown 41 A7
Sunland 78 J2
Sunny Side 71 I8, K12; 134 E2
Sunnylane 69 A8
Sunnyside 33 D9; 73 H7; 78 E3; 95 E9
Sunnyvale 46 G5; 107 K9; 115 A9
Sunray 29 A11
Sunray (airport) 29 A11
Sunrise 61 G7
Sunrise Acres 62 F2
Sunrise Beach 68 B5
Sunrise Beach (airport) 69 C7
Sunset 43 A11; 45 A10
Sunset (private airfield) 46 G6
Sunset Valley 69 G10; 92 K5
Sunshine 57 D8
Sunshine Lake 45 G10
Sunshine Yard 36 H6
Supplejack Creek 79 D8
Surf Oaks 81 A8
Surfside 80 G6
Surfside Beach 80 G6
Sutherland Creek 79 E11
Sutherland Springs 78 D3
Sutton 70 A5
Suttons Mill 60 G6
Swager Creek 43 F12
Swan 47 J12
Swan Lake 79 H11
Swan Point 79 K10
Swansons Landing 49 H7
Swartout 72 C2
Swauano Creek 48 D3
Swearingen 35 F9
Sweeny 80 F4
Sweet Home 79 C8
Sweetwater 43 I7
Sweetwater Creek 31 E7, F9; 43 I9, K7; 45 C12; 56 B6
Swenson 43 C8
Swift 60 F5
Swinney Switch 84 A3
Swiss Alp 70 J3
Sycamore 45 B12
Sycamore Creek 45 K9; 57 A9; 66 K6; 67 D12; 69 C8; 86 A5, D5
Sycamore Creek, East Fork 76 A1
Sycamore Creek, West Fork 66 K5
Sycamore Strip 46 H1
Sylvan 39 D12
Sylvester 43 G8

T

T P Mc Campbell (airport) 85 D7
T-Bar (airport) 41 C11
T-Ranch (private airfield) 77 D10
Tabbs Bay 94 E1
Table Rock Creek 57 I9, I10
Table Top Mountain 53 J10
Tabor 70 B6
Tacubaya 88 B1
Tadmor 60 G1
Taft 84 D6
Tahoka 41 C11
Tahoka Lake 41 C12
Tails Creek 59 D12
Tailspin Airpark (private) 45 H9
Talahone Creek 30 C4
Talbot Lake 67 A9
Talco 48 B1
Talking John Creek 35 F10
Talley Mountain 75 E10
Talpa 55 D11
Talty 46 H6
Tam Anne 33 C7
Tamberg 70 I4
Tamina 71 G12
Tampico 34 C5
Tampico Siding 34 C5
Tan Yard 59 J9
Tanglewood 70 D3
Tankersley 54 H6
Tankersley Creek 48 C2
Tankersley Lake 48 C2
Tanner Bayou 72 F3
Tanner Settlement 72 G4
Tanner's (private airfield) 79 J11
Tantabogue Creek 59 I11, J11
Tanyard 56 K6
Tapado Canyon 74 C4
Tarkington Bayou 72 E1
Tarpley 68 K2
Tarrant 46 F2
Tarrant Field 59 B12
Tarry Bank (private airfield) 68 K5
Tarzan 41 K10
Tascosa 29 E9
Tate Ranch (private airfield) 65 F9
Tate Springs 46 H2; 110 H4
Tatsie 70 B5
Tatum 48 K5
Tatum Ranch (private airfield) 68 G6
Tavener 80 A2
Taylor 69 D12
Taylor (private airfield) 44 G2; 47 E8
Taylor Bayou 154 J2
Taylor Bayou, North Fork 72 I6
Taylor Bayou, South Fork 72 J6
Taylor Creek 44 F2; 57 J9
Taylor Lake 146 C5
Taylor Lake Village 81 A8
Taylor Municipal (airport) 69 D12
Taylor Town 47 A11
Taylor's Air Park (private airfield) 45 J12
Taylorsville 69 I12
Tazewell 47 D11
Teague 59 F7
Teague Municipal (airport) 59 E7
Teaselville 59 A12
Tecifie 43 I8
Tecovas Creek 29 H10
Tecula 60 B1
Tee Pee Creek 34 G6
Tehuacana 58 E5
Tehuacana Creek 58 D6; 59 C7; 77 D8
Tejones Creek 82 E6
Telegraph 67 F10
Telephone 39 C8
Telferner 79 G9
Telico 46 J5
Tell 35 D7
Temco 73 E7
Temple 58 J1; 164 E5
Ten Mile Creek 46 I4
Tenaha 60 C6
Tenaha Creek 61 D7
Teneryville 48 I3
Tenmile 41 H11
Tenmile Draw 67 E7
Tennessee Colony 59 D9
Tenney Creek 69 J11
Tennyson 55 E8
Tepee Draw 54 H3, J3
Tequesquite Creek 86 E6
Terlingua 75 C7
Terlingua (private airfield) 75 C7
Terlingua Abaja 75 D7
Terlingua Creek 63 I12; 64 K1; 75 B7, D7
Terlingua Ranch (airport) 75 B8
Terneros Creek 74 A4
Terrapin Creek 60 E5
Terre Rouge Creek 39 D11
Terrell 47 G7
Terrell County (airport) 65 H9
Terrell Hills 77 B12; 157 K9; 159 A9
Terrell Municipal (airport) 47 G7
Terrell Plaza 77 B12
Terrell Wells 77 C12; 158 J6
Terrett Draw 67 B9
Terry 73 H8
Terry Chapel 58 K2
Terry County (airport) 41 C9
Terryville 79 D8
Tesco 43 I8
Tesnus 64 G5
Texarkana 49 A7; 163 J8
Texas A and M Flight Test Station (private airfield) 70 C6
Texas City 81 C9; 165 I11
Texas City Canal 165 K11
Texas City Junction 81 C8
Texas Menhaden Strip (private) 73 K8
Texas Point National Wildlife Refuge 73 K8
Texas State Railroad State Park 59 D12
Texhoma 27 B11
Texla 73 G8
Texline 26 C4
Texon 53 I12
Texroy 30 D2
Thalia 35 H12
The Big Tree 76 B5
The Bowl 50 C6
The Carter Memorial (airport) 69 K11
The Colony 46 D3
The Crossroads 70 B2
The Forks 72 G4
The Grove 57 I12
The Heights 80 B6
The Knobbs 70 E2
The Lake 97 H9
The Landing 146 H1
The Solitario 74 B6
Thedford 47 I12
Theis Hill 157 D10
Thelma 58 F5; 77 D12
Theon 69 B11
Thermo 47 D11
Theuvenins Creek 72 D6
Thicket 72 E4
Thicket Siding 72 E4
Thickety Creek 73 A8
Third Creek 27 I7
Thomas Creek 68 K2; 78 F5
Thomaston 79 F8
Thompson 128 B2
Thompson Chapel 80 A4
Thompson Creek 43 G10
Thompson Flyers (private airfield) 80 E1
Thompsons 80 B5
Thompsons Creek 70 B6
Thompsonville 70 K1; 83 J10
Thorn Hill 69 K8
Thornberry 37 G7
Thorndale 70 C1
Thorne 38 D4
Thornton 58 G5
Thorntonville 52 F5
Thorp (private airfield) 41 I11
Thorp Spring 45 I10
Thrall 70 C1
Threadgill Creek 68 E2
Three Bridges 71 A7
Three Corrals Creek 30 C5
Three Leagues 41 I10
Three Oaks 78 F2
Three Points 69 E9, E11
Three Rivers 78 K2
Three States 49 E8
Three Way 57 A9
Threemile Creek 70 B4; 71 H8
Threemile Mesa 64 A6
Thrift 36 F5
Thrifty 56 D3
Throckmorton 44 C2
Throckmorton Municipal (airport) 44 C2
Thurber 45 I7
Thurber Lake (private airfield) 45 I7
Thurmond Lake 80 C5
Thurston Canyon 65 H10
Tiawichi Creek 48 K3
Tidwell 47 C8
Tidwell Prairie 58 J5
Tierra Blanca Creek 29 K9; 32 A4; 33 A7
Tierra Linda Ranch (private airfield) 68 G2
Tiffin 44 I5
Tiger Creek 56 K2; 61 G8
Tigerbird Field (private) 58 E1
Tigertown 39 D9
Tigerville 72 B2
Tigua 62 G2
Tiki Island 81 D8
Tilden 77 K12
Tilmon 69 J12
Timber 71 F12
Timber Creek 38 E3; 46 D2; 145 G10
Timber Mountain 63 A11
Timberlane Acres 72 H1
Timesville 59 F10
Timpson 60 C5
Tin Top 45 H10; 80 H2
Tinaja 63 G11; 64 K5
Tinaja Mountains 64 I3
Tinsley Creek 79 A7
Tioga 46 A3
Tira 47 B11
Titley 64 D1
Tivoli 79 K9
Tivydale 68 F3
Tobacco Creek 41 G12; 42 G1
Toco 39 D10
Todd 71 F9
Todd City 59 C11
Todos Santos Creek 77 H7
Todville 81 A8; 146 C6
Togo 70 I1
Tokio 41 C7
Toland 43 J9
Tolar 45 J9
Tolbert 36 E1
Toledo 61 I10
Toledo Bend Reservoir 61 G9
Toliver Branch 60 E4
Tolosa 47 J7
Toluca 88 I3
Tom Ball Creek 34 F4
Tom Bean 38 E6
Tom Creek 60 G4
Tom Danaher (airport) 36 I6
Tom J Moore Farm (private airfield) 71 E7
Tomball 71 G10, H11
Tomlinson Hill 58 I3
Tompkins Mill Creek 72 A6
Tongue River 34 H4; 35 G7
Tonk Creek 57 G12
Tool 47 K7
Topsey 57 I9
Tordillo Creek 78 G2
Torian 84 F3
Tornillo 62 I4
Tornillo Creek 75 D10
Toro Creek 78 I3; 84 E1
Toronto 63 F12
Torres Creek 83 F9
Tortuga Creek 76 I5
Tours 58 D2
Tow 68 A6
Town & Country Airpark 41 A11
Town Bluff 73 B7
Town Branch 45 J12
Town Creek 59 E10; 68 H2
Town Lake 69 F11; 93 J9
Town Resaca 95 J8
Townsend Creek 38 E1
Toyah 51 H12
Toyah Creek 52 H3, I2, J1
Toyah Lake 52 H2
Toyahvale 51 K12
Tracy 70 B2
Tradewind (airport) 29 H11; 91 H10
Trading Post 69 F9
Tradinghouse Creek Airstrip (private) 58 F3
Tradinghouse Creek Reservoir 58 F3
Trammels 80 A5
Tramperos Creek 28 A3
Tranquitas Creek 84 G3
Tranquitas Lake 84 G3
Trap Travelstead Field (private) 48 J2
Travis 58 J3
Trawick 60 D4
Traylor Tick Farm (private airfield) 71 I7
Treichel 71 H10
Trent 43 I9
Trenton 46 A6
Tres Palacios Bay 80 I1
Tres Palacios River 80 E1, F1
Trevat 60 J2
Tri-County Aerodrome (private) 46 A6
Tri-Modal Air Park (private airfield) 69 C10
Triangle 58 I3
Triangle Ranch (private airfield) 35 G9
Tribune 38 E5
Trickham 56 F2
Trigg Street Yard 49 A7
Trinidad 59 A8
Trinidad Creek 84 G2
Trinidad Lake 59 A8
Trinity 59 K12
Trinity Bay 72 K3
Trinity Mills 46 E3; 152 J1
Trinity River 46 G3, I5; 47 K7; 59 A7, E10, I10; 71 A11; 72 E3, I3; 113 A8, D11; 114 G2, K5
Trinity River, Clear Fork 45 F10, G11, G12; 108 J5; 109 F8
Trinity River, East Fork 38 E4; 46 B5; 115 B12, K12
Trinity River, Elm Fork 37 K12; 38 E2; 46 A2, B3
Trinity River, South Fork 45 G11
Trinity River, West Fork 44 A5; 45 A7, B9, C11; 46 G2; 103 K11; 109 C7, D12; 110 B1, B5; 111 A9; 112 A5, C2
Trio 76 C6
Triple R (private airfield) 77 D12
Tripp 46 G5; 115 A9
Troup 60 A1
Trout Creek 61 K7; 73 C9
Troy 58 I1
Truby 43 H10
Truce 45 A9
True 44 C5
Trujillo Creek 28 G5
Trull (private airfield) 80 H1
Trulock Ranch Field (private) 42 J5
Trumbull 46 I5
Truscott 35 I11
Truscott Brine Control Lake 35 I10
Tschirhart Ranch (private airfield) 68 E4
TSTC Waco (airport) 58 F2
Tubbs Corner 53 H7
Tucker 59 E10
Tuckers Corner 48 A4
Tuff 68 J1
Tulane 73 H9
Tularosa (private airfield) 76 B2
Tule Creek 33 C12; 34 C1
Tule Lake Channel 98 B1
Tuleta 78 J4
Tulia 33 C12
Tulip 39 C8
Tulsita 78 I4
Tunas Creek 53 K9; 65 A8; 84 G5
Tundra 47 I9
Tunis 70 D5
Turcotte 88 A4
Turkey 34 D5
Turkey Creek 48 E4
Turkey Creek 34 E6; 36 B1; 37 H7; 45 A8, F8; 46 J1; 47 E9; 48 E5, J6; 55 D10; 56 B2; 57 D11, H8; 59 A9; 69 C12; 70 C1; 71 D12; 76 E4; 77 H11; 79 C7; 80 B2; 135 K11
Turkey Hill Wilderness 60 H6; 61 H1
Turkey Hollow 69 D10
Turkey Mountain 76 C2
Turkey Roost Creek 56 J4
Turkey Run Creek 57 J10
Turlington 59 E8
Turnbaugh Corner 52 C6
Turner Branch 73 C7
Turner Lake 48 A2
Turnersville 57 F10; 69 H10
Turney 60 C1
Turning Basin 165 K12
Turnpike Creek 60 C1
Turtle Bay 80 I1
Turtle Bayou 56 C1; 72 I4
Turtle Creek 68 I2; 80 H1
Turtle Hole Creek 34 F6
Tuscola 55 A11
Tuscosso Creek 60 F5
Tuxedo 43 E10
Twelvemile Creek 68 B3; 79 F7
Twelvemile Mesa 64 B5
Twichell 26 I5
Twin Bridges 51 J10; 58 G5
Twin Buttes Reservoir 55 H7
Twin City 38 D5
Twin Creek 85 A9
Twin Grove 27 I7
Twin Lakes 41 D10
Twin Mill 28 B6
Twin Mills 63 K9
Twin Mountains 44 D6
Twin Mountains 63 E12
Twin Oak Reservoir 58 I6
Twin Sisters 69 H7
Twin-Oaks (airport) 77 A12
Twitty 31 G8
Two Bush Branch 45 E9
Two Leggs (private airfield) 40 E5
Tye 43 J10
Tyler 47 J12; 165 C11
Tyler County (airport) 72 B5
Tyler Pounds Field 47 J12
Tyler State Park 47 I12
Tynan 84 B4
Tyson 58 D1

U

Uhland 69 I10
Umbarger 29 J10
Uncertain 49 G7
Underwood 33 G11
Union 41 A12, E9, H10; 42 G4; 47 D12; 71 A7; 78 C4
Union Center 56 A4
Union Grove 43 A10; 48 I3; 57 K11
Union High 58 D5
Union Hill 46 A2; 47 A7; 48 F2; 57 I12; 70 G5
Union Valley 47 F7, G7
Unity 39 C10; 78 D3
Universal City 78 A1; 166 C4
University Green 146 C2
University Heights 85 F7
University Park 46 F4; 105 H10; 156 E3
Upland 53 H10
Upland Island Wilderness 60 J6
Upper City Lake 151 C10
Upper Keechi Creek 59 E8, G9
Upper Meyersville 79 G7
Upper Nueces Reservoir 76 H5
Upper Sulphur Creek 60 J3
Upton 70 H1
Upton County (airport) 53 J9
Urbana 72 D2
Urebeno 87 B8
Urschel Ranch (private airfield) 31 B8
Utley 69 G12
Utopia 76 A6
Uvalde 76 D5; 164 I2

V

Vaden Creek 47 B11
Vahlsing 84 C4
Vair 60 I3
Val Verde 70 A1; 88 H3
Valdasta 46 B6
Valentine 63 D8
Valera 55 E12
Valley Acres Reservoir 88 H4
Valley Branch 79 A7
Valley Creek 55 A9, C9
Valley Creek, South Fork 55 A8
Valley Farm 52 I1
Valley Grove 60 C3
Valley Hi 77 C11
Valley Junction 70 A5
Valley Lake 38 D6
Valley Mills 57 E12
Valley Mills Municipal (airport) 57 F12
Valley Oaks (private airfield) 45 F10
Valley Plant (private airfield) 38 E6
Valley Ridge 46 H1
Valley Spring 68 A4
Valley View 35 G7; 36 H5; 37 H11; 42 I5; 46 A2; 55 D7; 58 F1; 69 J7
Valley Wells 76 J6
Van 47 I10
Van Alstyne 46 A5
Van Horn 50 K6
Van Horn Creek 62 C6
Van Horn Mountains 62 B6
Van Pelt 80 E6
Van Raub 68 K5
Van Vleck 80 F3
Vance 67 J10
Vancourt 55 H9
Vandalia 38 J2
Vanderbilt 79 H11
Vanderpool 67 K12
Vandyke 56 C6
Varisco 70 C5
Varisco (private airfield) 70 C5
Varner Creek 80 D4
Varner–Hogg Plantation State Historic Site 80 E4
Vasco 47 A11
Vashti 37 K9
Vasterling Creek 68 C4
Vattmannville 84 I4
Vaughan 58 C2
Veale Creek 44 F5
Vealmoor 42 I1
Vega 29 H8
Velasco Heights 80 F6
Velenzuela Creek 82 B5
Vemo 58 F2
Venable 61 G7
Venadito 88 I4
Venado Creek 79 H11; 83 D8
Venchoner Creek 45 B10
Venetia 59 J7
Ventura 71 G10
Venus 46 J2
Venus (private airfield) 46 J2
Vera 35 J12
Vera Cruz 84 H1
Verbena 42 C3
Verde Creek 68 I3; 77 B9
Verdi 78 F1
Verdolaga Lake 89 J7
Verhalen 52 J1
Verhelle 79 F8
Veribest 55 G8
Vernon 36 F2
Verona 46 C6
Vesrue 52 C4
Vessey 38 J2
Veterans Lake 164 G6
Viboras 87 D10
Vick 55 H9
Victor 56 A6; 72 I1
Victoria 58 F4; 79 H9; 166 J2
Victoria Barge Canal 79 I9
Victory 48 G5
Victory City 48 A6
Vidaurri 79 K8
Vidor 73 G8
Vienna 79 C10
View 43 K10
Vigo Park 34 B1
Vilas 70 A1
Vilbig Lake 112 A2
Villa 56 F5
Villa Cavazos 88 I5
Villa Creek 87 A9
Villa Nueva 88 J6
Village Creek 37 H11; 46 J5; 47 H11; 72 E6; 73 F7; 110 E5
Village Creek State Park 73 F7
Village Mills 72 D5
Vincent 42 I3
Vinegarone 66 I5
Vineyard 45 C9
Vinson 69 G10
Vinton 62 E1
Viola 84 E6
Violet 84 E5
Virginia Point 81 C9
Vista 57 F8
Vistula 59 J10
Vitek Field (private) 69 B12
Viterbo 73 I8
Voca 56 K2
Volente 69 E10
Von Ormy 77 D11
Voss 55 F12
Votaw 72 E4
Voth 73 G7
Vsetin 79 B10

W

W C Ranch (private airfield) 59 G10
W D Cornilius Ranch (private airfield) 80 F2
W J E (private airfield) 59 D9
W. Goodrich Jones State Forest 71 G11
Waco 58 F2; 167 E9
Waco Lake (USACE) 58 F1
Waco Lake 58 F2; 167 C7
Waco Regional (airport) 58 F1
Wadsworth 80 G3
Waelder 70 K1
Waffelow Creek 60 E5
Wagner 29 A7; 47 C7
Wagner-Braxdale (private airfield) 76 I5
Waka 26 J4
Wake 34 I3
Wake Village 49 A7
Wakefield 60 J3
Walburg 69 B11
Walcott 28 J6
Walda 72 A3
Waldeck 70 H4
Walden 73 H7
Walden Woods 72 H1
Waldrip 56 G1
Walhalla 70 H4
Walker Creek 46 K5; 60 F2
Walker Ranch (private airfield) 56 H1
Walker Village 57 J11; 142 A3
Walkers Mill 48 H5
Walkerton 69 D10
Wall 55 H8
Wallace 47 I9
Wallace Branch 60 B1
Wallace Canyon 66 H3
Wallace Creek 56 J4; 68 I2
Waller 71 H9
Waller Gully 78 K2
Walleye Creek 70 D2
Wallis 80 A2
Wallisville 72 J4
Walnut Creek 45 C11; 46 I2; 47 I7; 57 B7; 58 K5; 59 C11, D7; 68 E6; 70 H1; 71 G9; 93 B12
Walnut Forest 69 E11; 93 A11
Walnut Grove 48 K6; 60 A1; 68 J5
Walnut Ridge 39 D12
Walnut Run 73 B7
Walnut Springs 46 I5; 57 B10
Walton 37 I8; 49 E7
Waltonia 68 H2
Wampler 45 G10
Wanderers Creek 35 E11; 36 E1
Wanders Creek 60 D5
Waneta 59 F12
Waples 45 I11
Ward 46 I3; 59 C9
Ward Airpark 80 B3
Ward Creek 48 A4
Ward Mountain 75 D9
Ward Prairie 59 D8
Ward Spring 69 E11
Warda 70 H3
Wardlaw 58 F2
Wardswell Draw 40 F6; 41 H7
Ware 26 E6
Waresville 76 A6
Warfield 53 C9
Waring 68 I4
Waring Creek 57 D7
Warlock 48 F4
Warren City 48 I3
Warren Springs 48 D6
Warrenton 70 H4
Warsaw 46 I6
Warsaw Center 46 I6
Warschun Ranch (private airfield) 46 B2
Warwick 64 G4
Washboard Creek 56 E6
Washburn 30 H1
Washburn Draw 50 C3
Washer 76 F4
Washington 71 F7
Washington-on-the-Brazos State Historic Site 71 F7
Washita River 31 C11, D7
Waskom 49 I7
Wasp Creek 57 G12; 68 I5
Wasson 33 E12
Wastella 42 I6
Watauga 46 F1; 102 F2
Water Valley 54 E6
Waterford Park 149 E12
Waterhole Creek 157 A12
Waterloo 69 C12
Waterloo Lake 99 C11
Waters Bluff 48 I1
Waters Park 69 E11
Watkins 47 I8
Watson 56 D5; 69 A9
Watson Branch 70 D2
Watsonville 46 H2
Watt 58 E3
Watterson 69 I12
Watts 69 K11
Waukegan 71 F12
Waxahachie 46 J4; 167 J7
Waxahachie Country Club Lake 167 I7
Waxahachie Creek 46 K4; 167 K7
Wayland 44 H4
Wayside 34 A1; 41 B11
Wealthy 59 K7
Weatherford 45 G10
Weaver 47 C12
Weaver Creek 48 B4
Webb 46 H2
Webb Point 85 A10
Webb Village 54 A1
Webberville 69 G12
Webbville 56 B2
Weber Ranch (private airfield) 70 C5
Webster 81 A7; 146 E2
Weches 60 F1
Wedgewood 109 K8
Wedhaven 79 H12
Weedy Creek 78 I2
Weeks Settlement 61 J9
Weeping Mary 60 F1
Weesatche 78 G6
Weese Intl (private airfield) 47 E8
Wehdem 70 H6
Weide Creek 68 B3
Weiland 47 E8
Weimar 70 K4
Weinert 43 B11; 69 K10
Weir 47 B11; 69 C11
Weiser Air Park (airport) 71 I10
Weiss Canal 73 F7
Welch 41 E9
Welcome 70 H5
Welcome Valley 57 A8
Welder 70 K1
Weldon 59 K11
Welfare 68 I5
Wellborn 71 D7
Wellington 31 K8
Wellman 41 D8
Wells 41 E11; 60 G2
Wells Creek 59 D11
Wells Creek 59 D11
Welsh Reservoir 48 D3
Wendt 70 I3
Wentworth 47 I9
Wesco 30 F5
Weser 79 G7
Weslaco 88 H3; 168 B2
Wesley 70 H6
West 58 D2
West Academy 71 F8
West Airpark (private) 58 E2
West Amarillo Creek 29 G11
West Aransas Creek 84 A4
West Bay 81 D8
West Bear Creek 67 C10
West Bernard Creek 80 B2
West Bluff 73 G9
West Brook Creek 70 K2
West Brushy Creek 47 A12
West Buffalo Creek 45 J12
West Caddo Creek 47 C7
West Canal 131 F11
West Caney Creek 59 K8
West Carancahua Creek 79 F12, H12
West Carolina Creek 71 B12
West Cliff 57 J12
West Columbia 80 E4
West Copperas Creek 67 C9
West Creek 60 D6; 67 C11; 68 H2
West Deep Creek 56 K3
West Delta 47 B10
West Dixon Creek 30 F1
West Elm Creek 157 A10
West End Place 144 F1
West Farmers Creek 37 J11
West Frio River 67 I11, J11
West Houston (airport) 71 J10
West Kerr Ranch (private airfield) 67 G11
West Lake Hills 69 F10; 92 G5
West Las Moras Creek 67 A10
West Midway 48 D2
West Mill Creek 70 I6
West Mineola 47 H11
West Mountain 48 H3
West Mountain 150 B1
West Mud Creek 47 K12; 60 A1
West Mud Creek Lake 165 G12
West Mustang Creek 79 E12
West Navidad River 70 K3; 79 A9
West New Hope 48 C2
West Nolan River 45 I11
West Nueces River 67 I7, K7; 76 B3
West Oakland 73 H7; 95 F10
West Odessa 53 D8
West Orange 73 H9
West Oso Creek 84 F5
West Pinto Creek 76 B1
West Point 41 C10; 70 I2
West Port Arthur 73 J8; 154 K3
West Prong 29 G7
West Ranch (private airfield) 68 E6
West Rita Blanca Creek 26 C5
West Rocky Creek 54 F4
West Sabinal River 67 K12; 76 A6
West Saint Paul 84 C5
West Salt Creek 45 D7
West Sandy Creek 71 C10; 79 A10, B11
West Sinton 84 C5
West Sister Creek 68 H5
West Squirrel Creek 77 D7
West Sweden 56 I1
West Tawakoni 47 F8
West Tehuacana Creek 77 D8
West Tempe 72 B2
West Tempe Creek 72 B2
West Texas (airport) 62 G3
West Turkey Creek 79 C11
West University Place 71 K12; 133 B11
West Verde Creek 68 K2; 77 A8
West Weedy Creek 78 H2
West Yegua Creek 70 F2
Westbrook 42 J4; 45 D9; 48 F1
Westbury 72 H6
Westcott 72 E2
Westfield 71 H12
Westfield Estates 71 J12; 130 B3
Westhaven 69 J7
Westheimer Air Park (airport) 71 K10
Westhoff 78 D6
Westlake 46 E2
Westland 45 G12; 108 E2
Westminster 46 B6
Weston 46 B5
Westover 44 A3
Westover Hills 45 G12; 108 D6
Westphalia 58 J2
Westpoint 108 C2
Westville 60 J1
Westway 29 K7
Westwood Village 77 C11; 158 D1
Westworth Village 45 G12; 108 C6
Wet Marsh Pond 72 J3
Wetmore 78 A1; 157 E10
Wetsel 46 D5
Whalen Lake 40 J6
Whaley 48 A6
Whaley Corner 80 B4
Wharton 80 C2
Wharton Municipal (airport) 80 D1
Whatley Flying Service (private airfield) 79 J10
Wheat Creek 38 E1
Wheatland 35 E10; 45 H12; 113 K9
Wheeler 31 F8
Wheeler Municipal (airport) 31 F8
Wheeler Springs 59 H10
Wheelock 70 A6
Wheelock Creek 59 G9
Whiskey Ford 72 H5
Whispering Pines 60 D5
White City 36 E1; 61 I7
White Creek 68 D6; 70 D6; 78 K1; 84 A1
White Deer 30 F3
White Deer Creek 30 D3
White Lake 132 G1
White Mound 38 G5
White Oak 48 B2, F5, I3
White Oak (private airfield) 68 G3
White Oak Bayou 71 J11
White Oak Creek 47 D10; 48 B1, B3; 60 E1, K2; 68 G3; 73 B9
White Oak Junction 47 D11
White Oak Springs 48 D2
White River 34 H1, J3; 42 B4
White River Reservoir 42 A3
White Rock 38 J2; 46 F4; 47 C8; 58 I5; 61 F8; 106 F3
White Rock Creek 46 D4; 58 C1; 59 J12; 106 K1; 114 B1
White Rock Lake 46 F4; 106 I2
White Settlement 45 G12; 108 C4
White Shed 39 D7
White Stone 69 D10
White Wing Ranch (private airfield) 80 A3
White-Hall 57 F11
Whiteface 33 K7
Whitefish Creek 30 I6
Whiteflat 34 F5
Whitehall 71 F9
Whitehead 47 F7
Whitehouse 48 K1
Whiteland 55 J12
Whiteoak Creek 38 K3; 47 C12; 48 A1, A2
Whiterock 38 E6
Whites (private airfield) 79 G12
Whites Creek 46 B5; 59 K11
Whites Creek, West Prong 46 A5
Whitesboro 38 D3
Whiteway 57 E9
Whitewright 46 A6
Whitharral 33 J8
Whitney 34 D2; 58 C1
Whitney Lake 57 C12
Whitney Lake (USACE) 58 C1
Whiton 47 I8
Whitsett 78 I1
Whitson 57 H12
Whitt 45 E9
Whon 56 G2
Wichita Falls 36 H6; 168 H3
Wichita River 36 H5, J1; 37 G7; 168 H6, I2
Wichita River, Middle Fork 35 J8
Wichita Valley (airport) 36 H5
Wicker 71 D7
Wickett 52 F5
Wickson Creek 70 B6
Wied 79 B8
Wiedeville 70 G6
Wiergate 61 K9
Wiggins 58 D2
Wiggins Creek 48 J1
Wigginsville 71 F12
Wilbarger County (airport) 36 E2
Wilbarger Creek 56 H3; 69 F12
Wilber Farms (private airfield) 72 J6
Wilbourn Ranch (private airfield) 69 K12
Wilburn Creek 48 F6
Wilco 29 A9
Wilcox 70 E6
Wild Horse 51 K7
Wild Horse Creek 50 K6; 51 J7; 62 A6; 63 C7
Wild Horse Draw 51 D8, F8; 63 E8
Wild Horse Lake 91 D9
Wild Hurst 60 F2
Wild Peach 80 E5
Wildcat Creek 38 K1; 54 D6; 59 B9
Wilderville 58 J3
Wildhorse Creek 36 F6; 37 C11, C12; 42 J2, K4; 54 A4
Wildorado 29 H9
Wilds Creek 48 J2
Wildwood 72 D5
Wilhelm 30 E1
Wilkins 48 I2
Wilkinson 48 B2
Willamar 88 F5
Willawalla Creek 37 K11
William Penn 71 F7
Williams 35 C10; 56 B3; 72 F1
Williams (airport) 71 G12
Williams (private airfield) 69 C7
Williams Creek 37 K12; 47 I8; 58 E3; 70 J3
Williams Creek, East Fork 68 G6
Williams Creek, West Fork 68 G5
Williams Field (private) 32 G5
Williams Lake 143 F11
Williamsburg 79 C9
Williamson 69 G10
Williamson Creek 48 E3; 164 E6
Willie Slough Gully 73 K7
Willis 71 E11
Willis Creek 69 B12
Willis N Clark (private airfield) 30 C5
Willis-Isler (private airfield) 33 F11
Willman 70 I1
Willow 71 H11
Willow City 68 E5
Willow Creek 58 I6
Willow Creek 27 K9; 35 J8; 38 E2; 42 I3; 45 D10; 54 B4; 57 D12; 68 C3; 71 H10; 72 H5; 75 D7; 79 G9, K9; 80 E1; 85 A9
Willow Grove 58 F1
Willow Island 100 J4
Willow Lake 73 K8; 167 G12
Willow Oak Creek 47 B9
Willow Park 45 G11
Willow Point 45 D9
Willow Run (private airfield) 46 D1
Willow Springs 47 F10; 70 I5; 72 C1
Willowview 35 D11
Wills Point 47 G8
Wills Point Municipal (airport) 47 H8
Wilmer 46 H4
Wilmeth 55 C9
Wilsey 32 D5
Wilson 41 B12; 47 H7; 57 C7; 58 K2
Wilson (private airfield) 35 F9
Wilson Creek 45 J11; 46 B4, D5
Wimberley 69 I8
Winans Creek 68 K2
Winchell 56 G2
Winchester 70 H3
Windcrest 78 B1; 157 I12
Windmill Hill (private airfield) 46 E2
Windom 39 E8
Windsor 58 G1
Windthorst 37 K7
Windy Hill 26 E5
Windy Hill (private airfield) 46 B2
Winedale 70 H5
Winfield 48 C1
Winfree 72 J3
Wingate 55 B9
Wings For Christ Intl Flight Academy (airport) 58 F3
Wings Over Texas (private airfield) 47 G7
Wink 52 E4
Winkler 59 C7
Winkler County (airport) 52 D3
Winn Ranch (private airfield) 69 I8
Winnie 72 J6
Winningkoff 46 D5
Winnsboro 47 E12
Winnsboro Municipal (airport) 47 E12
Winona 48 I1
Winscott 45 I12
Winslow 58 B2
Winston Field 42 H4
Winter Haven 76 I4
Winterfield 47 D12
Winters 55 C10
Winters Bayou 71 C12; 72 D1
Winters Municipal (airport) 55 C10
Wire Hollow Creek 55 E11
Wisdom Temple 47 H11
Wise 47 I8
Witco 54 J2
Withers 77 C12; 158 I3
Witting 79 B8
Wizard Wells 45 C9
Woden 60 G5
Wolf Creek 72 C1
Wolf Creek 26 J6; 27 C11, D8; 38 E2; 46 A2; 47 C8; 57 I11; 59 B10; 68 G3; 72 A6
Wolfe Air Park (airport) 80 B6
Wolfe City 47 B8
Wolfforth 41 A10
Wolfpen Creek 47 C12
Wolters Village 45 F9
Womack 57 D12
Womack Farm (private airfield) 58 E1
Womack Plantation (private airfield) 39 C12
Wood 71 F8
Wood Crest Ranch (private airfield) 59 K7
Wood Lake 78 B6
Wood Springs 47 I12
Woodbine 38 E3
Woodbury 58 B1
Woodcreek Resort (private airfield) 69 H8
Woodcrest Acres 73 G7
Woodlake 60 K2
Woodlake Park 38 D5
Woodland 57 J12
Woodland Heights 56 E4; 97 E9
Woodland Hills 46 H3; 112 K6
Woodlands 71 G12
Woodlawn 48 H6; 60 H3
Woodrow 41 A11; 58 A1
Woods 60 B6
Woods Creek 72 B4
Woods Hollow Mountains 64 G3
Woods of Shavano 156 D4
Woodsboro 85 B7
Woodson 44 E3; 72 H4
Woodstock 38 K5
Woodville 72 B5
Woodville Lookout 72 B5
Woodward 77 J7
Woodway 58 G1
Woody Acres 72 H1
Wooland Siding 55 E8
Wooten Creek 60 C4
Worser Creek 45 H8
Worsham 52 H2
Worth Heights 109 G10
Wortham 58 D6
Worthing 79 C9
Worthington Lake 80 B4
Wright 33 E11; 45 F11
Wright City 60 A2
Wright Creek 59 F10; 71 A11
Wright Patman Lake (USACE) 49 B7
Wright Patman Lake 48 C6; 49 B7
Wrights Creek 68 B5
Wrightsboro 78 C5
Wuthrich Hill 70 C1
Wyatt (private airfield) 69 I9
Wye Siding 49 A7; 163 J8
Wyler Aerial Tramway 62 F2; 126 A4
Wylie 43 J11; 46 E5
Wylie Mountain 51 K7

XYZ

Y E Mesa 64 J3
Y O Ranch (private airfield) 67 G11
Yancey 77 E8
Yancey Creek 57 K7
Yantis 47 E11
Yarboro 71 F9
Yard 59 D9
Yarnall 30 H1
Yarrelton 58 K2
Yates 67 C12
Yates Creek 72 D2
Yates Field (private) 56 H4
Yeager Creek 77 K10
Yegua Creek 70 E6
Yellow Bayou 61 K9
Yellow House Draw 32 I6; 33 I8, J10
Yellow Lake 33 I8
Yellowpine 61 I9
Ygnacio Creek 83 D11
Yoakum 79 D8
Yoakum County (airport) 40 C6
Yoakum Municipal (airport) 79 C8
Yokum 78 E5
York Creek 69 J9
Yorktown 78 F6
Yorktown (private airfield) 78 F6
Youens 71 F12
Yougeen 84 A5
Young 59 D8
Youngs Creek 59 K10
Youngsport 57 K11
Yowell 47 B9
Ysleta 62 G3; 127 I11
Yturria 88 E4
Zabcikville 58 K2
Zachry Ranch (private airfield) 83 K10
Zapata 87 B8
Zapata County (airport) 87 A8
Zarzamora Creek 158 B2
Zavalla 60 J5
Zella 77 J10
Zephyr 56 E4
Ziler 42 A2
Zimmerle (private airfield) 43 K12
Zion Grove 60 D3
Zion Hill 73 A8
Zionville 70 G6
Zipp 78 A3
Zipperlandville 58 J2
Zita 29 I11
Zook Airfield (private airfield) 46 J3
Zorn 69 K9
Zuehl 78 B2
Zuehl (private airfield) 78 B2
Zummo 73 H7; 95 G12
Zunkerville 78 I3

National Lands

The federally owned lands listed in this chart total over three million acres and are managed by the US Army Corps of Engineers (USACE), the US Forest Service (USFS), the US Fish and Wildlife Service (USFWS) and the National Park Service (NPS).

For more information on national lands in Texas, contact the appropriate administrative agency. USACE, Recreation Resources Management Division: P.O. Box 17300, Fort Worth, TX 76102, (817) 886-1326; USFS, Southern Region: 1720 Peachtree Road NW, Atlanta, GA 30309, (404) 347-4177; USFWS, Region Two: P.O. Box 1306, Albuquerque, NM 87103, (505) 248-6911; NPS, Intermountain Region: 12795 Alameda Parkway, Denver, CO 80225, (303) 969-2500.

Many of the lands and bodies of water listed here appear in other categories. For more information, see Freshwater Fishing and Wildlife Viewing.

NAME, LOCATION	PAGE & GRID	ACREAGE	ADMINISTRATION	CAMPING	FISHING	BOATING	HIKING/NATURE TRAILS	HUNTING	SWIMMING	PICNIC SITES	VISITOR CENTER	COMMENTS
Addicks Reservoir, Houston	71 J11, 128 F3	13,693	USACE		●		●			●	●	Includes Bear Creek Park, with golf course, tennis courts and game fields; and Cullen–Addicks Park, with velodrome and hiking/biking trail. Dam is popular exercise area for bicyclists and joggers.
Alibates Flint Quarries National Monument, Fritch	29 E12	1,371	NPS				●				●	Significant archaeological site; provided early Native Americans with flint for trade and tools. Accessed only via guided tour. *(See Historic Sites.)*
Amistad National Recreation Area, Del Rio	86 B4	58,500	NPS	●	●	●	●	●	●	●	●	Portion of Amistad Reservoir located on US–Mexico border. 850 miles of shoreline. Limestone canyon walls rise over 200 feet. Archaeological sites, petroglyphs. Scuba diving, sailboarding. Interpretive displays, programs.
Anahuac National Wildlife Refuge, Anahuac	81 A11	30,162	USFWS		●		●	●			●	Sweeping coastal prairie, saltwater and freshwater marshes. Winter habitat for geese and various other waterfowl. Alligators, wood storks, peregrine falcons and bald eagles.
Angelina National Forest, Zavalla	60 J6	153,174	USFS	●	●	●	●	●	●	●		Rolling terrain in Neches River Basin; scattered tracts surround Sam Rayburn Reservoir. Longleaf, shortleaf and loblolly pines. Winter habitat for bald eagles. Horseback riding, ORV. *(See Hiking: Sawmill Hiking Trail.)*
Aquilla Lake, Vaughn	58 C2	10,212	USACE		●	●		●				Created on Aquilla Creek for flood control, water supply, and fish and wildlife enhancement. Some timbered areas along ends of lake's upper arms. Five recreation areas on 44 miles of shoreline.
Aransas National Wildlife Refuge, Austwell	85 A10	54,829	USFWS		●		●	●		●	●	On gulf coast's Blackjack Peninsula; wintering grounds for whooping crane *(see Unique Natural Features)*. Woodlands, marshlands, coastal grasslands. Observation tower, paved auto route.
Attwater Prairie Chicken National Wildlife Refuge, Eagle Lake	71 K7	7,984	USFWS				●			●	●	Prairie and wooded areas protect endangered Attwater prairie chicken. Species observation via blinds and guided tours. Birding popular fall–winter. Auto tour route. National Natural Landmark. *(See Unique Natural Features.)*
B. A. Steinhagen Lake/Town Bluff Dam, Jasper	73 A7	21,643	USACE	●	●	●		●	●	●	●	Lake created on Neches River. Noted habitat for black and largemouth bass. Eight recreation areas; 160 miles of shoreline. Waterskiing.
Bardwell Lake, Bardwell	46 K5	7,480	USACE	●	●	●	●	●	●	●	●	Created by impoundment of Waxahachie Creek. 25 miles of shoreline; six recreation areas and eight wildlife management areas.
Barker Reservoir, Houston	71 J10	12,583	USACE		●					●	●	Cullen–Barker Park, only developed recreation area along normally dry reservoir. Public shooting range, model airport, and baseball and soccer fields. Biking and jogging popular atop dam.
Belton Lake, Belton	57 J12	23,800	USACE	●	●	●	●	●	●	●	●	Over 135 miles of shoreline created on Leon River. Accessed via 13 recreation areas.
Benbrook Lake, Benbrook	45 H12, 108 K5	8,233	USACE	●	●	●	●	●	●	●	●	Impoundment on Clear Fork of Trinity River. 40 miles of shoreline, six recreation areas. 7.3-mile equestrian and nature trail.
Big Bend National Park, Study Butte	75 C9	801,163	NPS	●	●	●	●			●	●	Chisos Mountains, Chihuahuan Desert bounded by Rio Grande. Home to plant and animal species found nowhere else in world—including Chisos oak and Big Bend mosquitofish *(see Unique Natural Features)*. River floating, hiking, horseback riding. *(See Hiking—Big Bend National Park Trails.)*
Big Boggy National Wildlife Refuge, Matagorda	80 H3	4,216	USFWS		●	●		●				Coastal prairie and saltmarsh on East Matagorda Bay attracts various wintering waterfowl. Open during waterfowl hunting season.
Big Slough Wilderness, Davy Crockett National Forest	60 G1	3,639	USFS	●	●	●	●	●				Primitive, backcountry recreation in former logging region. Big Slough Canoe Trail follows scenic portion of Neches River.
Big Thicket National Preserve, Kountze	72 D6	84,550	NPS	●	●	●	●	●	●	●	●	12 individual units protect biologically diverse ecosystem. Combines virgin pine and cypress forest, hardwood forest, meadow and blackwater swamp. Various wildlife and carnivorous plants. Day-use recreation along Neches River. Horseback riding in Big Sandy Creek Unit. Designated International Biosphere Reserve.
Black Kettle National Grassland, Canadian	31 B9	31,300	USFS	●	●	●	●			●		Former Texas–Oklahoma farming region devastated by poor agricultural practices and drought in mid-1930s; rehabilitated into grasslands 1938–1953. 576 acres located in Texas; remaining 30,724 in Oklahoma.
Brazoria National Wildlife Refuge, Oyster Creek	81 E7	42,193	USFWS		●	●	●	●				Noted waterfowl wintering area along Central Flyway; Canada and white-fronted geese number 30,000–40,000 during December and January. Wading shorebirds, sandhill cranes and American alligators. Auto tour route.
Buffalo Lake National Wildlife Refuge, Umbarger	29 J10	7,664	USFWS	●			●			●		Semiarid landscape provides resting and feeding area for migrating waterfowl after rainfalls. Auto tour route.
Caddo National Grassland, Sash	39 D9	17,785	USFS	●	●	●	●	●		●		Three units of grazing land for privately owned livestock. Recreation areas located on Lake Crockett and Coffee Mill Lake. Scattered gas and oil wells. Horseback riding.
Canyon Lake, Canyon Lake	69 J8	10,990	USACE	●	●	●			●	●	●	Created by impoundment of Guadalupe River. One of state's deepest lakes; averages 47-foot depth. Stocked lake noted for cool water temperature. 80 miles of shoreline with eight recreation areas. Short walking trail.
Chamizal National Memorial, El Paso	62 F2, 126 D5	55	NPS							●	●	Recognizes 1963 US–Mexico settlement of long-standing international boundary dispute. Additional 193 acres located in Mexico's Chamizal Commemorative Park. Outdoor amphitheater, bike trail. *(See Historic Sites.)*
Davy Crockett National Forest, Apple Springs	60 I2	161,497	USFS	●	●	●	●	●	●	●	●	Named for Alamo hero. Contains recreation area, Alabama Creek Wildlife Management Area and Big Slough Wilderness *(see this section)*. Traversed by Four C Trail *(see Hiking)* and 52-mile-long Piney Creek Horse Trail.
Fort Davis National Historic Site, Fort Davis	63 C11	460	NPS				●			●	●	Ruins of 19th-century military post constructed to guard westward travel routes. Restored barracks, several miles of hiking trails. Museum, self-guiding tours. *(See Historic Sites—Historic Forts.)*
Granger Lake, Granger	70 B1	13,602	USACE	●	●	●	●	●	●	●		Created on San Gabriel River; provides flood control, water conservation. 36 miles of shoreline. Surrounded by four wildlife areas: Pecan Grove, San Gabriel, Willis Creek and Sore Finger. Fishing, hunting.
Grapevine Lake, Grapevine	46 E2, 103 A10	15,552	USACE	●	●	●	●	●	●	●	●	Impoundment on Denton Creek. Nine recreation areas on 60 miles of shoreline. Horseback riding, ORV and hiking *(See Hiking: Northshore Trail.)*
Guadalupe Mountains National Park, Salt Flat	50 C6	86,416	NPS	●			●			●	●	Canyons, Chihuahuan Desert plains and dense forest highlands. Surrounds portion of Guadalupe Mountains; contains 8,749-foot-high Guadalupe Peak, state's highest mountain. Collared lizards, mule deer, coyotes, mountain lions and elk. Hiking, horseback riding. *(See Unique Natural Features and Hiking—Guadalupe Mountains National Park Trails.)*
Guadalupe Mountains Wilderness, Guadalupe Mountains National Park	50 C6	46,850	NPS	●			●					Natural area within Guadalupe Mountains National Park *(see this section)*. Includes towering peaks of Hunter, Shumard, Bartlett and Bush mountains. Forested mountaintops, desert lowlands. Horseback riding.
Hagerman National Wildlife Refuge, Sadler	38 D4	11,320	USFWS		●	●	●	●		●	●	Popular fishing, birding destination along Lake Texoma. Marshes, woodlands and grasslands in waterfowl migration route. Home to over 7,500 Canada geese fall–spring. Auto tour route.
Hords Creek Lake, Coleman	55 D12	3,010	USACE	●	●	●	●	●	●	●	●	Impoundment on tributary of Pecan Bayou. 11 miles of shoreline; three recreation areas.
Indian Mounds Wilderness, Sabine National Forest	61 H9	10,917	USFS	●	●	●	●	●				Named for naturally occurring mounds located nearby. Once thought to be constructed by prehistoric inhabitants. Hiking along unmarked trails, horseback riding.
Joe Pool Lake, Cedar Hill	46 H3	15,192	USACE	●	●	●	●		●	●		Impoundment on Mountain Creek accessed via four recreation areas bordering lake. 60 miles of shoreline.
Laguna Atascosa National Wildlife Refuge, Rio Hondo	89 H7	45,187	USFWS				●	●		●	●	Open lagoons, coastal prairies. Large wintering concentration of redhead ducks. Year-round wildlife includes Texas tortoise, exotic Mexican birds. Two auto tour routes. *(See Hiking: Mesquite Trail.)*
Lake Georgetown, Georgetown	69 C10	5,317	USACE	●	●	●	●	●	●	●	●	Created by impoundment on North Fork of San Gabriel River. Accessed from four recreation areas situated along 25 miles of shoreline.
Lake Meredith National Recreation Area, Fritch	30 D1	44,978	NPS	●	●	●	●	●	●	●		Vast lake surrounded by High Plains of Panhandle region. 200-foot-high canyon breaks created by Canadian River erosion. Wind-eroded coves, scenic buttes. Scuba diving, waterskiing, ORV.
Lake O' The Pines, Ore City	48 F4	29,031	USACE	●	●	●	●	●	●	●	●	Popular fishing destination created by impoundment of Cypress Creek. 144 miles of shoreline bordered by boat ramps, pine and hardwood forests and 22 recreation areas. Waterskiing.
Lake Texoma, Denison	38 I4	193,000	USACE	●	●	●	●	●		●	●	Located on Red River, along Texas–Oklahoma border. 35 percent of acreage in Texas, remainder in Oklahoma. Over 20 recreation areas along 580 miles of Texas shoreline. Excellent angling for blue and flathead catfish. Waterskiing, horseback riding and hiking *(see Hiking: Cross Timbers Hiking Trail)*.
Lavon Lake, Wylie	46 E6	37,515	USACE	●	●	●	●	●	●	●	●	Impoundment on East Fork of Trinity River. 16 recreation areas scattered along 121 miles of shoreline. Three areas offer hunting and wildlife observation. Horseback riding, ORV.
Lewisville Lake, Lewisville	46 D3	45,944	USACE	●	●	●	●	●	●	●	●	183 miles of shoreline created on Elm Fork of Trinity River; popular destination for boating enthusiasts. Surrounded by 22 recreation areas, some offering horseback riding, waterskiing.
Little Lake Creek Wilderness, Sam Houston National Forest	71 D10	3,810	USFS	●	●		●	●				Undeveloped area within Sam Houston National Forest *(see this section)* named for perennial stream bisecting area. Contains portion of Lone Star Hiking Trail *(see Hiking)*.
Lyndon B. Johnson National Grassland, Alvord	45 B11	20,250	USFS	●	●	●	●	●		●		Grazing land for privately owned livestock. Over 400 small lakes offer fishing. Developed recreation area at Black Creek Lake. Hunting, horseback riding, hiking *(see Hiking: Cottonwood–Black Creek Trail)*.
Lyndon B. Johnson National Historical Park, Stonewall	68 F5	549	NPS								●	Contains reconstructed birthplace, boyhood home and ranch house of 36th US President. Composed of two distinct units: Johnson City and LBJ Ranch. Access by NPS tour bus from Lyndon B. Johnson State Park and Historic Site.
McClellan Creek National Grassland, Alanreed	30 H5	1,449	USFS	●	●	●	●			●		Agricultural area furnishes feed for domestic livestock and other wildlife. Horseback riding, ORV.
McFaddin National Wildlife Refuge, Sabine Pass	73 K7	41,682	USFWS	●	●	●	●	●				Marshland within state's upper gulf coast; home to one of state's densest alligator populations. Habitat for wintering waterfowl. Bald eagle and peregrine falcon sightings during fall and spring migrations.
Muleshoe National Wildlife Refuge, Muleshoe	32 H6	5,809	USFWS	●			●			●		Extensive population of wintering sandhill cranes and various waterfowl; nearly 100,000 sandhill cranes present December–mid-February. Prairie dog town. National Natural Landmark. *(See Unique Natural Features.)*
Navarro Mills Lake, Navarro Mills	58 C4	10,930	USACE	●	●	●	●	●	●	●	●	38 miles of shoreline created on impoundment of Richland Creek, tributary of Trinity River. Four recreation areas.
O. C. Fisher Lake, San Angelo	55 G7, 162 D2	17,876	USACE	●	●	●	●	●	●	●	●	Created by impoundment of North Concho River. 27 miles of shoreline; four recreation areas. 4,000 acres reserved for hunting and wildlife observation. Horseback riding, ORV, waterskiing, pavilion.
Padre Island National Seashore, Corpus Christi	85 H7	133,919	NPS	●	●	●	●		●	●	●	113-mile-long barrier island with one of longest stretches of undeveloped ocean beach in US. Dynamic landscape. Grasslands Nature Trail at Malaquite Beach area. Abundant birdlife. *(See Unique Natural Features.)*
Palo Alto Battlefield National Historic Site, Brownsville	88 I6	1,330	NPS				●				●	Scene of first major battle between US and Mexican troops in US–Mexican War. Site interprets battle and entire two-year-long conflict from both countries' perspectives. *(See Historic Sites.)*

NATIONAL LANDS, *continued*

NAME, LOCATION	PAGE & GRID	ACREAGE	ADMINISTRATION	CAMPING	FISHING	BOATING	HIKING/NATURE TRAILS	HUNTING	SWIMMING	PICNIC SITES	VISITOR CENTER	COMMENTS
Pat Mayse Lake, Powderly	39 C11	23,732	USACE	●	●	●		●	●	●	●	Impounded on Sanders Creek, tributary of Red River. Resting and feeding habitat for some migratory waterfowl. Upland game, white-tailed deer. 67 miles of shoreline; five recreation areas. Waterskiing.
Proctor Lake, Proctor	56 C6	9,009	USACE	●	●	●	●	●		●	●	Created along Leon River. 38 miles of shoreline; four recreation areas. Noted for hybrid striped bass.
Ray Roberts Lake, Tioga	46 A3	46,060	USACE	●	●	●	●	●	●	●		Created on Elm Fork of Trinity River. Noted for largemouth bass and crappie. Recreation facilities located at Ray Roberts Lake State Park—Isle du Bois Unit. Horseback riding.
Rita Blanca National Grassland, Texline	26 C6	77,463	USFS	●				●		●		Scattered tracts in Texas and over 15,000 acres in Oklahoma. Grassland furnishes food, cover and water for wildlife Recreation at Thompson Grove.
Sabine National Forest, Hemphill	61 H9	160,609	USFS	●	●	●	●	●	●	●		Located in Piney Woods region along Sabine River watershed. Indian Mounds Wilderness *(see this section)*. ORV, horseback riding, hiking *(see Hiking: Trail Between the Lakes)*.
Sam Houston National Forest, New Waverly	71 D11	161,154	USFS	●	●	●	●	●	●	●		East Texas Piney Woods interspersed with private land. Noted for colonies of red-cockaded woodpeckers. Includes Big Creek Scenic Area and Scotts Ridge Recreation Area. ORV, hiking *(see Hiking: Lone Star Hiking Trail)*.
Sam Rayburn Reservoir, Broaddus	61 J7	114,806	USACE	●	●	●	●	●	●	●	●	Constructed on Angelina River; state's largest reservoir. Accessed by 20 recreation areas along 560 miles of shoreline. 1,600 acres reserved for hunting and wildlife observation. Orchids, carnivorous plants.
San Antonio Missions National Historical Park, San Antonio	77 C12, 159 K9	860	NPS				●			●	●	Includes four missions constructed along San Antonio River over 200 years ago: Concepción, San José, San Juan and Espada *(see Historic Sites—Historic Missions)*. Auto tour route accesses all structures.
San Bernard National Wildlife Refuge, Jones Creek	80 G5	24,455	USFWS		●	●	●	●				Located along Central Flyway. Habitat for wintering Canada, snow and white-fronted geese. Small population of American alligators; numerous rattlesnakes and cottonmouth moccasins. Noted birding, photography spot.
Santa Ana National Wildlife Refuge, Alamo	88 I2	2,080	USFWS				●				●	Marsh areas and three lakes along Rio Grande at convergence of Central and Mississippi flyways. Sanctuary for endangered ocelot, jaguarundi and birds not found elsewhere in US. Photography blinds, auto tour route. National Natural Landmark. *(See Unique Natural Features.)*
Somerville Lake, Somerville	70 F5	29,800	USACE	●	●	●	●	●	●	●	●	Created on Yegua Creek for flood control. 85 miles of shoreline; seven recreation areas. Waterfowl hunting, horseback riding, ORV.
Stillhouse Hollow Lake, Nolanville	57 K12	15,271	USACE	●	●	●	●	●	●	●	●	Created on Lampasas River for flood control in Brazos River Basin. Six recreation areas; 58 miles of shoreline. 4,581 acres devoted to hunting and wildlife observation.
Texas Point National Wildlife Refuge, Sabine Pass	73 K8	8,952	USFWS		●	●		●				Marshland habitat for wintering waterfowl. Wildlife viewing area. Alligator sightings except in winter; bald eagle, peregrine falcon sightings during migrations. Access by foot or boat only.
Turkey Hill Wilderness, Angelina National Forest	60 H6	5,473	USFS	●	●		●	●				Primitive recreation area in former logging region; devoid of pines by 1930s and later reforested. Today covered with dense pine and hardwood forests. Home to rare red-cockaded woodpecker. Horseback riding.
Upland Island Wilderness, Angelina National Forest	60 J6	13,331	USFS	●	●		●	●				Pine and hardwood forests; former logging region. Rare and unusual plants include pitcher plants, champion longleaf pines and wild azaleas. Horseback riding.
Waco Lake, Waco	58 F1	14,219	USACE	●	●	●		●	●	●	●	Located at confluence of North, South and Middle Bosque rivers. 60 miles of shoreline; eight recreation areas. Two additional developed areas offer hunting and wildlife observation. ORV.
Whitney Lake, Laguna Park	58 C1	43,699	USACE	●	●	●		●	●	●	●	Created on Brazos River for hydropower production and flood control. 225 miles of shoreline; 15 recreation areas. Excellent year-round fishing.
Wright Patman Lake, Maud	49 B7	78,813	USACE	●	●	●	●	●	●	●	●	One of Texas' largest lakes; retains portion of Sulphur River. Premier catfish hatchery. Accessed via Atlanta State Park and 18 recreation areas on 165 miles of shoreline. ORV, waterskiing.

State Lands

Many of the lands and bodies of water listed here appear in other categories. For more information, see Freshwater Fishing and Wildlife Viewing.

For more specific information, including maps and brochures, contact the Texas Parks and Wildlife Department, 4200 Smith School Road, Austin, TX 78744, (800) 792-1112.

NAME, LOCATION	PAGE & GRID	ACREAGE	CAMPING	SWIMMING	BOATING	WATERSKIING	FISHING	FISHING PIER	HIKING TRAILS	NATURE/INTERPRETIVE TRAILS	BICYCLING TRAILS	EQUESTRIAN TRAILS	PICNIC SITES	PLAYGROUND	COMMENTS
Abilene State Park, Tuscola	43 K10	529	●	●			●		●	●			●	●	Located along limestone hills of Callahan Divide. Scenic woodlands, Texas longhorn herd. Swimming pool, game areas. Lake Abilene nearby.
Acton State Historic Site, Granbury	45 J11	0.01													Burial site of Elizabeth Crockett, second wife of frontiersman and Alamo hero Davy Crockett. *(See Historic Sites.)*
Admiral Nimitz State Historic Site–National Museum of the Pacific War, Fredricksburg	68 F4	9								●					Dedicated to War in the Pacific during WWII, Fleet Admiral Chester W. Nimitz and those who served under him. Allied and Japanese aircraft, tanks, guns and other WWII artifacts. *(See Historic Sites.)*
Atlanta State Park, Atlanta	48 C6	1,475	●	●	●	●	●		●	●			●	●	Pine forest bordering Wright Patman Lake. Bird and wildlife sightings.
Balmorhea State Park, Balmorhea	51 K12	46	●	●									●	●	One of world's largest spring-fed swimming pools (over 3.5-million-gallon capacity). Endangered Comanche Springs pupfish, Pecos mosquitofish. Scuba and skin diving.
Bastrop State Park, Bastrop	70 H1	5,770	●	●			●		●				●	●	Situated amongst Lost Pines of Texas—state's westernmost stand of loblolly pines. Swimming pool, scenic drive, golf course. *(See Hiking: Lost Pines Hiking Trail.)*
Bentsen–Rio Grande Valley State Park, Mission	88 H1	588	●		●		●		●	●			●	●	Natural preserve of subtropical woodlands. Some plant, animal species more commonly found in Mexico. Noted birding spot. *(See Hiking: Singing Chaparral Trail.)*
Big Bend Ranch State Park, Presidio	74 B3	298,029	●	●	●		●		●	●			●		Noted for rapids along Colorado Canyon portion of Rio Grande. Texas longhorn herd. Scenic drive, bus tours. Barton Warnock Environmental Education Center serves as east entrance visitor center. Primitive camping only.
Big Spring State Park, Big Spring	42 K1, 94 K1	382								●			●	●	Contains Scenic Mountain, 210-foot-high limestone mesa. Deep canyons. Scenic drive, prairie dog town and interpretive center. *(See Hiking: Scenic Mountain Trail.)*
Blanco State Park, Blanco	69 H7	105	●	●	●		●			●			●	●	Portion of Blanco River stocked with rainbow trout. Boat rentals, birding.
Boca Chica State Park, Brownsville	89 J8	1,055		●			●								Day-use area provides beach access to Gulf of Mexico. No facilities.
Bonham State Park, Bonham	39 E8	261	●	●	●		●	●					●	●	65-acre lake, wooded shoreline and prairie land. Wildlife, songbird viewing. Swimming beach. Boat rentals.
Brazos Bend State Park, Damon	80 C5	4,897	●				●	●	●		●		●	●	Wildlife observation tower, platforms. Observatory, interpretive center. Alligator viewing.
Buescher State Park, Smithville	70 H2	1,017	●	●			●		●				●	●	Located on eastern edge of Lost Pines of Texas, supposed pine forest remnant from Ice Age. Portion of Central Flyway. Wildlife observation platform. *(See Hiking: Buescher Trail.)*
Caddo Lake State Park, Karnack	49 H7	484	●	●	●	●	●	●	●	●			●	●	Accesses over 30,000 acres of cypress swamp, bayous and sloughs. Abundant sportfishing in Caddo Lake. Boat rentals. *(See Unique Natural Features.)*
Caddoan Mounds State Historic Site, Alto	60 F1	94								●					Southwesternmost ceremonial center of Mound Builder culture, who inhabited area around 1000 B.C.–A.D. 1500. Temple burial mounds and reconstructed dwelling. Interpretive center. *(See Historic Sites.)*
Caprock Canyons State Park, Quitaque	34 D4	15,314	●	●	●		●	●	●	●	●	●	●	●	Named for escarpment between tablelands and rolling plains. Features swimming on Lake Theo, rock climbing. Caprock Canyons Trailway, scenic drive, interpretive center, boat rentals. *(See Unique Natural Features and Hiking: Upper Canyon Trail.)*
Casa Navarro State Historic Site, San Antonio	159 D7	0.7													Three restored structures once belonging to early Texas statesman. Exhibits, period furnishings. Guided tours. *(See Historic Sites.)*
Cedar Hill State Park, Cedar Hill	46 H3	1,826	●	●	●	●	●	●	●		●		●	●	Accesses Joe Pool Lake. Upland forest and tall-grass prairie areas. Remnants of 1850s farmhouse. Swimming beach.
Choke Canyon State Park—Calliham Unit, Calliham	78 K1	1,100	●	●	●	●	●		●	●			●	●	Recreation area dominated by Choke Canyon Reservoir. Swimming beach. Westernmost common occurrence of American alligator.
Choke Canyon State Park—South Shore Unit, Three Rivers	78 K1	385	●	●	●	●	●						●	●	Unit located between Frio River and Choke Canyon Reservoir. Three recreation areas.

Continues on next page

STATE LANDS, *continued*

Many of the lands and bodies of water listed here appear in other categories. For more information, see Freshwater Fishing and Wildlife Viewing.
For more specific information, including maps and brochures, contact the Texas Parks and Wildlife Department, 4200 Smith School Road, Austin, TX 78744, (800) 792-1112.

NAME, LOCATION	PAGE & GRID	ACREAGE	CAMPING	SWIMMING	BOATING	WATERSKIING	FISHING	FISHING PIER	HIKING TRAILS	NATURE/INTERPRETIVE TRAILS	BICYCLING TRAILS	EQUESTRIAN TRAILS	PICNIC SITES	PLAYGROUND	COMMENTS
Cleburne State Park, Cleburne	45 K12	529	●	●	●		●		●	●	●		●	●	Spring-fed lake nestled in thickly wooded area. Sightings of white-tailed deer, turkeys. Boat rentals.
Colorado Bend State Park, Bend	56 K6	5,328	●	●	●		●		●		●		●		Includes six miles of Colorado River frontage. Armadillos, rare and endangered bird species. Scenic drive. Primitive camping only.
Confederate Reunion Grounds State Historic Site, Mexia	58 F5	77			●		●			●			●	●	Historic structures include 1872 Heritage House and 1893 dance pavilion. Oak-shaded paths, scenic footbridges. Picnic pavilion. *(See Historic Sites.)*
Cooper Lake State Park—Doctors Creek Unit, Cooper	47 B10	466	●	●	●	●	●	●	●	●	●		●	●	Located on north side of 19,300-acre Cooper Lake. 6.2 miles of shoreline features sandy beach.
Cooper Lake State Park—South Sulphur Unit, Sulphur Springs	47 B10	2,560	●	●	●	●	●	●	●	●	●	●	●	●	Larger of two park units located on south side of Cooper Lake. Rolling hills and 25.5 miles of shoreline. Equestrian camping.
Copano Bay State Fishing Pier, Rockport	85 C9	6		●	●		●	●							Fishing pier accesses Copano Bay. Boat ramp. No facilities.
Copper Breaks State Park, Crowell	35 F11	1,899	●	●	●		●		●	●		●	●	●	Named for copper deposits scattered throughout area. Rugged terrain, grass-covered mesas. Stocked lake with swimming beach. Texas longhorn herd. Visitor center, exhibits.
Daingerfield State Park, Daingerfield	48 E4	551	●	●	●		●	●	●				●	●	Spring-fed lake, pine forests and rolling hills. Sweetgum, oak and maple trees provide fall foliage. Boat rentals.
Davis Mountains State Park, Fort Davis	63 C11	2,709	●						●				●	●	Located in hills of extensive mountain range; habitat for rare Montezuma quail. Interpretive center, guided birdwalks. Scenic 75-mile loop drive. State-run Indian Lodge resembles Pueblo village.
Devil's Sinkhole State Natural Area, Rocksprings	67 H9	1,860													Named for geologic sinkhole created by collapsed cavern. Bat sightings. Tours by reservation only. Contact Kickapoo Cavern State Park *(see this section).*
Devils River State Natural Area, Comstock	66 I4	19,989	●		●				●		●				Noted site of ancient pictographs. Mountain-biking trails. Guided tours, limited use by reservation only.
Dinosaur Valley State Park, Glen Rose	45 K10	1,525	●	●			●		●		●	●	●	●	Dinosaur tracks along Paluxy River streambed. Fiberglass models, exhibits. Texas longhorn herd. *(See Unique Natural Features and Hiking: Dinosaur Valley Trail.)*
E. O. Siecke State Forest, Call	73 C9	1,722		●			●						●		Named for former state forester E. O. Siecke. Composed of two units; includes day-use area along Trout Creek.
Eisenhower Birthplace State Historic Site, Denison	38 D5, 99 C12	6							●	●			●		Two-story frame house birthplace for Dwight D. Eisenhower, 34th US president. Furnished with Eisenhower family quilt and period antiques. *(See Historic Sites.)*
Eisenhower State Park, Denison	38 C5	423	●	●	●	●	●	●	●	●	●		●	●	Borders Lake Texoma, one of state's largest reservoirs. Nationally recognized striper fishery. Marina.
Enchanted Rock State Natural Area, Fredericksburg	68 D4	1,644	●						●				●	●	Dome-shaped hills of pink granite. Location of one of largest known granite caves. Rock climbing. Primitive camping only. *(See Unique Natural Features and Hiking: Enchanted Rock Loop Trail.)*
Fairfield Lake State Park, Fairfield	59 D8	1,460	●	●	●	●	●	●	●	●			●	●	Noted fishing lake located along hardwood forests and rolling hills. Dogwoods, rosebuds and wildflowers provide seasonal color. Sandy swimming area. *(See Hiking: Big Brown Creek Trail.)*
Falcon State Park, Falcon	87 E9	573	●	●	●	●	●						●	●	Located on eastern shore of Falcon Reservoir. Bobcats, javelinas and tropical bird species.
Fanthorp Inn State Historic Site, Anderson	71 D8	1.4													Former hotel restored to 1850s appearance. Period furnishings. Operating stagecoach is on permanent exhibit. Guided tours. *(See Historic Sites.)*
Fort Boggy State Park, Centerville	59 I8	1,847		●	●		●		●				●		Named for former fort constructed 1840 by Republic of Texas. Wooded hills, pastures and meadows. Stands of endangered Centerville Brazos mint.
Fort Griffin State Park and Historic Site, Albany	44 F2	506	●				●		●	●			●	●	Structural remains, reconstructed buildings of outpost established mid-1800s during period of skirmishes with Native Americans. Sighting of white-tailed deer, mallard ducks, raccoons and armadillos. Texas longhorn herd. *(See Historic Sites—Historic Forts and Unique Natural Features: Texas Longhorn.)*
Fort Lancaster State Historic Site, Ozona	65 C12	82								●			●		Frontier post established along US military route during Apache conflicts of mid-1800s. Visitor center. *(See Historic Sites—Historic Forts.)*
Fort Leaton State Historic Site, Presidio	74 A3	23											●		Adobe fortress constructed late 1840s by farmer, trader and bounty hunter Benjamin Leaton. Cultural exhibits, artifacts, photographs. *(See Historic Sites—Historic Forts.)*
Fort McKavett State Historic Site, Fort McKavett	67 A9	80								●			●		Located on San Saba River overlook. Established 1852 by 8th Infantry. Reconstructed buildings, ruins. Interpretive center, historical trail. *(See Historic Sites—Historic Forts and Texas Travel Trails: Texas Forts Trail.)*
Fort Parker State Park, Mexia	58 F5	1,459	●	●	●		●	●	●				●	●	Oak woodlands surrounding Lake Fort Parker. Sightings of migrating bird species. Activity center, boat rentals.
Fort Richardson State Park and Historic Site, Jacksboro	45 C8	472	●		●		●		●	●			●	●	Military post noted for roles in Kiowa conflicts 1860–1870. Interpretive center, exhibits. Lost Creek Reservoir State Trailway terminus. *(See Historic Sites—Historic Forts and Texas Travel Trails: Texas Forts Trail.)*
Franklin Mountains State Park, El Paso	62 E2	24,248							●				●		Texas' largest state park; one of largest urban wilderness parks in US. Contains portion of Franklin Mountains, including 7,192-foot North Franklin Peak, highest point in range. Habitat for Chihuahuan Desert *(see Unique Natural Features)* plant and shrub species.
Fulton Mansion State Historic Site, Fulton	85 C8	2.3											●		19th-century home of Fulton family. Constructed 1874–1877 in French Second Empire style. Period furnishings, "modern" mechanical conveniences. Guided tours. *(See Historic Sites.)*
Galveston Island State Park, Galveston	81 D8	2,013	●	●	●	●	●		●	●	●		●		Spans width of Galveston Island; beach area extends over 1.5 miles along Gulf of Mexico. Observation platforms along nature trail, bird-viewing blinds. Shaded picnic sites.
Garner State Park, Concan	76 A5	1,420	●	●	●		●		●		●		●	●	Popular camping destination along spring-fed waters of Frio River. Tubing, boat rentals, miniature golf.
Goliad State Park, Goliad	78 I6	202	●	●	●		●		●	●			●	●	Reconstructed Mission Espiritu Santo and Mission Rosario ruins commemorate 1836 Goliad Massacre. Also includes state historic sites General Ignacio Zaragoza Birthplace and Fannin Battleground. *(See Historic Sites.)*
Goose Island State Park, Fulton	85 B9	321	●	●	●	●	●	●	●	●	●		●	●	Located at conjunction of Aransas, Copano and St. Charles bays. Contains the Big Tree, state champion coastal live oak *(see Unique Natural Features).* Excellent birding; home to endangered whooping cranes.
Guadalupe River State Park, Bulverde	68 J6	1,939	●	●	●		●		●				●	●	Rugged Texas Hill Country bisected by Guadalupe River. White-tailed deer, armadillos, mallard ducks. Canoeing, rafting and kayaking.
Hill Country State Natural Area, Bandera	77 A8	5,370	●	●			●		●		●	●			Over 30 miles of multiuse trails in backcountry area. Scenic hills, flowing springs, oak groves and canyons. Primitive and equestrian camping only. *(See Hiking: Hill Country Trail System.)*
Honey Creek State Natural Area, Spring Branch	68 J6	2,294								●					Diverse geology, flora and fauna. Nesting area for golden-cheeked warbler. Guided naturalist tours—contact Guadalupe River State Park for information *(see this section).*
Hueco Tanks State Historic Site, El Paso	62 E4	860	●						●	●			●		Named for rain-trapping natural rock basins. Native American petroglyphs, ruins of overland stagecoach station. Well-worn paths, old roads offer hiking opportunities. Rock climbing. *(See Historic Sites, Unique Natural Features and Hiking: North Mountain Trail.)*
Huntsville State Park, Huntsville	71 C11	2,083	●	●	●		●	●	●	●	●		●	●	Located within Sam Houston National Forest. Loblolly and shortleaf pines surround Lake Raven. Boat rentals, guided trail rides on horseback. Interpretive center. *(See Hiking: Huntsville Trail.)*
I. D. Fairchild State Forest, Rusk	59 D12	2,740					●		●				●		Five tracts within early-20th-century logging region. Day-use area located along US 84 S.
Inks Lake State Park, Burnet	69 B7	1,201	●	●	●	●	●	●	●				●	●	Cedar and oak woodland area bordering Inks Lake. Pink granite outcroppings, wildflowers. Boat rentals, golf course. Scuba diving.
John Henry Kirby State Forest, Woodville	72 D5	600											●		Demonstration forest; land donated by former lumberman John Henry Kirby. Access requires notification.
Kerrville–Schreiner State Park, Kerrville	68 I3	517	●	●	●		●	●	●	●			●	●	Area where bald cypress trees shade banks of Guadalupe River. Upland hills and arroyos. Opportunities for close-up wildlife viewing.
Kickapoo Cavern State Park, Brackettville	76 A1	6,368	●						●		●				Includes 1,800-foot-long Kickapoo Cavern. Location of Green Cave, home to over one million Mexican free-tailed bats at peak of migratory season. Guided tours by reservation. Primitive camping only.
Lake Arrowhead State Park, Wichita Falls	37 I7	524	●	●	●	●	●	●	●	●		●	●	●	160 miles of lake shoreline created on Little Wichita River. Major recreation site for North Central Plains. Waterfowl, wading birds. Boat rentals.
Lake Bob Sandlin State Park, Pittsburg	48 D2	640	●	●	●	●	●	●	●				●	●	Located on north shore of 9,460-acre Lake Bob Sandlin. Various tree species offer colorful fall foliage.
Lake Brownwood State Park, Brownwood	56 D3	538	●	●	●	●	●	●	●	●			●		Reservoir created by damming the Pecan Bayou. Home to white-tailed deer, ducks, raccoons and armadillos. Recreation areas scattered along shoreline.
Lake Casa Blanca International State Park, Laredo	83 H7, 143 A12	371	●	●	●	●	●	●					●	●	Recreation area along 1,656-acre Lake Casa Blanca. Basketball, volleyball and tennis courts. Golf course.
Lake Colorado City State Park, Colorado City	42 K4	500	●	●	●	●	●	●					●	●	Over five miles of shoreline and rocky outcrops. Warm water temperatures year-round. Prairie dog town.
Lake Corpus Christi State Park, Mathis	84 C4	14,112	●	●	●	●	●	●					●	●	Impounded portion of Nueces River, formerly disputed US–Mexico boundary. Boat rentals.
Lake Houston State Park, New Caney	72 G1	4,920		●			●		●		●		●		Day-use recreation area. Park boundaries follow Peach Creek and East Fork of San Jacinto River.
Lake Livingston State Park, Livingston	72 G2	636	●	●	●		●	●	●	●	●		●	●	Recreation area along eastern lakeshore. Loblolly pines and water oaks. Lakeside swimming pool.
Lake Mineral Wells State Park, Mineral Wells	45 F9	3,283	●	●	●		●	●	●	●	●	●	●	●	Rock-climbing area popular among rappelers, climbers. Excellent fishing. Equestrian camping, boat rentals. Lake Mineral Wells State Trailway access.
Lake Somerville State Park—Birch Creek Unit, Somerville	70 F5	640	●	●	●	●	●	●	●	●	●	●	●		Located on north shore; larger of two park units within landscape of dense yaupon holly. White-tailed deer, coyotes and various waterfowl. Equestrian camping, volleyball courts.
Lake Somerville State Park—Nails Creek Unit, Somerville	70 F5	300	●	●	●	●	●		●	●	●	●	●		South-shore park unit noted for abundant wildflowers, woodlands. Connected to Birch Creek Unit via 13-mile-long Lake Somerville Trailway *(see Hiking).* Equestrian camping, volleyball courts.

STATE LANDS, *continued*

NAME, LOCATION	PAGE & GRID	ACREAGE	CAMPING	SWIMMING	BOATING	WATERSKIING	FISHING	FISHING PIER	HIKING TRAILS	NATURE/INTERPRETIVE TRAILS	BICYCLING TRAILS	EQUESTRIAN TRAILS	PICNIC SITES	PLAYGROUND	COMMENTS
Lake Tawakoni State Park, Wills Point	47 F8	376	●	●	●	●	●		●				●		Located on south central shore of 36,000-acre Lake Tawakoni, popular water recreation destination. Rolling woodlands and small tract of tallgrass prairie.
Lake Texana State Park, Edna	79 F11	575	●	●	●	●	●	●					●	●	Lake created by damming of Navidad River. Mixed oak and pecan woodlands.
Lake Whitney State Park, Whitney	58 C1	1,281	●	●	●	●	●		●	●			●		One of Texas' largest lakes. Noted fishing for trophy-sized striped, white and smallmouth bass. Scattered groves of post and live oak. Excellent birding.
Landmark Inn State Historic Site, Castroville	77 C10	5		●	●		●			●			●		Historic 19th-century hotel. Gristmill on nearby Medina River. Milling equipment, exhibits. *(See Historic Sites.)*
Lipantitlan State Historic Site, Orange Grove	84 D4	5											●		Recreation area located in South Texas Brush Country. Named after Mexican fort that once stood on site. *(See Historic Sites.)*
Lockhart State Park, Lockhart	69 J11	264	●	●			●		●				●	●	Spring-fed stream. Wildlife includes bobcats, armadillos and snakes. Recreation hall, golf course, swimming pool.
Longhorn Cavern State Park, Burnet	69 C7	646							●	●			●		Limestone cavern in Backbone Ridge formed over 450 million years ago. History of animal and human habitation. More recently used as dance hall. Observation tower. Guided tours. *(See Unique Natural Features—Caverns.)*
Lost Maples State Natural Area, Vanderpool	67 J12	2,174	●	●			●		●	●			●		Scenic area named for stands of bigtooth maples. Diverse plant and bird life, colorful fall foliage. Rugged limestone canyons, wooded slopes. *(See Unique Natural Features and Hiking: East Trail.)*
Lyndon B. Johnson State Park and Historic Site, Stonewall	68 F5	718		●			●		●	●			●	●	Structures, exhibits relating to life of 36th US president Lyndon B. Johnson. Sauer–Beckmann Living History Farm. Texas longhorn herd, visitor center and garden. *(See Historic Sites.)*
Magoffin Home State Historic Site, El Paso	62 G2, 126 D4	1.5													19-room adobe structure designed and built by El Paso pioneer Joseph Magoffin. Family artifacts, furnishings and paintings. Guided tours. *(See Historic Sites.)*
Martin Creek Lake State Park, Tatum	48 K4	287	●	●	●	●	●	●	●		●		●	●	Scenic pine, hardwood forests particularly colorful during fall foliage. Common sightings of great blue herons, redheaded woodpeckers and great egrets. Historic pioneer trail used by early settlers.
Martin Dies, Jr. State Park, Jasper	73 A7	705	●	●	●	●	●	●	●	●	●		●	●	Heavily forested area located in East Texas Piney Woods; numerous creeks and stands of cypress, willows and beech trees. Adjacent B.A. Steinhagen Lake is site of winter bald eagle population. Boat rentals.
Matagorda Island State Park, Port O'Connor	85 A12	7,325	●	●	●	●	●		●		●				Over 39 miles of sandy beaches on isolated barrier island. Endangered wildlife species include whooping cranes, peregrine falcons. Primitive camping only. Unit of National Wildlife Refuge System.
McKinney Falls State Park, Austin	69 G11	744	●	●			●		●	●	●		●		Park and associated falls named for original settler Thomas F. McKinney, prominent horse breeder. Mid-1800s homestead ruins still visible. Visitor center, exhibits.
Meridian State Park, Meridian	57 C11	505	●	●	●		●		●	●	●		●	●	Abundant plants, wildflowers in woodland areas. Sightings of endangered golden-cheeked warbler during spring. *(See Hiking: Bosque Trail.)*
Mission Tejas State Park, Weches	60 F1	362	●				●		●	●			●	●	Abandoned Spanish Mission site contains relocated pioneer log home of early Houston County family. *(See Historic Sites—Historic Missions.)*
Monahans Sandhills State Park, Monahans	52 F6	3,840	●							●		●	●		Dynamic landscape containing over 3,800 acres of sand dunes *(see Unique Natural Features)*, some reaching 70 feet in height. Interpretive center.
Monument Hill and Kreische Brewery State Historic Sites, La Grange	70 I3	40								●			●	●	Homestead and brewery of former landowner Heinrich Kreische. Tomb of Texans killed during post-statehood conflicts with Mexico also located here. Visitor center. *(See Historic Sites.)*
Mother Neff State Park, Moody	57 H12	259	●		●		●		●				●	●	Oldest state park in Texas (developed in mid-1930s). Named for Mrs. Isabella Eleanor "Mother" Neff, who donated original six acres in 1916. Located along Leon River. Rock cliffs, diverse vegetation.
Mustang Island State Park, Corpus Christi	85 F8	3,954	●	●			●						●		Southern portion of coastal barrier island. Abundant shore birds; seasonal waterfowl, migratory birds. Aquatic life. Separate day-use area.
Palmetto State Park, Luling	78 A5	270	●	●	●		●	●	●	●			●	●	Named for wild dwarf palmetto growing throughout park. Eastern and western US plant species represented. Over 200 bird species identified within park. *(See Hiking: Palmetto Trail.)*
Palo Duro Canyon State Park, Canyon	29 J12	16,402	●				●		●		●	●	●	●	Spectacular geologic formations. Site of state's final battle with Native Americans in 1874. Guided tours via miniature railroad. Historical exhibits, scenic drive and horse rentals. Outdoor musical drama *TEXAS*. Texas longhorn herd. *(See Unique Natural Features and Hiking: Lighthouse Peak Trail.)*
Pedernales Falls State Park, Johnson City	69 F8	5,212	●	●			●		●	●	●		●		Portions of Texas Hill Country along scenic stretch of Pedernales River. Falls drop almost 50 feet over sloping limestone steps. Overlook at north end of park. *(See Hiking: Wolf Mountain Trail.)*
Port Isabel Lighthouse State Historic Site, Port Isabel	89 I7	0.9											●		Brick structure constructed to aid navigation along state's southern tip; lighthouse topped with mercury-vapor light. Only such lighthouse along Texas coast open to public. *(See Historic Sites.)*
Port Lavaca State Fishing Pier, Port Lavaca	79 I11	11			●		●	●							Former causeway of State Route 35 destroyed during 1961 hurricane. Converted to 3,200-foot-long pier.
Possum Kingdom State Park, Caddo	44 F6	1,529	●	●	●	●	●	●					●	●	Rugged canyon area in Palo Pinto Mountains. Home to Possum Kingdom Lake, one of southwestern Texas' clearest lakes. Texas longhorn herd. Boat rentals.
Purtis Creek State Park, Eustace	47 J8	1,582	●	●	●		●	●	●				●	●	Lake designed specifically for sportfishing. Largemouth bass fished on catch-and-release basis; large catfish, crappie may be retained.
Ray Roberts Lake State Park—Isle du Bois Unit, Pilot Point	46 B3	1,397	●	●	●	●	●		●		●	●	●	●	Several 19th- and early 20th-century farm sites designated State Archaeological Landmarks. Sandy beach, wooded terrain. Ray Roberts Lake/Lake Lewisville Greenbelt. Equestrian camping.
Ray Roberts Lake State Park—Johnson Branch Unit, Hemming	46 A2	1,514	●	●	●	●	●	●	●	●	●		●	●	Located on north shore of Ray Roberts Lake. Tours of 19th-century Jones Farm.
Rusk/Palestine State Park, Rusk	60 D1	136	●	●	●		●	●	●	●	●		●	●	Rusk Unit features mixed pine, hardwood forest and 15-acre lake stocked with bass, catfish and perch. Palestine Unit is designated day-use area. Both units are termini for Texas State Railroad.
Sabine Pass Battleground State Historic Site, Sabine Pass	73 K8	58	●		●		●						●		Important shipping, trade center during Civil War. Site of decisive skirmish protecting Texas from Union invasion. *(See Historic Sites.)*
Sam Bell Maxey House State Historic Site, Paris	39 D11, 151 J9	0.4													Restored Victorian Italianate–style mansion of former Confederate general. Maxey family furnishings, landscaped grounds. *(See Historic Sites.)*
San Angelo State Park, San Angelo	55 G7	7,677	●	●	●	●	●		●		●	●	●	●	Located along west shore of 5,440-acre O. C. Fisher Lake. Over 50 miles of multi-use trails. Guided tours to ancient Permian period animal tracks and Native American rock etchings. Texas longhorn herd.
San Jacinto Battleground State Historic Site, Deer Park	72 K2	1,168					●			●			●		570-foot-high monument commemorates heroes from 1836 Battle of San Jacinto. Steam-powered 1914 battleship USS *Texas* berthed at park. Museum, exhibits. *(See Historic Sites.)*
Sea Rim State Park, Sabine Pass	73 K7	15,094	●	●	●		●			●			●		Sandy beach area where tidal marsh meets waters from Gulf of Mexico. Biologically diverse area important to aquatic life, migrating waterfowl. Wildlife observation blinds. *(See Unique Natural Features: Sea Rim Marsh.)*
Sebastopol State Historic Site, Seguin	78 A3, 162 K5	2.2											●		Greek Revival home constructed of limecrete, a type of concrete made from gravel, lime and water. Antiques, exhibits. Guided tours. *(See Historic Sites.)*
Seminole Canyon State Historic Site, Comstock	66 K2	2,173	●						●	●	●		●		Limestone canyons noted for ancient pictographs. Caves accessed via one-hour ranger-guided tour. Visitor center, exhibits. *(See Historic Sites.)*
Sheldon Lake State Park and Environmental Education Center, Sheldon	72 J1, 131 A11	2,800			●		●	●	●	●			●		Major wintering spot for greater white-fronted, snow and Canada geese. Habitat for nesting bitterns, herons and egrets. Rest area for raptors and Neotropical bird species. Nature/ecology programs. Boating March–October.
South Llano River State Park, Junction	67 E11	524	●	●	●		●		●		●		●		Stream-fed South Llano River forms park's northern boundary. One of state's oldest and largest winter turkey roosts. Wildlife observation blinds. River tubing.
Starr Family Home State Historic Site, Marshall	48 I6, 147 B11	3.1													Late-19th-century homes previously inhabited by members of the prominent Starr family, headed by James Harper Starr, one-time treasurer of Republic of Texas. Maplecroft, complex centerpiece, shows architectural and decorative influence of New Orleans. Exhibits. *(See Historic Sites.)*
Stephen F. Austin State Park, San Felipe	71 J8	663	●	●			●		●				●	●	Historical townsite of San Felipe de Austin, early Texas colony founded by Stephen F. Austin 1824–1836. Forested grounds are natural habitat for deer, foxes. Swimming pool, golf course. Exhibits. *(See Historic Sites.)*
Texas State Railroad State Park, Rusk	60 D1	499													Dedicated to preserving steam locomotives and railroad's golden age. 50-mile round-trip through countryside aboard steam-powered *Iron Horse*. Exhibits. *(See Historic Sites.)*
Tyler State Park, Lindale	47 I12	985	●	●	●		●	●	●	●	●		●	●	Spring-fed lake within pine, hardwood forest. Abundant wildlife. Boat rentals.
Varner–Hogg Plantation State Historic Site, West Columbia	80 E4	66					●						●		Two-story Colonial Revival mansion acquired 1901 by James Stephen Hogg, state's first native-born governor. Historic furnishings, memorabilia. Guided tours. *(See Historic Sites.)*
Village Creek State Park, Lumberton	73 F7	1,004	●		●		●		●				●	●	Dense forest lands in region noted for heavy rainfall. Baygalls and cypress and water-tupelo swamps. Alligators, mink, snapping turtles and lizards. Renowned float stream.
W. Goodrich Jones State Forest, Conroe	71 G11	1,733								●			●		Site of devasting 1923 fire. Forest today is habitat for rare red-cockaded woodpecker. Picnic sites along small pond. *(See Hiking: Sweetleaf Nature Trail.)*
Washington-on-the-Brazos State Historic Site, Washington	71 F7	293							●				●	●	Site of March 2, 1836, signing of Texas Declaration of Independence. Historic townsite once capital of Republic of Texas. Reconstructed Independence Hall, museum and exhibits. Barrington Living History Farm. *(See Historic Sites.)*
Wyler Aerial Tramway, El Paso	62 F2, 126 A4	196													Tramway gondolas access summit of 5,632-foot Ranger Peak on east side of Franklin Mountains. Observation deck offers views of portions of Texas, New Mexico and Mexican state of Chihuahua. Interpretive panels.

Texas Travel Trails

The following Texas Travel Trails are officially designated state scenic drives. Each trail is traced on state maps in the Atlas with the dotted pattern indicated in the Legend. Most trails follow state highways and Farm to Market and Ranch roads, avoiding major highways whenever possible.

While traveling, look for trail signs at highway access points and intersections. Each route is marked with blue-and-white trail signs: rectangular signs designated with trail name and symbol or round signs designated with an arrow.

For copies of trail maps or additional information, contact the Texas Department of Transportation, Travel Division, 125 East 11th Street, Austin, TX 78701-2483, (800) 452-9292.

Note: All trails are loops, described in a clockwise direction from a designated starting location. However, trails may be accessed at any city or town located along the route.

TEXAS BRAZOS TRAIL – Waco – 461 miles – 58 F2, 167 G7 Route through fertile agricultural areas passes numerous geographic regions and state lands surrounding portions of Brazos River. Begins in Brazos River Valley, near Waco's single-span suspension bridge, and heads northeast past Balcones Fault, a surface fracture that extends into Oklahoma. Continues through Blackland Prairie, former marine bed noted for fossils, and post oak region near Mexia before turning south toward Wheelock. Short segment follows historic Old San Antonio Road—600-mile-long trail connecting Mexico with East Texas missions. Stretches south, offering side trips to Washington-on-the-Brazos State Historic Site and Somerville Lake. Continues north, affording scenic vistas en route to Belton Lake, habitat for freshwater jellyfish. Final return to Waco through ranches, pasture lands. Follows designated signs marked with an arrow or cotton tuft.

TEXAS FOREST TRAIL – Tyler – 835 miles – 47 J12, 165 A11 Route through East Texas' Piney Woods region connects four national forests. Travels north past Governor Jim Hogg City Park and oil fields. Continues along several short sections of highway renowned for impressive fall foliage. Heads south at Daingerfield, skirting Lake O' The Pines and Caddo Lake State Park en route to Sam Rayburn Reservoir, offering fishing and other recreation. Enters Angelina National Forest and heads east toward Pineland and Sabine National Forest. Turns west at B. A. Steinhagen Lake, cutting through deep forests and Big Thicket National Preserve, known for rare plants and birdlife, heading to Lake Livingston and Sam Houston National Forest. Skirts Lake Conroe and heads back to Tyler via Davy Crockett National Forest. Follows designated signs marked with an arrow or two pine trees.

TEXAS FORTS TRAIL – Abilene – 688 miles – 43 I11, 90 C5 Accesses eight frontier forts and one Spanish presidio in west central Texas. Begins near eastern shore of Lake Fort Phantom Hill and travels north, passing ruins and Texas longhorn herd at Fort Griffin State Park and Historic Site. Continues past Fort Belknap and Fort Richardson State Park and Historic Site, winding south through ancient river delta, ranching country and pecan orchards to Fort Mason. Passes ruins of Real Presidio de San Saba. Offers short side trip to restored buildings of Fort McKavett State Historic Site. Final stretch heads north to Fort Concho in San Angelo then passes Fort Chadbourne historical marker. Follows designated signs marked with an arrow or crossed swords. *(See Historic Sites—Historic Forts.)*

TEXAS HILL COUNTRY TRAIL – San Antonio – 623 miles – 77 B11, 158 B1 Abundant wildlife, vistas and historic sites located among geologic features formed millions of years ago. Leads through Castroville and broad coastal plains before turning sharply toward blue hills of Balcones Escarpment. Winds toward Bandera, noted dude ranch destination, passing panoramic landscapes dotted with sinkholes. Leaves hills south of Concan to travel through coastal plains, rich farmland. Heads north toward Bluffton, winding along portion of Pedernales River. Side trip accesses Enchanted Rock State Natural Area before arriving at Lyndon B. Johnson National Historical Park. Final portion passes through Inks Lake State Park, offers side trip to Longhorn Cavern State Park and returns to San Antonio through noted mineral region. Follows designated signs marked with an arrow or deer.

TEXAS INDEPENDENCE TRAIL – Houston – 712 miles – 72 K1, 135 B7 Accesses several historic sites critical to Texas' fight for independence and beach areas along Gulf of Mexico and Galveston Island. Trail begins at San Jacinto Battleground State Historic Site and loops into Baytown by way of the Lynchburg Ferry. Travels south along Galveston Island to Freeport, renowned area for fishing, industry and recreation. Continues along Gulf of Mexico toward Port Lavaca with optional side trip to "lost" city of Indianola. Egret sightings near Green Lake, one of state's largest natural freshwater lakes. Passes historical buildings and markers in Goliad State Park, site of 1836 massacre. Heads across San Antonio River, then northward through managed lands, livestock pastures and pastoral areas to Lockhart. Final stretch leads through historic Round Top and Stephen F. Austin State Park before returning to Houston. Follows designated signs marked with an arrow or rifle. *(See Historic Sites.)*

TEXAS LAKES TRAIL – Dallas – 644 miles – 46 E4, 105 B10 Links over 25 lakes and recreation areas offering exceptional fishing. Begins at lakes within Dallas and heads north past Lewisville and Ray Roberts lakes toward Lake Texoma. Side trip northwest of Gainesville leads to scenic Moss Lake. Continues east past Hagerman National Wildlife Refuge, which offers abundant birding, to Eisenhower Birthplace State Historic Site in Denison. Travels along portion of Texas–Oklahoma border to Chicota, accessing Pat Mayse Lake, before heading south to Lake Tawakoni (crossed by state's longest inland bridge), Cedar Creek Reservoir and Richland Chambers Reservoir. Final portion skirts Whitney Lake and returns to Dallas via Fort Worth. Side trip accesses dinosaur tracks *(see Unique Natural Features)* at Dinosaur Valley State Park in Glen Rose. Follows designated signs marked with an arrow or sailboat.

TEXAS MOUNTAIN TRAIL – El Paso – 658 miles – 62 F3, 126 C6 Figure-eight route through mountain and desert landscape skirts portion of border with Mexico. Originates in Franklin Mountains and continues past Hueco Tanks *(see Unique Natural Features)* and the volcanically formed Cornudas Mountains. Parallels portion of Butterfield–Overland stagecoach route, turning south near Guadalupe Mountains National Park, which contains four of the state's five highest peaks. Passes Mount Locke's McDonald Observatory *(see Museums)*. Heads toward Big Bend National Park and Big Bend Ranch State Park, passing Davis Mountains and other geological features used as landmarks by early explorers. Rock formations, canyons visible as route heads to Marfa. Continues northwest through Sierra Blanca then travels along portion of Rio Grande before returning to El Paso. Follows designated signs marked with an arrow or mountain peak.

TEXAS PECOS TRAIL – Odessa – 711 miles – 53 D8, 150 J4 Explores sunbaked southern region of Great Plains, traversing Pecos River and harsh landscape traveled by early American pioneers. Passes oil fields, drilling sites near Midland before turning southeast. Crosses Pecos River and winds through deep gorges en route to Iraan, one of the state's largest oil-producing fields. Accesses Fort Lancaster State Historic Site *(see Historic Sites—Historic Forts)* and offers side trip to Caverns of Sonora *(see Unique Natural Features—Caverns)*. Continues south to Brackettville, affording views of grazing ranch animals and other wildlife. Travels northwest toward Pecos, passing Amistad Reservoir; distant views of Mexico and Pecos Canyon while crossing Pecos River Bridge. Final portion skirts sand dunes at Monahans Sandhills State Park and ancient Odessa Meteor Crater. *(See Unique Natural Features.)* Follows designated signs marked with an arrow or boot.

TEXAS PLAINS TRAIL – Lubbock – 721 miles – 33 K10 Explores virtually flat landscape in Panhandle area once dominated by roaming buffalo and tall native grasses. Heads west to Whiteface, passing miles of pump jacks and oil fields before turning north toward Muleshoe National Wildlife Refuge. Continues north through agricultural regions featuring irrigation systems, feedlots and massive grain elevators. Turns east at Dumas; terrain changes from flat cropland to rolling pasture before plunging into Canadian River breaks near Stinnett. Travels south, crossing Lake Meredith via dam. Optional side trip accesses Alibates Flint Quarries National Monument on lake's south shore. Continues through Amarillo and Palo Duro Canyon *(see Unique Natural Features)*, with spectacular sculpted cliffs and buttes. Additional canyon views at Tule Canyon near Crosbyton. Final stretch leads south to Gail, before returning north to Lubbock. Follows designated signs marked with an arrow or windmill.

TEXAS TROPICAL TRAIL – Corpus Christi – 697 miles – 84 G6 Travels around state's southernmost tip, accessing gulf beaches and agricultural regions along Rio Grande. Heads south, passing enormous King Ranch *(see Museums)* and offering side trip to Laguna Atascosa National Wildlife Refuge. Turns inland at Port Isabel, following the Rio Grande from Brownsville to Laredo. Area noted for rich farmlands producing diverse crops—from grapefruit to sugarcane and cotton. Skirts Santa Ana National Wildlife Refuge, continues through rolling terrain toward Falfurrias, then turns north to Lake Corpus Christi. Next segment features wintering whooping crane population *(see Unique Natural Features)* at Aransas National Wildlife Refuge and arrives at Port Aransas and Mustang Island State Park via ferry. Final portion includes excursion to Padre Island National Seashore and developed areas along Gulf of Mexico. Follows designated signs marked with an arrow or palm tree.

Amusements

The following listings provide a variety of family-oriented activities and entertainment.

For more information, contact the Texas Economic Development, Tourism Division, P.O. Box 12728, Austin, TX 78711, (512) 462-9191.

ABILENE ZOOLOGICAL GARDENS AND DISCOVERY CENTER – Abilene – 43 J11, 90 F5 Over 500 mammals, birds and reptiles; many native and African species. Exhibits arranged according to animals' countries of origin. Bridge over giraffe habitat allows eye-to-eye viewing of residents.

ALAMO VILLAGE – Brackettville – 76 B1 Former movie set constructed 1959 for use in *The Alamo*. Replica expanded to include town complex; since used by other filmmakers. Open to public. Performances, attractions.

ALAMODOME – San Antonio – 77 C12, 159 D8 Multipurpose dome hosts sporting events, exhibitions, concerts and conventions. Seats over 72,000 people. Home to NBA's San Antonio Spurs basketball team. Facility tours.

ASTRODOME – Houston – 71 K12, 133 D12 One of world's largest domed stadiums. Large enough to contain an 18-story building; seating capacity in excess of 60,000. Home to National League's Houston Astros baseball team and NFL's Houston Oilers football team. Tours.

ASTROWORLD – Houston – 71 K12, 133 E12 Houston's largest amusement park; contains nine theme areas and over 100 rides. Famous roller coaster, Ultra-Twister, drops 92 feet and rotates backward and forward 360 degrees. Performances, nightly fireworks. Adjacent to WaterWorld *(see this section)*.

BALLPARK IN ARLINGTON – Arlington – 46 G2, 111 D9 Sports facility is home to American League's Texas Rangers baseball team. Accommodates 49,200 people. Museum, learning center, amphitheater and youth baseball field.

BILLY BOB'S TEXAS – Fort Worth – 46 G1, 109 A9 Considered "world's largest honky-tonk." Located on grounds of former cattle-holding area. Showcase facility for live bull riding, country-and-western performances. 10,000-square-foot dance floor.

DALLAS AQUARIUM – Dallas – 113 B12 One of country's largest inland aquariums. Features over 375 marine species; fish from Amazon and Hawaii exhibited. Endangered species. Located in Fair Park *(see this section)*.

DALLAS ARBORETUM AND BOTANICAL GARDEN – Dallas – 46 F4, 106 J2 Rolling landscape, gardens within city setting. Jonsson Color Garden especially beautiful when spring tulips bloom. Noted azalea collection, cascading water walls and hidden garden. Includes DeGolyer House, 1939 estate resembling Spanish colonial style. National Register of Historic Places.

DALLAS CIVIC GARDEN CENTER – Dallas – 113 B12 Flora from South America, Africa and Pacific Islands. Fragrance gardens for visually impaired. Miniature rose, Shakespearean gardens. Endangered species.

DALLAS ZOO – Dallas – 46 G4, 113 D9 One of Texas' largest zoos; approximately 1,600 animals. *Wilds of Africa* exhibit replicates six African habitats. Narrated journey through zoo via monorail. Simulated rain forest. Nature trail, gorilla-viewing area.

FAIR PARK – Dallas – 46 G4, 113 B12 Popular city park known for art deco architecture. Home to several museums, including The Science Place and Dallas Museum of Natural History *(see Museums)*. New Year's Day football classic held in park's Cotton Bowl Stadium. Hosts Texas State Fair, one of US' largest state fairs.

FAME CITY – Houston – 71 K10, 132 D3 Indoor amusement complex. Skating rink, bowling alley, cinemas and miniature golf course. Rides, playground and video games. Waterslides, other attractions at nearby Fame City Waterworks.

FIESTA TEXAS – San Antonio – 77 A12, 156 C2 Amusement park featuring four Texas towns: Mexican village, German settlement, 1920s boomtown and 1950s homecoming-weekend town. Musical entertainment, rides and food. Features one of world's tallest, steepest and fastest wooden roller coasters.

FORT WORTH BOTANIC GARDEN – Fort Worth – 46 G1, 109 E8 Oldest botanic garden in Texas; original rose garden constructed 1933. Native and exotic species. Republic of Texas rose garden, Japanese and fragrance gardens. 10,000-square-foot conservatory, exhibition greenhouse.

FORT WORTH WATER GARDENS – Fort Worth – 46 G1, 109 D10 4.3-acre plaza of plantings and molded concrete forming deep lakes. Numerous waterfalls, fountains and quiet pools. For viewing only—swimming, wading not permitted. Evening illumination.

FORT WORTH ZOO – Fort Worth – 46 G1, 109 F9 Houses over 4,400 specimens found worldwide; one of largest exhibits of reptiles and amphibians in US. Aquarium features extensive freshwater and saltwater fish collections. *Texas!* exhibit depicts turn-of-the-century Texas town with livestock corral and blacksmith shop.

FOSSIL RIM WILDLIFE CENTER – Glen Rose – 57 A10 Privately owned wildlife sanctuary; dedicated to protection of exotic and endangered species. Hundreds of animals viewed via 9.5-mile auto tour. Education center. Petting pasture, nature trail. Behind-the-scenes tour by reservation.

GLADYS PORTER ZOO – Brownsville – 88 J6, 95 K8 Over 1,500 animals grouped by geographic regions: Africa, Asia, Indo-Australia and Tropical America. Specimens situated on islands separated from spectators by moats. Train rides.

HOUSTON ZOOLOGICAL GARDENS – Houston – 71 K12, 134 B1 Contains several rare animal species, including albino reptiles. Vampire bat exhibit features bat feedings; tropical aviary contains free-flying exotic birds in simulated rain forest. Gorilla house, Hippo-Dome and large-cat facility. Located in Hermann Park.

INTERNATIONAL WILDLIFE PARK – Grand Prairie – 46 G3, 112 B1 Free-roaming animals from around the world viewed from 6.5-mile auto route. Feeding opportunities and possible close-up views of ostrich, camel, elk and other animals. Entertainment, rides.

MOODY GARDENS – Galveston – 81 D9, 126 K1 142-acre complex dominated by ten-story Rainforest Pyramid, habitat for thousands of exotic plant and animal species. IMAX theater. Paddle wheeler. Gardens, freshwater lagoons, sandy beach and jogging trails.

NATIONAL WILDFLOWER RESEARCH CENTER – Austin – 69 G10 Dedicated to study, preservation and reestablishment of native plants. Founded by Lady Bird Johnson in 1982. 60-acre grounds contain pollination garden, reconstructed prairie and demonstration beds. Tours.

NATURAL BRIDGE WILDLIFE RANCH – Comal – 69 K7 Drive-through park on privately owned ranch land features native and exotic animals. Rolling woodland setting home to ostriches, antelopes and zebras. Visitor center.

REUNION ARENA – Dallas – 113 B10 Home of NBA's Dallas Mavericks basketball team and NHL's Dallas Stars hockey team.

RIVER WALK – San Antonio – 77 B12, 159 D7 Also known as Paseo del Rio, 2.5-mile tree-lined footpath along San Antonio River. Bordered by restaurants, shops and hotels. Several river crossings and access points via staircases. River cruises.

SAN ANTONIO BOTANICAL GARDEN – San Antonio – 77 B12, 159 A8 Several theme gardens located on 33 landscaped acres. Japanese meditation, herb and children's vegetable gardens. Touch-and-smell garden for visually impaired. Extensive collection of native Texas plants.

SAN ANTONIO ZOO – San Antonio – 77 B12, 159 A8 One of largest animal collections in US. Sanctuary for whooping crane, snow leopard and white rhino. Exhibits include Monkey Island, outdoor hippopotamus pool and barless bear pits. Freshwater and saltwater aquariums, bird aviaries. Located in Brackenridge Park.

SCHLITTERBAHN – New Braunfels – 69 K8, 150 B5 65-acre water park located on Comal River shoreline. Spring-fed rides, chutes and slides. Pools, hot tubs, lagoon. Paddleboats, volleyball.

SEA WORLD OF TEXAS – San Antonio – 77 B11 One of world's largest marine parks; 250-acre complex. Killer whales, penguins, dolphins, walruses, otters, seals and sea lions. Re-created South Pacific coral reef. Water rides, shows and exhibits.

SEA-ARAMA MARINEWORLD – Galveston – 81 D9 38-acre complex provides home for marine life and other animals in tropical setting. Dolphins and exotic birds. Shark feedings, ski shows.

SIX FLAGS OVER TEXAS – Arlington – 46 G2, 111 C10 Opened 1961 as one of first US theme parks. Name refers to six countries that claimed land in what is now Texas. Over 100 rides, attractions and shows. Children's area, 200-foot parachute drop, 14-story roller coaster and Texas Cliff Hanger ride offering sensation of falling 10 stories.

SPLASHTOWN – San Antonio – 78 B1, 159 B10 Waterslides, wave pool and winding river ride on inner tubes. The Hydra, popular multislide attraction with twisting speed slides. Blue Lagoon, sand playground.

SPLASHTOWN USA – Spring – 71 H12 Water rides, attractions. Flumes, waterslides, wave pool. Sheer drops from The Hydra. Blue Lagoon, recreation pool, Kids Kove and children's area.

THE SUMMIT – Houston – 133 A11 Home court to NBA's Houston Rockets basketball team.

TEXAS SAFARI – Clifton – 57 D11 Exotic and native animals inhabit theme areas from plains to ponds. Over 800 acres. Baby-animal compound, petting zoo.

TEXAS STADIUM – Irving – 104 I5 Home stadium for NFC's Dallas Cowboys football team. Seats over 65,000 spectators.

TEXAS STATE AQUARIUM – Corpus Christi – 84 E6, 98 B4 Marine plants and animals indigenous to Gulf of Mexico. Indoor and outdoor exhibits display over 2,000 marine animals. Artificial reef community created by massive, steel-legged oil rigs. Touch pool contains starfish, crabs and sea urchins.

WATERWORLD – Houston – 71 K12, 133 E12 Water attractions, some simulating ocean waves. Waterslides, wave pool, inner-tube river ride. Features The Edge, 80-foot free-fall slide. Water playground, giant water maze. Adjacent to AstroWorld *(see this section)*.

WET 'N WILD – Arlington – 46 G2, 111 C9 Theme park featuring rides such as Corkscrew Flume and Kamikaze Waterslide. Lagoon pool, water playground. River floating.

ZILKER PARK – Austin – 69 F10, 93 H7 Lush landscaping in 400-acre city park. Spring-fed swimming hole, frisbee golf course. Rose gardens, lily ponds and walking trails within Zilker Botanical Gardens. Miniature-train rides. Zilker Hillside Theater.

Museums

For more information on museums, contact the Texas Economic Development, Tourism Division, P.O. Box 12728, Austin, TX 78711, (512) 462-9191.

AGE OF STEAM RAILROAD MUSEUM – Dallas – 113 B12 Passenger cars and steam locomotives depict American railroad history. World's largest steam engine and 1930s train with dining and sleeper cars.

AMERICAN AIRPOWER HERITAGE MUSEUM – Midland – 53 C9 Authentic WWII artifacts and memorabilia including uniforms, armament, photographs, weapons. Over 140 WWII-era aircraft represent US forces, British Royal Air Force, German Luftwaffe and Imperial Japanese Navy. Operated by Confederate Air Force.

AMERICAN QUARTER HORSE HERITAGE CENTER & MUSEUM – Amarillo – 29 H11, 91 F11 Devoted to history and development of American quarter horse, known as "America's fastest athlete." Heritage Gallery traces breed from colonial racing days to present. Performance Gallery illustrates racing, rodeos and ranching; contains American Quarter Horse Hall of Fame. Hands-on exhibits, artifacts, videos, live demonstrations.

AMON CARTER MUSEUM – Fort Worth – 109 D8 One of Fort Worth's largest contemporary art museums. Extensive collection of American Western art, including works by Remington and Russell. Modern sculpture, paintings and photography.

ANNIE RIGGS HOTEL MUSEUM – Fort Stockton – 64 A5 Adobe-style hotel built 1899 on popular Overland–Butterfield stagecoach route. 14 rooms illustrate pioneer life at turn of century and chronicle development of Fort Stockton. Historical furnishings, artifacts.

BIBLICAL ARTS CENTER – Dallas – 46 F4, 105 F11 Biblical artwork housed in building featuring early-Christian-era architecture. Religious relics and portraits of biblical figures. *The Garden Tomb of Christ* features life-sized replica of tomb in Calvary. Light-and-sound presentation.

CADILLAC RANCH – Amarillo – 29 H11 Brainchild of eccentric oil, banking and cattle magnate Stanley Marsh III. Ten Cadillacs buried nose-down in field at same angle as Pyramids at Giza. Graffiti-covered tribute to days of auto travel.

CATTLEMAN'S MUSEUM – Fort Worth – 109 D9 Commemorates American cowboys and 500-year development of cattle industry. Videotapes, movies and talking displays cover Western ranching, life on cattle trail and struggles between ranchers and cattle rustlers.

CHILDREN'S MUSEUM OF HOUSTON – Houston – 71 K12, 130 J1 Hands-on exhibits concerning science, history and the arts. Simulated anthropological dwellings and mechanical displays. Closed-circuit television station, costumes and stage for children to create productions.

CORPUS CHRISTI MUSEUM OF SCIENCE AND HISTORY – Corpus Christi – 84 E6, 98 B4 Portion of Bayfront Arts and Sciences Park devoted to prehistoric life, marine life and cultural development. *Shipwreck!* exhibit displays artifacts from three Spanish galleons wrecked on Padre Island in 1850s. Full-size galleon replica. Ranching and local history exhibits.

COWBOY ARTISTS OF AMERICA MUSEUM – Kerrville – 68 H3 Permanent and rotating collections of modern artwork in Old West tradition of Remington and Russell. Western art library, teaching facilities.

DALLAS MUSEUM OF ART – Dallas – 46 G4, 113 A10 City's largest art museum; contains African, pre-Columbian and 19th-century art. Sculpture garden with waterfalls and trees. Reves Collection of European art and furniture in re-created Mediterranean villa. Guided tours.

DALLAS MUSEUM OF NATURAL HISTORY – Dallas – 113 B12 Habitat displays of native plants, animals and minerals. Fossil exhibit of fish, reptile and dinosaur. 32-foot-high reconstructed mosasaur, one of world's largest prehistoric sea serpents. 20,000-year-old mammoth skeleton. Located in Fair Park *(see Amusements)*.

DEPOT MUSEUM – Henderson – 60 A3 Exhibits in restored 1901 Missouri–Pacific Railroad depot recount history of Rusk County. Restored 1841 T. J. Walling log cabin and Arnold Outhouse, first outhouse in Texas to receive historical marker. Children's learning center.

EAST TEXAS OIL MUSEUM – Kilgore – 48 J3 Development of East Texas Oil Field traced through audio-visual presentations, photographs, films and momentos. Re-created 1930s oil boomtown features general store, feed store and post office.

FORT WORTH MUSEUM OF SCIENCE AND HISTORY – Fort Worth – 109 D8 Highlights history of calculators and computers, geology and paleontology, rocks and fossils, and medicine. Planetarium features astronomy and laser light shows. Omni Theater with 80-foot screen.

FRONTIER TIMES MUSEUM – Bandera – 68 K3 Founded 1927 by author, newspaperman, printer and Texas historian J. Marvin Hunter. Estimated 30,000 items—prehistoric artifacts, pioneer clothes, weapons and household items. Paintings and photographs depict cowboy life. Works by local artists and craftsmen displayed in gallery.

FRONTIERS OF FLIGHT MUSEUM – Dallas – 46 F3, 105 H8 Located at Love Field. Highlights history of air travel. Newspaper and magazine articles, uniforms of famous aviators. Models and replicas of famous aircraft, modern passenger planes and space shuttles.

GREGG COUNTY HISTORICAL MUSEUM – Longview – 48 I4, 143 I11 Located in former 1910 bank building. Chronicles early agriculture and commerce, including railroads, timber and farming in western Texas. Refurbished 1900s banker's office, dentist's office and schoolroom. Audiovisual programs.

HERTZBERG CIRCUS MUSEUM – San Antonio – 159 D7 Over 20,000 items related to circus entertainment housed in 1930 art deco building. Exhibits of famous side-show performers. Artifacts, prints, memorabilia, posters, photographs, lithographs and handbills.

HOUSTON MUSEUM OF FINE ARTS – Houston – 71 K12, 134 A1 Works from Greece, Spain, Egypt and US represented. Includes van Gogh's *The Rocks* and pieces by Remington. Outdoor sculpture garden.

INSTITUTE OF TEXAN CULTURES – San Antonio – 159 D7 Located in former Texas Pavilion for 1968 HemisFair. Commemorates 26 ethnic and cultural groups that settled Texas. Hands-on activities, food, clothing, music and festivals depict various cultures. 38-screen audiovisual presentation.

INTERNATIONAL MUSEUM OF CULTURES – Dallas – 46 H3, 112 J3 Ethnographic museum part of International Linguistics Center. Life-size and miniature exhibits portray modern indigenous people living in remote areas of world. Guided tours.

KIMBELL ART MUSEUM – Fort Worth – 109 D8 Items in collection date from antiquity to 20th century. Works by Titian, Caravaggio, Rembrandt, Cézanne, Picasso and Matisse. Building designed by architect Louis Kahn; known for its excellent use of natural lighting and vaulted ceilings.

KING RANCH – Kingsville – 84 H3 Considered birthplace of American ranching. Founded 1853 by Captain Richard King. 15,500-acre land grant in Wild Horse Desert grew to 825,000-acre ranch, one of largest in US. Served as Confederacy back door through Union blockade and depot on Cotton Road to Mexico. Significant today for livestock and wildlife production and management. Home to 60,000 Santa Gertrudis cattle and 300 quarter horses. Museum, narrated bus tours.

LYNDON B. JOHNSON SPACE CENTER – Houston – 81 A8, 146 D3 Control center for all NASA manned spaceflights. Over 100 buildings include Mission Control Center, Mission Simulation and Training Facility. Space Center Houston offers exhibits, theme galleries and five-story movie screen. Guided tram tours of Johnson Space Center, space-flight simulation training devices, retired spacecraft *Apollo 17, Mercury 7, Gemini 5.*

LYNDON BAINES JOHNSON LIBRARY AND MUSEUM – Austin – 69 F11, 93 G9 Located on University of Texas campus. Library houses 35 million historical documents. Museum features replica oval office, gifts from heads of state and Johnson's 1968 Lincoln limousine.

MARION KOOGLER McNAY ART MUSEUM – San Antonio – 77 B12, 157 K9 Former residence of oil heiress houses Gothic and Flemish art, American and European watercolors. Sculpture, paintings, graphic arts, tapestries and stained glass. Works by Cézanne, Gauguin, van Gogh, El Greco, Toulouse-Lautrec and Homer.

McALLEN INTERNATIONAL MUSEUM – McAllen – 88 H2, 148 F2 Collection of 16th–19th century European oil paintings, Mexican folk art and 20th-century American and European prints. Natural science displays of fossils, minerals and artifacts.

McDONALD OBSERVATORY – Fort Davis – 63 C11 Built 1930s atop 6,791-foot Mount Locke at bequest of amateur astronomer William J. McDonald. 200-ton dome houses 107-inch telescope. Celestial bodies viewed through 14-inch and 24-inch telescopes at thrice-weekly star parties. Daily solar viewing. Guided tours.

MODERN ART MUSEUM OF FORT WORTH – Fort Worth – 109 D8 Permanent and traveling exhibits showcasing 20th-century art. Works by Picasso, Hockney, Rothko, Stella, Warhol and Pollock.

MUSEUM OF NATURAL SCIENCE – Houston – 71 K12, 134 A1 Highlights astronomy, geology, paleontology, anthropology and natural history. Dinosaur skeletons, large seashell collection and replica of space capsule used by John Glenn on first orbit around Earth. Over 600 mineral specimens. Planetarium and IMAX theater with six-story screen.

MUSEUM OF THE BIG BEND – Alpine – 64 E1 Located on Sul Ross State University campus. Artifacts of vast Big Bend region, where humans have lived for over 11,000 years. Contributions of Native American, Spanish, Mexican and pioneer cultures highlighted.

MUSEUM OF THE SOUTHWEST – Midland – 53 C10, 147 H10 Southwestern artwork and archaeological artifacts housed in former 1934 residence of early Midland oilman Fred Turner. Hogan Collection features works by founding members of Taos Society of Artists. Mansion boasts carved wooden friezes and hand-painted tile. Children's museum and Marian Blakemore Planetarium.

NATIONAL RANCHING HERITAGE CENTER – Lubbock – 33 K11, 144 E4 Chronicles ranching evolution on the Western frontier. Over 30 restored ranching structures from 19th and 20th centuries. Milk and meat houses, blacksmith shop, schoolhouse, windmills and corrals. Exhibits, craft demonstrations.

PANHANDLE–PLAINS HISTORICAL MUSEUM – Canyon – 29 J11 Located on campus of West Texas State University. Five-museum complex containing more than three million artifacts related to history of northwest Texas. Guns, prehistoric fossils and Southwestern art. Reconstructed pioneer town.

PERMIAN BASIN PETROLEUM MUSEUM – Midland – 53 C10, 147 J11 Traces history and development of oil industry and oil-rich Permian Basin. Re-created 1920s boomtown, walk-through diorama of ocean floor 230 million years ago and antique drilling and production equipment. Audiovisual displays and hands-on exhibits.

PRESIDENTIAL MUSEUM – Odessa – 53 D8, 150 J3 Dedicated to people who have run for or held the office of US president. Campaign memorabilia, medals and buttons, posters and political cartoons. Miniature replicas of inaugural gowns worn by first ladies.

RAILROAD MUSEUM/CENTER FOR TRANSPORTATION AND COMMERCE – Galveston – 81 C9, 126 I3 One of largest collections of restored vintage cars and steam engines in Southwest. Santa Fe Union Station restored to 1930s appearance. Audiovisual presentations illustrate Galveston's history and industry development. Port of Galveston miniature.

RED RIVER HISTORICAL MUSEUM – Sherman – 38 D5, 163 C11 Located in historic 1914 Carnegie Library building; illustrates development of northern Texas since mid-1800s. *Black Land, Red River* exhibits pictures, artifacts and memorabilia from Glen Eden, an early plantation house. Replica ranch room.

SAM HOUSTON MEMORIAL MUSEUM – Huntsville – 71 B11, 141 H11 Commemorates life of Sam Houston, who led defeat of Mexican army to gain Texas' independence. Includes two of Houston's homes: Steamboat House and Woodland. Memorabilia and exhibits depict Houston's private and public life. Guided tours.

SAN ANTONIO MUSEUM OF ART – San Antonio – 77 B12, 159 C7 Located in renovated, historic brewery. Pre-Columbian sculpture and pottery and Latin American folk art emphasize art of the Americas. Spanish colonial art, modern paintings and sculpture, Oriental art and Greek and Roman antiquities also represented. Sculpture garden.

THE SCIENCE PLACE – Dallas – 113 B12 Located in Fair Park *(see Amusements)*. Hands-on science exhibits highlighting technology, anatomy, physics and energy. Live demonstrations. Planetarium.

STARK MUSEUM OF ART – Orange – 73 H9, 151 C8 Devoted to traditional American art; collection includes Audubon prints, porcelain sculpture, Steuben crystal and works by Russell, Remington and Taos Society of Artists. Native American art and artifacts from Plains and Southwest regions.

TEXAS ENERGY MUSEUM – Beaumont – 73 H7, 95 D11 Traces history and technology of energy production since 18th century. Lifelike robots and exhibit of 1901 Spindletop Gusher illustrate evolution of Texas' petroleum industry.

TEXAS MARITIME MUSEUM – Rockport – 85 C8 Maritime development traced from early Spanish exploration through offshore oil drilling and commercial fishing. Boatbuilding tools, photographs, paintings and models.

TEXAS RANGER MUSEUM & HALL OF FAME – Waco – 58 F2, 167 D11 Located in 35-acre park around Fort Fisher replica. Represents history of Texas Rangers, law enforcement group founded 1823 by colonizer Stephen F. Austin. Antique firearms and weapons, Native American artifacts, Western artwork, wax figures. Hall of Fame commemorates noteworthy lawmen. Current headquarters of Company F, Texas Rangers.

WEST OF THE PECOS MUSEUM AND PARK – Pecos – 52 G2 Located in restored 1896 Orient Hotel. 30 theme rooms display artifacts, photographs, momentos and some original furnishings. Saloon site of famous 1896 killing of two outlaws. Adjacent park contains replica of Judge Roy Bean's 1930s saloon and grave of famous "Gentleman Gunfighter" Clay Allison.

WITTE MUSEUM – San Antonio – 159 A8 Depicts natural and cultural history of Texas. Dioramas and historic structures including a furnished log cabin and four early Texas houses. Multimedia presentation details San Antonio's cultural influences. Dinosaur program.

Information Centers

For general information about Texas, call (800) 452-9292. For regional information, call the appropriate office listed here. All information centers are open year-round. Call for holiday hours.

CITY	LOCATION	PHONE	PAGE & GRID
Amarillo	9400 I-40 E	(806) 335-1441	29 H12
Anthony	I-10 W	(915) 886-3468	62 D1
Austin	State Capitol	(512) 463-8586	69 F10, 93 H8
Denison	US 75 N	(903) 463-2860	38 C5
Gainesville	I-35 S	(940) 665-2301	38 D2
Langtry	State Loop 25 off US 90	(432) 291-3340	66 J1
Laredo	I-35 N	(956) 417-4728	82 G6
Orange	1708 I-10 E	(409) 883-9416	73 G9
Texarkana	I-30 W	(903) 794-2114	49 A7, 163 G8
Valley	2021 West Harrison Street	(956) 428-4477	88 H5, 141 D7
Waskom	1255 I-20 E	(903) 687-2547	49 I7
Wichita Falls	900 Central Freeway	(940) 723-7931	36 H6, 168 H3

Historic Sites

Most historic sites are in Texas' public lands (see State Lands and National Lands).

For more information on state sites, contact the Texas Parks and Wildlife Department, 4200 Smith School Road, Austin, TX 78744, (800) 792-1112. For national sites, contact the National Park Service, Intermountain Region, 12795 Alameda Parkway, Denver, CO 80025, (303) 969-2500.

ACTON STATE HISTORIC SITE – Granbury – 45 J11 Texas' smallest state park. Marks 1860 gravesite of Elizabeth Crockett, second wife of frontiersman and Alamo hero Davy Crockett.

ADMIRAL NIMITZ STATE HISTORIC SITE–NATIONAL MUSEUM OF THE PACIFIC – Fredericksburg – 68 F4 Dedicated to Fleet Admiral Chester W. Nimitz, commander in chief of the US Navy in the Pacific in WWII, as well as over two million people who served under him. Includes George Bush Gallery, History Walk of the Pacific War, Garden of Peace and Memorial Wall.

ALIBATES FLINT QUARRIES NATIONAL MONUMENT – Fritch – 29 E12 Preserves quarry that provided Native Americans of Southern Plains with flint supply for knives, arrows and spears for 12,000 years. Accessed via one-mile ranger-guided walking tour. Tours begin at Bates Canyon Information Station at Lake Meredith National Recreation Area.

BAYOU BEND – Houston – 71 K12, 129 J12 28-room mansion; former home of philanthropist Ima Hogg, daughter of first native-born Texas governor James Stephen Hogg. American decorative arts from late 17th, 18th and early 19th centuries. Fine American furniture. Gardens, landscaped grounds.

BISHOP'S PALACE – Galveston – 81 D9, 126 I4 Four-story stone Victorian mansion, home to Catholic Bishop Byrne from 1923 to 1950. Considered one of country's most outstanding buildings by American Institute of Architects. Completed 1893, after seven years and a final cost of $250,000. Hand-carved wooden staircase, art objects, jeweled-glass windows and 14 fireplaces. Guided tours.

BUFFALO GAP HISTORIC VILLAGE – Buffalo Gap – 43 K11 20 restored structures assembled in former village, buffalo-slaughtering headquarters. Log cabin, country store, two-room schoolhouse and doctor's office. Western artifacts include buggies, wagons and firearms.

CADDOAN MOUNDS STATE HISTORIC SITE – Alto – 60 F1 Southwesternmost ceremonial centers of Mound Builders, ancient Native American civilization. Culture dominated area from about A.D. 800 to 1300. Burial mound, two pyramid-like temple mounds and replica of Caddoan cane house. Exhibits and audiovisual presentation on Caddoan history and culture.

CHAMIZAL NATIONAL MEMORIAL – El Paso – 62 F2, 126 D5 Commemorates peaceful settlement of 99-year-long US–Mexico boundary dispute. Located on land affected by shifting channel of Rio Grande and claimed by both countries until 1963. Visitor center, theater and history museum.

CONFEDERATE REUNION GROUNDS STATE HISTORIC SITE – Mexia – 58 F5 Reunion site for Confederate States of America veterans until late 1940s. Features 1872 Heritage House, 1893 Dance Pavilion and two-story log cabin built by popular Methodist circuit preacher Mordecai Yell.

EISENHOWER BIRTHPLACE STATE HISTORIC SITE – Denison – 38 D5, 99 C12 Birthplace home of 34th US president, Dwight D. Eisenhower, born October 14, 1890. Encompasses two-story home, railroad trails and other historic structures. Visitor center, Eisenhower family furnishings, antiques.

FANNIN BATTLEGROUND – Goliad State Park – 79 I7 Site of 1836 surrender of Colonel J. W. Fannin and troops to Mexican army after Battle of Coleto Creek. Majority of men later executed when General Santa Anna overruled surrender terms set by General Urrea. *(See this section: Goliad State Park and Presidio La Bahia.)*

FANTHORP INN STATE HISTORIC SITE – Anderson – 71 D8 Typical 1850s wooden inn, owned and operated by Mr. and Mrs. Henry Fanthorp until 1867. Notable guests included Republic of Texas presidents Sam Houston and Anson Jones, Civil War generals Robert E. Lee and Stonewall Jackson and Jefferson Davis, who eventually became Confederate president. Restored to mid-19th-century appearance. Fanthorp family cemetery, barn and replica of 1850s Concord stagecoach. Guided tours.

FORT WORTH STOCKYARDS – Fort Worth – 46 G1, 109 A9 World's largest stockyard in early 1900s. Western-wear stores, art galleries, saloons, dance halls and restaurants. Live rodeo shows and weekly cattle and pig auctions. Designated National Historic District.

FULTON MANSION STATE HISTORIC SITE – Fulton – 85 C9 1876 mansion built in French Second Empire style by George W. Fulton. Designed to match splendor of eastern US homes; luxurious interior serviced by innovative systems: forced-air heat, gas lighting, water-cooled larder and gravity-fed water for toilets and bathtubs. Authentically restored and refurbished. Guided tours.

GOLIAD STATE PARK – Goliad – 78 I6 Commemorates Texans slain in 1836 Goliad Massacre, which inspired rallying cry "Remember Goliad!" Contains gravesites of Colonel Fannin and his men. Restored Mission Espiritu Santo *(see this section—Historic Missions)*, Mission Rosario ruins and birthplace of Mexican hero General Ignacio Zaragoza also part of park. Visitor center and mission museum. *(See this section: Fannin Battleground and Presidio La Bahia.)*

GOVERNOR JIM HOGG CITY PARK – Quitman – 47 G11 Dedicated to James Stephen Hogg, first native-born governor of Texas *(see this section: Jim Hogg City Historical Park)*. Stinson Home and Honeymoon Cottage contain family and period furnishings. Miss Ima Hogg Museum exhibits decorative arts and Texas artifacts. Guided tours.

GOVERNOR'S MANSION – Austin – 69 F10, 93 H8 25-room Greek Revival mansion, home to every Texas governor since 1856. Historically tight-fisted state legislators inadvertently preserved much of mansion in original condition. Period and historic furnishings. Guided tours. National Register of Historic Places.

HIGHLANDS MANSION – Marlin – 58 H3 Restored, late-19th-century mansion noted for stained-glass dome and windows and built-in glass china cabinet. Typifies elegant homes built during prosperous period in late 1800s. Some original furnishings. Guided tours.

HISTORIC FORTS

In the course of American history, forts have been established and used for various purposes, including fur-trading posts, overnight stage stops, supply stops for emigrants and for protection against Native American raids. Protection eventually became the primary purpose as pioneers emigrated to the state, settling the Texas frontier.

For more information on historic forts in Texas, see State Lands, National Lands and Texas Travel Trails: Texas Forts Trail.

FORT BLISS – El Paso – 62 F2, 126 A6 Founded 1848 to establish US control of eastern Texas. Currently largest air-defense installation in Western World. Museum in replica of mid-1800s adobe structure details fort's pioneer history. 3rd Armored Cavalry Museum devoted to mounted regiment that fought in US–Mexican and Indian wars.

FORT CONCHO – San Angelo – 55 G7, 162 D5 Located on critical travel route. Often used by Colonel Ranald Mackenzie during pursuit of Quanah Parker, last Comanche chief. More than 20 restored stone buildings; one of most complete forts in Texas. Museums on Fort Concho history, fine arts and history of telephone. National Historic Landmark.

FORT DAVIS – Fort Davis National Historic Site – 63 C11 Named for Confederate president Jefferson Davis. Preserves portions of important mid-1850s fort that protected travel and trade routes. During Indian Wars, served as headquarters of 9th Cavalry, one of two African American regiments nicknamed "Buffalo Soldiers." 25 restored, refurbished buildings. Many ruins. Visitor center, museum. Guided tours in summer.

FORT GRIFFIN – Fort Griffin State Park and Historic Site – 44 F2 Established 1867 to secure Southern Plains. Fort became trade center for buffalo and longhorn cattle. Visitor center, bakery, replica barracks and ruins of store, officers' quarters and powder magazine.

FORT LANCASTER – Fort Lancaster State Historic Site – 65 C12 Protected section of San Antonio–El Paso military road. Founded 1855, site had 25 permanent buildings by 1860. Abandoned 1861 at start of Civil War. Visitor center. Unrestored ruins.

FORT LEATON – Fort Leaton State Historic Site – 74 A3 Massive adobe structure built 1848 on site of 18th-century Spanish garrison. 25 of 40 original rooms restored. Exhibits feature history of local Native American, Spanish, Mexican and American populations. Guided tours.

FORT McKAVETT – Fort McKavett State Historic Site – 67 A9 15 restored limestone structures of 1850s fort overlooking San Saba River. Considered an attractive frontier fort because of stone buildings and location on river. Civilians occupied many buildings after army departure in 1883, aiding fort's preservation. Interpretive exhibits in 1870 hospital ward cover natural and cultural history of fort and area.

FORT RICHARDSON – Fort Richardson State Park and Historic Site – 45 C8 Northernmost frontier fort in Texas; played pivotal role in ending Comanche, Kiowa and Kiowa–Apache raids 1867–1874. Important campaigns included capture of Kiowa chiefs Santanta, Satank and Big Tree after Salt Creek Massacre. Abandoned 1878. Original buildings, replicas and interpretive center.

FORT SAM HOUSTON – San Antonio – 77 B12, 159 A9 Construction begun 1876 with well-known Quadrangle and tower; site today is Headquarters for 5th Army and US Army Health Services Command. Teddy Roosevelt, Pershing and Eisenhower served here. Site of first US military flight in 1910. Museums on history of US Army in Southwest and US Army medicine. National Historic Landmark.

OLD FORT PARKER – Groesbeck – 58 F5 Reconstructed 1834 pioneer fort built wooden-stockade style. Settlers' cabins and two blockhouses within walls. Cynthia Ann Parker was abducted by Comanches during 1836 Fort Parker raid. She adapted to life with Comanches, marrying Chief Peta Nacona and giving birth to last Comanche chief, Quanah Parker.

HISTORIC MISSIONS

During the 17th and 18th centuries, Spain constructed missions to spread Christianity and introduce European influences to the New World. These missions later served as strongholds for the Republic of Texas in her quest for independence from Mexico.

The following historic missions, well known for their Spanish Colonial architecture and innovative irrigation systems, offer glimpses into the cultural and anthropological foundations of Texas.

For more information on missions, see State Lands and National Lands.

THE ALAMO – San Antonio – 77 B12, 159 D7 Oldest mission in San Antonio. Marks site where 189 Texan soldiers fought 5,000-strong Mexican army in 1836. Although soldiers were defeated, "Remember the Alamo" became battle cry inspiring Texans to ultimate victory the following month. Two on-site museums, video presentation.

MISSION CONCEPCIÓN – San Antonio Missions National Historical Park – 77 C12, 159 F7 One of oldest unrestored stone churches in US; completed 1750s. Contains most original architectural and decorative detail of San Antonio missions. Only wall frescoes from Spanish Colonial period in San Antonio.

MISSION CORPUS CHRISTI – El Paso – 62 G3, 127 I10 Formerly named Ysleta, adobe pueblo replica marks site of Texas' first mission, founded 1680 by Franciscans and Christian Tiguas. Land once belonged to Mexico, but became US property due to change in course of Rio Grande. Nearby Tigua Indian Reservation offers museum, dances and crafts.

MISSION ESPADA – San Antonio Missions National Historical Park – 77 C12, 159 K9 Southernmost San Antonio mission. Rustic 1756 chapel with three-bell facade tower and "moorish" arched doorway. Still-functioning Espada Aqueduct, completed 1740, one of oldest in US and designated National Historic Landmark.

MISSION ESPIRITU SANTO – Goliad State Park – 78 I6 Restored church, granary and workshop. Mission and nearby Presidio La Bahia are rare examples of fully restored mission-presidio complex. Audiovisual presentations and museum. *(See this section: Presidio La Bahia.)*

MISSION SAN JOSÉ – San Antonio Missions National Historical Park – 77 C12, 159 H8 Largest and most richly decorated San Antonio mission; founded 1721. Elaborate stone carvings. Compound includes Indian quarters, soldiers' barracks, granary and mill. Exhibits. National Historic Site.

MISSION SAN JUAN – San Antonio Missions National Historical Park – 77 C12, 159 J9 Simple church converted from mission granary. Contains rare religious figures made by early Native American parishioners. Museum displays artifacts from archaeological digs.

MISSION TEJAS – Mission Tejas State Park – 60 F1 Replica log building commemorates Texas' first Spanish mission, established 1690 to counter French settlement. Original mission abandoned and destroyed 1693.

HUECO TANKS STATE HISTORIC SITE – El Paso – 62 E4 Unique natural basins, or *huecos*, in volcanic rock formations collect rainwater, forming only waterholes in area. Used by Native Americans beginning 8000 B.C. and westward migrators en route to California gold strikes. Estimated 5,000 petroglyphs, caves, rock shelters and ruins of stagecoach station. *(See Unique Natural Features: Hueco Tanks.)*

INDIANOLA – Indianola – 79 J12 Formerly bustling natural port in mid-1800s. Survived skirmishes and Union occupation during Civil War, but was leveled by massive hurricanes in 1866, 1875 and 1886. Today ghost town dominated by granite statue of French explorer La Salle, who landed here in 1685. Remains include courthouse foundation, concrete cisterns.

JIM HOGG CITY HISTORICAL PARK – Rusk – 60 D1 Established 1941 on birth land of James Stephen Hogg, Texas' first native-born governor. Birthplace replica fine example of southern "dog run" house. Museum, Hogg family cemetery and nature trail.

CASA NAVARRO STATE HISTORIC SITE – San Antonio – 159 D7 Dedicated to early Texas statesman who served as mayor of San Antonio. Attended convention at Washington-on-the-Brazos, signed Texas Declaration of Independence and helped draft Constitution of the Republic of Texas. Three stone and adobe buildings served as home, office and kitchen. Authentic period furnishings, personal memorabilia. Guided tours.

LA VILLITA – San Antonio – 159 D7 San Antonio's original settlement; characterized by narrow streets, shaded patios and adobe houses. Preserved buildings include Cos House, where commander of Mexico's military forces surrendered December 9, 1835, officially marking Texas' independence. Open-air theater, history museum, restaurants, arts and crafts shops.

LANDMARK INN STATE HISTORIC SITE – Castroville – 77 C10 1850s plastered stone structure resembling Alsatian farmhouse in northeastern France—origin of colonists. Later converted to hotel serving travelers on busy San Antonio–El Paso road. 1850s gristmill adapted to lumber milling, cotton ginning and finally electrical generation in 1920s. Exhibits on local history, milling and restoration of inn.

LIPANTITLAN STATE HISTORIC SITE – Orange Grove – 84 D4 Site of Fort Lipantitlan, Aztec-named adobe fort constructed by Mexican government in 1831. Fell to Texas forces after two-day battle in 1835.

LUBBOCK LAKE LANDMARK – Lubbock – 33 K11 Watering place attracting animals, hunters since 10,000 B.C. Excavations revealed human artifacts and remains of extinct animals. Believed to be only site in North America containing artifacts from all cultures known to have existed on Southern Plains. Interpretive center, children's educational center and two self-guiding trails. Guided tours. National Historic Landmark.

LYNDON B. JOHNSON NATIONAL HISTORICAL PARK – Stonewall – 68 F5 Birthplace, boyhood home, LBJ Ranch and gravesite of 36th US president. Period furnishings, memorabilia. Visitor center with exhibits and audiovisual presentation. Access to ranch and birthplace by NPS bus from Lyndon B. Johnson State Park and Historic Site *(see this section)*.

LYNDON B. JOHNSON STATE PARK AND HISTORIC SITE – Stonewall – 68 F5 Dedicated to 36th US president. Exhibits on LBJ Ranch, presidential years and Texas Hill Country. Sauer–Beckmann Living History Farm with costumed interpreters performing daily activities of early 1900s Texas–German farm. Departure point for bus tours of LBJ Ranch *(see this section: Lyndon B. Johnson National Historical Park)*.

MAGOFFIN HOME STATE HISTORIC SITE – El Paso – 62 G2, 126 D4 Rare, territorial-style adobe home built 1875 by founding El Paso family. One-story structure became social and civic center in Magoffinsville (later named El Paso). Classic architectural details, courtyard, two-and-a-half-foot-thick walls. Many original family furnishings in 19 rooms. Guided tours.

MONUMENT HILL AND KREISCHE BREWERY STATE HISTORIC SITE – La Grange – 70 I3 Dedicated to Texans killed in 1842 during Mexico–Texas skirmishes. Tomb contains remains of 41 prisoners killed at Battle of Salado Creek and Mier Expedition prisoners executed at Rancho Salado in Black Bean Episode (after execution orders from Santa Anna, prisoners drew white or black beans to determine who would die). 1870s commercial brewery and home belonging to Heinrich L. Kreische also on site. Visitor center. Guided tours.

NACOGDOCHES – Nacogdoches – 60 F4, 149 H11 One of Texas' oldest towns, named for Nacogdoche tribe who inhabited area. Historical sites include La Calle del Norte, believed to be oldest public thoroughfare in US; Oak Grove Cemetery, burial site for four signers of Texas Declaration of Independence. Caddoan burial mound.

OLD CITY PARK – Dallas – 46 G4, 113 B11 Site of Dallas' first city park. 37 restored structures dating 1840–1910 re-create turn-of-the-century Dallas village. Schoolhouse, bank, doctor's office, hotel, various houses. Authentic furnishings, living-history exhibits. Guided tours.

OLD TASCOSA – Boys Ranch – 29 E9 Ghost town once known as "Cowboy Capital of the Plains." Major shipping point for Texas ranches in 1870s. Town began decline when railroad lines bypassed site; completely deserted in 1930s. Remains include stone courthouse and adobe houses. Current site of Cal Farley's Boy's Ranch.

PALO ALTO BATTLEFIELD NATIONAL HISTORIC SITE – Brownsville – 88 I6 Site of first battle of US–Mexican War, which occurred May 8, 1846. Superior artillery gave victory to outnumbered US forces under General Zachary Taylor. Battle of Resaca de la Palma on May 9th forced General Mariano Arista's Mexican troops to retreat across Rio Grande. Commemorative markers.

PIONEER VILLAGE – Corsicana – 58 B6, 97 I11 Reconstructed and restored log buildings form typical mid-1800s village. Homes, blacksmith shop, trading post and doctor's office. Authentic furniture and artifacts.

PORT ISABEL LIGHTHOUSE STATE HISTORIC SITE – Port Isabel – 89 I7 1853 lighthouse guided vessels through Brazos Santiago Pass to Point Isabel. Over 70 feet tall, white-washed brick tower was used as observation post by Union and Confederate troops during Civil War. Only lighthouse on Texas coast open to public.

PRESIDIO LA BAHIA – Goliad State Park – 79 I7 Spanish fort established 1749 to protect nearby Mission Espiritu Santo *(see this section—Historic Missions)*. Site of 1836 imprisonment and execution of Colonel Fannin and more than 300 men. 1960s restoration revealed artifacts from nine levels of civilization at site. Museum. *(See this section: Goliad State Park and Fannin Battleground.)*

SABINE PASS BATTLEGROUND STATE HISTORIC SITE – Sabine Pass – 73 K8 Site of former Fort Griffin where, on September 8, 1863, Lieutenant Richard "Dick" Dowling and 46 fellow Texans defeated Union forces numbering 5,000, protecting Texas from Union invasion. Bronze statue of Dowling marks probable fort location. Concrete ammunition bunkers from WWII era also within park.

SAM BELL MAXEY HOUSE STATE HISTORIC SITE – Paris – 39 D11, 151 J9 Former home of Sam Bell Maxey, Confederate general and US senator. 1868 High Victorian Italianate home occupied by Maxey family members until 1966. Major renovations performed 1911. Main house, book house and stable. Period furnishings. Victorian garden. Guided tours.

SAN JACINTO BATTLEGROUND HISTORIC SITE – Deer Park – 72 K2 Site of battle of San Jacinto, historic victory April 21, 1836, that won Texas independence from Mexico. 570-foot-high San Jacinto Monument features elevator to observation windows and Museum of History. USS *Texas*, only surviving US Naval vessel to serve both world wars, berthed in park.

SEBASTOPOL STATE HISTORIC SITE – Seguin – 78 A3, 162 K5 Preserved and restored Greek Revival–style house innovatively constructed of limecrete (a type of concrete) in 1854—well before concrete construction became common in US. One of 20 remaining 19th-century limecrete buildings in Seguin. Exhibits recount original construction, restorations and history.

SEMINOLE CANYON STATE HISTORIC SITE – Comstock – 66 K2 Rugged limestone terrain noted for sparse vegetation, deep canyons. Site occupied over 8,000 years ago by ancient people, who drew pictographs on walls and ceilings of caves. Cave artwork believed to be earliest surviving in North America. Access only by one-hour ranger-guided tour. Visitor center.

STARR FAMILY HOME STATE HISTORIC SITE – Marshall – 48 I6, 147 B11 Four structures built by prominent Starr family represent elegant lifestyle of northeast Texas during late 1800s. Maplecroft, ancestral home, completed 1871 in Italianate style by James Franklin Starr. Ornately carved wooden beds, marble mantels and parlor draperies show strong New Orleans and St. Louis influences. Remodeled 1920s in Colonial Revival style. National Register of Historic Places.

STEPHEN F. AUSTIN STATE PARK – San Felipe – 71 J8 Named for "Father of Texas," Stephen F. Austin, who first colonized families in San Felipe de Austin townsite in 1824. Includes J. J. Josey General Store Museum, well dug by early colonists and statue and monument dedicated to Austin.

THE STRAND – Galveston – 81 C9, 126 I3 Historic district named for prominent street. Known as "Wall Street of the Southwest," formerly most important financial center beween San Francisco and St. Louis. Six-block section of iron-front buildings restored to mid-1800s appearance. Shops, restaurants and galleries. National Historic Landmark District.

STUDY BUTTE – Study Butte – 75 C8 Ghost town formerly retreat for bandits, smugglers, and Apache and Comanche warriors. Developed into mining town when mercury deposits discovered about 1900. Deserted early 1940s due to mine depletion. Old stone and adobe structures remain today.

SUNDANCE SQUARE – Fort Worth – 46 G1, 109 C10 Named for Sundance Kid, outlaw who came to Fort Worth between bank robberies. Historic district with several restored buildings dating from around 1900. Shops, restaurants, art galleries and Sid Richardson Collection of Western Art, noted for several paintings by Remington and Russell.

TERLINGUA – Terlingua – 75 C7 Ghost town formerly region's most prosperous mercury-mining town in early 1900s. Once home to Chisos Mining Company. Deserted after depletion of cinnabar deposits. Rock and adobe structures remain, some restored or converted to shops. International Championship Chili Cook-Off has been held here on first Saturday in November since 1967.

TEXAS SCHOOL BOOK DEPOSITORY – Dallas – 46 G4, 113 B10 Dallas' most photographed site. Building from which Lee Harvey Oswald allegedly assassinated 35th US president John F. Kennedy on November 22, 1963. Fatal shot reportedly came from sixth floor, which today features exhibits highlighting Kennedy's life. Photographs, artifacts.

TEXAS STATE CAPITOL – Austin – 69 F10, 93 H8 Largest state capitol in US and seven feet taller than US Capitol. Begun 1882, construction took nearly six years and required special, narrow-gauge railroad to transport pink granite quarried at Marble Falls. Rotunda displays paintings and historic documents, including Texas Declaration of Independence and Ordinance of Secession.

TEXAS STATE RAILROAD STATE PARK – Rusk/Palestine State Park – 60 D1 50-mile, round-trip rides aboard steam-powered trains from late 19th and early 20th centuries. Connects two units of Rusk/Palestine State Park. Railroad originally built 1896 to haul ore from Palestine area to Rusk. Spring–fall only.

THURBER – Thurber – 45 I7 Ghost town in former coal-mining and brick-manufacturing area founded late 1880s by Texas & Pacific Coal Company. Inhabitants once numbered 10,000. One of first towns in world to receive complete electrical service and be completely unionized. Town started decline when mines closed in 1920s. Abandoned after brick plant closed in 1930s.

USS *LEXINGTON* – Corpus Christi – 84 E6, 98 B4 Navy-blue-painted WWII aircraft carrier reported sunk four times, earning nickname "Blue Ghost" from Japanese. Historic carrier now floating naval museum with tours of flight deck, hangar deck, captain's quarters, sick bay and galley. Vintage aircraft.

VARNER–HOGG PLANTATION STATE HISTORIC SITE – West Columbia – 80 E4 Originally sugar plantation built 1830s by Columbus Patton on land previously owned by Texas Revolution veteran Martin Varner. Purchased 1901 by first native-born Texas governor James Stephen Hogg, who suspected oil reservoir on property. Remodeled in Colonial Revival style by Hogg children in 1920 after hitting West Columbia oilfield. Antebellum furnishings. Ceramics, prints, photographs and books.

WASHINGTON-ON-THE-BRAZOS STATE HISTORIC SITE – Washington – 71 F8 Site of March 2, 1836, signing of Texas Declaration of Independence. Encompasses much of historic townsite, including reconstructed Independence Hall and Barrington Living History Farm, restored cotton plantation of last Republic of Texas president Anson Jones. Star of the Republic Museum, auditorium, picnic area and amphitheater.

WAXAHACHIE – Waxahachie – 46 J4, 167 K8 Victorian homes, other structures built late 1800s by early cotton magnates. 1895 Ellis County Courthouse features arches, columns, turrets and cupola. Built of red sandstone and granite by Italian masons. Several buildings listed on National Register of Historic Places. Gingerbread Trail open house occurs first weekend each June. Site of Scarborough Faire, Renaissance-era country fair, weekends mid-April–early June.

Unique Natural Features

Many of the features listed in this category are found within Texas' public lands.

For more information on these areas, see National Lands and State Lands.

ATTWATER PRAIRIE CHICKEN NATIONAL WILDLIFE REFUGE – Eagle Lake – 71 K7 Rejuvenated critical habitat for Attwater prairie chicken, formerly abundant resident bird of Texas–Louisiana tall-grass prairie. Native prairie, potholes, sandy knolls and wooded areas. Birds, fur-bearing mammals and reptiles. Over 250 flowering plants recorded in refuge. National Natural Landmark.

BIG BEND MOSQUITOFISH – Big Bend National Park/ Rio Grande Village – 75 D11 Tiny fish with geographic range restricted to one pond within Big Bend National Park. Identified in 1928, species has often been threatened—world's only survivors once numbered two males and one female. Population replenished by stock raised at University of Texas at Austin. Feeds largely on mosquito larvae; gives birth to live offspring.

THE BIG TREE – Goose Island State Park – 85 B9 State champion coastal live oak tree over 1,000 years old. 44-foot height; 35-foot trunk circumference; 89-foot crown spread. Provides shelter and acorns for squirrels, raccoons, javelinas and deer.

BOQUILLAS CANYON – Big Bend National Park – 75 D11 Spectacular, 30-mile-long gorge through massive limestone of Sierra del Carmen. Cut by ancestral Rio Conchos 75–100 million years ago. Steep walls rise approximately 1,200 feet above river at highest points. Longest canyon in Big Bend National Park.

THE BOWL – Guadalupe Mountains National Park – 50 C6 High-country forest of pine and Douglas fir in two-mile-long depression atop Guadalupe Mountains. Located 2,500 feet above desert surrounding mountain range. 15,000-year-old relict from period of cooler and moister climate. Abundant wildlife.

CADDO LAKE – Caddo Lake State Park – 49 G7 State's largest natural lake; probably formed by great New Madrid earthquake of 1811. Over 30,000 acres. Coves, islands and cypress swamps.

CAPITAN REEF – Guadalupe Mountains National Park – 50 C6 400-mile-long, horseshoe-shaped ridge; world's largest fossil reef. Created approximately 250 million years ago by calcium-secreting marine organisms in tropical ocean that once covered most of Texas and New Mexico. Sea evaporated, burying reef beneath thick sediment for millions of years. Reef uplifted, exposing Guadalupe, Apache and Glass mountains.

CAPROCK CANYONS – Caprock Canyons State Park – 34 C3 Rugged escarpment separating western high plains from eastern rolling plains. Excellent examples of red Permian beds, eroded badlands and erosion-carved cliffs and canyons. Interpretive center.

CATFISH CREEK – Gus Engeling Wildlife Management Area – 59 C9 Free-flowing stream one of best riparian (streamside) habitats in Western Coastal Plain. Creek bottoms inhabited by rare, mostly undisturbed, forest and wetland ecosystems. Wildlife uncommon to Texas: swamp rabbits, American alligators, cattle egrets and several duck species.

CHIHUAHUAN DESERT – Cornudas – 50 D2 One of four North American deserts; partly situated in western Texas from Rio Grande to mountain ranges within Sierra Madre Occidental. Distinguished for animals and plants indigenous to this desert only, especially spined lechuguilla plant. Abundant wildlife, insects and reptiles. Woody and fiberous shrubs, cacti and other succulents.

CONGRESS AVENUE BRIDGE BAT COLONY – Austin – 69 F10, 93 I8 Home to nearly 750,000 Mexican free-tailed bats; largest urban bat colony in US. Bats leave bridge in search of insects almost every evening, spring–fall. Eat an estimated 20,000 pounds of bugs every night.

DINOSAUR TRACKS – Dinosaur Valley State Park – 45 K10 Fossil footprints of sauropod (four-legged vegetarian) and carnosaur (two-legged meat-eater) preserved in bed of Paluxey River. Tracks deeply impressed over 100 million years ago in limey mud. Depressions preserved when sediment filled tracks and hardened to rock. *(See Hiking: Dinosaur Valley Trail.)* National Natural Landmark.

EL CAPITAN – Guadalupe Mountains National Park – 50 C6 Imposing 8,085-foot cliff in Guadalupe Mountains; composed of limestone rocks from Capitan Reef *(see this section).*

ENCHANTED ROCK – Enchanted Rock State Natural Area – 68 D4 Massive, dome-shaped mountain of pink granite measuring 500 feet above surroundings. Portion of ancient igneous rock mass covering 90 square miles. Rock doughnuts, weather pits and channels on surface due to weathering. Creaking and groaning heard when granite rocks expand and contract from daytime heating and nighttime cooling. *(See Hiking: Enchanted Rock Loop Trail.)* National Natural Landmark.

FORT WORTH NATURE CENTER AND REFUGE – Fort Worth – 45 F12, 100 H3 Located on remnant of Fort Worth prairie; excellent examples of prairie, cross timbers, riparian (streamside) forest, limestone ledges and marshes. Unique trees include post oak, black willow, American elm, pecan and Mexican buckeye. Abundant wildlife. *(See Hiking: Fort Worth Nature Center and Refuge Trail System.)* National Natural Landmark.

GUADALUPE MOUNTAINS – Guadalupe Mountains National Park – 50 C6 State's highest range lies along Texas–New Mexico border. Exposed portion of Capitan Reef *(see this section).* Highest point, Guadalupe Peak, has 8,749-foot elevation.

GULF OF MEXICO – 85 E8 One of world's largest gulfs; covers 500,000-square-mile area and stretches over 300 miles in length. Depth ranges from very shallow to 17,000 feet. Dotted with refuges, fishing villages and resorts. Climate and terrain vary from saltwater marshes to grasslands and dunes. Rich in fish, oil and natural gas.

HUECO TANKS – Hueco Tanks State Historic Site – 62 E4 Natural rock basins, or *huecos,* in Chihuahuan Desert *(see this section).* Collect and store precious rainwater; seasonal explosions of tiny, translucent freshwater shrimp. Ancient Native American habitation. Strategic travel stop for archaic hunters, pioneers.

LOST MAPLES STATE NATURAL AREA – Vanderpool – 67 J12 Steep, rugged limestone canyons, grasslands, wooded slopes and clear streams. Renowned for strands of bigtooth or canyon maples, surviving relicts of Pleistocene epoch. Contains largest known nesting population of golden-cheeked warbler. Colorful fall foliage. National Natural Landmark.

McKITTRICK CANYON – Guadalupe Mountains National Park – 51 C7 Deep, sheer-sided canyon composed of desert region, lush canyon woodland and highland forest. Only canyon in park with perennial spring-fed stream. Impressive fall foliage. Abundant wildlife.

MULESHOE NATIONAL WILDLIFE REFUGE – Muleshoe – 32 H6 Habitat for large concentration of wintering waterfowl. Continent's largest wintering population of sandhill cranes. Playa lakes (shallow depressions), marsh areas, caliche outcroppings, native grasslands. National Natural Landmark.

ODESSA METEOR CRATER – Odessa – 53 E7 One of two known meteor craters in Texas. 550-foot-diameter crater formed 20,000 years ago when nickel–iron meteorite struck Earth, penetrating limestone bedrock and shattering surrounding rock. Originally 100 feet deep, crater filled to within six feet due to silt and sediment deposits. Crater today appears as shallow, circular depression surrounded by limestone rim. Various plants, birds, insects, horned toads and small lizards. National Natural Landmark.

PADRE ISLAND – Padre Island National Seashore – 85 H7 113-mile-long barrier island protecting Texas from onslaught of direct ocean storms. One of longest stretches of primitive, undeveloped ocean beaches in US. Site of shipwrecks, oil exploration and hurricanes. Dunes, coastal grasslands, tidal flats. Home to seasonal and year-round birds, other wildlife.

PALO DURO CANYON – Palo Duro Canyon State Park – 29 J12 120-mile-long canyon cut by Prairie Dog Fork of Red River over 200 million years ago. 800-foot-high canyon walls expose colorful geologic formations (Spanish Skirts and Lighthouse Rock); sedimentary rocks represent four geological periods. Home to various Native American tribes as far back as 12,000 years ago. *(See Hiking: Lighthouse Peak Trail.)* National Natural Landmark.

PERSIMMON GAP – Big Bend National Park – 64 K4 Gap in remnants of Santiago Mountains, oldest mountains in Big Bend National Park. Site of ancient ocean bed from sea once covering mountains. Fossils of sponges, brachiopods and simple marine organisms lie exposed.

RIO GRANDE – Big Bend National Park – 86 C4 Second longest river in US (after Mississipppi River) drains area of 172,000 square miles and forms international US–Mexico boundary. Originates in San Juan Mountains of Colorado; flows for total distance of 1,885 miles before emptying into Gulf of Mexico *(see this section).* Giant U-turn through Big Bend National Park creates deep-cut canyons, narrow valleys and towering cliffs. 191 miles designated National Wild and Scenic River.

SALT FLATS – Salt Flat – 50 E5 White salt deposits; remains of intermittent lakes fed by runoffs from Guadalupe Mountains. Site of 1870s Salt War between Mexicans and Americans, who both claimed rights to the salt.

SAND DUNES – Monahans Sandhills State Park – 52 F6 Portion of larger dune field containing stabilized and active dunes. Dynamic landscape; active dunes grow and change shape in response to seasonal winds. Stabilized dunes home to shinoak, acorn-bearing plant standing less than four feet tall at maturity.

SANTA ANA NATIONAL WILDLIFE REFUGE – Alamo – 88 I2 Preserves rapidly vanishing portion of Lower Rio Grande Valley. Woodlands, brushy areas, lakes and ponds. Habitat for over 300 bird species, some found nowhere else in US. Ocelots and jaguarundis, both rare in US. National Natural Landmark.

SEA RIM MARSH – Sea Rim State Park – 73 K8 Area where tidal marshlands meet Gulf of Mexico waters. Formed by longshore currents carrying silt from Sabine Delta. Rich with plankton and decomposing organic matter. Fertile grounds for aquatic life; essential for productivity of marine fisheries and migratory waterfowl.

TEXAS LONGHORN – Fort Griffin State Park and Historic Site – 44 F2 Descendents of herd assembled by well-known Western author J. Frank Dobie in early 1920s, when breed neared extinction. Known to withstand floods, cold, desert sun, and sparse food and water.

WHOOPING CRANES – Aransas National Wildlife Refuge – 85 A10 Endangered migratory birds. Principal wintering ground among saltwater marshes, tidal flats in Aransas National Wildlife Refuge November–March. Species once numbered as low as 15 in 1941; today numbers over 150.

CAVERNS

CASCADE CAVERNS – Boerne – 68 K5 Active, water-formed cavern extends to nearly 150 feet below surface. Named for 100-foot waterfall located within cave. Features delicate, crystal-clear formations. 0.5-mile guided tours. Stairs.

CAVE WITHOUT A NAME – Boerne – 68 I5 Water-formed cavern features massive stalactites and stalagmites, formed over hundreds of thousands of years. Remains at constant 66 degrees Fahrenheit year-round. 0.5-mile guided tours. Stairs.

CAVERNS OF SONORA – Sonora – 66 D5 Nearly eight miles of passages through seven levels. Unique and colorful stalactite, stalagmite and helictite formations. Remains at constant 70 degrees Fahrenheit. 1.5-mile guided tours. Stairs. National Natural Landmark.

INNER SPACE CAVERN – Georgetown – 69 C11 Water-formed cavern discovered 1963 during construction of Interstate 35. Stalactites, stalagmites and other natural formations. Sound-and-light shows. Accessed via cable car. 0.75-mile guided tours.

LONGHORN CAVERN – Longhorn Cavern State Park – 69 C7 450-million-year-old water-formed cavern site of secret gunpowder manufactory used during Civil War. Noted for its transparent crystal "rooms." Remains at constant 64 degrees Fahrenheit year-round. 1.25-mile guided tours. National Natural Landmark.

NATURAL BRIDGE CAVERNS – San Antonio – 69 K7 Formations in series of limestone caves resemble fried eggs, totem pole, king's throne and chandelier. Natural limestone bridge spans entrance to caverns. 0.5-mile guided tours.

WONDER CAVE – San Marcos – 69 J9, 163 C7 One of largest earthquake-formed caverns in US; actual crack of Balcones Fault viewed from inside cave. Although formed millions of years ago, dry-formed cave has no stalactites or stalagmites. Located in Wonder World. Guided tours. Stairs.

Wildlife Viewing

Texas takes part in the National Watchable Wildlife Program, a program in which state, federal and private organizations have joined forces and combined funds to promote wildlife viewing, conservation and education.

This chart includes wildlife sites in Texas, as listed and detailed in the Texas Wildlife Viewing Guide, *published by Falcon Press, P.O. Box 1718, Helena, MT 59624, (800) 582-2665.*

		WILDLIFE																	FACILITIES/RECREATION										
NAME, LOCATION	SIZE	SONGBIRDS	WATERFOWL	UPLAND BIRDS	WADING BIRDS	SHORE BIRDS	MARINE BIRDS	BIRDS OF PREY	HOOFED MAMMALS	CARNIVORES	SMALL MAMMALS	REPTILES/AMPHIBIANS	FRESHWATER MAMMALS	DOLPHINS	FISH	BATS	INSECTS	WILDFLOWERS	PARKING	RESTROOMS	BARRIER-FREE ACCESS	PICNIC AREA	RESTAURANT	LODGING	CAMPING	HIKING	BOAT RAMPS	LARGE BOATS	SMALL BOATS	PAGE & GRID
A. E. Wood Fish Hatchery, San Marcos	118 acres														●				●	●	●									69 J9, 163 D8
Alabama–Coushatta Indian Reservation, Livingston	4,600 acres	●			●				●		●								●	●	●	●	●		●	●	●		●	72 B4
Amistad National Recreation Area, Del Rio	58,500 acres	●	●		●			●				●							●	●	●	●			●	●	●	●		86 B4
Anahuac National Wildlife Refuge, Anahuac	30,162 acres	●	●		●			●				●							●	●						●	●			81 A11
Aransas National Wildlife Refuge, Austwell	54,829 acres	●			●				●	●		●							●	●		●				●				85 A10
Armand Bayou Nature Center, Pasadena	1,900 acres	●			●				●			●					●		●	●		●				●			●	81 A8
Atkinson Island, Morgan's Point	152 acres	●	●		●		●																					●		72 K2
Atlanta State Park, Atlanta	1,475 acres	●							●		●	●							●	●		●			●	●	●		●	48 C6
Attwater Prairie Chicken National Wildlife Refuge, Eagle Lake	7,984 acres	●	●		●			●				●						●	●	●		●				●				71 K7
Austin Area, Austin	—	●							●							●	●	●	●	●		●	●	●		●			●	93 H7
Balmorhea State Park, Balmorhea	46 acres	●													●				●	●		●	●	●	●					51 K12
Bastrop State Park and Lake Bastrop, Bastrop	3,504 acres	●	●								●	●						●	●	●		●		●	●	●	●		●	70 G1
Belton Lake, Belton	23,800 acres	●			●				●		●							●	●	●		●			●	●	●	●		57 J12
Benbrook Lake, Fort Worth	8,233 acres	●	●		●													●	●	●	●	●			●	●		●		45 H12, 108 K3
Bentsen–Rio Grande Valley State Park, Mission	588 acres	●		●				●		●		●					●		●	●		●			●	●			●	88 H1
Big Bend National Park, Study Butte	801,163 acres	●						●	●	●		●						●	●	●	●	●	●	●	●	●			●	75 C9
Big Bend Ranch State Park, Presidio	298,029 acres	●						●	●	●		●						●	●	●		●			●	●			●	74 B3
Big Creek Scenic Area, Cleveland	1,450 acres	●							●		●	●					●		●							●				72 D2
Big Spring State Park, Big Spring	382 acres	●						●			●	●							●	●	●	●				●				42 K1, 94 K1
Big Thicket National Preserve, Kountze	84,550 acres	●			●						●	●						●	●	●	●	●			●	●	●		●	72 D6
Black Gap Wildlife Management Area, Marathon	102,000 acres	●						●	●	●	●	●							●						●	●				75 A11
Boca Chica Beach, Brownsville	7 miles				●	●	●	●											●			●								89 J8
Bolivar Flats, Port Bolivar	550 acres	●			●	●	●																							81 C10
Boykin Springs Recreation Area, Jasper	300 acres	●									●								●	●		●			●	●				60 J6
Brazoria National Wildlife Refuge Complex, Lake Jackson	70,864 acres	●	●		●							●	●						●	●						●	●		●	81 F7
Brazos Bend State Park, Damon	4,897 acres	●	●		●				●			●							●	●	●	●			●	●				80 C5
Buffalo Lake National Wildlife Refuge, Umbarger	7,664 acres	●						●	●		●								●	●	●	●			●	●				29 J10
Caddo Lake State Park, Karnack	484 acres	●	●		●						●								●	●		●		●	●	●	●	●		49 H7
Caddo National Grassland, Sash	17,785 acres	●	●	●														●	●	●		●			●	●			●	39 D9
Cagle Recreation Area, New Waverly	5 acres				●								●						●											71 D11
Candy Abshier Wildlife Management Area, Smith Point	207 acres	●			●			●											●							●				81 A9
Caprock Canyons State Park, Quitaque	15,314 acres	●	●		●													●	●	●		●			●	●			●	34 D4
Chandler Independence Creek Preserve, Sheffield	701 acres	●		●				●	●						●				●	●		●				●				65 E12
Chaparral Wildlife Management Area, Artesia Wells	15,200 acres	●						●	●			●							●	●					●					83 A7
Choke Canyon State Park and James E. Daughtrey WMA, Three Rivers	12,500 acres	●						●	●		●								●	●		●			●	●	●	●		78 J1
Colorado Bend State Park, Bend	5,328 acres	●						●	●						●		●		●	●		●			●	●	●		●	56 K6
Comal Springs and Landa Park, New Braunfels	196 acres				●							●			●				●	●		●				●				69 K8, 150 B4
Copper Breaks State Park, Crowell	1,899 acres	●							●		●		●						●	●		●			●	●	●		●	35 F11
Corpus Christi Area, Corpus Christi	—	●	●		●	●												●	●	●	●	●	●			●				85 F7
Dallas Nature Center, Dallas	400 acres	●						●			●							●	●	●						●				46 H3
Davis Mountains Scenic Drive, Fort Davis	74 miles	●		●				●	●									●				●								63 C11
Davis Mountains State Park, Fort Davis	2,709 acres	●		●				●	●									●	●	●		●	●	●	●	●				63 C11
Devils River State Natural Area, Comstock	19,989 acres	●							●		●	●			●				●	●				●		●			●	66 I4
Diamond Y Springs Preserve, Fort Stockton	1,502 acres	●						●							●			●												52 K5
Dinosaur Valley State Park, Glen Rose	1,525 acres	●							●		●	●							●	●		●			●	●				45 K10
Double Lake Recreation Area, Cleveland	544 acres	●									●	●	●						●	●	●	●			●	●				72 D1
Drum Point and Kaufer–Hubert Memorial Park, Riviera	100 acres	●	●			●		●											●	●		●			●		●	●		84 I5
Eagle Lake, Eagle Lake	1,200 acres		●		●			●																						79 A12
Eckert James River Bat Cave, Mason	10 acres	●		●					●							●			●							●				68 D1
Enchanted Rock State Natural Area, Fredericksburg	1,644 acres							●	●		●	●							●	●		●			●	●				68 D4
Fairfield Lake State Park, Fairfield	1,460 acres	●						●	●		●								●	●		●			●	●	●	●		59 D8
Falcon State Park and Falcon Lake, Roma	573 acres	●						●	●										●	●		●			●		●	●		87 E8
Feather Lake Wildlife Sanctuary, El Paso	43.5 acres	●	●		●	●													●	●										62 G3, 127 I11
Fennessey Ranch, Refugio	4,000 acres	●	●		●			●	●										●								●		●	85 B7
Fort Parker State Park, Mexia	1,459 acres	●	●					●			●								●	●		●			●	●	●		●	58 F5
Fort Worth Nature Center and Refuge, Fort Worth	3,500 acres	●	●		●				●				●						●	●	●	●				●				45 F12, 100 H3
Fossil Rim Wildlife Center, Glen Rose	3,000 acres	●							●	●	●								●	●	●	●	●	●		●				57 A10
Four C National Recreation Trail, Kennard	20 miles	●						●	●		●								●	●		●			●	●			●	60 H1
Franklin Mountains State Park, El Paso	24,248 acres	●							●		●	●							●	●		●				●				62 E2
Freeport Area, Freeport	—	●	●		●	●		●											●	●			●	●						80 F6
Galveston Island, Galveston	30 miles	●			●	●	●							●					●	●		●	●	●	●	●	●	●		81 D8
Gambill Goose Refuge, Paris	674 acres	●	●															●	●											39 D10
Garner State Park, Concan	1,420 acres	●						●	●						●				●	●		●		●	●	●				76 A5
Gene Howe Wildlife Management Area, Canadian	5,821 acres	●		●						●			●												●	●			●	31 B8
Goliad State Park, Goliad	202 acres	●						●	●								●		●	●		●			●	●			●	78 I7
Goose Island State Park, Fulton	321 acres	●	●		●	●	●												●	●		●			●	●	●	●		85 B9
Guadalupe Mountains National Park, Salt Flat	86,415 acres	●						●	●	●	●								●	●	●	●			●	●				50 C6
Guadalupe River State Park and Honey Creek State Natural Area, Bulverde	4,232 acres	●		●					●						●			●	●	●		●			●	●			●	68 J6
Gus Engeling Wildlife Management Area, Palestine	10,941 acres	●	●								●	●	●						●						●	●				59 C9
Hagerman National Wildlife Refuge, Sadler	11,320 acres	●	●		●	●			●										●	●		●				●	●	●	●	38 D4
Hamilton Pool and Westcave Preserve, Bee Cave	260 acres	●							●			●			●			●	●	●		●				●				69 F8

WILDLIFE VIEWING, *continued*

NAME, LOCATION	SIZE	WILDLIFE																	FACILITIES/RECREATION												PAGE & GRID
		SONGBIRDS	WATERFOWL	UPLAND BIRDS	WADING BIRDS	SHORE BIRDS	MARINE BIRDS	BIRDS OF PREY	HOOFED MAMMALS	CARNIVORES	SMALL MAMMALS	REPTILES/AMPHIBIANS	FRESHWATER MAMMALS	DOLPHINS	FISH	BATS	INSECTS	WILDFLOWERS	PARKING	RESTROOMS	BARRIER-FREE ACCESS	PICNIC AREA	RESTAURANT	LODGING	CAMPING	HIKING	BOAT RAMPS	LARGE BOATS	SMALL BOATS	
Hawk Alley, Riviera	30 miles	●						●																						84 J3
Heard Natural Science Museum and Wildlife Sanctuary, McKinney	274 acres	●						●			●							●	●	●	●	●				●				46 D5
High Island, High Island	25 acres	●																	●	●						●				81 A12
Hill Country State Natural Area, Bandera	5,370 acres	●						●	●		●							●	●	●					●	●				77 A8
Hueco Mountains—Cornudas Drive, Cornudas	30 miles							●	●		●																			62 F4
Hueco Tanks State Historic Site, El Paso	860 acres	●						●			●	●					●		●	●		●			●	●				62 E4
Huntsville State Park, Huntsville	2,083 acres	●							●		●	●							●	●		●			●	●	●		●	71 C11
I. D. Fairchild State Forest and Texas State Railroad State Park, Rusk	3,239 acres	●									●							●	●			●				●				59 D12
Inks Lake State Park, Burnet	1,201 acres	●	●	●				●	●						●				●	●		●			●	●	●		●	69 B7
Jesse Jones Nature Center, Humble	225 acres	●							●		●	●							●	●	●	●				●			●	71 H12
Kerr Wildlife Management Area, Hunt	6,493 acres	●		●					●		●								●	●										67 H12
Kickapoo Cavern State Park, Brackettville	6,368 acres	●							●			●				●			●					●	●	●				76 A1
King Ranch, Kingsville	825,000 acres	●		●				●	●		●								●	●										84 H3
Kingsville Area, Kingsville	—	●	●			●		●											●	●		●			●	●				84 H4
Laguna Atascosa National Wildlife Refuge, Bayview	45,187 acres	●	●		●	●				●		●					●		●	●		●				●	●			89 H6
Lake Buchanan, Burnet	23,500 acres	●	●		●			●	●										●	●		●	●		●		●	●		69 A7
Lake Colorado City State Park, Colorado City	500 acres	●			●					●	●								●	●		●			●		●		●	42 K4
Lake Livingston/US 190 Causeway, Onalaska	2 miles	●	●																●								●	●		72 B1
Lake Marvin, Canadian	575 acres	●	●	●					●				●						●	●	●	●			●	●	●		●	31 B9
Lake McClellan and McClellan Creek National Grassland, Alanreed	1,449 acres	●	●	●					●	●									●	●		●			●	●	●		●	30 H5
Lake Meredith National Recreation Area, Fritch	44,978 acres	●	●		●			●	●										●	●	●	●			●	●	●	●		30 D1
Lake Mineral Wells State Park, Mineral Wells	3,283 acres	●		●					●	●									●	●		●			●	●	●		●	45 F9
Lake O' The Pines, Jefferson	29,031 acres	●	●		●			●											●	●		●			●	●	●	●		48 G5
Lake Ray Hubbard, Dallas	22,745 acres	●	●		●						●								●		●	●				●	●	●		46 F5, 107 E7
Lake Rita Blanca Park, Dalhart	1,668 acres		●					●	●	●									●			●			●	●				29 A7
Lake Somerville State Park, Somerville	940 acres	●	●					●			●								●	●		●			●	●	●	●		70 F5
Lake Travis Area, Austin	18,900 acres	●		●					●		●								●	●		●			●	●	●	●		69 E9
Lake Whitney State Park, Whitney	1,281 acres		●	●					●									●	●	●		●			●	●	●	●		58 C1
Las Palomas Wildlife Management Area—Ocotillo Unit, Presidio	2,082 acres	●		●				●				●							●											63 I7
Lost Maples State Natural Area, Vanderpool	2,174 acres	●		●				●	●						●			●	●	●		●			●	●				67 J12
Lower Neches Wildlife Management Area, Bridge City	6,200 acres		●		●	●						●	●						●							●	●	●		73 I9
Lyndon B. Johnson National Grassland, Alvord	20,250 acres	●	●	●	●			●										●	●	●		●			●	●			●	45 B11
Lyndon B. Johnson State Park and Historic Site, 10 mi. W of Johnson City	718 acres	●		●					●									●	●	●	●	●				●				68 F5
Marfa Area, Marfa	75 miles	●							●	●								●												63 F11
Martin Dies, Jr. State Park, Jasper	705 acres	●	●		●							●							●	●		●			●	●	●	●		73 A7
Matador Wildlife Management Area, Paducah	28,183 acres	●		●					●										●											35 F8
Matagorda Island, Port O'Connor	55,393 acres	●			●	●	●	●						●						●		●			●	●		●		85 A12
Meridian State Park, Meridian	505 acres	●	●		●						●	●							●	●		●			●	●	●		●	57 C11
Monahans Sandhills State Park, Monahans	3,840 acres	●							●	●	●								●	●	●	●			●	●				52 F6
Muleshoe National Wildlife Refuge, Muleshoe	5,809 acres	●	●		●													●	●	●		●			●	●				32 H6
Murphree Wildlife Management Area, Port Arthur	13,264 acres		●		●							●	●		●				●								●		●	73 J8
Mustang Island, Port Aransas	3,954 acres	●	●		●	●								●					●	●		●	●	●	●		●	●		85 F8
National Wildflower Research Center, Austin	60 acres	●						●									●	●	●	●	●	●								69 G10
Old Tunnel Wildlife Management Area, Fredericksburg	10.5 acres															●			●	●										69 G10
Padre Island National Seashore, Corpus Christi	133,919 acres	●			●	●		●						●					●	●	●	●	●		●	●	●	●		85 H7
Palmetto State Park, Luling	270 acres	●	●					●			●	●						●	●	●		●			●	●				78 A5
Palo Duro Canyon State Park, Canyon	16,402 acres	●							●	●	●								●	●		●	●	●	●	●				29 J12
Parkhill Prairie Preserve, Merit	436 acres	●						●				●					●	●	●	●		●				●				47 C7
Pedernales Falls State Park, Johnson City	5,212 acres	●		●				●	●									●	●	●		●			●	●				69 F8
Pine Park Rest Area, Hemphill	10 acres	●									●								●			●								61 H8
Playa Lakes Driving Tour, Dimmitt	42.1 miles		●		●	●						●																		33 C8
Possum Kingdom State Park, Caddo	1,529 acres	●							●		●								●	●		●			●		●	●		44 F6
Ray Roberts Lake, Sanger	43,000 acres		●		●	●												●	●	●		●			●	●	●	●		46 B2
Red-cockaded Woodpecker Interpretive Site, New Waverly	100 acres	●																●	●							●				71 D11
Rice–Osborne Bird and Nature Trail, La Grange	20 acres	●			●						●							●	●	●						●	●	●		70 I4
Richland Creek Wildlife Management Area, Corsicana	13,700 acres	●	●		●	●			●										●											59 C8
Rita Blanca National Grassland, Texline	77,463 acres	●						●	●		●							●				●			●					26 C6
Rockport and Live Oak Peninsula, Rockport	20,500 acres	●	●		●	●	●	●											●	●		●	●	●	●		●	●		85 C8
Roy E. Larsen Sandyland Sanctuary, Silsbee	2,380 acres	●								●	●	●						●	●							●			●	72 E6
Sabal Palm Grove Sanctuary, Brownsville	172 acres	●		●				●		●		●					●		●	●						●				88 K6
San Jacinto River Canoe Trail, Cleveland	10 miles	●			●						●		●																●	72 D1
San Marcos Springs, San Marcos	90 acres											●			●				●	●	●	●	●	●					●	69 I9, 163 B8
Santa Ana National Wildlife Refuge, Alamo	2,080 acres	●		●				●		●		●					●		●	●	●					●				88 I2
Sea Rim State Park, Sabine Pass	15,094 acres		●		●	●	●					●							●	●	●	●			●	●	●	●		73 K8
Seminole Canyon State Historic Site, Comstock	2,173 acres	●						●		●	●	●							●	●		●			●	●				66 K2
Sheldon Lake State Park and Environmental Education Center, Sheldon	2,800 acres		●		●				●			●	●									●				●	●		●	72 J1, 131 A11
South Llano River State Park and Walter Buck Wildlife Management Area, Junction	2,679 acres	●		●	●				●	●	●								●	●		●			●	●			●	67 E11
W. Goodrich Jones State Forest, Conroe	1,733 acres	●							●		●								●			●				●				71 G11
Waco Area, Waco	7,950 acres	●	●		●		●												●	●		●			●	●	●		●	58 F1
Welder Wildlife Refuge, Sinton	7,800 acres	●						●	●			●						●	●	●										84 C6

Hiking

Most of the hiking trails included in this section are located in state and national parks (see State Lands and National Lands). *Check with the appropriate park to obtain trail guides and additional information. Symbols on the map indicate the trailhead only; symbol orientation does not necessarily indicate trail direction.*

Note: All trail distances are one-way unless otherwise indicated.

BARTON CREEK TRAIL – Austin – 8-mile route – Trailhead: Zilker Park – Elevation Range: 465–880 feet – 69 F10, 93 H7 Trail follows creek-fed stream through lush forest, cavern and cliff areas. Path crosses stream several times; difficult crossings during heavy rains. Steep ascent at trail's end. Moderate.

BIG BROWN CREEK TRAIL – Fairfield Lake State Park – 2.5-mile route – Trailhead: park headquarters – Elevation Range: fairly level – 59 D8 Trail through woodlands and grasslands crosses Big Brown Creek, following portion of Fairfield Lake shoreline. Includes 1.5-mile interpretive trail. Some footbridges, benches. Easy.

BOSQUE TRAIL – Meridian State Park – 2-mile route – Trailhead: CCC building at picnic area – Elevation Range: 965–1,060 feet – 57 C11 Mostly shady route follows shoreline of Lake Meridian through stands of oak, pecan and cottonwood. Creek crossing via footbridge near 1.25-mile mark. Scenic overlook at limestone Bee Ledge. Armadillo sightings. Moderately easy.

BUESCHER TRAIL – Buescher State Park – 7.8-mile route – Trailhead: parking area off PR 1C – Elevation Range: 375–500 feet – 70 H2 Day-use trail within densely wooded area skirts University of Texas Science Park. Accesses Pine Gulch Trail at 2.2-mile mark. Noted grove of isolated loblolly pine. Moderately easy.

COTTONWOOD–BLACK CREEK TRAIL – Lyndon B. Johnson National Grassland – 4-mile route – Trailhead: Black Creek Recreation Site – Elevation Range: fairly level – 45 B11 Connects Cottonwood and Black Creek lakes; passes through some woodland areas. Colorful autumn foliage, spring wildflowers. Moderately difficult.

CROSS TIMBERS HIKING TRAIL – Lake Texoma – 14-mile route – Trailhead: Juniper Point Recreation Area – Elevation Range: 615–740 feet – 38 C4 Westward-winding trail along Lake Texoma's southern shore passes Cedar Bayou and Paw Paw Creek resort areas. Rocky ledges high above lake offer scenic views. Many elevation changes in first 2.5 miles. Additional 2-mile loop accesses peninsula. Moderately difficult.

DINOSAUR VALLEY TRAIL – Dinosaur Valley State Park – 6-mile network – Trailhead: park campground – Elevation Range: 650–850 feet – 45 K10 Series of short loop trails access scenic overlooks and fossilized dinosaur tracks *(see Unique Natural Features: Dinosaur Tracks).* Easy.

DOGWOOD TRAIL – Woodville – 1.5-mile route – Trailhead: Dogwood Drive – Elevation Range: fairly level – 72 B6 Double-loop trail winds beside Theuvenin Creek banks. Markers identify many tree, shrub species. Popular early spring destination when trees blossom. Easy.

EAST TRAIL – Lost Maples State Natural Area – 4.2-mile loop – Trailhead: picnic area – Elevation Range: 1,795–2,250 feet – 67 J12 Well-marked trail through noted Lost Maples *(see Unique Natural Features: Lost Maples State Natural Area).* Includes 0.4-mile paved Maple Trail along Sabinal River. Some steep grades, loose rocks as trail winds back along Can Creek to parking area. Especially colorful in autumn. Moderately difficult.

ENCHANTED ROCK LOOP TRAIL – Enchanted Rock State Natural Area – 4-mile loop – Trailhead: parking area past primitive camping area – Elevation Range: 1,355–1,825 feet – 68 D4 Winding trail encircles Enchanted Rock *(see Unique Natural Features)*, large pink granite outcropping. Spur trail has 425-foot elevation gain in 0.6 miles. Views of Freshman Mountain, Turkey Peak and Buzzard's Roost. Scenic overlook. Moderately difficult.

FORT WORTH NATURE CENTER AND REFUGE TRAIL SYSTEM – Fort Worth – 25-mile network – Trailhead: interpretive center – Elevation Range: fairly level – 45 F12, 100 H3 Trail system located in one of the largest nature centers in US. Includes Greer Island Trail, a 1.5-mile National Recreation Trail; and Limestone Ledge Trail, paved path accessible to wheelchairs and strollers. Additional trails skirt Lotus Marsh, Lake Worth. Sightings of buffalo, white-tailed deer and prairie dogs. Easy to moderate. *(See Unique Natural Features.)*

FOUR C TRAIL – Davy Crockett National Forest – 19-mile route – Trailhead: Ratcliff Lake Recreation Area parking area – Elevation Range: 205–390 feet – 60 H1 Follows abandoned tramways through woodlands. Crosses streams, portion of Big Slough Wilderness. Panoramic views of river bottomlands, forests at Neches Bluff Observation Area. Shorter hikes possible via connecting forest roads. National Recreation Trail. Moderate.

HILL COUNTRY TRAIL SYSTEM – Hill Country State Natural Area – 32-mile network – Trailhead: various sites – Elevation Range: 1,300–2,000 feet – 77 A8 Multiuse trails in scenic hill country for hiking, mountain biking and equestrian use. Backpacking, equestrian camping sites. Easy to moderately difficult.

HUNTSVILLE TRAIL – Huntsville State Park – 7.7-mile loop – Trailhead: interpretive center – Elevation Range: 240–350 feet – 71 C11 Encircles Lake Raven; begins along 0.25-mile interpretive trail and passes marshland, shoreline and dam. Final portion connects with hiking/biking trail back to trailhead. Easy.

LAKE SOMERVILLE TRAILWAY – Lake Somerville State Park – 13-mile route – Trailhead: interpretive center – Elevation Range: fairly level – 70 F5 Connects two units of Lake Somerville State Park. Hike passes through dense yaupon and oak forests. Scenic overlooks, water crossings, colorful wildflowers during spring. Abundant wildlife; bird checklist available. Barrier-free loop trails at termini. Easy.

GUADALUPE MOUNTAINS NATIONAL PARK TRAILS

Guadalupe Mountains National Park preserves over 86,000 acres of remote wilderness typical of the American West. Over 80 miles of trails access the peaks, canyons and desert of the Guadalupe Mountains.

For more information contact Guadalupe Mountains National Park, HC60, Box 400, Salt Flat, TX 79847-9400, (915) 828-3251.

BUSH MOUNTAIN TRAIL – 17-mile route – Trailhead: Pine Springs Campground – Elevation Range: 5,820–8,630 feet – 50 C6 Strenuous hike accesses 8,631-foot-high Bush Mountain, second highest peak in Texas. Rocky Tejas Trail ascends Pine Spring Canyon, where Bush Mountain trail continues along canyon's north rim to partially wooded mountain summit. Views of desert floor, mountain peaks and salt flats 4,000 feet below *(see Unique Natural Features).* Descends through West Dog Canyon. Difficult.

DEVILS HALL TRAIL – 2.1-mile route – Trailhead: Pine Springs Campground – Elevation Range: 5,825–6,360 feet – 50 C6 Named for rock formation within steep walls of Pine Canyon. Relatively easy climb follows portions of equestrian trail. Route along canyon bottom crosses stair-step formation and leads to narrow hall of limestone rock. Moderately easy.

EL CAPITAN TRAIL – 9.4-mile route – Trailhead: Pine Springs Campground – Elevation Range: 5,400–6,360 feet – 50 C6 Offers views of towering El Capitan cliff *(see Unique Natural Features).* Winds through grasslands and foothills before descending into Guadalupe Canyon. Good views of salt flats *(see Unique Natural Features)* from overlook via Salt Basin Trail loop. Terminus at Williams Ranch. Park permission necessary for ranch access. Moderately difficult.

GUADALUPE PEAK TRAIL – 4.2-mile route – Trailhead: Pine Springs Campground – Elevation Range: 5,819–8,749 feet – 50 C6 Accesses Guadalupe Peak, highest peak in Texas at 8,749 feet *(see Unique Natural Features).* Excellent views of surrounding area from rocky summit. Many switchbacks and optional routes via equestrian trails as hike ascends Pine Canyon. Small monument dedicated to transcontinental mail route at summit. Elevation gain over 2,900 feet. Difficult.

McKITTRICK CANYON TRAIL – 10.9-mile route – Trailhead: McKittrick Canyon Visitor Center – Elevation Range: 4,985–7,715 feet – 51 C7 Trail through steep-walled canyon in region noted for foliage and rugged landscape. Accesses Pratt Cabin, homestead of early settler. Some stream crossings, grotto picnic site with limestone formations. Especially steep section before reaching McKittrick Ridge. Trail ends at Tejas Trail access. Canyon open for day-use only. Difficult.

BIG BEND NATIONAL PARK TRAILS

Big Bend National Park has several hiking trails providing access to the natural beauty and unique geology of the Chisos Mountains, Chihuahuan Desert and portions of the mighty Rio Grande. Walks and hikes range from short, self-guided strolls to treks across the park.

For more information contact Big Bend National Park, P.O. Box 129, Big Bend National Park, TX 79834, (432) 477-2251.

EMORY PEAK TRAIL – 4.5-mile route – Trailhead: Basin Campground – Elevation Range: 5,395–7,825 feet – 75 D9 Steep spur trail leads to 7,825-foot-high Emory Peak, highest point in park. Begins with steady climb then switchbacks. Access to Pinnacle Pass located before final mile to summit. Last portion difficult ascent along sheer wall. Excellent panoramic views on clear days. Difficult.

GRAPEVINE HILLS TRAIL – 1.1-mile route – Trailhead: designated parking area – Elevation Range: 3,235–3,480 feet – 75 C9 Trail through desert region formed by volcanic action. Area noted for massive boulders, rock formations. Short route follows sandy wash. Mild ascent last 100 feet to arch formed by balanced rocks. Easy.

LOST MINE TRAIL – 2.4-mile route – Trailhead: parking area at Panther Pass – Elevation Range: 5,755–6,850 feet – 75 D9 Offers good views en route to rocky promontory adjacent to Pine Canyon. Steady climb through mixed forest; steep switchbacks after Juniper Canyon. Views of surrounding Chisos Mountains at terminus. Moderately difficult.

SOUTH RIM TRAIL – 13.5-mile loop – Trailhead: Basin Campground – Elevation Range: 5,395–7,460 feet – 75 D9 Longest trail within park. Strenuous trek with steep switchbacks skirts Toll Mountain, Emory Peak. Moderate climb to Pinnacle Pass, Boot Canyon. Distant views of Mexico, mountain ranges and desert floor before trail continues to Laguna Meadow. Final descent leads back to trailhead. Scenic portion along East Rim closed during falcon-nesting season. Difficult.

WINDOW VIEW TRAIL – 0.3-mile route – Trailhead: Chisos Basin – Elevation Range: fairly level – 75 D9 Paved trail with views of The Window—notch between Carter Peak and Vernon Bailey Mountain offering vista of distant valley. Bench at lookout point. Barrier-free. Easy.

LIGHTHOUSE PEAK TRAIL – Palo Duro Canyon State Park – 3-mile route – Trailhead: parking area off Palo Duro Drive – Elevation Range: 2,835–3,260 feet – 29 J12 Affords views of colorful rock formations and pinnacle named The Lighthouse. Passes through desert terrain within rugged canyon landscape along mild grade. Final steep ascent to pinnacle base. Moderate.

LONE STAR HIKING TRAIL – Sam Houston National Forest – 140-mile route – Trailhead: FR 219 & FM 149 – Elevation Range: some moderate grades – 71 D10 Transects Sam Houston National Forest. Begins in relatively flat area; becomes more rugged after first 15 miles. Some creek crossings require wading. Several loop trails and access points. National Recreation Trail. Moderately difficult.

LONGLEAF PINE TRAIL – Camden – 2-mile loop – Trailhead: FM 62 – Elevation Range: fairly level – 60 K4 Leads through stand of virgin pine timber. Many trees over 100 years old. Habitat for rare, red-cockaded woodpeckers. Easy.

LOST PINES HIKING TRAIL – Bastrop State Park – 8.5-mile loop – Trailhead: parking area – Elevation Range: 390–570 feet – 70 H1 Footpath through loblolly pine woodland. Trail crisscrosses creek at 3.9-mile mark along loop return. Last section back to trailhead accesses 0.4-mile spur trail at Overlook Junction. Moderately easy.

MESQUITE TRAIL – Laguna Atascosa National Wildlife Refuge – 1.5-mile loop – Trailhead: visitor center parking area – Elevation Range: fairly level – 89 H7 Figure-eight loop through recovering vegetation. Sightings of Texas tortoise, spiny lizard, white pelican and greater roadrunner. Easy.

NORTH MOUNTAIN TRAIL – Hueco Tanks State Historic Site – 1.5-mile loop – Trailhead: parking area near park headquarters – Elevation Range: fairly level – 62 E4 Well-worn path within region noted for petroglyphs, geologic formations known as *huecos (see Unique Natural Features).* Skirts North Mountain, one of three rock masses. Summit accessible via moderate climb. Easy.

NORTHSHORE TRAIL – Grapevine Lake – 9-mile route – Trailhead: Rockledge Park – Elevation Range: fairly level – 46 E2 Hiking/biking trail winds westward along Grapevine Lake, terminating at Twin Coves Park. Wildlife sightings include rabbits, foxes and waterfowl. Additional trail accesses along public roads. National Recreation Trail. Moderately easy.

PALMETTO TRAIL – Palmetto State Park – 0.3-mile route – Trailhead: PR 11 – Elevation Range: 300–315 feet – 78 A5 Short hike within former Ottine Swamp region skirts lagoon, passes small pools, flowering vegetation and dwarf palmetto stands. Stream crossings via bridges. Armadillo sightings. Easy.

SAWMILL HIKING TRAIL – Angelina National Forest – 5.5-mile route – Trailhead: Boulton Lake Recreation Area – Elevation Range: 95–150 feet – 60 K6 Trail through Piney Woods region. Follows Neches River bottom, passing two abandoned sawmill sites; Old Aldridge mill reached via 0.75-mile spur trail. Big Creek crossing via swinging footbridge. Ends at Boykin Springs Recreation Area. Moderate.

SCENIC MOUNTAIN TRAIL – Big Spring State Park – 2.5-mile loop – Trailhead: park entrance – Elevation Range: fairly level – 42 K1, 94 K1 Looped nature trail. Corresponding brochure identifies plant and animal species and geologic features. Prairie dog sightings. Easy.

SINGING CHAPARRAL TRAIL – Bentsen–Rio Grande Valley State Park – 1.5-mile loop – Trailhead: PR 43 – Elevation Range: fairly level – 88 H1 Short, looped trail through riparian (streamside) woodlands and brushlands called "chaparral." Trail named for songs heard from abundant birdlife in surrounding brush. Benches. Easy.

SWEETLEAF NATURE TRAIL – W. Goodrich Jones State Forest – 1-mile loop – Trailhead: off FM 1488 – Elevation Range: fairly level – 71 F11 Looped path through woodland setting. Booklet referencing plant species, geological points of interest is available. Easy.

TOWN LAKE WALK AND BIKEWAY TRAIL – Austin – 8.4-mile route – Trailhead: south shore parking area – Elevation Range: fairly level – 93 H8 Hike in urban park follows Town Lake shoreline; provides views of massive bald cypress trees. Many bridge crossings. National Recreation Trail. Easy.

TRAIL BETWEEN THE LAKES – Sabine National Forest – 28-mile route – Trailhead: Lakeview Recreation Area – Elevation Range: some steep grades – 61 I10 Extends along McLemore Hills from Toledo Bend Reservoir toward Sam Rayburn Reservoir. Several road crossings allow shorter hikes. Primitive campsites along route. Moderately difficult.

UPPER CANYON TRAIL – Caprock Canyons State Park – 7-mile loop – Trailhead: parking area adjacent to Little Red Tent Camp – Elevation Range: 2,435–3,160 feet – 34 D3 Loop trail highlights red sandstone formations and rugged canyons. Follows Canyon Loop Trail first 1.5 miles then climbs upstream along North Prong of Little Red River to Fern Cave. Ridge crossing, alternate trail access at Haynes Ridge Overlook. Steep descent into South Prong of Little Red River before final stretch back to trailhead. Moderately difficult.

WILD AZALEA CANYON TRAIL SYSTEM – Burkeville – 2-mile network – Trailhead: 1.8 mi. off FM 1414 – Elevation Range: fairly level – 73 A10 Series of short hiking trails within canyon noted for longleaf forest, rock cliffs and wild azaleas. Landscape especially colorful mid-March–early April. Some steep and slippery sections. Trail open March–April only. Moderately easy.

WOLF MOUNTAIN TRAIL – Pedernales Falls State Park – 7.7-mile loop – Trailhead: parking area adjacent to park headquarters – Elevation Range: 1,000–1,090 feet – 69 F8 Popular hiking trail leading to Pedernales River. Skirts both Wolf and Tobacco mountains. Some creek crossings. Boulder-strewn gorge and Twin Falls viewed from overlook. Moderately difficult.

Campgrounds

This chart includes a selected list of private campgrounds in Texas. To locate these campgrounds in the Atlas, look on the given page for the campground symbol and corresponding four-digit number. For more information on campgrounds, contact the Texas Association of Campground Owners (TACO), 4621 South Cooper Street, Suite 131-104, Arlington, TX 76017, (800) 657-6555; or the Texas Economic Development, Tourism Division, P.O. Box 12728, Austin, TX 78711, (512) 462-9191.

Developed public campsites located on state and national lands can be identified by the symbol shown in the legend. Undeveloped camping is permitted on many of these public tracts. For information on camping in state and national parks, see State Lands *and* National Lands.

NUMBER, NAME, LOCATION	TENT SITES	RV SITES	PAGE & GRID
2030 ABC RV & Mobile Home Park, Universal City		25	78 A1, 166 C4
2040 Abilene KOA, Abilene	18	54	43 I11, 90 C1
2050 Abilene RV Park, Abilene	50	66	43 J12
2060 Admiralty Park, San Antonio	25	240	77 B11
2070 Alamo Fiesta RV Park, Boerne	10	125	68 J5
2080 Almost Heaven Campground, Manvel	15	84	80 B6
2090 Amarillo KOA, Amarillo	23	100	29 H12
2100 American Campground, Del Rio	50	88	86 B4
2110 Amistad RV Park, Del Rio	20	50	86 B4
2120 Ancient Oaks Campground, Rockport	20	75	79 I8
2130 Autumn Acres Mobile Home & RV Park, Brownsville		16	88 J6
2140 Back Acre RV Park, Mineral Wells	12	60	45 F9
2150 Bass Lake RV Park, Zapata	10	77	87 B8
2160 Bayou Haven RV Resort, Galveston	40	84	81 D9, 126 K1
2170 Bayside Camper Park, Palacios		70	80 I1
2180 Bayside RV Park, Bacliff	4	83	81 B8
2190 Beachcomers Park, Bluffton		64	68 B6
2200 Bit-O-Heaven RV & Mobile Home Park, Donna		400	88 H2
2210 Bluebonnet RV Park, Perezville	220	220	88 G1
2220 Breeze Lake Campground, Brownsville	50	50	88 J6
2230 Bryan's Country RV Park, Seguin	10	40	78 A3
2240 Buxton's Diamond B RV Park, Weatherford	10	40	45 G10
2250 Camp Riverview, Concan	51	51	76 A5
2260 Campers Paradise, Bowie	8	85	45 A10
2270 Casa del Sol, Donna		332	88 H3
2280 Cascade Caverns Park, Boerne	50	100	68 J5
2290 Caverns of Sonora, Sonora	48	48	66 D5
2300 Chaparral RV Park, Blessing		32	80 G1
2310 Columbus RV Park & Campground, Columbus	10	44	70 K5
2320 Concho Valley KOA, San Angelo	15	60	55 H7
2330 Corral RV Park, Dalhart	8	35	29 A7
2340 Country Boy Mobile Home & RV Park, Harlingen		100	88 H5
2350 Country Pines RV Park, Marshall	50	100	48 H6
2355 The Country Place, Cut And Shoot	5	50	71 F12
2360 Countryside Mobile Home Park, Donna		180	88 H3
2370 Crooked Tree Camp, Brownsville	200	200	88 J6, 95 H8
2380 Dallas Hi-Ho Campground, Glen Heights	10	88	46 I3
2390 Dallas KOA, Corinth	9	140	46 D2
2400 Dallas West Mobile Home/RV Park, Dallas	2	109	113 B9
2410 Dellanera RV Park, Galveston		84	81 D9
2420 Dickinson RV Travel Park, Dickinson		66	81 B8
2430 Don Manuel RV Park, San Ygnacio	35	35	87 A7
2440 Dusty Oaks RV Park & Campground, Kingsbury	15	24	78 A4
2450 East Lucas RV Park, Beaumont	15	45	73 G7, 95 A10
2455 The Edgewater, Buchanan Dam		48	68 B6
2460 El Campo RV Park, Van Horn	5	48	50 K6
2470 Evening Shadows RV Park, Tool	10	85	47 K8
2480 Flagstop RV Park, Van Raub	10	10	68 K5
2490 Flame Mobile Home Park, Athens	70	19	59 A9
2500 Fontainebleau RV Park, Fort Davis	3	12	63 C11
2510 Forest Acres Park, Arlington		31	46 H2, 110 I5
2520 Forest Hollow Mobile Home & RV Community, Beaumont		60	73 G7
2530 Fort Stockton KOA, Fort Stockton	17	96	64 A6
2535 450 RV Hitchin Post, Hallsville	3	12	48 I4
2540 Four Seasons Mobile Home & RV Resort, Zapata		167	87 B8
2550 Four Seasons RV Resort, Brownsville	25	132	88 J6
2560 Fredericksburg KOA, Fredericksburg	20	52	68 G4
2570 Frontier Park Resort & Marina, Milam	25	76	61 G9
2580 Fun-N-Sun RV Park, San Benito	10	900	88 H5
2590 Gaslight Square Mobile Home Estates, Canutillo	3	23	62 E1
2600 Green Acres Travel Trailer Park, San Benito		88	88 H5, 141 E10
2610 Greentree Village North, San Antonio		144	78 A1, 157 F12
2620 Guadalupe River Resort, Kerrville		120	68 H2
2630 Gulf Holiday RV Park, Hitchcock	6	59	81 C8
2640 Happy Oaks RV Park, Columbus	15	49	70 K6
2650 Harborlight Campground & Marina, Hemphill	8	54	61 H9
2660 Hatch RV Park/Mobile Home Park, Corpus Christi		85	84 E6, 98 C3
2670 Hidden Valley Recreational Park, Von Ormy	100	44	77 D11
2680 Highway 155 RV Park, Palestine	2	22	59 D11
2690 Hillcrest RV Park, New Waverly	31	31	71 D12
2700 Hilltop RV Park, Marshall	100	47	48 I6
2710 Hilltop Trailer & RV Park, Palestine	2	15	59 E10
2720 Holiday Out RV Park, Los Fresnos		85	88 I6
2730 Holiday Trav-L-Park, Del Rio	50	114	86 B4
2740 Honeydale Mobile Home & RV Park, Brownsville		45	88 J6, 95 I7
2750 Houston East/Baytown KOA, Baytown	20	60	72 J3
2760 Houston Leisure Park, Houston	25	205	72 J2
2770 Houston West Campground, Brookshire	17	61	71 J9
2780 Island RV Resort, Port Aransas	127	127	85 E8
2785 "J" Five Mobile Home & RV Park, Mission		180	88 H1
2790 Junction KOA, Junction	20	50	67 D11
2800 Kampers Korner, Marble Falls	6	28	69 D7
2810 Kenwood RV & Mobile Home Plaza, La Feria	6	228	88 H4
2820 Kerrville KOA, Kerrville	8	42	68 H2
2830 King Parkway Mobile Home Community, Houston		11	72 J1, 131 B9
2840 KOA Houston Central RV Park, Houston	20	98	71 I12
2850 Lajitas RV Park, Lajitas	100	75	74 D6
2860 Lake Buffalo Campground, Oakwood	25	25	59 F9
2870 Lake Conroe Camping Grounds, Conroe	60	60	71 F11
2880 Lakefront Lodge, Zapata		430	87 B8
2890 Lakeside RV Resort & Marina, Onalaska	100	125	72 B1
2900 Lakewood RV Park, Harlingen		300	88 H4
2910 Last Chance Resort & RV Park, Burnet		24	69 B7
2920 Lazy-L-Ranch RV Park, Silver City		200	58 B5
2930 Leisure Camp & RV Park, Fentress	25	74	69 K10
2940 Li'l Thicket Travel Park, La Marque	2	48	81 C8, 165 J7
2950 Lighthouse Beach RV Park, Port Lavaca	10	40	79 I11
2960 Lubbock KOA, Lubbock	8	82	33 J11
2970 Lubbock RV Park, Lubbock	20	50	33 J11
2980 Midessa KOA, Odessa	12	173	53 C9
2990 Mission RV Park, El Paso	6	188	62 G3
3000 Mobil Village RV Park, Aransas Pass		14	85 D8
3010 Mobile Manor RV Park, Beaumont		39	73 H7
3020 Mockingbird Hill Mobile Home & RV Park, Burleson		27	46 I1
3030 Mt. Pleasant KOA, Mt. Pleasant	6	44	48 C2
3040 Murphy's RV Park, Childress	6	20	35 D9
3050 Oak Leaf Park, Orange	125	10	73 H9
3060 Oakwood RV Park, Fredericksburg	80	116	68 F4
3070 Oleander Acres, Mission	7	193	88 H1
3080 On the Beach RV Park, Port Aransas		60	85 E8
3090 Orange Grove RV Park, Edinburg		525	88 G2
3100 Outdoor Resorts of South Padre, Port Isabel		898	89 I8
3110 Overnite RV Park, Amarillo	2	86	29 H12
3120 Pan-American RV Park, San Benito		85	88 H5
3130 Paradise Park Mobile Home & RV Retirement Community, Pharr		244	88 H2, 148 I3
3140 Paradise Park RV Resort, Harlingen		294	88 H5, 141 B7
3150 Park Center, Port Isabel	5	170	89 I7
3160 Park Place Estates, Harlingen		686	88 H4
3170 Parkview RV Park, Fort Stockton	10	50	64 A5
3180 Paul's RV Park, Brownsville	30	135	88 J6
3190 Pecan Grove RV Park, Alpine	10	32	64 E1
3200 Pine Shadows RV Park, Houston	4	150	71 K12, 133 D12
3210 Pop's Place, Pipe Creek	21	20	77 A9
3220 Portobelo Village Mobile Home & RV Park, Aransas Pass	12	85	85 D8
3230 Posada del Sol, Harlingen		130	88 H5
3240 Post View RV Park, Post	35	39	42 C2
3250 Primrose Lane RV & Mobile Home Park, Bryan	5	55	70 B6, 96 B2
3260 Rio RV Park, Brownsville	15	100	88 J6
3270 Rio Vista Resort, Kingsland	10	57	69 C7
3280 River View RV Park, Marble Falls		42	69 D7
3290 Rocking "A" RV Park, Vernon	10	80	36 F2
3300 Royal Coach Mobile Village, Houston		193	71 I12
3310 RV Park at the Fish Pond, Esperanza	5	51	71 D11
3320 RV World, Harlingen		50	88 H5, 141 D7
3330 Salmon Lake Park, Grapeland	25	250	59 G11
3340 Sandpiper Trailer Park, Port Isabel	4	32	89 I7
3350 Sands Motel & RV Park, Cuero	5	18	79 E7
3360 Sandy Lake RV Park, Carrollton		200	46 E3, 152 K1
3370 Schulenburg RV Park, Schulenburg	49	49	70 K3
3380 Shady Grove Mobile Home & RV Park, Corpus Christi		63	85 G7
3390 Skyline Ranch RV Park, Bandera		75	68 K3
3400 Spring Creek RV Park, Victoria	6	30	79 G8
3410 Spring Creek Village Campground & RV Community, Plano		145	46 D4, 153 E12
3420 Spring Oaks Mobile Home & RV Community, Spring		49	71 H11
3430 Stillwell Store & RV Park, Alpine	100	80	75 A10
3440 Sun-Down Campground, Amarillo	18	66	29 H11
3450 Sunrise Beach, Mathis	100	140	84 C4
3460 Sunrise Cove, Ore City	30	36	48 F4
3470 Sunset RV Park, Fort Worth	10	70	45 G12, 109 C7
3480 Sunshine RV Park, Harlingen		869	88 H5
3490 Tejas Valley RV Park & Campground, San Antonio	200	100	77 B11
3495 1015 RV Park, Weslaco		130	88 H3, 168 B3
3510 Texas RV Park, Big Spring	12	103	54 A1
3520 Texas Safari RV Park, Clifton	158	158	57 D11
3530 Texas Trails RV Resort, Pharr		594	88 H2, 148 F4
3540 Texas 281 RV Park, Bulverde		150	69 J7
3560 Traveler's World RV Park, San Antonio	170	170	159 G7
3570 Travelers Paradise RV Park, Bay City	10	24	80 F3, 94 G2
3580 Treetop RV Village, Arlington		48	46 H2, 111 H7
3590 Tropic Star RV Resort, Pharr		1,144	88 H2, 148 K4
3600 Turtle Bayou RV Park, Wallisville	15	50	72 J4
3610 Twin Oaks RV Park, Appleby	6	24	60 E4
3620 Tye RV Park, Tye	100	38	43 I10
3630 Tyler 554 Campground, Tyler	25	80	47 I12
3640 United Campground of San Marcos, San Marcos	10	90	69 I10
3650 The Village East RV Park, Amarillo	4	100	29 H12
3660 Waco North KOA, West	4	72	58 D2
3670 Weatherford Kampground, Weatherford	30	70	45 G10
3680 West End RV Park, Garner	50	85	45 F9
3690 West 40 Camp Area, Shamrock	40	40	31 H8
3700 Western Villa Mobile Home Park, Longview		25	48 I3
3710 Whip-In Campground, Big Spring	10	48	42 K2
3720 Whispering Pines Campground, Tyler	10	100	48 I1
3730 Whispering Pines Mobile Home Park, Springdale		10	49 C7
3740 Whitewater Sports, Sattler	100	40	69 J8
3750 Windmill RV Park, McLean	6	30	30 H6
3760 Woodsy Hollow Campground, Goodrich	10	90	72 C2
3770 Yerby's Mobile Home & RV Park, Dumas		52	29 C10

Freshwater Fishing

To locate freshwater fishing spots in this Atlas, look on the given page for the freshwater fishing symbol and four-digit number.

It is most important to be thoroughly familiar with all rules, regulations and restrictions before fishing in any area. For a copy of the current Texas fishing regulations, contact the Texas Parks and Wildlife Department, 4200 Smith School Road, Austin, TX 78744, (800) 792-1112.

Note: Symbols on the map identify only the bodies of water; location does not necessarily indicate public access or the best fishing area.

ACCESS
1–good 4–poor
2–fair 5–none
3–adequate 6–undetermined

NUMBER, BODY OF WATER	ACREAGE	MEAN DEPTH (feet)	ACCESS			SPECIES																		PAGE & GRID
						BASS						CATFISH			CRAPPIE		SHAD							
			BOAT	BANK	BARRIER-FREE	GUADALUPE	HYBRID STRIPED	LARGEMOUTH	SMALLMOUTH	STRIPED	WHITE	BLUE	CHANNEL	FLATHEAD	BLACK	WHITE	GIZZARD	THREADFIN	BLUEGILL	RED DRUM	PADDLEFISH	RAINBOW TROUT	WALLEYE	
4001 Amistad Reservoir	67,000	45	1	3	2		●	●	●	●	●	●	●	●		●	●	●	●				●	86 B4
4004 Anzalduas Reservoir	1,750	20	1	3	5			●					●	●			●	●	●					88 H1
4007 Aquilla Lake	3,280	16	1	1	3			●			●	●	●	●		●	●	●	●					58 C2
4010 B. A. Steinhagen Lake	16,830	4	1	1	4		●	●		●	●	●	●	●	●	●	●	●	●		●			73 A7
4013 Balmorhea Lake	573	3	1	1	2			●		●			●		●	●	●		●					51 K12
4016 Bardwell Lake	3,570	12	1	3	2			●		●	●		●			●	●	●	●					46 K4
4019 Baylor Lake	600	15	1	3	2			●				●	●	●	●	●	●		●					35 C8
4022 Belton Lake	12,500	37	1	1	2		●	●	●		●		●	●		●	●	●	●					57 J12
4025 Benbrook Lake	3,770	23	3	1	2		●	●			●	●	●	●	●	●	●	●	●					45 H12
4028 Big Creek Reservoir	520	12	3	4	4			●				●	●	●	●	●	●	●	●					47 B10
4031 Brady Reservoir	2,020	15	1	3	2			●	●		●	●	●	●		●	●	●	●					56 J1
4034 Brandy Branch Cooling Pond	1,242	24	3	4	5			●					●	●	●		●	●	●					48 J5
4037 Braunig Lake	1,350	—	1	1	3		●	●				●	●	●	●	●	●	●	●	●				78 D1
4040 Bryan Utilities Lake	828	19	3	3	6			●			●		●		●	●	●	●	●					70 B6
4046 Caddo Lake	26,800	5	2	4	5			●			●	●	●	●	●	●	●	●	●		●			49 H7
4049 Calaveras Lake	3,450	18	1	1	3		●	●				●	●	●	●	●	●	●	●	●				78 D1
4052 Canyon Lake	8,240	43	1	1	2	●		●	●	●	●	●	●	●	●	●	●	●	●				●	69 I7
4058 Cedar Creek Reservoir	2,400	30	1	4	4			●				●	●	●	●	●	●	●	●					70 I4
4061 Cedar Creek Reservoir	34,300	20	3	4	4		●	●			●	●	●	●	●	●	●	●	●					47 K8
4064 Century Lake	555	5	4	4	4			●				●	●	●	●	●	●		●					47 D10
4067 Champion Creek Reservoir	1,560	22	1	1	2			●			●		●	●		●	●	●	●					42 K5
4070 Choke Canyon Reservoir	26,000	27	1	1	2			●			●	●	●	●	●	●	●	●	●					78 J1
4073 Coffee Mill Lake	650	12	1	4	5			●					●		●	●	●	●	●					39 D8
4076 Coleto Creek Reservoir	3,100	11	1	1	2		●	●				●	●	●		●	●	●	●					79 H8
4079 Cooper Lake	19,280	20	1	1	2			●			●	●	●	●	●	●	●		●					47 B10
4082 Cotton Lake	2,000	3	4	5	6			●					●		●									72 J3
4085 Delta Lake	2,371	4	5	4	5			●			●		●		●	●	●	●	●					88 F3
4088 Dixieland Reservoir	700	—	6	6	2							●	●			●	●							88 H5, 141 E7
4091 E. V. Spence Reservoir	14,950	33	1	1	2			●		●	●	●	●	●		●	●	●	●					54 C6
4094 Eagle Mountain Lake	9,200	22	3	3	4		●	●			●	●	●	●		●	●	●	●					45 F12, 100 F3
4097 Ellison Creek Reservoir	1,516	16	3	4	6			●			●		●		●	●	●	●	●					48 E4
4100 Fairfield Lake	2,353	22	1	3	1		●	●			●		●	●	●	●	●	●	●	●				59 D8
4103 Falcon Reservoir	78,300	31	1	3	2			●		●	●	●	●	●	●	●	●	●	●					87 D8
4106 Forest Grove Reservoir	1,500	10	5	5	5			●			●		●			●	●		●					47 K9
4109 Galveston County Reservoir	814	5	6	6	6							●	●	●		●	●	●	●					81 B8
4112 Gibbons Creek Reservoir	2,500	11	1	3	6			●				●	●	●	●	●	●	●	●					71 C8
4115 Granger Lake	4,400	9	1	1	4			●			●		●	●		●	●	●	●					70 B1
4118 Grapevine Lake	7,280	26	1	1	2		●	●			●	●	●	●		●	●	●	●					46 E2
4121 Greenbelt Reservoir	1,990	30	1	1	4			●	●		●	●	●	●		●	●		●				●	30 J4
4127 Holland Reservoir	840	—	3	6	6								●											83 A8
4130 Hords Creek Lake	510	17	1	1	3			●	●				●	●	●	●	●	●	●					55 D12
4133 Houston County Lake	1,500	12	1	3	6			●			●		●	●	●	●	●	●	●					59 G11
4136 Hubbard Creek Lake	15,250	21	1	3	4		●	●			●	●	●	●		●	●	●	●					44 F3
4142 Inks Lake	803	23	1	1	2	●		●		●	●		●	●		●	●	●	●					69 B7
4145 Joe Pool Lake	7,470	33	3	3	1			●			●	●	●	●		●	●	●	●					46 H3
4148 Kirby Lake	740	6	3	1	4			●					●	●		●	●		●					43 J11
4154 Lake Abilene	640	15	3	3	4		●	●					●	●		●	●							43 K10
4157 Lake Alice	700	2	4	1	2		●	●					●		●	●	●	●	●					84 E3
4160 Lake Alvarado	507	6	1	3	4			●			●		●			●	●	●	●					46 J1
4163 Lake Amon G. Carter	2,126	13	4	3	5			●					●	●	●	●	●	●	●					45 A10
4166 Lake Anahuac	5,300	4	3	3	6						●	●	●		●	●	●	●	●					72 J4
4169 Lake Arlington	2,275	20	3	2	2		●	●			●		●	●		●	●	●	●					46 G1, 110 G3
4172 Lake Arrowhead	16,200	16	1	1	2			●		●	●	●	●	●		●	●		●					37 J7
4175 Lake Athens	1,500	24	3	4	4			●			●		●	●	●	●	●	●	●					59 A10
4178 Lake Austin	1,830	12	1	4	4	●		●		●	●	●	●	●		●	●	●	●					69 F10, 93 E7
4181 Lake Bastrop	906	18	4	2	2	●		●				●	●	●	●	●	●	●	●					70 G1
4184 Lake Bob Sandlin	9,460	21	1	3	4			●			●		●	●	●	●	●	●	●					48 D2
4187 Lake Bonham	1,020	13	1	3	2			●				●	●		●	●	●		●					39 D8
4190 Lake Bridgeport	13,000	34	3	4	2		●	●	●		●		●	●		●	●	●	●				●	45 C10
4193 Lake Brownwood	7,300	22	1	2	4		●	●	●		●	●	●	●		●	●	●	●					56 D3
4196 Lake Buchanan	23,200	43	1	4	4	●	●	●		●	●	●	●	●		●	●	●	●					69 B7
4197 Lake Casa Blanca	1,656	12	1	1	2		●	●				●	●	●	●	●	●	●	●					83 G7
4199 Lake Charlotte	2,400	—	4	5	6			●			●	●	●	●	●	●	●	●	●					72 J4
4202 Lake Cisco	445	20	3	4	4		●	●				●	●	●		●	●		●					44 J3
4205 Lake Clyde	500	20	3	1	4			●				●	●	●		●	●	●	●				●	44 K1
4208 Lake Coleman	2,000	20	3	2	4		●	●					●	●		●	●		●					55 B12
4211 Lake Colorado City	1,618	12	1	1	1		●	●			●		●	●		●	●	●	●	●				42 K4
4214 Lake Conroe	21,000	20	1	4	2		●	●			●	●	●	●	●	●	●	●	●					71 E11
4217 Lake Corpus Christi	21,900	14	1	1	2		●	●		●	●	●	●	●	●	●	●	●	●					84 C4
4220 Lake Crook	1,226	10	3	3	4			●			●		●	●	●	●	●	●	●					39 D11
4223 Lake Cypress Springs	3,450	21	1	3	2			●			●	●	●		●	●	●	●	●					48 D1
4226 Lake Daniel	950	11	3	4	4			●					●	●		●	●		●					44 H4
4229 Lake Diversion	3,419	12	2	2	5		●	●		●	●	●	●	●		●	●		●					36 I4
4232 Lake Dunlap	410	25	1	4	5			●	●	●		●	●	●		●	●	●	●					69 K9
4235 Lake Fork Reservoir	27,690	12	1	4	4			●				●	●		●	●	●	●	●					47 F11
4238 Lake Fort Parker	700	4	3	1	2			●			●		●			●	●		●					58 F5
4241 Lake Fort Phantom Hill	4,246	18	1	2	4		●	●			●	●	●	●		●	●	●	●				●	43 H11
4244 Lake Georgetown	1,310	40	1	1	4	●	●	●	●		●		●	●		●	●	●	●					69 C10
4247 Lake Gladewater	800	9	3	4	4			●					●		●	●	●	●	●					48 I2
4250 Lake Gonzales	696	—	1	4	4	●		●					●	●	●	●	●	●	●					78 B5
4253 Lake Graham	3,000	21	3	2	4		●	●			●		●	●		●	●	●	●					44 D5

FRESHWATER FISHING, *continued*

ACCESS	
1–good	4–poor
2–fair	5–none
3–adequate	6–undetermined

NUMBER, BODY OF WATER	ACREAGE	MEAN DEPTH (feet)	ACCESS: BOAT	ACCESS: BANK	ACCESS: BARRIER-FREE	BASS: GUADALUPE	BASS: HYBRID STRIPED	BASS: LARGEMOUTH	BASS: SMALLMOUTH	BASS: STRIPED	BASS: WHITE	CATFISH: BLUE	CATFISH: CHANNEL	CATFISH: FLATHEAD	CRAPPIE: BLACK	CRAPPIE: WHITE	SHAD: GIZZARD	SHAD: THREADFIN	BLUEGILL	RED DRUM	PADDLEFISH	RAINBOW TROUT	WALLEYE	PAGE & GRID
4256 Lake Granbury	8,700	18	1	1	1			●		●	●		●	●	●	●	●	●	●					45 J10
4259 Lake Halbert	650	14	1	1	4			●			●		●	●		●	●	●	●					58 B6
4262 Lake Hawkins	800	15	1	3	4			●					●	●	●	●	●	●	●					48 H1
4265 Lake Holbrook	1,050	8	1	3	4			●					●	●	●	●	●	●	●					47 H11
4268 Lake Houston	12,240	12	1	1	1			●			●	●	●	●	●	●	●	●	●					72 I1
4271 Lake J. B. Thomas	7,820	13	1	1	3			●			●		●	●		●	●		●					42 H3
4274 Lake Jacksonville	1,352	23	1	3	4			●			●	●	●	●	●	●	●	●	●					59 C12
4277 Lake Kemp	16,540	19	2	2	5			●		●	●	●	●	●		●	●		●					36 I2
4280 Lake Kickapoo	6,200	17	2	2	4			●			●		●	●		●	●		●					36 J4
4283 Lake Kurth	800	15	3	4	2		●	●				●	●	●	●	●	●	●	●					60 G4
4286 Lake Leon	1,590	17	1	2	4			●				●	●	●		●	●	●	●					44 J5
4289 Lake Limestone	13,680	17	3	2	3		●	●			●	●	●	●	●	●	●	●	●					59 H7
4292 Lake Livingston	90,000	23	1	3	1			●		●	●	●	●	●	●	●	●	●	●					72 B1
4295 Lake Lyndon B. Johnson	6,375	22	2	2	4	●		●	●	●	●	●	●	●		●	●	●	●					69 D7
4298 Lake Marble Falls	780	11	1	4	4	●		●	●		●	●	●	●		●	●	●	●					69 D8
4301 Lake McClellan	405	4	3	1	4		●	●				●	●			●	●		●					30 H5
4304 Lake McQueeney	400	12	3	4	2			●			●		●	●		●	●	●	●					78 A3
4307 Lake Meredith	16,505	30	1	3	2			●	●		●	●	●	●		●	●		●				●	29 D12
4310 Lake Mexia	1,400	6	3	4	3			●			●	●	●	●		●	●	●	●					58 E5
4313 Lake Mineral Wells	663	11	1	3	1			●				●	●	●		●	●	●	●			●		45 F9
4316 Lake Monticello	2,000	20	3	3	4			●					●	●	●		●	●	●					48 D2
4319 Lake Murvaul	3,820	12	1	3	2			●					●	●	●	●	●	●	●					60 B5
4322 Lake Nacogdoches	2,200	15	1	3	5			●					●		●	●	●	●	●					60 F3
4325 Lake Nasworthy	1,598	4	1	1	1			●			●		●	●		●	●	●	●	●				55 H7
4328 Lake Nocona	1,470	17	3	3	5		●	●			●		●	●		●	●	●	●					37 I11
4331 Lake O' The Pines	18,700	14	1	1	3			●			●	●	●	●	●	●	●	●	●		●			48 G4
4334 Lake Palestine	25,500	16	1	3	4		●	●			●	●	●	●	●	●	●	●	●				●	59 A11
4337 Lake Palo Pinto	2,661	17	3	3	6			●			●		●	●		●	●	●	●					45 H7
4340 Lake Pat Cleburne	1,545	17	3	1	5			●			●	●	●	●		●	●	●	●					45 K12
4343 Lake Pauline	600	8	4	1	4		●	●				●	●	●		●	●		●					35 E11
4346 Lake Quitman	814	10	1	3	4			●					●	●	●	●	●	●	●					47 F12
4349 Lake Ray Hubbard	22,745	22	1	1	4		●	●		●	●		●	●	●	●	●	●	●					46 F6, 107 H11
4358 Lake Stamford	5,200	11	1	3	3		●	●				●	●	●		●	●	●	●				●	43 D12
4361 Lake Striker	2,400	15	4	4	4			●			●		●	●	●	●	●	●	●					60 C2
4364 Lake Sulphur Springs	1,340	11	1	3	4			●				●	●		●	●	●	●	●					47 C10
4367 Lake Sweetwater	630	19	1	3	4			●			●		●	●		●	●		●				●	43 J8
4370 Lake Tawakoni	36,700	12	1	1	4		●	●		●	●	●	●	●	●	●	●	●	●					47 F9
4373 Lake Texana	11,000	16	1	1	2			●			●	●	●	●	●	●	●	●	●					79 F11
4376 Lake Texoma	89,000	31	1	1	4		●	●	●	●	●	●	●	●	●	●	●	●	●					38 C4
4379 Lake Travis	18,930	62	1	2	4	●		●	●	●	●	●	●			●	●	●	●					69 E10
4382 Lake Tyler	2,450	18	1	3	4		●	●			●		●	●	●	●	●	●	●					48 K1
4385 Lake Tyler East	2,530	16	1	3	4			●			●		●	●	●	●	●	●	●					48 K1
4388 Lake Waxahachie	690	20	1	3	2			●			●		●		●	●	●	●	●					46 K4
4391 Lake Weatherford	1,144	17	4	1	1			●					●	●		●	●	●	●				●	45 G11
4397 Lake Wichita	1,578	7	2	2	5		●	●			●		●	●		●	●		●					36 I6
4400 Lake Winnsboro	1,100	11	1	3	4			●					●		●		●	●	●					47 F12
4403 Lake Worth	3,560	11	3	3	4			●			●	●	●	●	●	●	●	●	●					45 G12, 100 K4
4406 Lavon Lake	21,400	18	1	1	1		●	●		●	●	●	●	●	●	●	●	●	●				●	46 D6
4409 Lewisville Lake	29,592	20	3	1	2		●	●	●		●	●	●	●		●	●	●	●					46 D3, 145 C11
4412 Llano Grande Lake	1,400	—	6	2	6							●	●				●	●	●					88 I3
4415 Lost Creek Reservoir	500	30	1	1	4			●					●			●	●		●					45 C8
4418 Mackenzie Reservoir	900	52	1	2	4		●	●	●		●		●	●		●	●		●				●	34 C1
4421 Martin Lake	5,000	16	1	3	2			●					●	●	●	●	●	●	●					48 K5
4424 Medina Lake	5,575	46	1	1	6		●	●	●		●	●	●	●	●	●	●	●	●				●	77 A10
4427 Millers Creek Reservoir	1,900	13	1	1	2		●	●			●	●	●	●		●	●		●					44 A1
4433 Moss Lake	1,125	21	3	4	1			●	●		●		●			●	●	●	●				●	38 C1
4436 Mountain Creek Lake	2,710	9	4	2	5			●			●	●	●	●		●	●	●	●					46 G3, 112 F3
4448 Murphree WMA—Compartment #2	400	2	3	5	5			●					●		●		●		●					73 J8
4451 Murphree WMA—Compartment #3	500	2	3	5	5			●					●		●		●		●					73 J8
4454 Murphree WMA—Compartment #4	400	2	3	5	5			●					●		●		●		●					73 J8, 154 K1
4457 Murphree WMA—Compartment #5	600	2	3	5	5			●					●		●		●		●					73 J8
4460 Murphree WMA—Compartment #6	600	2	3	5	5			●					●		●		●		●					73 J8
4463 Murphree WMA—Compartment #7	400	2	3	5	5			●					●		●		●		●					73 J8
4466 Murphree WMA—Compartment #8	600	2	3	5	5			●					●		●		●		●					73 J8
4469 Murphree WMA—Compartment #9	800	2	3	5	5			●					●		●		●		●					73 J8
4470 Murphree WMA—Compartment #10	900	2	3	5	5			●					●		●		●		●					73 J8
4471 Murphree WMA—Compartment #11	1,000	2	3	5	5												●							73 J8
4472 Murphree WMA—Compartment #14	400	2	3	5	5												●	●		●				73 J8
4473 Navarro Mills Lake	5,070	11	1	1	6			●			●		●	●	●	●	●		●					58 C4
4475 New Ballinger Lake	575	10	1	3	2		●	●	●		●	●	●	●		●	●		●				●	55 E9
4478 North Fork Buffalo Creek Reservoir	1,392	10	3	4	5			●				●	●	●		●	●		●					36 G5
4481 North Lake	800	20	3	3	4			●			●		●	●		●	●	●	●					46 E3, 104 B2
4484 O. C. Fisher Lake	5,440	14	1	1	2			●			●	●	●	●		●	●	●	●				●	55 G7, 162 B2
4487 O. H. Ivie Reservoir	19,200	28	1	1	2			●	●		●	●	●	●	●	●	●	●	●				●	55 G11
4490 Oak Creek Reservoir	2,375	17	1	1	2			●	●		●	●	●	●		●	●	●	●					55 B8
4493 Old Marlin City Lake	453	6	2	2	5			●					●			●	●		●					58 H3
4496 Palo Duro Reservoir	2,413	30	1	1	1			●	●			●	●	●		●	●		●				●	26 I3
4499 Pat Mayse Lake	5,993	13	1	3	4		●	●			●		●	●	●	●	●	●	●					39 C10
4505 Pinkston Reservoir	560	20	3	3	5			●					●	●	●	●	●	●	●					60 E6
4508 Possum Kingdom Lake	19,800	37	2	1	2			●	●	●	●	●	●	●	●	●	●	●	●					44 F6
4511 Proctor Lake	4,610	13	1	1	2		●	●				●	●	●		●	●	●	●					56 C6

Continues on next page

FRESHWATER FISHING, *continued*

To locate freshwater fishing spots in this Atlas, look on the given page for the freshwater fishing symbol and four-digit number.

It is most important to be thoroughly familiar with all rules, regulations and restrictions before fishing in any area. For a copy of the current Texas fishing regulations, contact the Texas Parks and Wildlife Department, 4200 Smith School Road, Austin, TX 78744, (800) 792-1112.

Note: Symbols on the map identify only the bodies of water; location does not necessarily indicate public access or the best fishing area.

ACCESS
1–good 4–poor
2–fair 5–none
3–adequate 6–undetermined

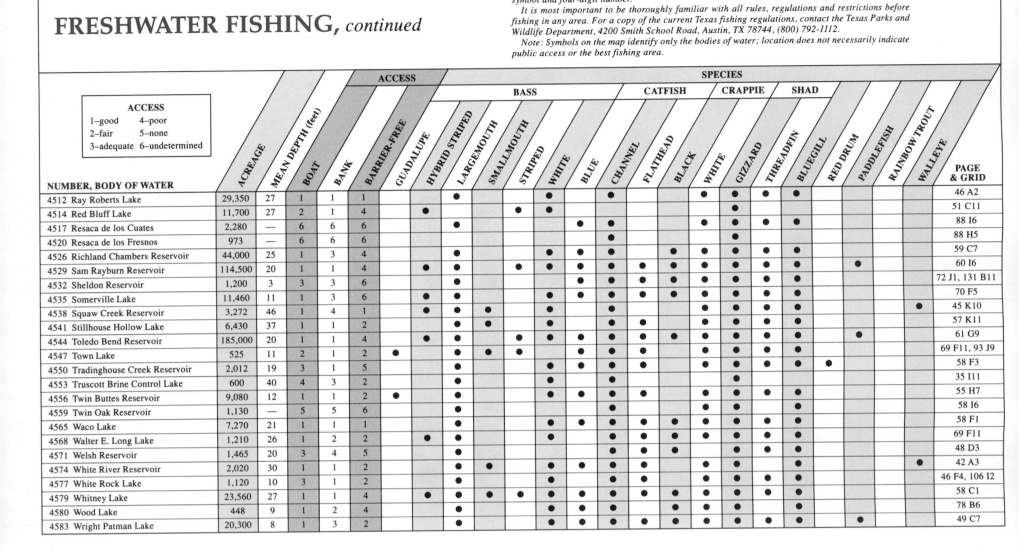

NUMBER, BODY OF WATER	ACREAGE	MEAN DEPTH (feet)	ACCESS: BOAT	ACCESS: BANK	ACCESS: BARRIER-FREE	BASS: GUADALUPE	BASS: HYBRID STRIPED	BASS: LARGEMOUTH	BASS: SMALLMOUTH	BASS: STRIPED	BASS: WHITE	CATFISH: BLUE	CATFISH: CHANNEL	CATFISH: FLATHEAD	CRAPPIE: BLACK	CRAPPIE: WHITE	SHAD: GIZZARD	SHAD: THREADFIN	BLUEGILL	RED DRUM	PADDLEFISH	RAINBOW TROUT	WALLEYE	PAGE & GRID
4512 Ray Roberts Lake	29,350	27	1	1	1			●			●		●			●	●	●	●					46 A2
4514 Red Bluff Lake	11,700	27	2	1	4		●			●	●						●							51 C11
4517 Resaca de los Cuates	2,280	—	6	6	6			●				●	●			●	●	●	●					88 I6
4520 Resaca de los Fresnos	973	—	6	6	6								●				●							88 H5
4526 Richland Chambers Reservoir	44,000	25	1	3	4			●			●	●	●		●	●	●	●	●					59 C7
4529 Sam Rayburn Reservoir	114,500	20	1	1	4		●	●		●	●	●	●	●	●	●	●	●	●		●			60 I6
4532 Sheldon Reservoir	1,200	3	3	3	6			●				●	●	●	●	●	●	●	●					72 J1, 131 B11
4535 Somerville Lake	11,460	11	1	3	6		●	●			●	●	●	●	●	●	●	●	●					70 F5
4538 Squaw Creek Reservoir	3,272	46	1	4	1		●	●	●		●		●			●	●	●	●				●	45 K10
4541 Stillhouse Hollow Lake	6,430	37	1	1	2			●	●		●		●	●		●	●	●	●					57 K11
4544 Toledo Bend Reservoir	185,000	20	1	1	4		●	●		●	●	●	●	●	●	●	●	●	●		●			61 G9
4547 Town Lake	525	11	2	1	2	●		●	●	●		●	●	●		●	●	●	●					69 F11, 93 J9
4550 Tradinghouse Creek Reservoir	2,012	19	3	1	5			●			●	●	●	●		●	●	●	●	●				58 F3
4553 Truscott Brine Control Lake	600	40	4	3	2			●			●		●				●							35 I11
4556 Twin Buttes Reservoir	9,080	12	1	1	2	●		●			●	●	●	●		●	●	●	●					55 H7
4559 Twin Oak Reservoir	1,130	—	5	5	6			●					●			●	●		●					58 I6
4565 Waco Lake	7,270	21	1	1	1			●			●	●	●	●	●	●	●	●	●					58 F1
4568 Walter E. Long Lake	1,210	26	1	2	2		●	●			●		●	●	●	●	●	●	●					69 F11
4571 Welsh Reservoir	1,465	20	3	4	5			●					●	●	●		●	●	●					48 D3
4574 White River Reservoir	2,020	30	1	1	2			●	●		●	●	●	●		●	●		●				●	42 A3
4577 White Rock Lake	1,120	10	3	1	2			●			●		●	●		●	●	●	●					46 F4, 106 I2
4579 Whitney Lake	23,560	27	1	1	4		●	●	●	●	●	●	●	●	●	●	●	●	●					58 C1
4580 Wood Lake	448	9	1	2	4			●			●	●	●		●	●	●		●					78 B6
4583 Wright Patman Lake	20,300	8	1	3	2			●			●	●	●	●	●	●	●	●	●		●			49 C7

Saltwater Fishing

Saltwater fishing areas are composed of coastal waters, tidal lakes, marshes and bogs. To locate saltwater fishing spots in this Atlas, look on the given page for the saltwater fishing symbol and four-digit number.

It is most important to be thoroughly familiar with all rules, regulations and restrictions before fishing in any area. For a copy of the current Texas fishing regulations, contact the Texas Parks and Wildlife Department, 4200 Smith School Road, Austin, TX 78744, (800) 792-1112.

Note: Symbols on the map identify only the bodies of water; location does not necessarily indicate public access or the best fishing area.

FISHING QUALITY
1–best chance for finding this species
2–good chance for finding this species
3–fair chance for finding this species
4–poor chance for finding this species
5–species not present

NUMBER, BODY OF WATER	BAY SYSTEM	GAFF-TOPSAIL CATFISH	ATLANTIC CROAKER	BLACK DRUM	RED DRUM	FLOUNDER	KING MACKEREL	SPANISH MACKEREL	SAND SEATROUT	SPOTTED SEATROUT	SHEEPSHEAD	RED SNAPPER	TARPON	PAGE & GRID
4601 Alazan Bay	Upper Laguna Madre	4	3	1	3	3	5	5	4	2	4	5	5	84 I6
4604 Aransas Bay	Aransas Bay	2	2	2	1	1	4	3	2	1	3	4	3	85 C9
4607 Army Hole	San Antonio Bay	4	4	2	1	3	4	4	4	1	3	4	4	85 A12
4610 Ayres Bay	San Antonio Bay	3	4	3	2	3	4	4	4	2	2	4	4	85 B10
4613 Baffin Bay	Upper Laguna Madre	4	3	1	2	2	5	5	4	1	3	5	5	84 J6
4616 Bastrop—Christmas Bay	Galveston Bay	2	1	2	1	1	4	3	3	1	1	4	4	81 E7
4619 Bessie Heights Marsh	Sabine Lake	3	3	2	1	2	5	5	3	3	1	5	5	73 H8
4622 Carancahua Bay	West Matagorda Bay	1	1	1	1	1	4	4	1	1	2	4	4	79 I12
4625 Carlos Bay	Aransas Bay	2	3	1	2	2	4	4	4	3	3	4	3	85 B9
4628 Cayo Del Grullo	Upper Laguna Madre	4	3	1	3	3	5	5	4	2	4	5	5	84 I5
4631 Cedar Lakes Complex	East Matagorda Bay	1	2	1	1	1	4	4	2	1	1	4	4	80 H5
4634 Chocolate Bay	Galveston Bay	2	1	1	1	1	4	4	2	1	2	4	4	81 E7
4637 Chocolate Bay	West Matagorda Bay	1	1	1	1	1	4	4	2	1	2	4	4	79 J11
4640 Copano Bay	Aransas Bay	2	2	1	1	3	4	3	4	1	3	4	2	85 C8
4643 Corpus Christi Bay	Corpus Christi Bay	2	3	2	2	2	4	3	1	1	2	4	4	85 E7
4646 Cox Bay	West Matagorda Bay	1	1	1	1	1	4	4	1	1	1	4	4	79 I11
4649 Dickinson Bay	Galveston Bay	3	3	3	3	3	4	4	3	2	3	4	4	81 B8
4652 East Bay	Galveston Bay	1	1	1	1	2	4	4	2	1	2	4	4	81 B10
4655 East Matagorda Bay	East Matagorda Bay	1	1	1	1	1	4	4	1	1	1	4	4	80 I3
4658 Espiritu Santo Bay	San Antonio Bay	1	3	2	1	1	4	4	3	1	1	4	4	85 A11
4661 Galveston Bay	Galveston Bay	3	1	2	2	2	4	2	1	1	1	4	4	81 A9
4664 Guadalupe Bay	San Antonio Bay	4	4	3	2	3	4	4	4	4	4	4	4	79 K10
4667 Gulf of Mexico	Aransas Bay	3	2	3	2	2	1	1	1	2	3	1	2	85 C10
4670 Gulf of Mexico	Corpus Christi Bay	4	2	3	2	2	1	1	1	2	2	1	3	85 F8
4673 Gulf of Mexico	East Matagorda Bay	2	1	2	1	1	1	1	1	1	1	1	3	80 I4
4676 Gulf of Mexico	Galveston Bay	1	2	1	1	2	1	1	1	2	1	1	1	81 C10
4679 Gulf of Mexico	Lower Laguna Madre	3	1	1	1	1	1	1	1	1	1	1	2	89 I8
4682 Gulf of Mexico	Sabine Lake	2	3	2	1	3	1	1	1	1	1	1	3	73 K10
4685 Gulf of Mexico	San Antonio Bay	3	4	2	2	4	1	1	1	3	1	1	1	85 B11
4688 Gulf of Mexico	West Matagorda Bay	2	1	2	1	2	1	1	1	1	1	1	2	80 K1
4691 Gulf of Mexico—Shore	San Antonio Bay	4	4	2	1	3	4	2	4	1	4	4	2	85 B10
4694 Gulf of Mexico—Shore	Upper Laguna Madre	3	3	3	2	3	1	1	3	2	3	1	1	85 J7
4697 Hynes Bay	San Antonio Bay	4	4	3	2	2	4	4	4	4	4	4	4	79 K10
4700 Jones Bay	Galveston Bay	3	1	1	1	1	4	4	3	1	3	4	4	81 C8
4703 Keith Lake Marsh	Sabine Lake	3	2	2	1	1	4	4	3	1	3	4	4	73 J8
4706 Keller Bay	West Matagorda Bay	1	1	1	1	1	4	4	1	1	1	4	4	79 I12
4709 Laguna Salada	Upper Laguna Madre	4	3	1	3	3	5	5	4	2	4	5	5	84 J5
4712 Lavaca Bay	West Matagorda Bay	1	1	1	1	1	4	4	1	1	1	4	4	79 I11
4715 Lavaca River Estuary	West Matagorda Bay	2	1	2	1	1	4	4	2	1	2	4	4	79 H11
4718 Lower Laguna Madre	Lower Laguna Madre	3	1	1	1	2	4	4	2	1	1	4	3	89 I7
4721 Lower Laguna Madre Jetties	Lower Laguna Madre	3	1	1	1	1	3	2	1	1	1	1	2	89 E7
4724 Mad Island Lake	West Matagorda Bay	4	2	2	1	2	4	4	3	3	3	4	4	80 I2
4727 Matagorda Bay	West Matagorda Bay	1	1	1	1	1	4	2	1	1	1	4	3	80 J1
4730 Matagorda Jetties	San Antonio Bay	3	3	1	1	3	3	1	2	1	1	3	2	79 K12
4733 Mesquite Bay	Aransas Bay	1	3	1	2	1	4	4	4	2	3	4	4	85 B10
4736 Mission Bay	Aransas Bay	3	2	1	1	3	4	4	4	3	3	4	3	85 B8
4739 Mission Lake	Aransas Bay	2	3	1	2	3	4	4	4	3	3	4	4	85 B8
4742 Mission Lake	San Antonio Bay	4	4	2	3	4	4	4	4	4	4	4	4	79 K10
4745 Moses Lake	Galveston Bay	4	1	1	2	2	4	2	2	2	3	4	4	81 B8
4748 Nueces Bay	Corpus Christi Bay	3	3	1	2	3	4	4	2	2	3	4	4	84 E6
4751 Oso Bay	Corpus Christi Bay	3	4	1	3	4	4	4	2	3	4	4	4	85 F7
4754 Oyster Lake	West Matagorda Bay	2	2	1	1	1	4	4	2	1	1	4	4	80 I1

SALTWATER FISHING, *continued*

FISHING QUALITY
1–best chance for finding this species
2–good chance for finding this species
3–fair chance for finding this species
4–poor chance for finding this species
5–species not present

NUMBER, BODY OF WATER	BAY SYSTEM	GAFF-TOPSAIL CATFISH	ATLANTIC CROAKER	BLACK DRUM	RED DRUM	FLOUNDER	KING MACKEREL	SPANISH MACKEREL	SAND SEATROUT	SPOTTED SEATROUT	SHEEPSHEAD	RED SNAPPER	TARPON	PAGE & GRID
4757 Pass Cavallo	San Antonio Bay	1	4	1	1	1	4	2	2	1	3	4	1	79 K12
4760 Port Bay	Aransas Bay	2	3	1	1	3	4	4	3	2	3	4	2	85 C8
4763 Powderhorn Lake	West Matagorda Bay	1	1	1	1	1	4	4	1	1	1	4	4	79 J11
4766 Pringle Lake	San Antonio Bay	4	4	3	1	3	4	4	3	1	3	4	4	85 A11
4769 Redfish Bay—North	Aransas Bay	2	2	2	1	3	4	3	3	1	2	4	3	85 D8
4772 Redfish Bay—South	Corpus Christi Bay	3	4	2	1	3	4	4	2	1	3	4	4	85 E8
4775 Rio Grande	Lower Laguna Madre	2	1	1	1	1	4	4	1	1	1	4	2	89 J8
4778 Sabine Lake	Sabine Lake	2	1	1	1	1	4	4	1	2	2	4	4	73 J8, 154 I6
4781 Sabine Pass Jetties	Sabine Lake	1	1	1	1	2	4	2	1	1	1	4	4	73 K9
4784 Salt Lake	Aransas Bay	2	3	1	2	2	4	4	4	3	3	4	3	85 C8
4787 San Antonio Bay	San Antonio Bay	1	3	3	1	1	4	4	3	1	3	4	4	85 A10
4790 Scott—San Jacinto Bay	Galveston Bay	4	3	2	1	2	4	4	1	1	4	4	4	72 K2
4793 Shoalwater Bay	San Antonio Bay	4	4	2	1	2	4	4	4	2	4	4	4	79 K11
4796 South Bay	Aransas Bay	2	2	2	1	2	4	3	2	1	2	4	3	85 D8
4799 South Bay	Lower Laguna Madre	3	1	1	1	2	4	4	2	1	1	4	3	89 I8
4802 St. Charles Bay	Aransas Bay	2	2	2	1	3	4	4	4	2	3	4	2	85 B9
4805 Swan Lake	West Matagorda Bay	3	2	2	1	1	4	4	2	1	2	4	4	79 H11
4808 Tres Palacios Bay	West Matagorda Bay	1	1	1	1	1	4	4	1	1	1	4	4	80 I1
4811 Trinity Bay	Galveston Bay	3	3	2	1	2	4	2	3	2	2	4	4	72 K3
4814 Turtle Bay	West Matagorda Bay	1	1	1	1	1	4	4	1	1	1	4	4	80 I1
4817 Upper Laguna Madre	Upper Laguna Madre	4	3	2	1	3	5	5	3	1	4	5	5	84 J6
4820 West Bay	Galveston Bay	1	1	2	1	1	4	3	3	1	2	4	4	81 D8

Hunting

While the majority of hunting occurs on private properties throughout the state, a number of public lands are available for hunting. The following chart identifies those wildlife management areas administered by the Texas Parks and Wildlife Department.

It is most important to be thoroughly familiar with all rules, regulations and restrictions before hunting in any area. For licensing and other information, contact the Texas Parks and Wildlife Department, 4200 Smith School Road, Austin, TX 78744, (800) 792-1112.

			BIG GAME			SMALL GAME								MIGRATORY GAMEBIRDS									
NAME	UNIT #	ACREAGE	WHITE-TAILED DEER	MULE DEER	JAVELINA	SQUIRREL	FERAL HOG	RABBIT/HARE	FURBEARERS	PREDATORY ANIMALS	FISH	FROGS	CRAYFISH	QUAIL	DOVE	SNIPE	WOODCOCK	GALLINULE	WATERFOWL	OTHER GAMEBIRDS	TEAL DUCK	RAIL	PAGE & GRID
Alabama Creek Wildlife Management Area	904	14,561	●			●	●	●	●	●	●	●	●	●	●				●	●	●		60 I2
Alazan Bayou Wildlife Management Area	747	1,973	●			●	●	●						●	●	●	●	●	●				60 G3
Angelina–Neches Scientific Area/Dam B Wildlife Management Area	707	13,445	●			●	●	●	●	●				●	●	●	●	●	●			●	73 A7
Aquilla Lake Wildlife Management Area	748	9,700	●			●	●	●						●	●				●	●			58 C2
Bannister Wildlife Management Area	903	28,307	●			●	●	●	●	●	●	●	●	●	●				●	●	●		60 H6
Black Gap Wildlife Management Area	701	106,915	●	●	●			●						●	●								75 A11
Caddo Lake State Park and Wildlife Management Area	730	6,929	●			●																	49 G7
Caddo Wildlife Management Area—Bois d'Arc Unit	901	13,370	●			●	●	●	●	●	●	●	●	●	●				●	●	●		39 C9
Caddo Wildlife Management Area—Ladonia Unit	901	2,780	●			●	●	●	●	●	●	●	●	●	●				●	●	●		47 A8
Chaparral Wildlife Management Area	700	15,200						●						●	●								83 A7
Cooper Lake Wildlife Management Area	731	14,480	●			●	●	●						●	●	●	●		●		●		47 B11
Elephant Mountain Wildlife Management Area	725	23,147						●						●	●								64 H2
Gene Howe Wildlife Management Area	755	5,373	●				●	●						●	●								31 B8
Granger Wildlife Management Area	709	11,116				●	●	●	●	●				●	●	●	●	●	●				69 C12
Guadalupe Delta Wildlife Management Area	720	6,078														●		●	●		●	●	79 J10
Gus Engeling Wildlife Management Area	754	10,941	●			●	●	●								●	●	●	●				59 C9
James E. Daughtrey Wildlife Management Area	713	8,714						●						●	●	●			●	●			78 K1
Keechi Creek Wildlife Management Area	726	1,500				●		●								●	●	●	●				59 G9
Las Palomas Wildlife Management Area—Anacua Unit	744	222													●								88 I4
Las Palomas Wildlife Management Area—Baird Unit	710	122													●								88 I3
Las Palomas Wildlife Management Area—Carricitos Unit	714	118													●								88 H5
Las Palomas Wildlife Management Area—Longoria Unit	741	200													●								88 G4
Las Palomas Wildlife Management Area—Penitas Unit	742	120													●								87 H12
Las Palomas Wildlife Management Area—Taormina Unit	715	325													●								88 I3
Lower Neches Wildlife Management Area—Old River Unit	728	6,200														●		●	●			●	73 H9
Mad Island Wildlife Management Area	729	7,200														●		●	●		●	●	80 I2
Matador Wildlife Management Area	702	28,183						●						●	●								35 F8
Matagorda Island Wildlife Management Area	722	43,900														●		●	●			●	85 A12
Moore Plantation Wildlife Management Area	902	26,347	●			●	●	●	●	●	●	●	●	●	●				●	●	●		61 I8
Murphree Wildlife Management Area	783	13,250														●		●	●		●	●	73 J8
North Toledo Bend Wildlife Management Area	224	2,818	●			●	●	●	●	●	●	●	●	●	●				●	●			61 D7
North Toledo Bend Wildlife Management Area	615	3,650	●			●	●	●	●	●	●	●	●	●	●				●	●	●		61 C8
Pat Mayse Wildlife Management Area	705	8,925	●			●	●	●	●	●				●	●	●	●	●	●				39 C10
Peach Point Wildlife Management Area	721	10,312														●		●	●		●	●	80 G6
Ray Roberts Lake Wildlife Management Area	501	41,220				●		●				●		●	●				●	●			46 A3
Resaca de la Palma State Park/Las Palomas Wildlife Management Area—Brasil Unit	743	1,175													●								88 J5
Richland Creek Wildlife Management Area	703	13,796	●			●	●	●						●	●	●	●	●	●				59 C8
Sabine River Authority Wildlife Management Area	630	7,044	●			●	●	●	●	●	●	●	●	●	●				●	●			61 B7
Sam Houston National Forest/Wildlife Management Area	905	161,154	●			●	●	●	●	●	●	●	●	●	●				●	●	●		71 B11
Sea Rim State Park—Marshlands Unit	746	10,000														●		●	●		●	●	73 J8
Somerville Wildlife Management Area	711	3,180	●			●	●	●						●	●	●	●	●	●			●	70 F4
White Oak Creek Wildlife Management Area	727	25,500	●			●	●	●						●	●	●	●		●				48 C4

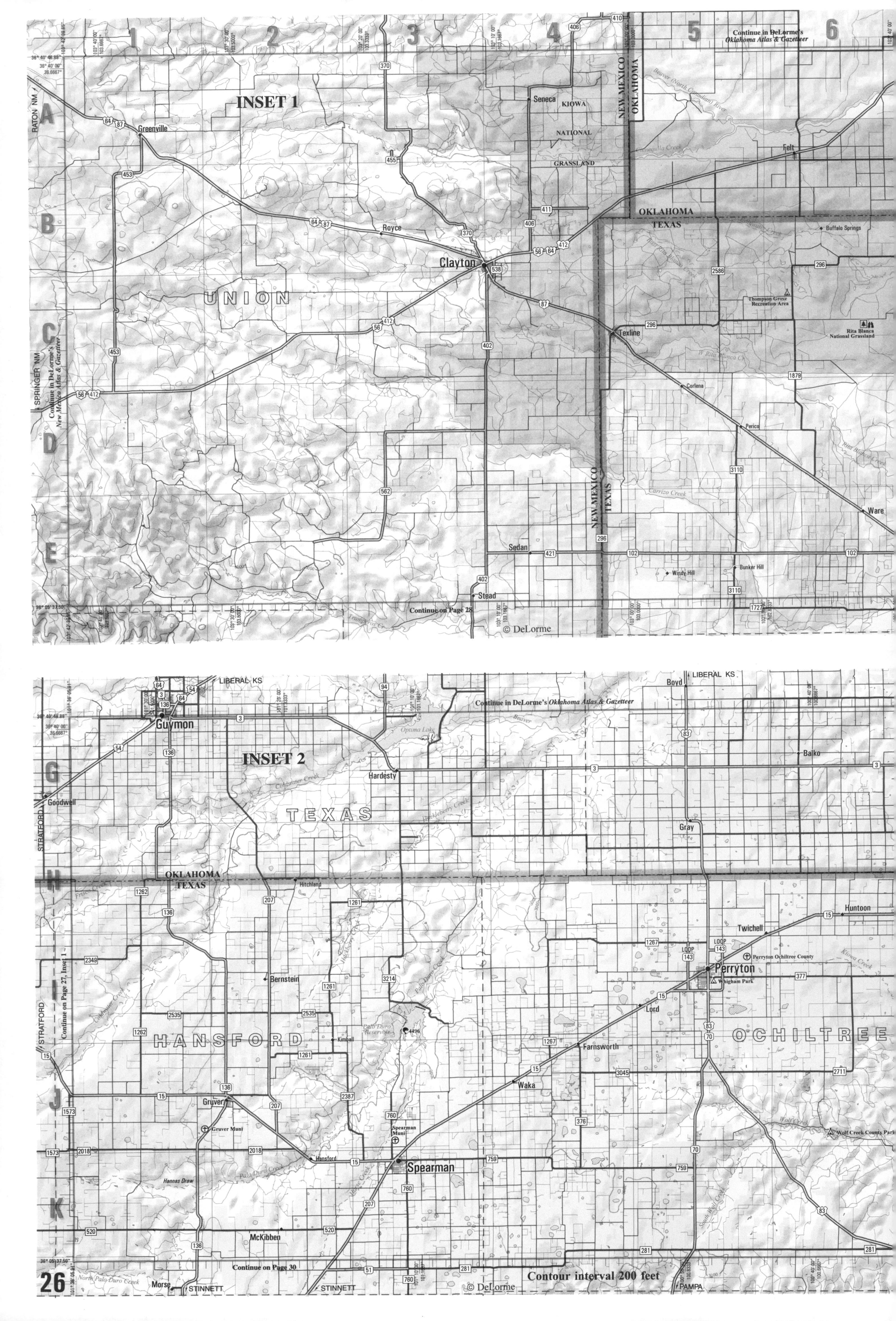
INSET 1
1
2
3
4
5
6
A
B
C
D
E
RATON NM
SPRINGER NM
Continue in DeLorme's New Mexico Atlas & Gazetteer
Continue in DeLorme's Oklahoma Atlas & Gazetteer
NEW MEXICO
OKLAHOMA
TEXAS
UNION
KIOWA
NATIONAL
GRASSLAND
Seneca
Greenville
Royce
Clayton
Texline
Corlena
Perico
Ware
Sedan
Stead
Windy Hill
Bunker Hill
Felt
Buffalo Springs
Thompson Grove Recreation Area
Rita Blanca National Grassland
Beaver (North Canadian) River
Carrizo Creek
Rita Blanca Creek
Continue on Page 28
© DeLorme
INSET 2
F
G
H
I
J
K
LIBERAL KS
STRATFORD
Continue in DeLorme's Oklahoma Atlas & Gazetteer
Continue on Page 27, Inset 1
Guymon
Goodwell
Hardesty
Optima Lake
Beaver
Coldwater Creek
Hackberry Creek
Boyd
Balko
Gray
TEXAS
OKLAHOMA
Hitchland
Huntoon
Twichell
Perryton
Perryton Ochiltree County
Whigham Park
Kiowa Creek
Bernstein
Lord
Farnsworth
Waka
Kimball
Palo Duro Reservoir
HANSFORD
OCHILTREE
Gruver
Gruver Muni
Hansford
Spearman
Spearman Muni
Pala Duro Creek
Hannas Draw
McKibben
Wolf Creek
Wolf Creek County Park
Morse
North Palo Duro Creek
STINNETT
PAMPA
Continue on Page 30
© DeLorme
Contour interval 200 feet
26

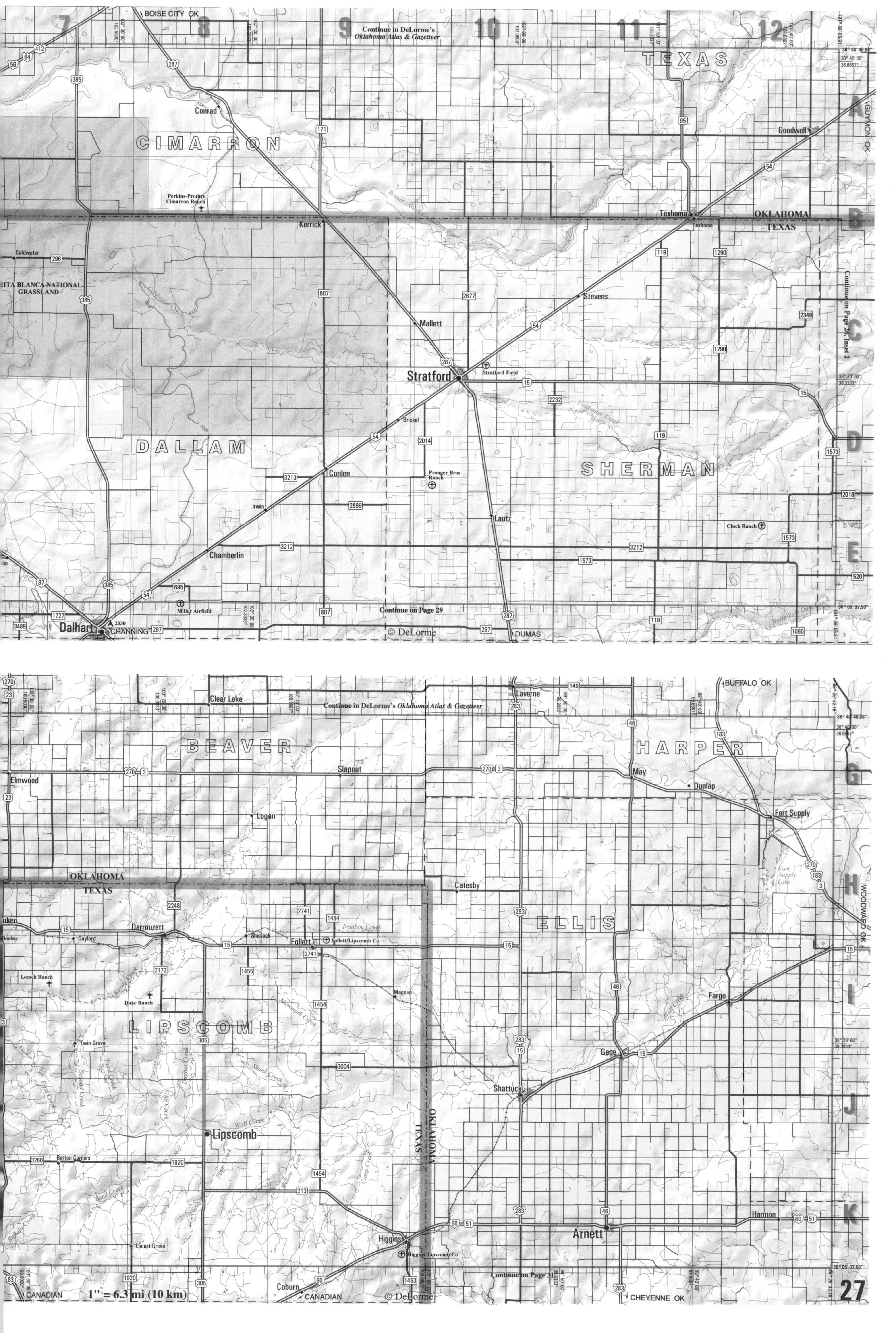
BOISE CITY OK
Continue in DeLorme's Oklahoma Atlas & Gazetteer
TEXAS
CIMARRON
Conrad
Perkins-Prothro Cimarron Ranch
Goodwell
GUYMON OK
Texhoma
OKLAHOMA
TEXAS
Kerrick
Coldwater
RITA BLANCA NATIONAL GRASSLAND
Stevens
Mallett
Continue on Page 26, Inset 2
Stratford
Stratford Field
Brickel
DALLAM
SHERMAN
Conlen
Pronger Bros Ranch
Irwin
Lautz
Cluck Ranch
Chamberlin
Miller Airfield
Continue on Page 29
Dalhart
CHANNING
DUMAS
© DeLorme
Clear Lake
Laverne
BUFFALO OK
Continue in DeLorme's Oklahoma Atlas & Gazetteer
BEAVER
HARPER
Elmwood
Slapout
May
Dunlap
Logan
Fort Supply
Fort Supply Lake
OKLAHOMA
TEXAS
Catesby
WOODWARD OK
ELLIS
Darrouzett
Gaylord
Sherlock
Follett
Follett/Lipscomb Co
Ivanhoe Creek
Loesch Ranch
Duke Ranch
Magoun
Fargo
LIPSCOMB
Twin Grove
Gage
Shattuck
Lipscomb
Barton Corners
OKLAHOMA
TEXAS
Harmon
Higgins
Arnett
Higgins-Lipscomb Co
Locust Grove
Continue on Page 31
Coburn
CANADIAN
CANADIAN
CHEYENNE OK
1" = 6.3 mi (10 km)
© DeLorme

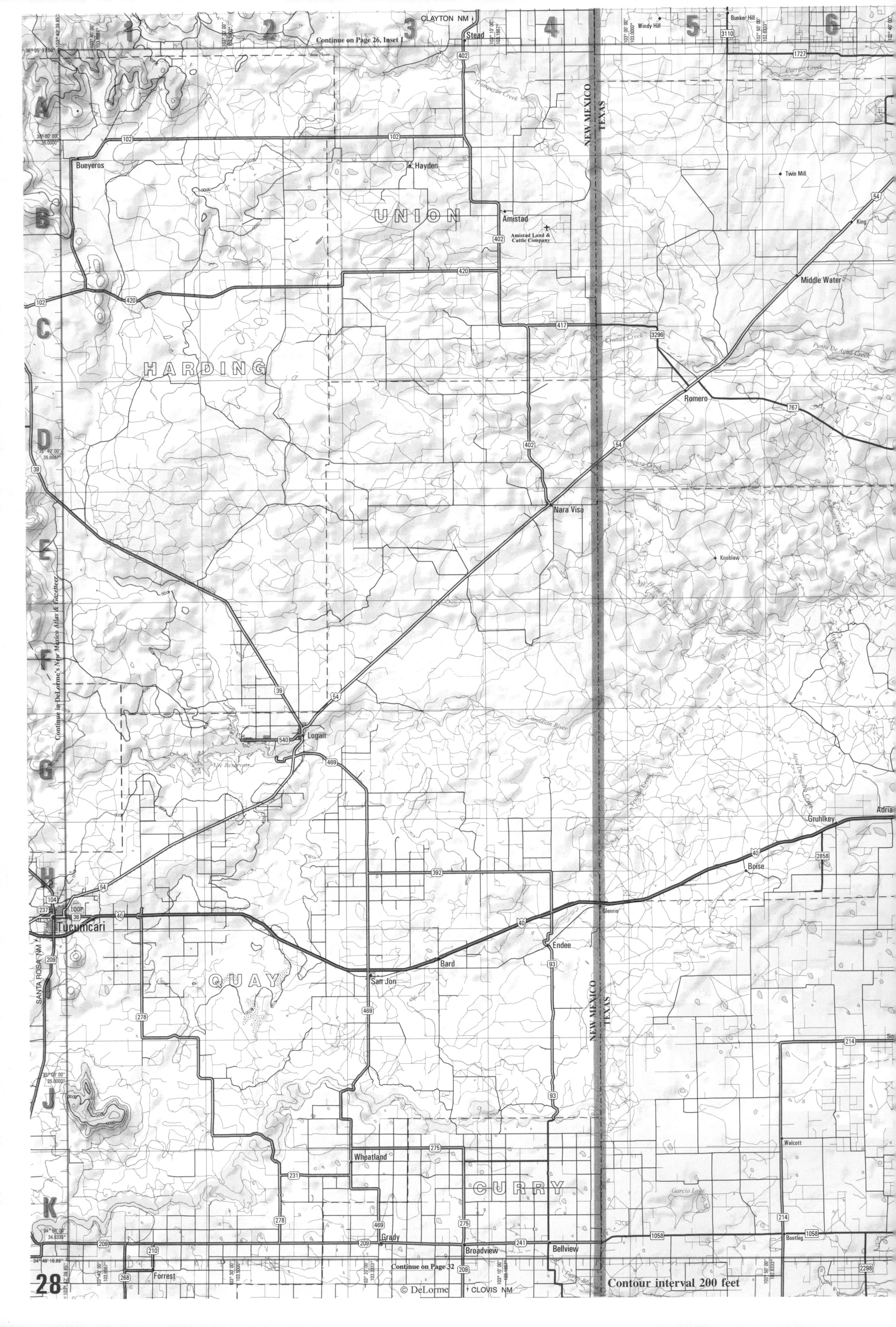

CLAYTON NM
Continue on Page 26, Inset I
Stead
Windy Hill
Bunker Hill
Tramperos Creek
Carrizo Creek
NEW MEXICO
TEXAS
Bueyeros
Hayden
Twin Mill
UNION
Amistad
Amistad Land & Cattle Company
King
Middle Water
HARDING
Punta De Agua Creek
Romero
Nara Visa
Knoblaw
Logan
Ute Reservoir
Canadian River
Gruhlkey
Boise
Tucumcari
Glenrio
Endee
Bard
San Jon
QUAY
SANTA ROSA NM
Continue in DeLorme's New Mexico Atlas & Gazetteer
Wheatland
CURRY
Walcott
Garcia Lake
Grady
Broadview
Bellview
Bootleg
Forrest
Continue on Page 32
CLOVIS NM
© DeLorme
Contour interval 200 feet

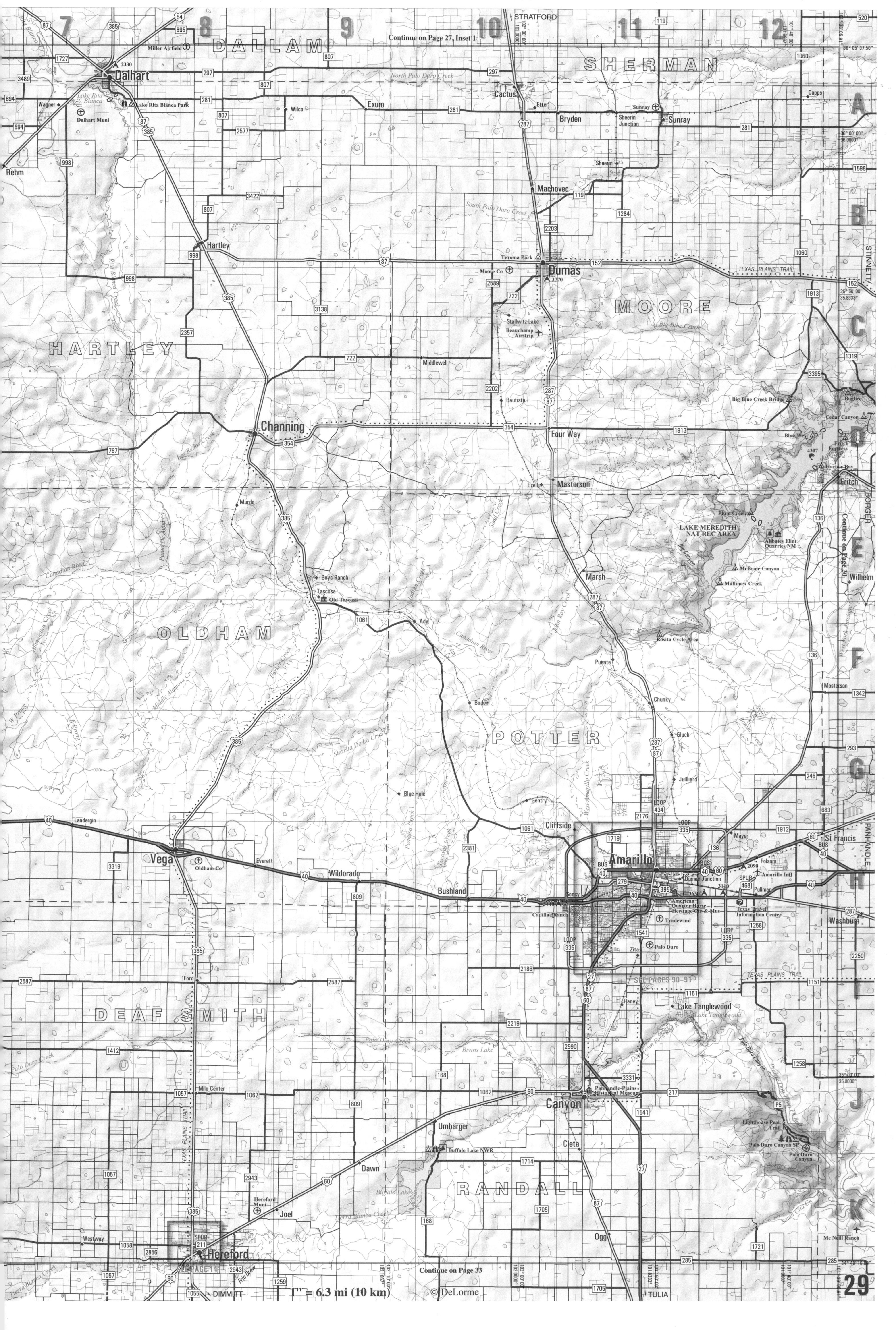

Continue on Page 27, Inset 1
Continue on Page 30
SEE PAGES 90–91
SEE PAGE 14
Continue on Page 33

1" = 6.3 mi (10 km)

© DeLorme

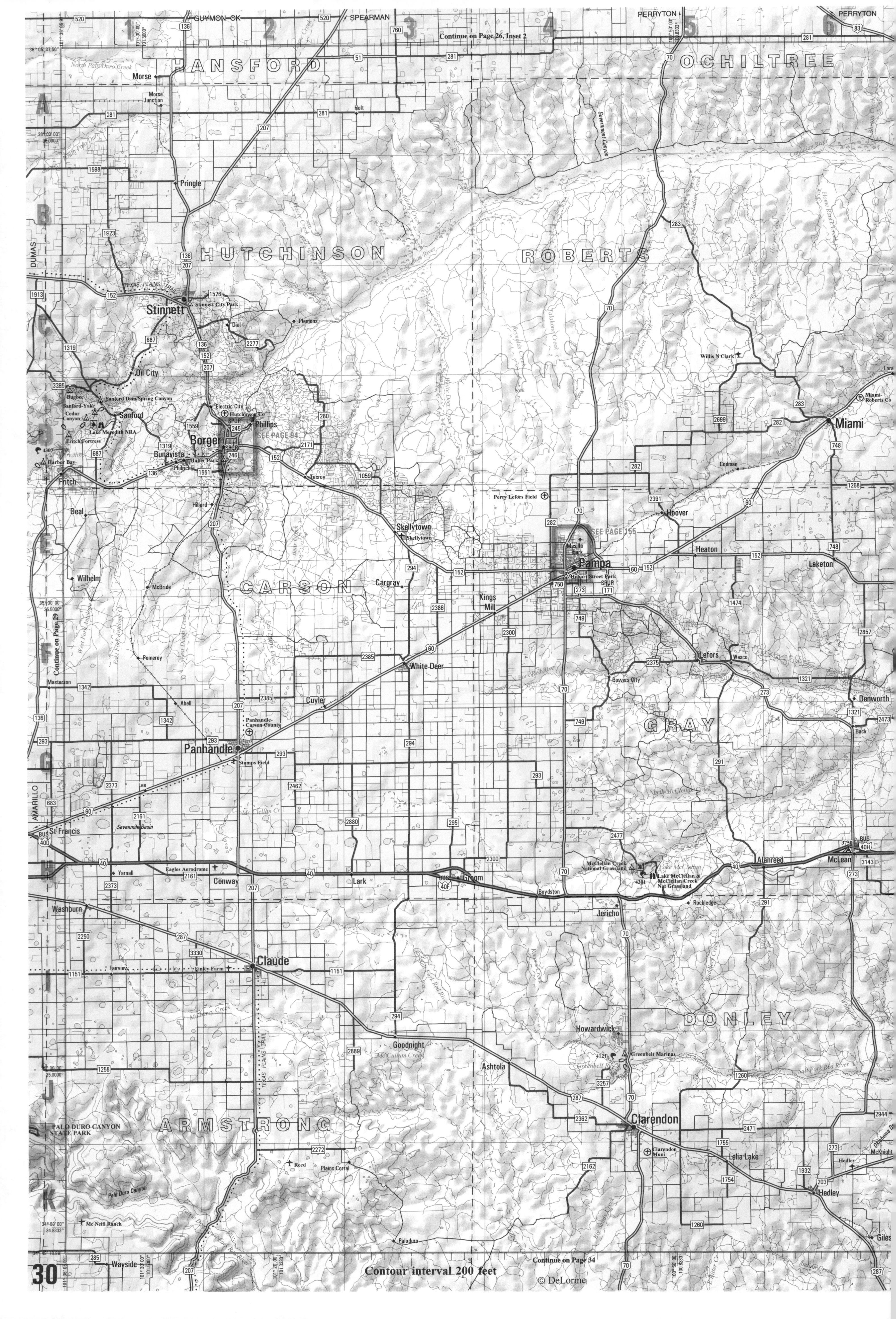
HANSFORD
OCHILTREE
HUTCHINSON
ROBERTS
CARSON
GRAY
DONLEY
ARMSTRONG
GUYMON OK
SPEARMAN
PERRYTON
Morse
Morse Junction
Holt
Pringle
Stinnett
Stinnett City Park
Dial
Plemons
Oil City
Sanford Dam/Spring Canyon
Sanford
Lake Meredith NRA
Fritch Fortress
Harbor Bay
Borger
Hutchinson Co
Phillips
Bunavista
Huber Park
Phillips
Fritch
Texroy
Deal
Hillard
Skellytown
Wilhelm
McBride
Cargray
Kings Mill
Pampa
Hobart Street Park
Perry Lefors Field
Hoover
Heaton
Laketon
Miami
Miami-Roberts Co
Codman
Willis N Clark
Pomeroy
White Deer
Lefors
Wesco
Bowers City
Denworth
Back
Masterson
Abell
Cuyler
Panhandle
Panhandle-Carson County
Stamps Field
Lee
Sevenmile Basin
St Francis
Yarnall
Eagles Aerodrome
Conway
Lark
Groom
Boydston
McClellan Creek National Grassland
Lake McClellan & McClellan Creek Nat Grassland
Rockledge
Jericho
Alanreed
McLean
Washburn
Fairview
Finley Farm
Claude
Goodnight
Howardwick
Greenbelt Marinas
Ashtola
Clarendon
Clarendon Muni
Lelia Lake
Hedley
McKnight
Giles
PALO DURO CANYON STATE PARK
Palo Duro Canyon
Reed
Plains Corral
Mc Neill Ranch
Paloduro
Wayside
TEXAS PLAINS TRAIL
Canadian River
Salt Fork Red River
DUMAS
AMARILLO
Continue on Page 26, Inset 2
SEE PAGE 94
SEE PAGE 155
Continue on Page 29
Continue on Page 34
Contour interval 200 feet
© DeLorme
30

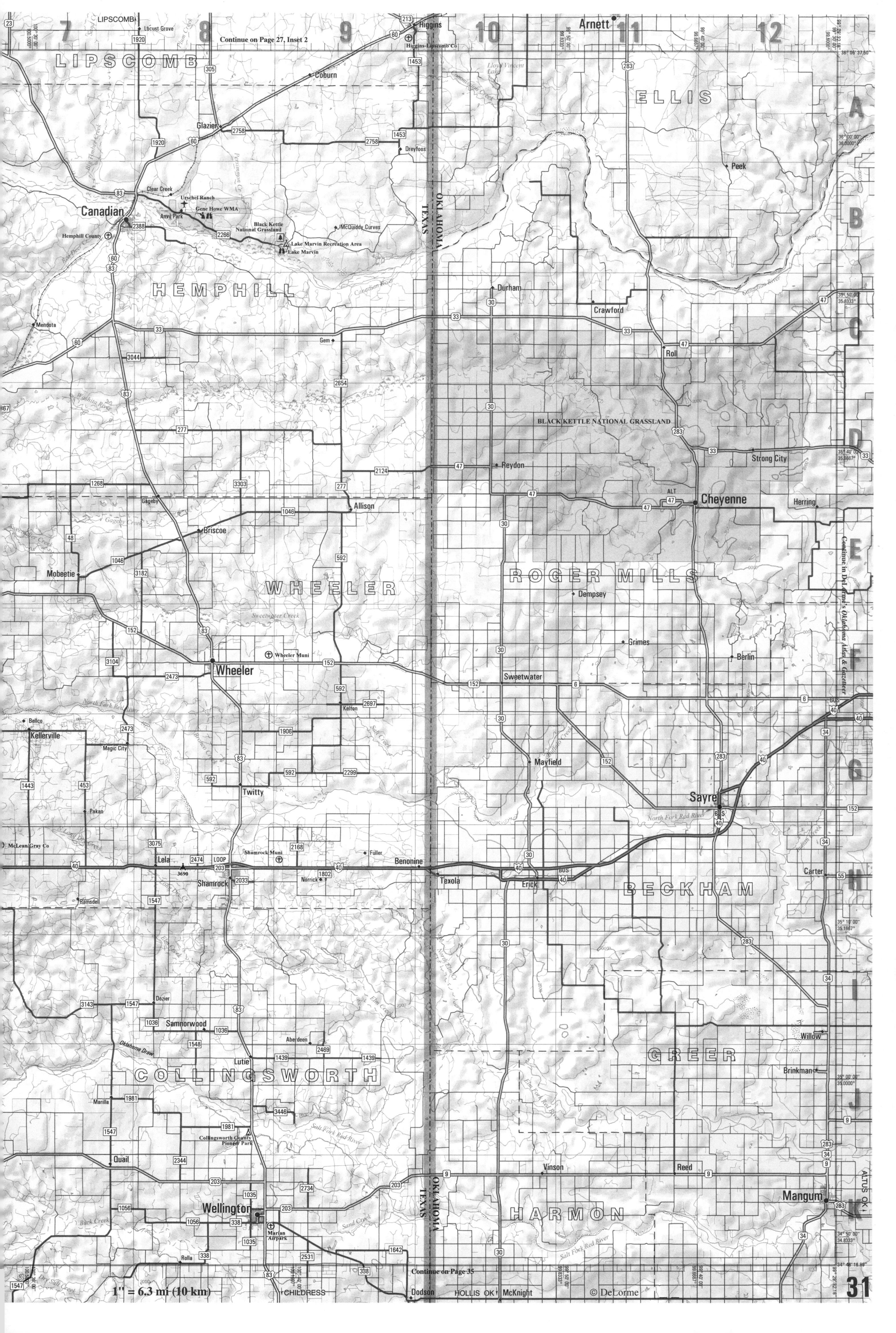

Continue on Page 27, Inset 2
Continue on Page 35

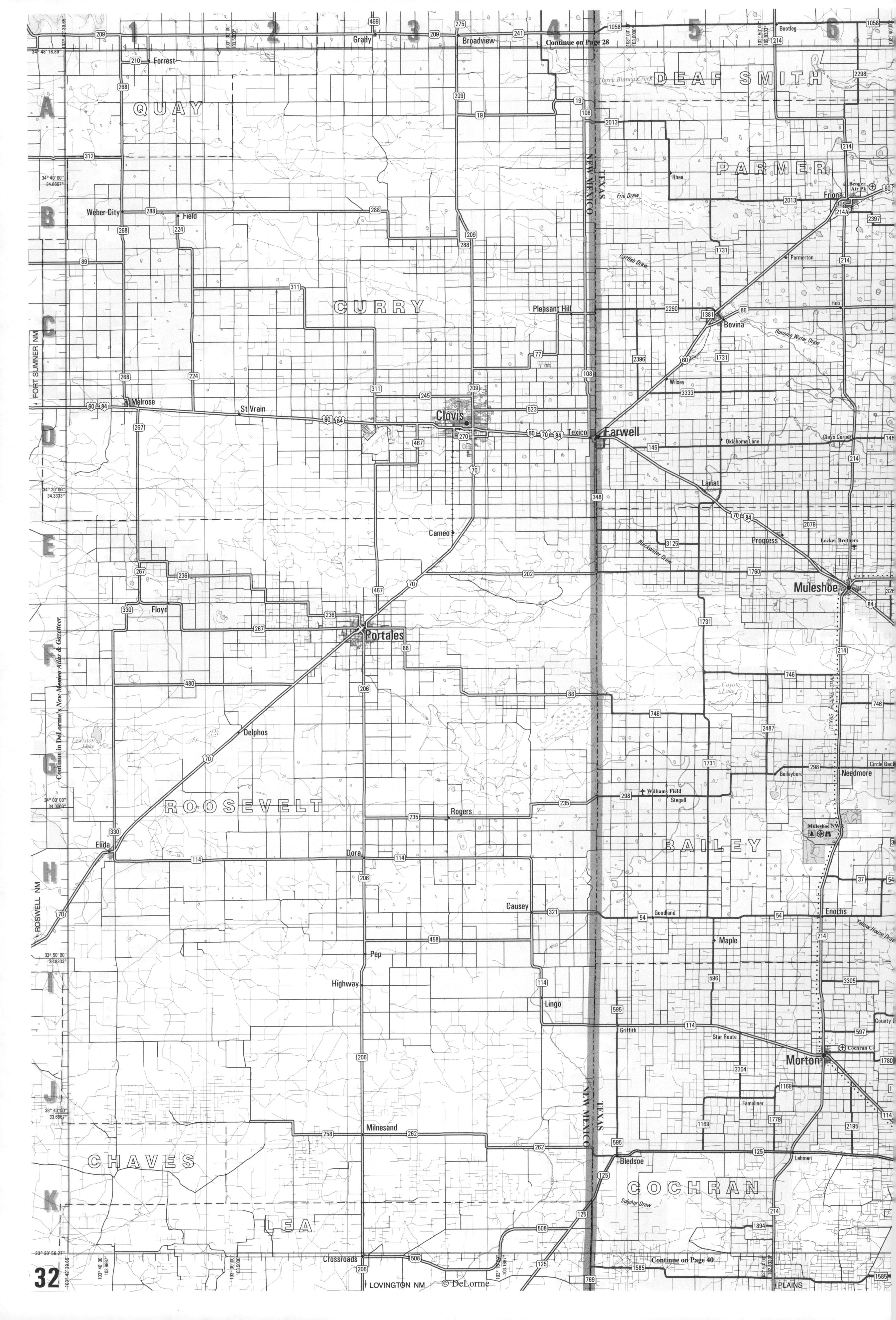
QUAY
CURRY
ROOSEVELT
CHAVES
LEA
DEAF SMITH
PARMER
BAILEY
COCHRAN
TEXAS
NEW MEXICO
Forrest
Grady
Broadview
Weber City
Field
Melrose
St Vrain
Clovis
Texico
Farwell
Pleasant Hill
Cameo
Floyd
Portales
Delphos
Rogers
Elida
Dora
Causey
Pep
Highway
Lingo
Milnesand
Crossroads
Bootleg
Rhea
Friona
Parmerton
Hub
Bovina
Wilsey
Oklahoma Lane
Clays Corner
Lariat
Progress
Muleshoe
Baileyboro
Needmore
Williams Field
Stegall
Goodland
Enochs
Maple
Griffith
Star Route
Morton
Bledsoe
Lehman
PLAINS
Continue on Page 28
Continue on Page 40
Continue in DeLorme's New Mexico Atlas & Gazetteer
FORT SUMNER NM
ROSWELL NM
LOVINGTON NM
© DeLorme

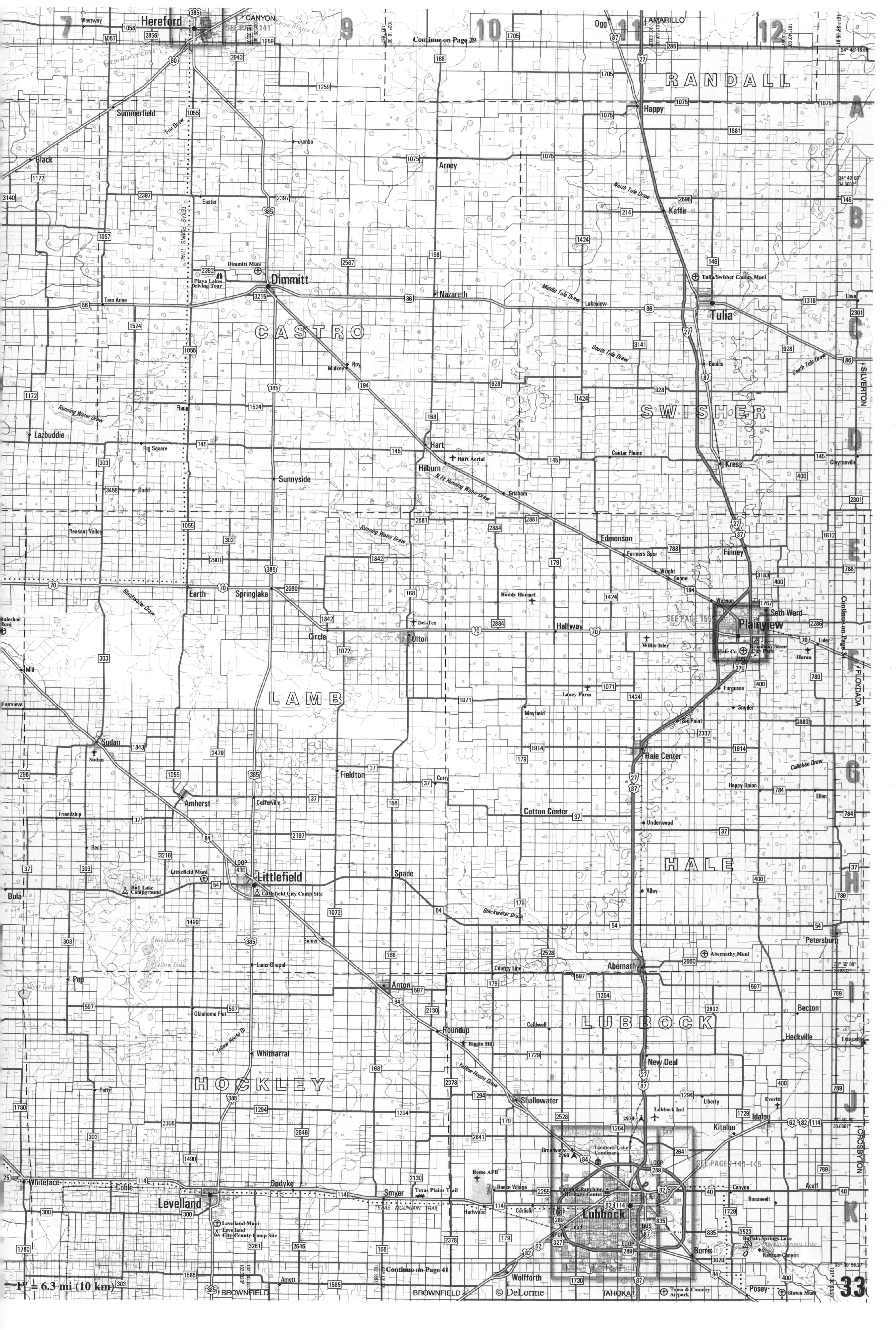

7
8
9
10
11
12
Hereford
Westway
CANYON
AMARILLO
Ogg
Continue on Page 29
RANDALL
Happy
Summerfield
Frio Draw
Jumbo
Black
Arney
North Tule Draw
Kaffir
Easter
TEXAS PLAINS TRAIL
Dimmitt Muni
Playa Lakes Driving Tour
Dimmitt
Tulia/Swisher County Muni
Tam Anne
Nazareth
Middle Tule Draw
Lakeview
Tulia
Love
CASTRO
South Tule Draw
Mulkey
Roy
Euoice
SILVERTON
SWISHER
Running Water Draw
Flagg
Lazbuddie
Big Square
Hart
Hart Aerial
Center Plains
Kress
Claytonville
Hilburn
N Fk Running Water Draw
Sunnyside
Dodd
Grisham
Pleasant Valley
Running Water Draw
Edmonson
Farmers Spur
Finney
Wright
Boone
Blackwater Draw
Earth
Springlake
Buddy Harmel
Wasson
Seth Ward
Mulesshoe Muni
Del-Tex
Circle
Olton
Halfway
SEE PAGE 155
Plainview
Continue on Page 34
Lide
Willis-Isler
Hale Co
Broadway Street City Park
Horan
Mill
FLOYDADA
LAMB
Laney Farm
Furguson
Snyder
Fairview
Mayfield
Six Point
Sudan
Hale Center
Callahan Draw
Fieldton
Corry
Happy Union
Amherst
Cofferville
Cotton Center
Ellen
Friendship
Underwood
Beck
HALE
Littlefield Muni
Littlefield
Spade
Bull Lake
Bull Lake Campground
Littlefield City Camp Site
Alley
Bula
Blackwater Draw
Petersburg
Bainer
Abernathy Muni
Lums Chapel
County Line
Abernathy
Pep
Anton
Becton
Oklahoma Flat
Caldwell
LUBBOCK
Heckville
Roundup
Biggin Hill
Estacado
Yellow House Dr
Whitharral
New Deal
Yellow House Draw
HOCKLEY
Pettit
Shallowater
Liberty
Everitt
Lubbock Intl
Idalou
Kitalou
CROSBYTON
Broadview
Lubbock Lake Landmark
Reese AFB
SEE PAGES 144-145
Whiteface
Coble
Opdyke
Texas Plains Trail
Reese Village
National Ranching Heritage Center
Canyon
Acuff
Smyer
Levelland
Hurlwood
TEXAS MOUNTAIN TRAIL
Carlisle
Lubbock
Roosevelt
Levelland Muni
Levelland City-County Camp Site
Buffalo Springs Lake
Ransom Canyon
Burris
Continue on Page 41
Wolfforth
Arnett
1" = 6.3 mi (10 km)
BROWNFIELD
BROWNFIELD
© DeLorme
TAHOKA
Town & Country Airpark
Posey
Slaton Muni
A
B
C
D
E
F
G
H
I
J
K

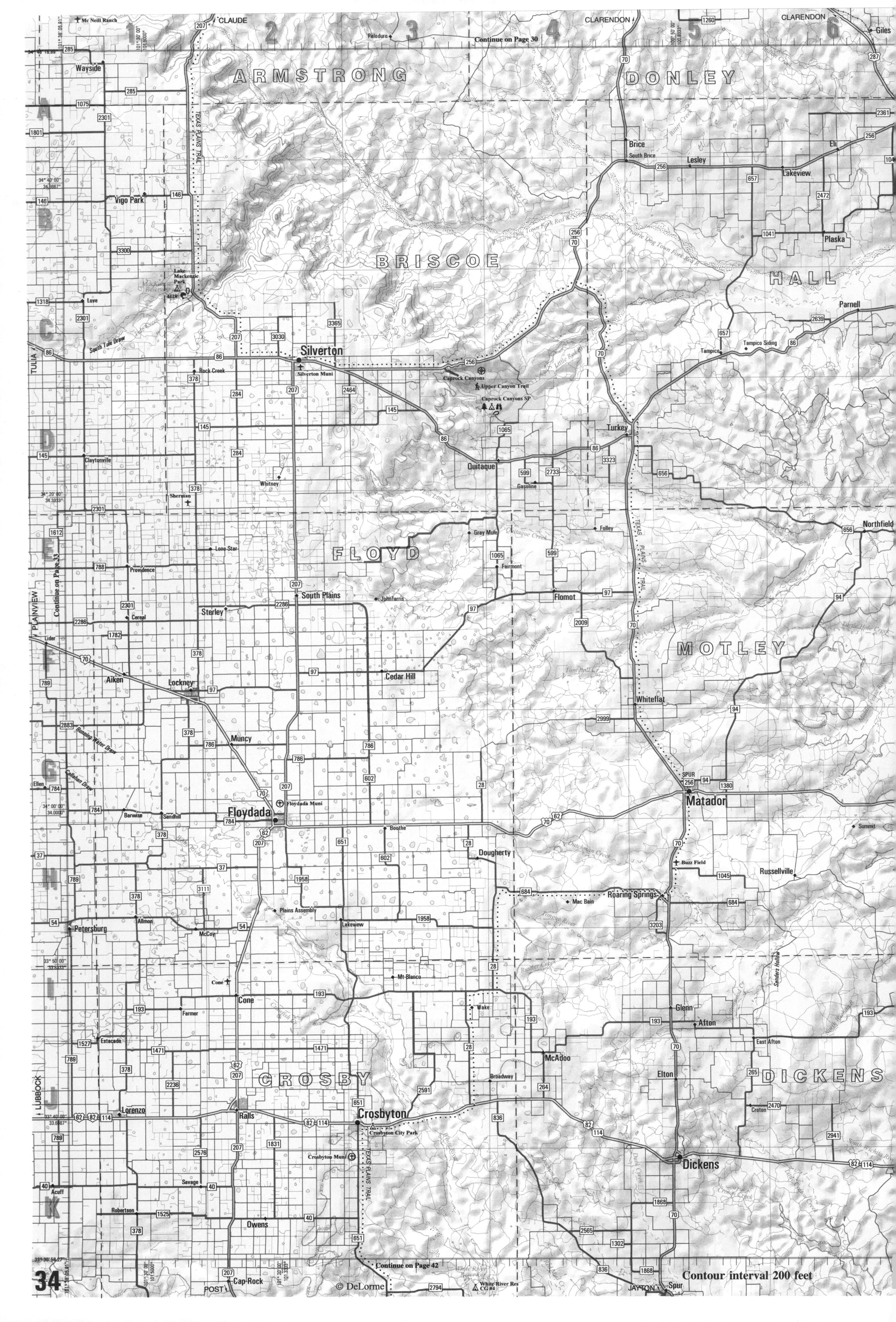

Continue on Page 30
Continue on Page 33
Continue on Page 42

Contour interval 200 feet

© DeLorme

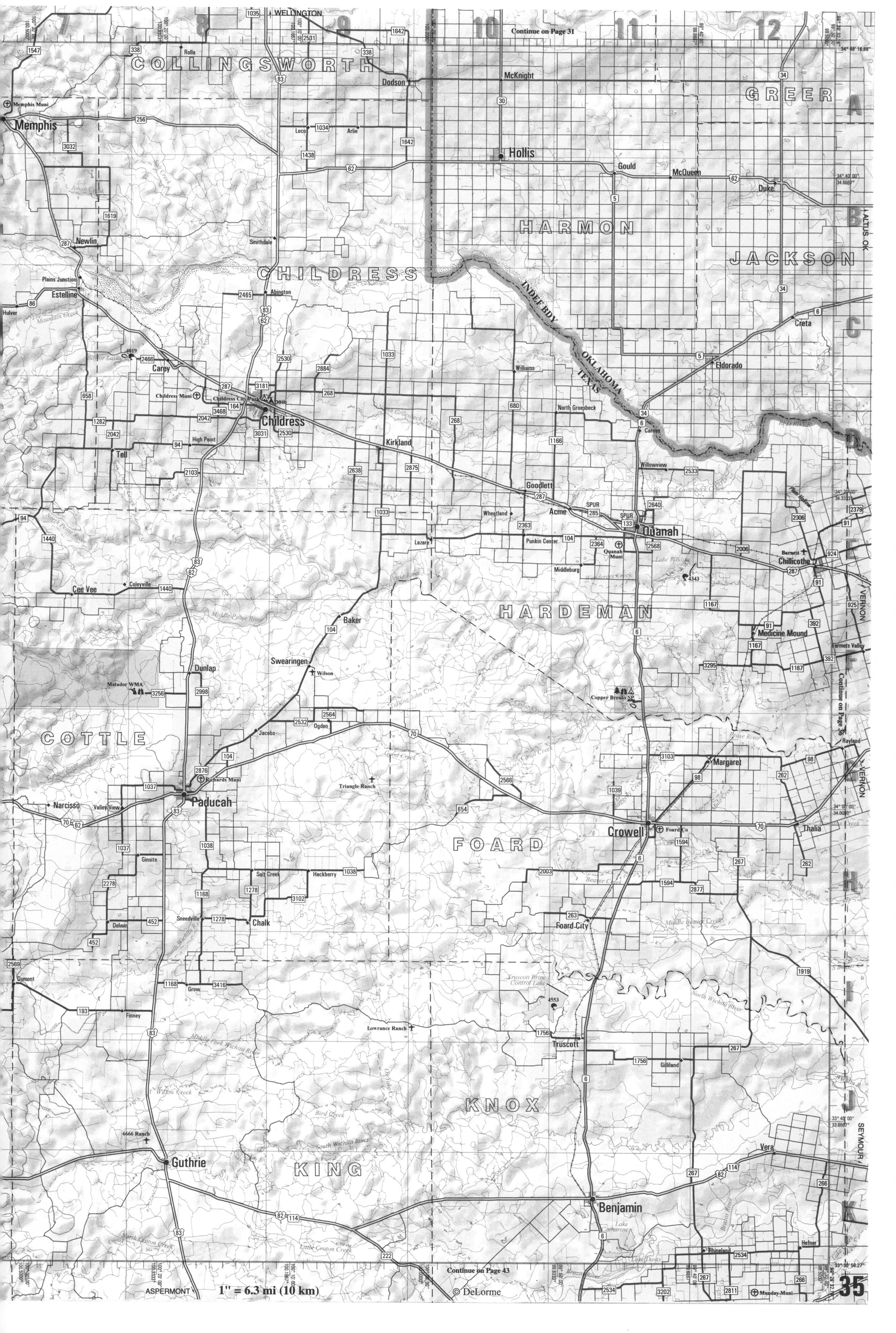

WELLINGTON
Continue on Page 31
COLLINGSWORTH
GREER
HARMON
JACKSON
CHILDRESS
HARDEMAN
COTTLE
FOARD
KNOX
KING
Memphis Muni
Memphis
Rolla
Dodson
McKnight
Loco
Arlie
Hollis
Gould
McQueen
Duke
ALTUS OK
Newlin
Smithdale
Plains Junction
Estelline
Hulver
Abington
Carey
Childress Muni
Childress City Park
Childress
High Point
Tell
Kirkland
Williams
North Groesbeck
INDEF BDY
OKLAHOMA
TEXAS
Creta
Eldorado
Carnes
Willowview
Goodlett
Wheatland
Acme
Quanah
Quanah Muni
Punkin Center
Lazare
Middleburg
Barnett
Chillicothe
VERNON
Cee Vee
Coleyville
Baker
Medicine Mound
Farmers Valley
Continue on Page 36
Swearingen
Wilson
Dunlap
Matador WMA
Copper Breaks SP
Jacobs
Ogden
Margaret
Rayland
Richards Muni
Paducah
Narcisso
Valley View
Triangle Ranch
Crowell
Foard Co
Thalia
Ginsite
Salt Creek
Hackberry
Sneedville
Chalk
Delwin
Foard City
Middle Beaver Creek
Truscott Brine Control Lake
North Wichita River
Dumont
Grow
Finney
Lowrance Ranch
Truscott
Gilliland
Middle Fork Wichita River
Bird Creek
South Wichita River
6666 Ranch
Guthrie
Vera
SEYMOUR
Benjamin
Lake Catharine
North Croton Creek
Little Croton Creek
Rhineland
Hefner
Lake Davis
Continue on Page 43
ASPERMONT
1" = 6.3 mi (10 km)
© DeLorme
Munday Muni

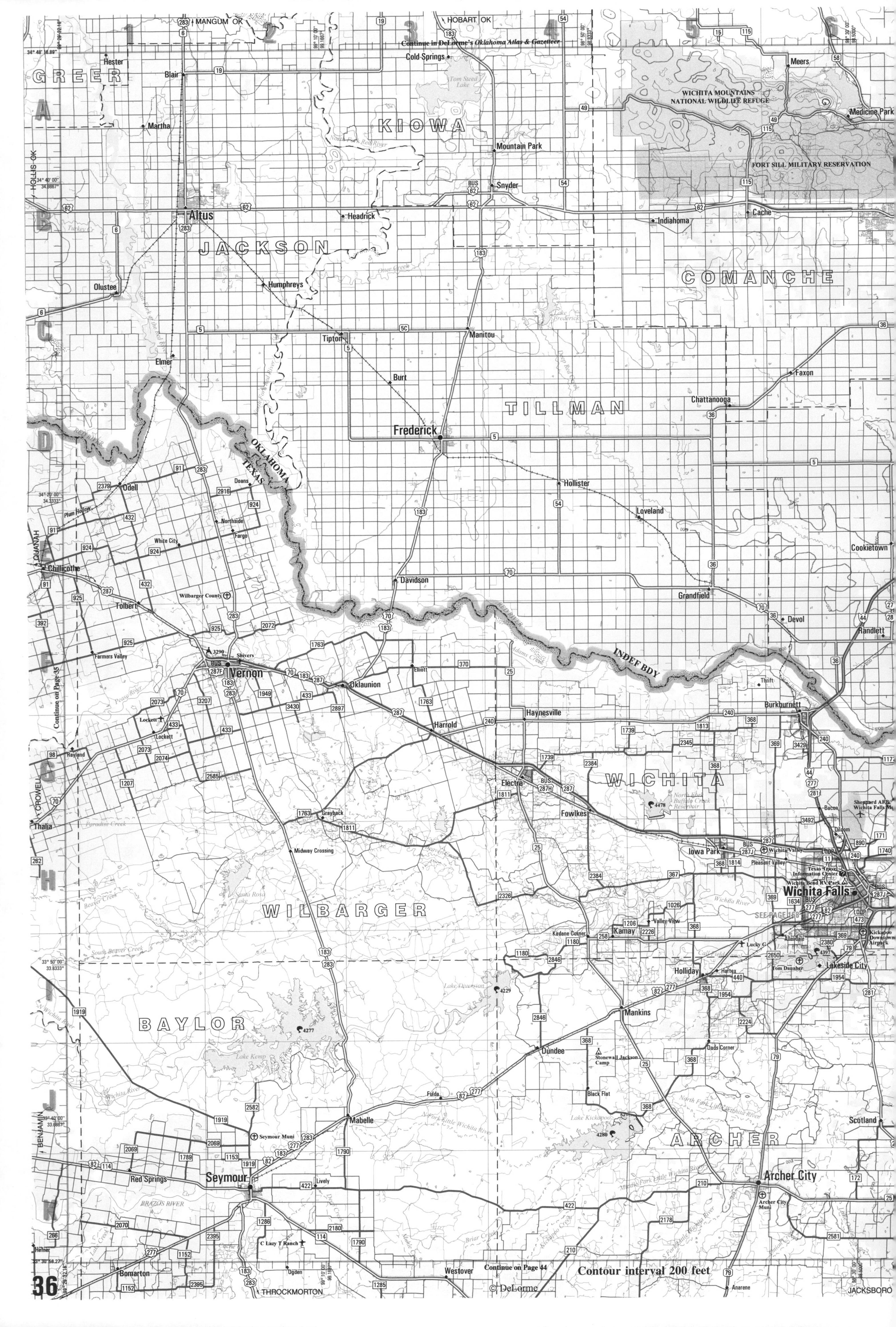

Continue in DeLorme's Oklahoma Atlas & Gazetteer
Continue on Page 35
Continue on Page 44
SEE PAGE 168

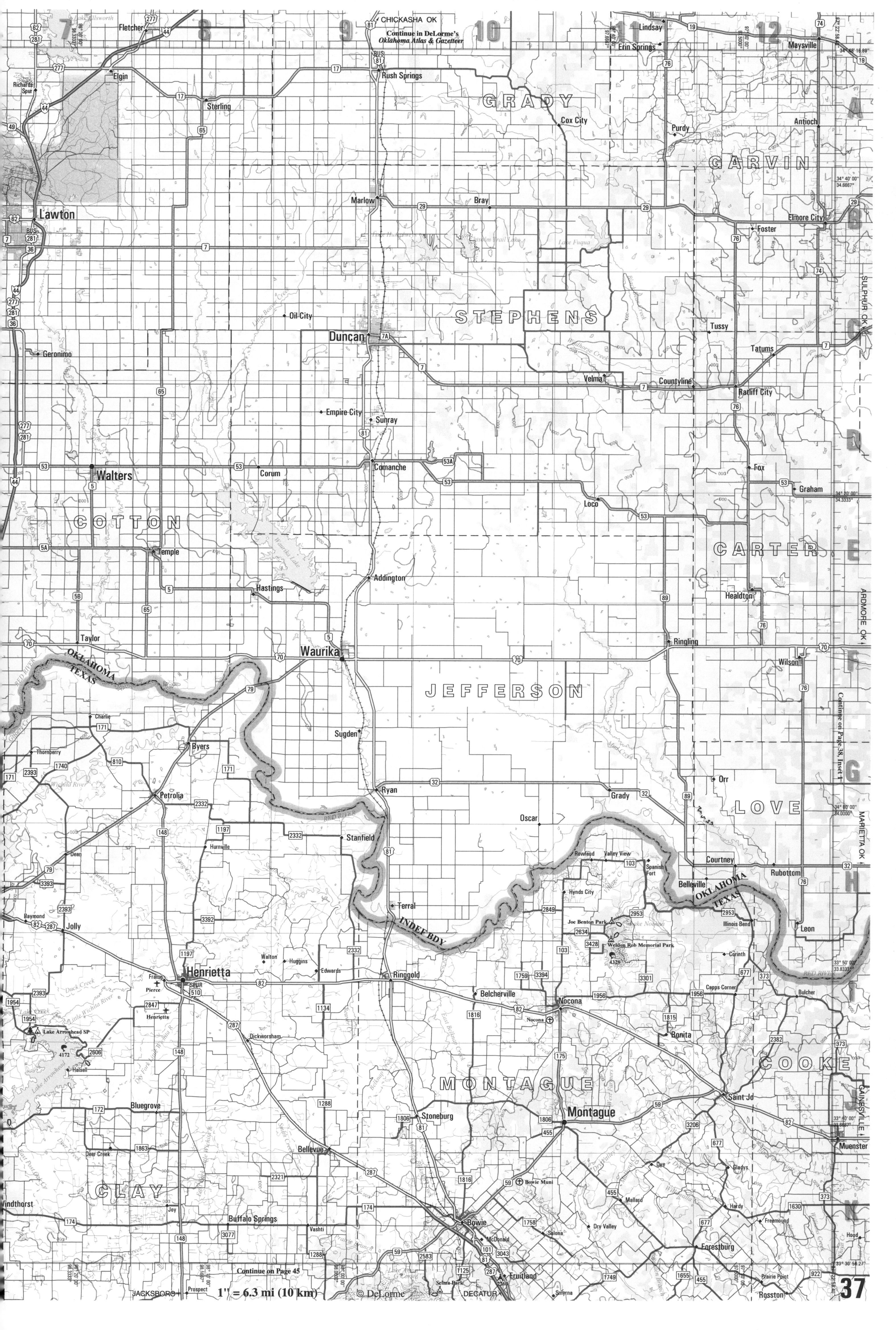

Continue on Page 45

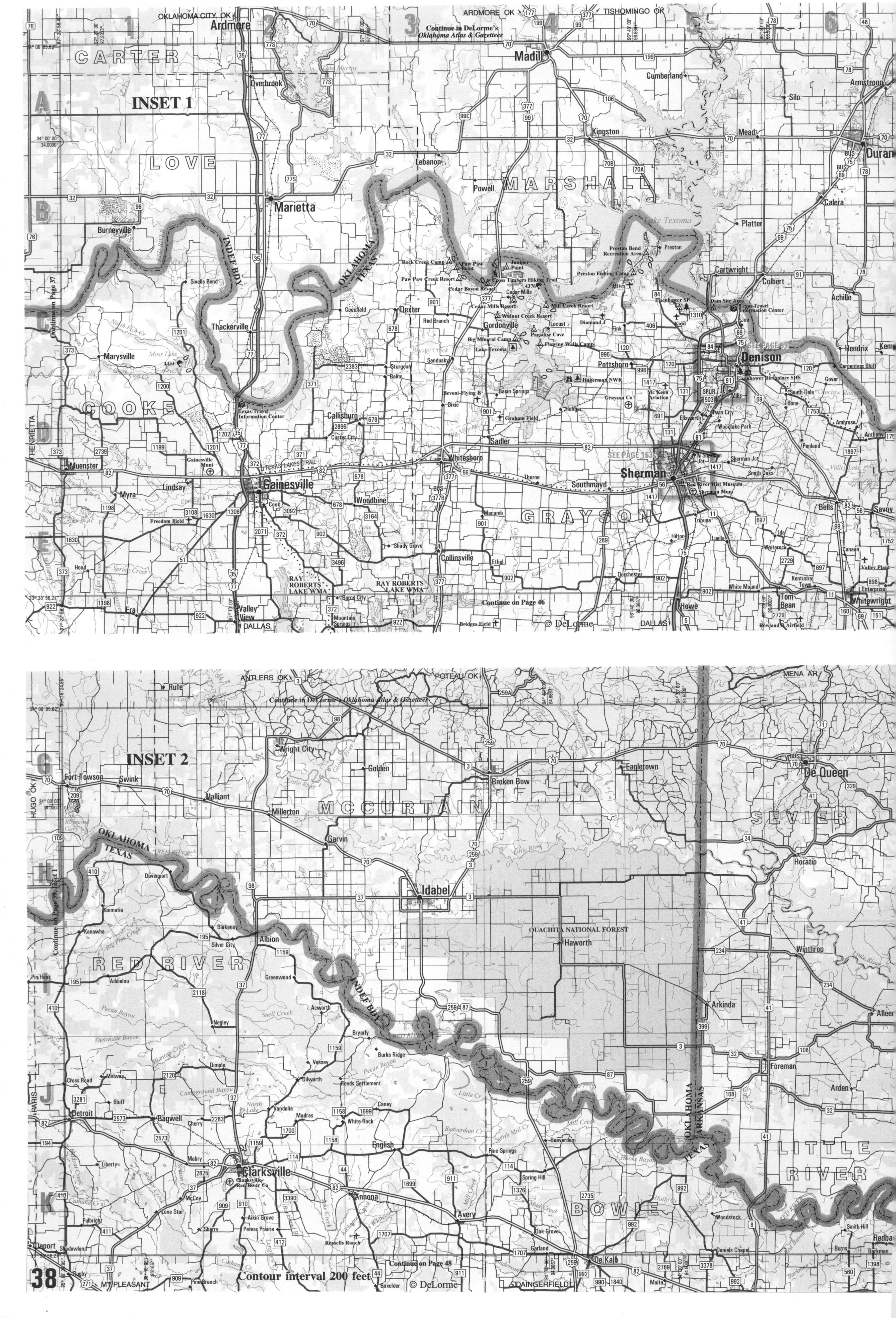

OKLAHOMA CITY OK
Ardmore
ARDMORE OK
TISHOMINGO OK
Continue in DeLorme's Oklahoma Atlas & Gazetteer
Madill
CARTER
Lake Murray
Overbrook
INSET 1
Cumberland
Armstrong
Silo
Kingston
Mead
Durant
LOVE
Lebanon
MARSHALL
Powell
Calera
Marietta
Lake Texoma
Platter
Burneyville
Preston
Preston Bend Recreation Area
INDEF BDY
OKLAHOMA
TEXAS
RED RIVER
Rock Creek Camp
Paw Paw Point
Juniper Point
Cross Timbers Hiking Trail
Preston Fishing Camp
Cartwright
Paw Paw Creek Resort
Cedar Bayou Resort
Cedar Mills
Hiles
Colbert
Achille
Sivells Bend
Eisenhower SP
Dam Site Area
Texas Travel Information Center
Continue on Page 37
Cedar Mills Resort
Mill Creek Resort
Walnut Creek Resort
Gordonville
Locust
Diamond
Fink
Kidd
Thackerville
Coesfield
Dexter
Red Branch
Paradise Cove
Flowing Wells Camp
Big Mineral Camp
Lake Texoma
Denison
SEE PAGE 89
Hendrix
Marysville
Moss Lake
Sturgeon
Balm
Sandusky
Pottsboro
Hagerman NWR
Eisenhower Birthplace SHS
Carpenters Bluff
Gover
COOKE
Basin Springs
Grayson Co
Mc Keon Aviation
Choctaw Slough
South Gale
Bona
Texas Travel Information Center
Callisburg
Bevoni-Flying B
Dixie
Graham Field
Hanger
Twin City
Ellsworth
Woodlake Park
Ambrose
Anthony
HENRIETTA
Custer City
Sadler
SEE PAGE 163
Gainesville Muni
Whitesboro
Sherman Jct
Penland
Muenster
TEXAS LAKES TRAIL
Smith Oaks
Valley Lake
Lindsay
Gainesville
Thorne
Southmayd
Sherman
Red River Hist Museum
Sherman Muni
Myra
Cook
Woodbine
Bells
Savoy
Freedom Field
Macomb
GRAYSON
Tribune
Lake Kiowa
Shady Grove
Hilton
Luella
Ida
Whiterock
Canaan
Collinsville
Ethel
Hood
Spring Creek
Kentucky Town
Dorchester
Whitewright
White Mound
Enterprise
RAY ROBERTS LAKE WMA
Burns City
Tom Bean
Fra
Valley View
Mountain Springs
Continue on Page 46
Rowland Airfield
Bridges Field
DALLAS
© DeLorme
ANTLERS OK
POTEAU OK
MENA AR
Rufe
Continue in DeLorme's Oklahoma Atlas & Gazetteer
Wright City
INSET 2
Golden
Broken Bow
Eagletown
De Queen
Fort Towson
Swink
Valliant
HUGO OK
Millerton
MCCURTAIN
SEVIER
Garvin
OKLAHOMA
TEXAS
RED RIVER
Horatio
Davenport
Idabel
Continue on Page 39 Inset 1
Kiomatia
Blakeney
OUACHITA NATIONAL FOREST
Kanawha
Silver City
Albion
Haworth
Winthrop
Big Pine Creek
RED RIVER
Pin Hook
Addielou
Greenwood
Pecan Bayou
Acworth
Arkinda
Alleene
Negley
Snell Creek
INDEF BDY
Denwidde Bayou
Bryarly
Burks Ridge
Foreman
Dimple
Vessey
Cross Road
Midway
Dilworth
Reeds Settlement
Arden
PARIS
Bluff
Campground Bayou
North Lake
Vandalia
Madras
Caney
Little Cr
OKLAHOMA
ARKANSAS
Detroit
Bagwell
Cherry
White Rock
Beaverdam Cr
Beaverdam
LITTLE
RIVER
English
North Mill Cr
Mill Creek
Liberty
Mabry
Pine Springs
Clarksville
Clarksville Red River Co
Spring Hill
McCoy
Annona
Avery
BOWIE
Lone Star
Aikin Grove
Peters Prairie
Woodstock
Smith Hill
Fulbright
Sherry
Oak Grove
Redbank
Deport
Shadowland
Russells Ranch
Garland
Daniels Chapel
Burns
Barkman
Continue on Page 48
De Kalb
Rugby
Contour interval 200 feet
MT PLEASANT
Pine Branch
Boxelder
© DeLorme
DAINGERFIELD
Malta

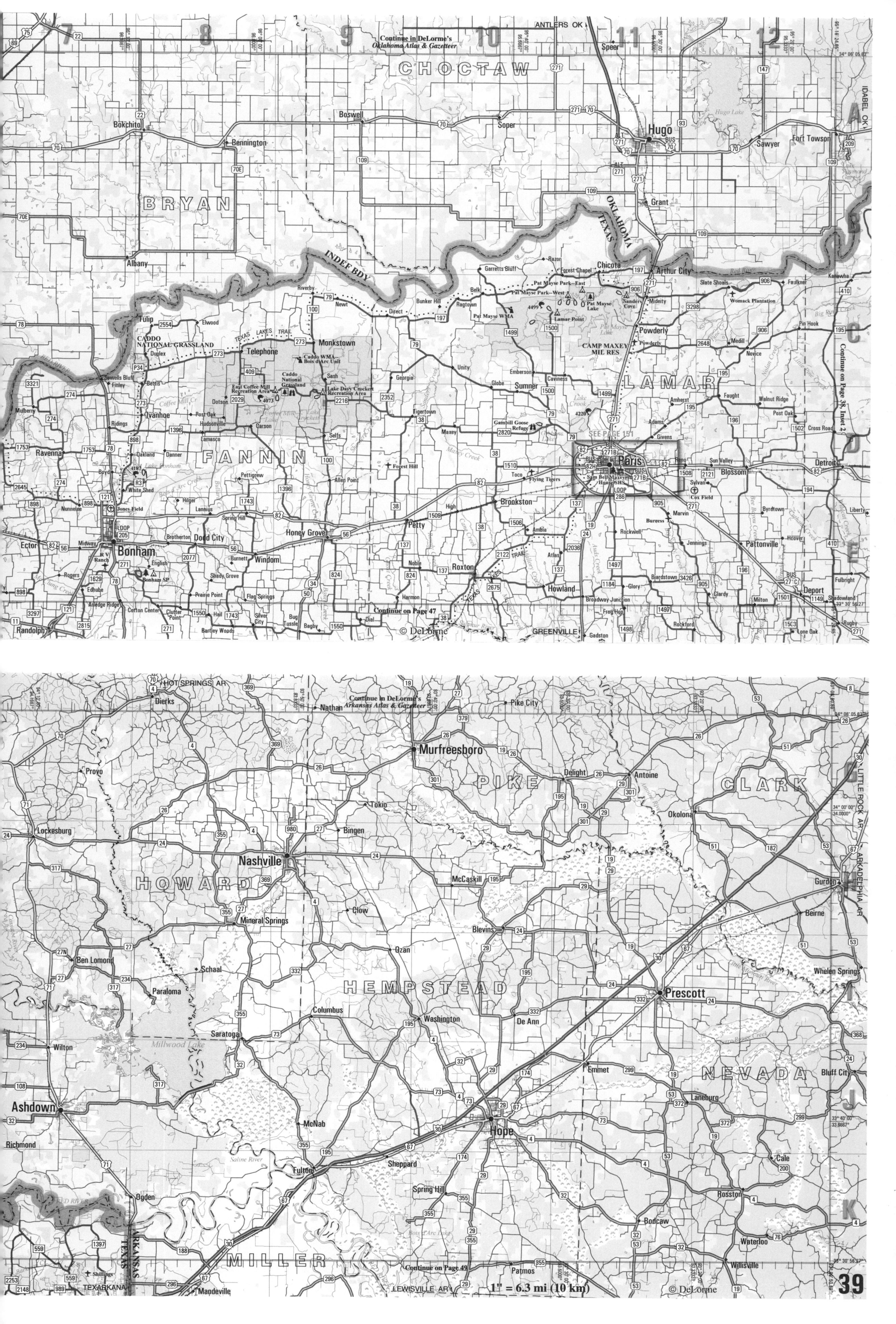

ANTLERS OK
Continue in DeLorme's Oklahoma Atlas & Gazetteer
CHOCTAW
BRYAN
Bokchito
Bennington
Boswell
Soper
Speer
Hugo
Sawyer
Fort Towson
Hugo Lake
IDABEL OK
Grant
Albany
OKLAHOMA
TEXAS
INDEF BDY
Red River
Garretts Bluff
Razor
Forest Chapel
Chicota
Arthur City
Slate Shoals
Faulkner
Kanawha
Womack Plantation
Pat Mayse Park–East
Pat Mayse Park–West
Pat Mayse Lake
Pat Mayse WMA
Lamar Point
Sanders Cove
Mideity
Riverby
Newt
Direct
Bunker Hill
Ragtown
Belk
Tulip
Elwood
CADDO NATIONAL GRASSLAND
TEXAS LAKES TRAIL
Telephone
Monkstown
Caddo WMA–Bois d'Arc Unit
Caddo National Grassland
Duplex
Powderly
CAMP MAXEY MIL RES
Pin Hook
Medill
Novice
Sowells Bluff
Finley
Bettis
East Coffee Mill Recreation Area
Lake Davy Crockett Recreation Area
Sash
Georgia
Unity
Emberson
Caviness
Globe
Sumner
LAMAR
Amherst
Faught
Walnut Ridge
Pest Oak
Cross Roads
Mulberry
Ivanhoe
Post Oak
Dotson
Hudsonville
Carson
Ridings
Tigertown
Maxey
Gambill Goose Refuge
Adams
Givens
Ravenna
Lamasco
Danner
Oakland
Lake Bonham
FANNIN
Selfs
Maxey Creek
SEE PAGE 151
Paris
Reno
Sun Valley
Blossom
Detroit
Boyd
Pettigrew
Forest Hill
Allen Point
Toco
Flying Tigers
Sam Bell Maxey House SHS
Sylvan
Cox Field
White Shed
Nunnelee
Jones Field
Holger
Lannius
Spring Hill
Brookston
High
Byrdtown
Liberty
Marvin
Bonham
Ector
Midway
RV Ranch
Brotherton
Dodd City
Honey Grove
Petty
Ambia
Rockwell
Bureess
Jennings
Pattonville
Hoover
English
Bonham SP
Burnett
Windom
Noble
Roxton
Atlas
Howland
Biardstown
Clardy
Deport
Fulbright
Shadowland
Rogers
Edhube
Shady Grove
Prairie Point
Flag Springs
Harmon
Glory
Broadway Junction
Milton
Arledge Ridge
Cotton Center
Clutter Point
Hail
Silver City
Bug Tussle
Bagby
Dial
Frog Hop
Rockford
Rugby
Lone Oak
Randolph
Bartley Woods
Gadston
GREENVILLE
Continue on Page 47
Continue on Page 38, Inset 2
© DeLorme
HOT SPRINGS AR
Dierks
Nathan
Continue in DeLorme's Arkansas Atlas & Gazetteer
Pike City
Murfreesboro
PIKE
Delight
Antoine
CLARK
Provo
Tokio
Okolona
LITTLE ROCK AR
Lockesburg
Bingen
Nashville
HOWARD
McCaskill
ARKADELPHIA AR
Gurdon
Beirne
Glow
Mineral Springs
Blevins
Ozan
Ben Lomond
Schaal
Whelen Springs
Paraloma
HEMPSTEAD
Prescott
Columbus
Washington
De Ann
Saratoga
Wilton
Millwood Lake
Emmet
NEVADA
Bluff City
Ashdown
McNab
Hope
Laneburg
Richmond
Saline River
Fulton
Sheppard
Cale
Ogden
RED RIVER
Spring Hill
Rosston
Bodcaw
Waterloo
ARKANSAS
TEXAS
MILLER
Willisville
Shillings
TEXARKANA
Mandeville
Continue on Page 49
Patmos
LEWISVILLE AR
1" = 6.3 mi (10 km)
© DeLorme

PORTALES NM
MORTON
Continue on Page 32
Crossroads
COCHRAN
Caprock
ROSWELL NM
YOAKUM
NEW MEXICO
TEXAS
Tatum
Gladiola
Bronco
Yoakum County
Plains
LEA
McDonald
Sulphur Draw
Lost Draw
Sulpher Springs Draw
Yoakum County Park
Sligo
Pleasant Hill
Mckenzie Draw
Allred
Denver City
Lovington
Two Leggs
Higginbotham
Continue in DeLorme's New Mexico Atlas & Gazetteer
ARTESIA NM
Wardswell Draw
GAINES
Humble City
OIL FIELDS
State Line
Paynes Corner
Hobbs
Seminole Draw
Gaines Co
Monument
Laguna Plata
CARLSBAD NM
OIL FIELDS
Monument Draw
Eunice
Frankel City
Whalen Lake
Contour interval 200 feet
Continue on Page 52
KERMIT
© DeLorme
1
2
3
4
5
6
A
B
C
D
E
F
G
H
I
J
K

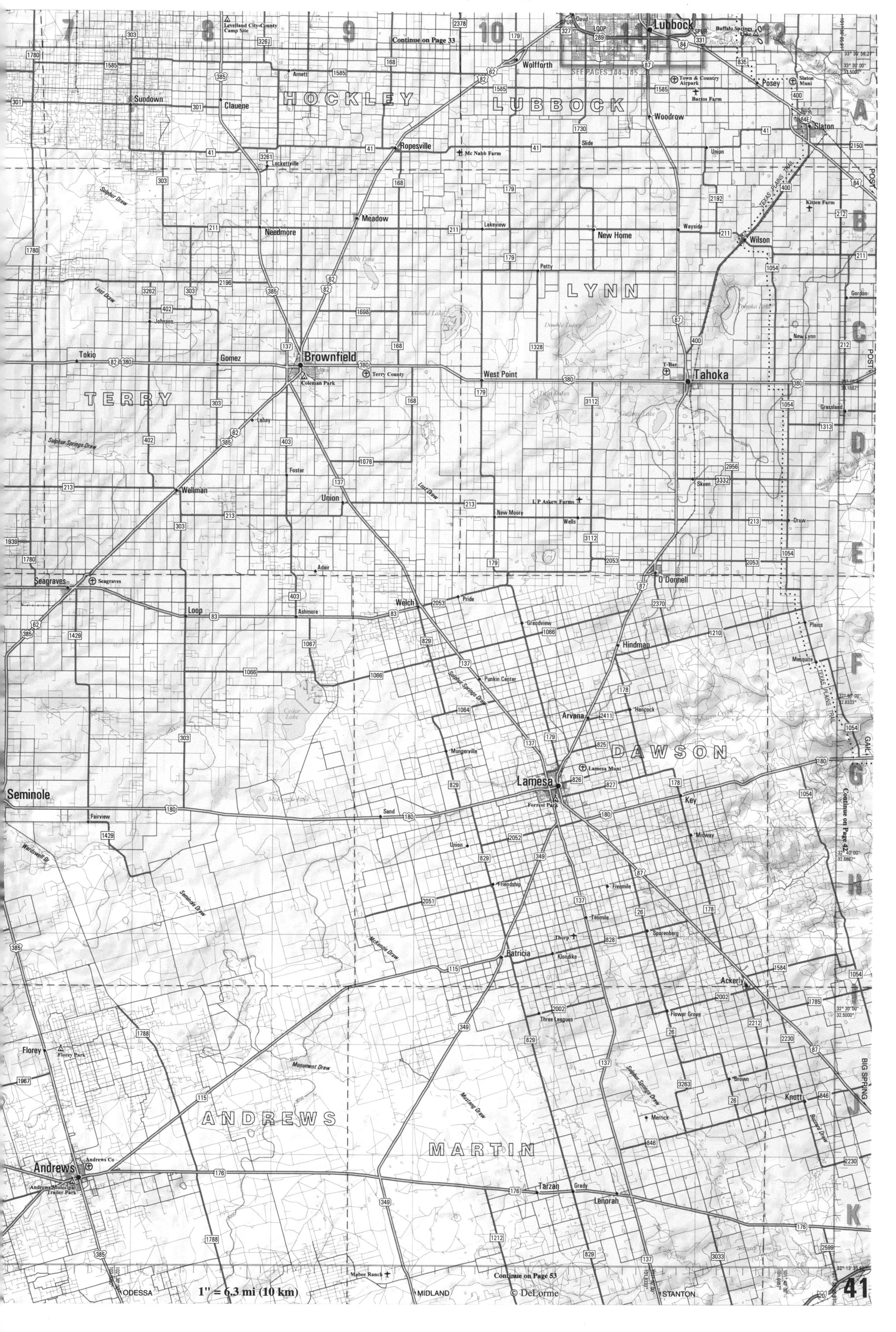

Continue on Page 33
SEE PAGES 144-145
Continue on Page 42
Continue on Page 53

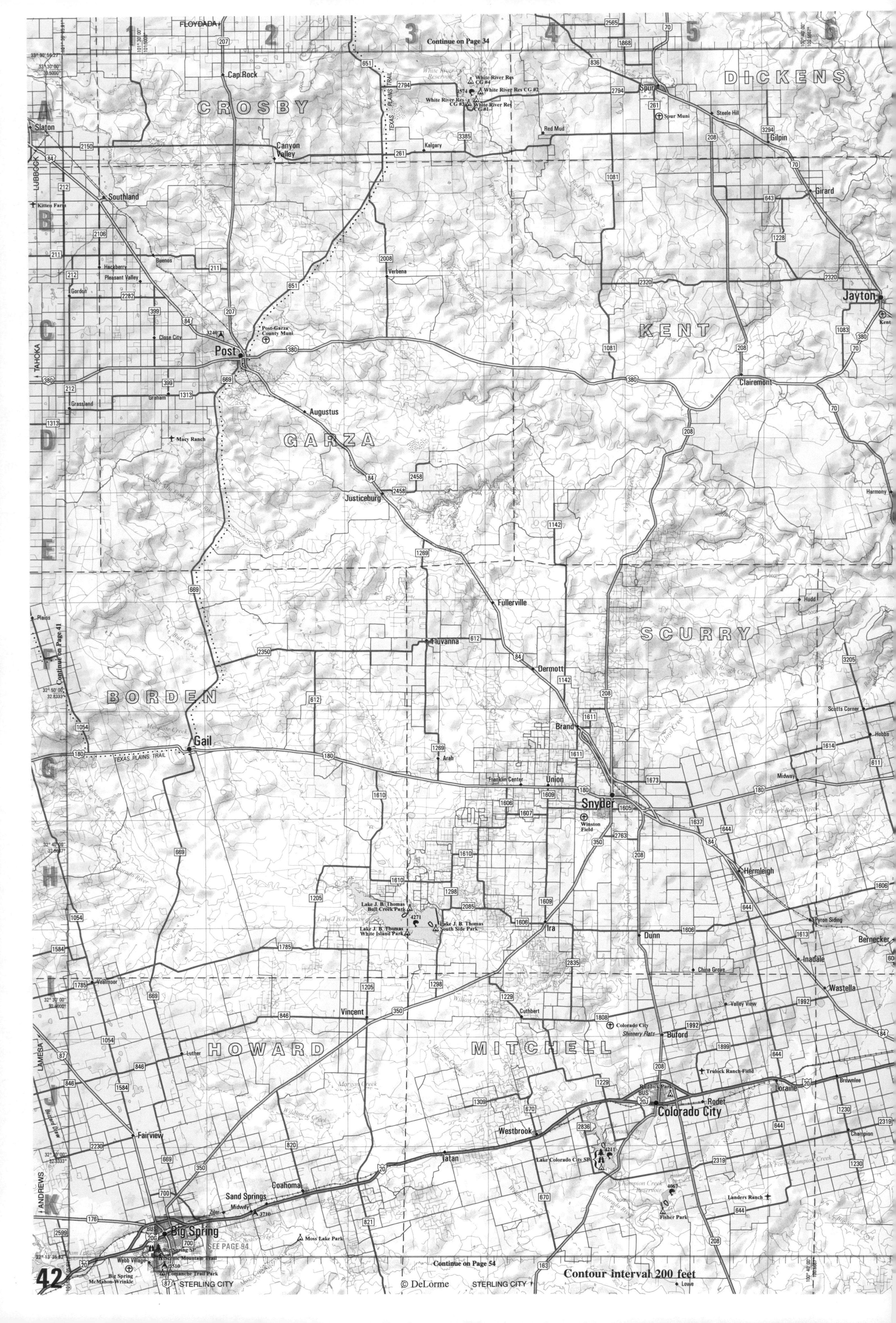

Continue on Page 34
Continue on Page 41
Continue on Page 54
SEE PAGE 94

Continue on Page 35

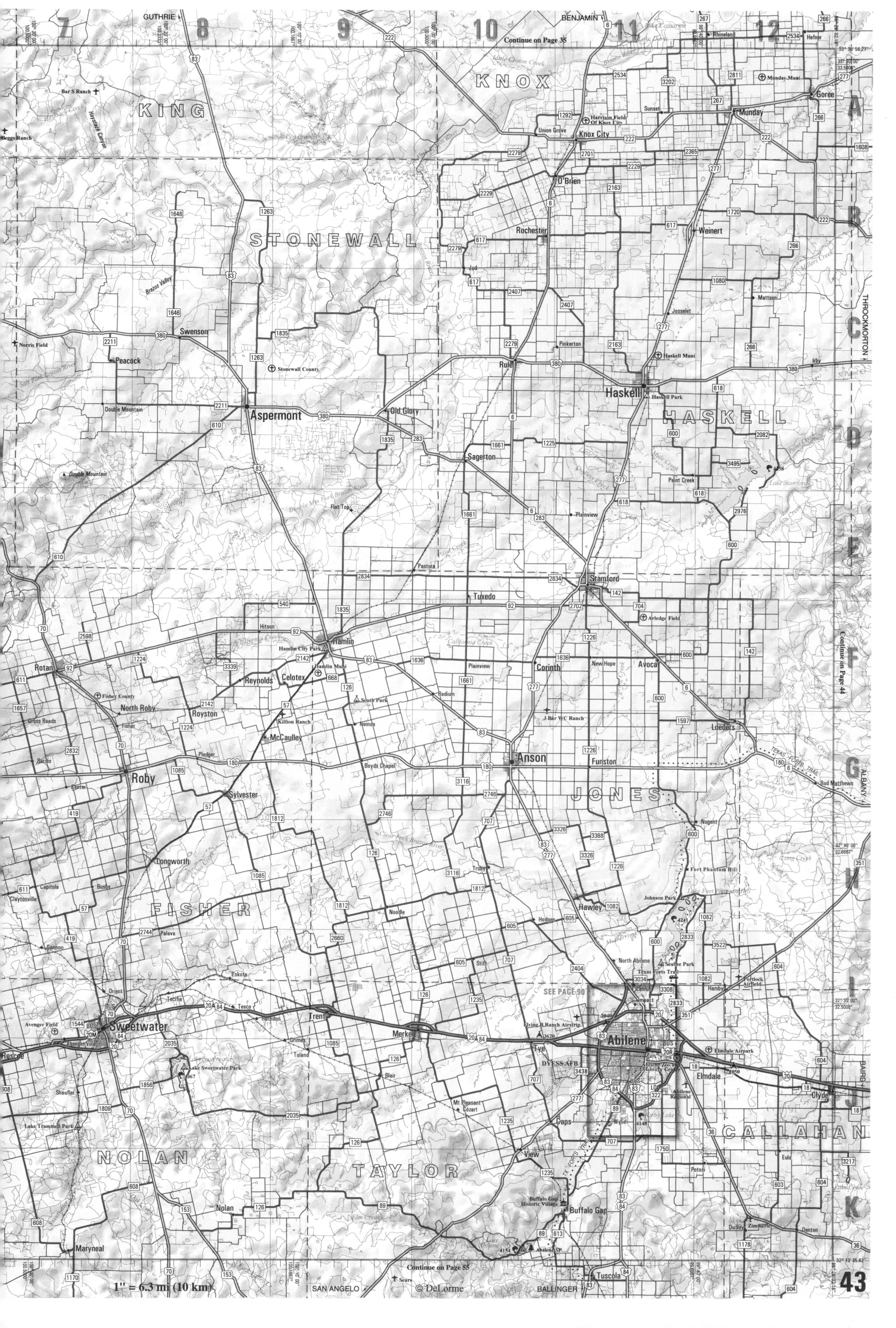

Continue on Page 44

Continue on Page 55

© DeLorme

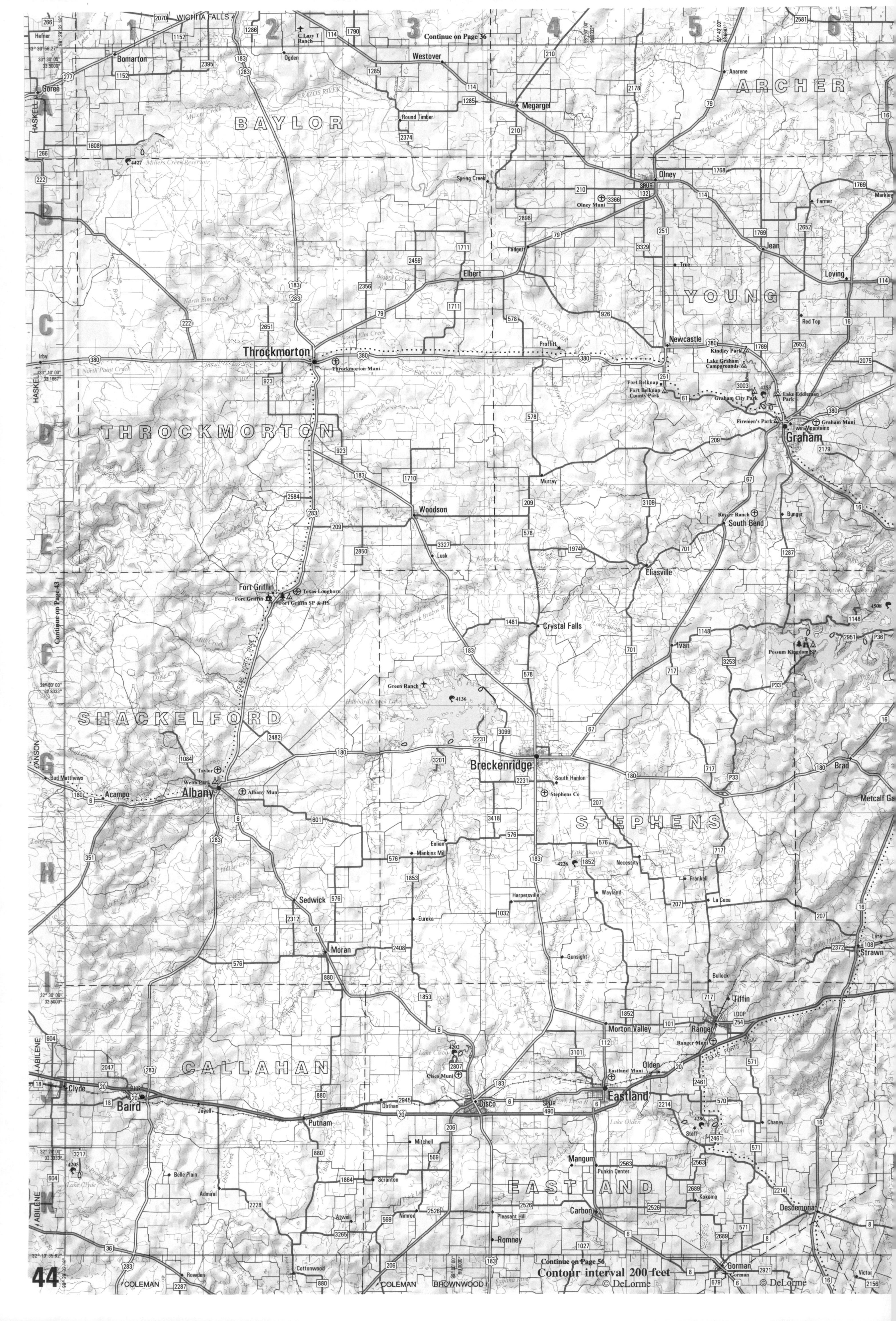

BAYLOR
ARCHER
YOUNG
THROCKMORTON
SHACKELFORD
STEPHENS
CALLAHAN
EASTLAND
Throckmorton
Olney
Graham
Breckenridge
Albany
Eastland
Cisco
Baird
Clyde
Ranger
Megargel
Westover
Newcastle
Woodson
Moran
Putnam
Gorman
Desdemona
Strawn
Continue on Page 36
Continue on Page 43
Continue on Page 56
Contour interval 200 feet
© DeLorme

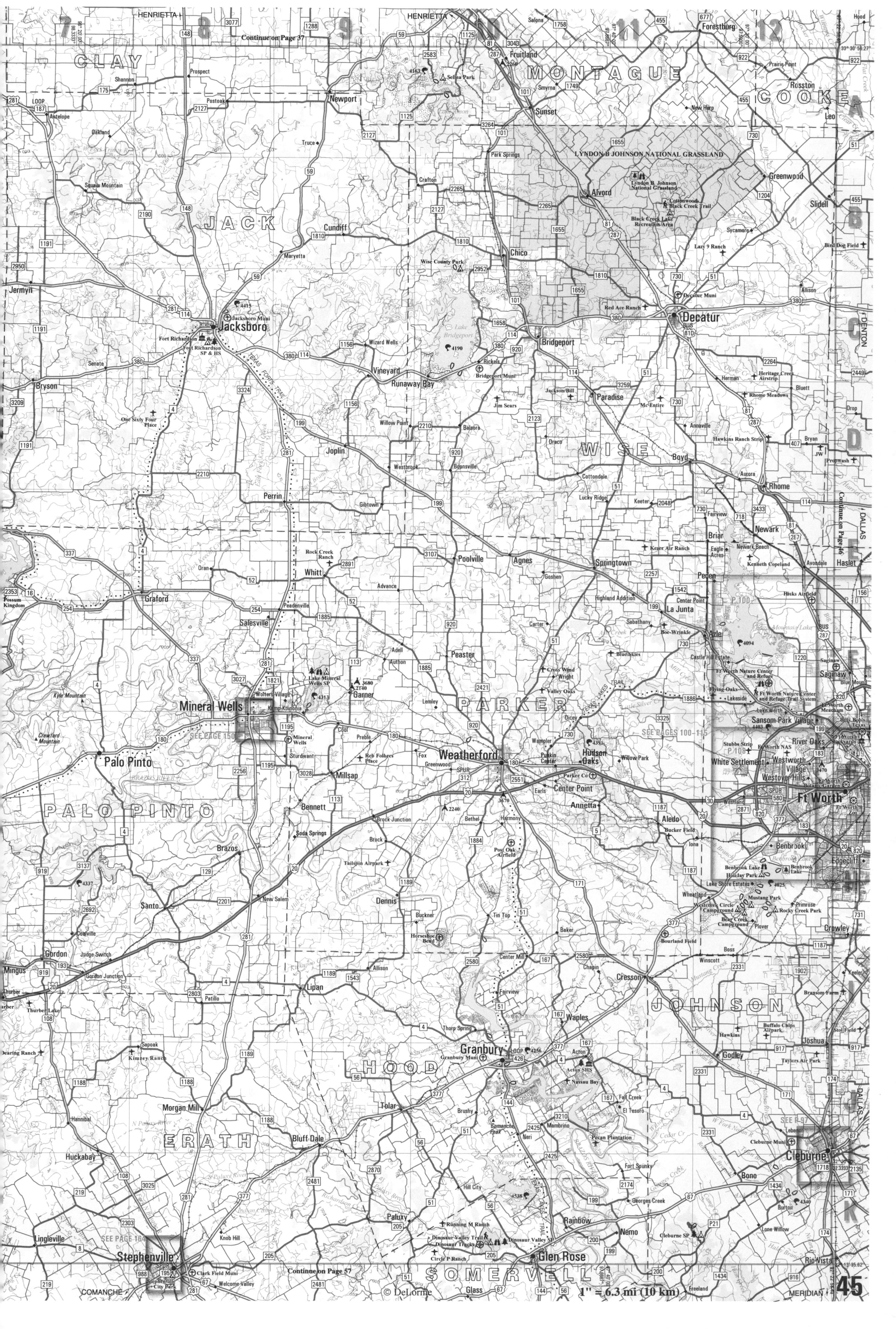

Continue on Page 37
Continue on Page 46
Continue on Page 57

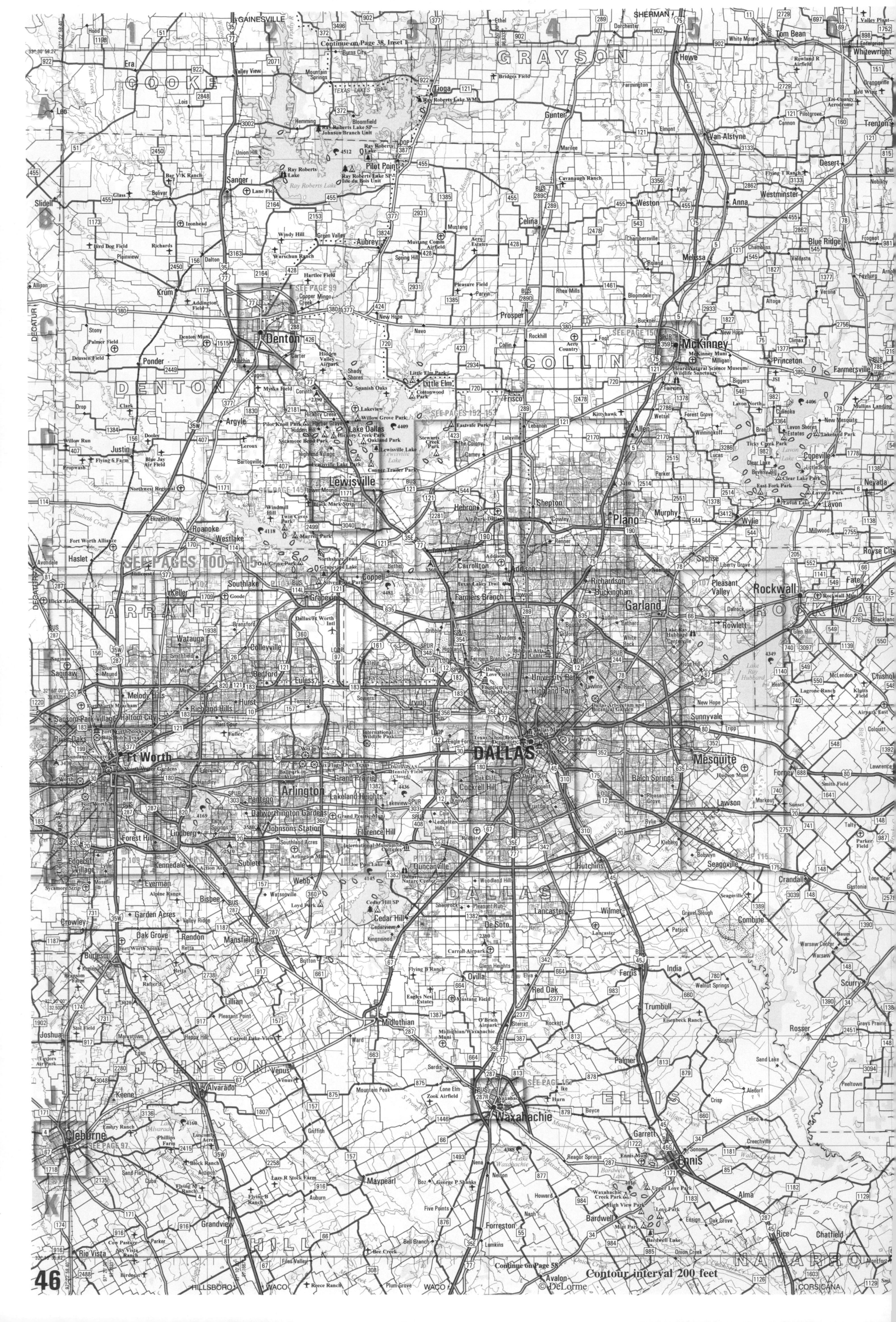

GAINESVILLE
SHERMAN
Continue on Page 38, Inset 1
GRAYSON
COOKE
DENTON
COLLIN
TARRANT
ROCKWALL
DALLAS
JOHNSON
ELLIS
HILL
NAVARRO
Tom Bean
Whitewright
Valley View
Era
Lois
Tioga
Howe
Gunter
Van Alstyne
Sanger
Pilot Point
Ray Roberts Lake
Celina
Weston
Anna
Westminster
Aubrey
Melissa
Blue Ridge
Krum
Denton
Ponder
Prosper
McKinney
Princeton
Farmersville
Frisco
Little Elm
Argyle
Lake Dallas
Lewisville
Allen
Lavon
Plano
Murphy
Wylie
Carrollton
Addison
Roanoke
Westlake
Southlake
Haslet
Keller
Grapevine
Coppell
Farmers Branch
Richardson
Garland
Rockwall
Fate
Rowlett
Watauga
Colleyville
Bedford
Euless
Irving
University Park
Highland Park
Sunnyvale
Saginaw
Richland Hills
Hurst
Haltom City
Ft Worth
DALLAS
Mesquite
Arlington
Grand Prairie
Balch Springs
Forney
Kennedale
Duncanville
Cedar Hill
De Soto
Lancaster
Wilmer
Hutchins
Seagoville
Crandall
Crowley
Burleson
Mansfield
Midlothian
Red Oak
Ferris
Alvarado
Venus
Waxahachie
Cleburne
Maypearl
Ennis
Palmer
Bardwell
Grandview
Rio Vista
Avalon
HILLSBORO
WACO
CORSICANA
SEE PAGE 99
SEE PAGE 150
SEE PAGE 145
SEE PAGES 152–153
SEE PAGES 100–115
SEE PAGE 97
SEE PAGE 157
Continue on Page 58
Contour interval 200 feet
© DeLorme

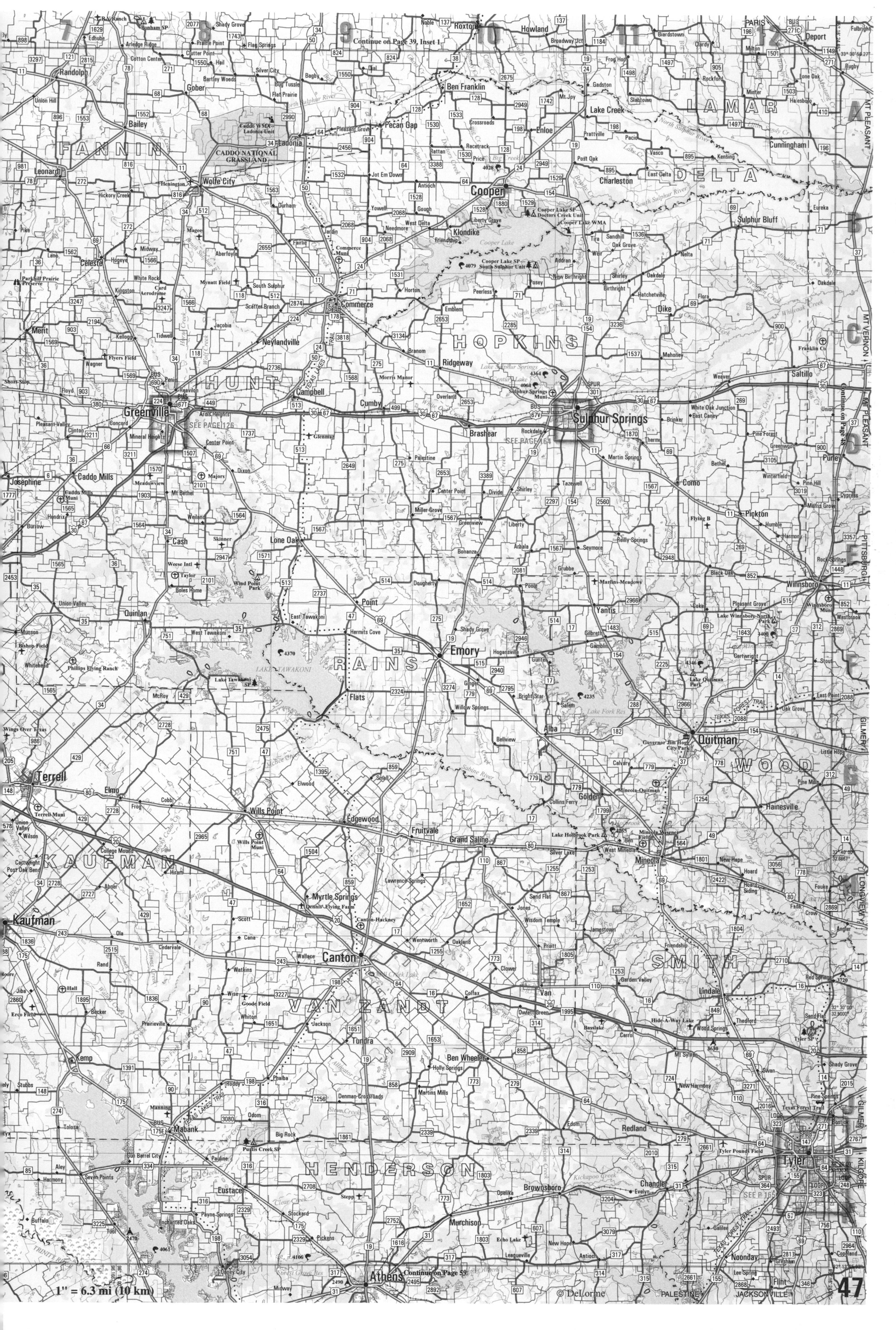

Continue on Page 39, Inset 1
FANNIN
HUNT
HOPKINS
LAMAR
DELTA
RAINS
WOOD
KAUFMAN
VAN ZANDT
SMITH
HENDERSON
CADDO NATIONAL GRASSLAND
Greenville
Commerce
Cooper
Sulphur Springs
Emory
Quitman
Terrell
Wills Point
Canton
Mineola
Kaufman
Tyler
Athens
Winnsboro
Lake Tawakoni
Cooper Lake
Lake Fork Res
SEE PAGE 126
SEE PAGE 164
Continue on Page 48
Continue on Page 59
1" = 6.3 mi (10 km)
© DeLorme
47

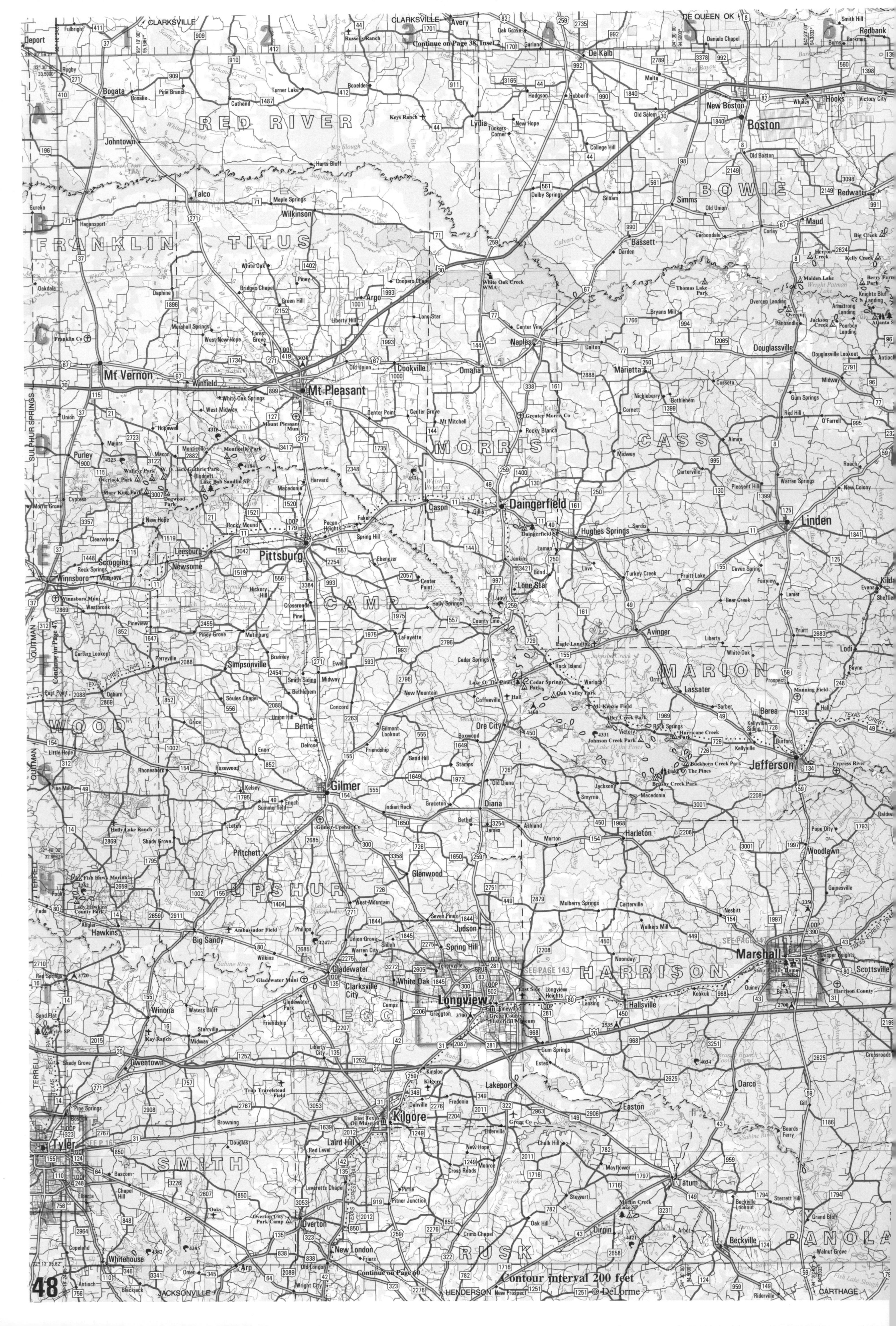

Continue on Page 38, Inset 2
Continue on Page 47
SEE PAGE 143
Continue on Page 60

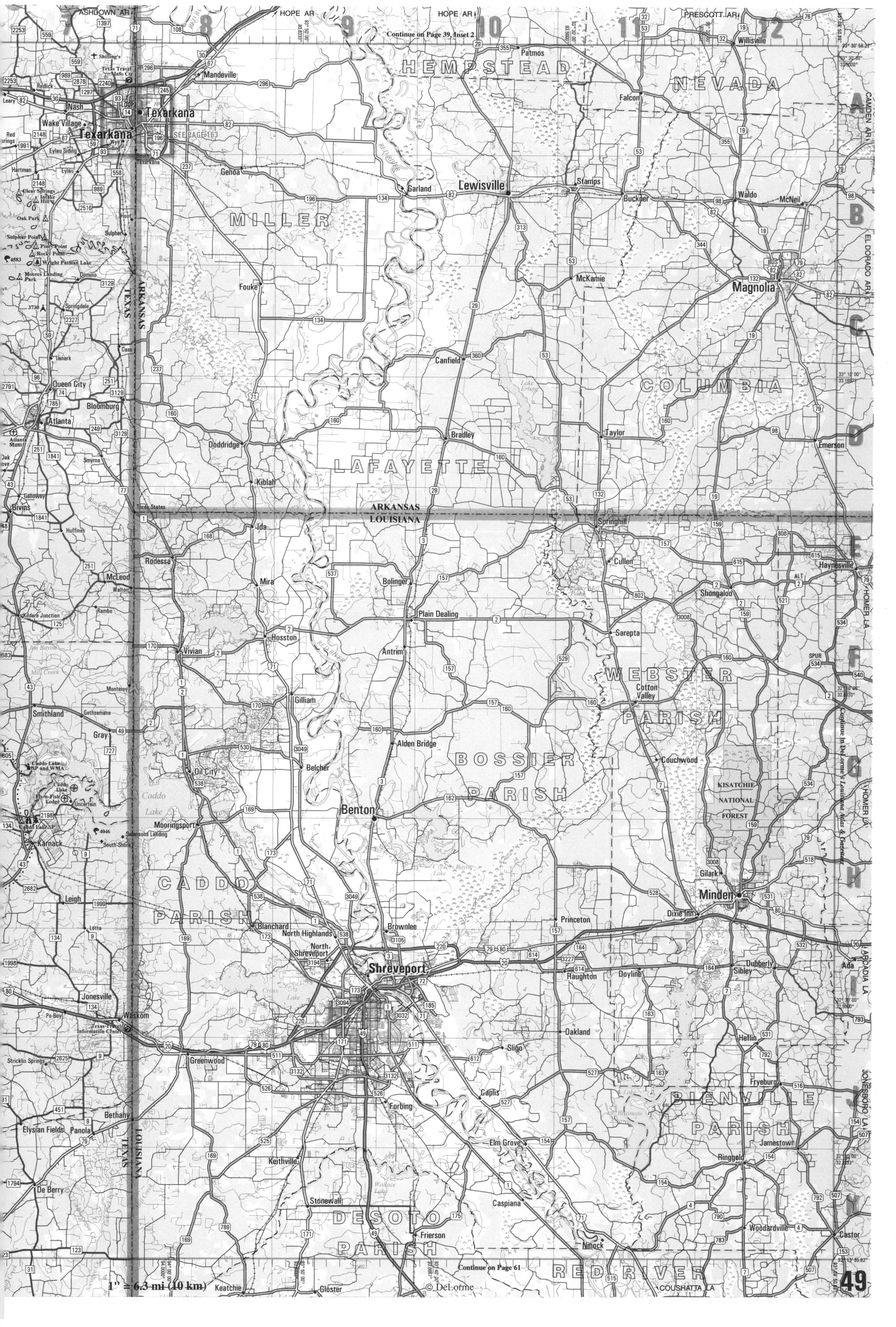
ASHDOWN AR
HOPE AR
HOPE AR
PRESCOTT AR
CAMDEN AR
EL DORADO AR
HOMER LA
ARCADIA LA
JONESBORO LA
COUSHATTA LA
HEMPSTEAD
NEVADA
MILLER
LAFAYETTE
COLUMBIA
WEBSTER PARISH
BOSSIER PARISH
CADDO PARISH
BIENVILLE PARISH
DESOTO PARISH
RED RIVER
ARKANSAS
TEXAS
LOUISIANA
ARKANSAS LOUISIANA
KISATCHIE NATIONAL FOREST
Texarkana
Patmos
Mandeville
Willisville
Falcon
Genoa
Garland
Lewisville
Stamps
Buckner
Waldo
McNeil
McKamie
Magnolia
Fouke
Canfield
Bradley
Taylor
Emerson
Doddridge
Kiblah
Three States
Ida
Springhill
Cullen
Haynesville
Rodessa
Bolinger
Shongaloo
Mira
Plain Dealing
Sarepta
Hosston
Vivian
Antrim
Cotton Valley
Gilliam
Alden Bridge
Couchwood
Belcher
Oil City
Benton
Mooringsport
Gilark
Minden
Dixie Inn
Princeton
Blanchard
North Highlands
Brownlee
North Shreveport
Shreveport
Haughton
Doyline
Dubberly
Sibley
Ada
Oakland
Sligo
Heflin
Greenwood
Fryeburg
Caplis
Forbing
Elm Grove
Jamestown
Keithville
Ringgold
Caspiana
Stonewall
Frierson
Woodardville
Ninock
Castor
Keatchie
Gloster
Nash
Wake Village
Queen City
Bloomburg
Atlanta
Bivins
McLeod
Vivian
Smithland
Gray
Karnack
Leigh
Jonesville
Waskom
Bethany
Elysian Fields
Panola
De Berry
Caddo Lake
Continue on Page 39, Inset 2
Continue on Page 61
1" = 6.3 mi (10 km)
© DeLorme

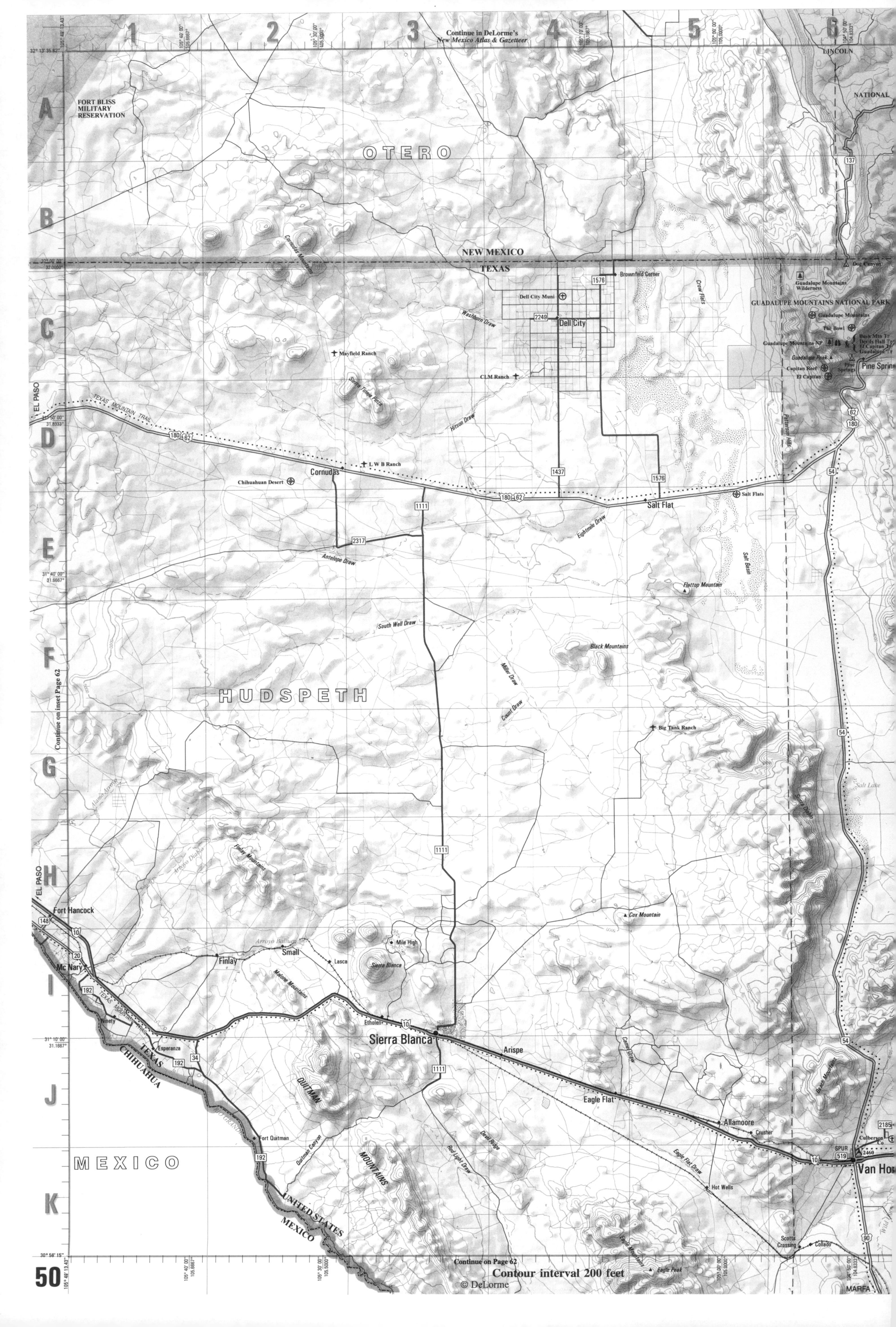
Continue in DeLorme's
New Mexico Atlas & Gazetteer
FORT BLISS
MILITARY
RESERVATION
OTERO
LINCOLN
NATIONAL
NEW MEXICO
TEXAS
Cornudas Mountains
Brownfield Corner
Dell City Muni
Dell City
Washburn Draw
Crow Flats
Dog Canyon
Guadalupe Mountains Wilderness
GUADALUPE MOUNTAINS NATIONAL PARK
Guadalupe Mountains
The Bowl
Guadalupe Mountains NP
Guadalupe Peak
Capitan Reef
El Capitan
Pine Springs
Pine Spring
Mayfield Ranch
Sierra Tinaja Pinta
CLM Ranch
Hitson Draw
EL PASO
TEXAS MOUNTAIN TRAIL
L W B Ranch
Cornudas
Chihuahuan Desert
Salt Flat
Salt Flats
Eightmile Draw
Patterson Hills
Antelope Draw
Salt Basin
Flattop Mountain
South Well Draw
Black Mountains
Miller Draw
Count Draw
HUDSPETH
Continue on inset Page 62
Big Tank Ranch
Sierra Diablo
Salt Lake
Alamo Arroyo
Arroyo Diablo
Finlay Mountains
Fort Hancock
Cox Mountain
Arroyo Balluco
Mile High
Mc Nary
Finlay
Small
Lasca
Sierra Blanca
Malone Mountains
Etholen
Esperanza
Arispe
Camel Draw
TEXAS
CHIHUAHUA
QUITMAN
Eagle Flat
Allamoore
Crusher
Baylor Mountains
Culberson Co.
Fort Quitman
Quitman Canyon
Devil Ridge
Red Light Draw
Eagle Flat Draw
Van Horn
MEXICO
MOUNTAINS
Hot Wells
UNITED STATES
MEXICO
Scotts Crossing
Collado
Eagle Mountains
Continue on Page 62
Contour interval 200 feet
Eagle Peak
© DeLorme
MARFA

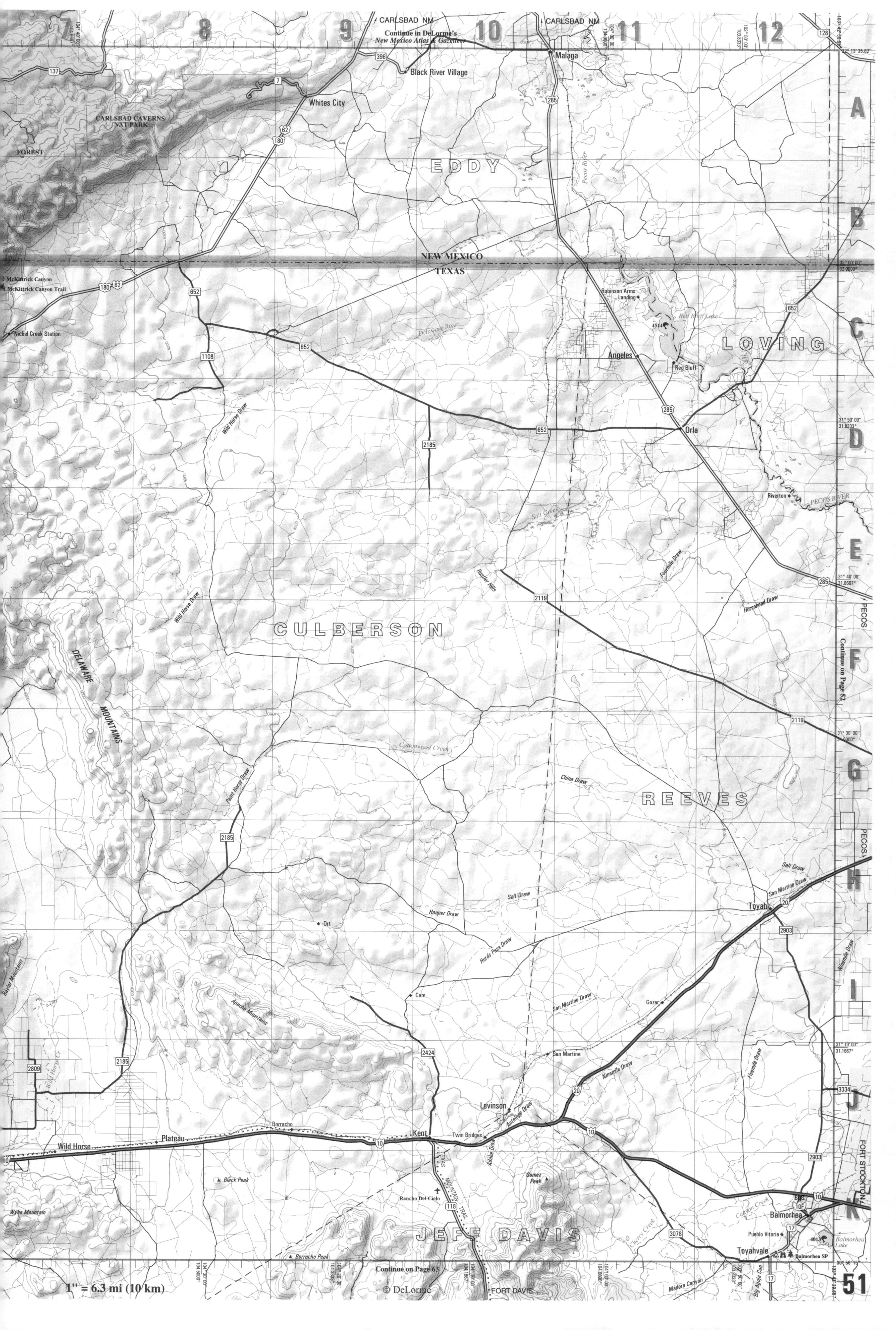

CARLSBAD NM
Continue in DeLorme's New Mexico Atlas & Gazetteer
Malaga
Black River Village
Whites City
CARLSBAD CAVERNS NAT PARK
FOREST
EDDY
NEW MEXICO
TEXAS
McKittrick Canyon
McKittrick Canyon Trail
Nickel Creek Station
Robinson Arms Landing
Red Bluff Lake
Angeles
Red Bluff
LOVING
Delaware River
Wild Horse Draw
Orla
Riverton
PECOS RIVER
Salt Creek
Rustler Hills
Fourmile Draw
Horsehead Draw
CULBERSON
DELAWARE MOUNTAINS
PECOS
Continue on Page 52
Cottonwood Creek
Chinu Draw
Paint Horse Draw
REEVES
Salt Draw
San Martine Draw
Toyah
Hooper Draw
Ort
Hurds Pass Draw
Cam
Gozar
Apache Mountains
Baylor Mountains
San Martine
Ninemile Draw
Fivemile Draw
Wild Horse Cr
Levinson
Antelope Draw
Borracho
Plateau
Wild Horse
Kent
Twin Bridges
Black Peak
Gomez Peak
Rancho Del Cielo
TEXAS MOUNTAIN TRAIL
Wylie Mountain
Balmorhea
Cherry Creek
Pueblo Vitoria
Balmorhea Lake
Borracho Peak
JEFF DAVIS
Toyahvale
Balmorhea SP
Continue on Page 63
FORT STOCKTON
FORT DAVIS
Madera Canyon
1" = 6.3 mi (10 km)
© DeLorme

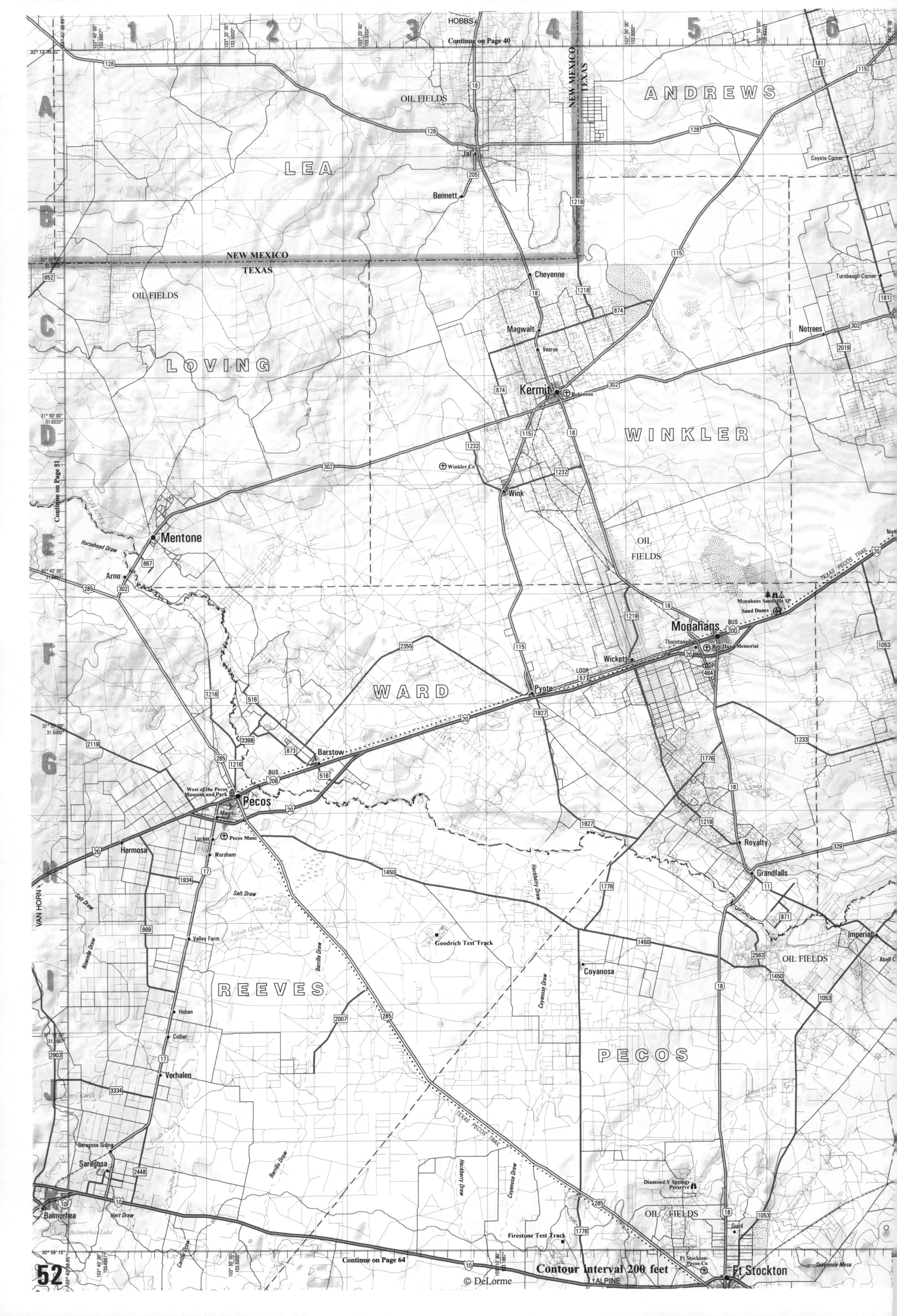

Continue on Page 40
Continue on Page 51
Continue on Page 64

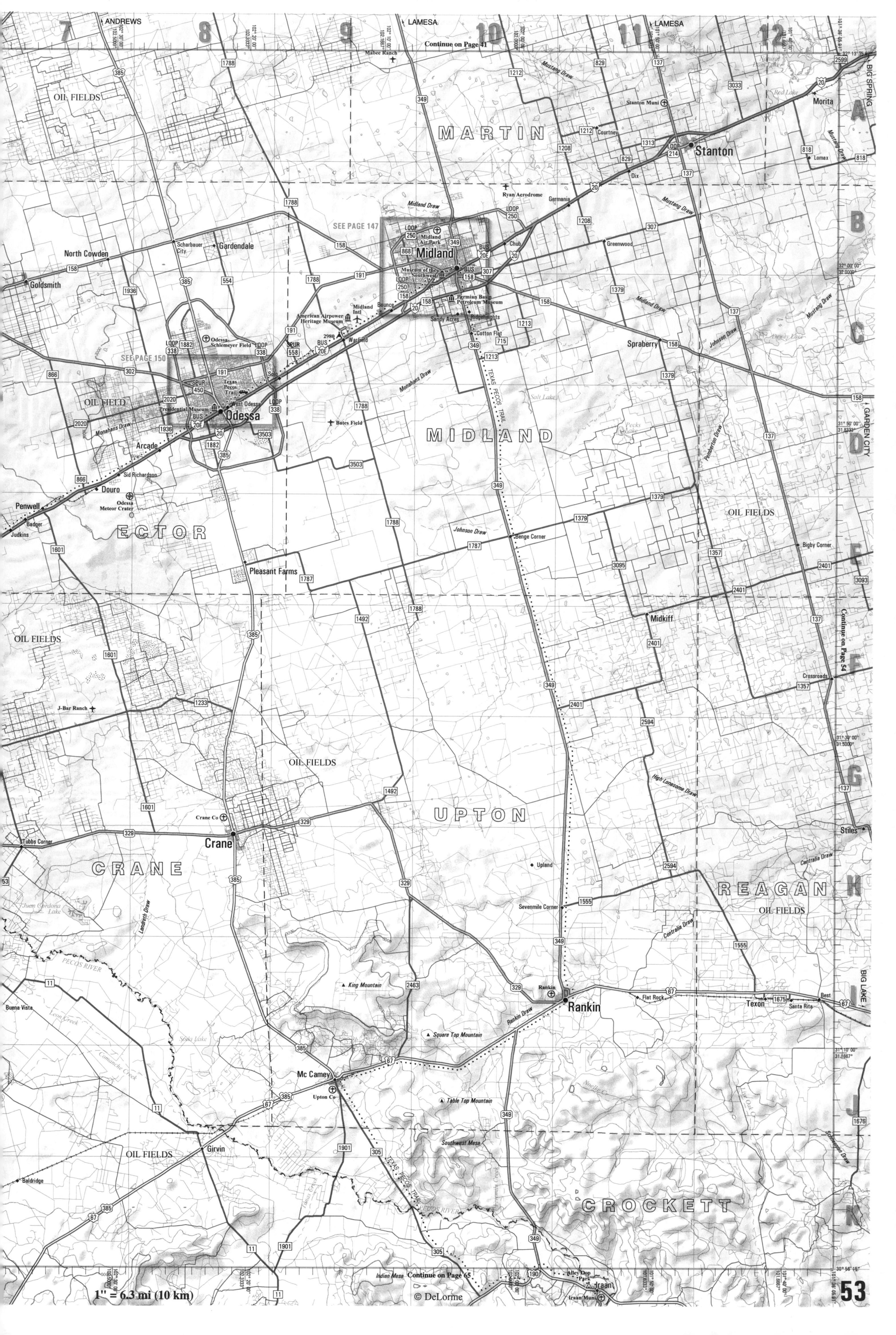

ANDREWS
LAMESA
LAMESA
Continue on Page 41
MARTIN
MIDLAND
ECTOR
UPTON
CRANE
REAGAN
CROCKETT
Midland
Odessa
Stanton
Rankin
Crane
Mc Camey
Iraan
Girvin
Goldsmith
North Cowden
Gardendale
Penwell
Pleasant Farms
Midkiff
Spraberry
Texon
Stiles
Continue on Page 54
Continue on Page 65
SEE PAGE 147
SEE PAGE 150
OIL FIELDS
BIG SPRING
GARDEN CITY
BIG LAKE
1" = 6.3 mi (10 km)
© DeLorme

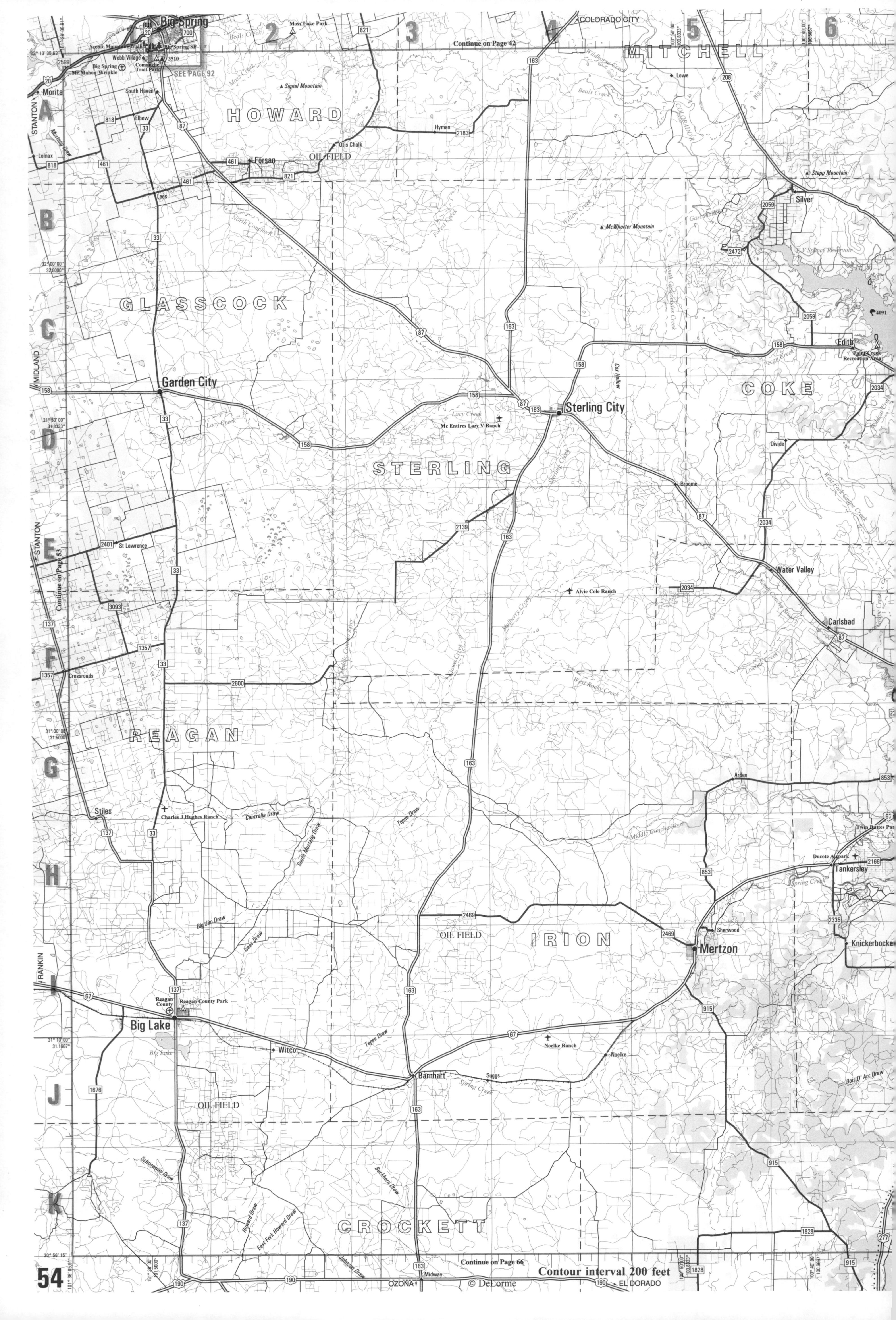

Big Spring
Moss Lake Park
COLORADO CITY
Continue on Page 42
MITCHELL
HOWARD
Signal Mountain
Scenic Mountain
Big Spring SP
Webb Village
Comanche Trail Park
SEE PAGE 92
Morita
South Haven
Elbow
Lomax
Forsan
Otis Chalk
OIL FIELD
Hyman
Lowe
Stepp Mountain
Silver
McWhorter Mountain
E V Spence Reservoir
Lees
GLASSCOCK
Edith
Paint Creek Recreation Area
COKE
Garden City
Sterling City
Mc Entires Lazy V Ranch
STERLING
Divide
Broome
St Lawrence
Continue on Page 53
Water Valley
Alvie Cole Ranch
Carlsbad
Crossroads
REAGAN
Arden
Stiles
Charles J Hughes Ranch
Twin Buttes Pat
Ducote Airpark
Tankersley
Sherwood
OIL FIELD
IRION
Mertzon
Knickerbocker
Reagan County
Reagan County Park
Big Lake
Witco
Noelke Ranch
Noelke
Barnhart
Suggs
OIL FIELD
CROCKETT
Continue on Page 66
Midway
OZONA
© DeLorme
Contour interval 200 feet
EL DORADO
STANTON
MIDLAND
RANKIN

SWEETWATER
ABILENE
ABILENE
Continue on Page 43
7
8
9
10
11
12
Maryneal
Dudley
Denton
TAYLOR
NOLAN
Sears
Tuscola
Ovalo
Rogers
Shep
Happy Valley
Hylton
Lawn
Blackwell
Bradshaw
Drasco
Goldsboro
Oak Creek Reservoir
Oak Creek Park
Fort Chadbourne
Wingate
Pumphrey
Lake Coleman
Press Morris Park
Sanco
Fort Chadbourne
OIL FIELDS
Kickapoo Mountain
Wilmeth
Winters
Novice
Winters Muni
Silver Valley
Robert Lee
Wildcat Creek Rec. Area
Robert Lee
Bronte
COLORADO RIVER
Norton
Hatchel
Glen Cove
Hamrick
Shawville
Lakeside Park
Friendship Park
Hords Creek Lake
Flat Rock Park
Maverick
Blanton
Valley View
RUNNELS
Benoit
Talpa
Valera
Old Ballinger Lake
Ballinger Lake Park
New Ballinger Lake
Ballinger City Park
Ballinger
Tennyson
COLEMAN
BROWNWOOD
Bruce Field
Fisk
Rowena
Olfen
Voss
Mozelle
Continue on Page 56
Wooland Siding
Orient
Miles
O.H. Ivie Reservoir
Leaday
Lowake
Gouldbusk
Harriet
Concho
SEE PAGE 162
Paint Rock
Alvery Junction
San Angelo
Fort Concho
Veribest
Mereta
COLORADO RIVER
Stacy
CONCHO
Goodfellow AFB
Eola
Millersview
Doole
Middle Concho
Lake Nasworthy
Spring Creek Marina Park
Mathis Field
Walker Ranch
Wall
Vancourt
Vick
Byrne
Reece Field
Salt Gap
Pear Valley
Brady Mountains
Eden
Pasche
TOM GREEN
Christoval
Melvin
Brown Field
Homer Junction
Whiteland
Live Oak
Marco
Lightner
BRADY
TEXAS FORTS TRAIL
Callan
SCHLEICHER
MENARD
Calf Creek
Adams
Menard Co
Continue on Page 67
1" = 6.3 mi (10 km)
© DeLorme
EL DORADO
Menard
A
B
C
D
E
F
G
H
I
J
K

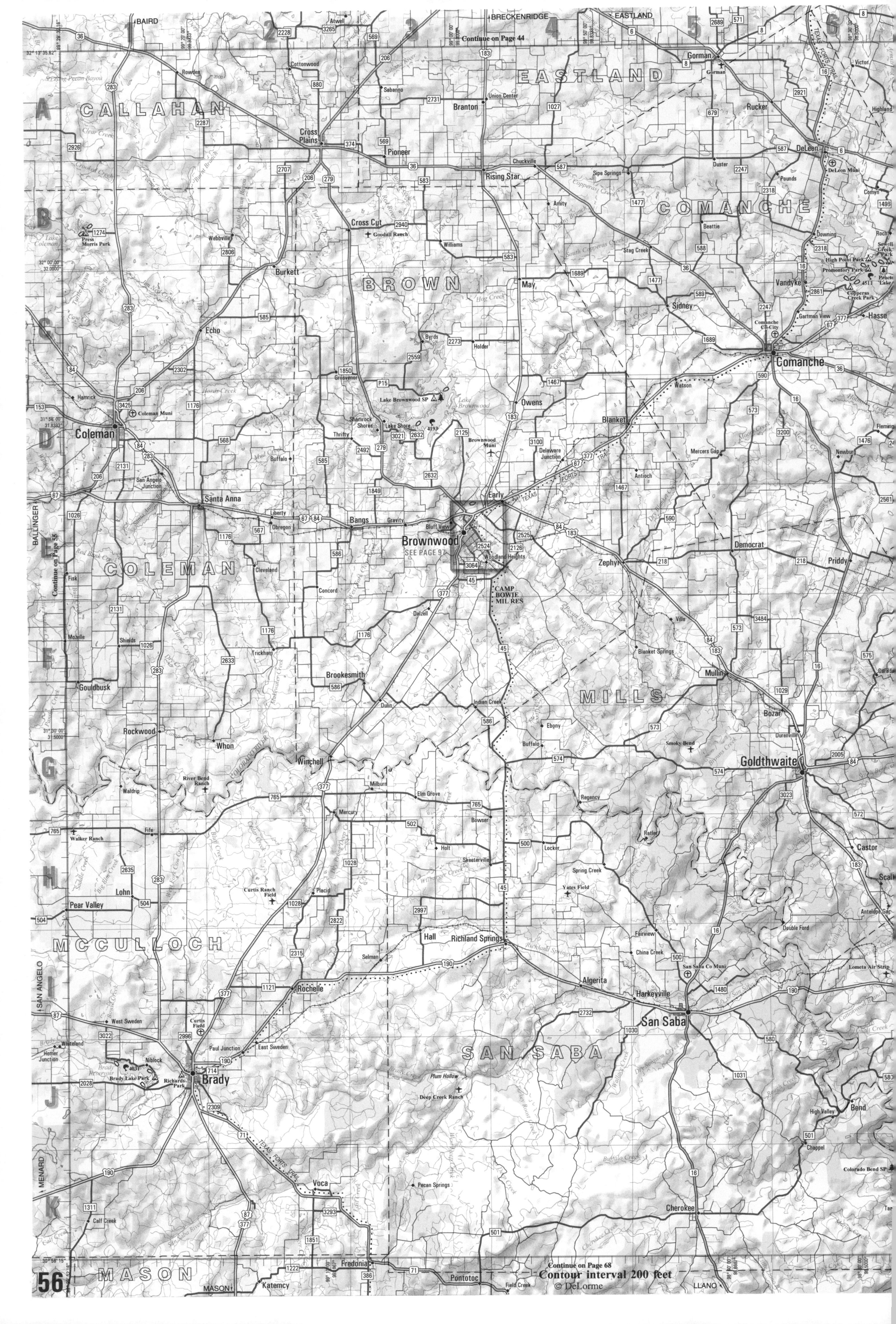

Continue on Page 44
BAIRD
BRECKENRIDGE
EASTLAND
CALLAHAN
EASTLAND
COMANCHE
BROWN
COLEMAN
MILLS
MCCULLOCH
SAN SABA
MASON
Gorman
Rowden
Cottonwood
Sabanno
Branton
Union Center
Rucker
Victor
Highland
Cross Plains
Pioneer
Rising Star
Chuckville
Sipe Springs
Duster
DeLeon
Pounds
Comyn
Amity
Cross Cut
Goodall Ranch
Williams
Press Morris Park
Lake Coleman
Webbville
Beattie
Downing
Stag Creek
High Point Park
Promontory Park
Burkett
May
Sidney
Vandyke
Copperas Creek Park
Hasse
Echo
Byrds
Holder
Gartman View
Comanche
Grosvenor
Lake Brownwood SP
Lake Brownwood
Owens
Watson
Hamrick
Coleman Muni
Coleman
Shamrock Shores
Lake Shore
Thrifty
Brownwood Muni
Blanket
Delaware Junction
Mercers Gap
Newburg
Fleming
Buffalo
Antioch
San Angelo Junction
Santa Anna
Liberty
Obregon
Bangs
Gravity
Bluff View
Early
Brownwood
SEE PAGE 97
Woodland Heights
Democrat
Priddy
Zephyr
BALLINGER
Continue on Page 55
Cleveland
Concord
CAMP BOWIE MIL RES
Fisk
Dalzell
Villa
Mozelle
Shields
Trickham
Blanket Springs
Brookesmith
Mullin
Gouldbusk
Indian Creek
Bozar
Dulin
Durenville
Ebony
Rockwood
Whon
Buffalo
Smoky Bend
Winchell
Goldthwaite
River Bend Ranch
Milburn
Waldrip
Elm Grove
Regency
Mercury
Bowser
Walker Ranch
Fife
Ratler
Castor
Holt
Locker
Skeeterville
Spring Creek
Yates Field
Lohn
Curtis Ranch Field
Placid
Pear Valley
Antelope Gap
Double Ford
Hall
Richland Springs
Fairview
China Creek
Selman
San Saba Co Muni
Lometa Air Strip
SAN ANGELO
Rochelle
Algerita
Harkeyville
West Sweden
Curtis Field
San Saba
Whiteland
Homer Junction
Paul Junction
East Sweden
Niblock
Brady Reservoir
Brady Lake Park
Richards Park
Brady
Plum Hollow
Deep Creek Ranch
Bend
High Valley
Chappel
Colorado Bend SP
MENARD
Voca
Pecan Springs
Calf Creek
Cherokee
Fredonia
Pontotoc
Field Creek
Katemcy
LLANO
Continue on Page 68
Contour interval 200 feet
© DeLorme
56

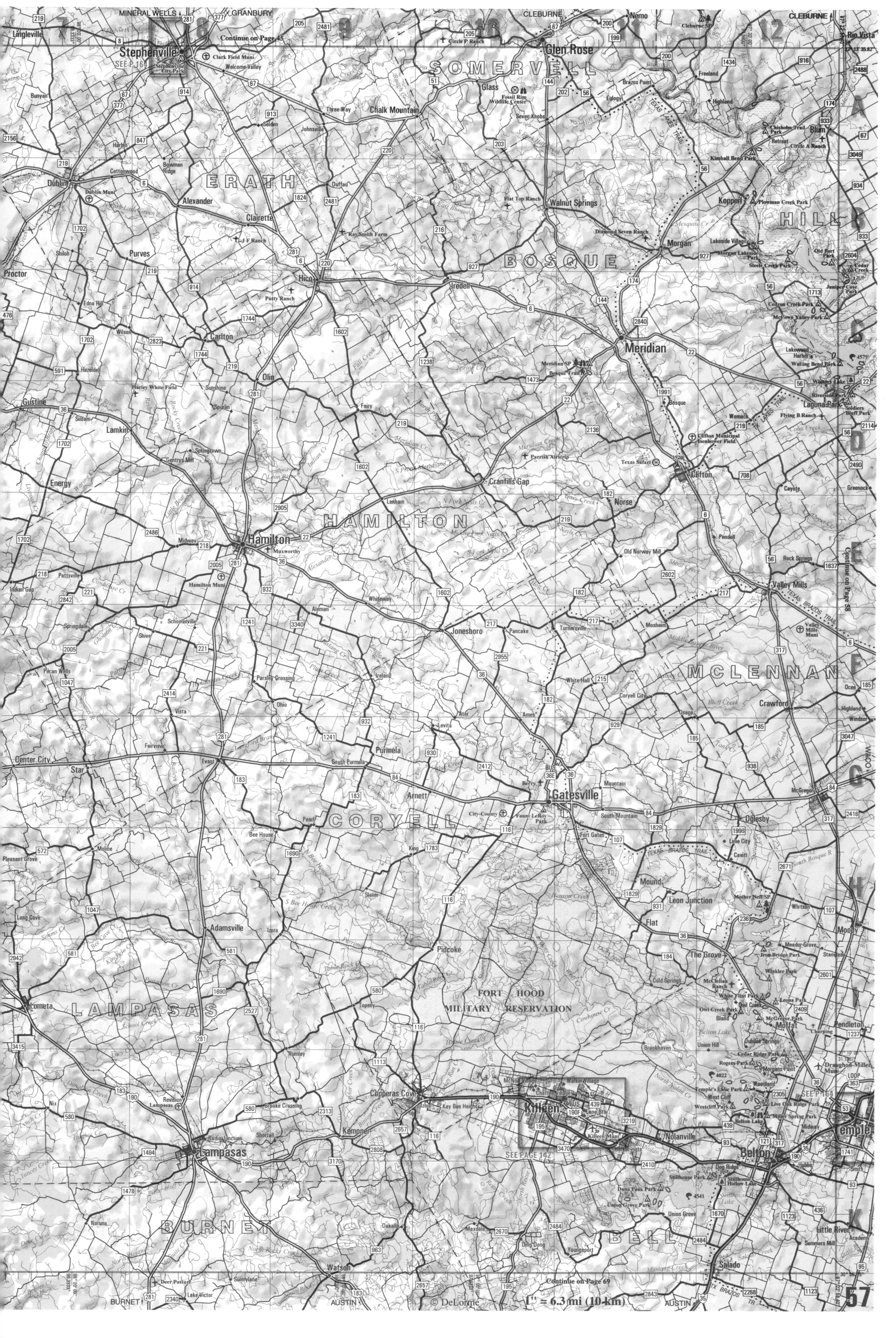

MINERAL WELLS
GRANBURY
CLEBURNE
Nemo
Continue on Page 45
Lingleville
Stephenville
SEE P. 164
Clark Field Muni
Welcome Valley
Circle P Ranch
Glen Rose
SOMERVELL
Cleburne SP
Rio Vista
Freeland
Brazos Point
Glass
Fossil Rim Wildlife Center
Eulogy
Highland
Bunyan
Three Way
Chalk Mountain
Seven Knobs
TEXAS LAKES TRAIL
Chisholm Trail Park
Blum
Retreat
Circle A Ranch
Selden
Johnsville
Harbin
Kimball Bend Park
Bowman Ridge
Cottonwood
Dublin
ERATH
Duffau
Dublin Muni
Alexander
Flat Top Ranch
Walnut Springs
Kopperl
Plowman Creek Park
HILL
Clairette
Diamond Seven Ranch
J F Ranch
Ray Smith Farm
Morgan
Lakeside Village
Morgan Lakeside Park
Old Fort Park
Steele Creek Park
Cedar Creek
Purves
BOSQUE
Proctor
Hico
Iredell
Putty Ranch
Juniper Cove Park
Edna Hill
Cedron Creek Park
McCown Valley Park
Wilson
Carlton
Meridian
Lakewood Harbor
Walling Bend Park
Hazeldell
Olin
Meridian SP
Bosque Trail
Whitney Lake
Harley White Field
Sunshine
Riverside Park
Gustine
Spurlin
Bosque
Laguna Park
Soldiers Bluff Park
Siloam
Flying B Ranch
Lamkin
Fairy
Womack
Clifton Municipal Isenhower Field
Springtown
Gentrys Mill
Parrish Airstrip
Texas Safari
Energy
Clifton
Cranfills Gap
Cayote
Greenock
Lanham
Norse
HAMILTON
Pendell
Midway
Hamilton
Muxworthy
Old Norway Mill
Rock Springs
Continue on Page 58
Pottsville
Hamilton Muni
Valley Mills
Indian Gap
Whiteway
Aleman
Schoolerville
Jonesboro
Pancake
Turnersville
Mosheim
Valley Mills Muni
TEXAS BRAZOS TRAIL
Springdale
Shive
Ireland
Parsley Grossing
MCLENNAN
Pecan Wells
White Hall
Ohio
Coryell City
Crawford
Oces
Vista
Ater
Ames
Usage
Highland
Windsor
Levita
Fairview
Purmela
WACO
Center City
Star
Evant
South Purmela
Arnett
Berry
Mountain
Gatesville
McGregor
Pearl
CORYELL
City-County
Faunt LeRoy Park
South Mountain
Oglesby
Bee House
Fort Gates
Pleasant Grove
Moline
King
Lime City
Cavitt
Mound
Slater
Leon Junction
Mother Neff SP
Long Cove
Whitson
Adamsville
Izoro
Flat
Moody
Pidcoke
The Grove
Meador Grove
Iron Bridge Park
Stampede
Winkler Park
Cold Springs
McClellan Ranch
FORT HOOD MILITARY RESERVATION
White Flint Park
Leona Park
Lometa
LAMPASAS
Topsey
Owl Creek Park
Owl Creek
Bland
McGregor Park
Moffat
Pendleton
Charping
Belton Lake
Brookhaven
Union Hill
Cedar Ridge Park
Rumley
Rogers Park
Morgans Point
Draughon-Miller Muni
Revision
Lampasas
Copperas Cove
Kay Bee Heights
Chaffin Village
Walker Village
Killeen
Temple's Lake Park
Woodland
West Cliff
Westcliff Park
Live Oak Ridge Park
Miller Spring Park
SEE P. 164
Nix
Brooke Crossing
Radios Junction
Shorthall
Kempner
Nolanville
Belton Lake
Midway
Temple
Lampasas
SEE PAGE 142
Killeen Muni
Belton
Dog Ridge
Stillhouse Park
Stillhouse Hollow Lake
Hobbs
Smith
Dana Peak Park
Union Grove Park
Union Grove
Naruna
BURNET
Oakalla
Maxdale
Ding Dong
Youngsport
BELL
Little River
Academy
Sommers Mill
Watson
Salado
Deer Pasture
Lake Victor
Sunnylane
Continue on Page 69
BURNET
AUSTIN
© DeLorme
1" = 6.3 mi (10 km)
AUSTIN
TX BRAZOS TR

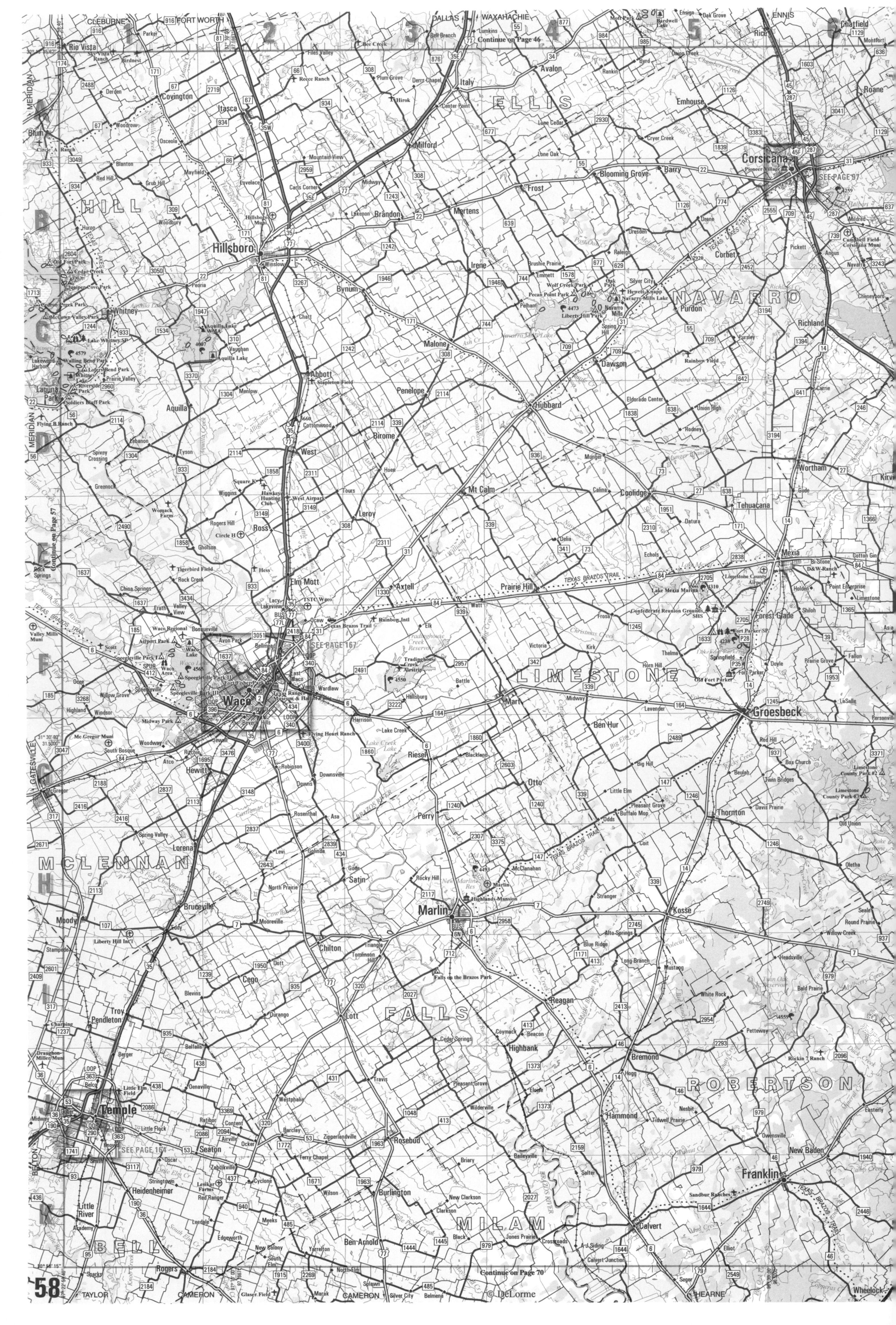

CLEBURNE
FORT WORTH
DALLAS
WAXAHACHIE
ENNIS
Continue on Page 46
Rio Vista
Covington
Itasca
Italy
Milford
ELLIS
Avalon
Emhouse
Corsicana
SEE PAGE 97
Blooming Grove
Barry
Frost
Mertens
Brandon
HILL
Hillsboro
Whitney
Lake Whitney SP
Aquilla Lake
Aquilla
Abbott
Penelope
Malone
Irene
Bynum
NAVARRO
Navarro Mills Lake
Dawson
Hubbard
Richland
Purdon
Corbet
West
Birome
Mt Calm
Coolidge
Wortham
Tehuacana
Leroy
Ross
Elm Mott
Axtell
Prairie Hill
Mexia
Continue on Page 57
TEXAS BRAZOS TRAIL
Waco
SEE PAGE 167
LIMESTONE
Mart
Groesbeck
Ben Hur
Riesel
Hewitt
Otto
Thornton
Perry
MCLENNAN
Lorena
Bruceville
Marlin
Kosse
Moody
Chilton
Cego
Troy
Lott
FALLS
Reagan
Bremond
Temple
SEE PAGE 164
ROBERTSON
Hammond
Rosebud
Franklin
Seaton
Heidenheimer
Burlington
Calvert
Little River
MILAM
BELL
Ben Arnold
Rogers
Continue on Page 70
TAYLOR
CAMERON
HEARNE
Wheelock
© DeLorme

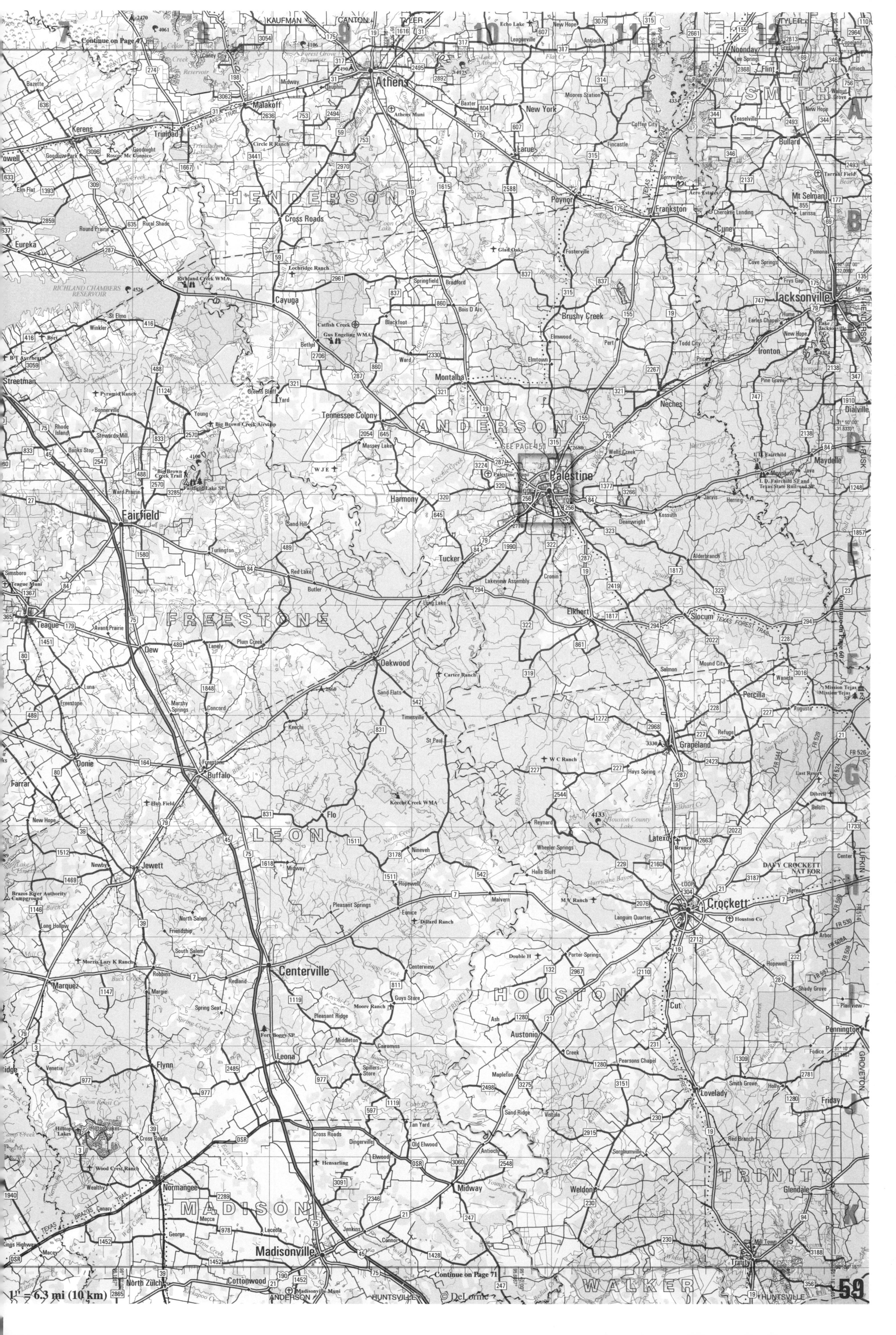

Continue on Page 47
KAUFMAN
CANTON
TYLER
Athens
Malakoff
Trinidad
Kerens
Goodlow Park
Roscoe Mc Connico
Elm Flat
Eureka
Round Prairie
Rural Shade
Circle R Ranch
Cross Roads
HENDERSON
Richland Creek WMA
RICHLAND CHAMBERS RESERVOIR
Lochridge Ranch
Cayuga
St Elmo
Winkler
Streetman
Pyramid Ranch
Catfish Creek
Gus Engeling WMA
Bethel
Blackfoot
Springfield
Bradford
Bois D Arc
Ward
Montalba
Tennessee Colony
Massey Lake
Greens Bluff
Yard
Young
Big Brown Creek Airstrip
Fairfield Lake SP
Ward Prairie
Fairfield
Turlington
Sand Hill
Red Lake
Butler
Harmony
Tucker
Palestine
Palestine Muni
SEE PAGE 151
ANDERSON
Elkhart
Slocum
TEXAS FOREST TRAIL
Echo Lake
New Hope
Antioch
Leagueville
Moores Station
Coffee City
Fincastle
New York
Larue
Poynor
Frankston
Berryville
Aero Estates
Cherokee Lending
Cuney
Reese
Fosterville
Glad Oaks
Brushy Creek
Elmwood
Elmtown
Pert
Todd City
Neches
Wells Creek
Noonday
Lee Springs
Flint
SMITH
Teaselville
Bullard
Tarrant Field
Mt Selman
Larissa
Pomona
Cove Springs
Frys Gap
Jacksonville
Mixon
Earles Chapel
Hume
New Hope
Ironton
Pine Grove
Dialville
Maydelle
Jarvis
Herring
Kossuth
Deanwright
Alderbranch
Cronin
Lakeview Assembly
Long Lake
FREESTONE
Teague
Teague Muni
Avant Prairie
Dew
Plum Creek
Luna
Freestone
Donie
Farrar
New Hope
Buffalo
Hub Field
Marshy Springs
Concord
Oakwood
Carter Ranch
Sand Flats
Timesville
Keechi
St Paul
Mound City
Salmon
Waneta
Percilla
Mission Tejas
Augusta
Refuge
Grapeland
Hays Spring
W C Ranch
Reynard
Houston County Lake
Wheeler Springs
Halls Bluff
Latexo
Bruner
Last Resort
Dibrell
Belott
Center
DAVY CROCKETT NAT FOR
Crockett
Houston Co
Langum Quarter
M Y Ranch
Keechi Creek WMA
Flo
LEON
Nineveh
Hopewell
Midway
Jewett
Newby
Brazos River Authority Campground
Long Hollow
North Salem
Friendship
South Salem
Morris Lazy K Ranch
Marquez
Robbins
Margie
Redland
Centerville
Spring Seat
Pleasant Springs
Eunice
Dillard Ranch
Malvern
Centerview
Guys Store
Moore Ranch
Pleasant Ridge
Middleton
Fort Boggy SP
Leona
Flynn
Venetia
Hilltop Lakes
Cross Roads
Wood Crest Ranch
Wealthy
Normangee
MADISON
Mecca
George
Madisonville
Madisonville Muni
North Zulch
Cottonwood
Jenkins
Connor
Midway
Dingerville
Elwood
Old Elwood
Hensarling
Antioch
Spillers Store
Double H
Porter Springs
HOUSTON
Ash
Austonio
Cut
Creek
Pearsons Chapel
Mapleton
Sand Ridge
Vistula
Lovelady
Smith Grove
Holly
Friday
Red Branch
Sorghumville
Weldon
TRINITY
Glendale
Mill Town
Trinity
Hopewell
Shady Grove
Plainview
Pennington
Fodice
GROVETON
LUFKIN
RUSK
WALKER
HUNTSVILLE
ANDERSON
Continue on Page 71
Continue on Page 60
1" = 6.3 mi (10 km)
© DeLorme

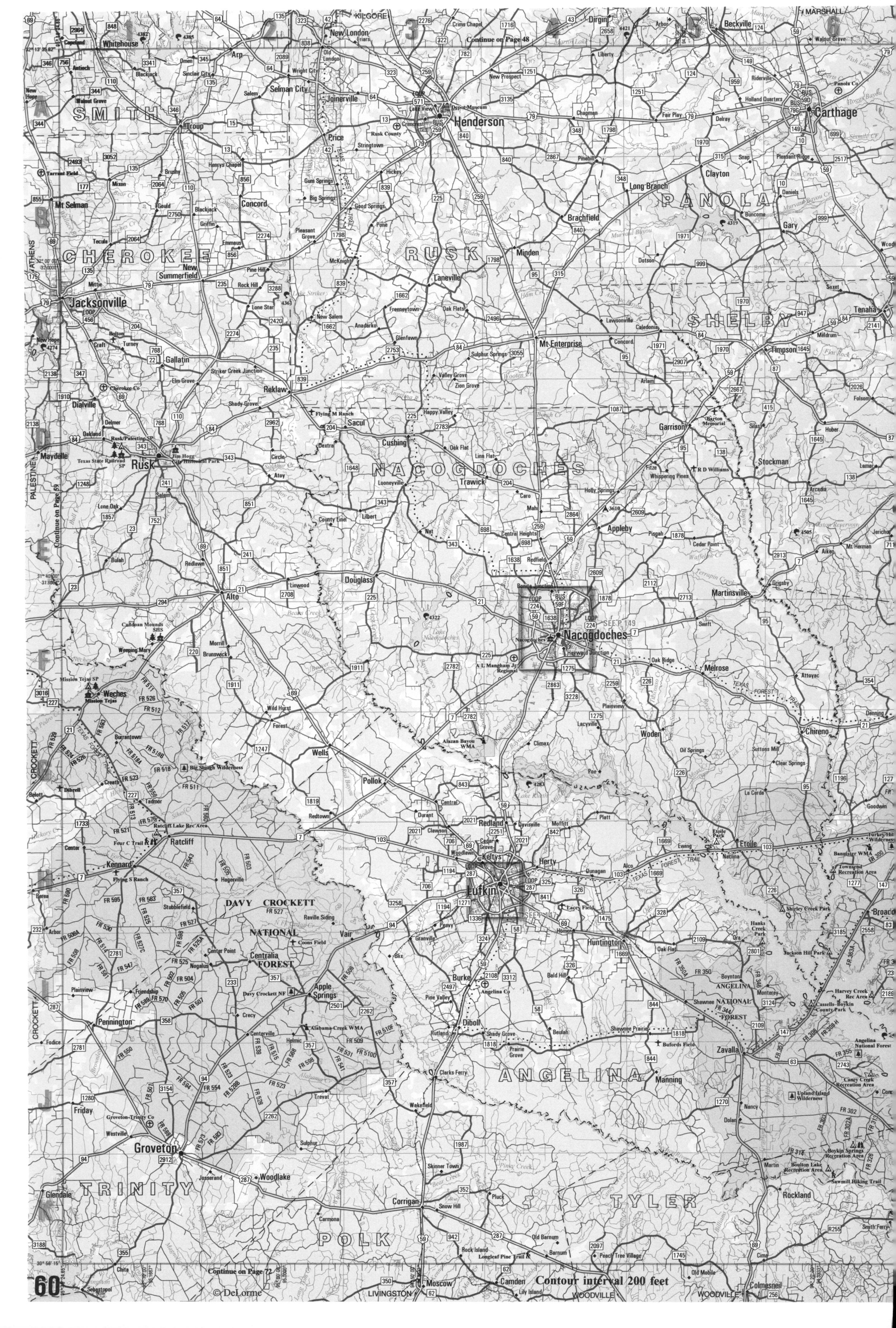

KILGORE
MARSHALL
Continue on Page 48
Continue on Page 59
Continue on Page 72
Contour interval 200 feet
SMITH
CHEROKEE
RUSK
PANOLA
SHELBY
NACOGDOCHES
ANGELINA
TRINITY
TYLER
POLK
HOUSTON
DAVY CROCKETT
NATIONAL
FOREST
ANGELINA NATIONAL FOREST
ATHENS
PALESTINE
CROCKETT
LIVINGSTON
WOODVILLE
Whitehouse
New London
Beckville
Arp
Troup
Henderson
Carthage
Selman City
Joinerville
Price
Mt Selman
Concord
Minden
Brachfield
Long Branch
Clayton
Gary
Jacksonville
New Summerfield
Caneville
Mt Enterprise
Tenaha
Timpson
Gallatin
Reklaw
Dialville
Sacul
Cushing
Garrison
Rusk
Trawick
Stockman
Appleby
Alto
Douglass
Martinsville
Nacogdoches
Melrose
Weches
Chireno
Wells
Woden
Pollok
Redland
Ratcliff
Kennard
Etoile
Lufkin
Huntington
Apple Springs
Centralia
Diboll
Zavalla
Pennington
Manning
Groveton
Woodlake
Corrigan
Rockland
Moscow
Camden
Colmesneil
Friday
Glendale

©DeLorme

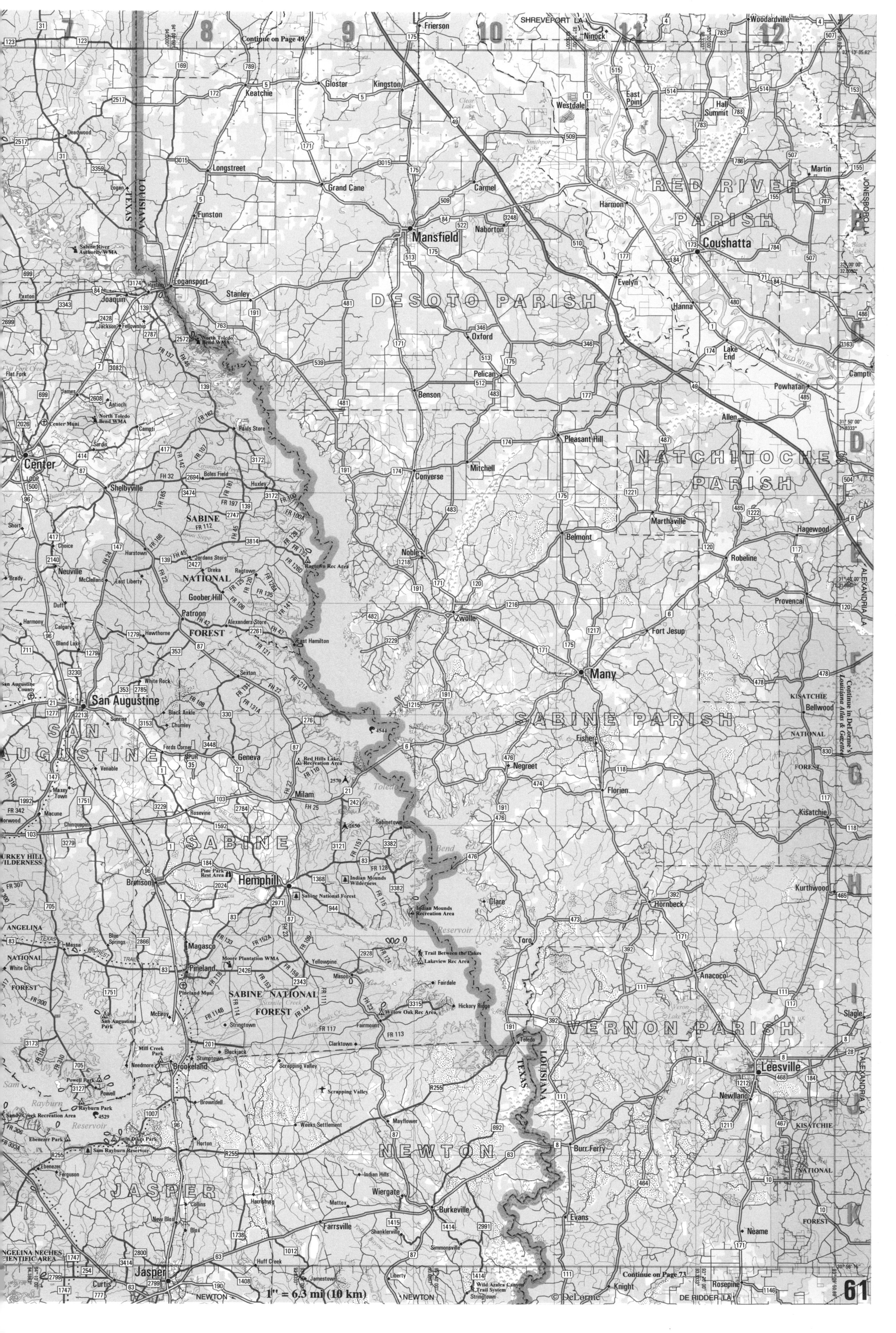

Continue on Page 49
Continue on Page 73
Continue in DeLorme's Louisiana Atlas & Gazetteer

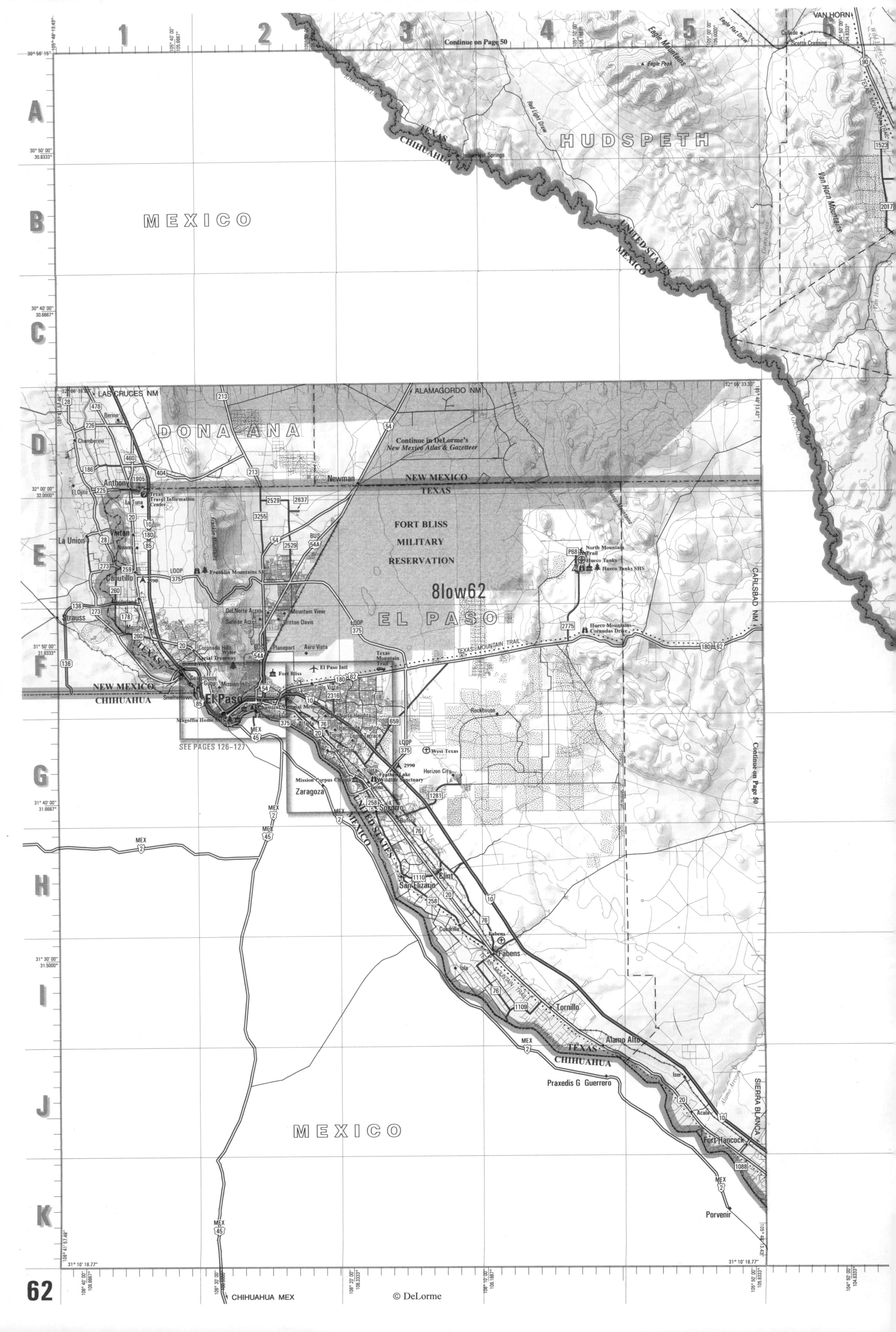

Continue on Page 50
Continue in DeLorme's New Mexico Atlas & Gazetteer
Continue on Page 50

© DeLorme

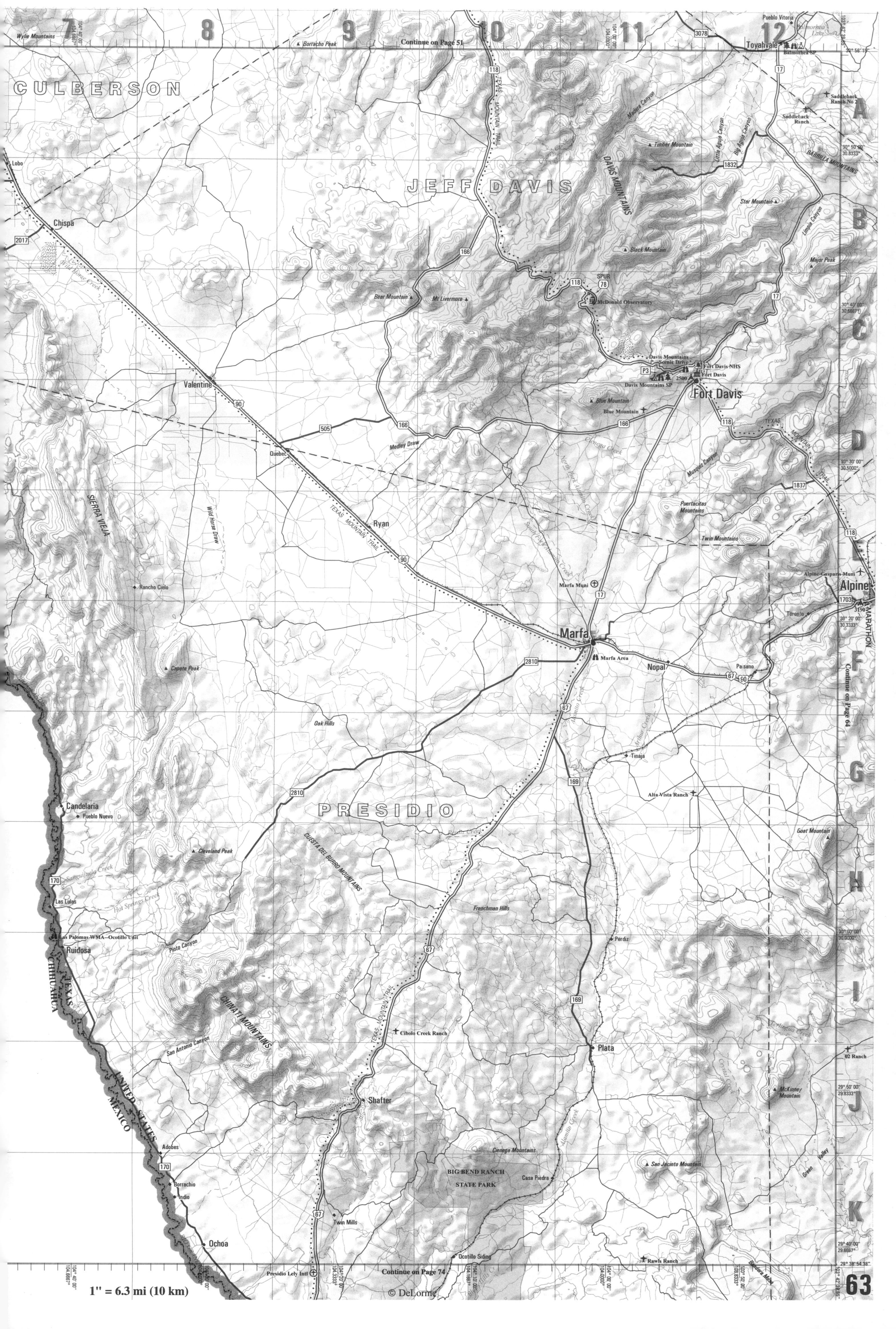

Continue on Page 51

Continue on Page 64

Continue on Page 74

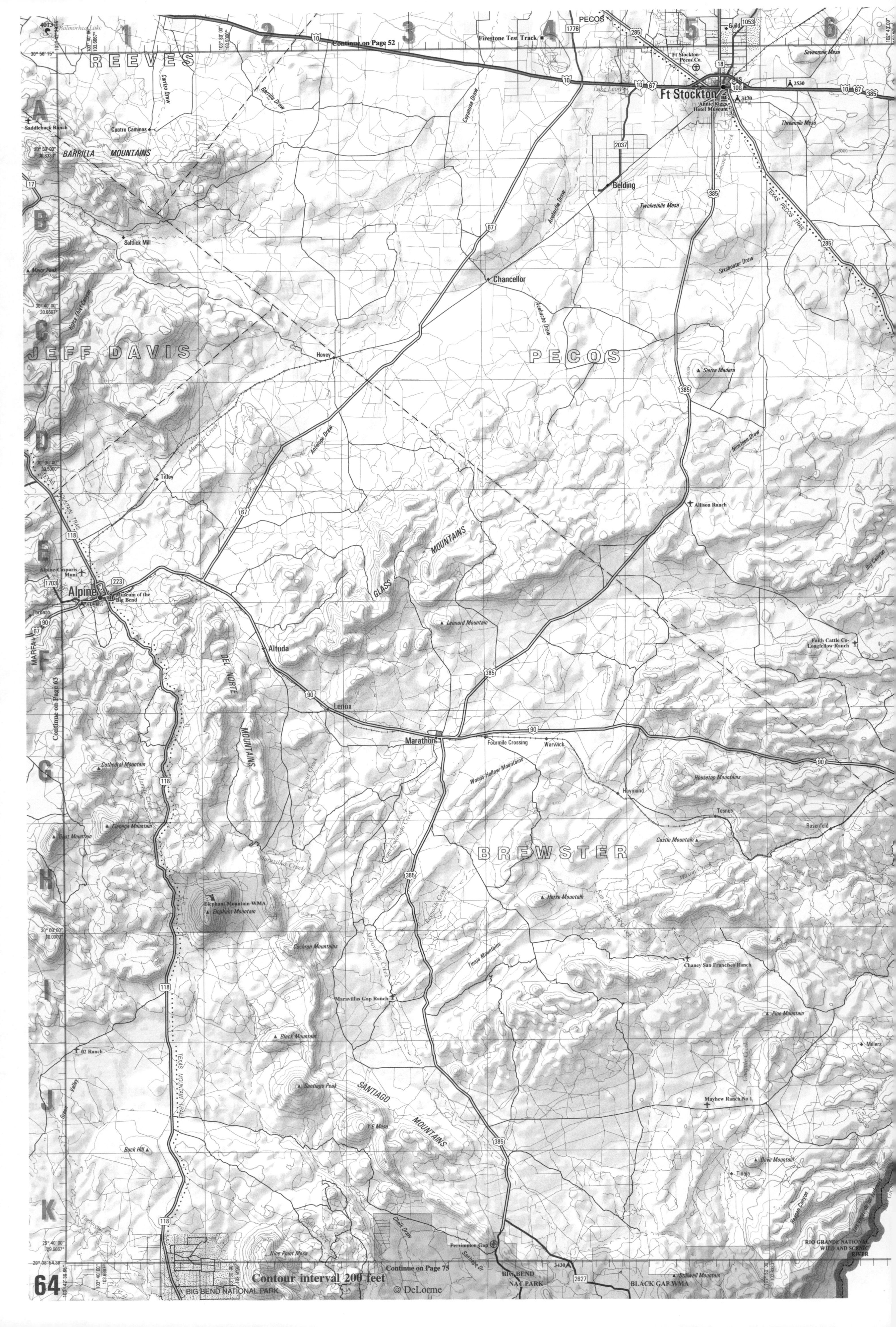
Continue on Page 52
Continue on Page 63
Continue on Page 75
Contour interval 200 feet
© DeLorme
REEVES
JEFF DAVIS
PECOS
BREWSTER
Ft Stockton
Ft Stockton-Pecos Co
Annie Riggs Hotel Museum
Firestone Test Track
Lake Leon
Sevenmile Mesa
Threemile Mesa
Twelvemile Mesa
Gold
Belding
Chancellor
Hovey
Sierra Madera
Sixshooter Draw
Nineteen Draw
Allison Ranch
Saddleback Ranch
Cuatro Caminos
BARRILLA MOUNTAINS
Barrilla Draw
Carrizo Draw
Coyanosa Draw
Saltlick Mill
Major Peak
Horse Thief Canyon
Antelope Draw
Titley
Alpine
Alpine-Casparis Muni
Museum of the Big Bend
MARFA
Altuda
GLASS MOUNTAINS
Leonard Mountain
DEL NORTE MOUNTAINS
Lenox
Marathon
Fourmile Crossing
Warwick
Woods Hollow Mountains
Housetop Mountains
Haymond
Tesnus
Rosenfeld
Castle Mountain
Faith Cattle Co-Longfellow Ranch
Big Canyon
Cathedral Mountain
Goat Mountain
Cienega Mountain
Maravillas Creek
Elephant Mountain WMA
Elephant Mountain
Horse Mountain
Cochran Mountains
Tinaja Mountains
Chaney San Francisco Ranch
Maravillas Gap Ranch
Pine Mountain
Black Mountain
Millers
02 Ranch
Santiago Peak
SANTIAGO MOUNTAINS
Y E Mesa
Mayhew Ranch No 1
Dove Mountain
Tinaja
Buck Hill
TEXAS MOUNTAIN TRAIL
TEXAS PECOS TRAIL
Persimmon Gap
Nine Point Mesa
Chalk Draw
Heath Canyon
RIO GRANDE NATIONAL WILD AND SCENIC RIVER
BIG BEND NAT PARK
BIG BEND NATIONAL PARK
BLACK GAP WMA
Stillwell Mountain

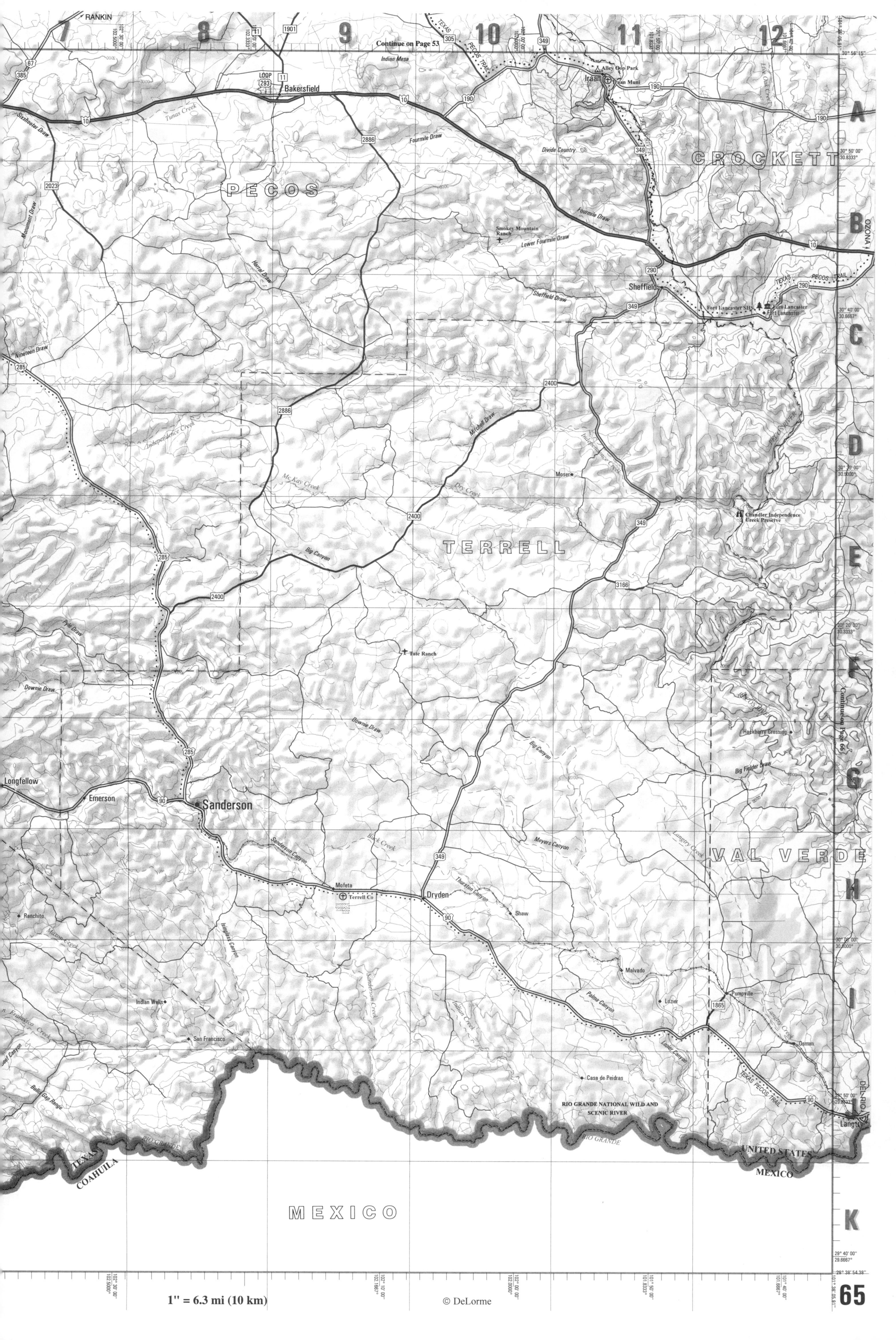

Continue on Page 53
Continue on Page 66
PECOS
CROCKETT
TERRELL
VAL VERDE
MEXICO
COAHUILA
TEXAS
UNITED STATES
RANKIN
Bakersfield
Iraan
Sheffield
Sanderson
Dryden
Longfellow
Emerson
Mofeta
Fort Lancaster SHS
Chandler Independence Creek Preserve
RIO GRANDE NATIONAL WILD AND SCENIC RIVER
Pumpville
Langtry
OZONA
DEL RIO
1'' = 6.3 mi (10 km)

© DeLorme

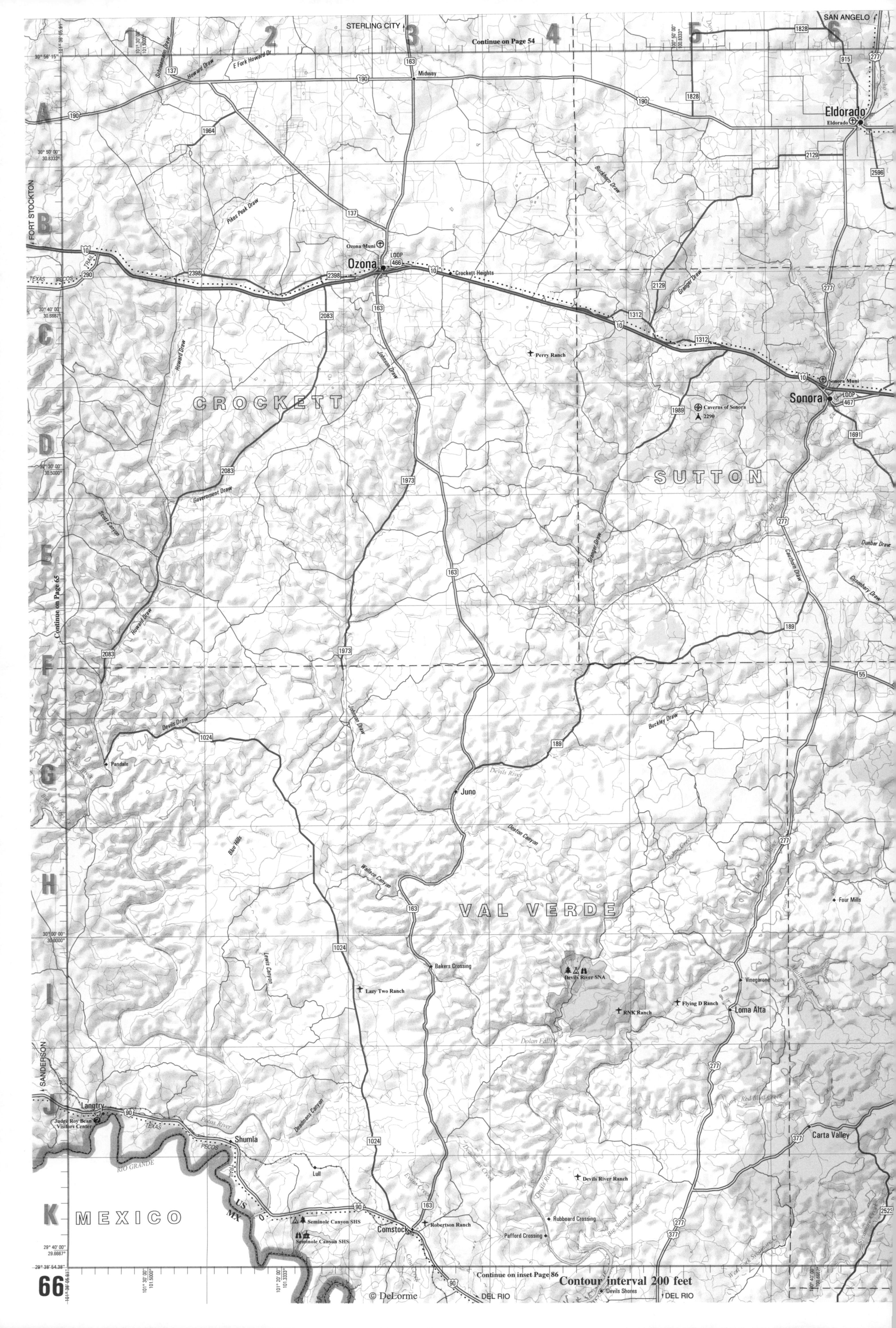

STERLING CITY
SAN ANGELO
Continue on Page 54
FORT STOCKTON
Continue on Page 65
SANDERSON
Eldorado
Ozona
Ozona Muni
Midway
Crockett Heights
Perry Ranch
Sonora
Sonora Muni
Caverns of Sonora
2290
CROCKETT
SUTTON
VAL VERDE
MEXICO
Howard Draw
E Fork Howard Dr
Pikes Peak Draw
Buckhorn Draw
Granger Draw
Johnson Draw
Government Draw
Scott Canyon
Dunbar Draw
Cusenbary Draw
Buckley Draw
Devils Draw
Pandale
Devils River
Juno
Dunlon Canyon
Blue Hills
Wallace Canyon
Lewis Canyon
Bakers Crossing
Lazy Two Ranch
Devils River SNA
RNK Ranch
Flying D Ranch
Vinegarone
Loma Alta
Four Mills
Dolan Falls
Langtry
Judge Roy Bean Visitors Center
Pecos River
Shumla
Deadmans Canyon
RIO GRANDE
Lull
Red Bluff Creek
Carta Valley
Devils River Ranch
Rubboard Crossing
Pafford Crossing
Big Satan Creek
Seminole Canyon SHS
Comstock
Robertson Ranch
Continue on inset Page 86
Contour interval 200 feet
Devils Shores
DEL RIO
© DeLorme

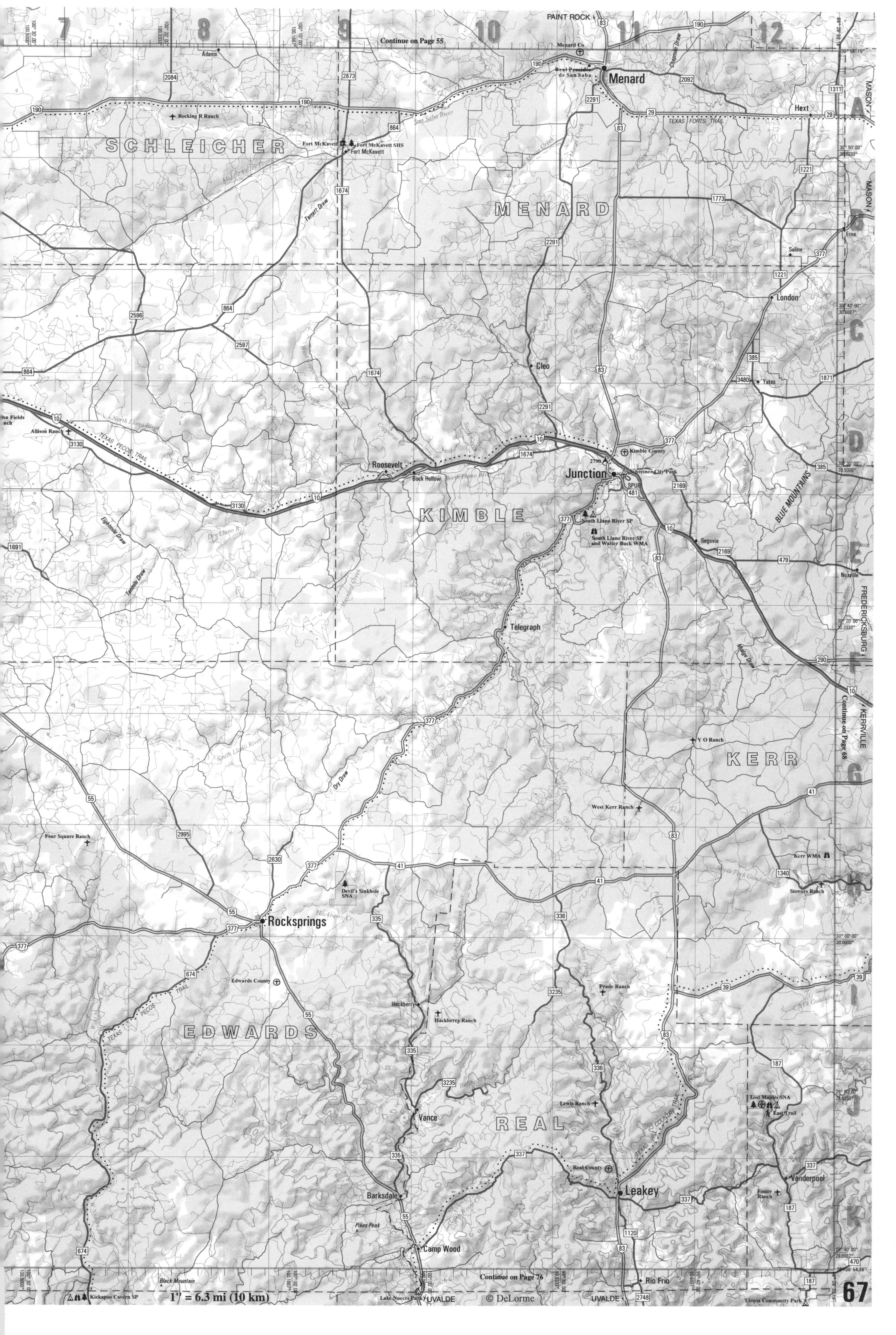
7
8
9
10
11
12
PAINT ROCK
Continue on Page 55
Adams
Menard Co
Real Presidio de San Saba
Menard
2084
2873
190
2092
2291
29
TEXAS FORTS TRAIL
Hext
1311
MASON
Rocking R Ranch
San Saba River
864
SCHLEICHER
Fort McKavett
Fort McKavett SHS
Middle Valley Prong
Terrett Draw
1674
1221
MENARD
1773
2291
Saline
377
Erna
1221
London
2596
864
2597
West Bear Creek
Cleo
385
3480
Yates
1871
1674
83
2291
Allison Ranch
3130
TEXAS PECOS TRAIL
North Llano River
10
377
Kimble County
Roosevelt
Buck Hollow
1674
Junction
Schreiner City Park
SPUR 481
2169
BLUE MOUNTAINS
385
3130
KIMBLE
377
South Llano River SP
South Llano River SP and Walter Buck WMA
Segovia
2169
479
Knoxville
1691
Eightmile Draw
Tenmile Draw
Dry Llano R.
South Llano R.
Little Paint Cr.
Telegraph
FREDERICKSBURG
290
10
Continue on Page 68
KERRVILLE
377
South Llano River
Dry Draw
Y O Ranch
KERR
55
41
West Kerr Ranch
Four Square Ranch
2995
83
2630
377
41
Kerr WMA
Devil's Sinkhole SNA
41
1340
Stowers Ranch
55
377
Rocksprings
Hackberry Cr.
335
336
377
674
39
TEXAS PECOS TRAIL
Edwards County
Prade Ranch
3235
39
Hackberry
Hackberry Ranch
55
EDWARDS
335
83
187
336
3235
Lewis Ranch
Lost Maples SNA
East Trail
Vance
REAL
TEXAS HILL COUNTRY TRAIL
335
337
Real County
337
Vanderpool
Barksdale
Leakey
337
Foster Ranch
187
Pikes Peak
55
1120
674
Camp Wood
83
470
Continue on Page 76
Rio Frio
187
Black Mountain
Kickapoo Cavern SP
1" = 6.3 mi (10 km)
Lake Nueces Park
UVALDE
© DeLorme
UVALDE
2748
Utopia Community Park
A
B
C
D
E
F
G
H
I
J
K

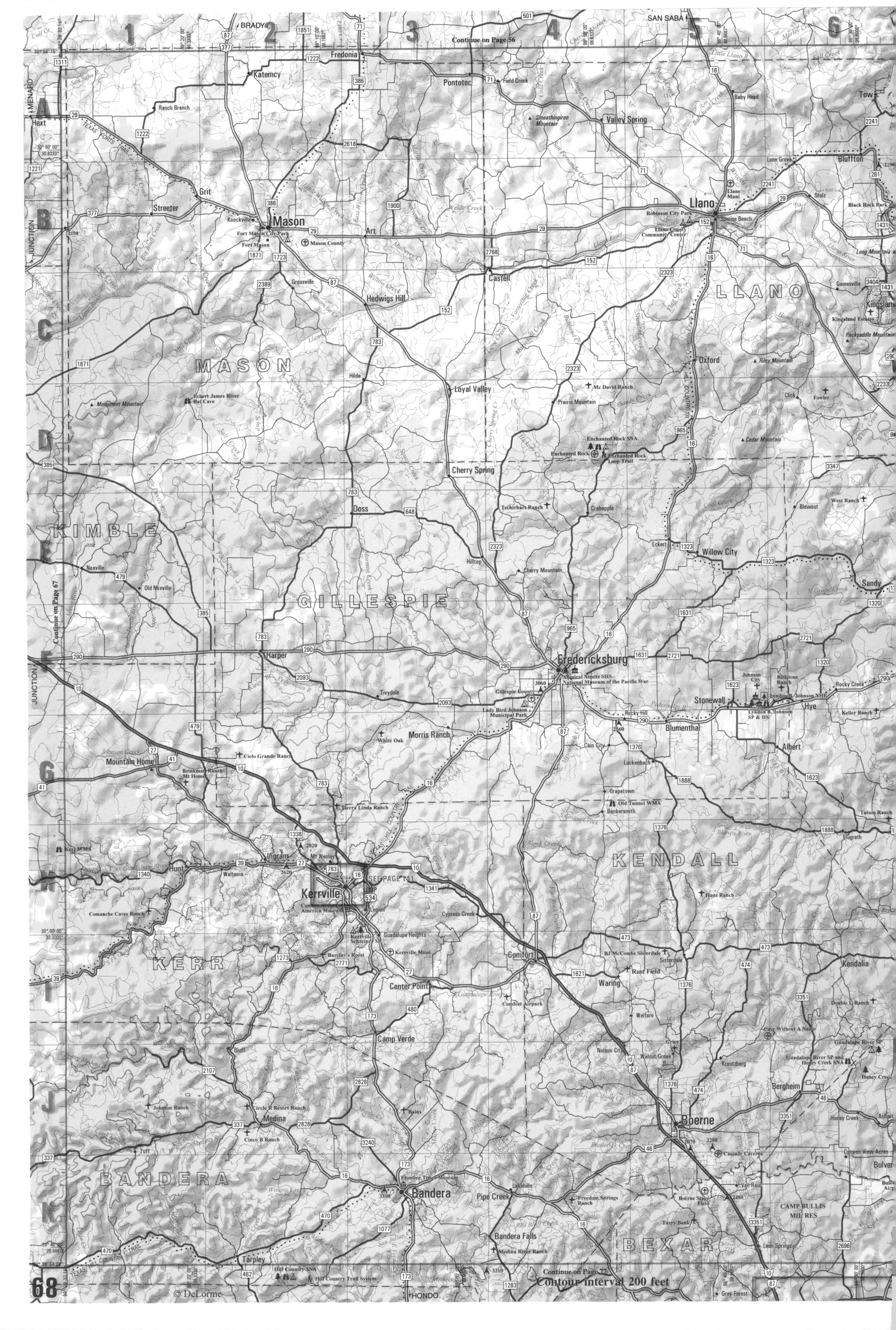

Continue on Page 56
MASON
LLANO
KIMBLE
GILLESPIE
KENDALL
KERR
BANDERA
BEXAR
Mason
Llano
Fredericksburg
Kerrville
Comfort
Boerne
Bandera
Continue on Page 67
Continue on Page 77
Contour interval 200 feet
© DeLorme

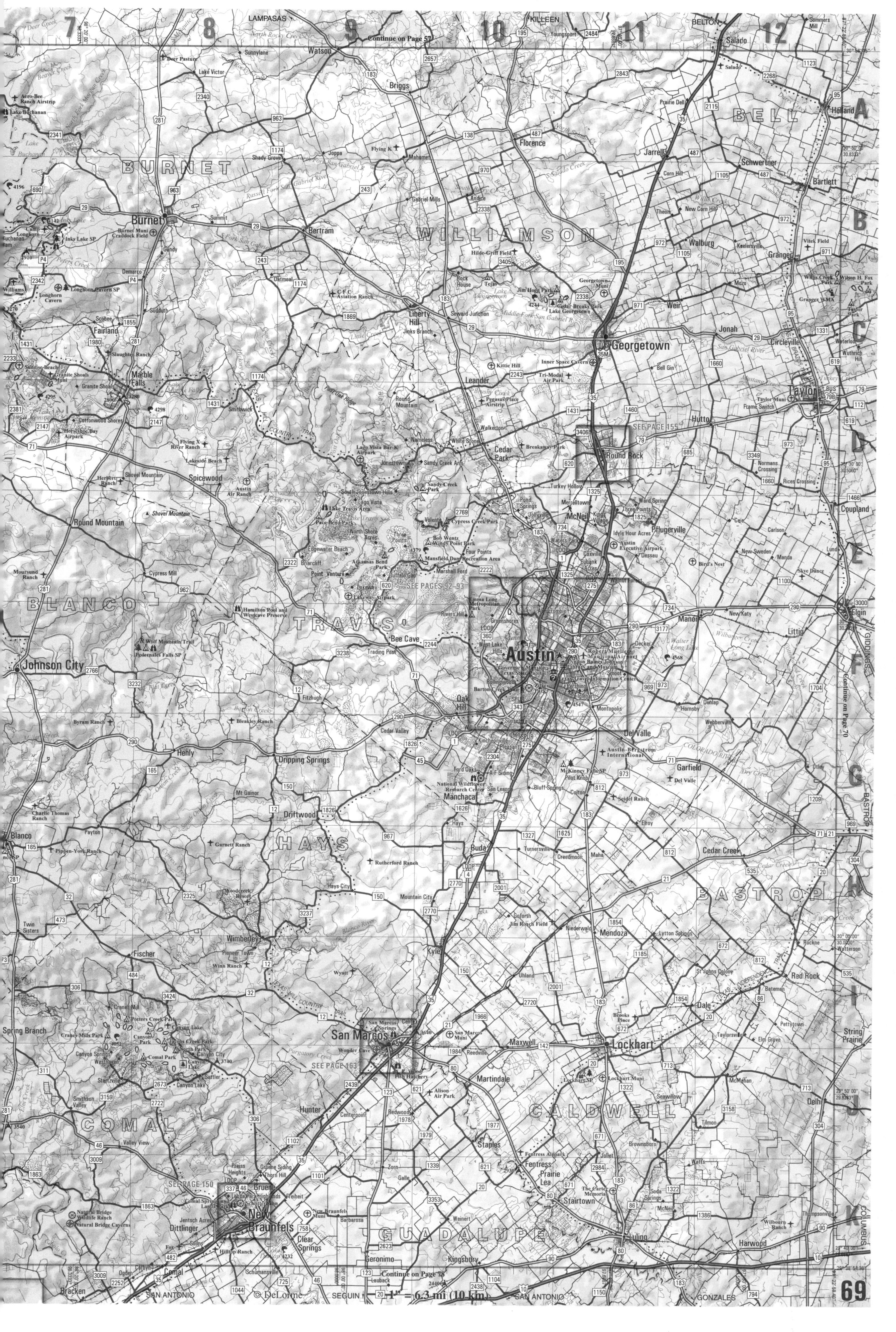
7
8
9
10
11
12
LAMPASAS
KILLEEN
BELTON
Continue on Page 57
Salado
Sommers Mill
Deer Pasture
Sunnylane
Watson
Youngsport
Lake Victor
Briggs
Acro-Bee Ranch Airstrip
Lake Buchanan
Prairie Dell
Holland
A
BELL
BURNET
Shady Grove
Joppa
Flying K
Mahomet
Florence
Jarrell
Schwertner
Corn Hill
Bartlett
Andice
Gabriel Mills
Burnet
Summit
Bertram
Burnet Muni Craddock Field
Inks Lake SP
WILLIAMSON
Theon
New Corn Hill
B
Hilde-Griff Field
Walburg
Keelersville
Vitek Field
Granger
Gandy
Demarco
Oatmeal
Longhorn Cavern SP
Longhorn Cavern
Williams
Rock House
Tejas
C F C Aviation Ranch
Jim Hogg Park
Cedar Breaks Park
Lake Georgetown
Georgetown Muni
Willis Creek Park
Wilson H. Fox Park
Granger WMA
Taylor Park
Sudduth
Seward Junction
Liberty Hill
Jinks Branch
Weir
Jonah
Circleville
Waterloo
Wuthrich Hill
C
Scobee
Fairland
Slaughter Ranch
Sunrise Beach
Granite Shoals
Marble Falls
Kittie Hill
Inner Space Cavern
Georgetown
Bell Gin
Tri-Modal Air Park
Leander
Round Mountain
Pegasus Place Airstrip
Taylor
Taylor Muni
Frame Switch
Smithwick
Cottonwood Shores
Horseshoe Bay Airpark
Walkerton
White Stone
Nameless
Hutto
SEE PAGE 155
Round Rock
Flying X River Ranch
Lakeside Beach
Lago Vista Bar-K Airpark
Jonestown
Sandy Creek Arpt
Cedar Park
Breakaway Park
D
Normans Crossing
Rices Crossing
Herbert Ranch
Shovel Mountain
Spicewood
Austin Air Ranch
South Jonestown Hills
Sandy Creek Park
Turkey Hollow
Round Mountain
Shovel Mountain
Lake Travis Area
Pace Bend Park
Lago Vista
Volente
Cypress Creek Park
Pond Springs
Jollyville
Merrelltown
McNeil
Kings Village
Ward Spring
Three Points
Pflugerville
Coupland
Cele
Carlson
North Shore Acres
Three Points
Bob Wentz Windy Point Park
Mansfield Dam Recreation Area
Four Points
Waters Park
Idyle Hour Acres
Austin Executive Airpark
Dessau
Bird's Nest
New Sweden
Manda
Lund
E
Moursund Ranch
Cypress Mill
Edgewater Beach
Briarcliff
Arkansas Bend Park
Point Venture
Buffalo Gap
Marshall Ford
Coxville
Eubank Acres
Walnut Forest
Skye Dance
Lakeway
Lakeway Airpark
SEE PAGES 92-93
Emma Long Metropolitan Park
BLANCO
Hamilton Pool and Westcave Preserve
TRAVIS
Rivers Hill
Greenshores
Manor
New Katy
Elgin
GIDDINGS
Bee Cave
West Lake Hills
Austin
Robert Mueller Municipal Airport
Decker
Littig
Wolf Mountain Trail
Pedernales Falls SP
Trading Post
Governor's Mansion
Texas State Capitol
Zilker Park
Barton Creek
Texas Travel Information Center
Walter E. Long Lake
F
Continue on Page 70
Johnson City
Fitzhugh
Rollingwood
Pershing
Montopolis
Dunlap
Hornsby
Oak Hill
Sunset Valley
Webberville
Byram Ranch
Bleakley Ranch
Cedar Valley
Lost Creek
Kinchenoville
Pleasant Valley
Del Valle
Henly
Dripping Springs
Austin-Bergstrom International
COLORADO RIVER
Garfield
Del Valle
Utley
Ford Oaks
National Wildflower Research Center
A-F Siding
McKinney Falls SP
Pilot Knob
Bluff Springs
Colton
Seidel Ranch
G
BASTROP
Mt Gainor
Manchaca
San Leanna
Charlie Thomas Ranch
Driftwood
Hays
Elroy
Blanco
Payton
Pippen-York Ranch
Garnett Ranch
HAYS
Rutherford Ranch
Buda
Turnersville
Creedmoor
Maha
Cedar Creek
Hays City
Mountain City
BASTROP
H
Woodcreek Resort
Goforth
Jim Ranch Field
Niederwald
Mendoza
Lytton Springs
Twin Sisters
Wimberley
Pioneer Town
Winn Ranch
Kyle
Rockne
Watterson
Fischer
Wyatt
Uhland
St Johns Colony
Red Rock
Batemen
Cranes Mill
Potters Creek Park
Canyon Lake
Canyon Park
Spring Branch
Cranes Mills Park
Jacobs Creek Park
North Park
Canyon City
Comal Park
Canyon Lake
Sattler
Canyon Springs West
Startzville
San Marcos Springs
San Marcos
Wonder Cave
SEE PAGE 163
Fish Hatchery
San Marcos Muni
Reedville
Maxwell
Lockhart
Brooks Place
Dale
Pettytown
Taylorsville
Elm Grove
String Prairie
I
Lockhart SP
Lockhart Muni
Martindale
Alison Air Park
Smithson Valley
COMAL
Hunter
Centerpoint
Redwood
CALDWELL
McMahan
Delhi
Tilmon
J
Valley View
Staples
Brownsboro
Fentress Airpark
Fentress
Prairie Lea
Zorn
Galle
Press Heights
Gruene Siding
Thorn Hill
Gruene
SEE PAGE 150
Freiheit
Jollet
The Carter Memorial
Watts
Soda Springs
McNeil
Stairtown
Natural Bridge Wildlife Ranch
Natural Bridge Caverns
Jentsch Acres
Dittlinger
New Braunfels
New Braunfels Muni
Barbarosa
Clear Springs
Weinert
GUADALUPE
Wilbourn Ranch
Thompsonville
Luling
Harwood
K
COLUMBUS
Hilltop Ranch
Fox
Solms
Comal
Ogden
Schumansville
Geronimo
Kingsbury
Continue on Page 28
Bracken
SAN ANTONIO
© DeLorme
SEGUIN
1" = 6.3 mi (10 km)
SAN ANTONIO
GONZALES

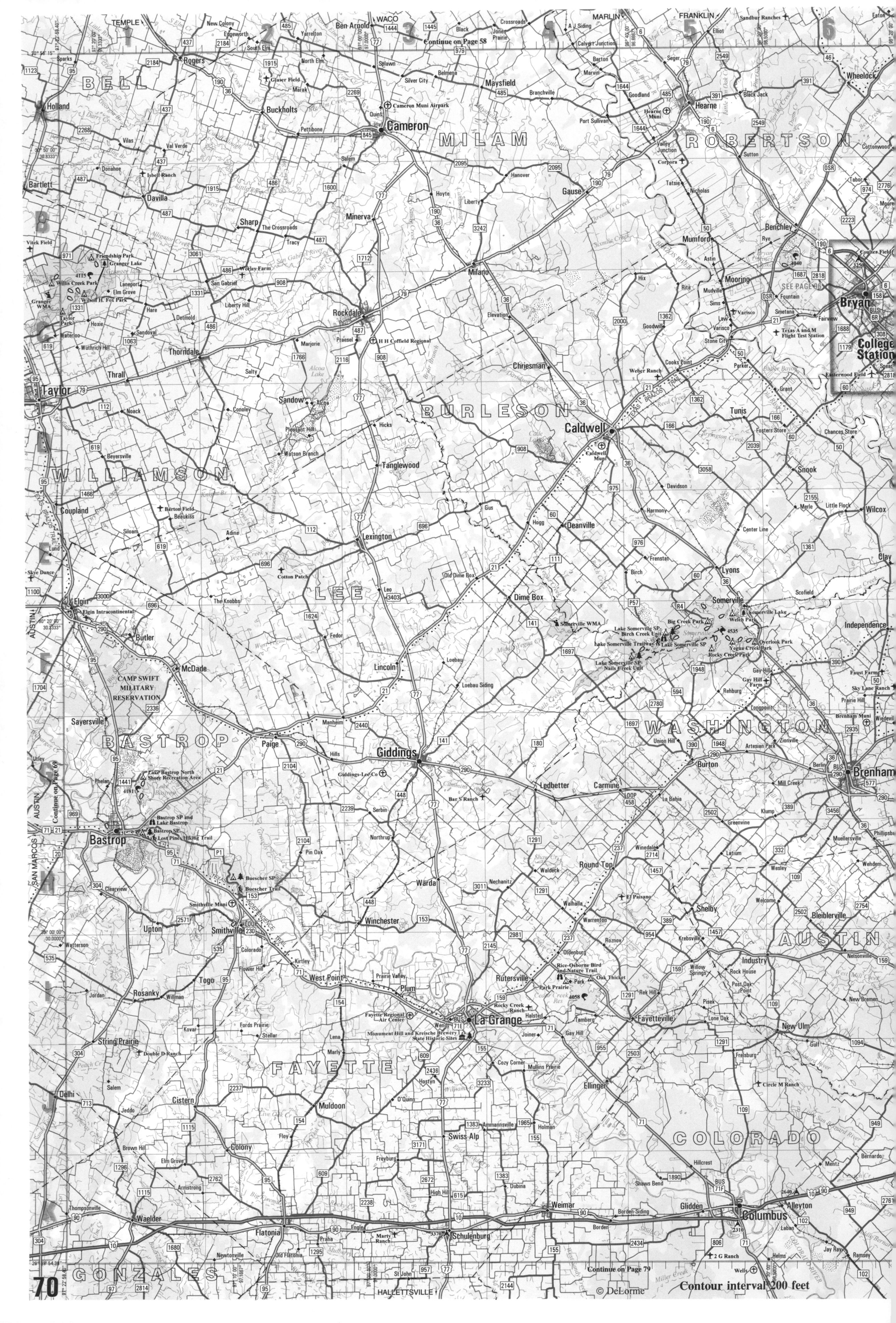
TEMPLE
WACO
MARLIN
FRANKLIN
Continue on Page 58
BELL
MILAM
ROBERTSON
BURLESON
WILLIAMSON
LEE
BASTROP
WASHINGTON
AUSTIN
FAYETTE
COLORADO
GONZALES
Holland
Rogers
Buckholts
Cameron
Maysfield
Hearne
Wheelock
Bartlett
Davilla
Sharp
Minerva
Gause
Mumford
Benchley
Milano
Rockdale
Thorndale
Taylor
Thrall
Sandow
Caldwell
Chriesman
Tunis
Snook
Bryan
College Station
Tanglewood
Coupland
Lexington
Deanville
Lyons
Somerville
Wilcox
Elgin
Dime Box
Butler
McDade
CAMP SWIFT MILITARY RESERVATION
Lincoln
Sayersville
Paige
Giddings
Independence
Brenham
Burton
Ledbetter
Carmine
Bastrop
Round Top
Shelby
Warda
Smithville
Upton
Winchester
West Point
Rosanky
La Grange
Rutersville
Fayetteville
Industry
New Ulm
Muldoon
Cistern
Ellinger
Swiss Alp
Colony
Waelder
Flatonia
Schulenburg
Weimar
Glidden
Columbus
Alleyton
HALLETTSVILLE
Continue on Page 79
Continue on Page 69
Contour interval 200 feet
© DeLorme

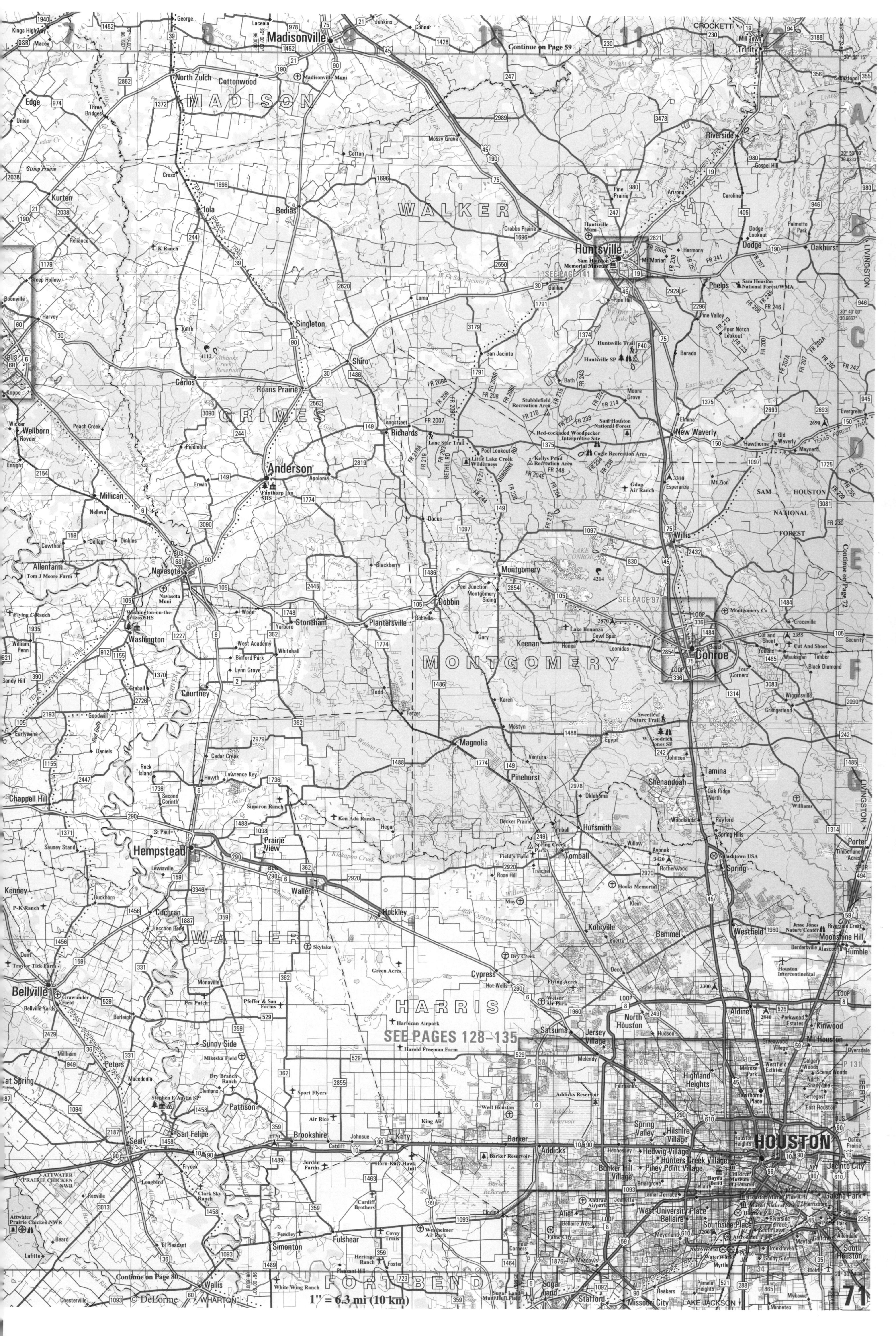

Continue on Page 59
SEE PAGE 141
SEE PAGE 97
Continue on Page 72
SEE PAGES 128–135
Continue on Page 80

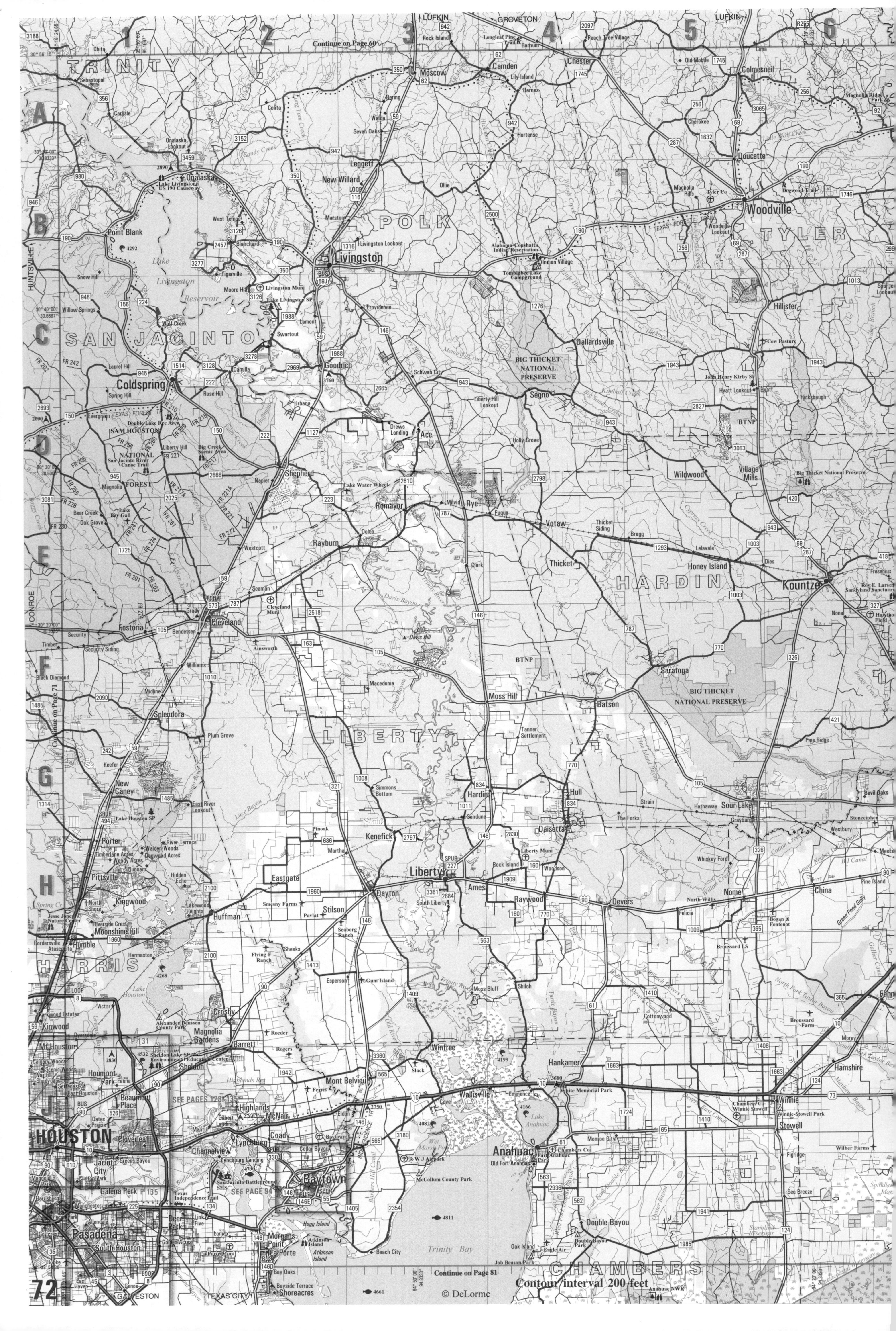
Continue on Page 60
LUFKIN
GROVETON
TRINITY
POLK
TYLER
SAN JACINTO
HARDIN
LIBERTY
HARRIS
CHAMBERS
Moscow
Camden
Chester
Colmesneil
Leggett
New Willard
Onalaska
Lake Livingston
Livingston
Woodville
Point Blank
Coldspring
Goodrich
Shepherd
Dallardsville
Segno
BIG THICKET NATIONAL PRESERVE
SAM HOUSTON NATIONAL FOREST
Hillister
Ace
Romayor
Rye
Votaw
Thicket
Kountze
Honey Island
Village Mills
Wildwood
Cleveland
Fostoria
Splendora
Saratoga
Batson
Moss Hill
Hardin
Hull
Daisetta
Sour Lake
New Caney
Porter
Kingwood
Humble
Liberty
Dayton
Ames
Raywood
Devers
Nome
China
Huffman
Crosby
Sheldon
Highlands
Mont Belvieu
Wallisville
Winnie
Stowell
Hankamer
Hamshire
Anahuac
Baytown
Channelview
HOUSTON
Pasadena
La Porte
Morgans Point
Shoreacres
Trinity Bay
Double Bayou
SEE PAGE 94
SEE PAGES 128-135
Continue on Page 71
Continue on Page 81
Contour interval 200 feet
GALVESTON
TEXAS CITY

© DeLorme

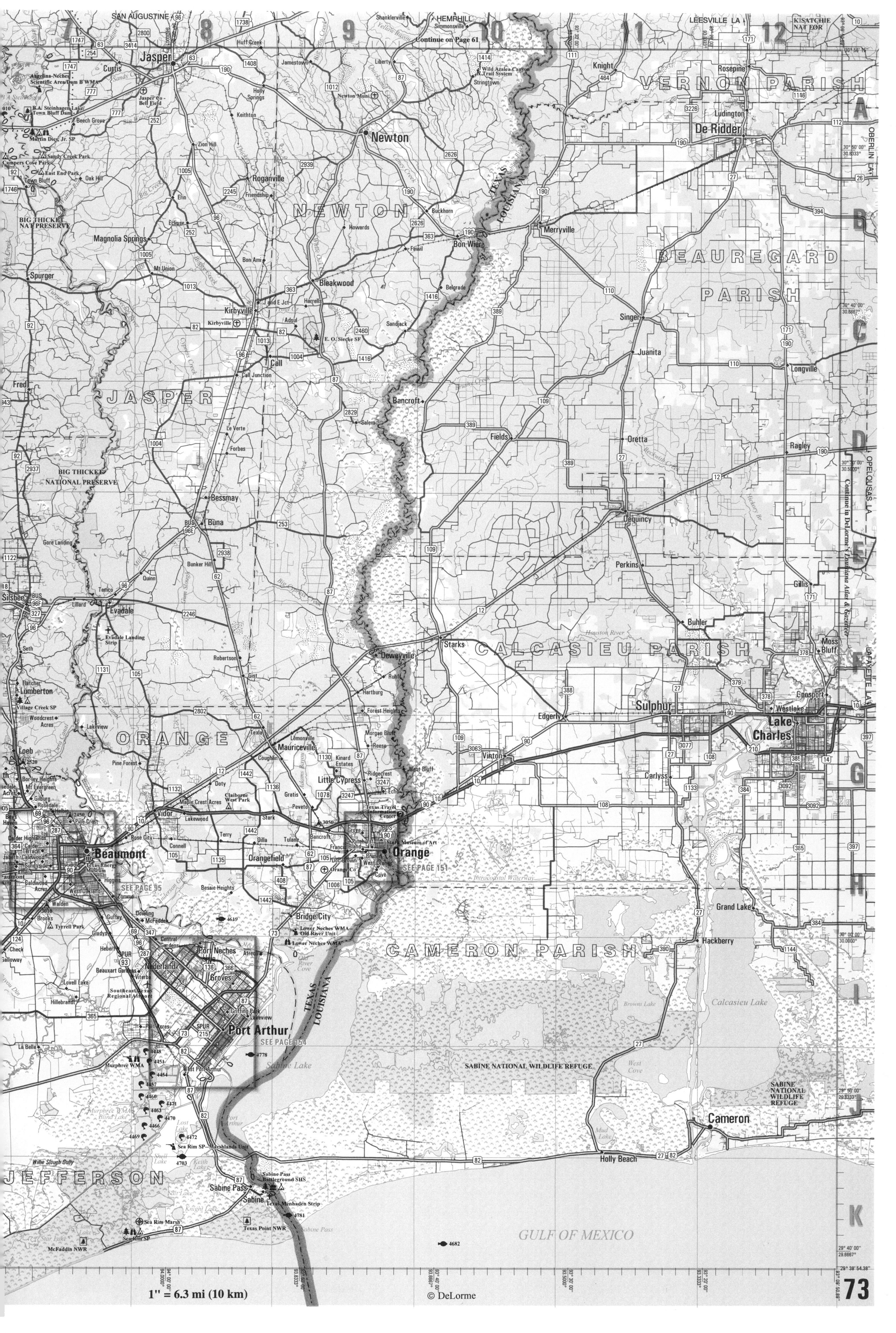

Continue on Page 61
VERNON PARISH
BEAUREGARD PARISH
NEWTON
JASPER
ORANGE
CALCASIEU PARISH
CAMERON PARISH
JEFFERSON
TEXAS
LOUISIANA
SAN AUGUSTINE
HEMPHILL
LEESVILLE LA
KISATCHIE NAT FOR
OBERLIN LA
OPELOUSAS LA
LAFAYETTE LA
Continue in DeLorme's Louisiana Atlas & Gazetteer
Jasper
Newton
De Ridder
Kirbyville
Bon Wier
Merryville
Singer
Longville
Ragley
Dequincy
Starks
Deweyville
Sulphur
Lake Charles
Vinton
Orange
Beaumont
Port Arthur
Nederland
Port Neches
Groves
Vidor
Mauriceville
Bridge City
Hackberry
Cameron
Holly Beach
Sabine Pass
Sabine
SEE PAGE 95
SEE PAGE 151
SEE PAGE 154
BIG THICKET NAT PRESERVE
BIG THICKET NATIONAL PRESERVE
SABINE NATIONAL WILDLIFE REFUGE
Sabine Lake
Calcasieu Lake
GULF OF MEXICO
1" = 6.3 mi (10 km)
© DeLorme

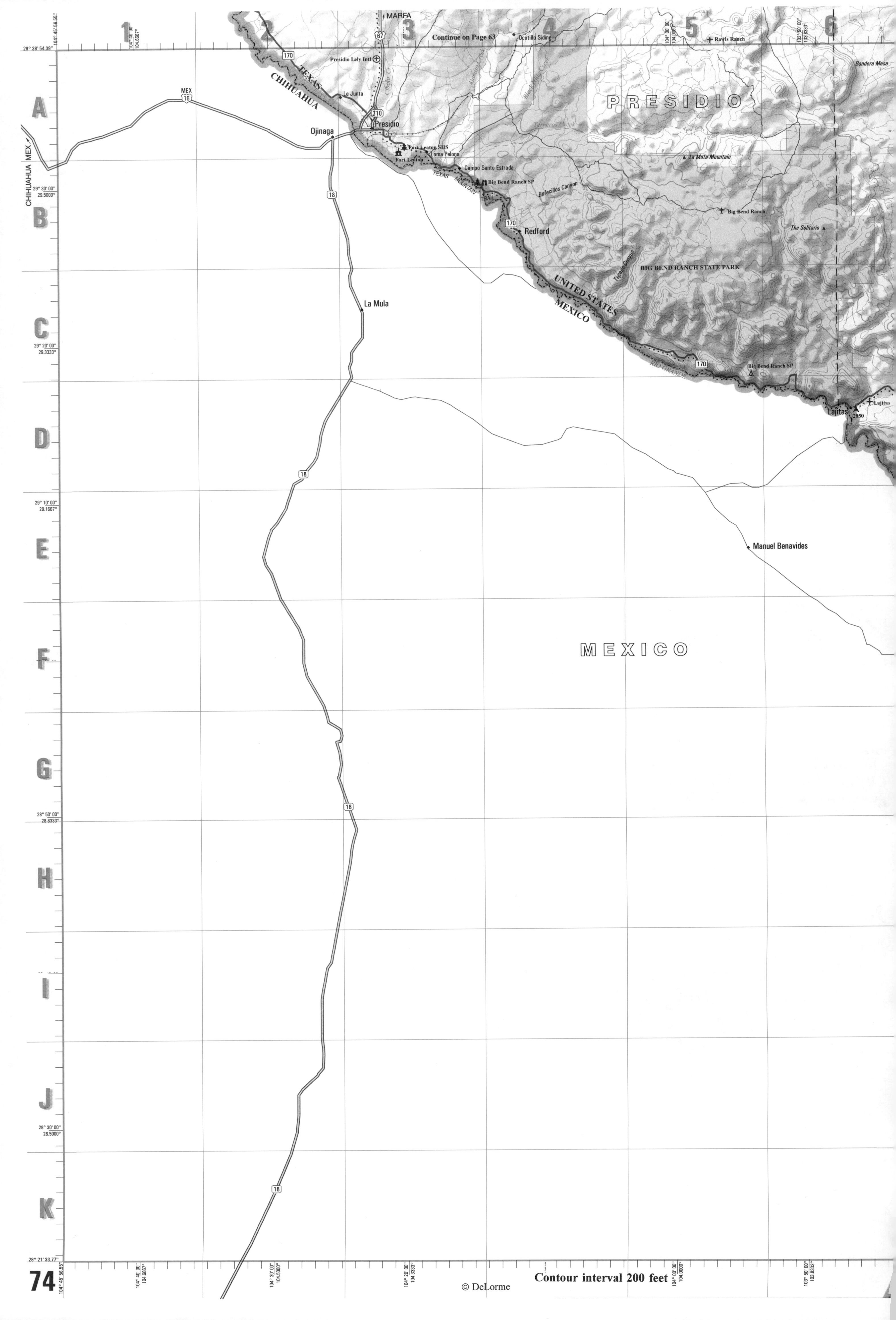

MARFA
Continue on Page 63
Ocotillo Siding
Rawls Ranch
Bandera Mesa
Presidio Lely Intl
TEXAS
CHIHUAHUA
La Junta
PRESIDIO
Presidio
Ojinaga
Fort Leaton SHS
Loma Pelona
Fort Leaton
Campo Santo Estrada
Big Bend Ranch SP
Bofecillos Canyon
La Mota Mountain
Big Bend Ranch
The Solitario
Redford
BIG BEND RANCH STATE PARK
UNITED STATES
MEXICO
La Mula
RIO GRANDE
Big Bend Ranch SP
Lajitas
Manuel Benavides
MEXICO
CHIHUAHUA MEX
MEX 16
18
170
67
310
A
B
C
D
E
F
G
H
I
J
K
1
2
3
4
5
6
Contour interval 200 feet
© DeLorme

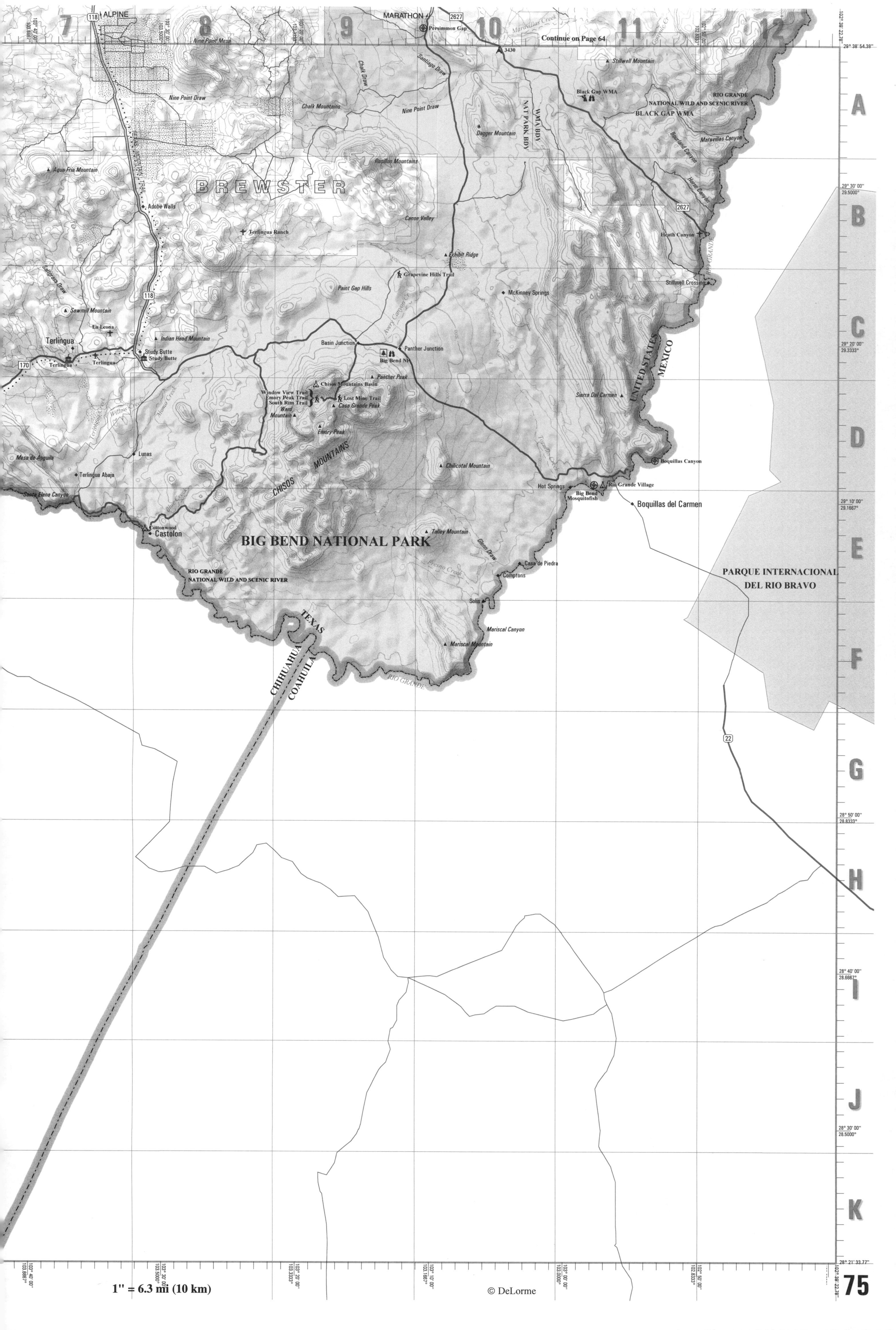

ALPINE
MARATHON
Persimmon Gap
Continue on Page 64
Nine Point Mesa
Stillwell Mountain
Black Gap WMA
RIO GRANDE
NATIONAL WILD AND SCENIC RIVER
BLACK GAP WMA
Chalk Mountains
Nine Point Draw
Dagger Mountain
NAT PARK BDY
WMA BDY
Agua Fria Mountain
Rosillos Mountains
BREWSTER
Adobe Walls
Terlingua Ranch
Canoe Valley
Heath Canyon
Exhibit Ridge
Grapevine Hills Trail
Stillwell Crossing
Paint Gap Hills
McKinney Springs
Sawmill Mountain
La Lcona
Indian Head Mountain
Terlingua
Study Butte
Basin Junction
Panther Junction
Big Bend NP
UNITED STATES
MEXICO
Panther Peak
Chisos Mountains Basin
Window View Trail
Emory Peak Trail
South Rim Trail
Lost Mine Trail
Casa Grande Peak
Ward Mountain
Emory Peak
Sierra Del Carmen
Lunas
Mesa de Anguila
Terlingua Abaja
CHISOS MOUNTAINS
Chilicotal Mountain
Boquillas Canyon
Hot Springs
Rio Grande Village
Big Bend Mosquitofish
Boquillas del Carmen
Santa Elena Canyon
Cottonwood
Castolon
Talley Mountain
BIG BEND NATIONAL PARK
Casa de Piedra
Comptons
RIO GRANDE
NATIONAL WILD AND SCENIC RIVER
PARQUE INTERNACIONAL
DEL RIO BRAVO
Solis
Mariscal Canyon
Mariscal Mountain
TEXAS
CHIHUAHUA
COAHUILA
RIO GRANDE
1" = 6.3 mi (10 km)
© DeLorme

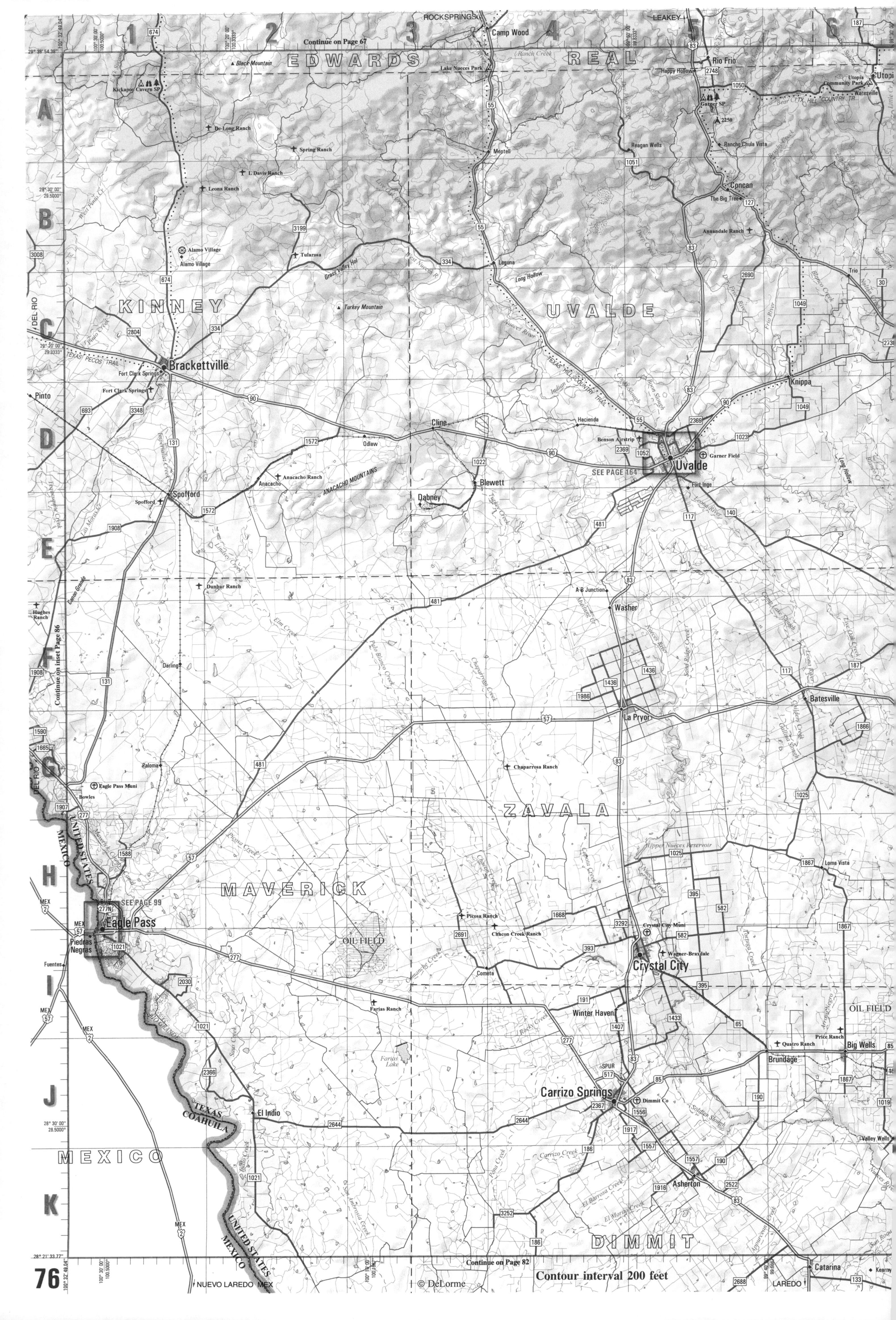

Continue on Page 67
ROCKSPRINGS
LEAKEY
Camp Wood
EDWARDS
REAL
Black Mountain
Lake Nueces Park
Rio Frio
Happy Hollow
Utopia
Kickapoo Cavern SP
De-Long Ranch
Spring Ranch
Montell
Garner SP
Reagan Wells
Rancho Chula Vista
L Davis Ranch
Leona Ranch
Concan
The Big Tree
Annandale Ranch
Alamo Village
Tularosa
Laguna
Long Hollow
Turkey Mountain
KINNEY
UVALDE
DEL RIO
Brackettville
Fort Clark Springs
TEXAS PECOS TRAIL
TEXAS HILL COUNTRY TRAIL
Pinto
Knippa
Cline
Odlew
Hacienda
Benson Airstrip
Garner Field
Uvalde
SEE PAGE 164
Anacacho Ranch
Anacacho
ANACACHO MOUNTAINS
Blewett
Dabney
Spofford
Fort Inge
Dunbar Ranch
A-B Junction
Washer
Hughes Ranch
Continue on inset Page 86
Darling
Batesville
La Pryor
Chaparrosa Ranch
Paloma
Eagle Pass Muni
Bowles
ZAVALA
Upper Nueces Reservoir
Loma Vista
MAVERICK
UNITED STATES
MEXICO
SEE PAGE 99
Eagle Pass
Piedras Negras
OIL FIELD
Picosa Ranch
Chacon Creek Ranch
Crystal City Muni
Wagner-Braxdale
Crystal City
Cometa
Fuentes
Farias Ranch
Winter Haven
Quatro Ranch
Price Ranch
Big Wells
Brundage
Farias Lake
SPUR
Carrizo Springs
Dimmit Co
El Indio
TEXAS
COAHUILA
Valley Wells
MEXICO
Asherton
DIMMIT
Continue on Page 82
Contour interval 200 feet
Catarina
Kearny
LAREDO
NUEVO LAREDO MEX
© DeLorme

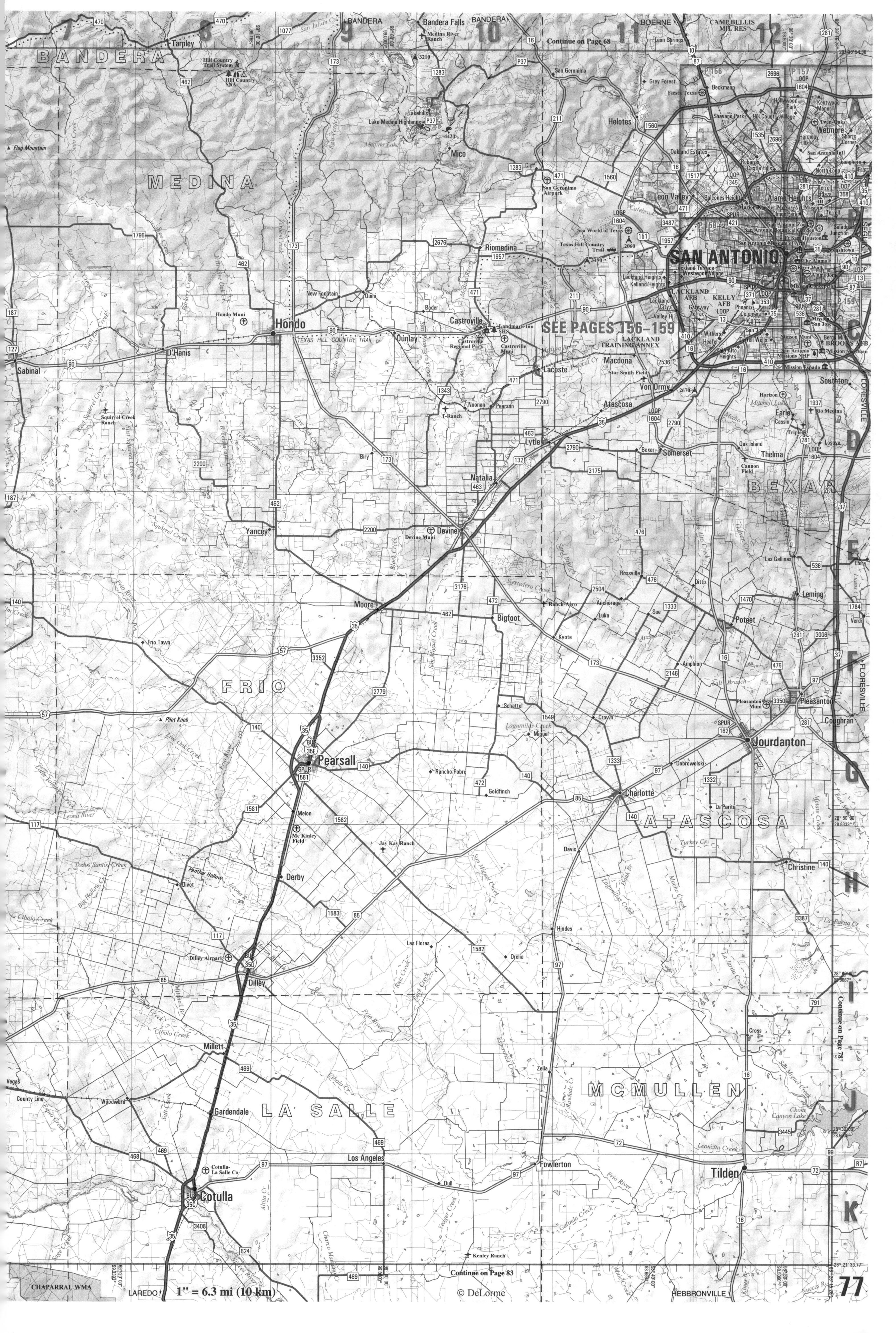

Continue on Page 68
Continue on Page 78
Continue on Page 83

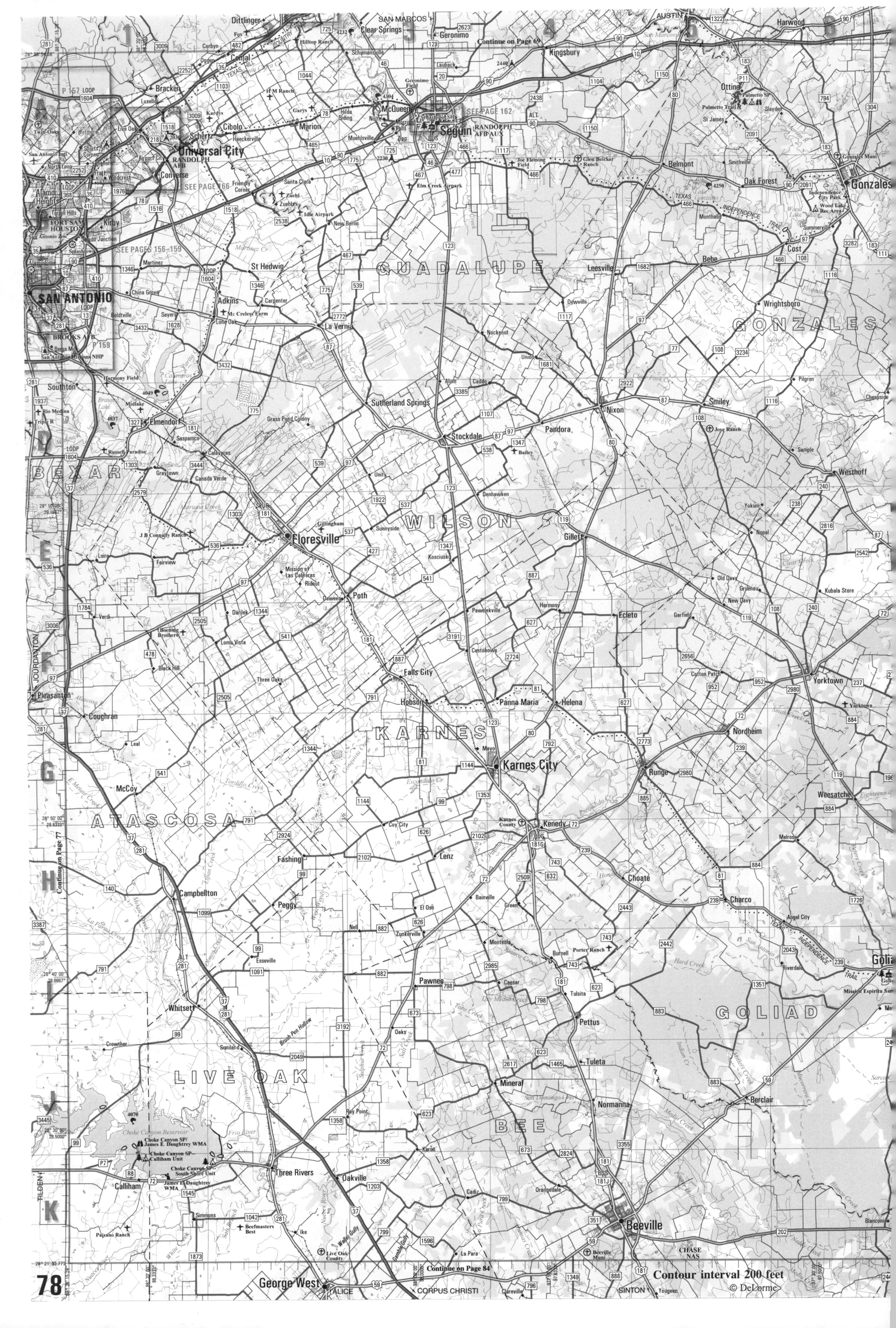
SAN MARCOS
AUSTIN
Continue on Page 69
Dittlinger
Clear Springs
Geronimo
Kingsbury
Harwood
Bracken
Comal
Cibolo
Schertz
Universal City
RANDOLPH AFB
Converse
Marion
McQueeney
Seguin
SEE PAGE 162
SEE PAGE 166
SEE PAGES 156–159
Santa Clara
Zuehl
New Berlin
Kirby
Otting
Palmetto SP
Belmont
Oak Forest
Gonzales
Cost
Bebe
Leesville
SAN ANTONIO
St Hedwig
Adkins
La Vernia
GUADALUPE
GONZALES
Wrightsboro
Nockenut
Union
Nixon
Smiley
Pilgrim
Sutherland Springs
Stockdale
Pandora
Elmendorf
Southton
BEXAR
Denhawken
Westhoff
WILSON
Floresville
Gillett
Poth
Pawelekville
Ecleto
Kubala Store
Cestohowa
Falls City
Hobson
Panna Maria
Helena
Yorktown
KARNES
Nordheim
Karnes City
Runge
Weesatche
Pleasanton
Coughran
McCoy
ATASCOSA
Kenedy
Coy City
Fashing
Lenz
Choate
Charco
Campbellton
Peggy
El Oso
Angel City
Pawnee
Whitsett
Tulsita
Pettus
GOLIAD
Tuleta
LIVE OAK
Mineral
Normanna
Berclair
BEE
Choke Canyon Reservoir
Three Rivers
Oakville
Calliham
Beeville
George West
ALICE
CORPUS CHRISTI
SINTON
Continue on Page 77
Continue on Page 84
Contour interval 200 feet
© DeLorme

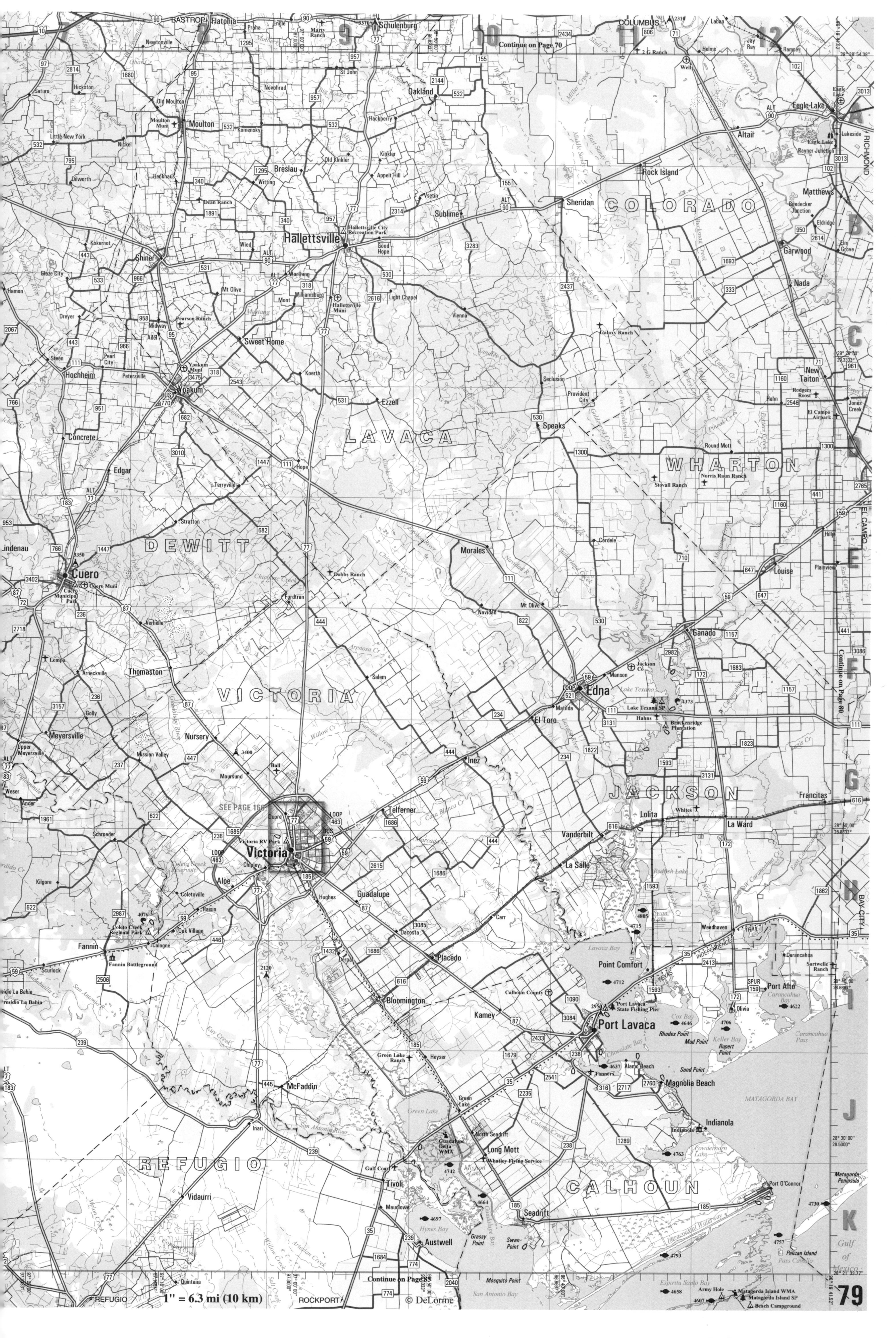

Continue on Page 70
Continue on Page 80
Continue on Page 85
SEE PAGE 166
COLORADO
LAVACA
WHARTON
DEWITT
VICTORIA
JACKSON
REFUGIO
CALHOUN
BASTROP
Flatonia
Praha
Engle
Schulenburg
COLUMBUS
Weimar
Laban
Jay Ray
Ramsey
Newtonville
St John
Oakland
Wells
2 G Ranch
Eagle Lake
Lakeside
Saturn
Hickston
Novohrad
Old Moulton
Moulton
Moulton Muni
Komensky
Hackberry
Altair
Rayner Junction
RICHMOND
Little New York
Nickel
Old Kinkler
Kinkler
Appelt Hill
Rock Island
Dilworth
Henkhaus
Breslau
Witting
Vsetin
Matthews
Dean Ranch
Sheridan
Sublime
Hallettsville City Recreation Park
Hallettsville
Good Hope
Garwood
Kokernot
Shiner
Wied
Glaze City
Worthing
Mont
Olive
Hamon
Williamsburg
Hallettsville Muni
Light Chapel
Nada
Dreyer
Pearson Ranch
Midway
Adel
Vienna
Sweet Home
Galaxy Ranch
Steen
Pearl City
Hochheim
Petersville
Yoakum
Yoakum Muni
Koerth
Seclusion
Provident City
New Taiton
Rodgers Roost
El Campo Airpark
Jones Creek
Hahn
Ezzell
Speaks
Concrete
Round Mott
Edgar
Hope
Norris Raun Ranch
Stovall Ranch
Terryville
Stratton
EL CAMPO
Hillje
Lindenau
Cuero
Cuero Muni
Cuero Municipal Park
Dobbs Ranch
Morales
Cerdele
Louise
Plainview
Fordtran
Verhelle
Mt Olive
Navidad
Ganado
Lempa
Arneckville
Thomaston
Salem
Jackson Co
Manson
Edna
Lake Texana SP
Lake Texana
Hahns
Brackenridge Plantation
Matilda
Golly
El Toro
Meyersville
Upper Meyersville
Mission Valley
Nursery
Inez
Weser
Ander
Moursund
Ball
Telferner
Francitas
Whites
Lolita
La Ward
Dupre
Schroeder
Vanderbilt
Victoria RV Park
Victoria
Chiltipin
Aloe
Kilgore
La Salle
Coletoville
Raisin
Hughes
Guadalupe
Redfish Lake
BAY CITY
Coleto Creek Regional Park
Oak Village
Fannin
Cologne
Fannin Battleground
Dacosta
Carr
Weedhaven
Placedo
Lavaca Bay
Point Comfort
Carancahua
Sartwelle Ranch
Scurlock
Dergal
Bloomington
Calhoun County
Port Alto
Carancahua Bay
Port Lavaca State Fishing Pier
Olivia
Kamey
Port Lavaca
Cox Bay
Rhodes Point
Mud Point
Keller Bay
Rupert Point
Carancahua Pass
Green Lake Ranch
Heyser
Chocolate Bay
Alamo Beach
Sand Point
Tanners
Magnolia Beach
McFaddin
Green Lake
MATAGORDA BAY
Indianola
Inari
North Seadrift
Guadalupe Delta WMA
Long Mott
Whatley Flying Service
Powderhorn Lake
Gulf Coast
Tivoli
Matagorda Peninsula
Port O'Connor
Vidaurri
Maudlowe
Seadrift
Hynes Bay
Austwell
Grassy Point
Swan Point
Intracoastal Waterway
Pelican Island
Pass Cavallo
Gulf of Mexico
Mosquito Point
San Antonio Bay
Espiritu Santo Bay
Army Hole
Matagorda Island WMA
Matagorda Island SP
Beach Campground
Quintana
REFUGIO
ROCKPORT
1" = 6.3 mi (10 km)
© DeLorme

HOUSTON
Continue on Page 71
SEE PAGES 132–135
AUSTIN
FORT BEND
BRAZORIA
WHARTON
MATAGORDA
Bellville
Simonton
Wallis
Orchard
Eagle Lake
Lissie
Richmond
Rosenberg
Sugar Land
Stafford
Missouri City
Brookside Village
Pearland
East Bernard
Beasley
Kendleton
Needville
Hungerford
Arcola
Manvel
Iowa Colony
Wharton
Glen Flora
New Taiton
Boling
Newgulf
Lane City
El Campo
Pierce
Pledger
Danciger
Damon
Guy
West Columbia
East Columbia
Angleton
Danbury
Rosharon
Sandy Point
Magnet
Danevang
Old Ocean
Sweeny
Brazoria
Lake Jackson
Clute
Oyster Creek
Freeport
Jones Creek
Van Vleck
Bay City
SEE PAGE 94
SEE PAGE 142
Markham
Midfield
Blessing
Elmaton
Francitas
Buckeye
Cedar Lane
Cedar Lake
Wadsworth
Collegeport
Palacios
Matagorda
San Bernard NWR
Big Boggy NWR
Mad Island WMA
East Matagorda Bay
Matagorda Bay
Tres Palacios Bay
Turtle Bay
Palacios Point
MATAGORDA PENINSULA
COLORADO RIVER
BRAZOS RIVER
Continue on Page 79
EDNA
PORT LAVACA
TEXAS INDEPENDENCE TRAIL

© DeLorme

Continue on Page 72
SEE PAGE 146
SEE PAGE 165
SEE PAGE 126

Continue on Page 76

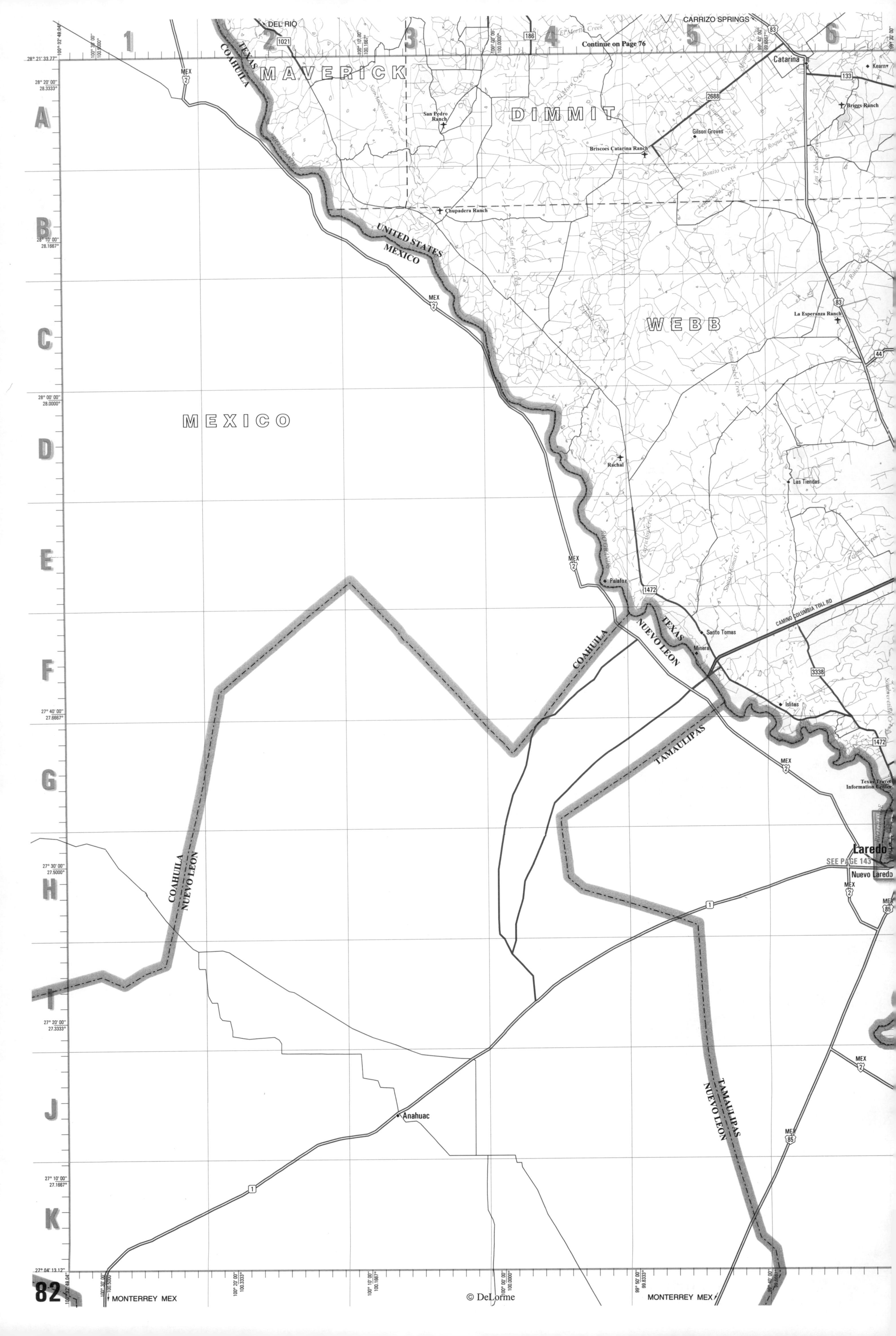

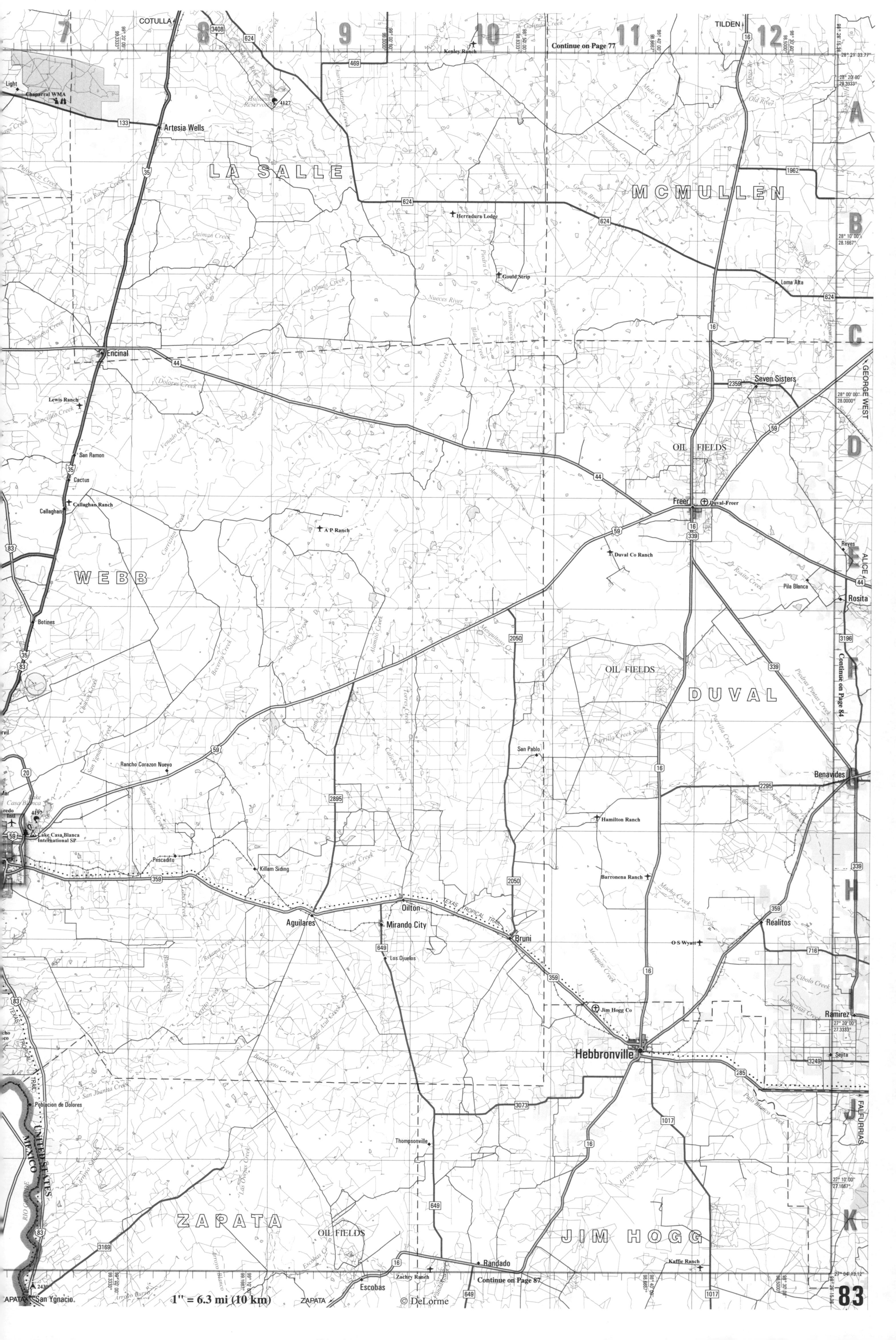

Continue on Page 77
Continue on Page 84
Continue on Page 87

Continue on Page 78
Continue on Page 83
Continue on Page 88

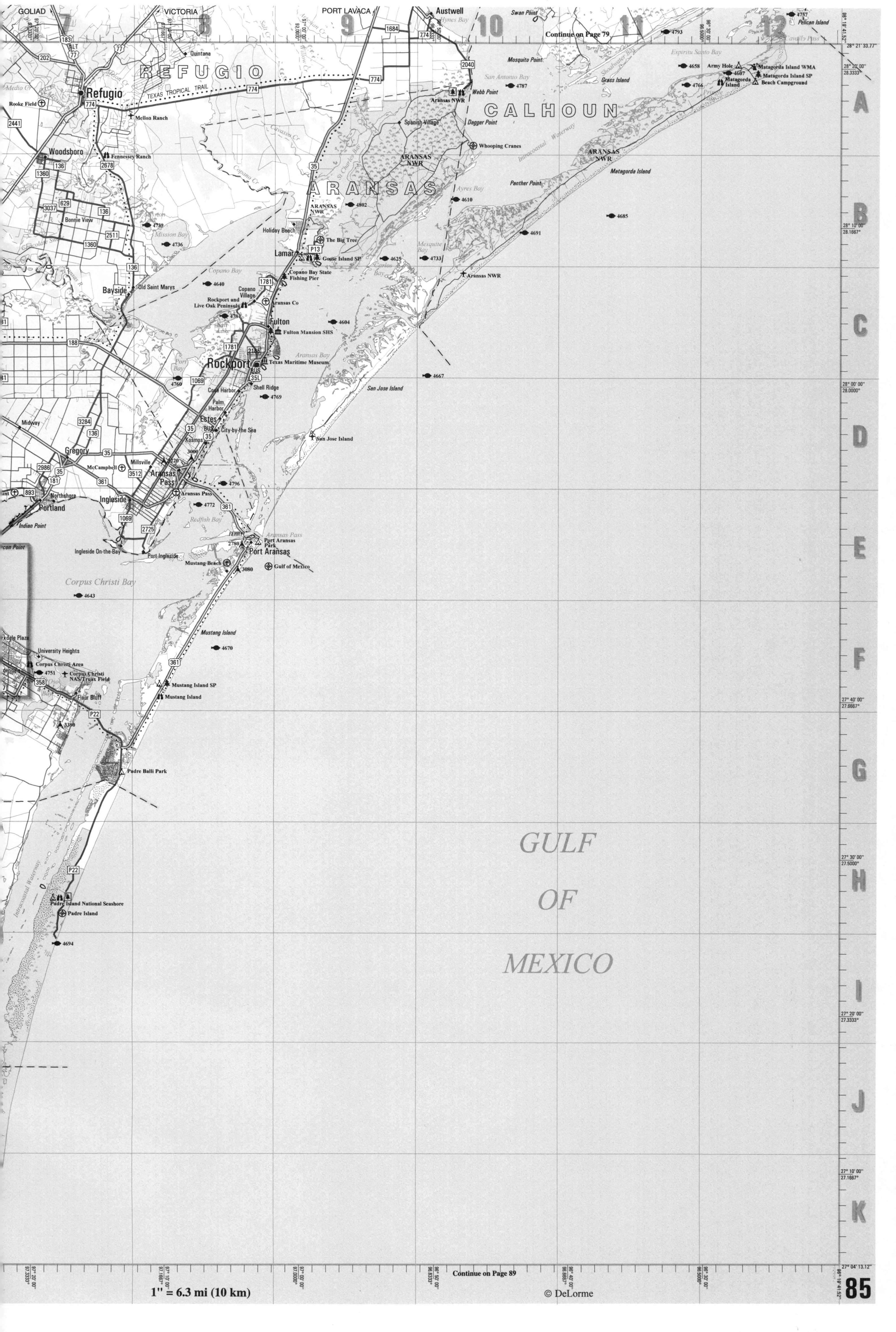

Continue on Page 89

© DeLorme

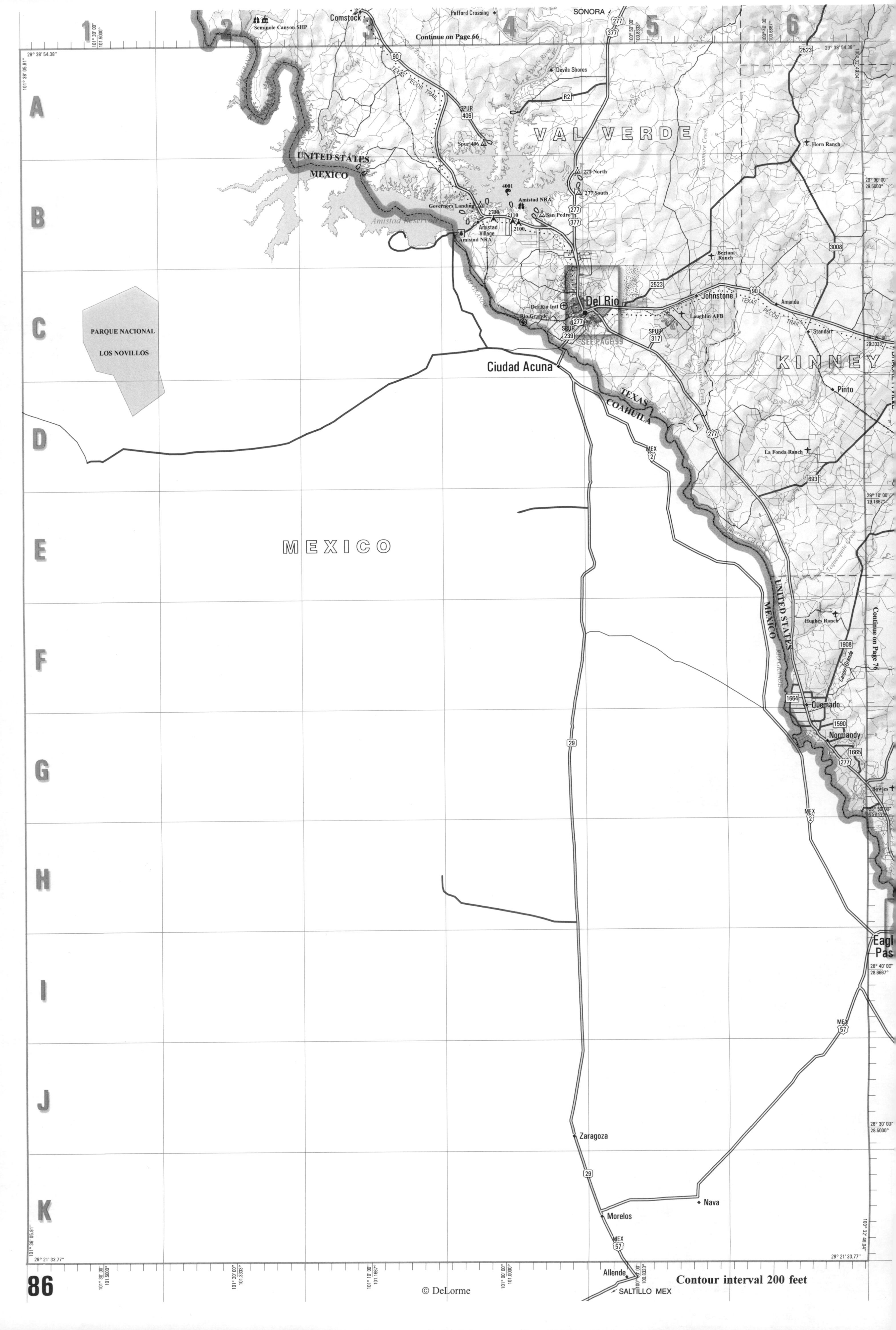

Continue on Page 66
Comstock
Seminole Canyon SHP
Pafford Crossing
SONORA
Devils Shores
VAL VERDE
UNITED STATES
MEXICO
Spur 406
277 North
277 South
Amistad NRA
Governors Landing
Amistad Village
San Pedro
Amistad Reservoir
Horn Ranch
Bertani Ranch
Del Rio
Johnstone
Amanda
Del Rio Intl
Rio Grande
Laughlin AFB
Standart
SEE PAGE 99
PARQUE NACIONAL
LOS NOVILLOS
Ciudad Acuna
KINNEY
Pinto
TEXAS
COAHUILA
La Fonda Ranch
MEXICO
Hughes Ranch
Quemado
Normandy
Bowles
Eagle Pass
Zaragoza
Nava
Morelos
Allende
SALTILLO MEX
Contour interval 200 feet
© DeLorme

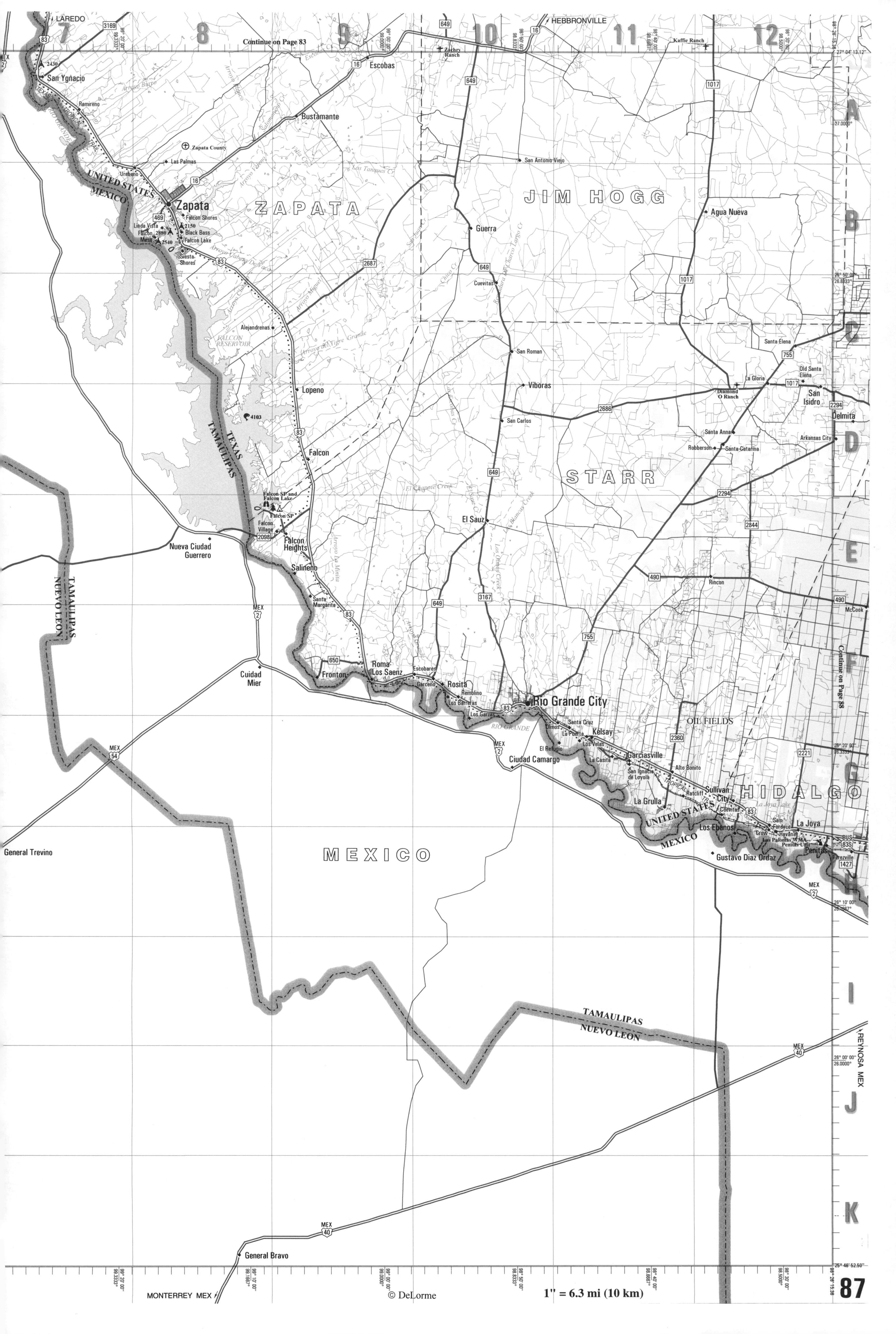

LAREDO
Continue on Page 83
HEBBRONVILLE
8
9
10
11
12
Kaffie Ranch
Zachry Ranch
San Ygnacio
Escobas
Ramireno
Bustamante
Zapata County
Las Palmas
San Antonio Viejo
Urebeno
UNITED STATES
MEXICO
Zapata
ZAPATA
JIM HOGG
Agua Nueva
Falcon Shores
Linda Vista
Falcon Mesa
Black Bass
Falcon Lake
Siesta Shores
Guerra
Cuevitas
Alejandrenas
FALCON RESERVOIR
Santa Elena
San Roman
La Gloria
Old Santa Elena
Diamond O Ranch
San Isidro
Viboras
Lopeno
Delmita
San Carlos
Santa Anna
Robberson
Santa Catarina
Arkansas City
TEXAS
TAMAULIPAS
Falcon
STARR
Falcon SP and Falcon Lake
Falcon SP
Falcon Village
El Sauz
Falcon Heights
Nueva Ciudad Guerrero
TAMAULIPAS
NUEVO LEON
Salineno
Rincon
McCook
Santa Margarita
Continue on Page 88
Cuidad Mier
Fronton
Roma-Los Saenz
Escobares
Garceno
Rosita
Remolino
Los Barreras
Los Garzas
Rio Grande City
RIO GRANDE
Santa Cruz
Olmos
La Puerta
Kelsay
OIL FIELDS
Los Velas
El Refugio
Ciudad Camargo
Garciasville
La Casita
San Ignacio de Loyola
Alto Bonito
La Grulla
Ratcliff
Sullivan City
HIDALGO
Cuevitas
UNITED STATES
Los Ebanos
La Joya
MEXICO
Penitas
Gustavo Diaz Ordaz
General Trevino
MEXICO
TAMAULIPAS
NUEVO LEON
REYNOSA MEX
General Bravo
MONTERREY MEX
© DeLorme
1" = 6.3 mi (10 km)

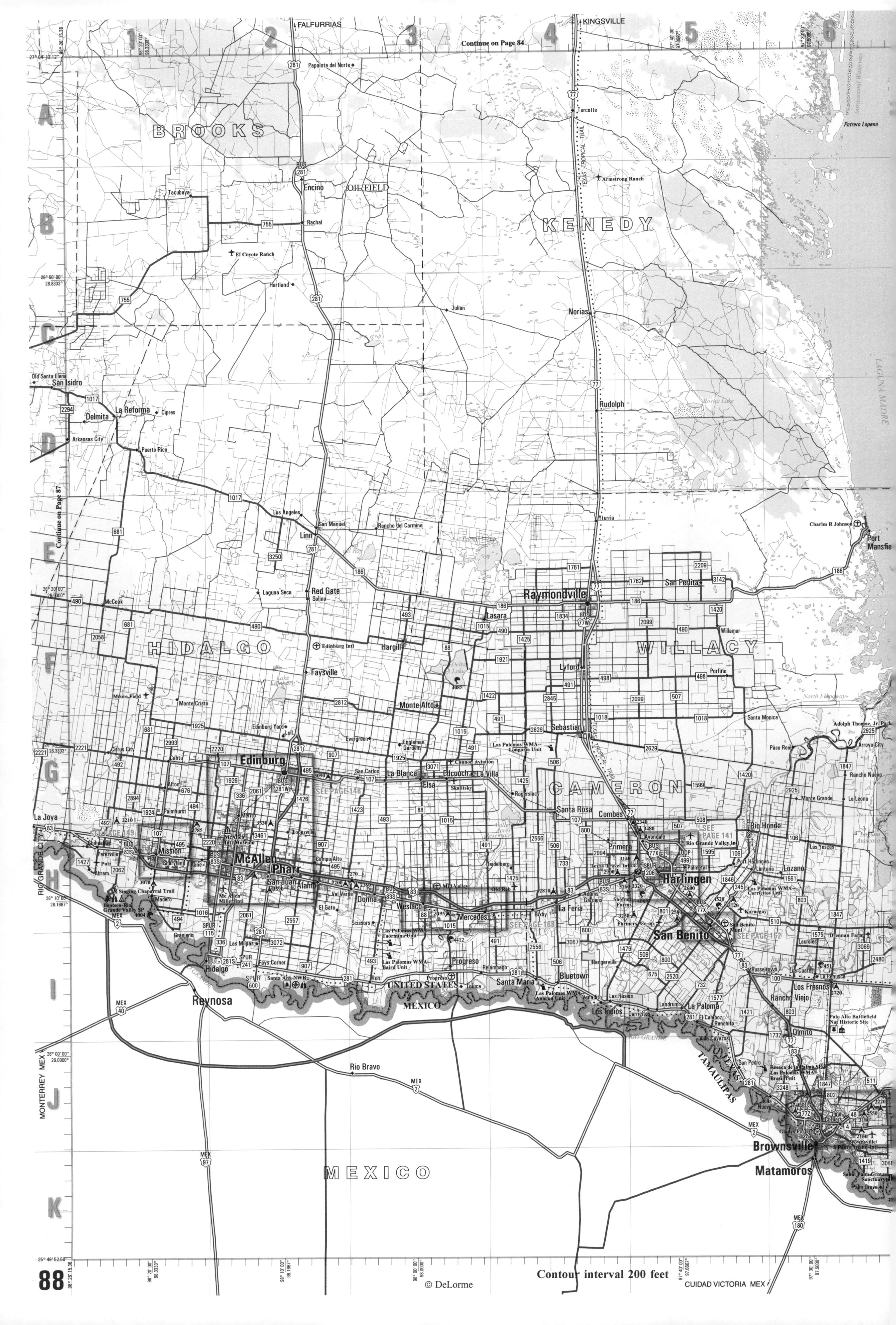
FALFURRIAS
KINGSVILLE
Continue on Page 84
Continue on Page 87
BROOKS
KENEDY
HIDALGO
WILLACY
CAMERON
MEXICO
TAMAULIPAS
TEXAS
LAGUNA MADRE
Intracoastal Waterway
Potrero Lopeno
Papalote del Norte
Turcotte
Armstrong Ranch
TEXAS TROPICAL TRAIL
Encino
OIL FIELD
Rachal
Tacubaya
El Coyote Ranch
Hartland
Julian
Norias
Rudolph
Old Santa Elena
San Isidro
Delmita
La Reforma
Cipres
Arkansas City
Puerto Rico
Los Angeles
San Manuel
Linn
Rancho del Carmine
Ytturria
Charles R Johnson
Port Mansfie
Laguna Seca
Red Gate
Solino
McCook
Raymondville
San Perlita
Lasara
Willamar
Edinburg Intl
Hargill
Faysville
Lyford
Porfirio
Moore Field
Monte Cristo
Monte Alto
Edinburg Yard
Lull
Sebastian
Santa Monica
Adolph Thomae, Jr. Park
Arroyo City
Citrus City
Evergreen
Engleman Gardens
Las Palomas WMA Longoria Unit
Paso Real
Cantu
Edinburg
San Carlos
La Blanca
Cannon Aviation
Edcouch
La Villa
Skalitsky
Rogerslacy
Rancho Nuevo
La Leona
Alton
Monte Grande
Palmhurst
Santa Rosa
Combes
La Joya
Merito
Lopezville
Avondale
Rio Grande Valley Intl
Rio Hondo
Sullivan City
Peñitas
Mission
Sharyland
Palmview
McAllen
Pharr
San Juan
Alamo
Campo Alto
Primera
Port Harlingen
Lantana
Lozano
Las Palomas WMA Carricitos Unit
Korneggy
Texas Travel Info Ctr
Harlingen
Palmetal
Abram
Singing Chaparral Trail
Madero
Bentsen-Rio Grande Valley SP
McAllen Miller Intl
Val Verde
Donna
Weslaco
Mid Valley
Old Rob
La Feria
Adams Gardens
Sholtex Farms
Farmers Co-op
San Benito Muni
San Benito
Mercedes
Heidelberg
El Gato
Scissors
Granjeno
Las Milpas
Las Palomas WMA Taormina Unit
Las Palomas WMA Baird Unit
Progreso
Relampago
Bixby
Bluetown
Rangerville
Laureles
Drennan Farm
Russelltown
Los Cuates
La Pomusca
Los Fresnos
Rancho Viejo
Hidalgo
Faysville
Reynosa
Santa Ana NWR
UNITED STATES
MEXICO
Santa Maria
Las Palomas WMA Anacua Unit
Las Rusias
Los Indios
Carricitos
La Paloma
Ranchito
El Calaboz
Palo Alto Battlefield Natl Historic Site
Olmito
Villa Cavazos
RIO GRANDE
Rio Bravo
San Pedro
Resaca de la Palma SP
Las Palomas WMA Brashl Unit
Villa Nueva
Brownsville
Brownsville/S Padre Island Intl
Matamoros
Sabal Palm Grove Sanctuary
Palm Grove
MONTERREY MEX
CUIDAD VICTORIA MEX
RIO GRANDE CITY
SEE PAGE 148
SEE PAGE 149
SEE PAGE 141
SEE PAGE 168
SEE PAGE 162
Contour interval 200 feet
© DeLorme

Continue on Page 85

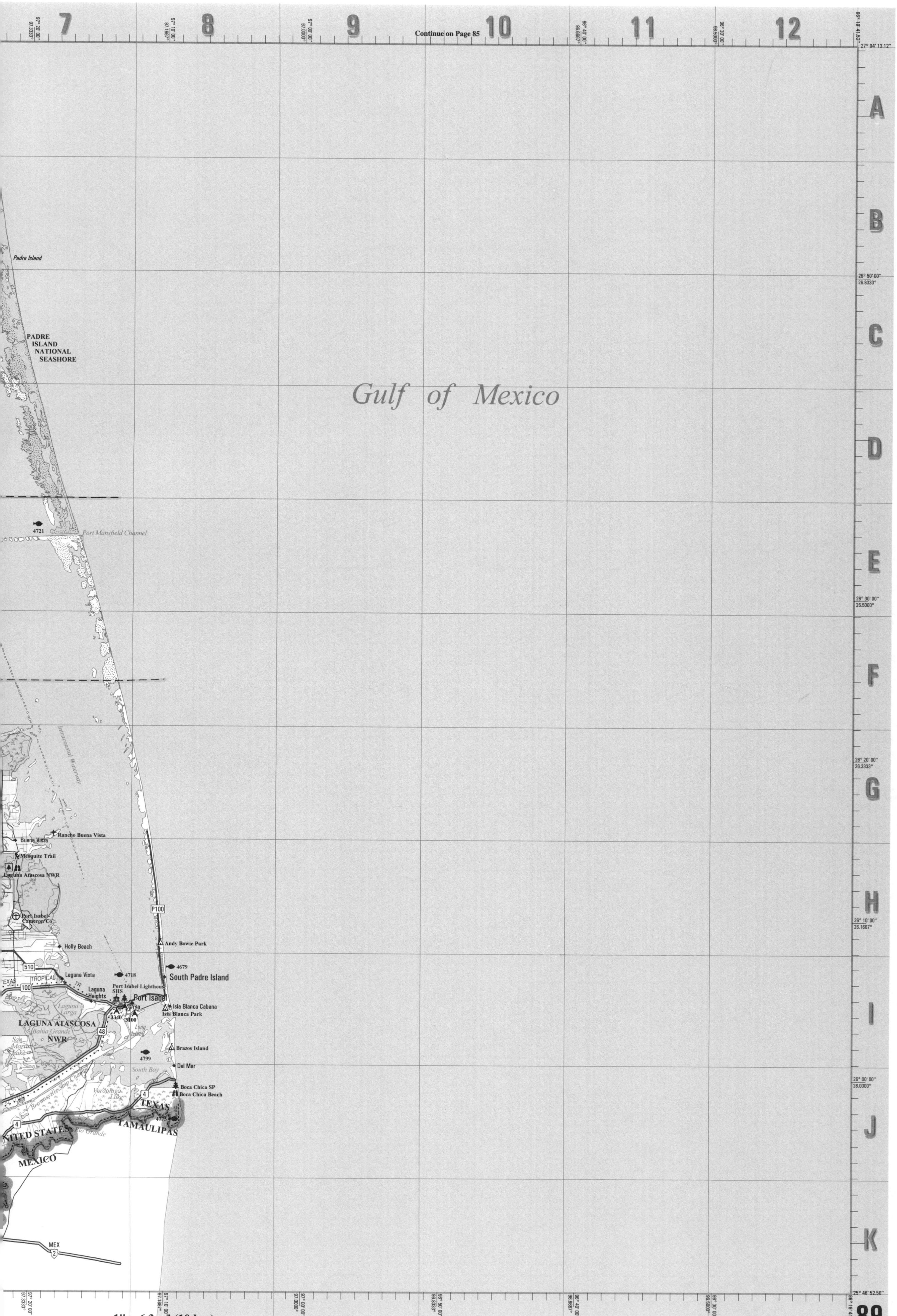
7
8
9
10
11
12
A
B
C
D
E
F
G
H
I
J
K
Gulf of Mexico
Padre Island
PADRE ISLAND NATIONAL SEASHORE
Port Mansfield Channel
4721
Intracoastal Waterway
Rancho Buena Vista
Buena Vista
Mesquite Trail
Laguna Atascosa NWR
P100
Port Isabel-Cameron Co
Andy Bowie Park
Holly Beach
4679
South Padre Island
Laguna Vista
4718
Laguna Heights
Port Isabel Lighthouse SHS
Port Isabel
Isle Blanca Cabana
Isla Blanca Park
LAGUNA ATASCOSA NWR
Laguna Larga
Bahia Grande
Long Island
Brazos Island
4799
South Bay
Del Mar
Boca Chica SP
Boca Chica Beach
TEXAS
TAMAULIPAS
UNITED STATES
MEXICO
Rio Grande
510
100
48
4
3340
3100
MEX 2

1" = 6.3 mi (10 km)

© DeLorme

ABILENE
SEE PAGE 43
Numbers replace street names where map space is limited
continue below
Abilene
Lanius
Impact
Hardin-Simmons Univ
Sears Park
Hair Park
Hendrick Med Ctr
Abilene Christian Univ
Cobb Park
Abilene HS
Civic Ctr
City Hall
C of C
Stevenson Park
Museums of Abilene
Conv and Visitors Bureau
Cisco Jr Coll
Taylor Co Courthouse
Rose Park
Young Park
Abilene Zoo and Discovery Center
Nelson Park
Taylor Co Expo Ctr
Scarborough Park
TX Rehab Ctr
Gill Park
McMurry Univ
Kirby Park
Lytle Lake
Abilene State School
Hendrick Home for Children
Red Bud Park
Maxwell Muni GC
Abilene Country Club
Cooper HS
Mall of Abilene
Vaughn Camp Park
West TX Regional Tech
Texas Forts Trail
Amarillo Med Ctr
Harrington Discovery Ctr
Northwest TX Hosp
Helium Mon
Med Ctr Park
Garden Ctr
High Plains Baptist Hosp
Southwest Reg Park
Southwest Pub GC
UNION PACIFIC
BURLINGTON NORTHERN
© DeLorme

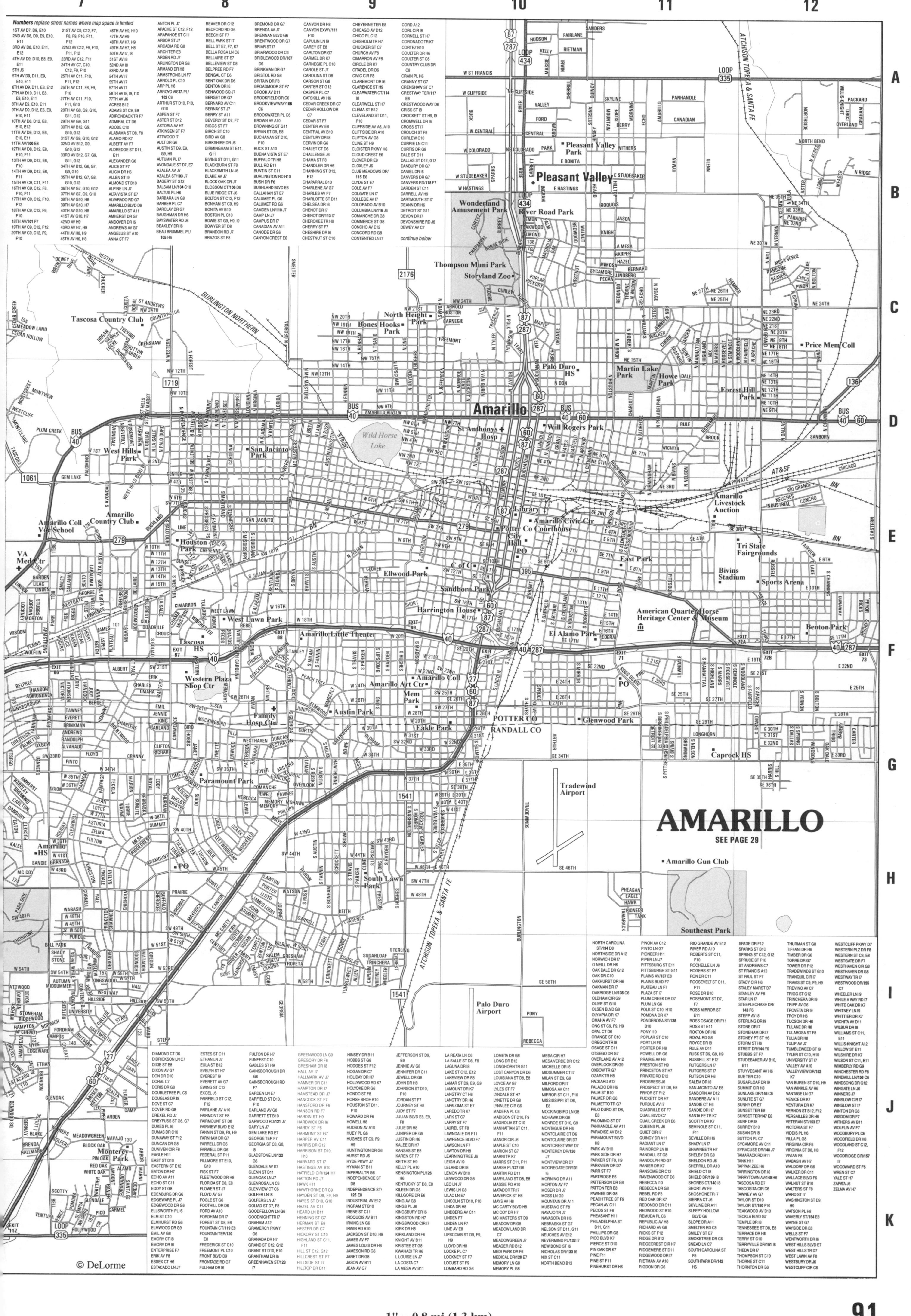
7
8
9
10
11
12
A
B
C
D
E
F
G
H
I
J
K
Numbers replace street names where map space is limited
continue below
AMARILLO
SEE PAGE 29
Amarillo
Pleasant Valley
Pleasant Valley Park
Wonderland Amusement Park
River Road Park
Thompson Muni Park
Storyland Zoo
Tascosa Country Club
North Height Park
Bones Hooks Park
Palo Duro HS
Martin Lake Park
Howe Park
Forest Hill Park
Price Mem Coll
Wild Horse Lake
St Anthonys Hosp
Will Rogers Park
West Hills Park
San Jacinto Park
Amarillo Country Club
Amarillo Coll Voc School
VA Med Ctr
Houston Park
Library
Amarillo Civic Ctr
Potter Co Courthouse
City Hall
PO
Amarillo Livestock Auction
Tri State Fairgrounds
Bivins Stadium
Sports Arena
Ellwood Park
C of C
Sandborn Park
Harrington House
East Park
American Quarter Horse Heritage Center & Museum
Benton Park
West Lawn Park
Tascosa HS
Amarillo Little Theater
El Alamo Park
Western Plaza Shop Ctr
Amarillo Coll
Amarillo Art Ctr
Mem Park
Austin Park
Family Hosp Ctr
Eakle Park
POTTER CO
RANDALL CO
Glenwood Park
Caprock HS
Paramount Park
Tradewind Airport
Amarillo HS
South Lawn Park
Amarillo Gun Club
Southeast Park
Palo Duro Airport
Monterey Park
BURLINGTON NORTHERN
ATCHISON TOPEKA & SANTA FE
© DeLorme

1" = 0.8 mi (1.3 km)

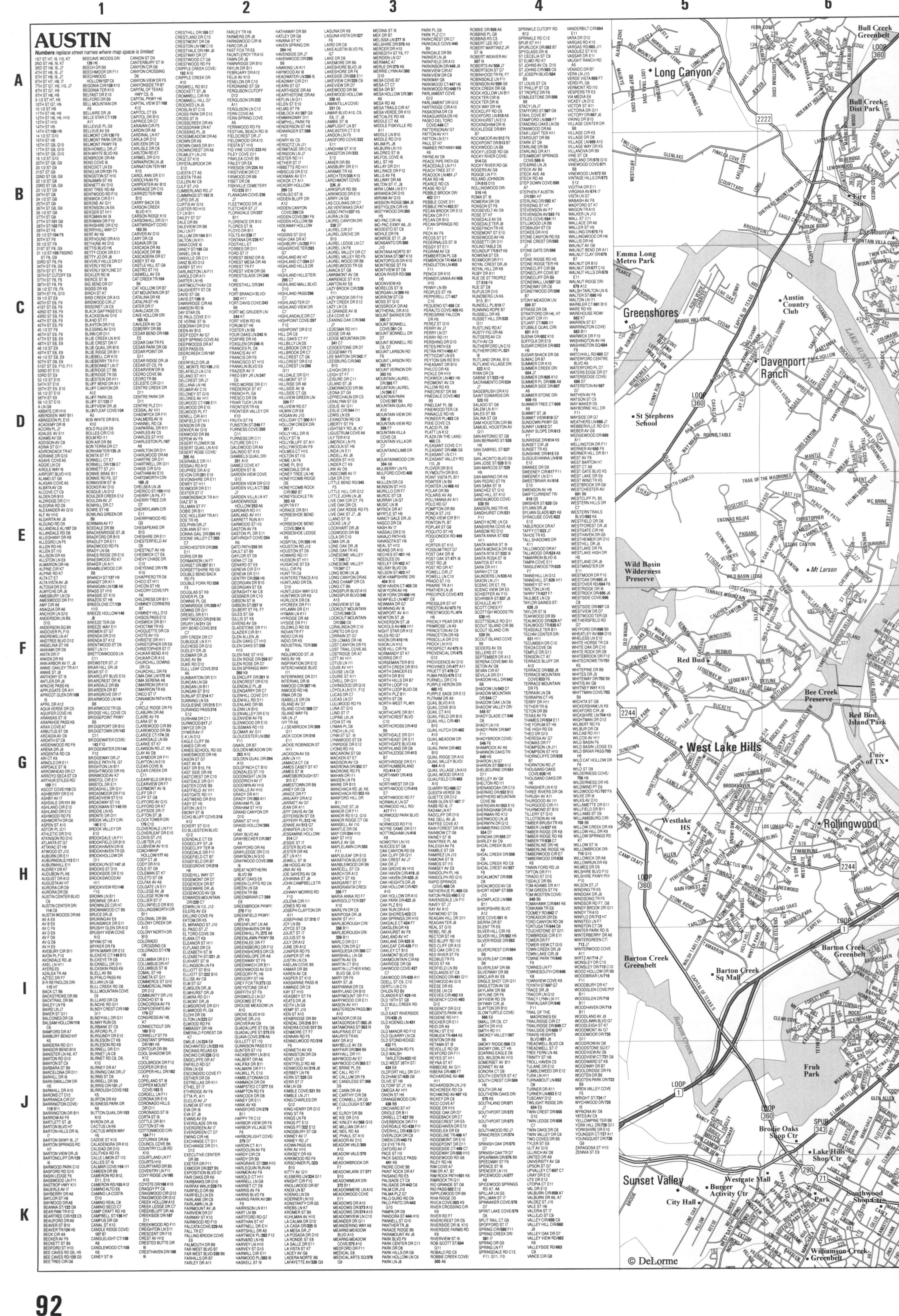

AUSTIN
Numbers replace street names where map space is limited
1
2
3
4
5
6
A
B
C
D
E
F
G
H
I
J
K
Long Canyon
Bull Creek Greenbelt
Bull Creek Dist Park
Emma Long Metro Park
Greenshores
Austin Country Club
Lake Austin
Davenport Ranch
St Stephens School
Wild Basin Wilderness Preserve
Mt Larson
Red Bud
Bee Creek Preserve
Red Bud Island Park
West Lake Hills
Univ of TX
Westlake HS
Rollingwood
Barton Creek Greenbelt
Barton Creek Sq Mall
Fruh Park
Brodie Oaks Shop Ctr
Lake Hills Shop Ctr
Sunset Valley
Westgate Mall
Burger Activity Ctr
City Hall
Southwood Shop Ctr
Williamson Creek Greenbelt
Barton Creek
© DeLorme

7
8
9
10
11
12
A
B
C
D
E
F
G
H
I
J
K
AUSTIN & VICINITY
SEE PAGE 69
AUSTIN
Northwest Hills
Quail Creek
Walnut Forest
Govalle
Montopolis
Frontier Valley
Bull Creek Greenbelt
Barrow Preserve
Anderson HS
North Oaks Park
Big Walnut Creek Greenbelt
Bachman Pioneer Settlement Farm
Village Shop Ctr
Northcross Mall
Library
Wooten Park
Lanier HS
Fire Sta
Allen Park
Brentwood Park
Brown Park
TX DOT
Northwest Rec Ctr
Shoal Creek Greenbelt
Perry Park
McCallum HS
TX Dept of Public Safety
Highland Mall
Buttermilk Br Greenbelt
Reagan HS
Nelson Stadium
Mt Bonnell Park
Camp Mabry Mil Res
TX School for the Blind
Capital Plaza Shop Ctr
Jordan Park
LBJ HS
Mayfield Park
Laguna Gloria Art Museum
Ramsey Park
Austin State School
Austin State Hosp
Shipe Park
Ney Museum
Reed Park
Shoal Creek Hosp
Seton Med Ctr
Bartholomew Dist Park
Northeast Dist Park
Bailey Park
Hancock Shop Ctr
Hancock GC
Patterson Park
Robert Mueller Municipal Airport
Adams-Hemphill Park
Concordia Lutheran Coll
Lions Muni GC
Westenfield Park
Eastwoods Park
St Davids Hosp
Williams GC
Neill-Cochran Museum
Lyndon Baines Johnson Library and Museum
Pease Dist Park
Univ of TX
Texas Mem Stadium
Johnson Creek Greenbelt
Clarksville Park
Disch-Faulk Field
Stadium
House Park
Eilers Park
W Austin Park
Austin Comm Coll
Downs Field
Fire Sta
Springdale Park
Givens Park and Rec Ctr
Austin Comm Coll Eastridge
Childrens Museum
Texas State Capitol
TX Travel Info Ctr
Hosp
Park
Travis State School
Austin Nature Ctr
Austin HS
Wooldridge Park
Governor's Mansion
Symphony Sq
Rosewood Park
Library
Town Lake Park
Treaty Oak
City Hall
Boggy Creek Greenbelt
Zilker Gardens
Austin Area Zilker Park
Republic Sq
Big Walnut Creek Greenbelt
Barton Creek Trail
Scott Theatre
Town Lake Walk and Bikeway Trail
O'Henry Museum
Conv Ctr
Colorado River Greenbelt
Huston Tillotson Coll
Zargosa Park
Govalle Park
City Coliseum
Palmer Auditorium
Congress Avenue Bridge Bat Colony
Johnston HS
Shop Ctr
TX State School for the Deaf
Fire Sta
Martin Park
Metz Park
Fiesta Gardens
Longhorn Dam
Town Lake
Kreig Field Complex
Guerrero Park
Little Stacy Park
Lakeshore Park
Colorado River Greenbelt
Montopolis Bridge
Blunn Creek Park
S Austin Park and Rec Ctr
Park
Big Stacy Park
Riverside GC
Civitan Park
Austin Comm Coll
Travis HS
Blunn Creek Preserve
Montopolis Park
St Edwards Univ
South Austin Med Ctr
Davis Dist Park
Colorado River
© DeLorme

1" = 0.8 mi (1.3 km)

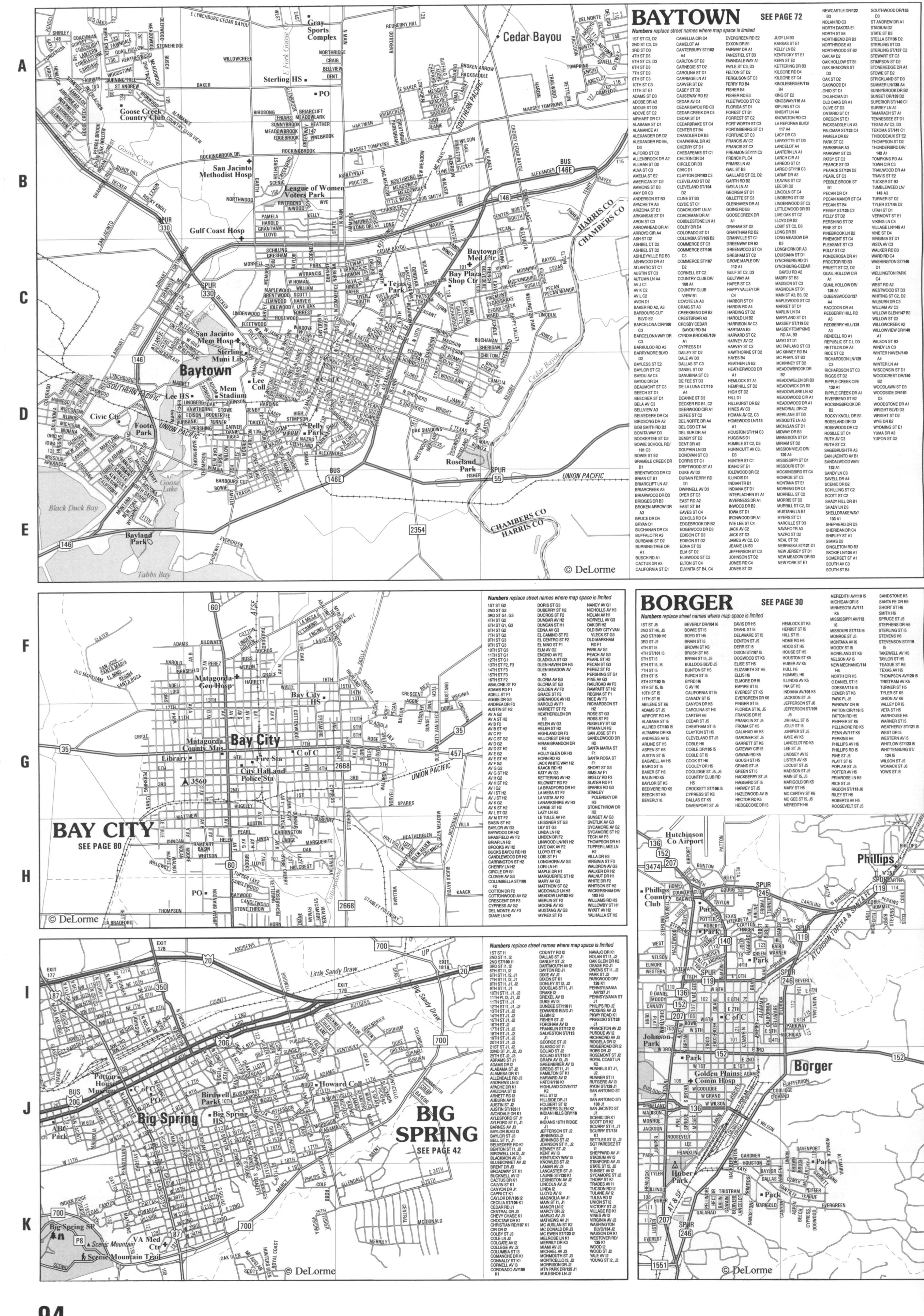
1
2
3
4
5
6
A
B
C
D
E
F
G
H
I
J
K
BAYTOWN
SEE PAGE 72
Numbers replace street names where map space is limited
Baytown
Cedar Bayou
Goose Creek Country Club
San Jacinto Methodist Hosp
League of Women Voters Park
Gulf Coast Hosp
Baytown Med Ctr
Bay Plaza Shop Ctr
Tejas Park
San Jacinto Mem Hosp
Sterling Muni Lib
Lee Coll
Mem Stadium
Lee HS
Civic Ctr
Foote Park
Pelly Park
Roseland Park
Bayland Park
Black Duck Bay
Tabbs Bay
Sterling HS
Gray Sports Complex
HARRIS CO
CHAMBERS CO
SOUTHERN PACIFIC
UNION PACIFIC
© DeLorme
BAY CITY
SEE PAGE 80
Numbers replace street names where map space is limited
Bay City
Matagorda Gen Hosp
Bay City HS
Matagorda County Mus
Library
Fire Sta
C of C
City Hall and Police Sta
UNION PACIFIC
© DeLorme
BORGER
SEE PAGE 30
Numbers replace street names where map space is limited
Hutchinson Co Airport
Phillips
Phillips Country Club
Borger
Golden Plains Comm Hosp
Johnson Park
Huber Park
ATCHISON TOPEKA & SANTA FE
© DeLorme
BIG SPRING
SEE PAGE 42
Numbers replace street names where map space is limited
Big Spring
Howard Coll
Birdwell Park
Big Spring HS
Potton House Museum
ABC Park
Big Spring SP
Scenic Mountain
Scenic Mountain Trail
VA Med Ctr
Little Sandy Draw
Big Sandy Draw
© DeLorme

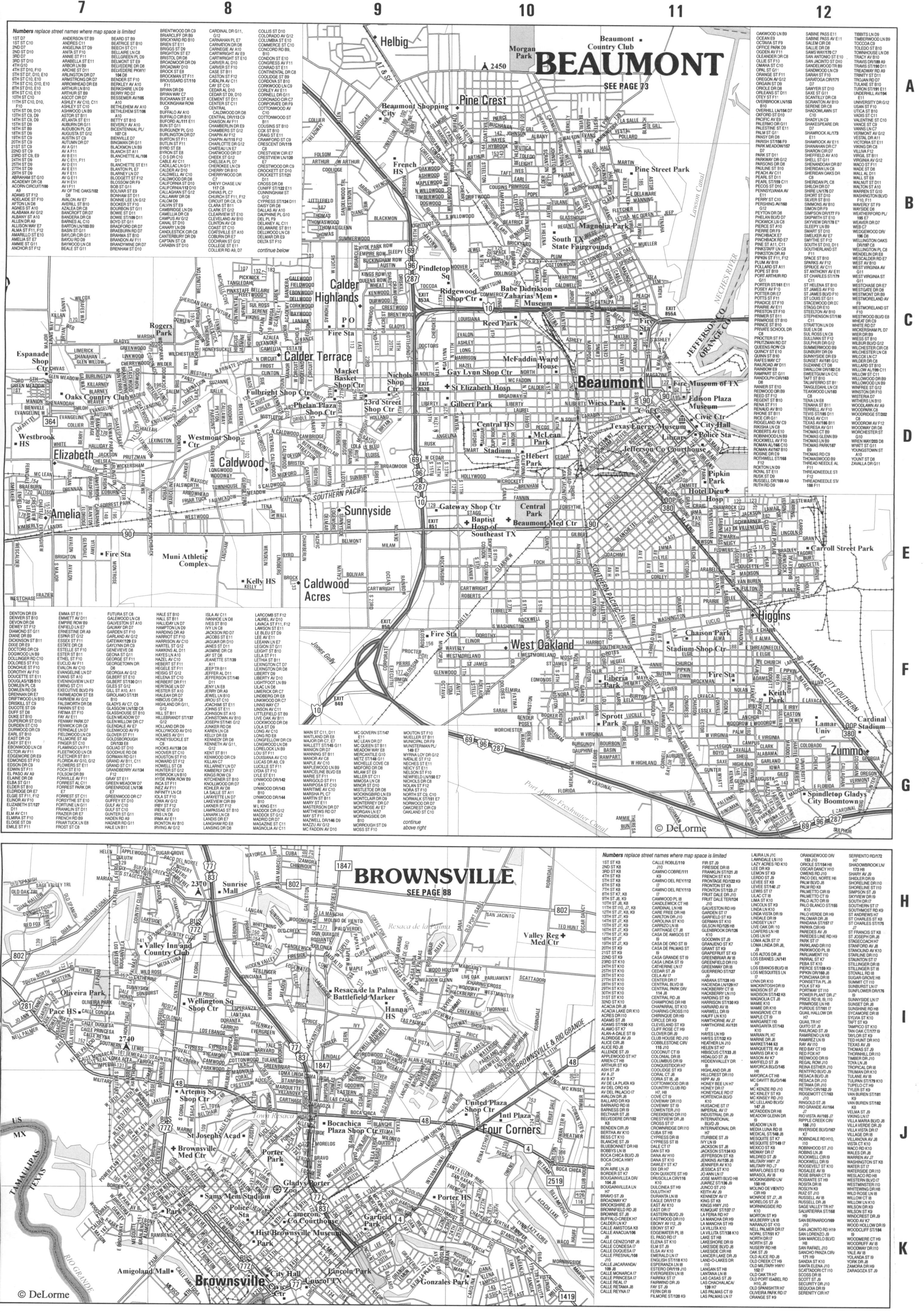
7
8
9
10
11
12
A
B
C
D
E
F
G
H
I
J
K
BEAUMONT
SEE PAGE 73
Beaumont Country Club
Morgan Park
Helbig
Pine Crest
Beaumont Shopping City
French HS
Pine Street Park
Magnolia Park
South TX State Fairgrounds
Pindletop Sq
Ridgewood Shop Ctr
Babe Didrikson Zaharias Mem Museum
Calder Highlands
Calder Terrace
Reed Park
McFaddin Ward House
Gay Lynn Shop Ctr
St Elizabeth Hosp
Market Basket Shop Ctr
Nichols Shop Ctr
Beaumont
Fire Museum of TX
Edison Plaza Museum
Rogers Park
Espanade Shop Ctr
Oaks Country Club
Fulbright Shop Ctr
Phelan Plaza Shop Ctr
23rd Street Shop Ctr
Gilbert Park
Wiess Park
Civic Ctr
City Hall
Police Sta
Texas Energy Museum
Library
Jefferson Co Courthouse
Central HS
McLean Park
Hebert Park
Pipkin Park
Hotel Dieu Hosp
Westbrook HS
Elizabeth
Westmont Shop Ctr
Caldwood
Amelia
Sunnyside
Gateway Shop Ctr
Baptist Hosp of Southeast TX
Central Park
Beaumont Med Ctr
Carroll Street Park
Muni Athletic Complex
Kelly HS
Caldwood Acres
Higgins
West Oakland
Chaison Park
Stadium Shop Ctr
Liberia Park
Fire Sta
Keith Park
Sprott Park
Lamar Univ
Cardinal Stadium
Zummo
Spindletop Gladys City Boomtown
Port Arthur Freshwater Canal
Neches River
Lawson Canal
© DeLorme
BROWNSVILLE
SEE PAGE 88
Sunrise Mall
Valley Inn and Country Club
Valley Reg Med Ctr
Resaca de la Palma
Resaca de la Palma Battlefield Marker
Hanna HS
Oliveira Park
Pace HS
Wellington Sq Shop Ctr
Artemis Sq Shop Ctr
United Plaza Shop Ctr
Intl Plaza
Four Corners
Bocachica Plaza Shop Ctr
St Josephs Acad
Brownsville Med Ctr
Porter Park
Gladys Porter Zoo
Sams Mem Stadium
Police Sta
Porter HS
Cameron Co Courthouse
Garfield Park
Hist Brownsville Museum
City Hall
Amigoland Mall
Brownsville
Civic Ctr
Lincoln Park
Gonzales Park
Rio Grande
TAMAULIPAS
TEXAS
US
MX
© DeLorme

1" = 0.8 mi (1.3 km)

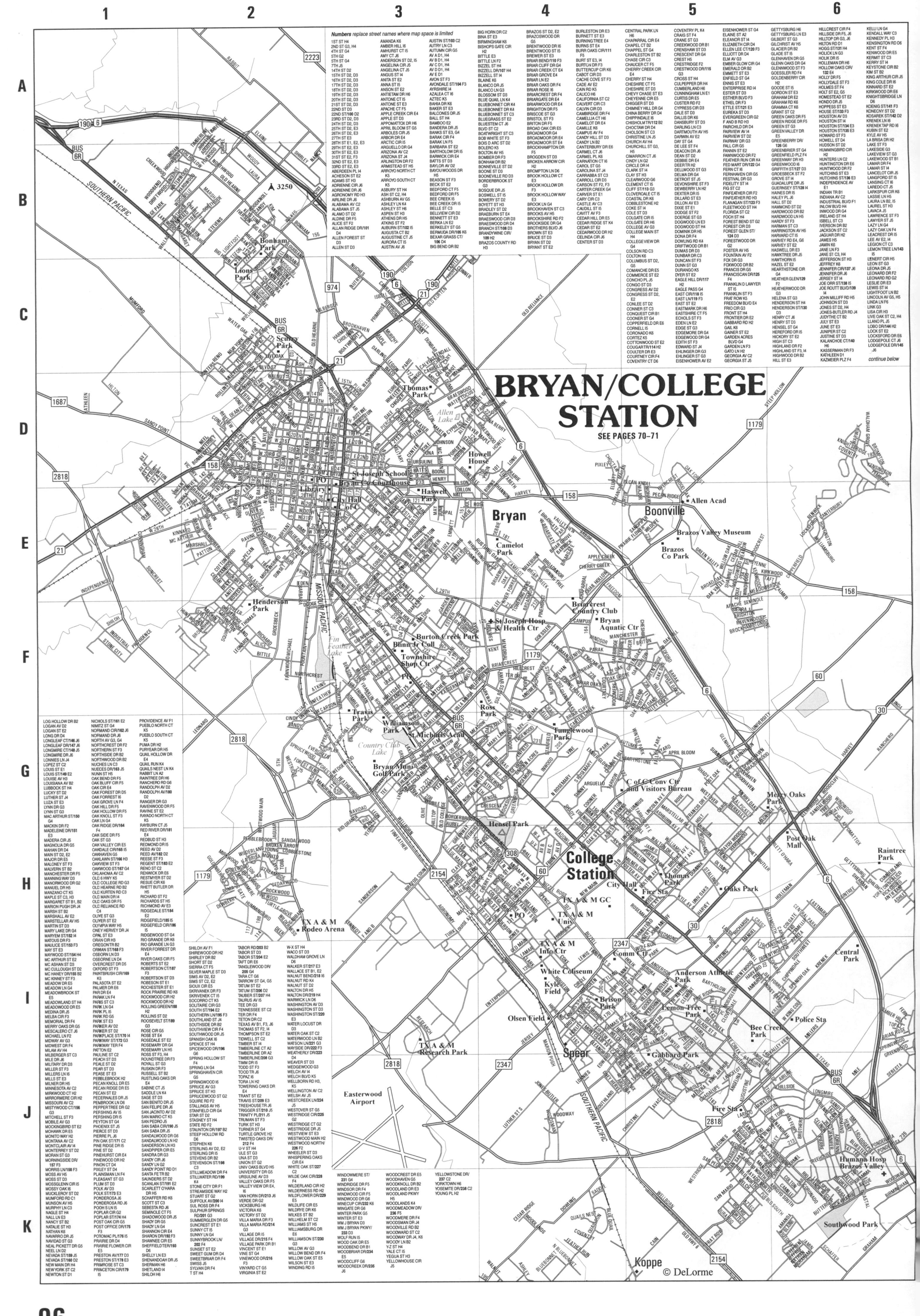
BRYAN/COLLEGE STATION
SEE PAGES 70–71
Bryan
College Station
Boonville
Koppe
Spear
Numbers replace street names where map space is limited
continue below
© DeLorme

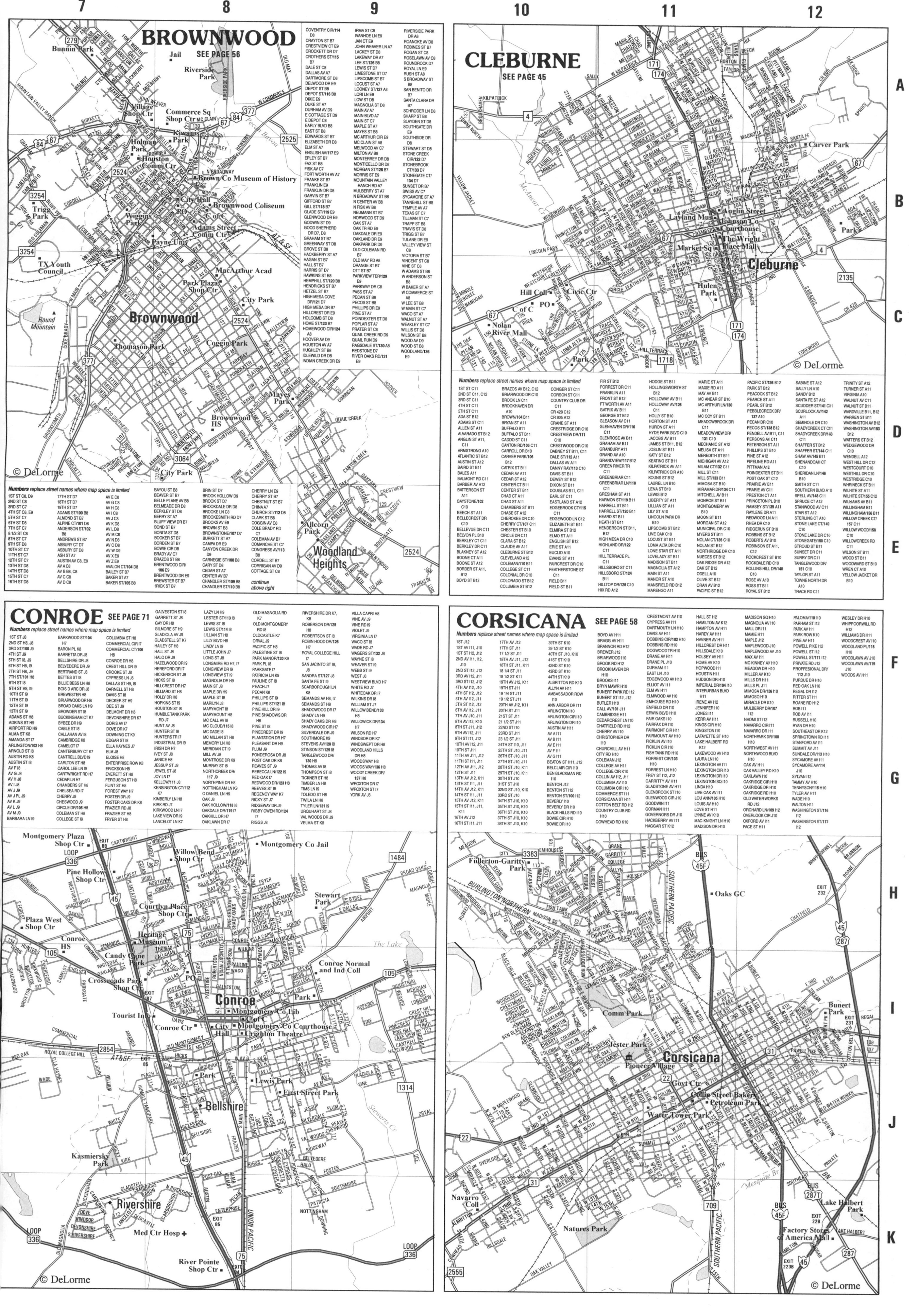
7
8
9
10
11
12
A
B
C
D
E
F
G
H
I
J
K
BROWNWOOD
SEE PAGE 56
CLEBURNE
SEE PAGE 45
CONROE
SEE PAGE 71
CORSICANA
SEE PAGE 58
Numbers replace street names where map space is limited
Brownwood
Cleburne
Conroe
Corsicana
© DeLorme

1" = 0.8 mi (1.3 km)

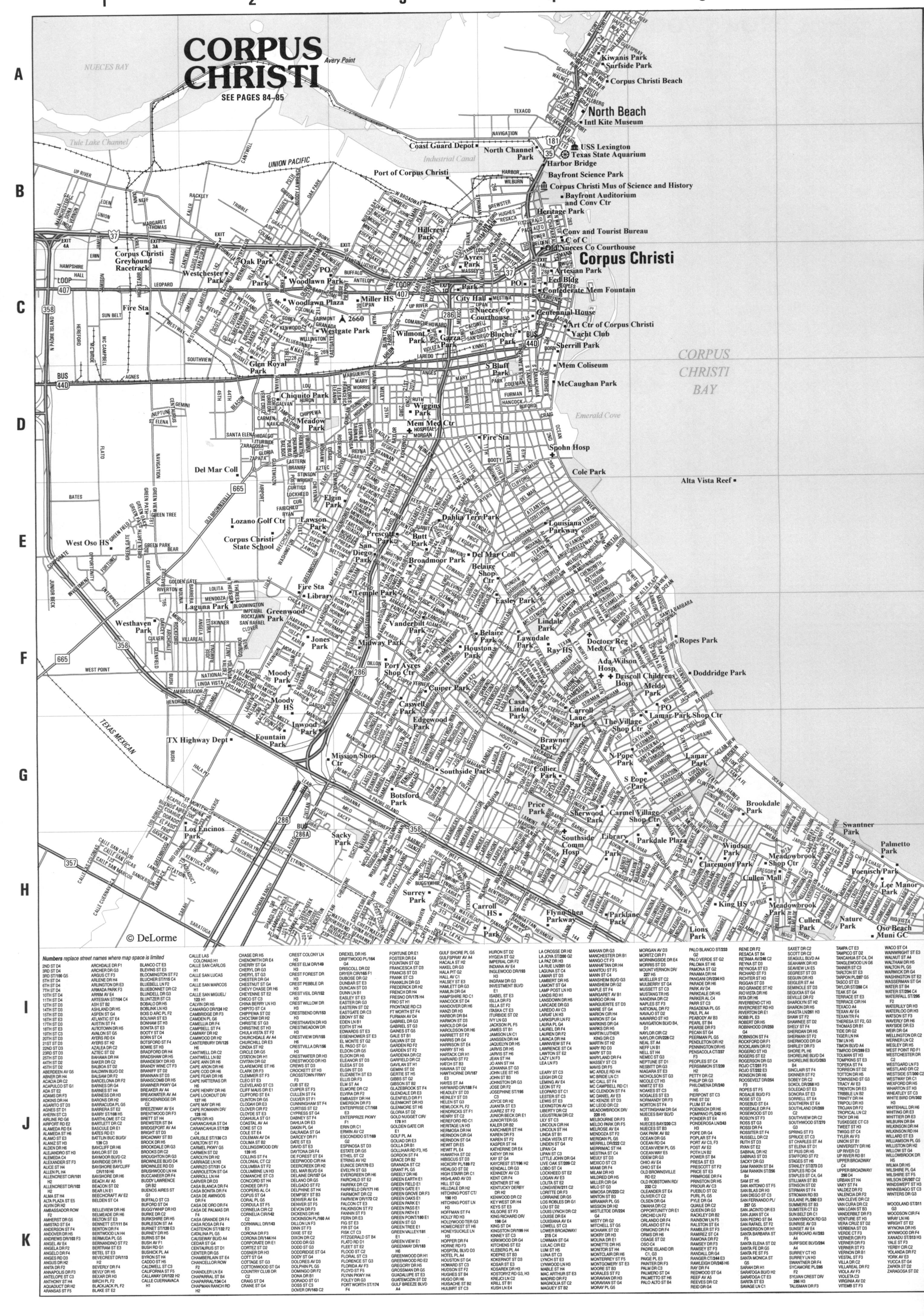

CORPUS CHRISTI
SEE PAGES 84–85
1
2
3
4
5
6
A
B
C
D
E
F
G
H
I
J
K
NUECES BAY
Avery Point
Tule Lake Channel
UNION PACIFIC
Industrial Canal
Coast Guard Depot
North Channel Park
USS Lexington
Texas State Aquarium
Harbor Bridge
Port of Corpus Christi
Kiwanis Park
Surfside Park
Corpus Christi Beach
North Beach
Intl Kite Museum
Bayfront Science Park
Corpus Christi Mus of Science and History
Bayfront Auditorium and Conv Ctr
Heritage Park
Conv and Tourist Bureau
C of C
Old Nueces Co Courthouse
Corpus Christi
Artesian Park
Fed Bldg
Confederate Mem Fountain
Centennial House
Art Ctr of Corpus Christi
Yacht Club
Sherrill Park
CORPUS CHRISTI BAY
Mem Coliseum
McCaughan Park
Emerald Cove
Spohn Hosp
Cole Park
Alta Vista Reef
Corpus Christi Greyhound Racetrack
Westchester Park
Oak Park
Woodlawn Park
Woodlawn Plaza
Miller HS
Hillcrest Park
Ayres Park
City Hall
Nueces Co Courthouse
Westgate Park
Wilmont Park
Garza Park
Blucher Park
Fire Sta
Glen Royal Park
S Bluff Park
Chiquito Park
Meadow Park
Wiggins Park
Mem Med Ctr
Del Mar Coll
Elgin Park
Lozano Golf Ctr
Corpus Christi State School
Lawson Park
West Oso HS
Dahlia Terr Park
Louisiana Parkway
Prescott Park
Butt Park
San Diego Park
Broadmoor Park
Belaire Shop Ctr
Library
Temple Park
Laguna Park
Westhaven Park
Greenwood Park
Easley Park
Vanderbilt Park
Lindale Park
Jones Park
Midway Park
Belaire Park
Lawndale Park
Ray HS
Doctors Reg Med Ctr
Ropes Park
Houston Park
Port Ayres Shop Ctr
Ada Wilson Hosp
Driscoll Childrens Hosp
Doddridge Park
Moody Park
Moody HS
Cuiper Park
Meldo Park
Casa Linda Park
Caswell Park
Edgewood Park
Carroll Lane Park
Lamar Park Shop Ctr
The Village Shop Ctr
Inwood Park
Fountain Park
TX Highway Dept
Mission Shop Ctr
Brawner Parkway
Southside Park
Collier Park
N Pope Park
Lamar Park
S Pope Park
Botsford Park
Price Park
Brookdale Park
Sherwood Park
Carmel Village Shop Ctr
Los Encinos Park
Sacky Park
Southside Comm Hosp
Library
Parkdale Plaza
Swantner Park
Palmetto Park
Windsor Park
Meadowbrook Shop Ctr
Claremont Park
Poenisch Park
Cullen Mall
Lee Manor Park
Surrey Park
Carroll HS
Flynn Shea Parkway
Parklane Park
King HS
Meadowbrook Park
Cullen Park
Nature Park
Lions Park
Oso Beach Muni GC
TEXAS MEXICAN
© DeLorme

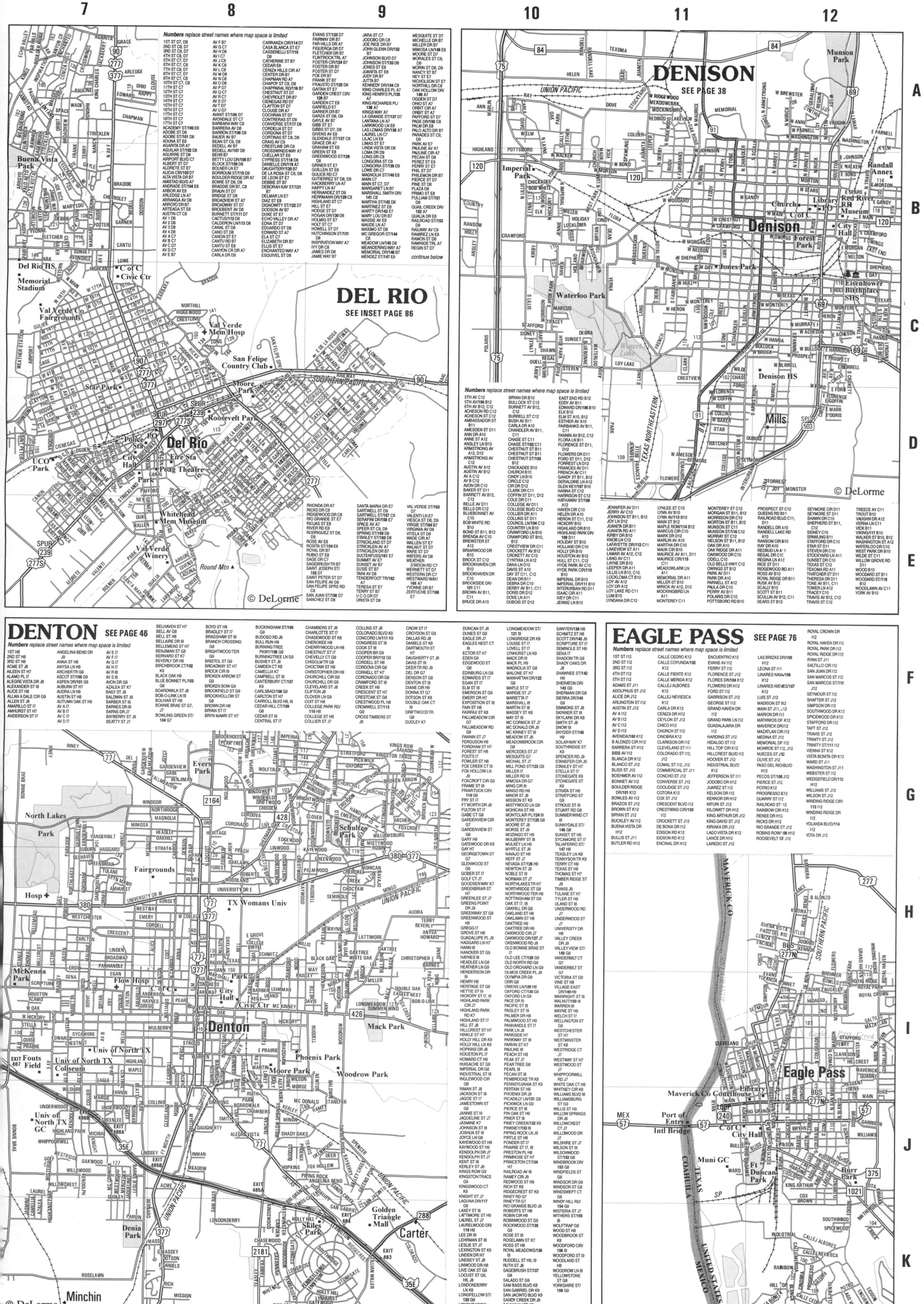

7
8
9
10
11
12
A
B
C
D
E
F
G
H
I
J
K
DEL RIO
SEE INSET PAGE 86
Numbers replace street names where map space is limited
continue below
Del Rio
Del Rio HS
Memorial Stadium
Val Verde Co Fairgrounds
Val Verde Mem Hosp
San Felipe Country Club
Moore Park
Star Park
Roosevelt Park
Buena Vista Park
Police Sta
Fire Sta
City Hall
Poag Theatre
UCO Park
Whitehead Mem Museum
Val Verde Winery
C of C
Civic Ctr
Round Mtn
SOUTHERN PACIFIC
© DeLorme
DENISON
SEE PAGE 38
Denison
Munson Park
Imperial Park
Waterloo Park
Waterloo Lake
Randall Annex
Red River RR Museum
Library
Church
C of C
City Hall
Forest Park
Jones Park
Eisenhower Birthplace SHS
Denison HS
Mills
UNION PACIFIC
TEXAS NORTHEASTERN
Numbers replace street names where map space is limited
© DeLorme
DENTON
SEE PAGE 46
Numbers replace street names where map space is limited
Denton
North Lakes Park
Evers Park
Fairgrounds
Hosp
TX Womans Univ
McKenna Park
Flow Hosp
C of C
City Hall
Civic Ctr
Mack Park
Phoenix Park
Moore Park
Woodrow Park
Univ of North TX
Univ of North TX Coliseum
Fouts Field
Univ of North TX GC
Golden Triangle Mall
Skiles Park
Denia Park
Carter
Minchin
UNION PACIFIC
© DeLorme
EAGLE PASS
SEE PAGE 76
Numbers replace street names where map space is limited
Eagle Pass
Maverick Co Courthouse
Library
Port of Entry
Intl Bridge
C of C
City Hall
Muni GC
Ft Duncan Park
Burr Park
MAVERICK CO
COAHUILA
TEXAS
UNITED STATES
MEXICO
SOUTHERN PACIFIC
© DeLorme

1" = 0.8 mi (1.3 km)

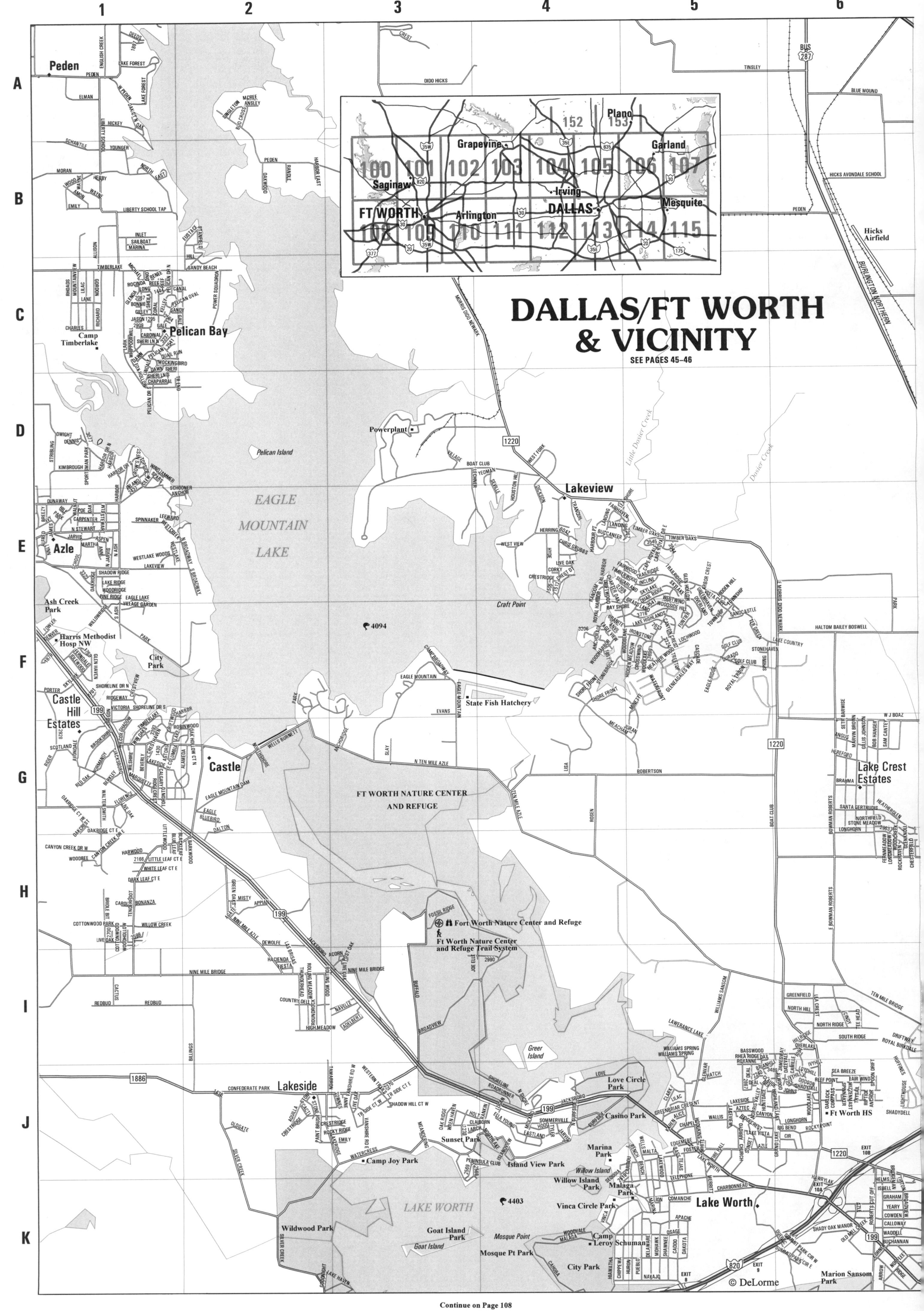

Continue on Page 108

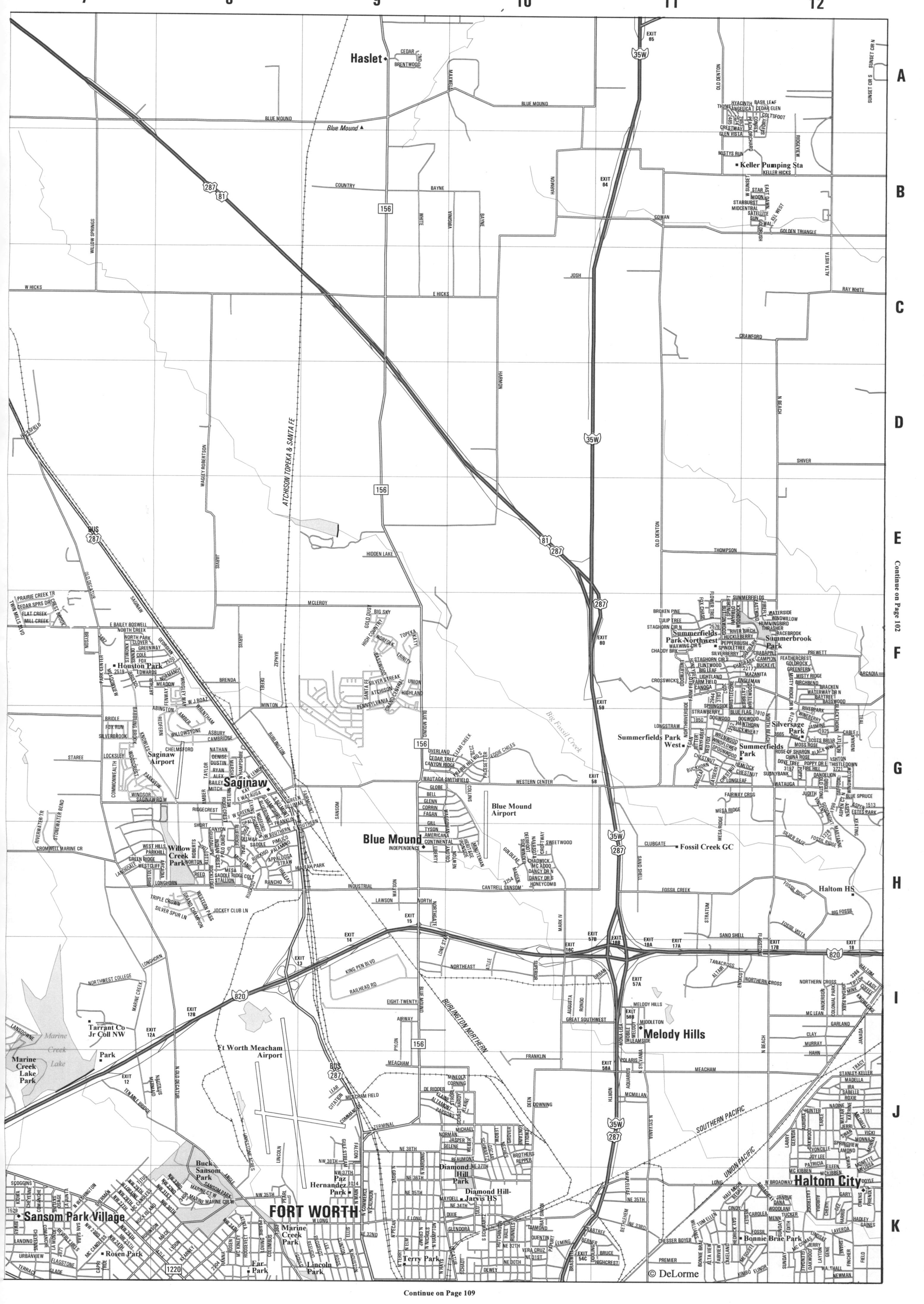

Continue on Page 102
Continue on Page 109

1" = 0.8 mi (1.3 km)

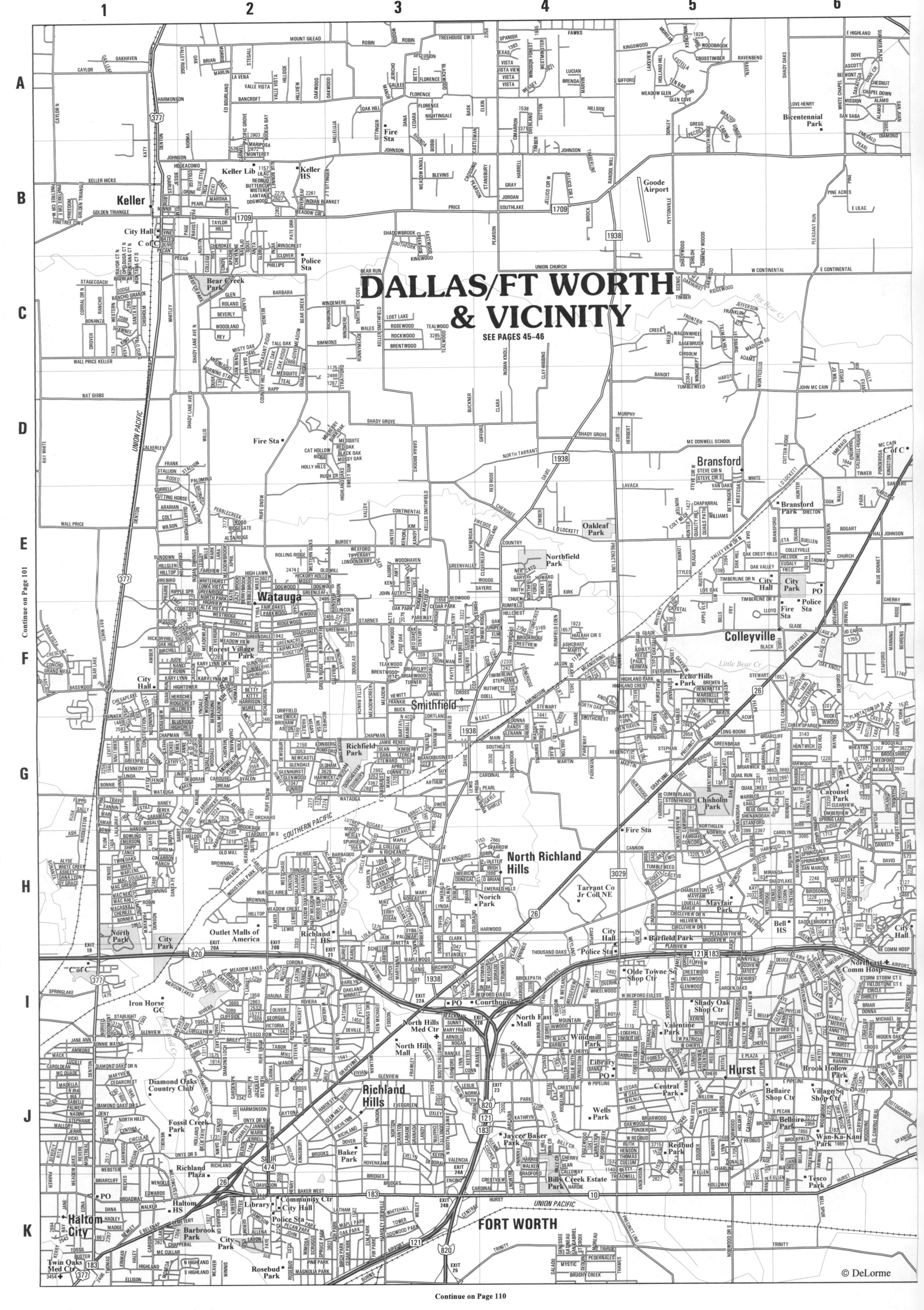

Continue on Page 101
Continue on Page 110

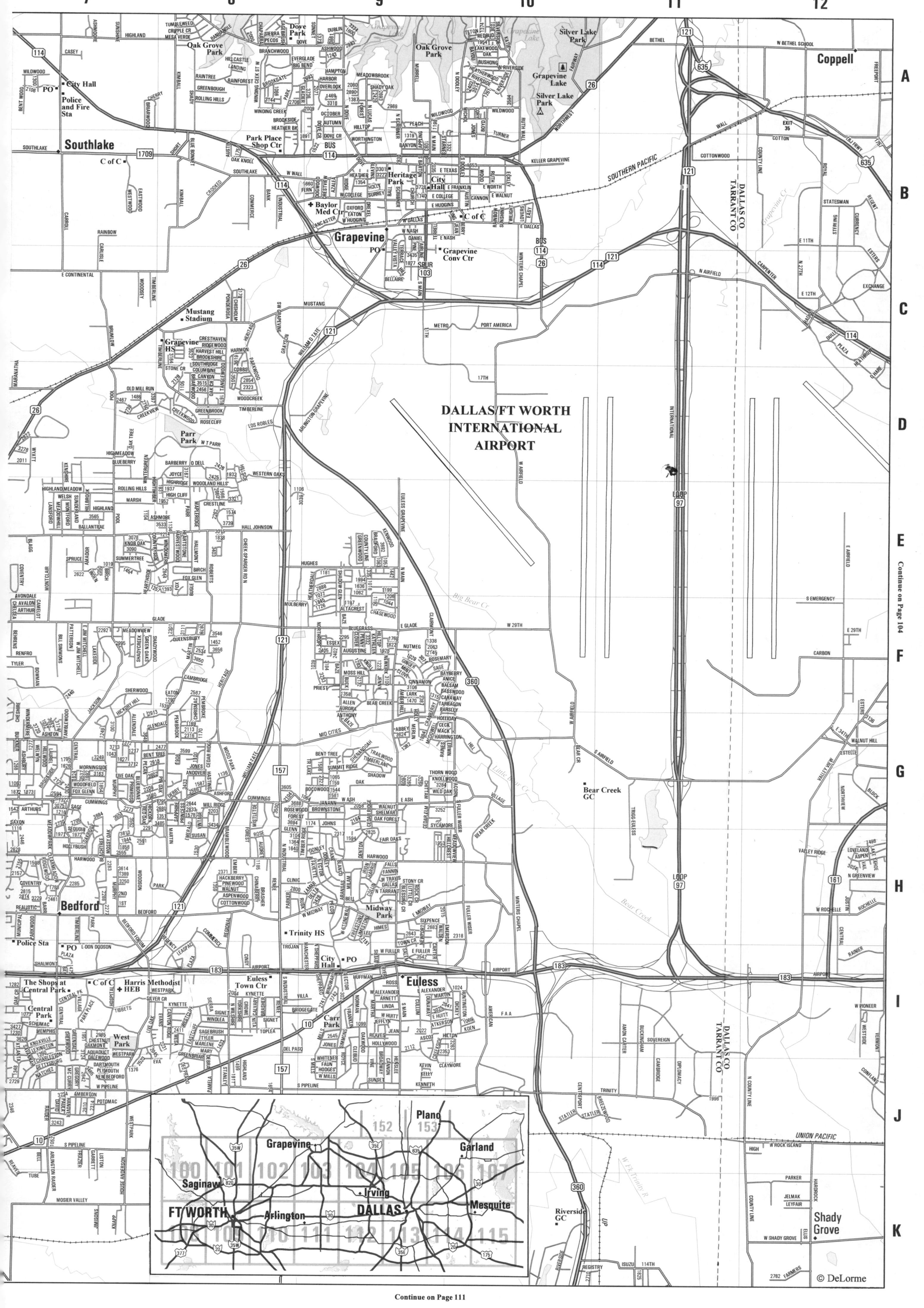

Continue on Page 104

Continue on Page 111

1" = 0.8 mi (1.3 km)

Continue on Page 152

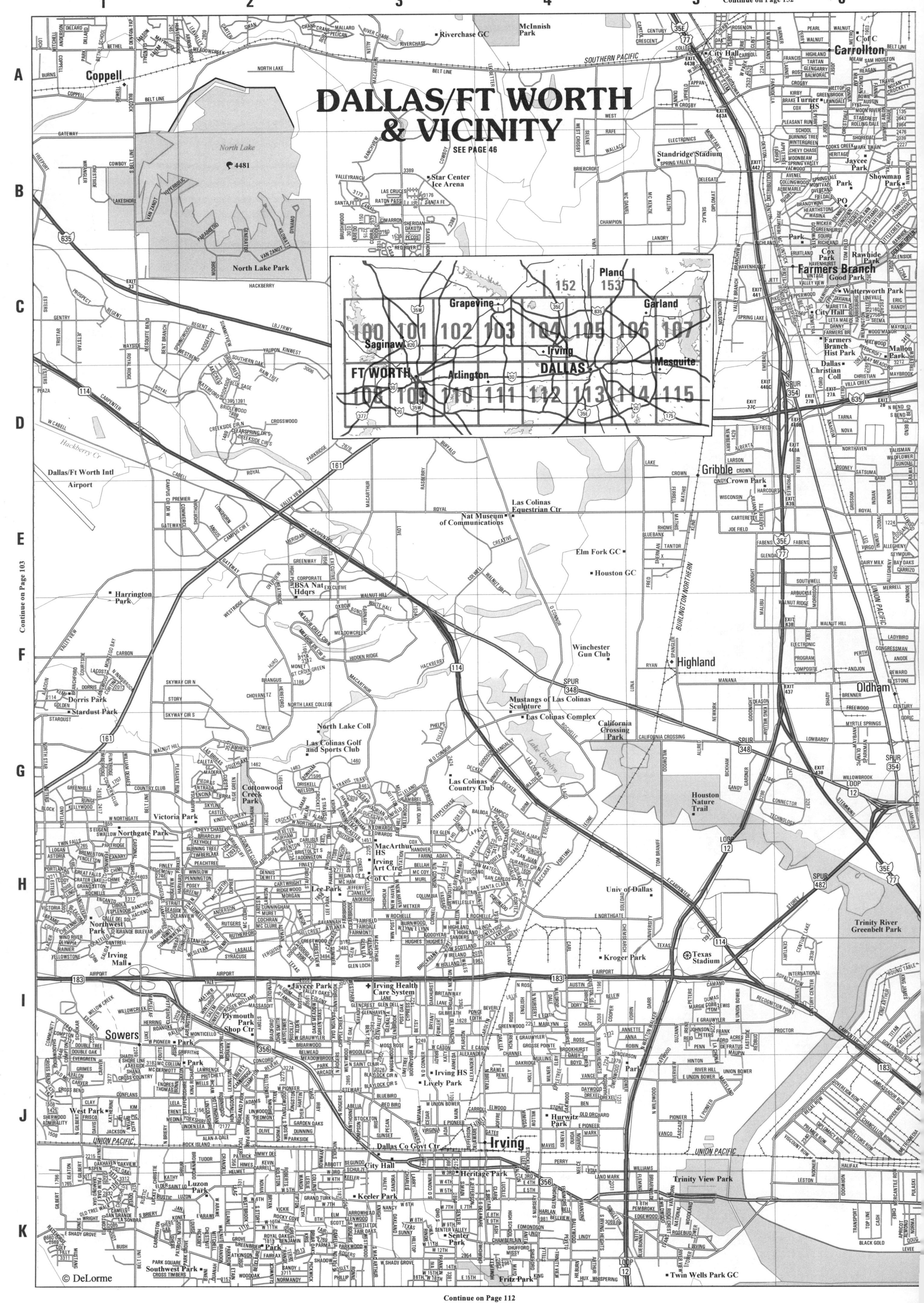

Continue on Page 103

Continue on Page 112

Continue on Page 152

Continue on Page 153

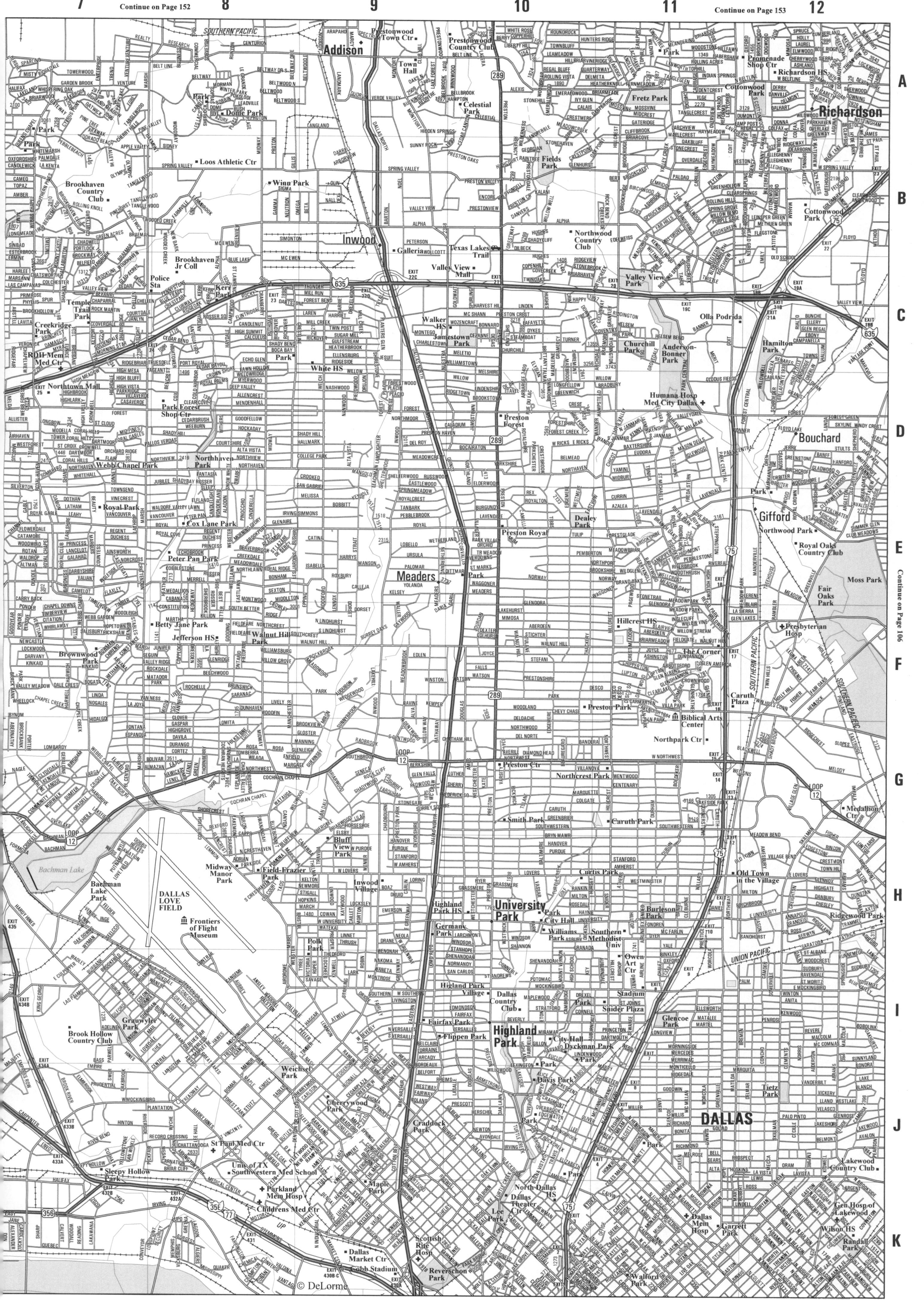

Continue on Page 106

Continue on Page 113

1" = 0.8 mi (1.3 km)

Continue on Page 153

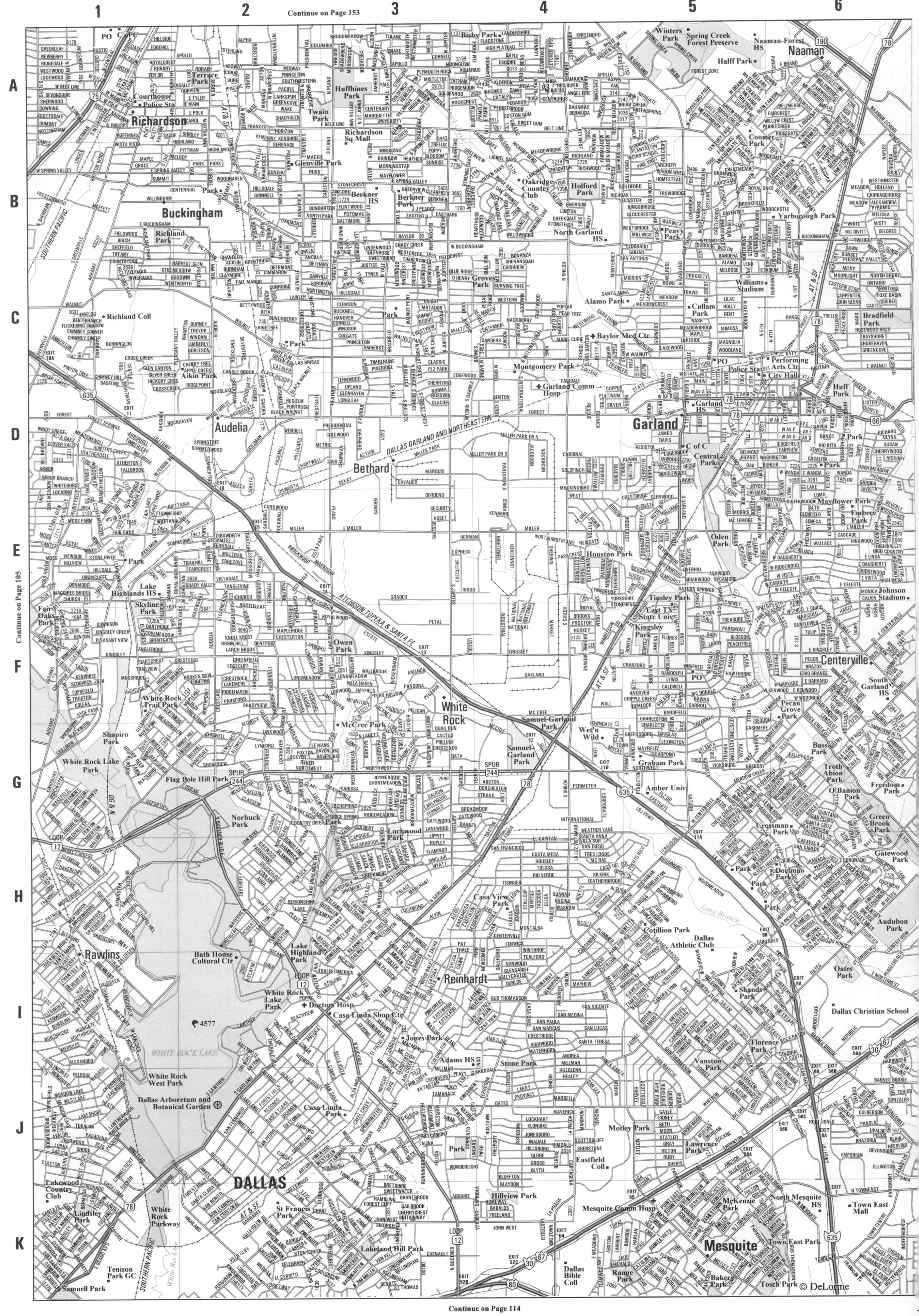

Continue on Page 105

Continue on Page 114

7 8 9 10 11 12

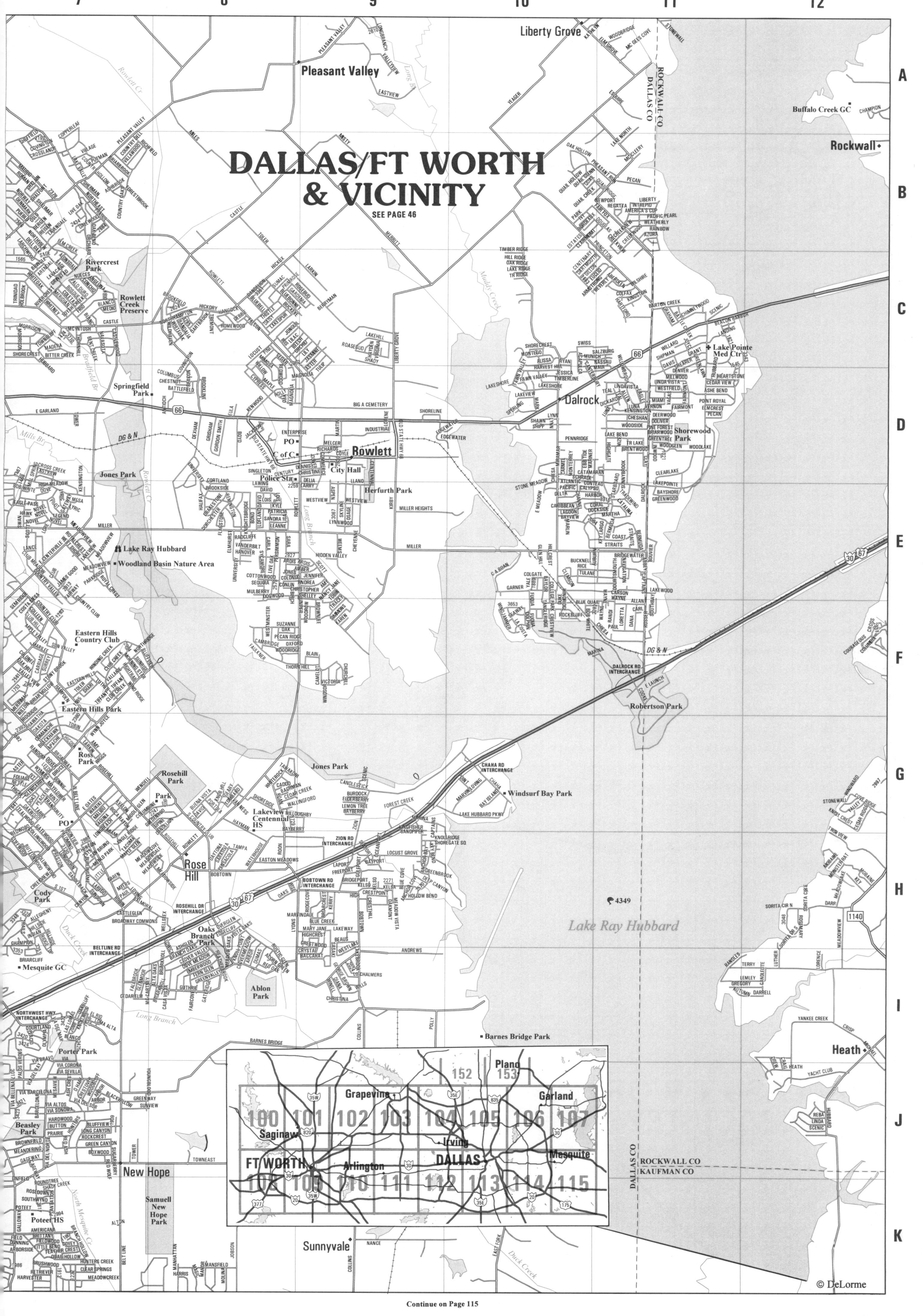

A B C D E F G H I J K

Continue on Page 115

1" = 0.8 mi (1.3 km)

Continue on Page 100

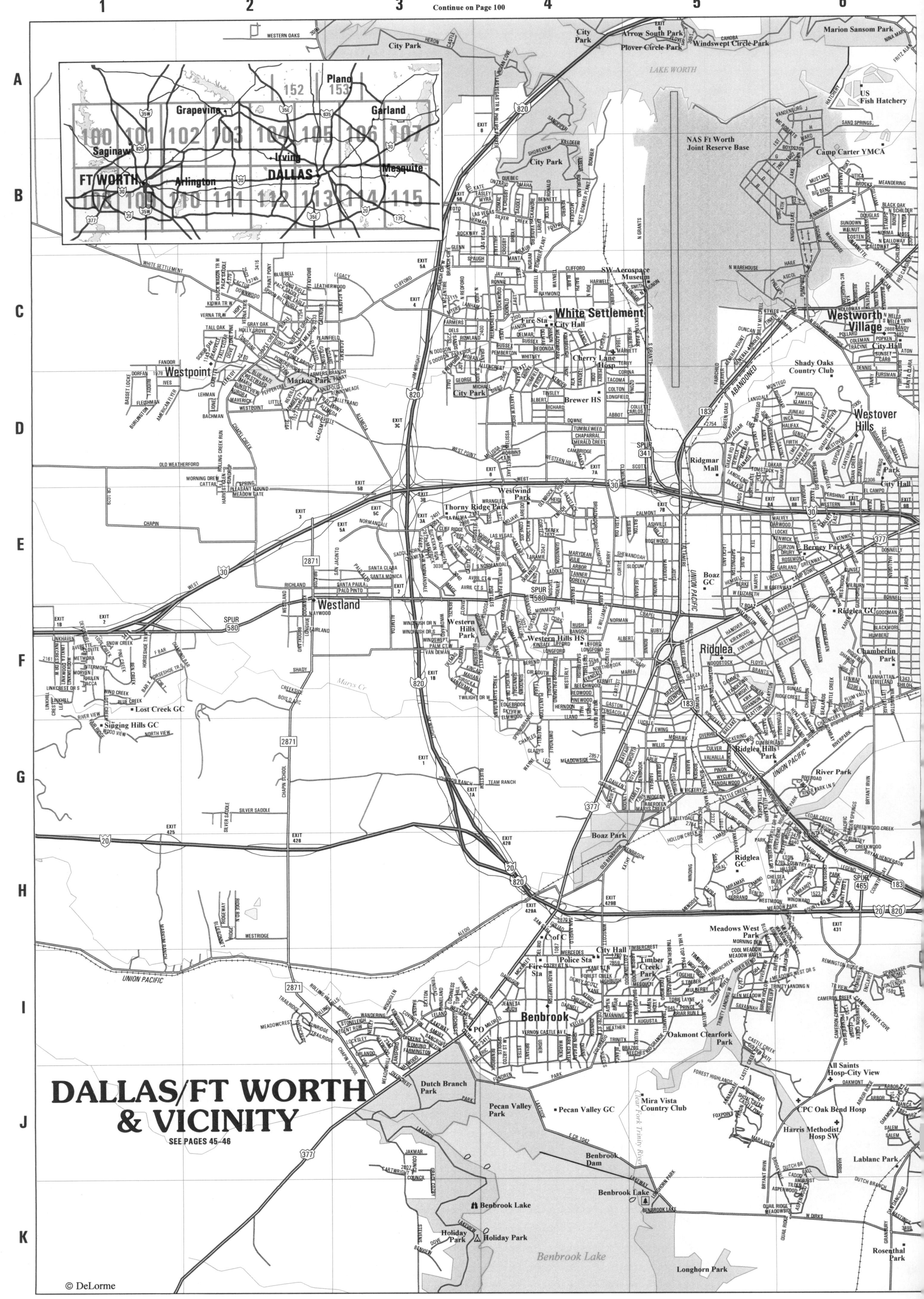

Continue on Page 101

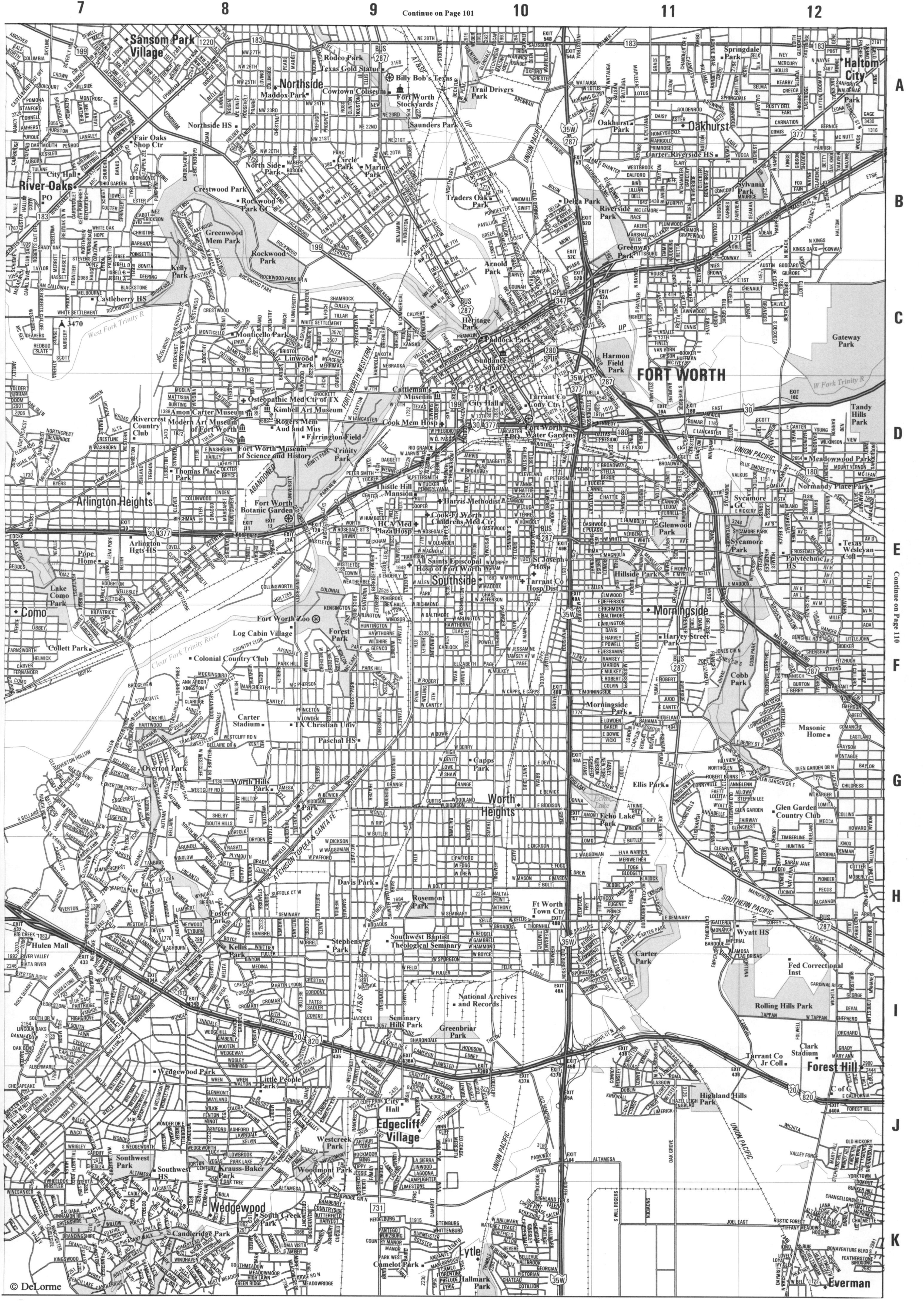

Continue on Page 110

A B C D E F G H I J K

1" = 0.8 mi (1.3 km)

Continue on Page 102

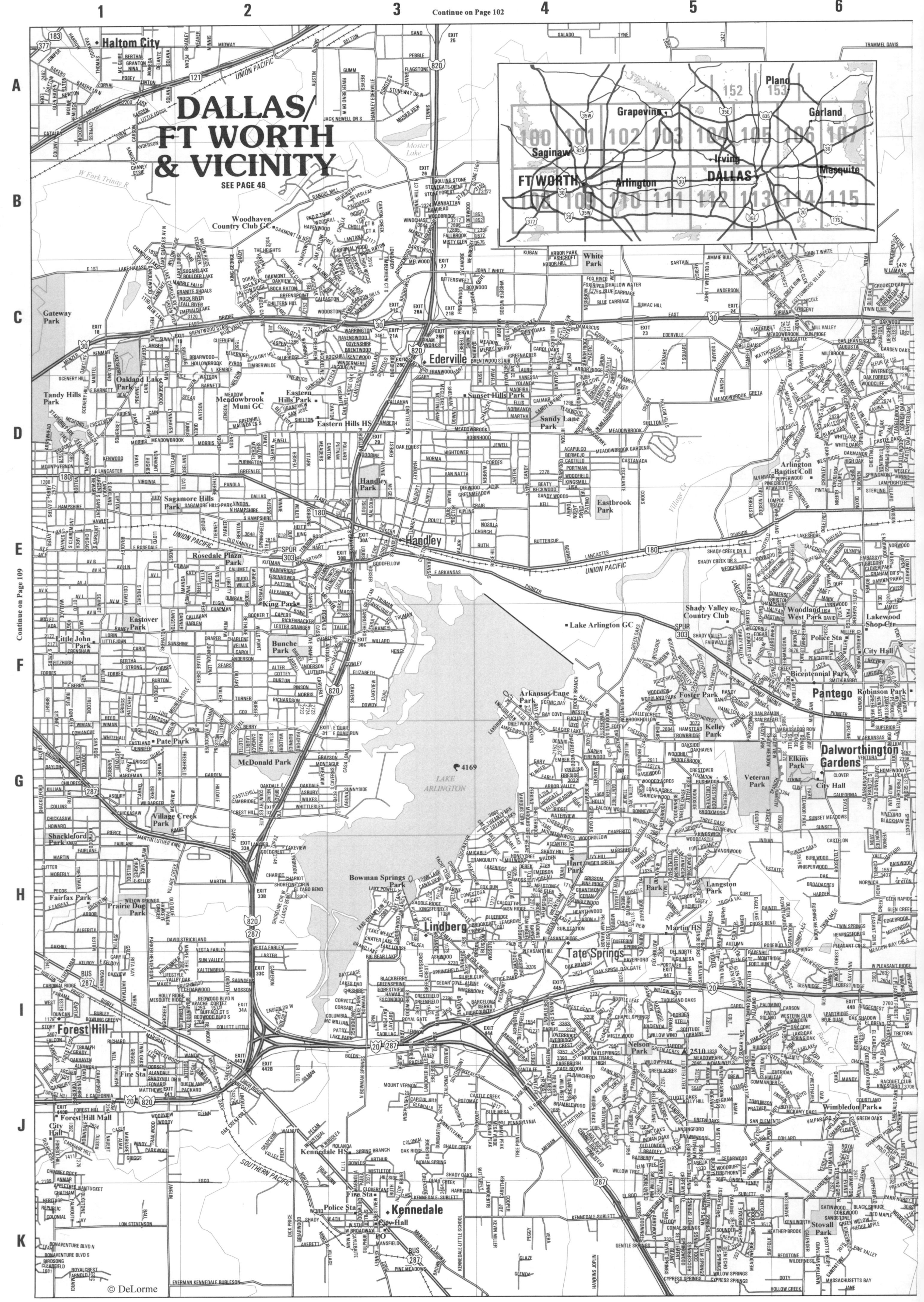

Continue on Page 109

Continue on Page 103

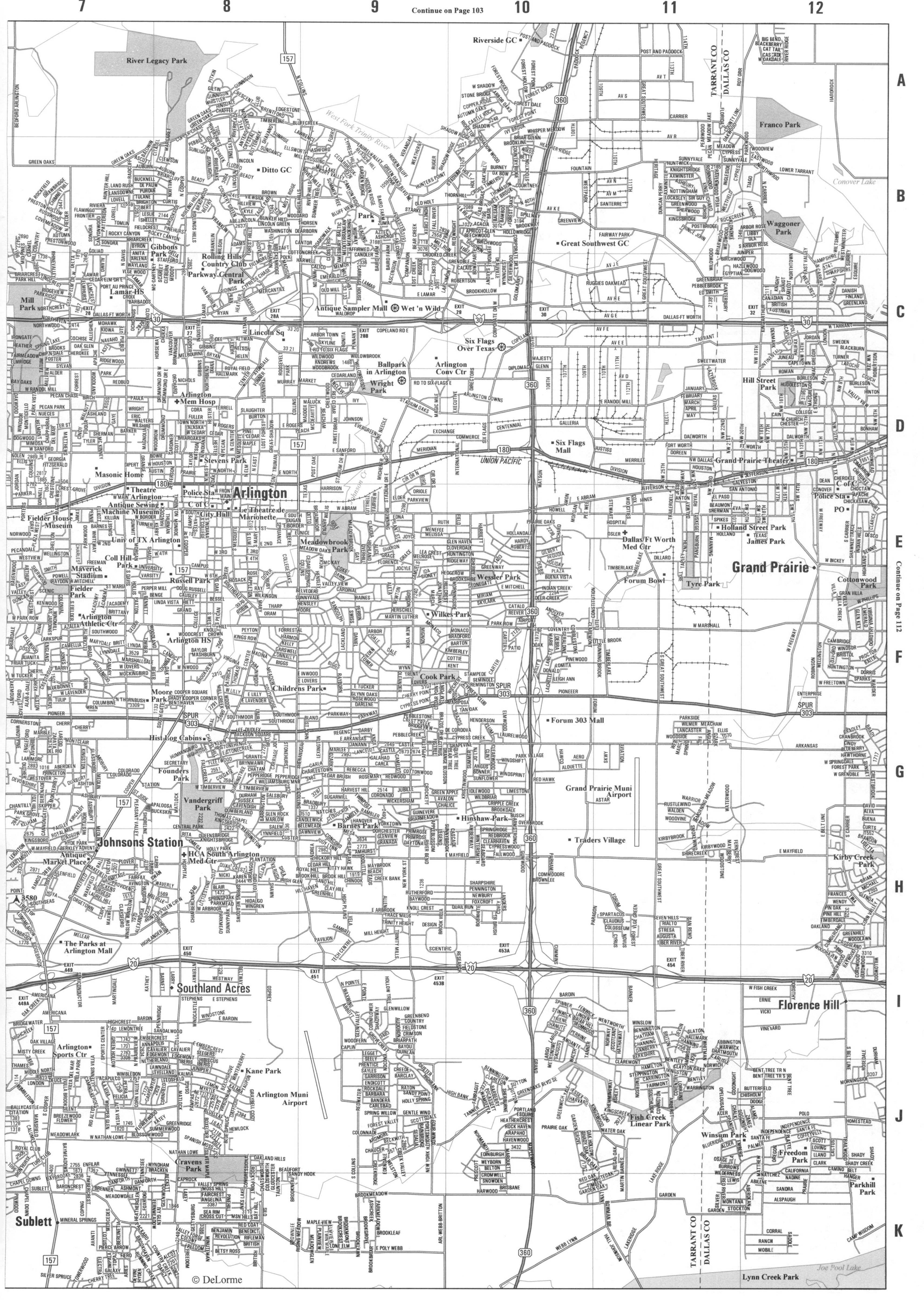

Continue on Page 112

Continue on Page 104

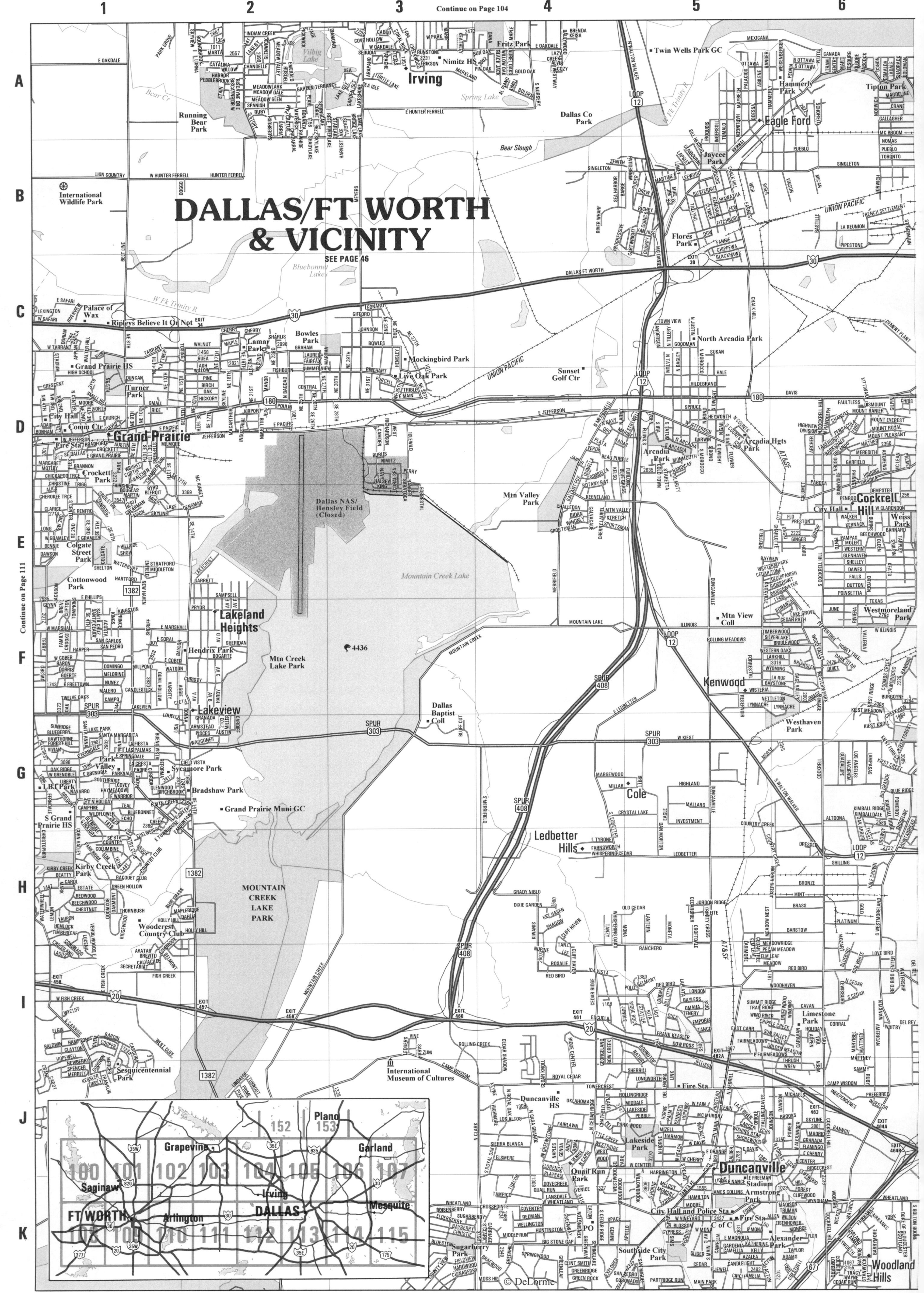

Continue on Page 111

Continue on Page 105

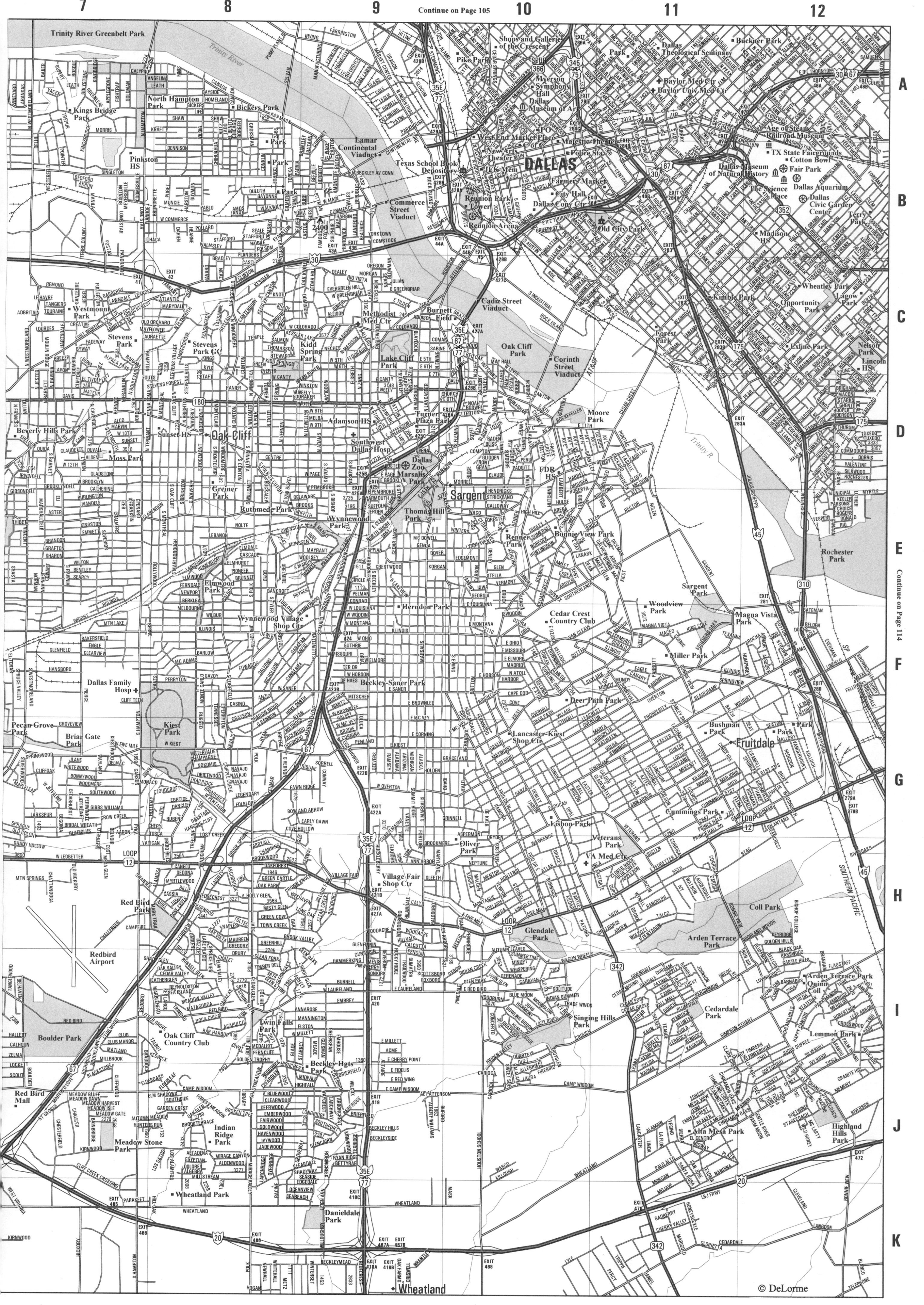

Continue on Page 114

1" = 0.8 mi (1.3 km)

Continue on Page 106

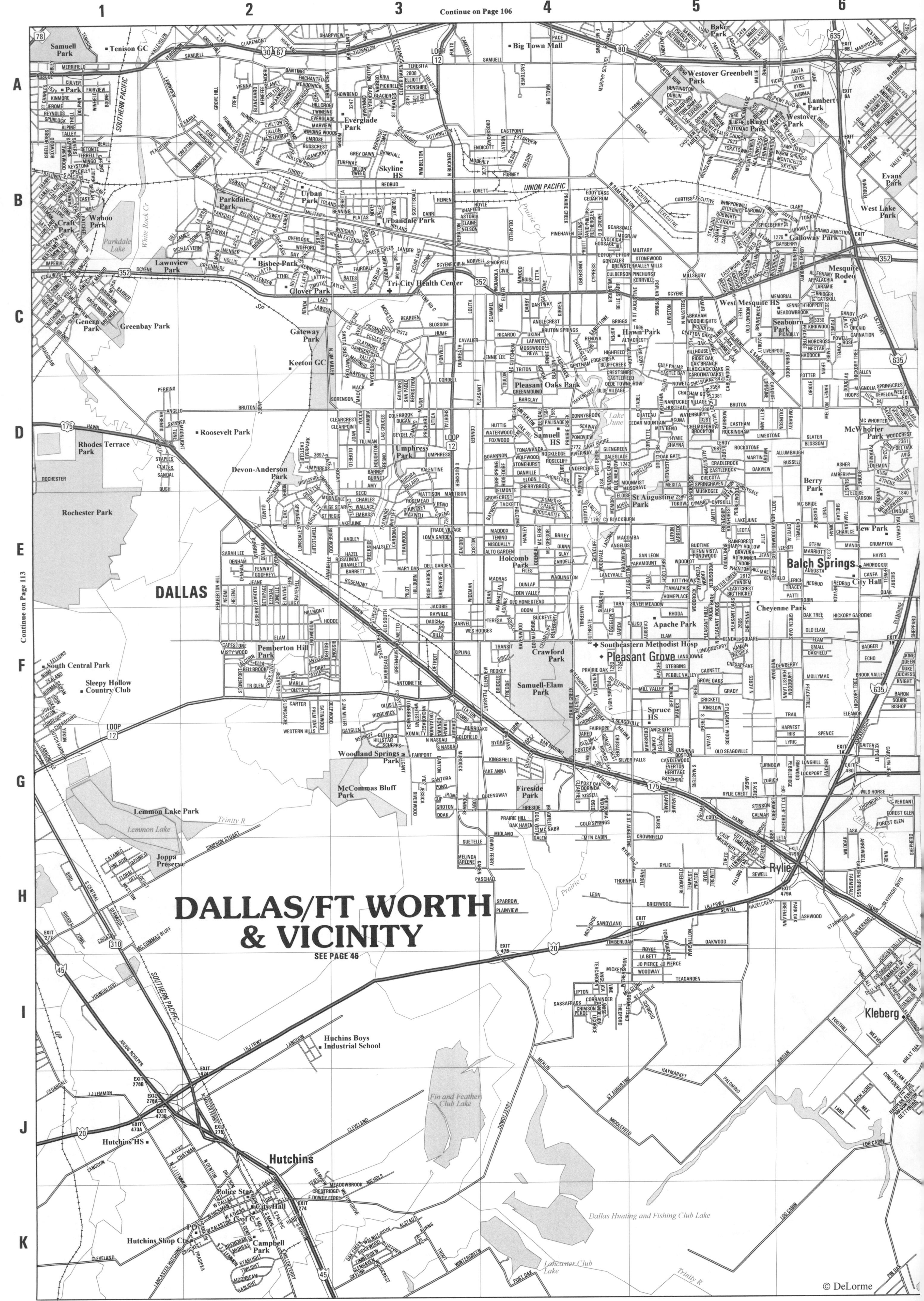

Continue on Page 113

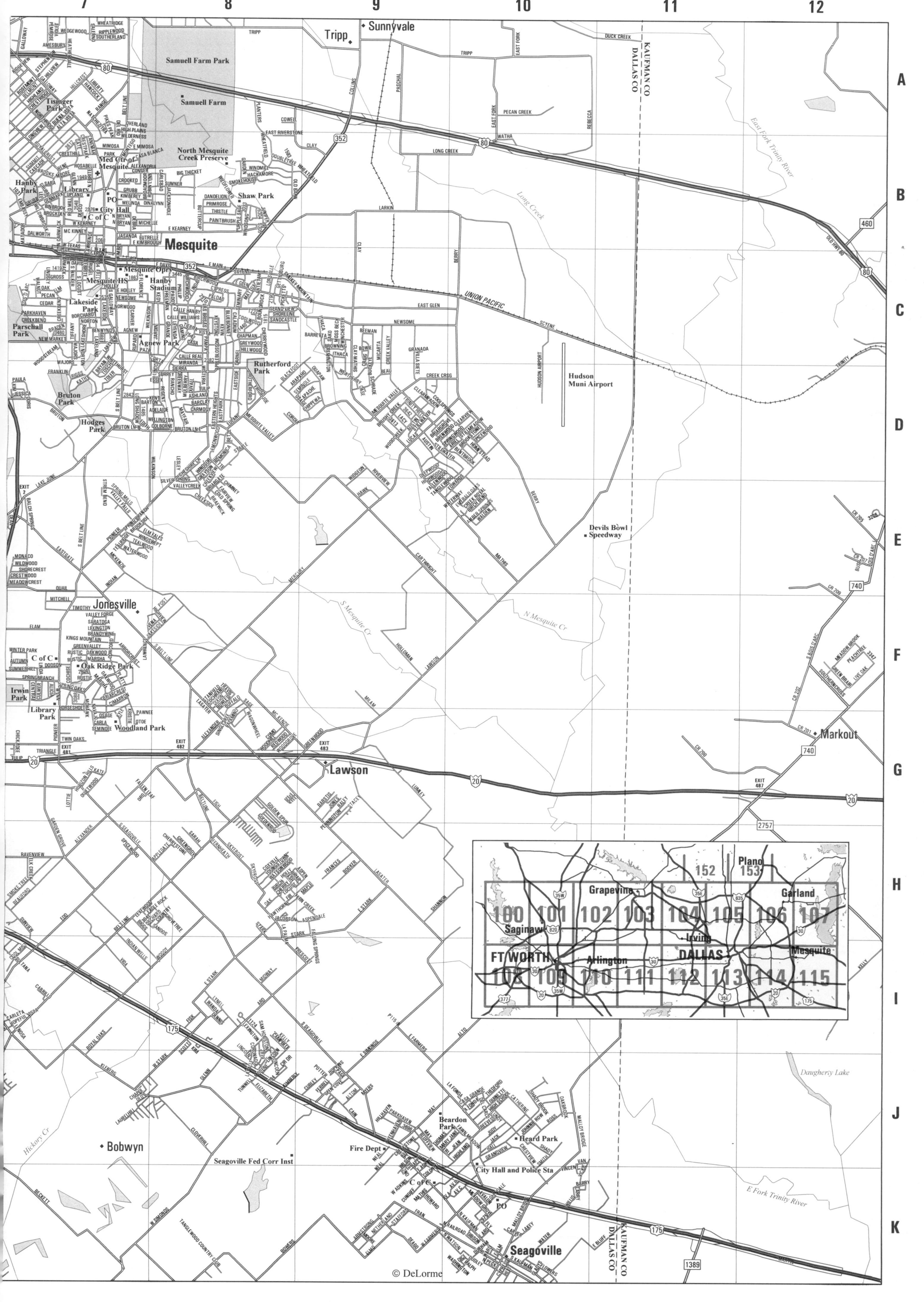
7
8
9
10
11
12
A
B
C
D
E
F
G
H
I
J
K
Sunnyvale
Tripp
Samuell Farm Park
Samuell Farm
North Mesquite Creek Preserve
Med Ctr of Mesquite
Shaw Park
Tisinger Park
Hanby Park
Library
PO
C of C
City Hall
Mesquite
Mesquite Opry
Mesquite HS
Hanby Stadium
Lakeside Park
Parschall Park
Agnew Park
Rutherford Park
Bruton Park
Hodges Park
UNION PACIFIC
Hudson Muni Airport
KAUFMAN CO
DALLAS CO
Long Creek
East Fork Trinity River
Devils Bowl Speedway
Jonesville
C of C
Oak Ridge Park
Irwin Park
Library Park
Woodland Park
S Mesquite Cr
N Mesquite Cr
Markout
Lawson
Daugherty Lake
Hickory Cr
Bobwyn
Seagoville Fed Corr Inst
Fire Dept
Beardon Park
Heard Park
City Hall and Police Sta
C of C
PO
Seagoville
E Fork Trinity River
© DeLorme
152
Plano
153
Grapevine
Garland
100
101
102
103
104
105
106
107
Saginaw
Irving
FT WORTH
Arlington
DALLAS
Mesquite
108
109
110
111
112
113
114
115

1" = 0.8 mi (1.3 km)

DALLAS/FT WORTH & VICINITY INDEX

***Numbers** replace street names where map space is limited; municipality abbreviations appear in parentheses.*

AD Addison
AR Arlington
AZ Azle
BB Benbrook
BE Bedford
BM Blue Mound
BR Briar
BS Balch Springs
BU Buckingham
CA Carrollton
CK Cockrell Hill
CO Colleyville
CP Coppell
DA Dallas
DG Dalworthington Gardens
DU Duncanville
ED Edgecliff Village
EM Eagle Mountain
EU Euless
EV Everman
FB Farmers Branch
FH Forest Hill
FW Fort Worth
GA Garland
GP Grand Prairie
GR Grapevine
HA Haslet
HC Haltom City
HE Heath
HP Highland Park
HR Hurst
HU Hutchins
IR Irving
KD Kennedale
KE Keller
LA Lancaster
LS Lakeside
LW Lake Worth
ME Mesquite
NR North Richland Hills
PB Pelican Bay
PT Pantego
RH Richland Hills
RI Richardson
RL Rowlett
RO River Oaks
RW Rockwall
SE Seagoville
SG Saginaw
SL Southlake
SP Sansom Park Village
SU Sunnyvale
UP University Park
WA Watauga
WH Westover Hills
WS White Settlement
WW Westworth Village

continue on next page

DALLAS/FT WORTH, *continued*

***Numbers** replace street names where map space is limited; municipality abbreviations appear in parentheses.*

AD	Addison	CO	Colleyville	FB	Farmers Branch	HR	Hurst	PB	Pelican Bay	SP	Sansom Park Village
AR	Arlington	CP	Coppell	FH	Forest Hill	HU	Hutchins	PT	Pantego	SU	Sunnyvale
AZ	Azle	DA	Dallas	FW	Fort Worth	IR	Irving	RH	Richland Hills	UP	University Park
BB	Benbrook	DG	Dalworthington Gardens	GA	Garland	KD	Kennedale	RI	Richardson	WA	Watauga
BE	Bedford	DU	Duncanville	GP	Grand Prairie	KE	Keller	RL	Rowlett	WH	Westover Hills
BM	Blue Mound	ED	Edgecliff Village	GR	Grapevine	LA	Lancaster	RO	River Oaks	WS	White Settlement
BR	Briar	EM	Eagle Mountain	HA	Haslet	LS	Lakeside	RW	Rockwall	WW	Westworth Village
BS	Balch Springs	EU	Euless	HC	Haltom City	LW	Lake Worth	SE	Seagoville		
BU	Buckingham	EV	Everman	HE	Heath	ME	Mesquite	SG	Saginaw		
CA	Carrollton			HP	Highland Park	NR	North Richland Hills	SL	Southlake		
CK	Cockrell Hill										

continue on next page

DALLAS/FT WORTH, *continued*

***Numbers** replace street names where map space is limited; municipality abbreviations appear in parentheses.*

AD	Addison	CO	Colleyville	FB	Farmers Branch	HR	Hurst	PB	Pelican Bay	SP	Sansom Park Village
AR	Arlington	CP	Coppell	FH	Forest Hill	HU	Hutchins	PT	Pantego	SU	Sunnyvale
AZ	Azle	DA	Dallas	FW	Fort Worth	IR	Irving	RH	Richland Hills	UP	University Park
BB	Benbrook	DG	Dalworthington Gardens	GA	Garland	KD	Kennedale	RI	Richardson	WA	Watauga
BE	Bedford	DU	Duncanville	GP	Grand Prairie	KE	Keller	RL	Rowlett	WH	Westover Hills
BM	Blue Mound	ED	Edgecliff Village	GR	Grapevine	LA	Lancaster	RO	River Oaks	WS	White Settlement
BR	Briar	EM	Eagle Mountain	HA	Haslet	LS	Lakeside	RW	Rockwall	WW	Westworth Village
BS	Balch Springs	EU	Euless	HC	Haltom City	LW	Lake Worth	SE	Seagoville		
BU	Buckingham	EV	Everman	HE	Heath	ME	Mesquite	SG	Saginaw		
CA	Carrollton			HP	Highland Park	NR	North Richland Hills	SL	Southlake		
CK	Cockrell Hill										

HAMPTON DR/**1873** (BE) 103 G7
HAMPTON LN (AR) 110 K6
HAMPTON RD (DA) 113 A7, C7, G7, K7
HAMPTON RD (GR) 103 A9
HAMPTON ST (FW) 101 K9; 109 C10
HAMPTON ST/**1874** (FW)

HARTFORD DR (RO) 109 B7
HARTFORD DR/**1886** (GA) 106 G6
HARTFORD ST (DA) 105 K9
HARTIN CIR (IR) 104 J2
HARTLINE DR (DA) 106 I4
HARTMAN RD (FH) 110 J1
HARTMAN ST (FW) 110 I1
HARTS HOLLOW RD/**1887**

HAYS ST (FW) 101 K9; 109 C10
HAYSTACK (FW) 108 E4
HAYWOOD CT (BB) 108 J3
HAYWOOD DR (BB) 108 I3
HAYWOOD PKWY/**1904** (DA) 113 H9
HAYWORTH AV (DU) 112 K6
HAZEL LEIGH LN (FW) 109

HENSLEY ST (AR) 111 F9
HENSLEY TER (AR) 111 E9
HENSON DR (HR) 102 J5
HENSON ST/**1918** (DA) 105 K9
HERALD DR (GA) 106 A4
HERALD ST (DA) 113 D12
HERBERT DR (WS) 108 C5
HERBERT RD (CO) 102 D5

HIGH LAWN TER (FW) 109 K8
HIGH LAWN TER (WA) 102 E2
HIGH MEADOW CIR (GA) 107 E7
HIGH MEADOW CIR/**1934** (DA) 105 C7
HIGH MEADOW DR (DA) 105 D7

HIGHTOWER PL (DA) 105 C8
HIGHTRAIL LN (GA) 107 F7
HIGHVIEW DR (GA) 106 B4; 115 F8
HIGHVIEW DR/**1953** (EU) 103 H9
HIGHVIEW LN/**1954** (GR) 103 A10
HIGHVIEW ST (AR) 110 F5

continue on next page

***Numbers** replace street names where map space is limited; municipality abbreviations appear in parentheses.*

AD Addison
AR Arlington
AZ Azle
BB Benbrook
BE Bedford
BM Blue Mound
BR Briar
BS Balch Springs
BU Buckingham
CA Carrollton
CK Cockrell Hill
CO Colleyville
CP Coppell
DA Dallas
DG Dalworthington Gardens
DU Duncanville
ED Edgecliff Village
EM Eagle Mountain
EU Euless
EV Everman
FB Farmers Branch
FH Forest Hill
FW Fort Worth
GA Garland
GP Grand Prairie
GR Grapevine
HA Haslet
HC Haltom City
HE Heath
HP Highland Park
HR Hurst
HU Hutchins
IR Irving
KD Kennedale
KE Keller
LA Lancaster
LS Lakeside
LW Lake Worth
ME Mesquite
NR North Richland Hills
PB Pelican Bay
PT Pantego
RH Richland Hills
RI Richardson
RL Rowlett
RO River Oaks
RW Rockwall
SE Seagoville
SG Saginaw
SL Southlake
SP Sansom Park Village
SU Sunnyvale
UP University Park
WA Watauga
WH Westover Hills
WS White Settlement
WW Westworth Village

POST OAK DR (NR) 102 F3
POST OAK DR (RI) 106 C2
POST OAK RD (HU) 114 K4
POST OAK RD (KE) 102 C2
POST OAK RD/**2626** (GA) 106 A4
POST OAK ST (AR) 111 D9
POST OAK ST/**2627** (HR) 102 K5
POST OAK/**2624** (RL) 107 C8
POST OAKS DR/**2628** (BE) 103 H7
POST RD (BE) 115 F8
POSTAL WAY (DA) 113 B7
POSTBRIDGE DR (GP) 111 B11
POSTGLEN DR/**2629** (DA) 113 I10
POTEET DR (ME) 107 K7
POTOMAC AV (FW) 109 C8
POTOMAC AV (HP) 105 I10
POTOMAC AV (ME) 114 A5
POTOMAC DR (EU) 103 J7
POTOMAC DR (RI) 106 B3
POTOMAC PKWY (KD) 110 J3
POTOMAC PL/**2630** (GA) 106 B4
POTTER LN (ME) 114 D6
POTTER ST (SE) 115 J9
POULIN AV (GP) 112 D2
POWDERHORN RD (FW) 108 C2
POWELL AV (FW) 109 F10, F11
POWELL CIR (ME) 114 C6
POWELL DR (AR) 111 E7
POWELL DR (ME) 114 C6
POWELL RD (ME) 114 C6
POWER CT (IR) 104 G2
POWER DR (DA) 114 B2
POWER DR (DU) 112 J6
POWER SQUADRON RD (DU) 100 C2
POWERS ST/**2631** (HR) 102 J4
POWHATTAN ST (DA) 113 B10
PRAIRIE AV (DA) 105 K11
PRAIRIE AV (FW) 101 K8; 109 A8
PRAIRIE AV/**2632** (DA) 113 A12
PRAIRIE CIR (GA) 107 B7
PRAIRIE CREEK RD (DA) 114 B4, D4, F4
PRAIRIE DR (WA) 102 E1
PRAIRIE HILL LN (DA) 114 G4
PRAIRIE HILL RD (FW) 101 G10
PRAIRIE LN (GP) 111 K12
PRAIRIE LN (ME) 107 J7
PRAIRIE OAK BLVD (GP) 111 J10
PRAIRIE OAK DR (DA) 114 F4
PRAIRIE OAKS DR (AR) 111 E10
PRAIRIE ST (AR) 111 D8
PRAIRIE VIEW DR/**2633** (DA) 105 J8
PRAIRIE VISTA DR (DA) 114 F4
PRAIRIEVIEW CT (AR) 111 I7
PRAIRIEVIEW CT/**2634** (AR) 111 I7
PRASIFKA ST (HU) 114 K2
PRATER ST (DA) 114 H5
PRATHER CT (AR) 110 J5
PRATT ST (DA) 113 E9
PREAKNESS CT (AR) 110 K6
PREAKNESS LN/**2635** (DA) 112 D5
PREAKWOOD DR (GA) 106 B4
PRECINCT LINE RD (FW) 102 K5
PRECINCT LINE RD (NR) 102 E4
PRECINCT LINE RD/**2636** (FW) 110 A5
PRECINCT RD (HR) 102 G5
PREFERRED PL (DA) 112 J6
PRELUDE DR (DA) 106 G3
PRELUDE DR (FW) 109 K10
PREMIER CT (FW) 108 I6
PREMIER DR (IR) 104 E1
PREMIER ROW (DA) 104 J6
PREMIER ST (FW) 101 K11; 109 A11
PRENTICE ST (AR) 111 J9
PRENTICE ST (DA) 105 H11
PRESCOTT AV (DA) 105 J10
PRESCOTT DR (AR) 111 K10
PRESCOTT DR (GA) 106 F6
PRESCOTT LN (SE) 115 I9
PRESIDENTIAL DR (DA) 106 D3
PRESIDENTIAL DR (RI) 106 A2
PRESIDENTIAL ROW (ME) 114 A5
PRESIDENTS CORNER DR/**2637** (AR) 111 B8
PRESIDIO AV (DA) 113 G10
PRESIDIO DR (GA) 106 H6
PRESIDIO ST (FW) 109 D9, D11
PRESTON CIR (CK) 112 E6
PRESTON CREEK DR (DA) 105 B10
PRESTON CREST LN (DA) 105 C10
PRESTON DALE DR (HR) 102 G5
PRESTON DR (FW) 110 G2
PRESTON HAVEN DR (DA) 105 D9
PRESTON HOLLOW CT (AR) 111 B7
PRESTON HOLLOW LN/**2638** (DA) 105 F10
PRESTON HOLLOW RD/**2639** (FW) 109 G8
PRESTON OAKS RD (DA) 105 B10
PRESTON PARK DR (DA) 105 G9
PRESTON PKWY (HP) 105 I10
PRESTON RD (DA) 105 A10, E10, G10
PRESTON RD (UP) 105 H10
PRESTON TR (GA) 107 H7
PRESTON TRAIL DR (ME) 106 I5
PRESTON VALLEY DR (DA) 105 B10
PRESTONDALE DR (DA) 105 B10
PRESTONDELL DR (DA) 105 B10
PRESTONLAKE CT/**2640** (AR) 111 C7
PRESTONRIDGE RD/**2641** (DA) 105 D10
PRESTONSHIRE LN (DA) 105 F10
PRESTONVIEW BLVD (DA) 105 B10
PRESTONWOOD BLVD (DA) 105 A9
PRESTONWOOD DR (AR) 111 B7
PRESTONWOOD DR (RI) 106 B1
PRESTWICK CIR (FB) 105 B7
PRESTWICK ST/**2642** (BE) 103 J7
PREVOST ST (FW) 109 E7
PREWETT RD (FW) 101 F12; 102 F1
PRICE DR (NR) 102 G3
PRICE ST (KE) 102 B3
PRICHARD LN (DA) 114 D3
PRIDDY LN (FW) 109 C7
PRIEST DR (EU) 103 F9
PRIME LN (DA) 112 J2
PRIMROSE AV (FW) 109 B11
PRIMROSE CT (AR) 111 H9
PRIMROSE HILL ST/**2643** (EU) 103 H9
PRIMROSE LN (AR) 111 H9
PRIMROSE LN (BE) 103 G7
PRIMROSE LN (FB) 105 C7
PRIMROSE LN (RL) 107 C8
PRIMROSE ST (ME) 115 B8
PRINCE CT (FW) 109 G11
PRINCE CT (GP) 112 F1
PRINCE CT/**2644** (BE) 103 G8
PRINCE CT/**2645** (FW) 108 I5
PRINCE DR (BB) 108 I5
PRINCE EDWARD ST/**2646** (AR) 110 J6
PRINCE HALL CT/**2647** (DA) 113 G11
PRINCE HALL LN (DA) 113 G11
PRINCE HALL SQ (DA) 113 G11
PRINCE JOHN CT (GP) 111 B11
PRINCE ST (FW) 109 H11
PRINCESS ANNE/**2648** (AR) 110 J6
PRINCESS CIR (DA) 105 E8
PRINCESS LN (DA) 105 E7
PRINCESS LN (HR) 102 I4
PRINCESS PL/**2649** (AR) 111 G9
PRINCESS ST (BE) 103 G8
PRINCETON AV (HP) 105 I11
PRINCETON DR (AR) 111 G7
PRINCETON DR (GA) 106 C3
PRINCETON DR (RI) 106 A2
PRINCETON RD (RL) 107 C11
PRINCETON ST (FW) 109 F9
PRINCEWOOD CT (AR) 110 H5
PRINCEWOOD CT/**2650** (GA) 106 A6
PRINCEWOOD DR/**2651** (GA) 106 A6
PRISCILLA DR (IR) 104 I2
PRITCHETT DR (IR) 104 J2
PRO LN (DA) 105 I12
PROCTOR DR (GP) 111 F12
PROCTOR PL (AR) 111 E8
PROCTOR ST (FW) 110 E3
PROCTOR ST (GA) 106 F4
PROCTOR ST (IR) 104 I6
PRODUCTION DR/**2652** (DA) 105 K9
PROFIT DR (DA) 104 J6
PROFIT ST (GA) 106 C6
PROGRAM DR (DA) 104 F6
PROGRESSIVE DR (DA) 112 B4
PROSPECT AV (DA) 105 J12
PROSPECT AV (FW) 101 K9; 109 A9
PROSPECT DR (IR) 104 C1
PROSPER ST (DA) 105 H9
PROSPERITY AV (DA) 113 F11
PROTHROW ST/**2653** (FW) 110 F3
PROTON DR (AD) 105 A8
PROTON RD (FB) 105 B8
PROVIDENCE CT (AR) 111 H7
PROVIDENCE DR (GA) 106 G6
PROVINCE LN (DA) 106 J4
PROVINE ST (FW) 110 D1
PRUDENTIAL DR (DA) 105 J7
PRUITT AV (DA) 114 B4
PRUITT ST (FW) 109 E9
PRYOR PL (GP) 112 F2
PRYOR ST (DA) 113 A11
PUEBLO AV (DA) 112 B6
PUEBLO CT (AR) 111 C7
PUEBLO DR (GA) 107 B7
PUEBLO ST (DA) 112 B6
PUEBLO TR (LW) 100 K5
PUERTO RICO DR (DA) 106 H5
PUERTO ST (FW) 109 K7
PUERTO VALLARTA DR (NR) 102 H2
PUGET ST (DA) 113 B8
PULASKI (DA) 104 K6
PULASKI ST (FW) 109 E11
PUMP PLANT B RD (DA) 113 A8
PUMPHREY RD (WW) 108 C6
PUMPKIN DR (FW) 109 B8
PURCELL DR (GA) 106 A6
PURCELL ST (GP) 112 D3
PURCEY ST (FW) 109 C9
PURDUE AV (DA) 105 H9
PURDUE AV (RO) 109 A7
PURDUE DR (AR) 111 B7
PURDUE DR (GA) 106 C3, D3
PURDUE ST (UP) 105 H10
PURINGTON AV (FW) 110 D2
PURINGTON AV/**2654** (FW) 109 D12
PURITAN DR/**2655** (DA) 113 E10
PURITAN DR/**2656** (IR) 104 I2
PURPLE SAGE RD (DA) 105 B11
PURPLE SAGE TR (ME) 115 B8
PURSELLEY DR (FW) 110 D3
PUTMAN (GA) 107 B7
PUTNAM DR (DA) 105 H7
PUTNAM ST (FW) 110 D3
PUTTING GREEN DR/**2657** (DA) 113 J8
PYKA DR (DA) 113 G7
PYLON ST (FW) 101 I9
PYRAMID DR (FB) 104 B6
PYRAMID DR (GA) 106 B6
PYRAMID DR (ME) 114 D6
PYRON AV (FW) 110 C2
QAK PATH LN (DA) 105 D12
QUAIL COVE CT/**2658** (HR) 102 G5
QUAIL CREEK CT (KD) 110 K3
QUAIL CREEK ST/**2659** (BB) 108 I4
QUAIL CREEK TR (RL) 107 B10
QUAIL CREST CT/**2660** (GR) 103 E8
QUAIL CREST DR (AR) 111 H8
QUAIL CREST DR (CO) 102 G5
QUAIL CT (AR) 110 G4
QUAIL CT (RL) 107 B10
QUAIL DR (BS) 114 E6
QUAIL DR (FW) 110 G3
QUAIL GLENN CT (RL) 107 B10
QUAIL HOLLOW DR (GP) 112 F1
QUAIL HOLLOW DR (ME) 107 K7
QUAIL HOLLOW DR (RL) 107 B10
QUAIL HOLLOW DR/**2661** (GA) 106 F6
QUAIL HOLLOW RD (FW) 109 K7
QUAIL LN (AR) 110 H4
QUAIL MEADOW DR/**2662** (WA) 102 G2
QUAIL RD (BS) 115 E7
QUAIL RD (FW) 110 F3
QUAIL RIDGE CT (FW) 108 K6
QUAIL RIDGE DR (EM) 100 E5
QUAIL RIDGE DR/**2663** (NR) 102 I2
QUAIL RIDGE RD (FW) 108 K6
QUAIL RIDGE RD (KE) 102 D2
QUAIL RIDGE RD (RL) 107 B11
QUAIL RUN (DA) 106 G3
QUAIL RUN (DU) 112 K4
QUAIL RUN (FW) 109 D7
QUAIL RUN (PB) 100 C1
QUAIL RUN/**2664** (GA) 107 B7
QUAIL RUN/**2665** (NR) 102 H4
QUAIL RUN DR (FW) 110 G3
QUAIL RUN DR (WA) 102 F1
QUAIL RUN RD (AR) 111 H10
QUAIL RUN RD/**2666** (KE) 102 C2
QUAIL RUN ST (CO) 102 G5
QUAIL TR (FW) 109 B7
QUAIL VALLEY ST/**2667** (IR) 112 A2
QUAILS LN (FW) 110 G1
QUAILS PATH RD (CO) 102 E5
QUAKER ST (DA) 105 K8
QUALITY HILL RD (CO) 102 E5
QUALITY LN/**2668** (DA) 105 G12
QUANAH ST (DA) 106 H4
QUANAH ST (IR) 104 K2
QUAPAW (ME) 115 D9
QUARRY ST (DA) 112 B5
QUARTER HORSE (KE) 102 E2
QUARTER HORSE DR/**2669** (GP) 104 K1
QUARTERWAY DR (DA) 105 A10
QUARTET DR (DA) 113 I10
QUEBEC DR (GA) 106 C6
QUEBEC DR (WS) 108 B4
QUEBEC ST (DA) 105 K7
QUEBEC ST (FW) 100 K6
QUEEN ANN CT (FH) 110 J2
QUEEN ANN/**2670** (AR) 110 J6
QUEEN CT (FW) 110 D2
QUEEN DR (BS) 114 F6
QUEEN ELIZABETH/**2671** (AR) 110 J6
QUEEN ST (FW) 110 D2
QUEENLILY CT/**2672** (AR) 111 J8
QUEENS CHAPEL RD (FB) 105 A7
QUEENS CT (GA) 106 G6
QUEENS CT/**2673** (AR) 111 G9
QUEENS CT/**2674** (AR) 111 G9
QUEENS WAY (BE) 102 I6
QUEENSBOROUGH DR/**2675** (AR) 111 H7
QUEENSBRIDGE RD (AR) 111 H8
QUEENSBURY WAY CT (CO) 103 F8
QUEENSBURY WAY/**2676** (CO) 103 F8
QUEENSVIEW CT/**2677** (DA) 105 F11
QUEENSWAY ST (DA) 114 G4
QUEENSWOOD LN (DA) 106 F2
QUEENSWOOD LN (GA) 106 A6
QUENTIN CT (FW) 101 K10
QUETA ST (FW) 109 K7
QUIET LN (DA) 112 F6
QUIETWOOD DR (DA) 115 G7
QUINCY DR (GA) 106 D6
QUINCY LN (DA) 105 D10
QUINCY ST (DA) 112 B5
QUINELLA DR (DA) 112 D4
QUINETTE DR (SE) 115 J10
QUINLAN CT (AR) 111 I9
QUINN ST (DA) 114 E4
QUINN ST (FW) 109 F12
QUINTANA DR (GA) 106 G6
QUINTO DR (DA) 114 C3
QUORUM DR (AD) 105 A9
R L THORNTON FRWY (DA) 113 A12, B10; 114 A3
RACE ST (DA) 113 A11
RACE ST (FW) 109 B11, K12
RACEBROOK CT (FW) 101 F12
RACEHORSE DR (GP) 104 K1
RACELL ST (DA) 114 C1
RACINE DR (DA) 113 K8
RACQUET CLUB CT (AR) 110 J6
RACQUET CLUB DR (AR) 110 I6
RACQUET CLUB DR (GP) 112 H1
RADAR WAY (DA) 112 D4
RADBROOK PL (DA) 105 G9
RADCLIFF DR (AR) 111 B7
RADCLIFFE DR (RL) 107 E8
RADFORD RD (FW) 110 G2
RADIO RD (IR) 103 C12
RADSTOCK CT/**2678** (FW) 109 J7
RAFE (CA) 104 B4
RAIDER DR (FW) 103 K7
RAIDER RD (EU) 103 J7
RAILRIDGE CIR (FW) 109 K9
RAILROAD AV (DA) 113 D12
RAILROAD AV (SE) 115 K10
RAIN TREE (IR) 104 D2
RAINBOW (RL) 107 B11
RAINBOW DR (DA) 113 C8
RAINBOW DR (RI) 106 B3
RAINBOW DR/**2679** (GP) 112 G1
RAINBOW ST (SL) 103 B7
RAINBOW TR (GR) 103 B10
RAINER DR (DG) 110 H6
RAINES CT (EU) 103 G9
RAINES ST (AR) 111 F9
RAINFOREST CT (DA) 114 E5
RAINFOREST CT (SL) 103 A8
RAINFOREST DR (DA) 114 E5
RAINIER ST (IR) 103 I12; 104 I1
RAINTREE CT (DA) 105 B10
RAINTREE CT/**2680** (BE) 103 G8
RAINTREE DR (SL) 103 A8
RAINTREE RD (FW) 110 C1
RAINWOOD CT/**2681** (AR) 110 J6
RALEIGH CIR (IR) 104 I1
RALEIGH PL (DA) 105 J9
RALEIGH ST (DA) 105 J9
RALEY DR (DA) 115 G9
RALL CIR (FW) 108 J6
RALL CT (AR) 111 H7
RALPH ST (SE) 115 K10
RALPH ST (WS) 108 C4
RALSTON AV (DA) 105 I8
RAMBLER CT (AR) 111 G9
RAMBLER RD (AR) 111 G9
RAMBLER RD (DA) 105 F12
RAMBLEWOOD TR (DA) 105 B12
RAMBLING CREEK CT/**2682** (AR) 110 I5
RAMBLING DR (DA) 106 K3
RAMBLING LN/**2683** (EU) 103 H9
RAMEY AV (FW) 110 F3
RAMEY ST (FW) 110 F1
RAMHEAD DR (FW) 110 B3
RAMONA AV (DA) 113 G10
RAMONA DR (FW) 108 E5
RAMOS DR (AR) 111 H7
RAMPART ST (DA) 105 J9
RAMPART ST (FW) 109 E12
RAMSEY AV (DA) 113 G9
RAMSEY AV (FW) 109 F10, F11
RAMSGATE DR/**2684** (AR) 110 G5
RANA LN (AR) 110 F5
RANCH DR (GA) 106 F5
RANCH LN (FW) 110 D5
RANCH RD (GP) 111 K12
RANCH RD (HC) 102 H1
RANCH VIEW RD (FW) 109 G7
RANCH VIEW TER (FW) 109 G7
RANCHERO CIR (IR) 104 H1
RANCHERO CT (AR) 110 J4
RANCHERO RD (DA) 112 I5
RANCHO DR (ME) 102 C1; 115 D8
RANCHO DR (SG) 101 H8
RANCHO GRANDE DR/**2685** (AR) 110 J4
RANCHO GRANDE TR/**2686** (KE) 102 C1
RANCHVIEW (IR) 104 B3
RANCHVIEW CT (FW) 109 G7
RANCHWAY DR (ME) 114 E6
RAND AV (DA) 113 H10
RAND AV (FW) 110 D1
RAND ST (FW) 110 D1
RANDALL ST/**2687** (DA) 113 A10
RANDELL AV (ED) 109 J9
RANDELL ST (FW) 109 J9
RANDI RD (RL) 107 F11
RANDLE DR (NR) 102 I3
RANDLE LN (EM) 100 B2
RANDLES RD (HE) 107 I11
RANDOL LN (FW) 110 C6
RANDOL MILL RD (AR) 111 D7, D11
RANDOL MILL RD (FW) 110 B3
RANDOL MILL RD (SL) 102 B4
RANDOLPH CT/**2688** (WW) 108 C6
RANDOLPH DR (DA) 112 D6
RANDOLPH DR (GA) 106 F5
RANDOLPH ST (AR) 111 F9
RANDOLPH ST (DA) 113 H11
RANDOM CIR (GA) 107 G7
RANDOM RD (EM) 100 E4
RANDY DR (AR) 110 F5
RANDY DR (IR) 104 K2
RANDY DR (NR) 102 G4
RANDY LN (FB) 104 C6
RANGE DR (GA) 106 C6
RANGE DR (ME) 115 A7
RANGER (GP) 112 D3
RANGER DR (DA) 112 A6
RANGEWAY DR/**2689** (DA) 106 K2
RANIER CIR (GA) 106 F5
RANIER CT (FW) 109 H8
RANIER ST (DA) 113 D8
RANKIN AV (UP) 105 H10
RANKIN DR (BE) 102 J6
RANKIN RD (LS) 100 J4
RANSOM TER (FW) 110 E2
RAPHAEL DR (FW) 110 G2
RAPP RD (KE) 102 D2
RASBERRY RD (IR) 104 E3
RASHTI CT (FW) 109 H8
RATLIFF RIDGE CT/**2690** (AR) 111 B7
RATON DR (AR) 111 J9
RATON DR (FW) 108 E5
RATON PASS (IR) 104 B3
RATTIKIN RD (FW) 109 G12
RAVEHILL LN (DA) 114 D3
RAVEN CT (SL) 102 A5
RAVEN CT/**2691** (CO) 102 G6
RAVENBEND CT (SL) 102 A5
RAVENCROFT DR/**2692** (GA) 106 H6
RAVENDALE LN (DA) 105 I12
RAVENHILL LN (AR) 110 I5
RAVENS WAY (BB) 108 I3
RAVENSWAY DR (DA) 106 E2
RAVENSWOOD DR (BE) 102 I6
RAVENSWOOD DR (FW) 110 C3
RAVENSWOOD DR/**2693** (GR) 103 A9
RAVENVIEW RD (DA) 115 H7
RAVENWOOD DR (AR) 111 E7
RAVENWOOD DR (DA) 114 F4
RAVENWOOD DR (GP) 111 B11
RAVINA DR (AR) 110 D6
RAVINA DR (GA) 106 F5
RAVINE DR (DA) 105 F9
RAVINE RD (FW) 109 E12
RAVINIA DR (DA) 113 D7, E7
RAWHIDE (IR) 112 A2
RAWHIDE DR (FB) 104 C6
RAWHIDE PKWY (FB) 104 B6
RAWLINS ST (DA) 105 I9
RAWLS CIR (IR) 104 J4
RAY ALVIN ST (FW) 109 H12
RAY DR (HC) 102 K1
RAY DR/**2694** (HC) 102 K1
RAY SIMON DR (FW) 101 K10
RAY ST (AR) 111 E8
RAY WHITE RD (FW) 101 C12; 102 D1, F1
RAYBORN DR (AR) 111 F9
RAYBURN AV (ME) 114 A6
RAYBURN CT (FW) 109 J8
RAYBURN DR (FW) 109 J8
RAYBURN ST/**2695** (GA) 106 D6
RAYDON DR (AR) 111 E7
RAYENELL AV (DA) 114 E2
RAYMOND AV (WS) 108 C4
RAYNER ST (FW) 109 C11
RAYOR CT (KE) 102 C1
RAYVILLE DR (DA) 114 F3
RAYWOOD DR (GP) 111 I12
READING RD (AR) 111 B9
READING ST (DA) 105 K7
REAGAN AV (DA) 105 K9
REAGAN BLVD (CA) 104 A6
REAGAN DR (FW) 108 E5
REAGAN RD (CO) 102 E5
REALISTIC DR (BE) 103 H7
REALTY RD (CA) 105 A7
REAUMUR DR (DA) 105 E8
REAVES (FW) 103 J7
REAVES CT (EU) 103 I9
REAVES LN/**2696** (HR) 102 J5
REBA CT (FW) 109 H11
REBA RD (HE) 107 J12
REBECCA LN (AR) 111 G9
REBECCA LN/**2697** (WA) 102 G2
REBECCA RD (SU) 115 A10
RECOGNITION POINT DR (IR) 104 I6
RECORD CROSSING RD (DA) 105 J8
RECORD ST (DA) 113 B10
RECTOR AV (FW) 109 I9
RECTOR ST (DA) 113 E11
RED ASH CIR (ME) 107 J7
RED BIRD CENTER DR (DA) 112 I6
RED BIRD DR (IR) 104 J3
RED BIRD LN (DA) 112 I4, I6; 113 I8, I10
RED BIRD RD (DA) 113 I7
RED BIRD RD (DU) 112 I5
RED CACTUS CT/**2698** (AR) 110 J4
RED CARDINAL LN (FW) 108 C6
RED CEDAR LN (AR) 111 D9
RED CLOUD DR (DA) 114 D5
RED COAT LN (AR) 111 K8
RED CYPRESS CT/**2699** (AR) 111 C7
RED ELM RD (DA) 106 D2
RED FERN LN (DA) 105 C11
RED FOX TR (FW) 101 G11
RED HAWK DR (GP) 111 G10
RED MAPLE CT (AR) 110 K6
RED MILL LN (ME) 115 B7
RED OAK (KE) 102 D3
RED OAK CIR (KE) 100 G1
RED OAK CT/**2700** (KE) 100 H1
RED OAK DR (GA) 107 I8
RED OAK DR (GP) 111 K10
RED OAK LN (AR) 110 D6
RED OAK LN (BE) 103 G7
RED OAK LN (RO) 109 B7
RED OAK ST (DA) 113 C10
RED OAK ST (NR) 102 F3
RED RIVER DR (AR) 110 J4
RED RIVER DR (GA) 106 A4
RED RIVER ST (ME) 106 K6
RED RIVER TR (GP) 111 K11
RED RIVER TR (IR) 104 C3
RED ROSE TR (NR) 102 E4
RED WING DR (DA) 113 J9
RED WOLF DR (ME) 107 J7
RED WRIGHT RD (AR) 111 B10
REDBIRD CT (DA) 113 I7
REDBIRD LN (WW) 108 C6
REDBIRD LN/**2701** (AZ) 100 F1
REDBROOK CT (AR) 111 H10
REDBROOK DR (GA) 106 B6
REDBUD (GA) 100 I1
REDBUD DR (AR) 111 D7
REDBUD DR (BS) 114 E6
REDBUD DR (DA) 114 B3
REDBUD DR (DU) 112 K5
REDBUD DR (HR) 102 J5
REDBUD DR (KE) 102 B2
REDBUD LN (BS) 114 E6
REDBUD LN (FW) 109 C7
REDBUD LN (GR) 100 I1; 103 A10
REDBUD LN (IR) 104 I5
REDELLE ST (GA) 106 C5
REDFIELD DR/**2702** (FW) 109 K7
REDFIELD ST (DA) 105 J8
REDFORD LN (WS) 108 C3
REDKEY ST (DA) 114 F4
REDMAN AV (ME) 114 B6
REDMAN LN (DU) 112 K4
REDONDA ST (WS) 108 C4
REDONDO DR (DA) 106 J2
REDONDO ST (NR) 102 I2
REDROCK DR/**2703** (AR) 110 I6
REDSTART LN (DA) 106 I1
REDSTONE DR (AR) 110 K6
REDWATER DR (AR) 111 J9
REDWOOD BLVD (FW) 110 I2
REDWOOD CIR (DA) 106 I2
REDWOOD CIR/**2704** (FW) 110 I2
REDWOOD CT (NR) 102 F3
REDWOOD DR (BB) 108 F4
REDWOOD DR (GA) 107 H7
REDWOOD DR (GP) 112 H1
REDWOOD DR (ME) 115 G8
REDWOOD LN (DA) 105 G9
REDWOOD LN (RL) 107 D8
REDWOOD ST (AR) 111 G9
REDWOOD ST/**2705** (BE) 103 G7
REDWOOD TR/**2706** (GR) 103 A8
REED AV (SG) 101 H8
REED DR (FW) 110 G1
REED LN (DA) 113 C12
REED ST (FW) 109 F12; 110 F1
REED ST (HR) 102 J5
REEDCROFT DR (FB) 104 C6
REEDER RD (DA) 104 D6
REEF CT (IR) 112 A3
REEF CT (PB) 100 C1
REEF DR (PB) 100 C1
REEF POINT LN (FW) 100 J6
REESE DR (DA) 114 C1
REESE LN (HR) 102 F5
REESLING DR (ME) 106 J6
REEVER ST (AR) 111 F10
REEVES (FW) 110 A3
REEVES LN (SE) 115 J10
REEVES ST (DA) 105 H7
REEVES ST (HC) 102 K1
REFLECTION BAY DR/**2707** (AR) 110 F4
REFLECTION ST (FW) 110 C1
REFORMA DR (DA) 105 A11
REFORMA DR (GP) 112 G1
REFUGIO AV (FW) 101 K9; 109 A9
REGAL BLUFF DR (DA) 105 A10
REGAL CT (RI) 105 A12
REGAL DR (AR) 110 H4
REGAL DR (FW) 108 I6
REGAL DR (RI) 105 A12
REGAL OAK (GP) 111 J11
REGAL PARK LN (DA) 105 F11
REGAL RD (FH) 110 J2
REGAL RD (FW) 101 K12
REGAL ROW (DA) 104 J6
REGATTA (RL) 107 B11
REGATTA CIR/**2708** (DA) 113 I8
REGATTA CT/**2709** (EM) 100 E4
REGENCY CT (AR) 111 G9
REGENCY DR (GP) 111 A10
REGENCY DR (IR) 104 I6
REGENCY DR (NR) 102 G4
REGENCY DR (RI) 105 B12
REGENCY DR/**2710** (GP) 103 K10
REGENCY PL (DA) 105 B10
REGENCY WAY (BE) 103 I8
REGENT BLVD (IR) 103 B12; 104 C2
REGENT CIR (DA) 105 E8
REGENT CIR (IR) 104 C1
REGENT DR (DA) 105 E7
REGENT ROW (BB) 108 I3
REGENT ST (ME) 115 D8
REGENTS PK DR (BE) 102 I6
REGINA CT (IR) 104 H3
REGINA CT/**2711** (IR) 104 H3
REGINALD RD (FW) 110 F2
REGIONAL HWY (BE) 103 H8
REGISTRY DR (GP) 103 K11
REID ST (IR) 104 I5
REIGER AV (DA) 105 K12
REINOSA DR (GA) 106 H6
REISEN DR (GA) 107 B7
REMINGTON CIR (FW) 108 I6
REMINGTON DR (AR) 111 F10
REMINGTON DR (RL) 107 E8
REMINGTON DR/**2712** (FW) 108 D5
REMINGTON LN/**2713** (DA) 105 E8
REMINGTON RIDGE PL (FW) 108 I6
REMINGTON TR (ME) 115 C9
REMOND DR (DA) 113 C7
RENCH DR (LW) 100 J5
RENCH RD (LW) 100 J5
RENDA DR (DA) 114 C2
RENEE (BE) 103 H8
RENEE CT (PB) 100 C1
RENEE DR (EU) 103 I8
RENEE DR (HR) 102 H6
RENEE DR (IR) 104 J4
RENFRO RD (CO) 103 F7
RENFRO ST (GP) 112 E1
RENFRO ST (WS) 108 B4
RENFRO ST/**2714** (GP) 112 E1
RENNER AV (FW) 109 F11
RENNER DR (DA) 113 E10
RENO CT (DA) 114 E3
RENO RD (FW) 108 E4
RENOIR LN (DA) 105 C10
RENOVA DR (DA) 114 C4
RENZEL BLVD (FW) 108 F3
REPPER ST (FW) 101 J10
REPUBLIC DR (FH) 110 K1
REPUBLIC PKWY (ME) 106 I6
REPUBLIC ST (DA) 113 B9
RESCUE ST (GA) 106 D4
RESEARCH BLVD (AR) 111 I10
RESEARCH DR (AD) 105 A8
RESERVE ST (GA) 106 E3
RESERVOIR ST (DA) 112 G5
RESISTOL RD (GA) 106 D5
RETRIEVER LN (ME) 107 K7
RETTA AV (FW) 109 B11, C11
RETTA ST (FW) 109 C11
REUNION BLVD (DA) 113 B10
REVA ST (DA) 114 C4
REVEILLE RD (FW) 108 D2
REVERCHON DR/**2716** (AR) 110 J6
REVERCHON DR/**2717** (DA) 113 D7
REVERE DR (FW) 109 K10
REVERE DR (IR) 104 J2
REVERE PL (DA) 105 I12
REVERE ST (HC) 102 J1
REVOLUTION LN (AR) 111 K8
REWARD LN (DA) 104 F6
REX DR (DA) 105 E10
REX LN (GA) 106 C6
REXFORD DR (DA) 105 G8
REXLAWN DR (DA) 114 C3
REXTON LN (DA) 105 H12
REY CT (KE) 102 C2
REYNOLDS AV (DA) 114 A1
REYNOLDS RD/**2718** (NR) 102 I2
REYNOLDSTON LN (DA) 113 I8
RHAPSODY LN (DA) 113 I10
RHEA RIDGE DR (FW) 100 I5
RHEIMS AV (HP) 105 J10
RHINELAND RD (BB) 108 I3
RHINEVALLEY DR (AR) 111 C7
RHOADS ST (AZ) 100 C1
RHODA LN (DA) 114 F5
RHODES LN (DA) 114 H1
RHOME ST (DA) 104 E5
RHONDA DR (ME) 114 A5
RHONDA RD (KE) 102 B3
RHULEN CT (FW) 108 F1
RIALTO DR (DA) 105 C12
RIALTO WAY (GP) 111 H11
RIATA RIVER RD (FW) 109 I7
RIBELIN WAY (GA) 106 D3
RICARDO DR (DA) 114 C4
RICE CT (AR) 111 B7
RICE DR (GA) 106 B3
RICE DR (RL) 107 E10
RICE LN (FW) 110 D2
RICE ST (GP) 112 D1
RICHACRES DR (DA) 114 J6
RICH ST (DA) 114 B2
RICH ST (FW) 110 E3
RICHARD AV (DA) 105 J11
RICHARD CREEK RD (HC) 102 K2
RICHARD DR (AR) 111 E10
RICHARD DR (GA) 106 D6
RICHARD DR/**2719** (WA) 102 G1
RICHARD LN (AZ) 100 C1
RICHARD RD (FH) 110 I1
RICHARD ST (ME) 114 A6
RICHARD ST (WS) 108 D4
RICHARDS ST (RL) 107 D9
RICHARDS TER (FW) 109 I11
RICHARDSON AV/**2720** (DA) 113 B11
RICHARDSON BRANCH TR/**2721** (DA) 105 E12
RICHARDSON CT/**2722** (FW) 110 F2
RICHARDSON CT/**2723** (FW) 110 F2
RICHARDSON CT/**2724** (FW) 110 F2
RICHARDSON DR (GP) 112 D3
RICHARDSON DR (WA) 102 F2
RICHARDSON ST (FW) 110 F2
RICHBROOK DR/**2725** (GA) 106 B4
RICHCREEK DR (GA) 106 B4
RICHEY ST (DA) 112 B5
RICHFIELD DR (GA) 107 B7
RICHFIELD DR (NR) 102 G2
RICHLAND AV (FB) 104 C6
RICHLAND BLVD (NR) 102 H3
RICHLAND DR (GA) 106 B4
RICHLAND OAKS DR (RI) 106 C1
RICHLAND PARK DR (RI) 106 B1
RICHLAND PLZ DR (NR) 102 J2
RICHLAND RD (RH) 102 J3
RICHLAND ST (FB) 104 C6
RICHLAND ST (FW) 108 E2
RICHLAND ST/**2726** (IR) 104 I5
RICHLYNN TER (RH) 102 J3
RICHMAN DR/**2727** (ME) 106 J5
RICHMOND (KE) 102 C3
RICHMOND AV (DA) 105 J11
RICHMOND AV (FW) 109 F9, F11
RICHMOND DR/**2728** (AR) 111 G8
RICHMOND DR/**2729** (BE) 103 J7
RICHOAK DR (GA) 106 B4
RICHVIEW CT (GA) 106 B4
RICHWOOD CIR/**2730** (BE) 103 H7
RICHWOOD DR (DA) 113 J7
RICHWOOD DR (GA) 106 B4
RICKEE CT (WA) 102 G1
RICKEE DR (FW) 109 I11
RICKEE DR (WA) 102 G2
RICKENBACKER DR/**2731** (DA) 106 K3
RICKENBACKER ST (FW) 110 F2
RICKOVER CIR (DA) 105 C8
RICKOVER CT (DA) 105 C8
RICKOVER DR (DA) 105 C9
RICKS CIR (DA) 105 D10
RICKSHAW DR (DA) 105 F7
RIDAN LN (DA) 112 E4
RIDDINGTON PL (DA) 105 C11
RIDDLE DR (NR) 102 G4
RIDER CIR/**2732** (IR) 104 I4
RIDER RD (IR) 100 G1
RIDGE (KE) 102 D2
RIDGE CENTER RD (DA) 112 I4
RIDGE DR (AR) 110 G4
RIDGE DR (BE) 102 H6
RIDGE DR (WS) 108 D4
RIDGE HAVEN DR/**2733** (AR) 111 C9
RIDGE LN (SP) 100 K6
RIDGE OAK CT/**2734** (GA) 106 B4
RIDGE OAK DR (GA) 106 B4
RIDGE OAK PL/**2735** (GA) 106 B3
RIDGE OAK ST (DA) 114 C5
RIDGE OAK ST (FW) 110 D3
RIDGE RD (DA) 105 F8
RIDGE RD (FW) 108 H2; 109 K9
RIDGE RD (GR) 103 B9
RIDGE RD/**2736** (FW) 109 K8
RIDGE ROCK LN (DU) 112 I5
RIDGE SPRING CT/**2737** (AR) 110 I4
RIDGE SPRING DR (DA) 106 G3
RIDGE ST (DA) 113 D10
RIDGE TOP DR (GA) 107 H7
RIDGE WAY (GA) 106 C4
RIDGEBEND DR/**2738** (GR) 103 D7
RIDGEBRIAR DR (DA) 105 C7
RIDGEBROOK DR (AR) 111 H7
RIDGECOVE DR (GA) 107 H9
RIDGECOVE DR/**2739** (DA) 105 C7
RIDGECREST AV (ME) 114 A6
RIDGECREST CIR (LW) 100 J5
RIDGECREST CIR (SG) 101 G8
RIDGECREST CT (AZ) 100 G1
RIDGECREST DR (AR) 110 I6
RIDGECREST DR (DU) 112 J6
RIDGECREST DR (FW) 108 F6
RIDGECREST DR (GA) 106 E5
RIDGECREST DR (IR) 104 K5
RIDGECREST DR (SG) 101 G8
RIDGECREST DR (WA) 102 F2
RIDGECREST DR/**2741** (EU) 103 I9
RIDGECREST DR/**2742** (EU) 103 I9
RIDGECREST LN/**2743** (FW) 108 J6
RIDGECREST RD (DA) 105 G12
RIDGECREST WAY/**2744** (FW) 108 J6
RIDGEDALE AV (DA) 105 J11
RIDGEDALE DR (CA) 105 A7
RIDGEDALE DR (GA) 106 F5
RIDGEDALE DR (ME) 106 J5
RIDGEDALE DR (RI) 106 A1
RIDGEDALE DR/**2745** (AR) 110 G5
RIDGEDALE ST (IR) 104 H1
RIDGEDORF DR (DA) 114 D4
RIDGEFAIR PL (FB) 105 C7
RIDGEFIELD CIR (ME) 114 C5
RIDGEFIELD ST/**2746** (IR) 104 H1
RIDGEFROST CIR/**2747** (DA) 106 H4
RIDGEGATE (KE) 102 E2
RIDGEGATE DR (GA) 106 A6, B6
RIDGEGATE PL/**2748** (GA) 106 B6
RIDGEHAVEN DR (DA) 106 F2
RIDGEHAVEN RD (FW) 108 F6
RIDGEHEAVEN CT (FW) 108 F6
RIDGELAKE DR (DA) 106 G3
RIDGELAND DR (FW) 109 F11
RIDGELAWN DR (DA) 105 H12
RIDGELINE DR (AR) 110 I4
RIDGELINE DR (HR) 102 J4
RIDGEMAR BLVD (FW) 108 D6
RIDGEMAR MEADOW RD/**2754** (FW) 108 D5
RIDGEMAR PLZ (FW) 108 E6
RIDGEMEADE DR/**2749** (GA) 106 B5
RIDGEMEADOW DR (DA) 106 G3
RIDGEMONT CT (AR) 110 B6
RIDGEMONT DR (DA) 105 H12
RIDGEMONT ST (IR) 104 H1
RIDGEMOOR DR (GA) 106 A3
RIDGEOAK WAY (FB) 105 C8
RIDGEPOINT BLVD (DA) 106 D2
RIDGEPOINT DR (DA) 112 E6
RIDGEPOINT DR (IR) 104 C2
RIDGEROCK RD (FW) 109 I7
RIDGEROW DR/**2750** (GR) 103 D7
RIDGESIDE CT (AR) 110 F5
RIDGESIDE DR (AR) 110 F5
RIDGESIDE DR (DA) 105 C9
RIDGETON RD (FW) 108 G5
RIDGETOP DR (NR) 102 F2
RIDGETOP LN (AR) 111 B10
RIDGETOWN CIR (DA) 105 D10
RIDGETREE LN (AR) 110 J3
RIDGEVALE ST (FW) 108 G5
RIDGEVIEW CIR (DA) 101 B12; 105 C10
RIDGEVIEW CT/**2751** (NR) 102 I2
RIDGEVIEW DR (AR) 111 C7
RIDGEVIEW DR (WA) 102 G1
RIDGEVIEW LN (IR) 104 H1
RIDGEVIEW PLZ (ME) 115 A7
RIDGEVIEW ST (FW) 109 G11
RIDGEVIEW ST (ME) 114 A6
RIDGEWAY (FW) 108 H2
RIDGEWAY AV (AZ) 100 F1
RIDGEWAY AV (NR) 102 F3
RIDGEWAY DR (RI) 105 B12
RIDGEWAY ST (AR) 111 E10
RIDGEWAY ST (DA) 105 K12
RIDGEWAY ST (FW) 108 F6
RIDGEWICK DR (DA) 114 F3
RIDGEWOOD CIR (SL) 102 C5
RIDGEWOOD CIR/**2752** (HR) 102 F5
RIDGEWOOD DR (DA) 114 E3
RIDGEWOOD DR (GA) 106 E6
RIDGEWOOD DR (GP) 112 H1
RIDGEWOOD DR (GR) 103 C8
RIDGEWOOD DR (NR) 102 F2
RIDGEWOOD LN (HU) 114 K3
RIDGEWOOD RD (FW) 109 C8
RIDGEWOOD ST (BE) 103 H7
RIDGEWOOD ST (IR) 104 H2
RIDGEWOOD TER (AR) 111 C7
RIDGLEA AV (FW) 108 E6
RIDGLEA COUNTRY CLUB DR/**2753** (BB) 108 H5
RIDGLEA DR (WA) 102 F2
RIDGLEA LN (FW) 108 F6
RIDINGS PL (AR) 111 C8
RIFLEMAN TR (AR) 111 K8
RIGGS CIR (ME) 115 D7
RIGGS ST (DA) 113 C11
RILEY ST (FW) 109 G11
RILLA DR (GA) 106 F6
RILLA ST (DA) 114 F3
RIMBEY RD (FW) 110 G2
RIMCREST DR/**2755** (AR) 111 J7
RIMDALE DR (DA) 106 J4
RIMWOOD DR (BS) 114 G6
RINCON WAY (DA) 105 H12
RINDIE ST (IR) 104 K3
RINEHART ST (GP) 112 D3
RING ST (DA) 113 A12
RIO ALTOS DR (AR) 111 J7
RIO BRANCO ST/**2756** (FB) 104 C6
RIO BRAVO DR/**2757** (AR) 111 J7
RIO GRANDE AV (FW) 109 D9
RIO GRANDE CIR (DA) 112 G6
RIO GRANDE DR (BB) 108 I5
RIO GRANDE PASS (ME) 106 K6
RIO GRANDE ST (GA) 106 F6
RIO HONDO DR (DA) 106 H3
RIO RITA DR (GA) 106 D6
RIO ST (DA) 113 E12
RIO VERDE WAY (DA) 106 H4
RIO VISTA DR (DA) 113 C9
RIO VISTA LN/**2758** (AR) 111 J7
RIO VISTA RD (FW) 108 E4
RIPLEY ST (DA) 105 K11
RIPPLE CREEK CT/**2759** (FW) 110 C4
RIPPLE RD (DA) 113 I11
RIPPLE SPR DR (WA) 102 E2
RIPPLEWOOD DR (DA) 106 J3
RIPPLEWOOD DR (ME) 115 A7
RIPTIDE CT (FW) 100 J6
RIPY CT (FW) 109 G9
RIPY ST (FW) 109 G9, G11
RISER ST (DA) 112 B5
RISING MEADOW DR (AR) 111 K9
RITA BETH LN (NR) 102 J2
RITA DR (GA) 106 C5
RITA KAY LN (FW) 110 I1
RITA LN (AR) 111 H8
RITA LN (DU) 112 I5
RITA LN (HC) 102 J1
RITA RD (DA) 106 C2
RITTER LN (FW) 101 G11
RIVE LN (AD) 105 A8
RIVER BEND DR (AR) 111 H9
RIVER BEND DR (DA) 105 J7
RIVER BEND DR (FW) 110 A3
RIVER BEND RD (FW) 108 I5
RIVER BIRCH RD (FW) 101 F12
RIVER BLUFF DR (FW) 108 I5
RIVER CHASE DR (CP) 104 A3
RIVER FOREST DR/**2760** (AR) 110 I6
RIVER HILL RD (IR) 104 J5
RIVER HILLS CIR (AR) 111 B9
RIVER HILLS CT (AR) 111 B9
RIVER HILLS DR (AR) 111 B9
RIVER OAKS LN (ME) 106 I6
RIVER OAKS LN (RI) 106 C1
RIVER OAKS RD (RO) 109 B7
RIVER PARK LN (FW) 108 G6
RIVER PARK LN/**2761** (FW) 108 G6
RIVER RD (FW) 108 B6
RIVER RIDGE BLVD (GP) 111 A12
RIVER RIDGE BLVD/**2762** (GP) 103 K12
RIVER RIDGE RD (AR) 110 J6
RIVER VALLEY BLVD (FW) 109 I7
RIVER VALLEY CT/**2763** (AR) 111 B8
RIVER VALLEY CT/**2764** (BB) 108 G5
RIVER VIEW (FW) 108 F1
RIVER VIEW CT/**2765** (BB) 108 H6
RIVER VIEW RD (IR) 104 K5
RIVER WHARF DR (DA) 112 B4
RIVERBEND DR (BB) 108 H6
RIVERBROOK DR (DA) 105 E11
RIVERCHASE RD (CP) 104 A3
RIVERCREST DR (AR) 111 B8
RIVERCREST DR (DA) 106 K3
RIVERCREST DR (FW) 109 C8
RIVERCREST LN (GA) 107 C7
RIVERDALE DR/**2767** (FW) 108 I5
RIVERFALL DR (DA) 105 E11
RIVERIDGE CT/**2768** (FW) 109 H7
RIVERIDGE RD (FW) 108 G6
RIVERLAKE CT (IR) 112 A3
RIVEROAD CT (FW) 108 G6
RIVEROAKS DR (AR) 111 B8
RIVEROAKS DR (DA) 113 H12
RIVEROAKS DR/**2769** (IR) 104 K2
RIVERPARK DR (FW) 101 F12; 108 G6
RIVERPLACE DR (AR) 111 A8
RIVERPORT DR (ME) 106 I6
RIVERPORT RD (FW) 108 G5
RIVERSIDE DR (DA) 105 J7
RIVERSIDE DR (FW) 109 B11, D11, E11, F11
RIVERSIDE DR (GR) 103 A10
RIVERSIDE PKWY (GP) 103 K10
RIVERSIDE PKWY/**2770** (GP) 111 A10
RIVERSIDE RD (DA) 113 J12
RIVERTON RD (DA) 106 H2
RIVERVIEW (GP) 112 C1
RIVERVIEW DR (AR) 110 C6
RIVERVIEW DR (FW) 108 I5
RIVERVIEW DR (IR) 104 J5
RIVERVIEW DR (ME) 115 E9
RIVERVIEW DR/**2771** (NR) 102 I2
RIVERWAY CIR/**2772** (DA) 114 D4
RIVERWAY DR (DA) 114 D4
RIVERWAY PL (DA) 114 D4
RIVERWOOD DR (DA) 114 G3
RIVIERA CT (AR) 111 B7
RIVIERA DR (DA) 112 F6
RIVIERA DR (GA) 106 B6
RIVIERA DR (NR) 102 I2
ROADRUNNER CIR (FW) 100 J4
ROAD RUNNER LN (DA) 114 E5
ROAD TO SIX FLAGS DR (AR) 111 C8, C9, D9
ROAN RD (GA) 107 G8
ROANOKE AV (DA) 105 I7
ROANOKE ST (FW) 108 G5
ROANOKE ST (IR) 104 I1
ROANOKE ST/**2773** (AR) 111 H9
ROARING SPRINGS ACCESS RD/**2774** (WW) 108 C6
ROARING SPRINGS LN (DA) 105 C11
ROARING SPRINGS RD (WH) 108 D6
ROARING SPRINGS RD (WW) 108 C6
ROBBINS DR (WS) 108 D4
ROBERT AV (FW) 109 F11
ROBERT B CULLUM BLVD (DA) 113 B12
ROBERT BURNS DR (FW) 109 G11
ROBERT JONES DR (ME) 106 J6
ROBERT ST (FW) 109 F9, F11
ROBERTA DR (NR) 102 H3
ROBERTA ST (DA) 113 E10
ROBERTS AV (IR) 104 K2
ROBERTS AV/**2775** (DA) 113 C12
ROBERTS CIR (AR) 111 E10
ROBERTS CUT OFF RD (FW) 109 C7
ROBERTS CUT OFF RD (LW) 100 K6
ROBERTS CUT OFF RD (RO) 109 B7
ROBERTS DR (SG) 101 H8
ROBERTS RD (GR) 103 E8
ROBERTSON DR (DA) 113 I12
ROBERTSON RD (AR) 111 C10
ROBERTSON RD (EM) 100 G5
ROBERTSON RD (GP) 111 D12
ROBIN AV (FW) 109 B8
ROBIN CIR (NR) 102 H4
ROBIN CT (HC) 102 H1
ROBIN DR (KE) 102 A3
ROBIN DR (WA) 102 F1
ROBIN HILL CIR (DA) 106 F2
ROBIN HILL LN (DA) 106 F2
ROBIN HOOD BLVD (ME) 114 C6
ROBIN LN (AR) 111 F8
ROBIN LN (BS) 114 F6
ROBIN LN (GA) 106 E4
ROBIN LYNN RD (ME) 115 B7
ROBIN MEADOW DR/**2776** (DA) 106 D1
ROBIN OAKS DR/**2777** (DA) 113 G11
ROBIN RD (DA) 105 I9
ROBIN RD (GA) 107 H7
ROBIN RD (IR) 104 I5
ROBIN RD (PT) 110 F6
ROBINCREEK DR (DA) 113 J9
ROBINDALE DR (DA) 106 F2
ROBINDALE DR/**2778** (BE) 102 I6
ROBINDALE RD (FH) 110 J1
ROBINGLEN DR/**2779** (DA) 113 I8
ROBINGREEN LN/**2780** (DA) 113 J8
ROBINHOOD CT/**2781** (BE) 102 G6
ROBINHOOD DR (GP) 111 B11
ROBINHOOD LN (FW) 110 D4
ROBINHOOD LN (IR) 104 J2
ROBINS LAIR CT/**2782** (AR) 111 E7
ROBINSON RD (GP) 111 F12
ROBINSON ST (FW) 101 K8
ROBINWOOD CT/**2783** (AR) 111 I7
ROBINWOOD DR/**2784** (FW) 109 A11
ROBINWOOD LN (AZ) 100 G2
ROBINWOOD ST (FW) 109 A11
ROBOTICS PL (FW) 110 A3
ROBT JONES DR (ME) 106 J6
ROBY ST (DA) 113 C12
ROCHDALE ST (GA) 106 B5
ROCHELLE BLVD (IR) 104 G4, H4
ROCHELLE DR (AR) 110 H5
ROCHELLE DR (DA) 105 F8
ROCHELLE RD (IR) 103 H12; 104 H1, H2, H3, H4
ROCHESTER ST (DA) 113 D12; 114 D1
ROCINDA CT (PB) 100 C1
ROCK BEND PL (DA) 105 B11
ROCK CANYON TR/**2785** (DA) 113 I8
ROCK CLIFF PL (DA) 105 G9
ROCK CREEK DR (EU) 103 H9
ROCK HAVEN ST (AR) 111 J10
ROCK ISLAND (DA) 113 B9
ROCK ISLAND RD (IR) 103 J12; 104 J2
ROCK ISLAND ST (DA) 113 C10
ROCK ISLAND ST (FW) 101 K7
ROCK MARTIN DR (FB) 105 C7
ROCK QUARRY RD (FW) 109 I7
ROCK RIDGE TER (FW) 109 F9
ROCK RIVER DR (FW) 110 C2
ROCK SPRINGS RD/**2786** (DU) 112 K4
ROCKAWAY DR/**2787** (DA) 106 H1
ROCKAWAY DR/**2788** (DU) 112 J5
ROCKBLUFF DR (DA) 114 C3
ROCKBLUFF DR (RL) 107 F10
ROCKBROOK CT/**2789** (AR) 111 B10
ROCKBROOK DR (DA) 105 F9
ROCKBROOK DR/**2790** (AR) 111 C9
ROCKCRAFT ST (DA) 106 H3
ROCKCREEK DR (DA) 105 J10
ROCKCREEK DR (GP) 111 B12
ROCKCREEK DR/**2791** (AR) 111 F8
ROCKCREEK DR/**2792** (GA) 106 D5
ROCKCREST DR (DA) 113 C7
ROCKCREST DR (GA) 106 A3
ROCKCREST DR (ME) 107 J7
ROCKDALE DR (AR) 111 J9
ROCKDALE DR (DA) 105 F8
ROCKDALE DR/**2793** (NR) 102 F4
ROCKDALE RD (FW) 109 K10
ROCKEFELLER BLVD (DA) 113 D10
ROCKFIELD CT (AR) 111 B7
ROCKFORD DR/**2794** (DA) 112 F6
ROCKHAVEN (FW) 100 H6
ROCKHAVEN PL (DA) 106 D1
ROCKHILL RD (FW) 110 C3
ROCKINGHAM ST (DA) 114 D5
ROCKLAKE CT/**2795** (IR) 112 A2
ROCKLAND DR (DA) 106 C2
ROCKLAND DR/**2796** (AR) 110 I3
ROCKLEDGE DR (DA) 114 D4
ROCKLEDGE DR (GA) 106 H5
ROCKLEDGE DR (SG) 101 H8
ROCKMOOR DR (ED) 109 J9
ROCKMOOR DR/**2797** (DA) 105 F7
ROCKMOOR LN (FW) 108 G5
ROCKNE LN (ME) 106 J5
ROCKPORT DR (DA) 113 H9
ROCKRIDGE TR/**2798** (FW) 109 F9
ROCKSPRINGS CT/**2799** (DA) 105 B10
ROCKSPRINGS DR (AR) 110 K5
ROCKSTONE DR (BS) 114 D5
ROCKVIEW LN (DA) 106 H1
ROCKWALL DR/**2800** (EU) 103 H8
ROCKWALL RD (DA) 106 E2
ROCKWAY ST (WS) 108 B4
ROCKWOOD DR (FW) 109 C7
ROCKWOOD DR (KE) 102 C3
ROCKWOOD LN (FW) 109 B8
ROCKWOOD PARK DR (FW) 109 C8
ROCKWOOD TR (AR) 110 I4
ROCKY BRANCH CT (AR) 110 F4
ROCKY BRANCH DR/**2801** (DA) 106 E1
ROCKY CANYON DR (AR) 111 B8
ROCKY CANYON RD (AR) 111 B7
ROCKY COVE (IR) 104 K2
ROCKY COVE CIR/**2802** (DA) 106 E1
ROCKY DR/**2803** (ME) 114 C6
ROCKY LEDGE/**2804** (BS) 115 F7
ROCKY LN/**2805** (IR) 104 K2
ROCKY PLACE CT (DA) 114 D3
ROCKY POINT DR (AR) 111 K8
ROCKY POINT TR (LW) 100 J6
ROCKY RD (DA) 105 C8
ROCKY RIDGE (LS) 100 J3
ROCKY RIDGE RD (DA) 113 I9
ROCKY TR (GA) 106 B4
ROCKYGLEN DR (DA) 106 K3
RODANDO DR/**2806** (GA) 106 D5
RODEO DR (CO) 102 G6
RODEO DR (IR) 104 B3
RODEO DR (KE) 102 D1
RODEO ST (FW) 109 H12
RODNEY LN (BS) 114 E6
RODNEY LN (DA) 104 D6
ROE ST (DA) 113 C10
ROE ST (WS) 108 C4
ROGAN DR (NR) 102 I3
ROGENE ST (NR) 102 J2
ROGER WILLIAMS DR (IR) 104 I2
ROGERS AV (FW) 109 G8
ROGERS PL (IR) 104 K3
ROGERS RD (FW) 109 E8
ROGERS RD (IR) 104 I3, J3, K3
ROGERS RD/**2807** (BB) 108 J3
ROGERS ST (AR) 111 D8
ROGERS ST (DA) 113 E12
ROGNER DR (FW) 108 B6
ROGUE WAY (DA) 106 H3
ROKY CT (FW) 108 B6
ROLAND AV (HP) 105 J9
ROLAND CT (FW) 109 K12
ROLAND DR (KE) 102 C2
ROLANDA LN (KD) 110 J3
ROLANDO DR (GA) 106 E6
ROLINDA DR (DA) 113 F7
ROLLING ACRES DR (DA) 105 A11
ROLLING CREEK LN (DA) 112 I4
ROLLING CREEK RUN DR (FW) 108 D2
ROLLING DALE LN (FB) 104 A6
ROLLING FORK DR/**2808** (DA) 114 A3
ROLLING HILL CT (BB) 108 I2
ROLLING HILLS DR (BB) 108 I2
ROLLING HILLS DR (FW) 109 G11
ROLLING HILLS LN (DA) 105 B11
ROLLING HILLS LN (GR) 103 E7
ROLLING HILLS LN (SL) 103 A8
ROLLING HILLS RD/**2809** (CP) 104 A2
ROLLING HILLS TR (AR) 111 B8
ROLLING KNOLL CT/**2810** (FB) 105 B7
ROLLING KNOLL DR (FB) 105 B7
ROLLING KNOLL PL/**2811** (FB) 105 B7
ROLLING MEADOW TR (FB) 100 I2
ROLLING MEADOWS DR/**2812** (BE) 103 G7
ROLLING MEADOWS LN (DA) 112 F5
ROLLING OAK LN (GA) 106 B4
ROLLING RIDGE DR (NR) 102 E2
ROLLING ROCK LN (DA) 106 G3
ROLLING SPRINGS CT (FW) 110 C6
ROLLING STONE DR (FW) 110 B3
ROLLING VISTA DR (DA) 105 A10
ROLLING WOOD TR (DA) 100 I2
ROLLINGHILLS CIR/**2813** (GA) 107 E7
ROLLINGRIDGE LN (DU) 112 J5
ROLLINGRIDGE LN (GA) 106 G6
ROLLINGS HILLS TR (AR) 111 B8
ROLLINGSHIRE CT/**2814** (BE) 103 H7
ROLLINGWOOD CT/**2815** (BE) 103 H7
ROLLINGWOOD DR (GA) 107 H7
ROLLINGWOOD DR (ME) 114 C5
ROLNICK DR (GA) 106 D4
ROLSTON RD (IR) 104 K2
ROMA DR (DU) 112 J4
ROMA DR (GA) 106 F6
ROMA LN (FW) 109 J11
ROMACK CT/**2817** (AR) 111 D7
ROMAN CT (DG) 110 G6
ROMAN RD (GP) 111 D12
ROMAN WAY (GA) 107 B7
ROMFORD WAY (NR) 102 G2
ROMINE AV (DA) 113 D11
RONALD ST (WS) 108 B4
RONDO DR (FW) 101 I10
RONNE DR (IR) 104 K3
RONNIE ST (WS) 108 C4
ROON RD (GA) 107 H8
ROOSEVELT AV (FW) 101 K8; 109 A8
ROOSEVELT DR (DG) 110 H6
ROOSEVELT ST (AR) 111 D8
ROPER ST (DA) 105 I9
RORARY CIR (RI) 106 A2
RORARY DR (RI) 106 A1
ROSA CT (DA) 105 G8
ROSA RD (DA) 105 G8
ROSABELLE DR (ME) 115 B7
ROSALIE DR (DA) 112 I4
ROSALINDA LN (DA) 114 E3
ROSALYN DR (WA) 102 G1
ROSCOE AV (DA) 114 A1
ROSE CT (FH) 110 J1
ROSE GARDEN AV (DA) 114 E3
ROSE HILL DR (FW) 110 E4
ROSE LN (FW) 110 E2
ROSE LN (IR) 104 I4
ROSE LN (ME) 114 C6
ROSE OF SHARON LN (FW) 101 G12
ROSE PL (BE) 103 H8
ROSE ST (AR) 111 E8
ROSE ST (CO) 102 F6
ROSE ST (IR) 104 I4
ROSEBUD (RL) 107 C9
ROSEBUD DR (IR) 104 K5
ROSEBUD DR (RH) 102 K2
ROSEBUD DR (RL) 107 C9
ROSEBUD LN (DG) 110 H6
ROSECLIFF DR (DA) 114 D4
ROSECLIFF TER (GR) 103 D8
ROSEDALE AV (UP) 105 H10
ROSEDALE ST (FW) 109 E8, E9, E12; 110 E1
ROSEDALE ST (GP) 111 J12
ROSEDOWN ST (ME) 107 K7
ROSEHILL RD (GA) 107 G7, H8
ROSELAND AV (DA) 105 K11
ROSELAND ST (FW) 110 D2
ROSELANE ST/**2818** (FW) 110 E2
ROSELANE ST/**2819** (FW) 110 E2
ROSEMARY DR (AR) 111 G9
ROSEMARY DR (HE) 107 H12
ROSEMARY LN (EU) 103 F9
ROSEMEAD DR (DA) 114 E3
ROSEMON AV (CA) 104 A5
ROSEMONT AV (DA) 113 D8
ROSEMONT AV (FW) 108 E6
ROSEMONT RD (DA) 114 E3
ROSEMONT ST (ME) 115 A7
ROSEN AV (FW) 101 K8; 109 A8
ROSEN RD (EM) 100 G4
ROSEVILLE DR/**2820** (DA) 113 I12
ROSEWOOD AV (DA) 105 K9
ROSEWOOD AV (FW) 108 E5
ROSEWOOD CT (EU) 103 G8
ROSEWOOD DR (KE) 102 C3
ROSEWOOD DR (ME) 106 J5
ROSEWOOD HILLS DR (GA) 106 C6
ROSEWOOD LN (AR) 111 F9
ROSEWOOD ST/**2821** (GP) 112 C2
ROSINE AV (DA) 113 C12
ROSITA ST (IR) 104 H4
ROSS AV (CA) 104 A6
ROSS AV (DA) 105 K12; 113 A10
ROSS AV (EU) 103 I9
ROSS AV (FW) 101 K9; 109 A9
ROSS DOWNS DR/**2822** (CO) 103 D7
ROSS DR (IR) 104 I4
ROSS LN (SE) 115 J10
ROSS RD (NR) 102 H3
ROSS TR (AR) 111 D7
ROSSER (RL) 107 F11
ROSSER CIR (DA) 105 E8
ROSSER CT (DA) 105 D8
ROSSER RD (DA) 105 E8
ROSSER SQ (DA) 105 C8
ROSSER ST (FW) 110 E3
ROSSFORD DR (FB) 104 C6
ROSSFORD ST/**2823** (FB) 104 C6
ROSSLYN CHAPEL CT (AR) 110 D6
ROSWELL ST (DA) 105 K10
ROTA CIR (FW) 109 K7
ROTAN LN (DA) 105 E7
ROTHINGTON RD (DA) 114 A3
ROTHINGTON RD (FW) 108 F5
ROUGH BARK DR (DA) 114 E5
ROUGH CREEK RD/**2824** (FH) 110 J1
ROUND TABLE DR (DA) 104 I6
ROUND TREE DR/**2825** (EU) 103 H9
ROUNDROCK RD (DA) 105 A10
ROUNDROCK RD/**2826** (AR) 111 G8
ROUNDROCK TR (ME) 100 I2; 115 C8
ROUNDTOP BLVD (DU) 112 I5
ROUNDTREE ST (ME) 107 K7
ROUSE ST (FW) 109 C11
ROUTH ST (DA) 113 A10
ROUTH ST/**2827** (DA) 105 K10
ROUTT ST (FW) 110 E3
ROWAN AV (DA) 113 A12
ROWAN DR (FW) 108 F5
ROWCROP DR/**2828** (AR) 111 J8
ROWENA ST (DA) 105 K11
ROWLAND AV/**2829** (DA) 114 F3
ROWLAND DR (WS) 108 C3
ROWLETT RD (GA) 107 H8
ROWLETT RD (RL) 107 C8, E9
ROWLETT ST/**2830** (RL) 107 D9
ROXANNE WAY (FW) 100 J5
ROXBURY LN (DA) 105 E9
ROXIE ST (HC) 101 J12; 102 J1
ROY LN (KE) 102 C2
ROY ORR BLVD (GP) 111 A11
ROYAL AV (GP) 111 E11
ROYAL AV/**2831** (DU) 112 K5
ROYAL CEDAR LN (DA) 112 J4
ROYAL CHAPEL DR (DA) 105 E7
ROYAL CIR (AR) 110 J6
ROYAL CIR (DA) 105 E11
ROYAL CLUB CT (AR) 111 J7
ROYAL CLUB LN (DA) 105 E7
ROYAL COACH LN/**2832** (GP) 104 K1
ROYAL COVE DR (DA) 105 E8
ROYAL CREST CIR (GA) 107 E7
ROYAL CROWN DR (DA) 105 E12
ROYAL CT/**2833** (BE) 103 G8
ROYAL DR (FW) 108 G5
ROYAL DR (GA) 106 F4
ROYAL FIELD DR (AR) 111 D8
ROYAL GABLE DR (DA) 105 E7
ROYAL GATE DR (AR) 110 I3
ROYAL HARBOR (EM) 100 F4
ROYAL HAVEN LN (DA) 105 E7
ROYAL HIGHLANDS DR (DA) 106 E2
ROYAL HILL LN (AR) 111 H9
ROYAL LN (BB) 108 H6
ROYAL LN (DA) 104 E6; 105 E8, E9; 106 E1
ROYAL LN (HR) 102 J4
ROYAL LN (IR) 103 B12; 104 D1, D2, E3
ROYAL MILE DR (AR) 111 H7
ROYAL OAK DR (DU) 112 J4
ROYAL OAKS CIR/**2834** (GA) 106 B5
ROYAL OAKS DR (DA) 115 I7
ROYAL OAKS DR (FH) 110 J2
ROYAL OAKS DR (GA) 106 B5
ROYAL OAKS DR (IR) 104 K2
ROYAL OAKS DR/**2835** (NR) 102 G4
ROYAL PALMS ST (DA) 105 D8
ROYAL PARK (DA) 105 E11
ROYAL PL (DA) 105 E11
ROYAL RIDGE DR (DA) 105 E8
ROYAL RIDGE LN (IR) 104 D1
ROYAL SPRINGS DR (AR) 110 K5
ROYAL TER (HR) 102 I4
ROYAL WAY (DA) 105 E10
ROYALCREST DR (DA) 105 E9
ROYALCREST DR (FW) 110 K1
ROYALCREST DR (GA) 107 E7
ROYALCREST DR (ME) 115 B7
ROYALCREST DR (RI) 106 A1
ROYALCREST DR/**2836** (AR) 111 K7
ROYALOAK DR/**2837** (AR) 110 F4
ROYALPINE DR (DA) 106 G1
ROYALSHIRE DR (DA) 105 D10
ROYALTON DR (DA) 105 E10
ROYALTY FARROW ROW RD/**2838** (IR) 104 I6
ROYALTY ROW (IR) 104 I6
ROYALWOOD DR (DA) 106 F2
ROYALWOOD DR/**2839** (AR) 111 B9
ROYCE DR (AR) 110 G4
ROYCE DR (DA) 114 I5
ROYCE DR (EU) 103 J9
ROYSTER RD (FW) 109 K9
RUBENS DR (DA) 113 G8
RUBY (KE) 102 B1
RUBY DR (DA) 112 J6
RUBY DR (ME) 106 J5
RUBY PL (FW) 108 F5
RUBY RD (GP) 112 C1
RUBY RD (IR) 112 A2
RUBY ST (AR) 111 E8
RUDD ST (FW) 110 E2
RUDER ST (DA) 112 B5
RUE CHALEAU/**2840** (BB) 108 H6
RUE CIR (ME) 114 B6
RUE DU LAC RD (DA) 105 D10
RUEA ST (GP) 112 C2
RUFE SNOW DR (KE) 102 E2
RUFE SNOW DR (NR) 102 I2
RUFE SNOW RD (NR) 102 J2
RUFE SNOW RD (WA) 102 G2
RUFUS ST (FW) 110 F1
RUGBY LN (FB) 104 B6
RUGEL ST (ME) 115 C7
RUGER DR (AR) 111 B9
RUGGED DR (DA) 113 G8
RUGGIES OAKMEAD DR (AR) 111 C11
RUIDOSA AV (DA) 106 H4
RUIDOSA TR (FW) 108 F4
RUIDOSO CT (AR) 110 I5
RUIDOSO CT (SG) 101 H8
RUIDOSO DR (AR) 110 I5
RUIDOSO DR (SG) 101 H8
RUMFIELD EDEN RD (NR) 102 F4
RUMFIELD RD (NR) 102 F4
RUMFIELD RD (WS) 108 D4
RUNGE CT (IR) 104 G1
RUNNELS ST (FW) 101 K10
RUNNELS ST/**2841** (FW) 109 A10
RUNNEMEDE LN (DA) 105 I12
RUNNING BROOK DR (AR) 111 F11
RUNNING CREEK DR (AR) 111 K8
RUNNING RIVER RD (GA) 106 B5
RUNNINGBROOK LN (DA) 106 J3
RUNNINGBROOK LN/**2842** (ME) 115 D7
RUNNYMEADE (KE) 102 C3
RUNNYMEADE PL (FW) 108 D3
RUNNYMEDE DR (GA) 106 C3
RUNSTONE DR (IR) 112 A3
RUNYON RD (AD) 105 A8
RUPARD (ME) 115 C7
RUPERT ST (DA) 113 A7
RUPERT ST (FW) 109 C9
RUPLEY LN (DA) 106 H3
RUSDELL DR (IR) 112 A2
RUSH CIR (AD) 105 A8
RUSH CREEK (KE) 102 D3
RUSH SPRINGS CT (AR) 110 I6
RUSH ST (BB) 108 F4
RUSH VALLEY CT (AR) 110 G5
RUSHING MEADOW CT (DG) 110 H6
RUSHMOOR DR (AR) 110 G5
RUSK AV (DA) 105 K11
RUSK DR (EU) 103 H9
RUSK DR (ME) 114 D6
RUSK DR (RI) 106 B2
RUSK ST (HC) 102 G1
RUSKIN ST (DA) 113 C12
RUSS CT (IR) 112 A2
RUSSCREST DR (DA) 114 B2
RUSSELL AL (DA) 105 K10
RUSSELL DR (BS) 114 D6
RUSSELL DR (GA) 106 E5
RUSSELL GLEN LN (DA) 113 I8
RUSSELL LN (BE) 102 I6
RUSSELL ST (WS) 108 C4
RUSSWIN DR (GA) 106 D3
RUSSWOOD CIR (DA) 105 D9
RUSSWOOD DR (AR) 111 B7
RUSSWOOD LN (GA) 106 A4
RUST WOOD CT/**2843** (FW) 109 G7
RUSTIC CIR (BS) 115 F7
RUSTIC CIR (RI) 106 A1
RUSTIC CT (IR) 104 K1
RUSTIC DR (FH) 110 J1
RUSTIC DR (IR) 104 K1
RUSTIC DR/**2844** (GR) 103 E8
RUSTIC FOREST RD (FW) 109 K12
RUSTIC GLEN DR (GA) 107 I8
RUSTIC MEADOW DR (GA) 106 A4
RUSTIC PL (BS) 115 F7
RUSTIC RIDGE DR (GA) 106 A6
RUSTIC TR (BS) 115 F7
RUSTIC TR (CO) 102 E5
RUSTLE LEAF DR (AR) 110 I4
RUSTLELEAF DR (DA) 106 F2
RUSTLEWIND LN (GP) 111 G11
RUSTON AV (FW) 109 I9
RUSTOWN DR (DA) 106 J4
RUSTY DELL RD (HC) 109 A12
RUTAN ST (FW) 110 G1
RUTGERS CT/**2845** (AR) 111 G7
RUTGERS DR (DA) 106 H1
RUTGERS DR (IR) 104 H2
RUTH DR (GA) 106 E5
RUTH DR (KD) 110 K3
RUTH LN (HR) 102 J5
RUTH RD (RH) 102 J3
RUTH ST (AR) 111 E9
RUTH ST (FW) 110 E4
RUTH ST (GR) 103 B10
RUTH WALL RD (GR) 103 A10
RUTHANN DR (DA) 106 I4
RUTHANN DR (FW) 110 F2
RUTHDALE DR (DA) 105 C8
RUTHERFORD DR (ME) 115 D8
RUTHERFORD LN (AR) 111 H9
RUTHERFORD ST (IR) 104 H2
RUTHERGLEN DR (DA) 114 B4
RUTHETTE DR (NR) 102 F4
RUTLAND AV (FW) 109 H8
RUTLEDGE ST (DA) 113 C12
RUTLEDGE ST (FW) 109 E8
RUTZ ST (DA) 113 A8
RYAN AV (FW) 109 F9
RYAN CIR (DA) 113 G8
RYAN PL DR (FW) 109 F10
RYAN PLZ DR (AR) 111 C8
RYAN RD (DA) 104 F5; 113 F9
RYAN RD (RL) 107 C10
RYAN RIDGE DR (DA) 113 J9
RYAN ST (IR) 104 J2
RYE GLEN DR/**2846** (AR) 110 J5
RYKER DR (DA) 106 G2
RYLIE CREST DR (DA) 114 G5
RYLIE RD (DA) 114 H5
RYLIE ST (DA) 114 H5
RYOAK DR (DA) 114 G4
RYODINGTON PL (DA) 105 C11
SABELLE ST (HC) 101 J12
SABELLE ST/**2847** (HC) 102 J1
SABINE PASS/**2848** (ME) 106 K6
SABINE ST (DA) 113 C9
SABINE ST (FH) 109 H12
SABLE ST/**2849** (FB) 104 C6
SABROSA CT/**2850** (FW) 109 K7
SABROSA CT/**2851** (FW) 109 K7
SACRO MONTE DR/**2852** (DA) 105 A10
SADDLE HORSE LN/**2853** (FH) 109 J12
SADDLE RD (GP) 111 K12
SADDLE RD (WS) 108 B4
SADDLE RIDGE DR/**2854** (GR) 103 D8
SADDLE RIDGE LN (SG) 101 H8
SADDLE RIDGE RD (AR) 110 H3
SADDLE TR (FW) 108 E4
SADDLE TR (SG) 101 H8
SADDLEBACK CIR/**2855** (HC) 102 H1
SADDLEBACK RD (GA) 107 H7
SADDLEBACK RD/**2856** (AR) 110 J5
SADDLEBROOK DR (CO) 102 F6
SADDLEBROOK DR/**2857** (BB) 108 G4
SADDLEBROOK ST (BE) 102 H6
SADDLEBROOK ST/**2858** (BE) 102 H6
SADDLEHORN DR (FW) 108 E3
SADDLEHORN DR (IR) 104 B3
SADLER AV (FW) 109 I9
SADLER CIR (DA) 105 J8
SAFARI PKWY (GP) 112 C1
SAFARI PKWY/**2859** (GP) 111 C12
SAFARI TR/**2860** (AR) 111 J9
SAFETY CT (DA) 113 A12
SAFFRON CIR (ME) 114 B6
SAGAMORE HILLS PARK (FW) 110 E2
SAGE BLOOM DR (AR) 110 J4
SAGE CANYON CT/**2861** (AR) 110 H5
SAGE CIR (GA) 107 C7
SAGE DR (GA) 107 C7; 115 F8
SAGE LN (BE) 103 G7
SAGE LN (EU) 103 F9
SAGE TR (HR) 102 H5
SAGE VALLEY LN (DA) 112 F6
SAGEBRUSH RD (BB) 108 F4
SAGEBRUSH ST (CO) 102 C5
SAGEBRUSH ST (IR) 112 A2
SAGEBRUSH TR (AR) 110 I4
SAGEBRUSH TR (EU) 103 I8
SAGEBRUSH TR (GR) 103 A8
SAGECREST TER (FW) 109 G7
SAGINAW RD (SG) 101 F7, G8
SAHARA PL (FW) 109 H11
SAHARA WAY (DA) 106 H3
SAHARAH DR/**2862** (GA) 106 A4
SAILBOAT DR (PB) 100 B1
SAINT ANDREWS CT/**2863** (AR) 111 C8
SAINT ANDREWS CT/**2864** (AR) 111 C8
SAINT CLAIR DR (IR) 104 J3
SAINT CLAIR DR/**2865** (IR) 104 J3
SAINT LO DR (IR) 104 K1
SAINT LOUIS ST (FW) 109 G10
SAINT PATRICK ST/**2866** (NR) 102 H4
SAINT THOMAS PL/**2867** (FW) 100 J5
SAIPAN ST (DA) 114 F1
SAKO LN (ME) 115 C9
SALADO TR (FW) 102 K4; 110 A4
SALAZAR ST/**2868** (GA) 106 C6
SALDANA DR (FW) 109 K7
SALE ST (DA) 105 K10
SALEM CIR (FW) 108 J6
SALEM CT (CP) 104 A1
SALEM CT (FW) 109 K10
SALEM DR (AR) 111 G8
SALEM DR (EU) 103 I9
SALEM DR (ME) 106 I5
SALEM DR/**2869** (HR) 102 H5
SALEM ST (IR) 104 I2
SALEM TR (FW) 108 J6
SALERNO DR (DA) 113 F8
SALERNO DR (ME) 115 A7
SALIDA ST (IR) 104 I1
SALISBURY DR (DA) 105 F7
SALISBURY ST (FW) 109 A10
SALIX CT (FW) 109 H7
SALLIE CT (RI) 106 A1
SALLY ST (HC) 102 G1
SALMON DR (DA) 113 C8
SALSBURY CIR (AR) 111 G8
SALZBURG DR (RL) 107 C11
SAM CALLOWAY RD (RO) 109 C7
SAM CANTEY ST (EM) 100 G6
SAM HILL ST (IR) 104 G3
SAM HOUSTON BLVD (CA) 104 A6
SAM HOUSTON DR (GA) 106 B5
SAM HOUSTON DR (SE) 115 I8
SAM HOUSTON RD (ME) 114 B4, B5, C5
SAMMY CIR (DA) 112 J6
SAMPSELL DR (GP) 112 E2
SAMUELL BLVD (DA) 113 A12; 114 A2
SAMUELL BLVD (ME) 114 A4
SAMUELS AV (FW) 109 B10
SAMUELS LN (AR) 111 E9
SAN ANGELO AV (BB) 108 H4
SAN ANTONIO LN (GA) 106 C5
SAN ANTONIO ST (GP) 111 E12
SAN ANTONIO ST/**2870** (BB) 108 H4
SAN BAR LN (HR) 102 G5
SAN BENITO ST/**2871** (SP) 101 K7
SAN BENITO WAY (DA) 106 K2
SAN BRUNO DR (GA) 107 H7
SAN CARLOS CT (IR) 104 H4
SAN CARLOS DR (GA) 106 H6
SAN CARLOS DR (GP) 112 F1
SAN CARLOS DR (UP) 105 I10
SAN CLEMENTE/**2872** (KE) 102 B2
SAN CLEMENTE DR (AR) 110 J5
SAN CLEMENTE DR/**2873** (GA) 106 H6
SAN CRISTOBAL DR (DA) 106 K2
SAN DIEGO DR (DA) 106 H4
SAN DIEGO DR/**2874** (AR) 111 G7
SAN FELIPE DR/**2875** (DA) 106 H3
SAN FERNANDO WAY (DA) 106 J2
SAN FRANCISCO CT (AR) 110 C6
SAN FRANCISCO DR (DA) 106 H4
SAN GABRIEL CT (FW) 102 K4
SAN GABRIEL DR (DA) 105 E9
SAN GABRIEL DR/**2876** (GA) 106 G6
SAN GRANADA TR/**2877** (IR) 104 J1
SAN GRANDE CT (GP) 104 K1
SAN JACINTO DR (FW) 108 E3
SAN JACINTO DR/**2878** (IR) 104 D3
SAN JACINTO DR/**2879** (SE) 115 I8
SAN JACINTO ST (DA) 105 K11
SAN JACINTO ST/**2880** (DA) 113 A10
SAN JOSE AV (DA) 113 J11
SAN JOSE DR (FW) 110 D2
SAN JUAN (SL) 102 A6
SAN JUAN AV (DA) 106 I4
SAN JUAN CT (AR) 110 D6
SAN JUAN CT (IR) 104 H4
SAN JUAN DR/**2881** (DU) 112 J6
SAN LEA DR (DA) 106 J4
SAN LEANDRO DR (DA) 106 K2
SAN LEON AV (DA) 114 E5
SAN LORENZO DR (DA) 106 I4
SAN LUCAS AV (DA) 106 I4
SAN MARCOS CT/**2882** (FW) 108 E3
SAN MARCOS DR/**2883** (FW) 108 E4
SAN MARCOS LN (BE) 102 H6
SAN MARCUS AV (DA) 106 I4
SAN MARCUS AV (ME) 106 J5
SAN MARINO AV (DA) 114 G4
SAN MATEO BLVD (DA) 106 K1
SAN MATEO CT (IR) 104 H4
SAN MATEO DR/**2884** (GA) 107 H7
SAN MEDINA AV (DA) 106 I4
SAN MIGUEL CT (AR) 110 H4
SAN MIGUEL DR/**2885** (SL) 102 A6
SAN MIGUEL ST (DU) 112 K5
SAN PABLO DR (DA) 114 D3
SAN PATRICIO DR (DA) 106 I3
SAN PAULA AV (DA) 106 I4
SAN PAULO CT (AR) 110 D6
SAN PEDRO (DU) 112 K4
SAN PEDRO DR (GA) 106 G6
SAN PEDRO DR (GP) 112 F1
SAN PEDRO PKWY (DA) 106 J2
SAN RAFAEL DR (AR) 110 G5
SAN RAFAEL DR (DA) 106 J2
SAN RAMON CT/**2886** (AR) 110 G6
SAN RAMON DR (AR) 110 F5
SAN REMO DR (GP) 111 H11
SAN ROSE DR (FW) 110 G1
SAN SABA DR (DA) 106 J3
SAN SABA DR (SL) 102 A6
SAN SABA DR (SP) 101 K7
SAN SABA ST (BB) 108 H4
SAN SABA ST (ME) 106 K6
SAN SOUCI DR/**2887** (DA) 106 G2
SAN VICENTE AV (DA) 106 I4
SANBORN ST (FW) 109 D12
SAND HILL CT (AR) 111 H9
SAND SHELL DR (FW) 101 H11
SAND SHELL RD (FW) 101 H11
SAND SPRINGS AV (DA) 114 C5
SAND SPRINGS RD (FW) 108 A6
SAND ST (FW) 110 A3
SANDAGE AV (FW) 109 H9
SANDAL ST (DA) 114 D1
SANDALWOOD DR (DA) 106 I4
SANDALWOOD LN (AR) 111 I8
SANDALWOOD LN (FW) 108 G5
SANDALWOOD LN/**2888** (GR) 103 E9
SANDCASTLE (ME) 115 C8
SANDCASTLE CT (EM) 100 F5
SANDCASTLE TR (AR) 110 C6
SANDELL DR (WS) 108 D4
SANDEN DR (DA) 106 E3
SANDERS DR (GA) 106 C4
SANDERS LN (CO) 102 E6
SANDERS PL (IR) 104 H3
SANDERS ST (FW) 110 B1
SANDERS ST (GP) 112 E1
SANDERSON AV (FW) 109 D12
SANDERSON AV/**2889** (DA) 113 D10
SANDHILL RD (DA) 106 E2
SANDHURST CT/**2890** (GR) 103 A9
SANDHURST LN (DA) 105 H12
SANDHURST LN (NR) 102 G3
SANDHURST LN/**2891** (NR) 102 G3
SANDHURST LN/**2892** (NR) 102 G3
SANDOS DR (DA) 115 H8
SANDPEBBLE CT (DA) 105 B10
SANDPIPER CIR (FW) 108 A4
SANDPIPER LN (DA) 105 E11
SANDPIPER LN (GA) 107 H9
SANDRA DR (FW) 109 J9
SANDRA DR (IR) 104 K3
SANDRA KAY LN/**2893** (AR) 111 G7
SANDRA LN (GP) 111 K12
SANDRA LN (RL) 107 E8
SANDRA LYNN DR (ME) 106 I5
SANDRA ST (FW) 109 J8
SANDS CT (WS) 108 C3
SANDSPRINGS CT/**2894** (AR) 110 I6
SANDSTONE CT (AR) 110 K6
SANDSTONE CT/**2895** (FW) 110 B3
SANDSTONE DR (AR) 110 K6
SANDSTONE DR (DA) 114 C4
SANDUSKY CT (AR) 110 J5
SANDY BEACH RD (BR) 100 C2
SANDY HOOK LN (AR) 111 K8
SANDY LN (DA) 104 G5
SANDY LN (FW) 110 D4
SANDY LN (IR) 104 K2
SANDY LN (ME) 114 C6
SANDY LN (PB) 100 C1
SANDY LN (WW) 108 C6
SANDY LN PARK DR (FW) 110 D4
SANDY POINT CT (AR) 111 J9
SANDY WOODS CT (FW) 110 E4
SANDYBROOK DR/**2896** (FW) 110 B3
SANDYLAND BLVD (DA) 114 H4
SANER AV (DA) 113 F8, F9
SANFORD AV (DA) 106 J2
SANFORD ST (AR) 111 D7, D9
SANFORD ST (HC) 109 A12
SANGAMON DR/**2897** (DA) 106 I2
SANGER AV (DA) 113 C11
SANGUINET CT/**2898** (FW) 109 F7
SANGUINET ST (FW) 109 F7
SANSHIRE AV/**2899** (DA) 106 F1
SANSOM BLVD (SG) 101 G9
SANSOM CIR (RO) 109 A7
SANSOM PARK DR (FW) 101 K8
SANTA ANITA DR/**2900** (DA) 106 H1
SANTA ANNA AV (DA) 106 H4
SANTA ANNA DR (GA) 106 C5
SANTA ANNA DR (GP) 112 G1
SANTA BARBARA AV/**2901** (FW) 109 D7
SANTA BARBARA DR (DA) 106 I1
SANTA BARBARA DR/**2902** (GP) 112 G1
SANTA BARBARA RD/**2903** (KE) 102 A2
SANTA CLARA CT (GP) 112 F1
SANTA CLARA DR (DA) 106 J2, K2
SANTA CLARA DR (FW) 108 D6, E3
SANTA CLARA ST (IR) 104 H4
SANTA CLARA ST/**2904** (IR) 104 H3
SANTA CRUZ CIR (GP) 112 F1
SANTA CRUZ DR (DA) 114 C3
SANTA CRUZ DR (GA) 106 G6
SANTA FE (SG) 101 F9
SANTA FE AV (DA) 105 K12; 106 K1; 113 A12
SANTA FE CT (AR) 110 J4
SANTA FE CT (GP) 111 J12
SANTA FE DR (AR) 110 J4
SANTA FE ST (GA) 106 D5
SANTA FE ST/**2905** (GA) 106 D5
SANTA FE TR (DU) 112 K5
SANTA FE TR (FW) 108 E4
SANTA FE TR (GP) 111 J12
SANTA FE TR (HC) 102 H1
SANTA FE TR (IR) 104 B3
SANTA FE TR (KE) 102 C1
SANTA GARZA DR (DA) 106 J4
SANTA GERTRUDIS (EM) 100 G6
SANTA MARGARITA (GP) 112 G1
SANTA MARIA LN (DA) 106 I1
SANTA MARIE ST/**2906** (FW) 109 D7
SANTA MONICA DR (DA) 106 K1
SANTA MONICA DR (FW) 108 E3
SANTA PAULA DR (FW) 108 E3
SANTA PAULA/**2907** (GP) 112 G1
SANTA ROSA WAY (DA) 113 J11
SANTA TERESA AV (DA) 106 I4
SANTERRE AV (DA) 113 C7
SANTERRE DR (GP) 111 B11
SANTIAGO AV (FW) 109 K8
SANTIAGO CT (IR) 104 H4
SANTIAGO DR/**2908** (GA) 106 H6
SAPLING WAY (DA) 105 B12
SAPPHIRE CT (AR) 110 J6
SAPPHIRE ST (BE) 103 G8
SAPPHIRE ST (DA) 114 B1
SAPPINGTON PL (FW) 108 E5
SARA DR (ME) 115 B7
SARA DR (RL) 107 E8
SARA DUNN DR (GA) 106 C4
SARA NELL CT/**2909** (PB) 100 C1
SARAH BROOKS (KE) 102 D3
SARAH JANE LN (FW) 109 H12
SARAH LEE DR (DA) 114 E2
SARAH LN (DA) 112 I3; 115 H8
SARAMAC DR (WA) 102 G1
SARANAC DR (DA) 105 F8
SARASOTA CIR (DA) 106 K1
SARASOTA DR (GA) 107 H8
SARATOGA (GP) 112 D3
SARATOGA (SL) 102 A6
SARATOGA CIR (DA) 105 H12
SARATOGA LN (BS) 115 F7
SARATOGA ST/**2910** (EU) 103 J7
SARAZEN DR (ME) 106 J5
SARGENT AV (FW) 110 D1, E1
SARGENT RD (DA) 113 E11
SARGENT ST (FW) 110 E1
SARITA CT (FW) 109 H7
SARITA DR (FW) 109 H7
SARITA PARK (FW) 109 H7
SARTAIN DR (FW) 110 C5
SASAKI (GA) 107 I9
SASANQUA LN (DA) 106 H3
SASSAFRASS (DA) 114 I4
SATELLITE DR (FW) 101 B12
SATINWOOD CT (AR) 110 K6
SATINWOOD DR (DA) 114 F2
SATSUMA DR (DA) 104 D6
SATURN RD (GA) 106 E5, G5
SATURN SPRINGS DR (GA) 106 E5
SAUGUS DR (GP) 111 I10
SAUNDERS RD (FW) 110 I2
SAUSALITO DR/**2911** (AR) 110 G5
SAVAGE DR (FW) 109 J11
SAVAGE DR (ME) 114 D6
SAVAGE ST (DA) 105 I9
SAVANNAH DR (GA) 106 G5
SAVANNAH DR (IR) 104 H2
SAVANNAH LN (FW) 108 I5
SAVANNAH ST/**2912** (DA) 113 C11
SAVANNAH WAY (BE) 103 J7
SAVORY DR (BE) 101 A12
SAVOY ST (DA) 113 F8
SAXON DR (BE) 103 G7
SAXON ST (DA) 106 H3
SAXONY (AR) 111 C10
SAXONY RD (FW) 108 D6
SAYERS LN (NR) 102 E4
SAYLES AV (AR) 111 J9
SCAMMEL DR (DA) 114 C4
SCARBOROUGH LN/**2913** (CO) 103 G7
SCARLET CT (AR) 111 C8
SCARLET OAK CT/**2914** (FB) 105 A7
SCARLET OAK DR/**2915** (RI) 106 A3
SCARLET SAGE CT/**2916** (FW) 110 C3
SCARSDALE LN (DA) 114 B4
SCENERY HILL CT (FW) 110 D1
SCENERY HILL RD (FW) 110 D1
SCENIC BAY CT (AR) 110 F4
SCENIC CIR (DA) 113 F11
SCENIC CIR (GA) 107 G9
SCENIC DR (AR) 107 J12; 111 E7
SCENIC DR (RL) 107 C11
SCENIC DR (SL) 102 C5
SCENIC FOREST TR/**2917** (AR) 110 H4
SCENIC HILLS CT/**2918** (BE) 103 G8
SCHADT CT (FW) 101 J10
SCHADT ST (FW) 101 K10
SCHADT ST/**2919** (FW) 109 A10
SCHANTILE (BR) 100 B1
SCHARF CT (FW) 108 F5
SCHEPPS PKWY (DA) 114 G3
SCHIEFFER ST (FW) 109 G10
SCHIEME ST (RO) 109 C7
SCHILDER DR (RO) 108 B6
SCHILLER DR (NR) 102 I3
SCHIRRA WAY (ME) 106 K5
SCHMIDT ST (FW) 110 E1
SCHOFIELD DR (DA) 112 A6
SCHOOL HILL CIR/**2920** (AR) 110 J5
SCHOOL RD (CA) 104 B6
SCHOOL ST (AZ) 100 E1
SCHOOL ST (GA) 106 C4
SCHOONER DR (AZ) 100 E2
SCHRADE DR (ME) 115 D9
SCHRADE RD (RL) 107 D10
SCHREIBER DR/**2921** (DA) 105 C9
SCHREIBER ST (GA) 106 B6
SCHROEDER RD (DA) 105 D12
SCHUKAR CT (IR) 104 I1
SCHULL ST (DA) 113 B12
SCHULZE DR (IR) 104 J3
SCHUMAC LN (BE) 103 I7
SCHUSTER DR/**2922** (DA) 112 A6
SCHWARTZ AV (FW) 101 J10, K10
SCHWARTZ AV/**2923** (FW) 109 A10
SCIENTIFIC DR (AR) 111 I9
SCIO DR (DU) 112 I5
SCOGGINS ST (SP) 101 K7
SCOTLAND (GP) 111 I11
SCOTLAND AV (GP) 100 G1
SCOTLAND CT (IR) 104 I4
SCOTLAND DR (DA) 113 G11
SCOTLAND DR (LA) 112 K6
SCOTLAND DR (IR) 104 I3
SCOTLAND DR/**2924** (IR) 104 I4
SCOTS BRIAR LN (FW) 101 G12
SCOTSMEADOW DR/**2925** (DA) 106 G3
SCOTSWOOD DR (GA) 106 E4
SCOTT AV (FW) 109 D12
SCOTT CT (IR) 104 K3
SCOTT CT/**2926** (WA) 102 G2
SCOTT DR (AR) 111 D8
SCOTT DR (GA) 107 E7
SCOTT DR (HR) 102 I4
SCOTT DR (RL) 107 E9
SCOTT PL (SE) 115 I8
SCOTT RD (FW) 109 C7
SCOTT RD/**2927** (RL) 107 E8
SCOTT ST (DA) 113 D12
SCOTT ST (WS) 108 D5
SCOTTLAND AV/**2928** (WS) 100 G1
SCOTTS BLUFF CT (AR) 110 K6
SCOTTSBLUFF DR (DA) 106 J4
SCOTTSBORO LN (DA) 113 I9
SCOTTSDALE DR (AR) 111 J9
SCOTTSDALE DR (ME) 106 J5
SCOTTSDALE DR (RI) 106 A1
SCOTTSDALE DR/**2929** (RI) 105 A12
SCOTTSDALE ST (DA) 114 B3
SCOUT AV (DA) 113 J7
SCRANTON DR (RH) 102 J3
SCRIBNER ST (GR) 103 A9, B9
SCRIBNER ST/**2930** (GR) 103 B9
SCRUB OAK CT (FW) 108 C2
SCRUGGS DR (RH) 102 K2
SCURRY ST (DA) 105 K11
SCYENE (ME) 115 C8
SCYENE CIR (DA) 114 C1, C3
SCYENE RD (DA) 114 C5
SCYENE RD (SU) 115 C10
SCYENE RD C (DA) 114 C3
SEA BREEZE LN (FW) 100 J6
SEA HARBOR RD (DA) 112 B4
SEA ISLAND DR (DA) 113 I8
SEA ISLE DR (IR) 112 A3
SEA MEADOW DR/**2931** (FW) 108 H6
SEA PINES ST/**2932** (ME) 106 J6
SEA RIM DR (AR) 111 K8
SEA TER DR (IR) 112 A3
SEABEACH RD (DA) 113 K9
SEABOARD DR (AR) 111 H10
SEABROOK DR (FW) 108 H6
SEAFORD DR (DA) 114 E3
SEAGO DR (DA) 115 K9
SEAGOVILLE RD (DA) 114 F4, G4; 115 H7
SEAGOVILLE RD (SE) 115 I9
SEAGULL CT (IR) 112 A3
SEALANDS LN (FW) 108 G6
SEALE ST (DA) 113 B8
SEAMAN ST (FW) 109 B12
SEAN CT (HR) 102 J4
SEAN DR (NR) 102 G3
SEAPORT DR (GA) 107 H9
SEARCY DR (DA) 113 E7
SEARS ST (DA) 105 J11
SEARS ST (FW) 110 F2
SEASIDE DR (DA) 113 J9
SEASIDE ST (IR) 104 H1
SEATON DR (DA) 113 G12
SEATON RD (GP) 104 J1
SEATTLE SLEW DR (FW) 110 C4
SEAWAY DR (DA) 114 D4
SEAWAY DR (RL) 107 F10
SEAY DR (DA) 113 G12
SEBRING DR (DA) 113 J12
SECLUSION (KE) 102 A3
SECO BLVD (DA) 114 E3
SECRET CT (AR) 111 C9
SECRETARIAT (GP) 112 I1
SECRETARY DR (AR) 111 G8
SECURITY DR (DA) 105 K8
SECURITY ST (GA) 106 E3
SEDALIA DR (AR) 111 J9
SEDALIA ST (DA) 113 G12
SEDGEMOOR AV/**2933** (DA) 113 K9
SEDGEWICK DR/**2934** (DA) 106 F1
SEDGWICK DR (DA) 106 F1
SEDONA LN (DA) 113 H8
SEEDLING LN (ME) 106 J6
SEEGAR ST (DA) 113 C11
SEEGERS DR (AR) 111 I8
SEELCCO ST (DA) 105 H7
SEELY ST (AR) 111 J9
SEEVERS AV (DA) 113 G9
SEGRAM CT (AR) 110 J5
SEGUIN DR (DA) 105 F8
SEGUNDO ST (IR) 104 J3
SEGURA CT (FW) 109 I7
SELDON WAY (DA) 114 B4
SELENE (CA) 104 B4
SELENE ST (FW) 101 J10
SELF PLAZA DR (DA) 106 G4
SELK AV (HC) 109 A12
SELKIRK DR (FW) 109 H7, I8
SELMA LN (FB) 104 C6
SELMA ST (HC) 109 A12
SELVA DR (DA) 106 I3
SEM RIDGE DR (GA) 107 F7
SEMICONDUCTOR DR (AR) 111 I7
SEMINARY (ME) 115 C8
SEMINARY DR (FW) 109 H8, H10, H11
SEMINARY RIDGE/**2935** (GA) 106 F6
SEMINOLE (ME) 115 D9
SEMINOLE DR (AR) 111 F10
SEMINOLE DR (BS) 115 G7
SEMINOLE DR (DA) 114 G3
SENATE ST (DA) 106 K3
SENDERO DR (GA) 106 D6
SENECA DR (DA) 105 G9
SENECA DR (GA) 106 E6
SENLAC DR (FB) 104 B5
SENTER RD (IR) 104 K3
SENTER VALLEY DR (IR) 104 K3
SEPTEMBER LN (DA) 114 F5
SEQUIN TR (FW) 102 K4
SEQUOIA CIR (RL) 107 E8
SEQUOIA CT (LW) 100 J4
SEQUOIA DR (GA) 106 G5
SEQUOIA LN (AR) 111 E10
SEQUOIA LN (BE) 103 H7
SEQUOIA TR (IR) 112 A3
SERENADE CT (AR) 111 G7
SERENADE LN (DA) 113 I10
SERENADE LN (RI) 106 B2
SERENO DR (DA) 105 I3
SERRANO DR (FW) 108 H5
SERRANO ST/**2936** (BE) 102 I6
SESAME DR (ME) 114 B5
SESAME PL (ME) 114 B5
SESAME ST (DA) 106 E2
SETH BARWISE ST (EM) 100 G6
SETTLEMENT DR (AR) 110 K5
SEVEN HILLS DR (GP) 111 H11
SEVERIGE CT/**2937** (FW) 107 F12
SEVILLA DR (GA) 106 H6
SEVILLA RD (FW) 108 D5
SEVILLA ST/**2938** (DA) 106 K1
SEVILLE CT (DG) 110 G6
SEVILLE DR (EM) 100 E4
SEWANEE AV (HP) 105 I11
SEWELL AV (FW) 109 A7
SEWELL CIR (DA) 114 H5
SEWELL CT/**2939** (IR) 104 G3
SEWELL RD (DA) 114 H5
SEXTON DR (AR) 110 H6
SEXTON LN (BB) 108 I3
SEXTON LN (DA) 105 E8
SEYDEL ST (DA) 114 D3
SEYMOUR DR (DA) 104 E6
SHACKELFORD DR/**2940** (ME) 106 J6
SHACKELFORD ST (FW) 110 G1
SHACKLEFORD ST/**2941** (FH) 110 I1
SHADOW CT (AR) 111 A10
SHADOW DR (AR) 111 A10
SHADOW DR (FW) 108 F6
SHADOW GLEN RD/**2942** (GR) 103 E9
SHADOW HILL CT (LS) 100 J3
SHADOW LN (AZ) 100 G1
SHADOW LN (DA) 112 H4
SHADOW LN (EU) 103 G9
SHADOW LN (HC) 109 B12
SHADOW LN (IR) 104 K2
SHADOW RIDGE CT (AR) 111 A10
SHADOW RIDGE DR (AR) 111 B10
SHADOW RIDGE DR (AZ) 100 E1
SHADOW WAY (DA) 106 D2
SHADOW WOOD CT (AR) 111 B10
SHADOW WOOD DR (DA) 113 F8
SHADOW WOOD DR/**2943** (HR) 102 G5
SHADOWBEND DR (RI) 106 A3
SHADOWBEND DR/**2944** (FW) 101 F11
SHADOWBROOK DR (KE) 102 B3
SHADOWBROOK LN/**2945** (HR) 102 J5
SHADOWHILL DR/**2946** (FW) 110 C4
SHADOWRIDGE (IR) 104 J1
SHADRACK DR (DA) 112 A6
SHADWELL DR/**2947** (GA) 106 G5
SHADWELL LN/**2948** (ME) 114 A5
SHADY (RL) 107 C9
SHADY BEND DR (DA) 105 C8
SHADY BROOK CT/**2949** (BE) 102 H6
SHADY BROOK LN (DA) 105 G12
SHADY BROOK LN (SE) 115 J10
SHADY CREEK (KD) 110 J3
SHADY CREEK DR (AR) 110 E5
SHADY CREEK DR (GA) 106 B3
SHADY CREEK DR (GP) 111 J12
SHADY CREEK ST (ME) 107 K7
SHADY CREST TR/**2950** (DA) 113 I9
SHADY DOWNS CT/**2951** (DA) 106 F3
SHADY GLEN LN (DA) 113 I8
SHADY GLEN LN/**2952** (BE) 102 H6
SHADY GROVE DR (BE) 102 H6
SHADY GROVE DR/**2953** (BE) 101 A11
SHADY GROVE RD (GP) 103 K12; 104 K1
SHADY GROVE RD (IR) 104 K3
SHADY GROVE RD (KE) 102 D3
SHADY GROVE RD (NR) 102 D4
SHADY GROVE RD/**2954** (IR) 104 K3
SHADY HILL DR (DA) 105 D8, D9
SHADY HILL LN (AR) 110 H4
SHADY HOLLOW CT/**2955** (NR) 102 F3
SHADY HOLLOW LN (DA) 113 H7
SHADY LAKE DR (BE) 102 H6
SHADY LAKE DR (NR) 102 I2
SHADY LANE AV (KE) 102 C2, D2
SHADY LANE DR (FW) 110 B2
SHADY LN (AR) 111 E7
SHADY LN (DA) 113 C8
SHADY LN (FW) 108 F2
SHADY LN (GP) 111 J12
SHADY LN (IR) 104 J1
SHADY LN (KD) 110 K2
SHADY LN (SE) 115 J10
SHADY LN (SL) 103 A8
SHADY LN/**2956** (HR) 102 J6
SHADY MEADOW (NR) 102 H2
SHADY MEADOW CT (AR) 110 G5
SHADY OAK DR (GR) 103 A9
SHADY OAK DR (RO) 109 B7
SHADY OAK MANOR DR (FW) 100 K6
SHADY OAK TR (GP) 111 J10
SHADY OAKS CT/**2957** (AR) 110 D6
SHADY OAKS CT/**2958** (GA) 106 B4
SHADY OAKS DR (KD) 110 J3
SHADY OAKS DR (SL) 102 A6
SHADY OAKS DR/**2959** (KE) 102 D2
SHADY OAKS LN (WH) 108 D6
SHADY PARK DR (AR) 110 G5
SHADY PT (AR) 111 F8
SHADY REST CT/**2960** (BE) 102 H6
SHADY RIDGE LN (FB) 105 C7
SHADY RIVER CT (BB) 108 I5
SHADY SPRING CT/**2961** (IR) 104 K4
SHADY SPRING CT/**2962** (IR) 104 K4
SHADY SPRINGS/**2963** (FW) 100 H6
SHADY SPRINGS CT/**2964** (AR) 110 I4
SHADY ST (FW) 109 C11
SHADY TIMBERS DR (DA) 113 I11
SHADY TR (DA) 104 E6, F6
SHADY TR (GP) 111 J12
SHADY TURF DR/**2965** (BE) 103 I7
SHADY VALLEY CT (AR) 110 F5
SHADY VALLEY DR (AR) 110 F5
SHADY VALLEY DR (DA) 106 E2
SHADY VIEW CT (AR) 110 G6
SHADYBAY CIR (DA) 105 D8
SHADYBROOK CIR/**2966** (DA) 105 G12
SHADYBROOK CIR/**2967** (GA) 107 F7
SHADYBROOK DR/**2968** (BE) 102 H6
SHADYBROOK DR/**2969** (GR) 103 A9
SHADYCLIFF DR (DA) 105 B10
SHADYCREEK DR (FW) 109 G8
SHADYCREEK DR/**2970** (EU) 102 J6
SHADYCREEK LN (CO) 103 F7
SHADYDALE DR (NR) 102 F2
SHADYDALE LN (DA) 106 G2
SHADYDELL DR (FW) 100 J6
SHADYGLEN CIR (RI) 106 A2
SHADYGLEN DR (GA) 106 G6
SHADYGLEN DR/**2971** (AR) 111 H7
SHADYHILL DR (FH) 110 J1
SHADYLAKE CT (HR) 102 H6
SHADYLAKE CT (IR) 112 A2
SHADYMEADOW DR (DA) 113 J8
SHADYMEADOW DR/**2972** (BE) 102 H6
SHADYSIDE LN (DA) 106 K1
SHADYVIEW DR (DA) 106 F2
SHADYVIEW DR/**2973** (BE) 102 H6
SHADYWAY DR (AR) 111 I9
SHADYWAY DR (DA) 113 J9
SHADYWOOD (SL) 102 C5
SHADYWOOD CT (ME) 106 K5
SHADYWOOD CT/**2974** (AR) 110 D6
SHADYWOOD LN (CO) 103 F7
SHADYWOOD LN (DA) 105 G9
SHADYWOOD LN (RI) 105 A12
SHADYWOOD LN/**2975** (SE) 115 K10
SHADYWOOD PL/**2976** (RI) 105 A12
SHAFTER DR (DA) 114 B3
SHAGBARK CT (FW) 101 F12
SHAGBARK ST (FW) 101 F12
SHAGROCK LN (DA) 106 G3
SHAHAN DR (FB) 105 C7
SHAIOT CIR (GP) 111 C12
SHALAIN DR (GA) 107 B7
SHALAKO DR/**2977** (FW) 108 E3
SHALAKO PASS/**2978** (FW) 108 E3
SHALFONT LN (GA) 107 B7
SHALIMAR DR (GA) 107 B7
SHALLOW WATER CT (FW) 110 C4
SHALMONT RD (BE) 103 I7
SHALON AV (FW) 110 D2
SHAMROCK AV (FW) 109 C9
SHAMROCK BEND LN/**2979** (AR) 111 C7
SHAMROCK LN/**2980** (FH) 109 I12
SHAMROCK PL/**2981** (RI) 106 A3
SHAMROCK RD (AR) 110 H4
SHANA CT/**2982** (AR) 111 H9
SHANA LN (IR) 104 J1
SHANDS DR (ME) 106 I5
SHANE DR (HC) 101 K12
SHANNON DR (FW) 108 F5
SHANNON LN (UP) 105 H10
SHANNON RD (SE) 115 H9

continue on next page

DALLAS/FT WORTH, *continued*

Numbers *replace street names where map space is limited; municipality abbreviations appear in parentheses.*

AD	Addison	CO	Colleyville	FB	Farmers Branch	HR	Hurst	PB	Pelican Bay	SP	Sansom Park Village
AR	Arlington	CP	Coppell	FH	Forest Hill	HU	Hutchins	PT	Pantego	SU	Sunnyvale
AZ	Azle	DA	Dallas	FW	Fort Worth	IR	Irving	RH	Richland Hills	UP	University Park
BB	Benbrook	DG	Dalworthington Gardens	GA	Garland	KD	Kennedale	RI	Richardson	WA	Watauga
BE	Bedford	DU	Duncanville	GP	Grand Prairie	KE	Keller	RL	Rowlett	WH	Westover Hills
BM	Blue Mound	ED	Edgecliff Village	GR	Grapevine	LA	Lancaster	RO	River Oaks	WS	White Settlement
BR	Briar	EM	Eagle Mountain	HA	Haslet	LS	Lakeside	RW	Rockwall	WW	Westworth Village
BS	Balch Springs	EU	Euless	HC	Haltom City	LW	Lake Worth	SE	Seagoville		
BU	Buckingham	EV	Everman	HE	Heath	ME	Mesquite	SG	Saginaw		
CA	Carrollton			HP	Highland Park	NR	North Richland Hills	SL	Southlake		
CK	Cockrell Hill										

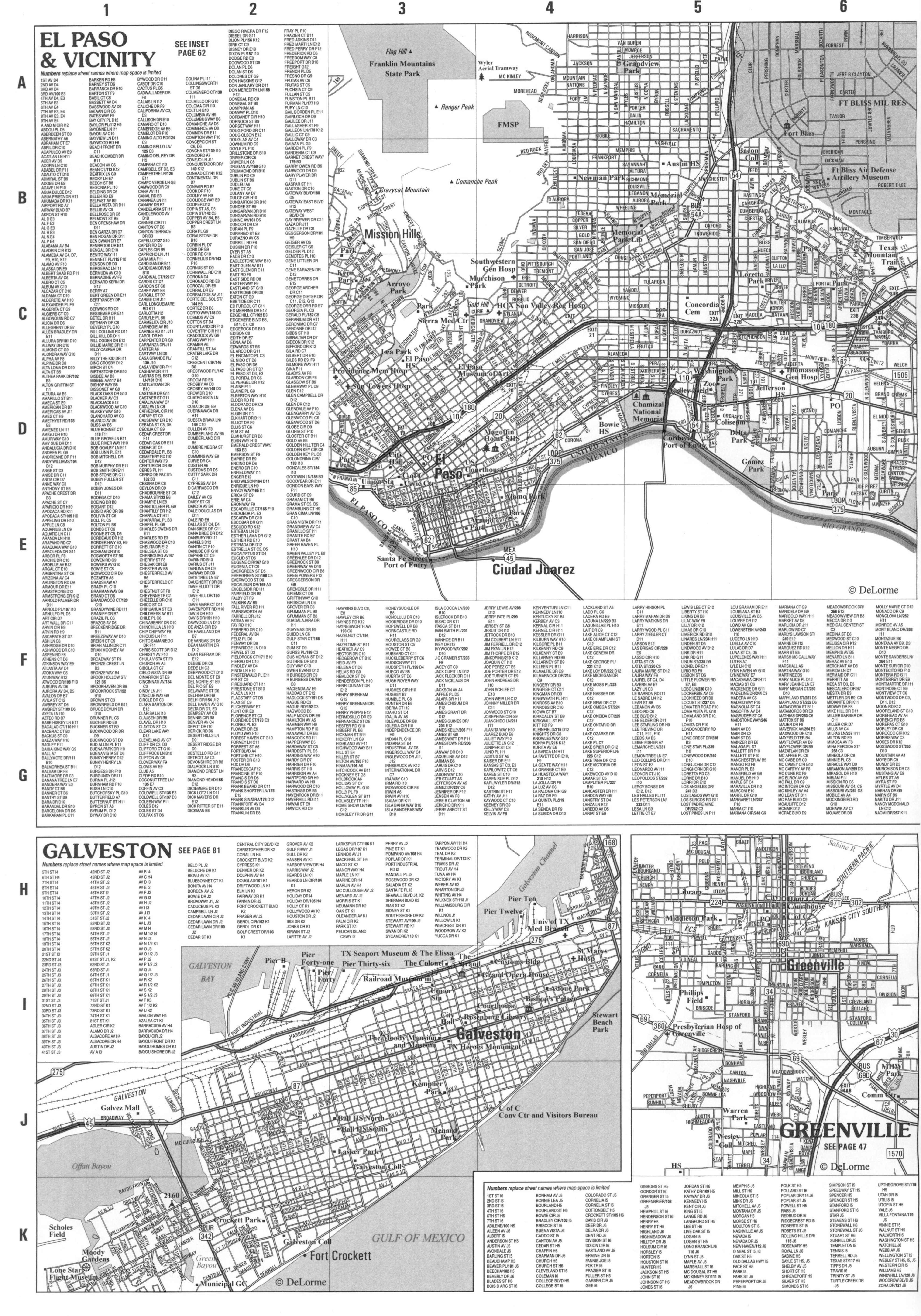
EL PASO & VICINITY
SEE INSET PAGE 62
Numbers replace street names where map space is limited
Franklin Mountains State Park
Flag Hill
Wyler Aerial Tramway
Ranger Peak
FMSP
Comanche Peak
Crazycat Mountain
Mission Hills
FT BLISS MIL RES
Fort Bliss
Ft Bliss Air Defense Artillery Museum
Grandview Park
Newman Park
Austin HS
Memorial Park
Memorial Park Lib
Texas Mountain Trail
Southwestern Gen Hosp
Murchison Park
Arroyo Park
HCA Sun Valley Reg Hosp
Sierra Med Ctr
Concordia Cem
Providence Mem Hosp
Sun Towers Hosp
El Paso Museum of Art
Washington Park
Zoo
Thomason Gen Hosp
Jefferson HS
Chamizal National Memorial
Bowie HS
Coliseum
Delta Park
Magoffin Home SHS
Cordova Port of Entry
Gomez Park
City Hall
El Paso
Courthouse
Union Sta
Alamo Park
Armijo Park
Santa Fe Street Port of Entry
Ciudad Juarez
UNITED STATES
MEXICO
RIO GRANDE
© DeLorme
GALVESTON
SEE PAGE 81
Numbers replace street names where map space is limited
Galveston Channel
Pier Ten
Pier Twelve
Univ of TX Med Branch
Pier B
Pier Forty-one
TX Seaport Museum & The Elissa
Pier Thirty-six
The Colonel
The Strand
Customs Bldg
St Marys Hosp
Grand Opera House
GALVESTON BAY
Railroad Museum
Union Sta
Adoue Park
Bishop's Palace
Courthouse
City Hall
Rosenburg Library
Stewart Beach Park
The Moody Mansion and Museum
Galveston
TX Heroes Monument
Kempner Park
C of C Conv Ctr and Visitors Bureau
Galvez Mall
Ball HS North
Ball HS South
Menard Park
Offatt Bayou
Lasker Park
Galveston Coll
Crockett Park
Scholes Field
Moody Gardens
Lone Star Flight Museum
Galveston Coll
Fort Crockett
GULF OF MEXICO
Municipal GC
© DeLorme
Sabine R
Library
Courthouse
Middleton Park
City Hall
C of C
Greenville
Phillips Field
Presbyterian Hosp of Greenville
MHV Park
Comm Ctr
Warren Park
Wesley Coll
GREENVILLE
SEE PAGE 47
© DeLorme
Numbers replace street names where map space is limited

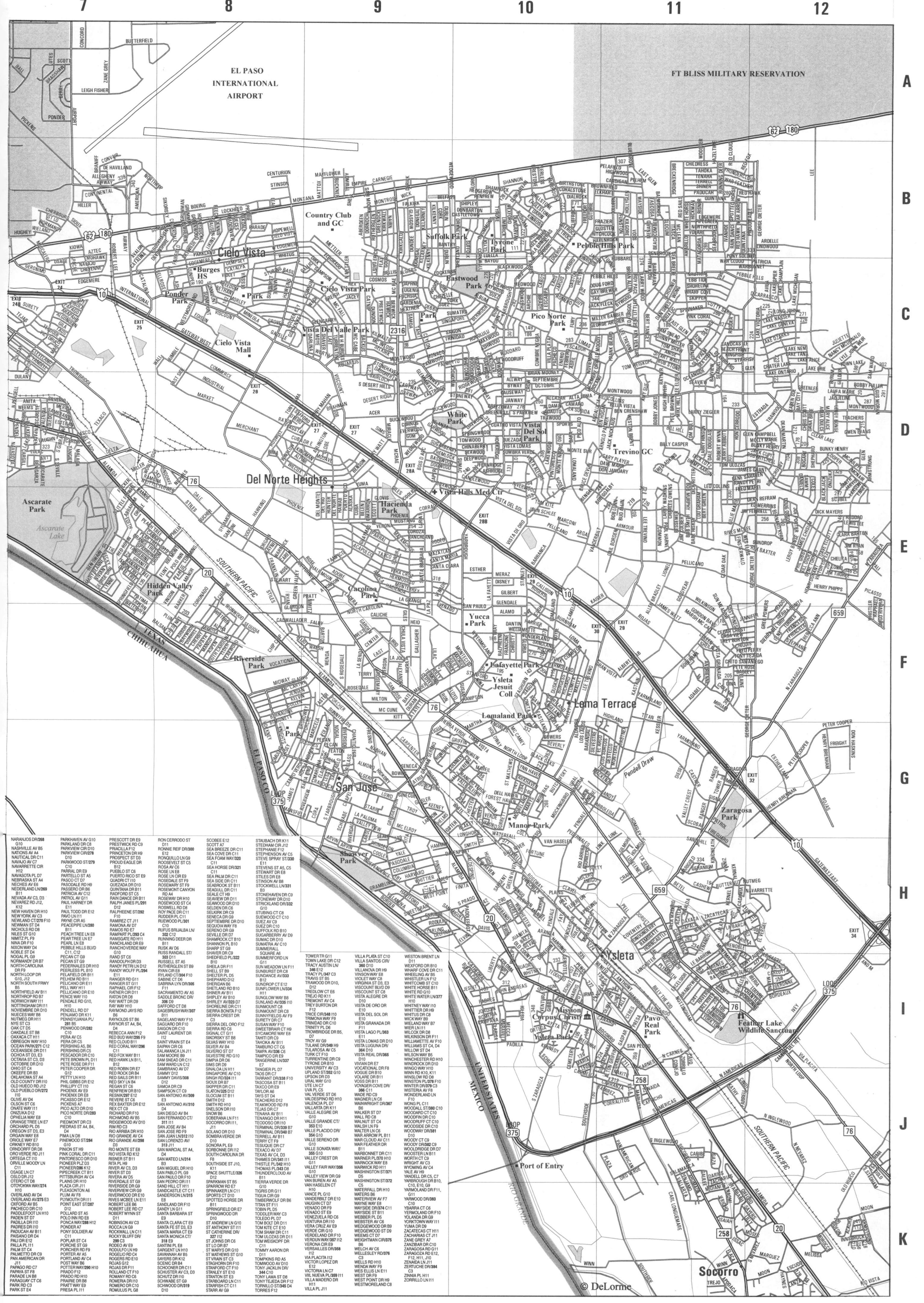
EL PASO
INTERNATIONAL
AIRPORT
FT BLISS MILITARY RESERVATION
Country Club and GC
Cielo Vista
Burges HS
Ponder Park
Cielo Vista Park
Cielo Vista Mall
Vista Del Valle Park
Suffolk Park
Tyrone Park
Eastwood Park
Pebble Hills Park
Pico Norte Park
White Park
Vista Del Sol Park
Trevino GC
Del Norte Heights
Vista Hills Med Ctr
Hacienda Park
Ascarate Park
Ascarate Lake
Hidden Valley Park
Carolina Park
Yucca Park
SOUTHERN PACIFIC
TEXAS
CHIHUAHUA
Riverside Park
Lafayette Park
Ysleta Jesuit Coll
Loma Terrace
Lomaland Park
Park
San Jose
Manor Park
Shawver Park
Zaragosa Park
Ysleta
Mission Corpus Christi
Pavo Real Park
Ysleta Park
Feather Lake Wildlife Sanctuary
UNITED STATES
MEXICO
RIO GRANDE
Port of Entry
Socorro
© DeLorme
A
B
C
D
E
F
G
H
I
J
K

1" = 0.8 mi (1.3 km)

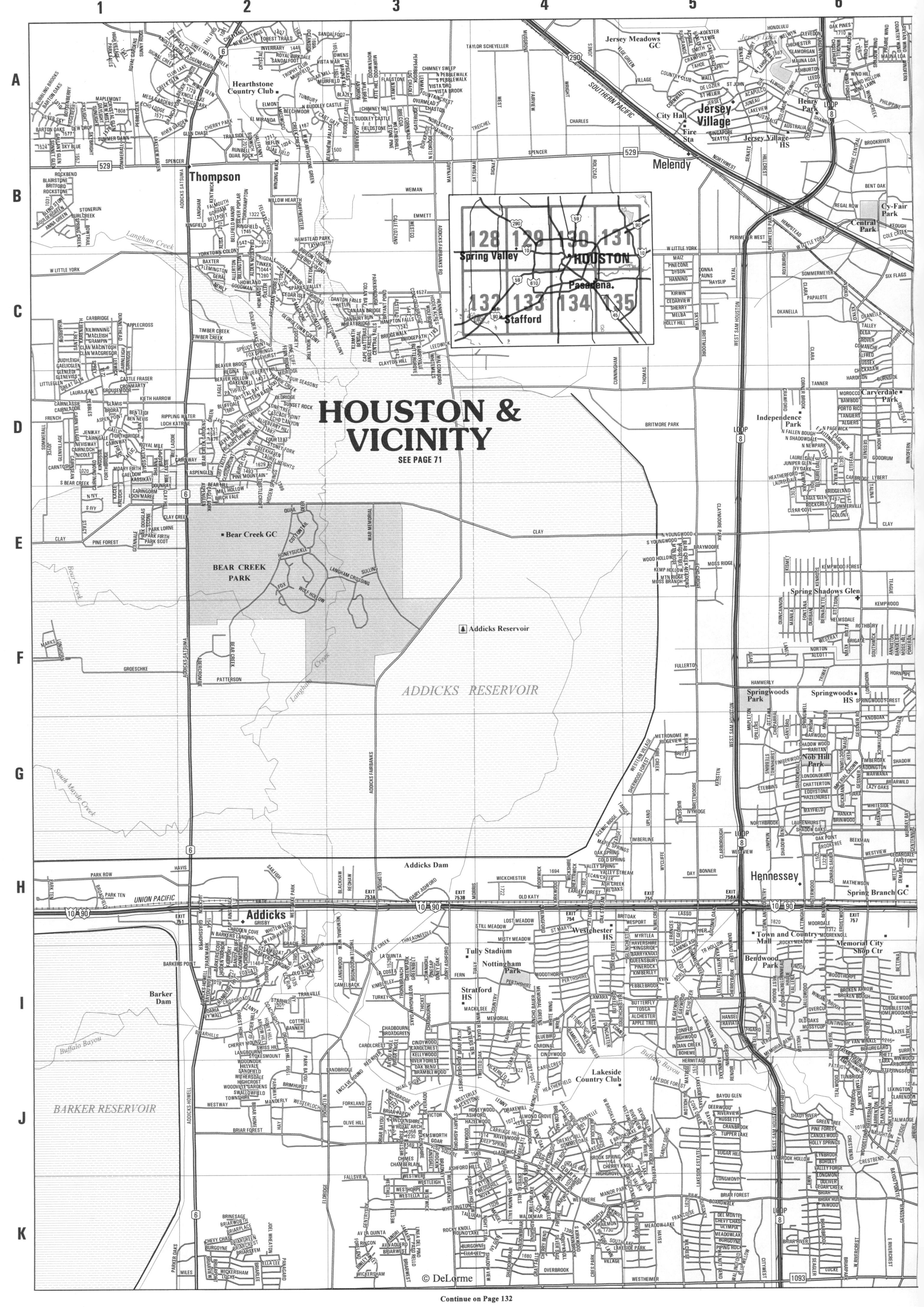

Continue on Page 132

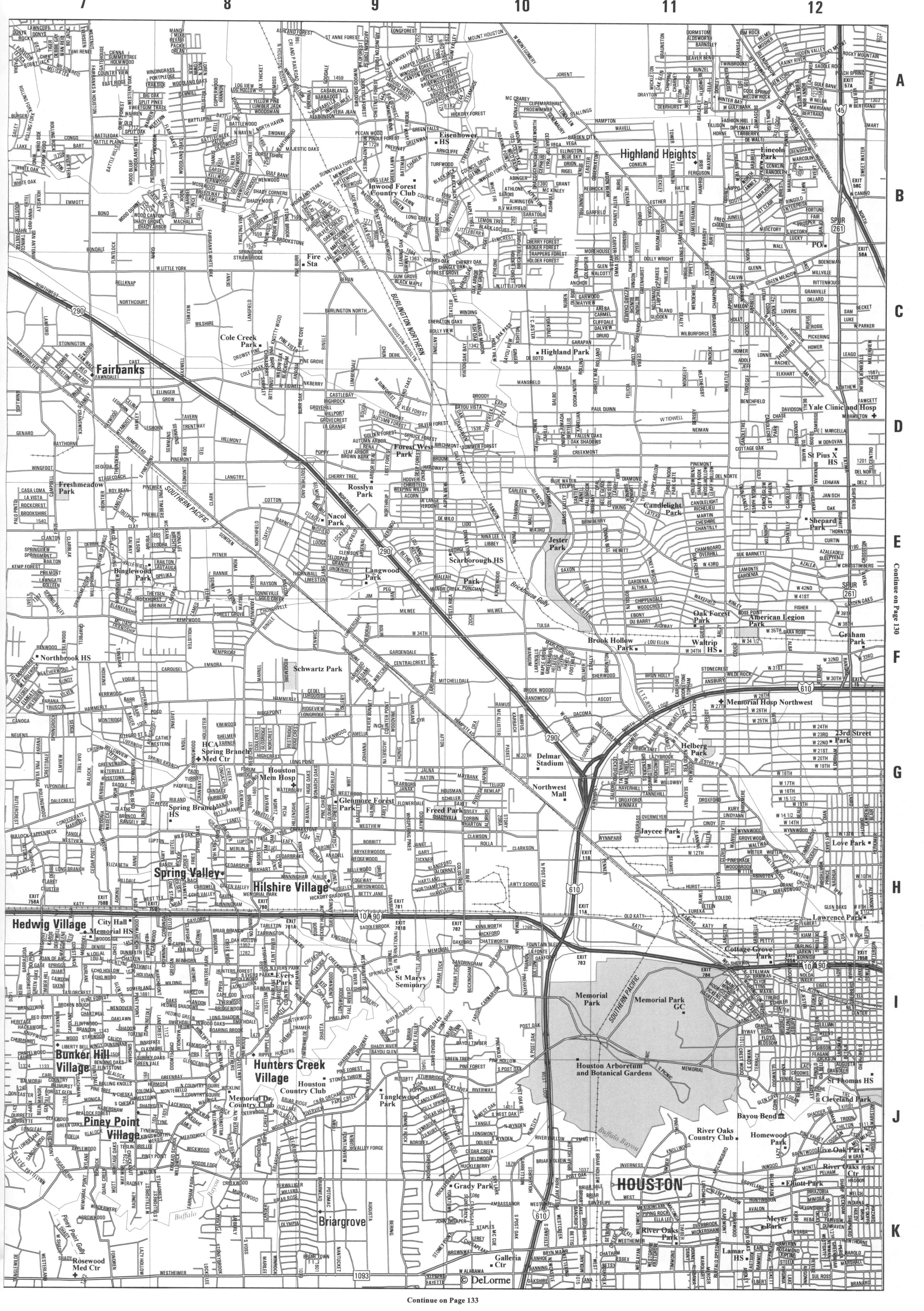

Continue on Page 133

1'' = 0.8 mi (1.3 km)

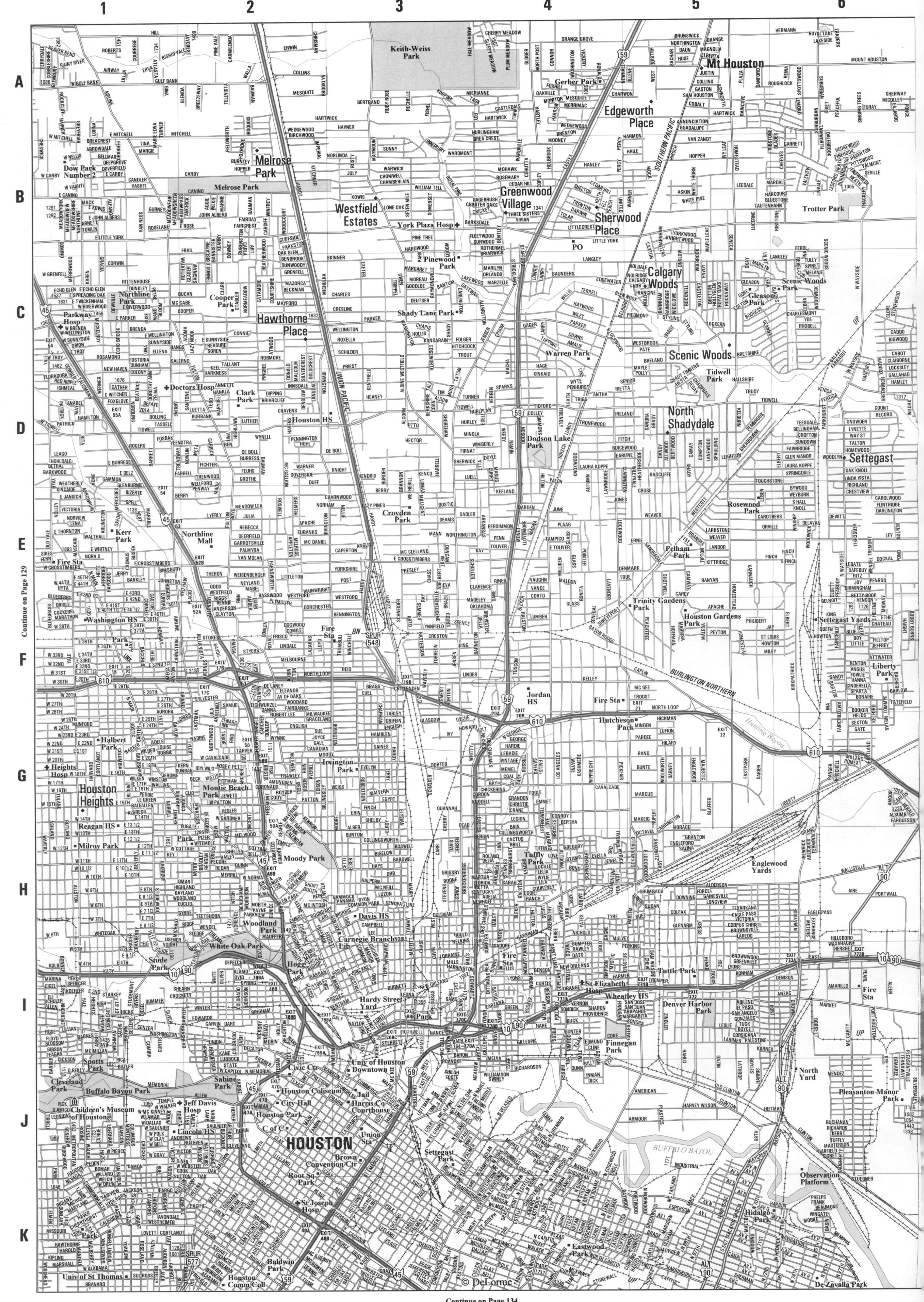

Continue on Page 129

Continue on Page 134

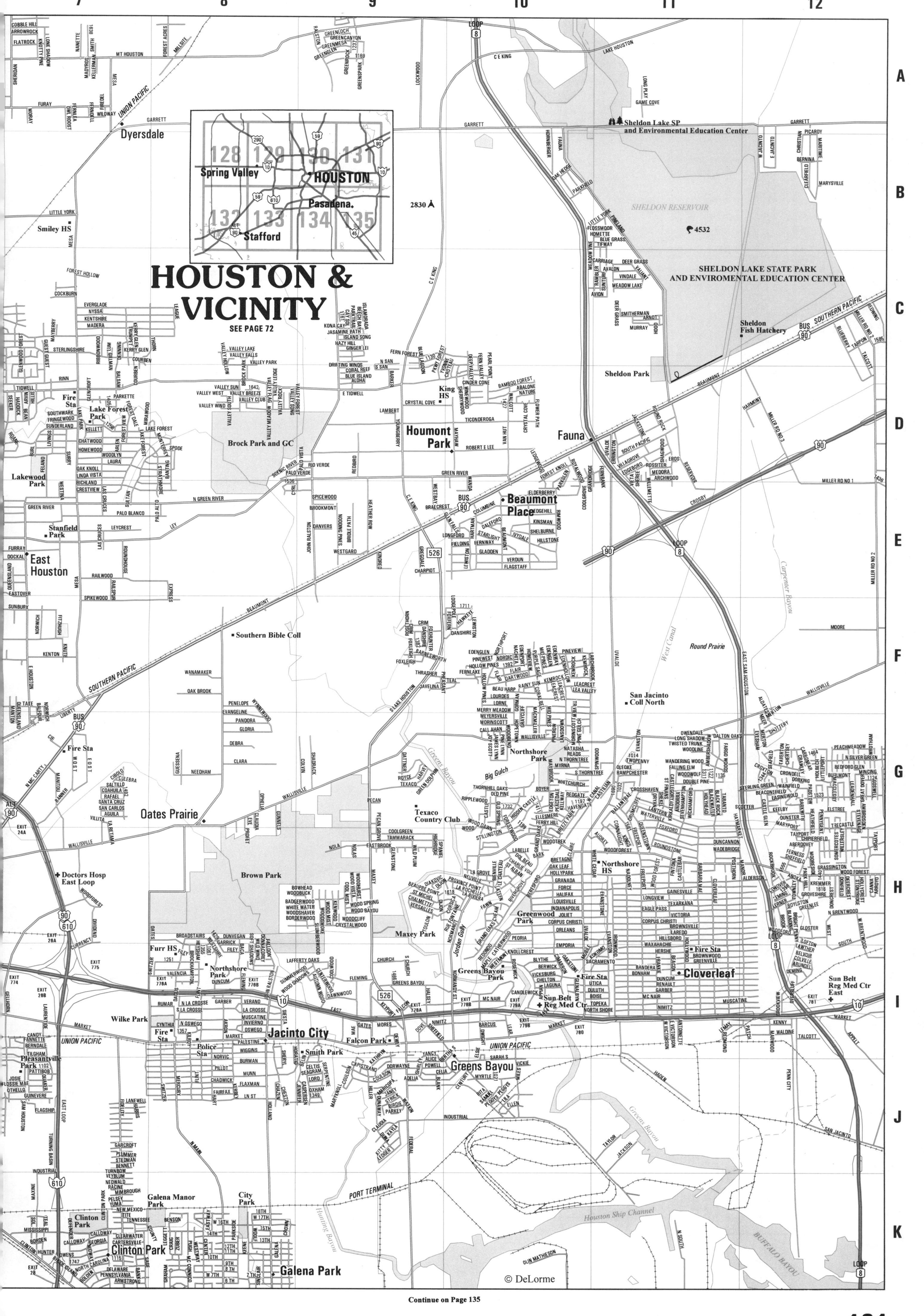

Continue on Page 135

1'' = 0.8 mi (1.3 km)

1 2 3 4 5 6

Continue on Page 128

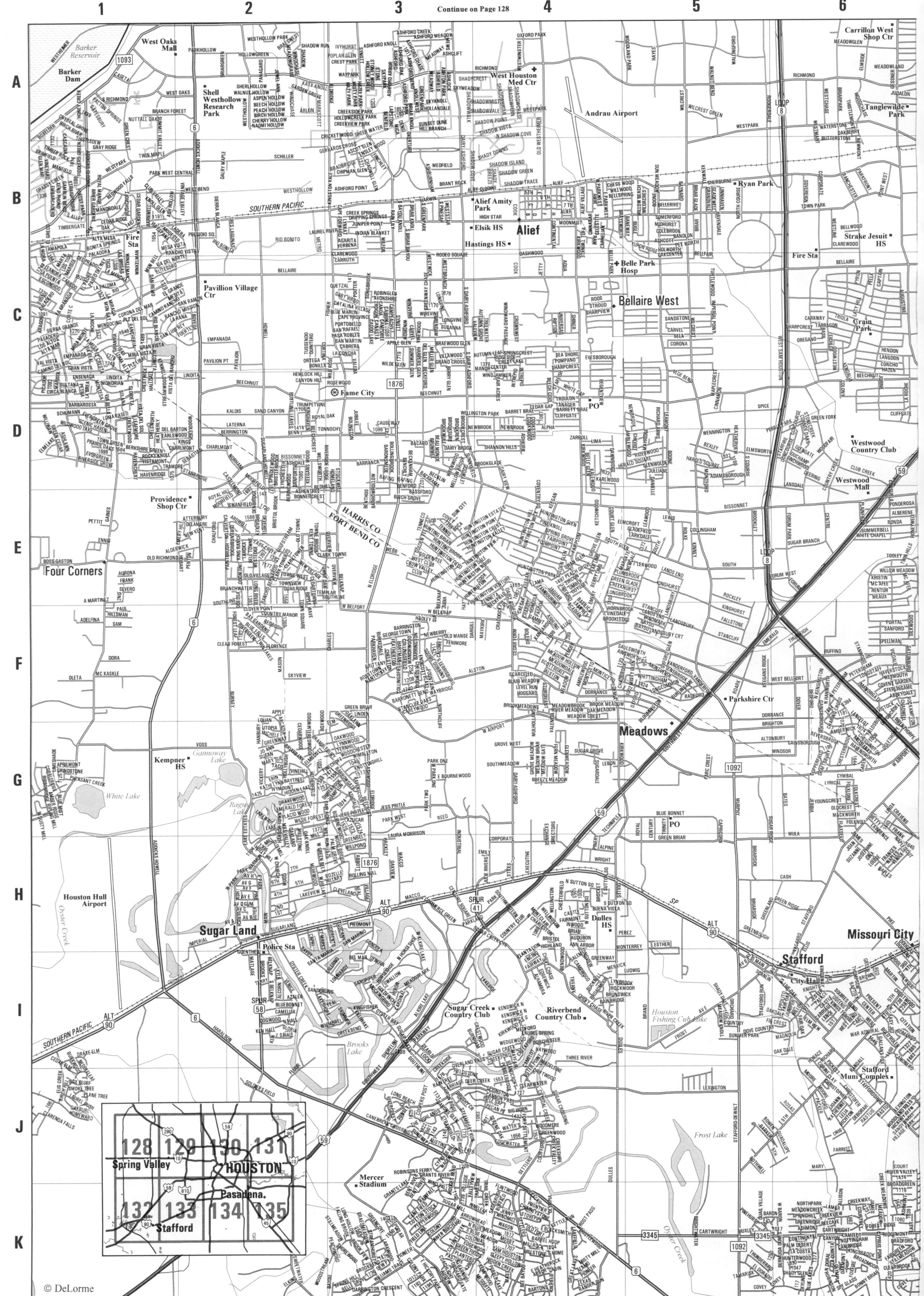

Continue on Page 129

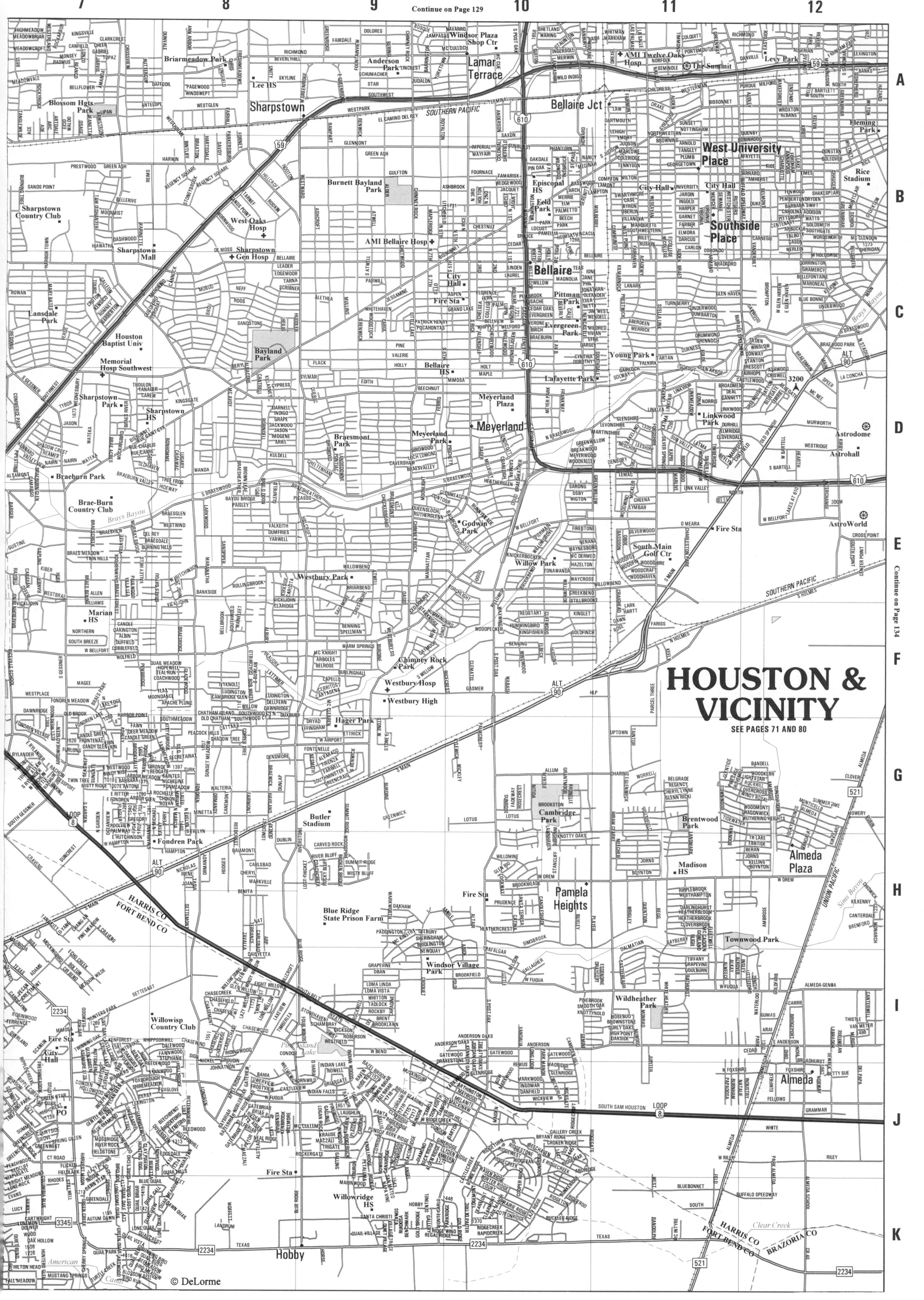

Continue on Page 134

1" = 0.8 mi (1.3 km)

Continue on Page 130

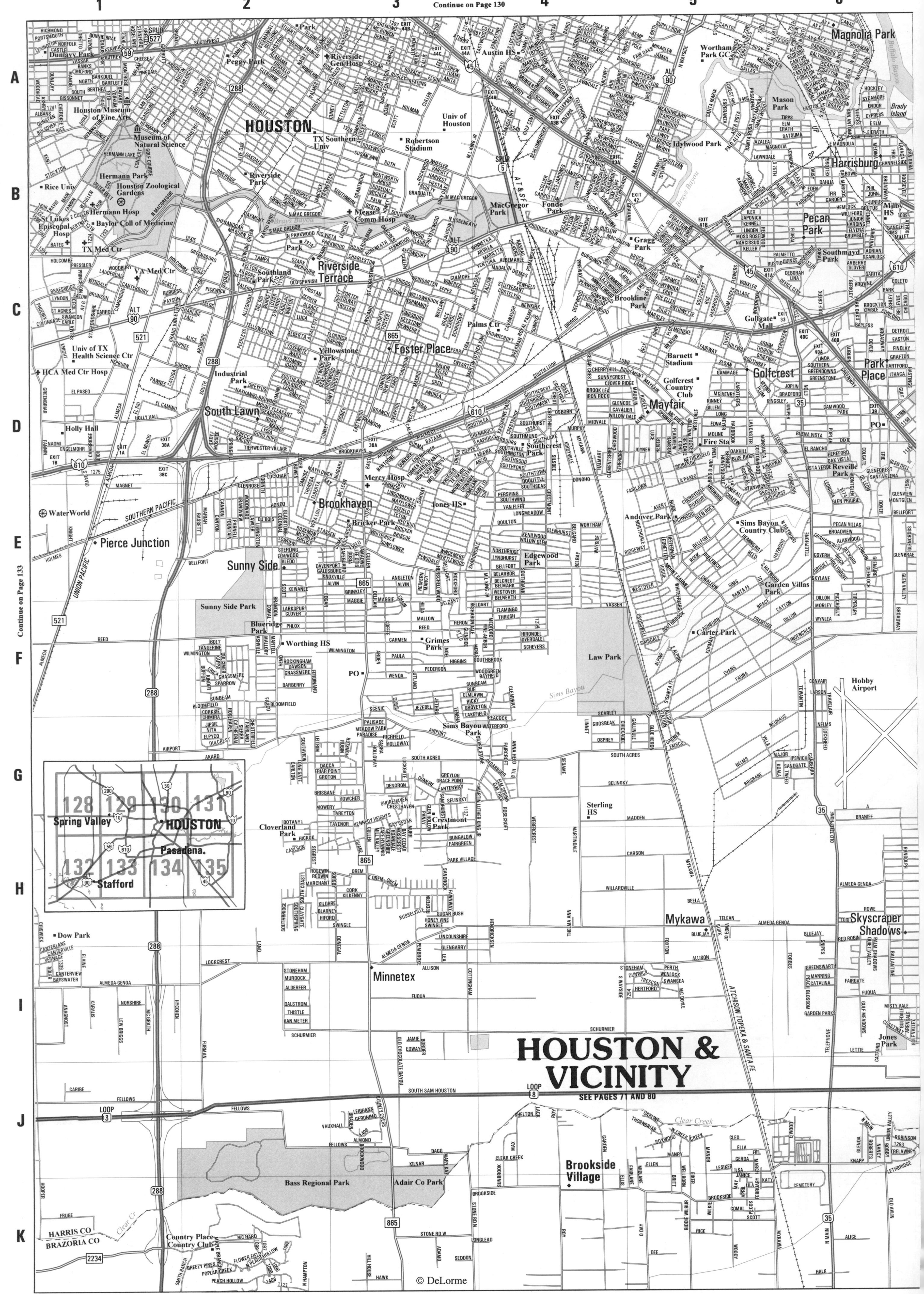

Continue on Page 131

7 8 9 10 11 12

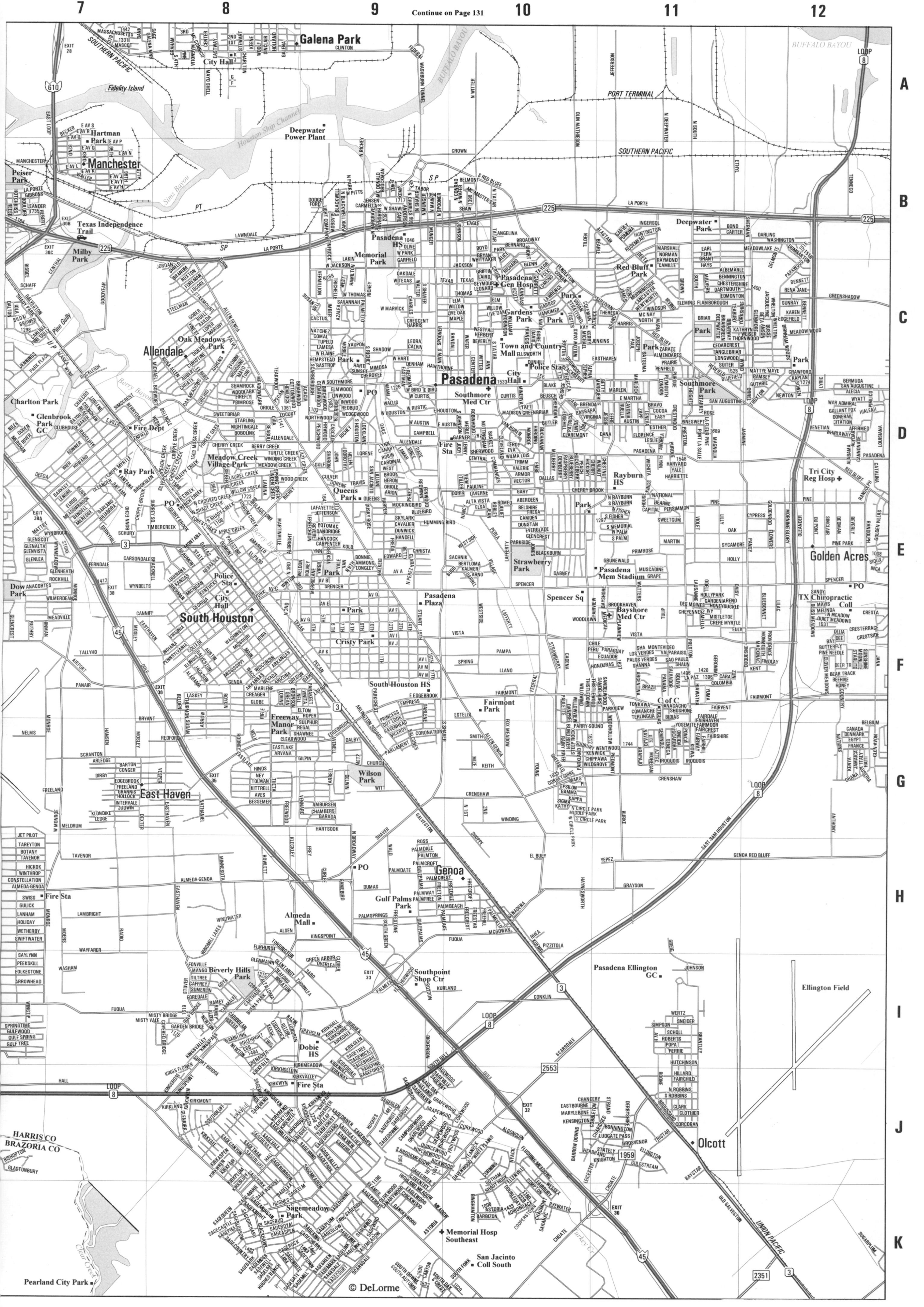

A B C D E F G H I J K

1" = 0.8 mi (1.3 km)

HOUSTON & VICINITY INDEX

***Numbers** replace street names where map space is limited; municipality abbreviations appear in parentheses.*

AL	Aldine	GP	Galena Park	MC	Missouri City	SP	Southside Place
BA	Bellaire	HC	Hunters Creek Village	ME	Meadows	ST	Stafford
BH	Bunker Hill Village	HL	Hilshire Village	PA	Pasadena	SV	Spring Valley
BV	Brookside Village	HO	Houston	PL	Pearland	WU	West University Place
CV	Channelview	HW	Hedwig Village	PP	Piney Point Village		
FC	First Colony	JC	Jacinto City	SH	South Houston		
		JV	Jersey Village	SL	Sugar Land		

1ST ST (BA) 133 B10, C10
1ST ST (GP) 135 A8
1ST ST (HO) 135 G10
1ST ST (SL) 132 H2
1ST ST (ST) 132 I6
2ND ST (BA) 133 B10, C10
2ND ST (GP) 132 E1; 135 A8
2ND ST (HO) 130 I1; 135 G10
2ND ST (SH) 135 F8
2ND ST (SL) 132 H2
3RD ST (BA) 133 B10, C10
3RD ST (GP) 135 A8
3RD ST (HO) 130 H4
3RD ST (MC) 132 I6
3RD ST (SH) 135 E8, E9
4TH ST (GP) 135 A8
4TH ST (HO) 130 I1
4TH ST (MC) 132 I6
4TH ST (SH) 135 F9
4TH ST (SL) 132 H2
4 1/2 ST (HO) 130 I1
5TH ST (BA) 133 B10, C10
5TH ST (HO) 130 I1; 132 B4
5TH ST (MC) 132 I6
5TH ST (SH) 132 J6; 135 F9
5TH ST (SL) 132 H2
5 1/2 ST (HO) 130 H1
6 TH ST (GP) 131 K8
6 TH ST (HO) 132 B4
6 TH ST (SH) 135 F9
6TH ST (BA) 133 B9, C9
6TH ST (HO) 129 H12; 130 H1
6TH ST (SL) 132 H2
6TH ST (ST) 132 I6
6 1/2 ST (HO) 130 H1
7 TH ST (GP) 131 K8
7 TH ST (HO) 132 B4
7 TH ST (SH) 135 F9
7TH ST (BA) 133 C9
7TH ST (GP) 131 K8
7TH ST (HO) 130 H1
7TH ST (SL) 132 H2
7 1/2 ST (HO) 129 H12; 130 H1
8TH ST (GP) 131 K8
8TH ST (HO) 129 H12; 130 H1
8TH ST (HO) 134 G4
8TH ST (SH) 135 E9, F9
8 1/2 ST (HO) 130 H1
9TH ST (GP) 131 K8
9TH ST (HO) 130 H1
9TH ST (SH) 135 F9
10TH ST (GP) 131 K8
10TH ST (HO) 129 H12; 130 H1
10TH ST (SH) 135 F9
10 1/2 ST (HO) 130 H1
11TH ST (GP) 131 K8
11TH ST (HO) 129 H12; 130 H1
11TH ST (SH) 135 F9
11 1/2 ST (HO) 130 H1
12TH ST (GP) 131 K8
12TH ST (HO) 129 H11; 130 H1
12TH ST (SH) 135 F9
12 1/2 ST (HO) 130 H1
13TH ST (GP) 131 K8
13TH ST (HO) 129 H12; 130 H1
13TH ST (SH) 135 F9
13 1/2 ST (HO) 130 G1
14TH ST (GP) 131 K8
14TH ST (HO) 129 G12; 130 G1
14TH ST (SH) 135 F9
14 1/2 ST (HO) 129 G12
15TH ST (GP) 131 K8
15TH ST (HO) 129 G12; 130 G1
15TH ST (SH) 135 F9
15 1/2 ST (HO) 129 G12
16TH ST (GP) 131 K8
16TH ST (HO) 129 G12; 130 G1
16TH ST (SH) 135 F9
17TH ST (GP) 131 K8
17TH ST (HO) 129 G12; 130 G1
17TH ST (SH) 135 F9
18TH ST (GP) 131 K8
18TH ST (HO) 129 G12; 130 G1; 134 E3
19TH ST (HO) 129 G12; 130 G1
20TH ST (HO) 129 G10, G12; 130 G1
21ST ST (HO) 129 G12; 130 G1
22ND ST (HO) 129 G12; 130 G1
23RD ST (HO) 129 G12; 130 G1
24TH ST (HO) 129 G12; 130 G1
25TH ST (HO) 129 G12; 130 G1
26TH ST (HO) 129 F12; 130 F1
27TH ST (HO) 129 F11; 130 F1
28TH ST (HO) 129 F12; 130 F1
29TH ST (HO) 130 F1
30TH ST (HO) 129 F12; 130 F1
31ST ST (HO) 129 F12; 130 F1, F2
31 1/2 ST (HO) 130 F1
32ND ST (HO) 129 F12; 130 F1
32 1/2 ST (HO) 130 F1
33RD ST (HO) 129 F12; 130 F1
34TH ST (HO) 129 F9; 130 F1
34 1/2 ST (HO) 129 F12
35TH ST (HO) 129 F12; 130 F1
36TH ST (HO) 130 F1
37TH ST (HO) 130 F1
38TH ST (HO) 129 F12; 130 F1
39TH ST (HO) 129 F12; 130 F1
40TH ST (HO) 130 F1
40 1/2 ST (HO) 130 F1
41ST ST (HO) 129 E12; 130 F1
42ND ST (HO) 129 E12; 130 E1
42 1/2 ST (HO) 130 E1
43RD ST (HO) 129 E10, E11; 130 E1
44TH ST (HO) 130 E1
45TH ST (HO) 130 E1
66TH ST (HO) 130 K5; 134 A5
67TH ST (HO) 130 K5
69TH ST (HO) 130 J5, K5
70TH ST (HO) 130 K5; 134 A5
71ST ST (HO) 130 K5
72ND ST (HO) 130 K5; 134 A5
73RD ST (HO) 130 K6; 134 A5
74TH ST (HO) 130 K6; 134 A6
75TH ST (HO) 130 K6; 134 A6, B6
76TH ST (HO) 130 K6; 134 A6
77TH ST (HO) 130 K6
78TH ST (HO) 134 A6
79TH ST (HO) 134 A6
80TH ST (HO) 134 A6
92ND ST (HO) 135 B7
93RD ST (HO) 135 B7
95TH ST (HO) 135 B7
96TH ST (HO) 135 B7
97TH ST (HO) 135 B7
A AV (HO) 134 G6
A K J ST (ST) 132 I6
A MARTINEZ ST (ST) 132 E1
ABALONE WAY (ST) 131 D10
ABBA WOOD (HO) 129 B8
ABBEYDALE DR (HO) 132 F6
ABBOTT CIR (SL) 132 H3
ABBOTT ST (HO) 130 I1
ABERCROMBIE (HO) 128 F2
ABERDEEN RD (PA) 135 E10
ABERDEEN WAY (HO) 133 C11
ABERDEEN/**1000** (ST) 132 H4
ABERDOVEY LN (CV) 131 H12
ABERNATHY ST (HO) 130 H4
ABIDE DR (HO) 133 I10
ABILENE AV (HO) 130 I5
ABINGER LN (HO) 129 B10
ABINGTON WAY (HO) 129 H12
ACACIA DR (PA) 135 D9
ACACIA ST (BA) 133 B10
ACADEMY ST (SP) 133 C11
ACADIAN DR (HO) 132 F4
ACAPULCO DR (JV) 128 A5
ACE (HO) 133 A7
ACHGILL ST (JV) 128 A5

ACME CT (HO) 130 D1
ACOMA DR (HO) 130 C2
ACORN (HO) 129 E9
ACORN FOREST DR (HO) 129 B9
ADA ST (HO) 130 H2
ADAIR ST (HO) 134 A3
ADAMO ST (PL) 134 K3
ADAMS AV (MC) 133 I7
ADAMS ST (HO) 130 K4
ADAMSBOROUGH DR (HO) 132 D5
ADDICKS CLODINE RD (HO) 132 B1
ADDICKS FAIRBANKS RD (HO) 128 B3, G3
ADDICKS HOWELL RD (HO) 128 I2, 132 B2, H1
ADDICKS SATSUMA RD (HO) 128 B2, F2
ADDISON RD (HO) 133 B12
ADDISON RD/**1001** (HO) 134 B1
ADE ST (HO) 133 A7
ADELBERT ST (HO) 130 E3
ADELE ST (HO) 130 G1
ADELFINA ST (HO) 132 F1
ADELIA CT (HO) 131 J9
ADELIA ST (HO) 130 H4
ADELLE ST (HO) 130 E3
ADIRONDACK DR (HO) 135 K10
ADKINS RD (HO) 129 H7
ADLER DR (HO) 134 I1
ADOLF DR (HO) 129 C12
ADRIAN ST (HO) 134 C6
AFFIRMED RD (PA) 135 D12
AFTON ST (HO) 129 G9
AGAR LN (HO) 128 F5
AGARITA LN (HO) 132 B3
AGGIE LN (HO) 130 B2
AGNES ST (HO) 134 C5
AGUILA (HO) 131 G7
AHRENS DR (HO) 135 C8
AINSDALE DR (HO) 128 J3
AINSWORTH DR (HO) 132 F5
AINSWORTH/**1002** (ME) 132 F5
AIRE (HO) 130 H6
AIRLINE RD (HO) 130 A1, D1, F1
AIRPORT BLVD (HO) 132 G6; 133 G9; 134 G1, G3; 135 F7
AIRPORT BLVD (SL) 132 G4
AIRWAY AV (HO) 130 A1
AJAX ST (HO) 130 F1
AKARD ST (HO) 134 G2
AKRON ST (JC) 131 I8
ALABAMA (HO) 129 K10; 130 K1, K2; 134 A2
ALABAMA (SH) 135 F8
ALABAMA CT (HO) 129 K11
ALABAMA ST (PA) 135 D12
ALABONSON RD (HO) 129 A9
ALAMO AV (FC) 132 K4
ALAMO ST (HO) 130 I2
ALANWOOD ST (HO) 134 E6
ALASKA ST (HO) 135 C7
ALASTAIR DR (PA) 135 B11
ALBA RD (HO) 129 F12
ALBACORE DR (HO) 133 D8
ALBANS RD (HO) 134 A1
ALBANS RD (WU) 133 A12
ALBANY ST (HO) 130 K2
ALBEMARLE DR (PA) 135 C11
ALBEMARLE LN (HO) 134 C4
ALBER ST (HO) 130 G3
ALBERENE DR (HO) 132 E6
ALBERTA AV (HO) 134 C2
ALBIN LN (HO) 133 F7
ALBRIGHT DR (HO) 135 E8
ALBURY DR (HO) 133 F8
ALCHESTER LN (HO) 128 I5
ALCOMITA DR (HO) 132 C1
ALCONBURY LN (HO) 134 C3
ALCORN ST (HO) 130 D3
ALCORN ST (SL) 132 I2
ALCOTT DR (HO) 128 F6
ALDATES DR (CV) 131 F12
ALDEN RIDGE DR (HO) 133 J9
ALDEN ST (HO) 128 C2
ALDER DR (HO) 133 B9
ALDERBROOK DR/**1003** (SL) 132 G2
ALDERFER ST (HO) 134 I2
ALDERNEY DR (HO) 129 H10
ALDERSON ST (CL) 131 H12
ALDERSON ST (HO) 130 H5
ALDERSY CT (HO) 129 I9
ALDERWICK (HO) 132 E2
ALDINE WESTFIELD RD (HO) 130 D3
ALDIS (HO) 135 I8
ALDON ST (HO) 130 D3
ALDRICH ST (HO) 129 G10
ALDSWORTH DR (HO) 129 A11
ALECIA DR (PA) 135 D12
ALEDO ST (HO) 134 E2
ALEEN ST (HO) 130 I6
ALEJO DR (HO) 129 B9
ALETHEA LN (HO) 133 C9
ALEXANDER ST (HO) 129 H12
ALFANO ST (HO) 130 B1
ALFRED LN (HO) 128 C6
ALGER DR (HO) 133 J8
ALGERIAN WAY (HO) 133 A12
ALGIERS RD (HO) 128 D6
ALGONQUIN DR (HO) 135 J10
ALGREGG ST (HO) 130 G1
ALHAMBRA CT (SL) 132 I4
ALICE LN (HO) 131 J9
ALICE ST (HO) 134 C2
ALICE ST (PA) 135 C10
ALICE ST (PL) 134 K6
ALIEF CLODINE RD (HO) 132 B4
ALIEF PL DR (HO) 132 B4
ALIEF RD (HO) 132 B4
ALIEF VILLAGE DR (HO) 132 B4
ALINE (HO) 134 D5
ALISA LN (HO) 128 B2
ALKAY ST (HO) 133 I11
ALKIRE LAKE DR (SL) 132 I3
ALLBRITTON DR (HO) 130 C4
ALLEGHENY ST (HO) 134 C2
ALLEGRO ST (HO) 129 G7, G8
ALLEGRO ST/**1004** (HO) 129 G7
ALLEN LN (HO) 133 E7
ALLEN PKWY (HO) 129 J12; 130 J2
ALLEN ST (HO) 129 I12; 130 I1
ALLEN-GENOA RD (HO) 135 C8
ALLEN-GENOA RD (PA) 135 G10
ALLENDALE RD (HO) 135 D8
ALLENDALE RD (PA) 135 D9
ALLENDALE ST (BA) 133 C10
ALLENSBY ST (HO) 130 F2
ALLERTON DR (MC) 133 J7
ALLERTON ST (MC) 128 C2
ALLISON CT (MC) 132 K6
ALLISON RD (HO) 134 I3, I5
ALLSTON ST (HO) 130 H1
ALLSUP ST (HO) 134 G5
ALLUM RD (HO) 133 G10
ALLWOOD ST (HO) 130 D5
ALMA ST (HO) 130 H2
ALMEDA PLZ DR (HO) 133 G12
ALMEDA RD (HO) 133 G12, J11; 134 D1, F1
ALMEDA SCHOOL RD (HO) 133 K12
ALMEDA-GENOA RD (HO) 133 I12; 134 H6, I1, I3; 135 H7, H8
ALMEECE ST (HO) 133 I11
ALMENDARES AV (PA) 135 C11
ALMINGTON LN (HO) 129 B10
ALMOND (HO) 134 J3
ALMOND GROVE CT (HO) 128 J4
ALMOND GROVE DR (HO) 128 J4
ALMONT DR/**1005** (HO) 130 B6
ALOE (HO) 129 J12

ALOHA TR DR (HO) 131 D9
ALPERTON DR (HO) 129 B10
ALPHA (HO) 132 D4
ALPHA DR (PA) 135 C10
ALPHA ST (HO) 129 J12
ALPINE CT (BA) 133 B10
ALPINE DR (HO) 134 F5
ALPINE DR (ST) 132 H4
ALROVER ST (HO) 133 I11
ALSACE ST (HO) 134 C2
ALSEN ST (HO) 135 H8
ALSTEAD CT (HO) 133 J8
ALSTEAD DR (HO) 128 C3
ALSTON (ME) 132 F4
ALSTON RD (SL) 132 F4
ALSUMA ST (HO) 130 G6
ALTA LOMA WAY (HO) 135 I8
ALTA MAR (HO) 132 C1
ALTA MESA DR (HO) 132 B1
ALTA VISTA DR (PA) 135 E10
ALTA VISTA ST (HO) 134 A5
ALTAIR WAY (HO) 133 H10
ALTAMONT DR (HO) 133 D7
ALTHEA DR (HO) 129 E11
ALTIC ST (HO) 130 K4
ALTON ST (HO) 134 A6
ALTONBURY LN (HO) 132 G6
ALTOONA ST (HO) 130 H4
ALVARADO DR (HO) 133 G9
ALVIN AV (HO) 134 E3
ALVIN ST (HO) 134 E3
ALVIN ST (PA) 135 C10
ALYDAR DR (PA) 135 D12
AMADWE ST (HO) 134 E3
AMALIE ST (HO) 130 C4
AMANDA LN (HO) 133 A7
AMAPOLA DR (HO) 132 B1
AMARILLO ST (HO) 130 I6
AMARILLO ST (SH) 135 E8
AMASA ST (HO) 130 F2
AMBASSADOR WAY (HO) 129 K10
AMBER RIDGE (HO) 132 G1
AMBER ST (HO) 130 F2
AMBERGATE DR (HO) 128 J4
AMBERLY CT (HO) 129 K8
AMBERN DR (HO) 133 J10
AMBERSHADOW DR (CL) 131 G11
AMBERWICK DR (HO) 132 G6
AMBLE LN (HO) 133 H10
AMBLEWOOD (ME) 132 F4
AMBLEWOOD DR (HO) 132 D5
AMBOY ST (HO) 130 H4
AMBROSDEN LN (CV) 131 G12
AMBROSE (HO) 133 H12
AMBROSE ST (HO) 133 G12
AMBURSEN ST (HO) 135 G9
AMELIA RD (HO) 129 G9
AMERICAN (HO) 130 J5
AMES CIR (PP) 129 J8
AMESWOOD RD (PP) 128 A2
AMHERST ST (WU) 133 B12
AMIR ST (HO) 132 B4
AMMONS (SH) 135 E9
AMOCO DR (HO) 128 H2
AMOOR AV (HO) 130 G6
AMOS ST (HO) 134 D2
AMSTERDAM DR/**1006** (HO) 135 K10
AMUNDSEN ST (HO) 130 G2
AMY ST (HO) 130 F6
ANABEL LN (HO) 130 D1
ANACACHO ST (PA) 135 F11
ANACORTES ST (HO) 135 E7
ANADELL ST (HL) 129 H9
ANAGNOST RD (HO) 134 I1
ANAQUA DR (HO) 129 D8
ANCHICK ST (HO) 130 B2
ANCHOR (HO) 129 C10
ANCHORAGE LN (HO) 128 I2
ANDERSON OAKS CT (HO) 133 I10
ANDERSON OAKS ST (HO) 133 I10
ANDERSON RD (HO) 133 I10, I12
ANDERSON ST (BA) 133 A10
ANDERSON ST (HO) 130 F2
ANDERSON ST (PA) 135 B9
ANDIRON CIR (HO) 128 A3
ANDORRA LN (CL) 131 G11
ANDREA LN (PA) 135 D11
ANDREA ST (HO) 134 D3
ANDREWS ST (HO) 130 J1
ANDWOOD ST (HO) 134 E5
ANDY DR (HO) 129 C12
ANGEL WAY (HO) 133 J9
ANGELINA (PA) 135 B10
ANGELINA ST (HO) 130 F2
ANGELO ST (HO) 130 G2
ANGLE FALLS LN (HO) 128 C3
ANGLETON ST (HO) 134 E3
ANGLIN ST (HO) 130 E3
ANGUS ST (HO) 130 F6
ANITA ST (HO) 130 K2; 134 A3
ANN (HO) 130 J3
ANN (PA) 135 C10
ANN ARBOR CT (SL) 132 H4
ANN ARBOR DR (HO) 133 A8
ANNA GREEN (HO) 128 B1
ANNA HELD (HO) 134 G4
ANNAPOLIS ST (WU) 133 B12
ANNE ST (HO) 129 H7
ANNETTE LN (HO) 130 D2
ANNEX DR (HO) 129 B12
ANNISTON DR (HO) 128 F6
ANNUNCIATION ST (HO) 130 A5
ANOKA DR (CV) 131 H12
ANSBURY DR (HO) 129 F11
ANSON CIR (PA) 135 C12
ANTELOPE ST (HO) 133 A7
ANTHA ST (HO) 130 D4
ANTHONY LN (PA) 135 G12
ANTOINE DR (HO) 129 C9
ANTOINETTE LN (HO) 131 I11
ANTOINETTE ST (HO) 134 C5
ANTONE CIR (MC) 133 G7
ANTONE CIR/**1007** (MC) 133 G7
ANZAC ST (HO) 130 I6
ANZIO RD (HO) 134 D4
APACHE DR/**1008** (PA) 135 E12
APACHE PLUME DR (HO) 133 F8
APACHE ST (HO) 130 E2, F5
APOLLO (HO) 129 C11
APPELT (HO) 131 I12
APPIAN WAY (HO) 131 I10
APPLE CREEK RD (HO) 135 E8
APPLE DR (SL) 132 F2
APPLE GLEN LN (HO) 132 C3
APPLE RIDGE DR (HO) 133 J8
APPLE TREE RD (HO) 128 I5
APPLEBY DR/**1009** (HO) 132 G6
APPLECROSS LN (HO) 128 C1
APPLETON ST (HO) 130 E2
APPLEWOOD ST (BH) 129 J7
APRIL LN (HO) 129 F9
APRIL ST (BV) 134 K5
APRIL WAY (HC) 129 I8
APRILMONT DR (HC) 132 G1
AQUA LN (HO) 132 C4
ARABELLA ST (HO) 129 C12
ARABELLE ST (HO) 129 B12, H12
ARAGON (HO) 132 C1
ARAI (HO) 133 I12
ARANSAS DR (HO) 129 A11
ARAPAHOE ST (HO) 130 I5
ARAPAJO ST (PA) 135 G11
ARBERRY ST (HO) 134 C6
ARBOLES DR (HO) 133 F9
ARBOR GLEN RD (MC) 133 G7
ARBOR MEADOW DR (MC) 133 G7
ARBOR OAK DR (HO) 129 C10
ARBOR PL (FC) 132 K4
ARBOR PL (HO) 134 A1
ARBOR RIDGE ST (MC) 133 G7
ARBOR ST (HO) 134 B3
ARBOR VITAE DR (HO) 129 D9
ARBOR WOOD DR (HO) 129 B8

ARBORDALE LN (BH) 129 J7
ARBORWAY (HO) 129 I9
ARBUCKLE ST (WU) 133 B12
ARC ST (HO) 133 A7
ARCADIA (HO) 130 H4
ARCADIA DR (SL) 132 G2
ARCADIAN SHORES DR (SL) 128 C2
ARCHER ST (HO) 130 G2
ARCHLEY DR (HL) 129 H9
ARCHWOOD ST (HL) 131 D11
ARCIDIAN FOREST DR (HL) 129 A9
ARCRIDGE CIR (HO) 133 J10
ARDEN CT (HO) 134 F3
ARDENNES RD (HO) 134 D3
ARDMORE ST (HO) 134 C2
ARDWELL DR (HO) 132 E2
AREBA ST (HO) 129 C11
ARENDALE (HO) 134 I6
ARGENTINA (JV) 128 A6
ARGENTINA CIR (PA) 135 F11
ARGONNE ST (HO) 129 K12
ARIEL ST (HO) 133 D8
ARION LN (PA) 135 E9
ARIZONA ST (SH) 135 F8
ARKANSAS ST (HO) 130 E4, H4
ARKANSAS ST (SH) 135 F8
ARLEDGE (HO) 135 G7
ARLEN (HO) 131 D7
ARLICIOUS ST (HO) 130 H6
ARLINGTON (HO) 130 E1
ARLINGTON FOREST DR (HO) 129 A9
ARLINGTON SQUARE DR (HO) 135 G9
ARMADA DR (HO) 129 C10
ARMAND (HO) 133 C11
ARMOR AV (PA) 135 D10
ARMOUR DR (HO) 130 J5
ARMSTRONG (HO) 133 A7
ARMSTRONG ST (HO) 131 K7
ARNCLIFFE DR (HO) 129 B9
ARNELL DR (HO) 129 E10
ARNETT LN (HO) 130 B1
ARNIM ST (HO) 134 C5
ARNO ST (PA) 135 E10
ARNOLD (HO) 129 J12
ARNOLD ST (WU) 133 B11
ARNOT RD (WU) 131 C11
ARNOT ST (HO) 129 I12
ARP ST (HO) 133 H8
ARROW (HO) 135 G8
ARROW HILL RD (HO) 128 I2
ARROWDALE DR (HO) 130 B1
ARROWHEAD DR (FC) 132 K3
ARROWHEAD GLEN DR (HO) 133 G7
ARROWHEAD LN (HO) 135 I7
ARROWPOINT DR (HO) 130 E1
ARROWROCK TR (HO) 131 A7
ARROWWOOD CIR (PP) 129 K7
ARROYO DR (CV) 131 H12
ARSENAL (HO) 129 E9
ART ST (HO) 130 B2
ARTDALE ST (HO) 133 A7
ARTESIAN PL (HO) 130 J2
ARTHINGTON AV (HO) 133 J10
ARTHUR ST (HO) 130 J2
ARTO ST (HO) 130 F3
ARTWOOD DR (HO) 133 K7
ARUBA DR (HO) 129 E7
ARUNDEL DR (CV) 131 I12
ARVANA (HO) 135 G8
ARVILLA LN (HO) 134 C4
ARVIN ST (HO) 131 D7
ASBURY AV (HO) 129 I12
ASCOT GLEN LN (HO) 132 B3
ASCOT LN (HO) 129 F11
ASH CREEK DR (HO) 128 H4
ASH HOLLOW DR (HO) 132 B1
ASH OAK DR (HO) 129 C10
ASH OAK DR (MC) 133 I7
ASH PL (HO) 130 I2
ASH ST (SL) 132 H2
ASHBROOK DR (HO) 133 B10
ASHBURN AV (HO) 134 F5
ASHBURN SPUR/**1010** (HO) 134 E5
ASHBURNHAM DR (HO) 132 B3
ASHBURTON (JV) 128 A6
ASHBY ST (HO) 134 A1
ASHCLIFT DR (HO) 132 A3
ASHCOTT DR (HO) 132 B5
ASHCROFT DR (HO) 133 B9
ASHDALE DR (SL) 132 G3
ASHDALE LN (SL) 132 D2
ASHENTREE WAY (SL) 132 E2
ASHFIELD DR (HO) 132 A3
ASHFORD ARBOR DR (HO) 132 A3
ASHFORD BEND DR (HO) 132 A3
ASHFORD CHASE DR (HO) 132 A3
ASHFORD CREEK DR (HO) 132 A3
ASHFORD FOREST DR (HO) 128 I3
ASHFORD HILLS DR (HO) 128 J3
ASHFORD HOLLOW LN (HO) 128 K3
ASHFORD KNOLL DR (HO) 132 A3
ASHFORD MEADOW DR (HO) 132 A3
ASHFORD OAK DR (HO) 132 A3
ASHFORD PARK DR (HO) 132 A3
ASHFORD PINE DR/**1011** (HO) 132 A3
ASHFORD PKWY (HO) 128 J3
ASHFORD POINT DR (HO) 132 B3
ASHFORD TRAIL DR (HO) 132 A3
ASHGROVE DR (HO) 128 K4
ASHKIRK DR (HO) 132 D4
ASHLAND FOREST DR (HO) 129 A8
ASHLAND ST (HO) 130 G1
ASHLAWN DR (HO) 132 D1
ASHLEY AV (HO) 134 C6
ASHLEY CIR DR (HO) 133 G7
ASHLING DR (HO) 132 F4
ASHLOCK DR (HO) 132 A3
ASHMOLE LN (HO) 129 B10
ASHMONT CT (MC) 132 K6
ASHMONT DR (MC) 132 K6
ASHMORE DR (MC) 133 J7
ASHTON (HO) 129 C10
ASHTON PARK DR (HO) 132 A3
ASHVILLE DR (HO) 134 F2
ASHWOOD DR (SL) 132 G3
ASHWOOD ST (HO) 133 D12
ASHWORTH RD (HO) 130 A5
ASKEW ST (HO) 134 C5
ASKINS LN (HO) 130 B5
ASPEN GROVE DR (HO) 128 K4
ASPEN HOLLOW LN (HO) 132 A2
ASPEN POINT DR (HO) 128 D1
ASPEN ST (BA) 133 C10
ASPEN VIEW CT (HO) 129 E10
ASPENGLEN DR (HO) 128 D2, E2
ASTON ST (HO) 129 D7
ASTORIA BLVD (HO) 135 K9, K10
ATHENS (HO) 134 A3
ATHLONE CT (HO) 129 B10
ATHLONE DR (HO) 129 C10
ATHOS ST (HO) 134 B6
ATLANTIC ST (HO) 130 H2
ATLASTA LN (HO) 130 A1
ATLAW DR (HO) 133 G7
ATTERBURY (HO) 132 E2
ATTINGHAM DR (HO) 128 H6
ATTLEE DR (HO) 128 K4
ATTRIDGE RD (HO) 129 F12
ATTUCKS ST (HO) 134 B3

ATTWATER ST (HO) 130 F6
ATWELL DR (HO) 133 B9, C9, E9
ATWOOD LN (HO) 130 C2
AUBERT ST (HO) 135 D8
AUBIN (HO) 130 F2
AUBURN AV (HO) 134 C6
AUBURNDALE ST (HO) 134 B4
AUDEN DR (HO) 133 A11
AUDEN ST (SP) 133 C11
AUDLEY (HO) 129 K12; 133 A12
AUDREY LN (CL) 131 H11
AUDUBON CT (SL) 132 H4
AUDUBON PL (HO) 130 K1
AUGUSTA AV (HO) 129 J12
AUGUSTA DR (HO) 129 K9
AUGUSTINE DR (HO) 132 C6
AULINE LN (HO) 129 G9
AURONA ST (HO) 132 E1
AURORA ST (HO) 130 F1
AUSTIN (PA) 135 D11
AUSTIN AV (PA) 135 D9, D10
AUSTIN PKWY (FC) 132 K3
AUSTIN ST (HO) 130 K2; 134 A2
AUSTIN ST (SH) 135 F8
AUSTINS PL (SL) 132 J3
AUSTRALIA ST (JV) 128 A6
AUSTRIA DR (PA) 135 G12
AUTAUGA ST (HO) 129 E8
AUTREY ST (HO) 134 A1
AUTUM DAWN CT (MC) 133 K7
AUTUMN ARBOR DR (HO) 129 D9
AUTUMN FOREST DR (HO) 129 D9
AUTUMN GROVE DR (HO) 132 C4
AUTUMN LEAF LN (HO) 132 C4
AUTUMN LN (HO) 130 E4
AUTUMN OAKS DR (HO) 128 H5
AUTUMN RUN CIR/**1012** (FC) 132 K3
AUTUMN WOOD DR (HO) 131 I9
AV A (SH) 135 E9
AV A (SL) 132 H2
AV B (BA) 133 B10, C10
AV B (HO) 134 A6
AV B (SH) 135 E9
AV B (SL) 132 H2
AV B (ST) 132 I5
AV C (HO) 130 K5; 134 A6
AV C (SH) 135 E8
AV C (SL) 132 H2
AV D (SH) 135 E9
AV D (SL) 132 H2
AV D (ST) 132 I5
AV E (HO) 130 K5; 134 A6
AV E (SH) 135 F9
AV E (SL) 132 H2
AV E (SL) 132 I5
AV F (HO) 130 K5; 134 A6
AV F (SH) 135 F9
AV F (SL) 132 H2
AV F (ST) 132 I6
AV G (HO) 134 C1
AV G (SH) 135 F9
AV G (SL) 132 H2
AV G (ST) 132 I6
AV H (HO) 130 K6; 135 B7, I11
AV H (SL) 132 H2
AV H (ST) 132 I6
AV I (HO) 130 K5; 135 B7
AV I (SH) 135 F9
AV I (ST) 132 I6
AV J (HO) 130 K5; 135 B7
AV J (SH) 135 F9
AV K (HO) 130 K5, K6; 135 B7
AV K (SH) 135 F9
AV L (HO) 130 K5; 135 B7
AV L (SH) 135 F9
AV M (SH) 135 F9
AV N (HO) 130 K5; 135 B7
AV N (SH) 135 F9
AV O (HO) 130 K6; 135 B7
AV P (HO) 130 K6; 135 B7
AV Q (HO) 130 K5; 135 B7
AV R (HO) 130 K5; 135 A7
AV S (HO) 130 K5; 135 A7
AV T (HO) 130 K5
AV U (HO) 130 J5
AV V (HO) 130 J5
AV W (HO) 130 J5
AVALON CT (HO) 131 C11
AVALON PL (HO) 129 K12
AVENELL RD (HO) 135 G9
AVENS (HO) 129 E12
AVENUE LA QUINTA (HO) 128 K3
AVENUE OF OAKS ST (HO) 130 F2
AVENUE VAQUERO (HO) 128 K3
AVERILL ST (HO) 130 G2
AVERNUS (HO) 130 F2
AVERT CT (HO) 129 B12
AVERY (HO) 134 E5
AVES ST (HO) 135 G8
AVIE ST (HO) 130 I1
AVION (HO) 131 C11
AVONDALE AV (HO) 130 K1
AVONELLE LN (HO) 133 G10
AVONSHIRE DR (HO) 132 C3
AWTY SCHOOL LN (HO) 129 H10
AXILDA AV (HO) 135 C8
AZALEA CT (PA) 135 C9
AZALEA ST (HO) 129 E12; 134 B5
AZALEA ST (SL) 132 I2
AZALEADELL DR (HO) 129 E12
AZTEC ST (PA) 135 G11
AZUCAR CT (SL) 132 G3
B ST (HO) 132 B4
BACA ST (HO) 131 I8
BACARD DR (HO) 132 D3
BACCHUS ST (HO) 130 F1
BACE DR (SV) 129 H8
BACHER ST (HO) 130 F6
BACON ST (HO) 134 D2
BADE ST (SV) 129 H7
BADEN ST (HO) 130 G2
BADGER FOREST DR (HO) 129 B10
BADGERWOOD DR (HO) 131 H9
BAER ST (HO) 130 I3
BAFING CT (HO) 132 D3
BAFING DR (HO) 132 D3
BAGBY ST/**1013** (HO) 130 I2
BAGGETT LN (HO) 129 G9
BAGPIPE (HO) 128 D1
BAHIA LN (HO) 133 J8
BAIAMONTE (HO) 133 H8
BAILEY ST (HO) 130 J2
BAIN ST (HO) 130 G4
BAINBRIDGE CT (SL) 132 I4
BAINBRIDGE ST (HO) 130 C5
BAIRD ST (HO) 134 A4
BAKER DR (HO) 135 D7
BALARAMA DR (HO) 132 D3
BALBO (HO) 129 D10
BALBO ST (HO) 129 D10
BALCONES DR (HO) 135 G9
BALDINGER (HO) 134 A5
BALDWIN (HO) 130 J2
BALFOUR (HO) 131 G7
BALKIN (HO) 134 D3
BALL (HO) 130 J4
BALLANTINE (HO) 134 I6
BALLANTRAE CT/**1014** (CL) 131 G11
BALLANTRAE LN (CL) 131 G11
BALMFORTH LN (HO) 133 E10
BALMORAL LN (BH) 129 J7
BALSAM LN (HO) 131 D7
BALTIMORE ST (HO) 134 A6
BALZY RD (HO) 129 F11
BAMBOO FOREST TR (HO) 131 D10
BAMBOO RD (HO) 128 D6
BAMMEL LN (HO) 129 K12
BANBURY PL (HO) 133 A10
BANBURY PL/**1015** (HO) 129 K10
BANCROFT LN (HO) 129 K10
BANDELIER DR (HO) 128 F6
BANDELL DR (HO) 133 G12
BANDERA ST (CL) 131 I11
BANDLON DR (HO) 132 B5
BANEWAY DR (HO) 132 B5
BANGLE ST (HO) 134 B6
BANGS RD (HO) 130 C1
BANJO ST (HO) 129 B12
BANK DR (GP) 131 K7; 135 A7
BANKS ST (HO) 133 A12; 134 A1
BANKSIDE DR (HO) 133 E8
BANNER DR (HO) 131 G7
BANNER PKWY CT (HO) 128 I2
BANNING (HO) 129 K10
BANNISTER LN (HO) 130 B2
BANTA DR (HO) 133 J9
BANTING ST (HO) 131 D8
BANTUM ST (HO) 130 C3
BANYAN ST (HO) 130 E5

BANZER ST (HO) 129 G8
BAPTIST ST (ST) 132 I6
BARADA ST (HO) 135 G9
BARBADOS DR (HO) 129 A9
BARBARA CIR (MC) 133 G7
BARBARA CIR/**1016** (MC) 133 G7
BARBARA LN (PA) 135 D10
BARBARA LN (WU) 133 B12
BARBARA MAE BLVD (CL) 131 H11
BARBARELLA CT (HO) 129 A9
BARBAROSSA (HO) 132 D1
BARBEE ST (HO) 134 A2
BARBER ST (HO) 130 J1
BARBERRY DR (HO) 134 F2
BARBERTON DR (HO) 133 C7
BARBIZON DR (HO) 135 K10
BARCELONA CT/**1017** (MC) 132 K6
BARCUS LN (HO) 131 I10
BARDWELL ST (HO) 130 H3
BARGER RD (HO) 133 E7
BARK LN (HO) 131 H10
BARKDULL ST (HO) 134 A1
BARKER (MC) 132 J5
BARKER DR (MC) 131 D9
BARKER RD (HO) 130 G1
BARKERS COVE (HO) 128 I2
BARKERS LANDING RD (HO) 128 H2, I2
BARKERS POINT LN (HO) 128 I2
BARKLEY DR (HO) 135 E7
BARKLEY ST (HO) 130 E1
BARKSDALE DR (HO) 130 B4
BARKWITH LN (CV) 131 G12
BARKWOOD (HO) 130 D1
BARLOW ST (HO) 130 F6
BARNES ST (HO) 130 I1
BARNESWORTH DR (HO) 131 F9
BARNEY RD (HO) 129 E8
BARNHAM (HO) 130 B5
BARNHAM ST (HO) 130 C5
BARNHILL LN (FC) 132 K3
BARNSLEY LN (FC) 129 A11
BARNSTON ST (HO) 130 F4
BARNWELL DR (HO) 132 B1
BARON (HO) 130 I3
BARON LN (MC) 132 K5, K6
BARONS GLEN (SL) 132 J3
BARONSMEDE DR (SL) 132 D3
BARR CIR (HO) 129 F7
BARR ST (HO) 129 F7
BARRACUDA CT (HO) 129 I7
BARRANCA DR (HO) 132 D3
BARREL HOOP CIR (FC) 132 K4
BARREMORE ST (HO) 134 A4
BARRET BRAE DR (HO) 132 D4
BARRETT (HO) 130 D1
BARRETT BRAE DR (HO) 132 D4
BARRINGTON CT (SL) 132 F3
BARRINGTON PL DR (SL) 132 F3
BARRINGTON RD (HO) 133 A9
BARRONETT BEND (SL) 132 F3
BARROW DOWNS WAY (HO) 135 J10
BARROWGATE DR (SL) 132 G3
BARROWHOLLOW DR (SL) 132 D3
BARRYKNOLL LN (HO) 128 I5
BART LN (HO) 129 B7
BARTELL DR (HO) 133 D12
BARTLETT ST (HO) 133 A12; 134 A1
BARTON (HO) 130 F6; 135 G7
BARTON OAKS CT (HO) 128 A1
BARTON OAKS DR (HO) 128 A1
BARTONS LN (FC) 132 K4
BARWOOD DR (HO) 128 G6
BARZIZA ST (HO) 130 K5
BASCOM LN (HO) 129 E8
BASH PL (HO) 133 A10
BASIL (HO) 130 J4
BASIL LN (HO) 132 C6
BASILICA ST (HO) 132 F4
BASIN (HO) 130 K6
BASKET ST (PA) 135 D10
BASKING DR (HO) 128 G6
BASS ST (HO) 130 I1
BASSETT ST (HO) 134 E2
BASSFORD DR (HO) 132 E3
BASSOON DR (HO) 133 E11
BASSWOOD LN (BA) 133 B10
BASSWOOD ST (HO) 130 E2
BASTIAN (HO) 134 D3
BASTOGNE RD (HO) 134 D3
BASTROP ST (HO) 130 K3; 134 A2
BASTROP ST (PA) 135 C9
BATAAN RD (HO) 134 D3
BATEMAN LN (HO) 129 B9
BATES (HO) 134 B1
BATES LN (ST) 132 G6
BATHURST DR (HO) 133 I11
BATON ROUGE ST (HO) 130 F4
BATTERSON (HO) 130 F3
BATTLE HILLS DR (HO) 129 B7
BATTLE PLAINS DR (HO) 129 B7
BATTLECREEK DR (HO) 129 B8
BATTLEOAK DR (HO) 129 B7
BATTLEPINE CT (HO) 129 A8
BATTLEPINE DR (HO) 129 A8
BATTLEWOOD DR (HO) 129 A8
BAUER DR (HO) 129 G7
BAUMAN RD (HO) 130 A2, B2, D2
BAXTER AV (HO) 128 C2
BAY CEDAR CT (HO) 134 G3
BAY CEDAR DR (HO) 134 H3
BAY GARDENS DR (SL) 132 F2
BAY OAKS RD (HO) 129 H12
BAY ST (HO) 130 G4
BAYARD LN (HO) 134 A1
BAYBERRY DR (HO) 133 H11
BAYBRIAR DR (HO) 133 J8
BAYFIELD DR (HO) 134 F4
BAYHURST DR (BH) 129 J7
BAYLAND ST (HO) 130 H2
BAYLESS DR (HO) 134 C6
BAYLOR ST (HO) 130 G1
BAYNARD DR (HO) 132 B5
BAYOU BEND CT (HO) 134 B2
BAYOU BRIDGE DR (HO) 133 E8
BAYOU COVE CT (HO) 128 J5
BAYOU DR (HO) 130 F2; 135 D7
BAYOU FOREST DR (HO) 129 B9
BAYOU GLEN RD (HO) 128 J5; 129 I9
BAYOU KNOLL DR (HO) 128 I3; 132 B3
BAYOU PKWY (FC) 132 K3
BAYOU PLACE DR (HO) 132 F5
BAYOU PLACE LANE (HO) 132 F5
BAYOU POINTE DR (HO) 128 K6
BAYOU RIVER CT/**1018** (HO) 128 I2
BAYOU RIVER DR (HO) 128 I2
BAYOU SHADOWS ST/**1019** (HO) 128 J6
BAYOU ST (HO) 130 I4
BAYOU TIMBER LN (HO) 129 I10
BAYOU VIEW DR (HO) 129 C10
BAYOU VISTA DR (HO) 129 D10
BAYRAM DR (HO) 129 G8
BAYSHORE DR (PA) 135 E11
BAYSTAR (HO) 135 J11
BAYSWATER DR (HO) 134 I1
BAYTHORNE DR (HO) 129 D7
BAYTREE DR (SL) 132 G2
BAYWOOD (HO) 130 K4
BAZEL BROOK DR (HO) 133 J9
BAZELBRIAR DR (HO) 133 J8
BAZIN ST (HO) 135 I8
BEACHTON (HO) 130 I2
BEACHWOOD ST (HO) 134 D3
BEACON ST (CL) 131 I11
BEACONRIDGE DR (HO) 133 J9

BEACONSFIELD DR (CV) 131 G12
BEACONSHIRE RD (HO) 128 J3
BEALL ST (HO) 129 D12, G12
BEAMER RD (HO) 135 K9
BEAN ST (HO) 131 D7
BEAR CREEK (HO) 128 F2
BEAR CREEK DR (HO) 128 E1
BEAR CREEK DR/**1020** (HO) 128 D1
BEAR CREEK GARDENS ST (HO) 128 D2
BEAR CREEK MEADOWS LN (HO) 128 E5
BEAR HILL DR (HO) 128 E2
BEAR TRACK LN (PA) 135 F12
BEARD CT/**1021** (HO) 130 J1
BEARLE ST (PA) 135 B11
BEATRICE RD (HO) 130 D1
BEATTY ST (HO) 134 B5
BEAU GESTE DR (HO) 129 B9
BEAU HARP DR (HO) 131 F10
BEAU MONDE DR (HO) 132 D3
BEAUCHAMP AV (HO) 130 H2
BEAUDRY DR (HO) 133 F8
BEAUJOLAIS LN (HO) 128 J4
BEAUMONT (HO) 130 K6
BEAUMONT (SH) 135 E8
BEAUMONT PL (HO) 131 E10
BEAUPRE POINT DR (HO) 131 H9
BEAUREGARD DR (HO) 128 I6
BEAVER BEND RD (HO) 129 A11; 130 A1
BEAVER BEND/**1022** (HO) 129 A12
BEAVER BROOK DR (HO) 128 C2
BEAVER DR/**1023** (HO) 130 G6
BEAVER HOLLOW DR (HO) 128 D2
BECK (HO) 130 G2
BECK RIDGE DR (HO) 133 J9
BECKENHAM DR (HO) 132 D3
BECKER AV (HO) 135 A7
BECKET (HO) 129 C12
BECKFIELD CT/**1024** (HO) 132 F4
BECKFIELD DR (HO) 132 E4
BECKFORD DR (HO) 132 D3
BECKLEY ST (HO) 129 B11
BECKLIN LN (HO) 132 D3
BECKMAN ST (HO) 130 C2
BECONS CASTLE LN/**1025** (HO) 128 C2
BEDFORD (HO) 132 F6
BEDFORD GLEN DR (CV) 131 G12
BEDFORD ST (HO) 134 A6
BEDWORTH LN (HO) 129 A11
BEE BAYOU LN (FC) 132 K4
BEECAVE DR (MC) 132 K6
BEECH BAY (MC) 131 C9
BEECH COVE (HO) 132 D4
BEECH HOLLOW LN (HO) 132 A2
BEECH ST (BA) 133 B10
BEECHAVEN DR (HO) 133 J10
BEECHBEND DR (MC) 133 J8
BEECHBEND DR/**1026** (HO) 128 K4
BEECHCREST ST (HO) 132 D2
BEECHMONT RD (HO) 129 J7
BEECHMOOR DR (HO) 128 A2
BEECHNUT BLVD (HO) 132 D2, D3
BEECHNUT ST (HO) 132 D6; 133 D9
BEECROFT DR (SL) 132 G3
BEEHIVE DR (PA) 135 F12
BEEKMAN PL DR (HO) 128 H6
BEEKMAN RD (HO) 134 C4
BEELA RD (HO) 134 H5
BEEMEADOW LN (HO) 133 K8
BEFAYE RD (HO) 130 D1
BEGGS ST (HO) 130 G2
BEGONIA ST (BA) 133 C10
BEHAN DR (HO) 129 C9
BEINHORN RD (HW) 129 I8
BEL MAR (SL) 132 I3
BELARBOR ST (HO) 134 E4
BELASCO LN/**1027** (HO) 132 E3
BELBAY ST (HO) 134 E4
BELCREST ST (HO) 134 E4
BELDART CT (HO) 134 F3
BELDART ST (HO) 134 F4
BELDEN (HO) 135 F8
BELFORT AV (HO) 132 F3
BELGARD ST (HO) 134 E4
BELGIUM DR (PA) 135 G12
BELGRADE DR (HO) 133 G11
BELIN DR (JC) 131 J9
BELIN MANOR DR (BH) 129 J7
BELK ST (HO) 134 C5
BELKNAP CT (SL) 132 I2
BELKNAP PL (HO) 132 F3
BELKNAP RD (HO) 132 E3, F3
BELKNAP ST (SL) 132 I2
BELL AV (HO) 130 K3
BELL ST (HO) 130 J1, K4; 134 A4
BELL TOWNE (SL) 132 E2
BELLA VISTA ST (HO) 130 F2
BELLAIRE BLVD (BA) 132 C2; 133 C10
BELLAIRE BLVD (HO) 132 C6; 133 C8
BELLAIRE CT (BA) 133 C10
BELLBROOK DR (HO) 133 F8
BELLE GLADE DR (HO) 129 E11
BELLE GLEN DR (HO) 132 D4
BELLE GROVE LN (FC) 132 K3
BELLE PARK DR (HO) 132 C4
BELLEFONTAINE (HO) 133 C12
BELLERIVE DR (HO) 132 B5; 133 B7
BELLEVUE ST (HO) 134 C6
BELLEWOOD DR (HO) 129 H9
BELLFAIR DR (HO) 132 C5
BELLFIELD MANOR LN (HO) 128 B2
BELLFLOWER ST (HO) 133 A7
BELLFORT AV (HO) 133 E10, F7; 134 E2, E4, E5, E6
BELLFORT CT (HO) 134 E3
BELLFORT ST (HO) 133 E12
BELLGREEN DR (HO) 133 C12
BELLINGHAM DR (HO) 130 D6
BELLIS LN (HO) 133 J9
BELLKNAP RD (HO) 129 C7
BELLMAR DR (HO) 130 B1
BELLMEADE ST (HO) 129 J12
BELLNOLE DR (HO) 135 D8
BELLPORT DR (HO) 128 B2
BELLSPRING DR (HO) 132 B4
BELLVIEW DR (BA) 133 C10
BELLWOOD LN (HO) 132 B6
BELMARK ST (HO) 134 E4
BELMONT ST (PA) 135 B10
BELMONT ST (WU) 133 B12
BELMORE (HO) 129 E9
BELNEATH ST (HO) 134 F4
BELRIDGE ST (HO) 130 C5
BELROIT ST (HO) 130 F6
BELROSE DR (HO) 133 F9
BELSHIRE ST (PA) 135 E10
BELVEDERE (HO) 134 C4
BELVOIR DR (CV) 131 I12
BEN DR (HO) 130 D2
BEN HUR DR (SV) 129 H8
BEN LEIDI DR (SV) 128 D1
BEN NEVIS DR (SV) 128 D1
BENBOW WAY (HO) 129 G7
BENBROOK DR (HO) 130 C2
BENCHFIELD DR (HO) 129 D12
BENCHLY DR (HO) 132 D3
BENCHMARK DR (HO) 133 K9
BEND ST (HO) 133 I9
BENDELL DR (HO) 135 E7
BENDING OAKS LN (PP) 129 J7
BENDWOOD DR (HO) 128 I6
BENDWOOD DR (SL) 132 I4
BENFIELD DR (HO) 132 A3
BENFORD DR (HO) 132 E3

BENGAL CT (HO) 128 C3
BENIGNUS RD (HO) 128 H6
BENITA ST (HO) 133 H8
BENNETT DR (PA) 135 C12
BENNETT ST (HO) 131 J7
BENNIE ST (HO) 130 F2
BENNING (HO) 133 F10
BENNING DR (HO) 133 F9
BENNINGTON DR (PA) 135 C11
BENNINGTON ST (HO) 130 F3
BENSON CT (HO) 130 I4
BENSON DR (GP) 131 K8
BENSON ST (HO) 130 I4
BENT BOUGH LN (HO) 129 B10
BENT BRANCH DR (HO) 129 B9
BENT OAK DR (MC) 128 B6; 133 J7
BENT RIVER CT (FC) 132 K3
BENT RIVER DR (FC) 132 K3
BENTHOS DR (FC) 132 E3
BENTLEY ST (HO) 130 B4
BENTWORTH DR (HO) 128 K4
BENWICH CIR (HO) 128 B2
BERAN DR (HO) 133 H12
BERENDO (HO) 129 E9
BERESFORD DR (HO) 131 H10
BERETTA CT (HO) 133 J8
BERGIN (HO) 130 H4
BERING DR (HO) 129 K9; 133 A9
BERING ST (HO) 130 J4
BERINGWOOD DR (HO) 132 D2
BERK RIDGE DR (HO) 133 J9
BERKLEY ST (HO) 134 C6
BERKSHIRE GREEN DR (HO) 132 D1
BERKSHIRE ST (HO) 130 D3
BERMUDA DR (PA) 135 D12
BERMUDA DUNES DR (MC) 132 K6
BERNADETTE LN (HO) 128 F6
BERNARD ST (PA) 135 B10
BERNDALE ST (HO) 131 I7
BERNICE ST (HO) 134 D5
BERNINA LN (HO) 131 B12
BERRINGTON DR (HO) 132 D2
BERRY BROOK DR (HO) 135 E8
BERRY CREEK DR (HO) 135 D8
BERRY GLEN LN (HO) 132 C3
BERRY LIMB DR (HO) 132 E4
BERRY RD (HO) 130 E2, E3
BERRY ST (HO) 130 K2; 134 A3
BERRYDALE RD (HO) 135 D7
BERRYFIELD DR (HO) 128 K4
BERRYHILL CT (HO) 135 E7
BERRYWOOD LN (HO) 128 J3
BERSEY LN (HO) 129 D11
BERTELLIS LN (HO) 129 D10
BERTHA S LN (HO) 131 I10
BERTHA ST (HO) 130 G4
BERTHEA ST (HO) 134 A1
BERTLOMA ST (PA) 135 E10
BERTNER AV (HO) 134 B1
BERTRAND (HO) 129 A12; 130 A3
BERTWOOD RD (HO) 130 D5
BERWICK ST (HO) 131 I10
BERWYN DR (HO) 129 A12
BERYL ST (HO) 133 C8
BESSEMER ST (HO) 135 G8
BETA CIR (PA) 135 C12
BETHEL BLVD (HO) 129 E9
BETHJE (HO) 129 I12
BETHLEHEM (HO) 129 E12
BETHUNE DR (HO) 129 C11
BETRAL ST (HO) 130 D1
BETSY LN (HO) 129 K11
BETTINA CT (HO) 128 I6
BETTIS DR (HO) 129 K10
BETTY BOOP (HO) 130 F6
BETTY JANE LN (HO) 129 H9
BETTY LN (PA) 135 D11
BETTY LN (ST) 132 G6
BETTY ST (BA) 133 C10
BETTY ST (SH) 135 E9
BETTY SUE LN (HO) 133 J12
BEULAH ST (HO) 134 A3
BEUSCH DR (PA) 135 D10
BEUTEL DR (SV) 129 H8
BEVERLY AV (PA) 135 C10, E12
BEVERLY LN (BA) 133 C10
BEVERLY ST (HO) 130 H1
BEVERLYHILL ST (HO) 133 A8
BEVERSBROOK DR (HO) 132 G6
BEVIS ST (HO) 129 G12
BEVLYN DR (HO) 133 D11
BEXLEY DR (HO) 132 D5
BICKWOOD DR (HO) 135 J9
BIDDIE WILBUR RD (PL) 134 K5
BIDIAS ST (PA) 135 F11
BIENVILLE LN (PA) 131 H10
BIG BEND DR (HO) 129 G7
BIG HOLLOW LN (HO) 128 J5
BIG HORN CT (SL) 132 J4
BIG LAKE DR (HO) 128 J5
BIG OAK TRAIL DR (HO) 129 A7
BIGELOW ST (HO) 130 H3
BIGGS CT (HO) 134 E6
BIGWOOD ST (HO) 130 C6
BIHIA FOREST DR (HO) 129 A9
BILLINGS DR (HO) 129 G7
BILLINGSLEY ST (HO) 130 G2
BILLINGTON ST (HO) 128 C2
BILLY ST (HO) 130 J4
BILOXI ST (HO) 135 C7
BINGHAM ST (HO) 130 I2
BINGHAMTON (HO) 135 K10
BINGLE RD (HO) 129 G8
BINLEY CT (HO) 128 K3
BINLEY DR (HO) 128 K3
BINTLIFF DR (HO) 133 B8
BINZ ST (HO) 134 B2
BIRCH COVE (HO) 128 D2
BIRCH GROVE DR (HO) 132 E3
BIRCH HILL DR (HO) 132 J1
BIRCH HOLLOW LN (HO) 132 A2
BIRCH RIVER DR (HO) 132 A1
BIRCH ST (BA) 133 C10
BIRCH VALE DR (BA) 128 E2
BIRCHCROFT DR (HO) 129 B10
BIRCHDALE DR/**1028** (MC) 132 K6
BIRCHMONT DR (HO) 129 D10
BIRCHTON (HO) 129 E8
BIRCHTREE FOREST DR (HO) 129 C10
BIRCHWOOD DR (PA) 135 D9
BIRCHWOOD ST (PA) 130 A2
BIRD (PA) 135 D9
BIRD DOG DR (HO) 133 J7
BIRD FOREST DR (HO) 129 A9
BIRD MEADOW LN (HO) 133 K7
BIRD RD (PA) 135 D9
BIRD RUN DR (HO) 133 K7
BIRDIE LN (GP) 131 J9
BIRDSALL ST (HO) 129 I12
BIRDWOOD CT (HO) 133 D9
BIRDWOOD RD (HO) 133 D9
BIRMINGHAM ST (HO) 130 E6
BIRNHAM WOODS BLVD (PA) 135 C12
BISBEE ST (HO) 135 C7
BISCAYNE WAY (HO) 130 B2
BISHOP ST (HO) 130 I2
BISHOPTON ST (PL) 135 J7
BISHOPVALE DR (AL) 130 A2
BISLEY LN (AL) 129 A11
BISON DR (HO) 128 I3
BISSONET ST (HO) 132 E5
BISSONNET ST (BA) 133 C10
BISSONNET ST (HO) 133 A11, D7; 134 A1
BITRIDGE CIR/**1029** (HO) 133 J10
BITTERNUT DR (HO) 129 D8
BIZERTE ST (HO) 130 E1
BLACK LOCUST DR (HO) 129 B10
BLACK MAPLE LN (HO) 129 C9
BLACK ROCK RD (CL) 131 G11
BLACK ST (HO) 134 B4
BLACKBERRY DR (PA) 135 D10
BLACKBURN DR (PA) 135 E10

BLACKGUM DR (HO) 129 D8
BLACKHAW (HO) 128 H3
BLACKHAWK BLVD (HO) 135 K8
BLACKJACK CT (HO) 129 B10
BLACKJACK LN (HO) 129 B9
BLACKSHEAR ST/**1030** (HO) 130 F1
BLACKSMITH LN (FC) 132 K4
BLACKSTONE CT (HO) 128 J3
BLACKWATER LN (CL) 131 G11
BLACKWELL ST (PA) 135 B9
BLADES (HO) 130 B6
BLADES ST (HO) 130 C6
BLAFFER (HO) 130 G5
BLAIR MEADOW DR (ME) 132 F4
BLAIR ST (HO) 129 G12
BLAIRSTONE (HO) 128 B1
BLAKE AV (PA) 135 D10
BLAKE RD (SL) 132 F3
BLALOCK CIR (PP) 129 J7
BLALOCK FOREST (BH) 129 J7
BLALOCK LN (BH) 129 J7
BLALOCK RD (HO) 129 G7
BLANCHE ST (HO) 130 K4
BLANCO ST (HO) 133 A7
BLAND ST (HO) 129 C11
BLANDCROFT CT (SL) 132 I4
BLANDFORD LN (HO) 129 H9
BLANDING DR (CV) 131 H12
BLANK (HO) 131 J9
BLANKENSHIP DR (HO) 129 F7
BLANTON BLVD (HO) 129 E10
BLARNEY DR (HO) 134 H2
BLAZEY DR (HO) 128 A3
BLEKER ST (HO) 130 F4, H4
BLEND STONE (HO) 128 B1
BLENHEIM PALACE LN (HO) 128 B3
BLIGH ST (HO) 133 H11
BLIND RIVER DR (PA) 135 G10
BLISS MEADOWS DR (PA) 135 F12
BLISS ST (HO) 135 E7
BLISS TR/**1031** (HO) 128 B1
BLODGETT AV (HO) 134 A2
BLOOM DR (HO) 130 C1
BLOOMFIELD ST (HO) 134 F2
BLOOMINGTON LN (ME) 132 F5
BLOSSOM BELL LN (HO) 133 K7
BLOSSOM ST (HO) 129 I12; 130 I1
BLOUNT ST (HO) 130 G1
BLUE (HO) 130 F6
BLUE BONNET (ST) 132 G5
BLUE BONNET BLVD (HO) 133 C12
BLUE CASTLE LN/**1032** (CL) 131 G11
BLUE DIAMOND DR (MC) 133 J7
BLUE FALLS DR (SL) 132 F2
BLUE GRASS LN (SL) 131 B11
BLUE HERON LN (HO) 134 G5
BLUE ISLAND DR (HO) 131 D9
BLUE LAGOON (HO) 131 C9
BLUE LAKES LN (MC) 132 K6
BLUE MARLIN LN (MC) 132 C3
BLUE MEADOW CIR (FC) 132 K3
BLUE MIST DR (MC) 132 G1
BLUE QUAIL DR (HO) 133 K8
BLUE RIDGE DR (HO) 133 I9; 134 D5
BLUE RIDGE RD (HO) 133 K9
BLUE SKY (HO) 129 B10
BLUE WATER LN (HO) 129 D10
BLUE WILLOW DR (HO) 128 K5
BLUEBERRY HILL CT (HO) 128 D2
BLUEBERRY HILL DR (HO) 128 D2
BLUEBERRY LN (PA) 135 D10
BLUEBERRY LN (SH) 131 C12
BLUEBERRY ST (HO) 130 E1
BLUEBIRD (HO) 128 I4
BLUEBIRD LN (PA) 135 E9
BLUEBONNET DR (PA) 133 K11
BLUEBONNET ST (PA) 135 E12
BLUEBONNET ST (SL) 132 I2
BLUEFIELD DR (PA) 135 D11
BLUEGATE DR (HO) 133 D12
BLUEGRASS ST (HO) 130 F1
BLUEJAY LN (HO) 134 H6
BLUEJAY ST (HO) 134 H5
BLUERIDGE AV (PA) 135 D9
BLUESTEM DR/**1033** (HO) 129 B10
BLUESTONE DR (HO) 130 B6
BLUFFDALE DR (HO) 128 D2
BLUFFRIDGE CIR/**1034** (HO) 128 B2
BLYTHE ST (HO) 131 I10
BLYTHEWOOD ST (HO) 134 B3
BO JACK DR (HO) 129 A7
BOARDWALK ST (HO) 128 K5
BOB ST (HO) 130 K4
BOB WHITE DR (HO) 133 F8
BOBBITT LN (HO) 129 H9
BOBBY BURNS ST (HO) 130 F6
BOBBY DR (PL) 134 J6
BOBBY JACK LN (PL) 129 A7
BOBBY LEE LN (HO) 134 B5
BOBOLINK (HO) 135 D8
BOCA CT (HO) 132 E3
BODEGA DR (HO) 133 K9
BOENEMAN DR (HO) 129 C12
BOGGESS RD (HO) 130 C5
BOHEME CT (HO) 128 I6
BOHEME DR (HO) 128 I5
BOICEWOOD ST (HO) 130 D4
BOIS D ARC ST (HO) 134 D5
BOISE (HO) 131 I11
BOLD RULER RD (ST) 132 I6
BOLDEN ST (HO) 131 K7
BOLDFOREST DR (HO) 129 A9
BOLERO CT (ME) 132 F4
BOLIN RD (HO) 129 F9
BOLINGTON DR (HO) 132 D3
BOLIVAR ST (BA) 133 C10
BOLIVIA BLVD (HO) 129 C10
BOLIVIA DR (PA) 135 F11
BOLLING LN (HO) 130 D1
BOLLINGBROOK DR (HO) 132 D3
BOLSOVER RD (HO) 133 B12; 134 A1
BOLT AV (HO) 134 F2
BOLTON DR (MC) 133 I7
BOLTON PL (HO) 129 I10
BOMAR ST (HO) 130 J1
BOMBAY ST (HO) 130 F1
BONAIRE ST (HO) 130 F6
BONAZZI BLVD (HO) 129 A10
BOND (HO) 129 B7
BOND ST (HO) 130 H4
BOND ST (PA) 135 B11
BONDALE (HO) 129 B7
BONHAM ST (CL) 131 I11
BONHAM ST (HO) 130 I5
BONHOMME RD (HO) 133 D8
BONILLA LN (HO) 132 C2
BONITA SPRINGS DR (HO) 132 B1
BONITA ST (HO) 130 E4
BONN ECHO CIR (HO) 135 E7
BONNER (HO) 128 H5
BONNER DR (HO) 135 D7
BONNER ST (HO) 130 I1
BONNERCREST (HO) 132 E2
BONNIE (SH) 135 E9
BONNIE BRAE ST (HO) 134 A1
BONNINGTON DR (HO) 135 J11
BONNO PL (HO) 130 I4
BONNY BRIAR LN (MC) 132 K6
BONSRELL ST (HO) 134 A4
BOOKER ST (HO) 130 F6, I4
BOONE (HO) 132 B5; 135 J11
BOONE RD (HO) 130 H3; 132 D5
BOONRIDGE RD (HO) 133 J10
BOONWAY DR (HO) 133 H11

BOOTH ST (HO) 130 H2
BOOTS RD (HO) 129 D12
BORDEN (HO) 131 K7
BORDER (HO) 134 I3
BORDERWOOD DR (HO) 131 H9
BORDLEY DR (HO) 128 J6; 129 J9
BOROS DR (HC) 129 H9
BOSQUE ST (HO) 133 A9
BOSS-GASTON RD (HO) 132 E1
BOSTIC ST (HO) 130 E3
BOSTON ST (HO) 130 K1
BOSWELL ST (HO) 130 H3
BOSWORTH (HO) 135 D8
BOTANY LN (HO) 134 G2; 135 H7
BOTHWELL WAY (PP) 129 I7
BOUGH CT (HO) 129 D9
BOULDER OAKS DR (HO) 128 C2
BOULDER ST (HO) 135 B7
BOULDERGREEN (HO) 128 B1
BOUNDARY ST (HO) 130 H2
BOURNEMOUTH DR/**1035** (PA) 135 G10
BOURNEWOOD (SL) 132 G3
BOURNEWOOD DR (SL) 132 H3
BOVEDA DR (SL) 132 C2
BOW LN (HO) 133 J10
BOWEN DR (PA) 135 D12
BOWEN LN (PA) 132 J5
BOWEN ST (HO) 134 D2
BOWHEAD DR (HO) 131 H9
BOWIE RIDGE LN (HO) 133 J10
BOWIE ST (HO) 134 B6
BOWLAN LN (HO) 133 F8
BOWLING GREEN ST (HO) 134 B2
BOWRIDGE LN (HO) 133 J9
BOWTRAIL (HO) 128 B1
BOX BLUFF CT (HO) 132 J1
BOXELDER DR (HO) 132 A1
BOXWOOD CT (SL) 132 G2
BOXWOOD DR (BV) 134 J5
BOY (HO) 130 F6
BOYCE AV (HO) 130 I5
BOYD (HO) 130 E2
BOYD CT (PA) 135 B10
BOYER LN (PA) 131 G10
BOYKIN ST (HO) 135 F8
BOYLES ST (HO) 130 J5
BOYLSTON DR (CV) 131 H12
BOYNTON (HO) 133 H12
BOYNTON DR (HO) 133 H11
BOYSENBERRY (HO) 128 A1
BRACE AV (HO) 134 F5
BRACHER (SV) 129 H8
BRACKENRIDGE ST (HO) 130 H3
BRACKLEY LN (HO) 129 A11
BRACKNELL (HO) 135 E8
BRADBRIDGE LN (HO) 132 B3
BRADEN (HO) 134 J3
BRADFORD COLONY DR (HO) 128 C2
BRADFORD DR (MC) 132 K6
BRADFORD ST (HO) 133 C11; 134 D6
BRADLEY ST (HO) 130 H2
BRADMAR (HO) 129 B11
BRADNEY DR (HO) 128 J3
BRADSHAW ST (HO) 130 G1
BRADY ST (HO) 130 K5
BRAE ACRES RD (HO) 133 D7
BRAEBURN BEND DR (HO) 133 E7
BRAEBURN DR (BA) 133 C10
BRAEBURN GLEN BLVD (HO) 133 E7
BRAEBURN VALLEY DR (HO) 133 D7
BRAECREST LN (HO) 131 E9
BRAES BAYOU DR (HO) 133 E8
BRAES BEND DR (HO) 133 E7
BRAES BLVD (SP) 133 C11
BRAES FOREST DR (HO) 133 F7
BRAES MEADOW DR (HO) 133 E7
BRAES PARK DR (HO) 133 F7
BRAES RIVER DR (HO) 133 D7
BRAESCREEK DR (HO) 133 E7
BRAESDALE LN (HO) 133 E8
BRAESGLEN DR (HO) 133 E8
BRAESHEATHER CT (HO) 133 D10, E8
BRAESHEATHER DR (HO) 133 E9
BRAESMAIN DR (HO) 133 C12
BRAESMEADOW LN (FC) 132 K3
BRAESMONT DR (HO) 133 E9
BRAESRIDGE DR (HO) 133 F8
BRAESVALLEY DR (HO) 133 D9
BRAESVIEW LN (HO) 133 E7
BRAESWEST DR (HO) 132 A2
BRAESWOOD BLVD (HO) 133 C12, D10; 134 C1
BRAEWICK DR (HO) 133 G8
BRAEWOOD GLEN LN (HO) 132 C3
BRAEWOOD PARK DR (HO) 133 C12
BRAGG ST (HO) 130 F3
BRAILSFORT ST (HO) 134 A3
BRAMBLEBURY DR (SL) 132 G3
BRAMBLEWOOD DR (HO) 128 J3
BRANARD ST (HO) 129 K12; 130 K1
BRANCH (HO) 134 D3
BRANCH FOREST DR (HO) 132 A1
BRANCH POINT DR (HO) 128 A2
BRANCHWATER LN (SL) 132 E2
BRAND RD (SL) 132 I5
BRANDON ST (HO) 134 F2
BRANDON WAY (BH) 129 I7
BRANDT ST (HO) 130 K2; 134 A2
BRANDYWINE LN (BH) 129 I7
BRANDYWYNE DR/**1036** (HO) 128 K4
BRANFORD ST (HO) 129 C11
BRANIFF AV (HO) 134 G6
BRANNON ST (HO) 130 D3
BRANT ROCK DR (HO) 132 B3
BRANTLEY (HO) 135 I11
BRANUM ST (HO) 135 C8
BRASHEAR ST (HO) 130 I1
BRAUNSTON LN (HO) 129 A11
BRAVO (PA) 135 D11
BRAXTON DR (HO) 133 B8
BRAYMOORE (HO) 128 E5
BRAYS ST (HO) 134 A6
BRAYSWORTH (HO) 132 B4
BRAZIL CIR (PA) 135 F11
BRAZIL ST (HO) 130 F3
BRAZORIA (HO) 129 K12
BRAZOS ST (HO) 130 K2
BREA CREST (HO) 130 B4
BREA CREST ST (HO) 130 B1
BREAKWOOD DR (HO) 133 D10
BRECCIA DR (HO) 128 A3
BRECON HALL DR (HO) 128 J4
BREEZE PARK DR (HO) 131 G10
BREEZEWAY ST (HO) 129 B8; 130 A2
BREEZY MEADOW DR (ST) 132 G4
BREEZY PINES LN (PL) 134 K2
BRELAND ST (HO) 130 C5
BREMOND AV (HO) 130 K2; 134 A3
BRENDA LN (PA) 135 D10
BRENDA ST (HO) 130 C1
BRENDAM LN (HO) 132 C3
BRENFORD DR (HO) 133 H12
BRENT DR (HO) 133 I9
BRENTON ST (HO) 130 A4
BRENTWOOD DR (CV) 131 H12
BRENTWOOD DR (HO) 129 J12
BRETAGNE DR (CL) 131 H10
BRETSHIRE DR (HO) 130 C5
BRETTON DR (HO) 130 C5
BREWSTER ST (HO) 130 F4

BRIAN HAVEN DR (HO) 129 E12
BRIAR BAYOU DR (HO) 128 J3; 132 B3
BRIAR BRANCH DR (HC) 129 H8
BRIAR CT (SL) 132 H4
BRIAR DALE CT (HO) 129 K11
BRIAR DR (HO) 128 K6; 129 I9
BRIAR DR (PA) 135 C11
BRIAR FOREST RD (HO) 128 J2, K5
BRIAR GLADE DR (HO) 132 B5
BRIAR HILL DR (HO) 128 J6
BRIAR HOLLOW LN (HO) 129 J10, J11
BRIAR HOLLOW LN/**1037** (HO) 129 J10
BRIAR HOLLOW PL (HO) 129 J10
BRIAR HOME DR (HO) 128 J2
BRIAR KNOLL DR (HO) 128 I3; 132 A3, B3
BRIAR MEADOW/**1038** (HO) 132 F4
BRIAR OAKS LN (HO) 129 K10
BRIAR PATCH DR (HO) 128 J3
BRIAR PATH DR (HO) 128 I3
BRIAR RIDGE DR (HO) 129 J8
BRIAR RIVER DR (HO) 128 K6
BRIAR ROSE DR (HO) 128 K6; 129 K8
BRIAR RUN CT (HO) 133 J8
BRIAR SEASONS DR (HO) 133 J9
BRIAR SPRING CT (HO) 133 J9
BRIAR TERRACE DR (HO) 132 B5
BRIAR TOWN LN (HO) 129 K9
BRIAR TR (HO) 129 I10
BRIAR WAY (HO) 129 K11
BRIARBANK DR (SL) 132 G2
BRIARBEND DR (HO) 133 E9
BRIARBROOK DR (HO) 128 K6
BRIARCLIFF DR (HO) 130 D2
BRIARCREST DR (HO) 128 K2
BRIARGATE DR (HO) 133 J9
BRIARGLEN DR (HO) 129 K10
BRIARGREEN DR (HO) 128 K2; 132 A2
BRIARGREEN DR (PA) 135 C11
BRIARGROVE DR (HO) 129 J8
BRIARHILLS (HO) 128 I2
BRIARHURST DR/**1039** (HO) 129 K9
BRIARLEE DR (HO) 128 K2
BRIARMEAD DR (HO) 129 K9
BRIARPARK DR (HO) 128 K6; 132 A6
BRIARPLACE DR (HO) 128 K2
BRIARPORT DR (HO) 128 K2
BRIARSIDE DR (ST) 132 H5
BRIARSTEAD DR/**1040** (HO) 133 J9
BRIARSTEM DR (HO) 128 K2
BRIARVIEW DR (HO) 128 K2
BRIARWAY ST (PA) 135 C11
BRIARWEST BLVD (HO) 128 K3
BRIARWEST CIR (HO) 128 K3
BRIARWICK LN (HO) 130 C4
BRIARWILD LN (HO) 128 G6
BRIARWOOD CT (HO) 129 K11
BRIARWOOD DR (PA) 135 D8
BRIARWOOD FOREST DR (PA) 129 A9
BRIARWORTH DR (HO) 128 K2
BRICKER ST (HO) 134 E3
BRIDGE FOREST DR (HO) 129 A9
BRIDGELAND LN (HO) 128 E6
BRIDGEPATH LN (HO) 128 C3
BRIDGEPORT RD (HO) 133 I12
BRIDGEWALK LN (HO) 128 C3
BRIDGEWOOD ST (HC) 129 I8
BRIDLE PATH DR (HC) 131 E9
BRIDLE SPUR/**1041** (HL) 129 H9
BRIDLEWOOD ST (HC) 129 I8
BRIDLINGTON ST (HO) 133 H9
BRIEFWAY AV (HO) 134 C5
BRIER GARDENS DR (HO) 132 B1
BRIG O DOON CIR (HO) 133 E8
BRIGADE (HO) 128 F6
BRIGHT MEADOWS DR (MC) 133 K7
BRIGHT PENNY LN (CV) 131 H12
BRIGHTON LN (CV) 132 G6
BRIGHTON/**1042** (MC) 132 K5
BRIGHTWATER (MC) 132 K5
BRILEY ST (HO) 130 K3; 134 A2
BRILL ST (HO) 130 H4
BRIMBERRY ST (HO) 129 E11
BRIMFIELD DR (HO) 132 B1
BRIMHURST DR (HO) 128 J2
BRINESAGE CT (HO) 128 K2
BRINGHURST ST (HO) 130 H4
BRINKLEY AV (HO) 134 E3
BRINKMAN ST (HO) 129 D12
BRINWOOD DR (HO) 128 G6
BRISBANE RD (HO) 134 G2, G5
BRISCOE ST (HO) 134 E3
BRISTLEBROOK DR (HO) 132 D2
BRISTO CT (HO) 128 C2
BRISTOL BROOK DR (HO) 132 E2
BRISTOL CT (SL) 132 H4
BRISTOL HARBOUR CIR/**1043** (SL) 128 C2
BRISTOL ST (HO) 130 G2
BRITFORD (HO) 128 B1
BRITMORE PARK (HO) 128 D5
BRITOAK LN (HO) 128 H5
BRITON COVE DR (HO) 128 C2
BRITT RD (BV) 134 K5
BRITT WAY (HO) 128 G5
BRITTANY DR (SL) 132 F3
BRITTERIDGE ST/**1044** (SL) 128 C2
BRITTMOORE RD (HO) 128 C5, G5
BROAD OAKS CIR (HO) 129 I9
BROAD OAKS DR (HO) 129 I9
BROAD OAKS DR/**1045** (HO) 129 J9
BROAD ST (HO) 134 B5
BROADFIELD BLVD (HO) 128 H1
BROADGREEN DR (HO) 128 I3
BROADGREEN DR (MC) 132 K6
BROADHURST DR (HO) 133 J12
BROADLEY DR (HO) 132 E2
BROADMEAD DR (HO) 133 D11
BROADMOOR CIR (MC) 132 K6
BROADMOOR DR (SL) 132 I4
BROADMOOR ST (HO) 134 A4
BROADSTAIRS ST (HO) 131 H8
BROADVIEW DR (HO) 134 E6
BROADWAY (HO) 135 H9
BROADWAY BLVD (HO) 134 B6, C6, F6
BROADWAY BLVD (PA) 135 B10
BROADWAY/**1046** (PA) 135 B9
BROCK PARK DR (HO) 131 D8
BROCK ST (HO) 134 C5
BROCKET PL (ST) 132 H4
BROCKHAMPTON ST (HO) 131 I8
BROCKLEY LN (HO) 134 E6

BROCKMAN ST (PA) 135 B9
BROCKTON ST (HO) 134 C6
BROCKWOOD (HO) 134 J3
BROGDEN RD (HC) 129 H8
BROKEN ARROW (HO) 128 I6
BROKEN BOUGH CIR (BH) 129 I7
BROKEN BOUGH DR (HO) 128 I6
BROKEN BOUGH DR/**1047** (MC) 132 K6
BROKEN BRIDGE DR (HO) 133 H9
BROMLEY RD (HL) 129 H9
BROMPTON RD (HO) 133 C12
BRON HOLLY DR (HO) 129 F11
BRONCO DR (HO) 129 G7
BRONSON ST (HO) 135 F8
BRONTON ST (HO) 129 F11
BROODING OAK CIR/**1048** (HO) 133 E8
BROOK DR (PA) 135 D9
BROOK HOLLOW DR/**1049** (SL) 132 G3
BROOK LEA DR (HO) 134 D4
BROOK MEADOW LN (ME) 132 F4
BROOK SPRING DR (HO) 128 J4
BROOK SPRINGS DR (HO) 128 A2
BROOK ST (CV) 131 H12
BROOK VIEW LN (FC) 132 K3
BROOK WOODS DR (HO) 129 F10
BROOKBEND DR (HO) 133 E10
BROOKBEND LN (FC) 132 K3
BROOKCREST CIR (HO) 132 D3
BROOKFIELD ST (HO) 133 I10
BROOKFORD DR (MC) 133 J8
BROOKGLADE CIR (HO) 132 D4
BROOKGLEN DR (HO) 135 D7
BROOKHAVEN AV (HO) 134 D3
BROOKHAVEN AV (PA) 135 F11
BROOKLAKE CT/**1050** (HO) 128 J4
BROOKLAKE DR (HO) 128 J4, J5
BROOKLAWN DR (HO) 133 I9
BROOKLEDGE DR (HO) 132 F4
BROOKLET DR (HO) 132 E5
BROOKLYN (HO) 130 A2
BROOKMEADE DR (HO) 133 H10
BROOKMEADOW CIR/**1051** (HO) 135 J9
BROOKMEADOW CT/**1052** (HO) 135 J9
BROOKMEADOW DR (HO) 135 J9
BROOKMEADOWS LN (ME) 132 F4
BROOKMERE DR (HO) 129 G11
BROOKMONT LN (HO) 131 E9
BROOKREN CIR (HO) 132 D3
BROOKRIVER DR (HO) 128 B6
BROOKS ST (HO) 130 I3
BROOKS ST (SL) 132 I2
BROOKSHIRE DR (HO) 129 E7
BROOKSIDE DR (HO) 134 A5
BROOKSIDE RD (BV) 134 K5
BROOKSIDE RD (PL) 134 K4
BROOKSTON ST (HO) 133 G10
BROOKSTONE DR (HO) 129 B8
BROOKSURE CIR (HO) 132 D3
BROOKTREE DR (HO) 128 H6; 129 G11
BROOKVALLEY DR (HO) 133 G7
BROOKVIEW DR (HO) 131 I12
BROOKWULF DR (HO) 132 D3
BROOM (HO) 129 D9
BRORA CT (HO) 128 D1
BROU LN (HO) 133 C8
BROUSSARD (HO) 135 J11
BROWER ST (HO) 135 C7
BROWN (HO) 130 I1
BROWN BARK DR (HO) 129 D9
BROWN DR (PA) 135 C11
BROWN LEAF CIR (HO) 133 E8
BROWN SADDLE RD (HO) 129 J9
BROWN ST (MC) 132 I6
BROWNCROFT ST (HO) 134 C4
BROWNE (HO) 134 C6
BROWNING ST (WU) 133 B11
BROWNSTONE LN (HO) 133 I11
BROWNSVILLE ST (CL) 131 H11
BROWNSVILLE ST (HO) 130 H5
BROWNWAY RD (HO) 129 K10
BROWNWOOD ST (CL) 131 I11
BROWNWOOD ST (HO) 130 I5
BROYLES ST (HO) 130 G4
BRUCE ST (HO) 130 H2
BRUMBLEY ST (HO) 134 B6
BRUMMEL DR (HO) 132 D3
BRUN ST (HO) 129 K12
BRUNSON ST (HO) 134 C1
BRUNSWICK (HO) 130 A5
BRUNSWICK DR (SL) 132 I4
BRUSH WOOD DR (HO) 129 B9
BRUSHY CREEK DR (SL) 132 J3
BRUSHY CT (HO) 129 B9
BRUTUS ST (HO) 134 B6
BRYAN ST (HO) 130 K4
BRYAN ST (PA) 135 C10
BRYANT POND DR (HO) 128 C3
BRYANT RIDGE RD (HO) 133 J10
BRYANT ST (HO) 135 G7
BRYCE (HO) 129 H12
BRYKERWOODS DR (HO) 129 H9
BRYN MAWR DR (HC) 129 I8
BRYN MAWR LN (HO) 129 K10
BRYONWOOD DR (HO) 129 H9
BUBBLING BROOKS LN (HO) 128 A1
BUCAN DR (HO) 130 C2
BUCHANAN ST (HO) 130 J6
BUCHANAN ST (PA) 135 D10
BUCK ST (HO) 130 I4
BUCKINGHAM DR (HO) 129 I10
BUCKINGHAM/**1053** (ST) 132 H4
BUCKLER RIDGE (HO) 133 K10
BUCKMANN CT (HO) 128 G6
BUCKNELL CT (SL) 132 I4
BUCKNELL RD (HO) 130 C5
BUCKNER ST (HO) 130 J2
BUCROFT ST/**1054** (HO) 130 J6
BUDD (PA) 135 E10
BUEL CT (HO) 130 J1
BUELOW ST (HO) 134 B4
BUENA PARK DR (HO) 135 I8
BUENA VISTA ST (HO) 134 D6
BUENA VISTA ST (ST) 132 H4
BUESCHER DR (HO) 128 G5
BUFFALO RIDGE CIR (HO) 129 I9
BUFFALO SPEEDWAY (HO) 129 K11; 133 C11, K12
BUFFALO SPEEDWAY (WU) 133 B11
BUFFALO TER/**1055** (HO) 130 J1
BUFFALO TR (FC) 132 K4
BUFFUM ST (HO) 134 F2
BUFORD ST (HO) 134 B5
BUGLE RD (HO) 132 B5
BULL LN (MC) 133 H7
BULLFINCH (HO) 134 E5
BULLOCK LN (HO) 129 H7
BUNCHE DR (HO) 129 C11
BUNDICK DR (HO) 129 C11
BUNDY LN (HO) 129 F7

BUNGALOW LN (HO) 134 H3
BUNKER HILL RD (BH) 129 I7
BUNKERIDGE RD (HO) 133 K10
BUNNINGHAM LN (SV) 129 H8
BUNNY RUN DR (HO) 129 A12
BUNTE ST (HO) 130 G5
BUNTON ST (HO) 130 H3
BUNZEL ST (HO) 129 A11
BURBANK ST (HO) 130 D2
BURCH ST (HO) 130 J4
BURDEN ST (HO) 130 D3
BURDINE ST (HO) 133 F9, G9
BURFORD LN (HO) 129 A11
BURFORD PVT ST/**1056** (HO) 128 J3
BURG LN (HO) 129 B11
BURGER LN (HO) 129 A7
BURGESS ST (HO) 134 C1
BURGOYNE DR (HO) 128 K3
BURGOYNE RD (HO) 128 K2, K5
BURGUNDY LN (HO) 134 C4
BURK (HO) 134 H5
BURKE RD (PA) 135 G11
BURKEDALE DR (SL) 132 F3
BURKETT ST (HO) 134 C2
BURKHART RD (SV) 129 H8
BURKRIDGE DR (SV) 128 A3
BURKWOOD CT (SV) 132 I1
BURL ST (HO) 131 D7
BURLCREEK (HO) 128 B1
BURLINGAME DR (HO) 132 F5
BURLINGHALL DR (HO) 133 F9
BURLINGTON NORTH DR (HO) 129 C9
BURLMONT LN (CV) 131 G12
BURLWOOD DR (CV) 135 J10
BURMA RD (HO) 134 D3
BURMAN ST (JC) 131 J8
BURNETT ST (HO) 130 I3
BURNEY RD (SL) 132 F2
BURNHAM (SL) 132 I3; 133 J11
BURNING HILLS DR (HO) 133 E8
BURNING TREE DR (HO) 133 B7
BURNINGBUSH LN (HO) 130 B6
BURNLEY (HO) 130 B2
BURNSIDE LN (HO) 128 D6
BURR OAK DR (HO) 129 D9
BURR ST (HO) 130 K4
BURRESS AV (HO) 130 D2
BURRESS ST (HO) 130 D1
BURT RD (HO) 129 B11
BURWELL (HO) 134 B4
BUSIEK CT (HO) 130 E1
BUSSE CIR (PA) 135 C12
BUTE ST (HO) 130 K1
BUTLER DR (PA) 135 D10
BUTLER ST (HO) 130 J1
BUTLERCREST (HO) 129 G7
BUTTERCUP ST (HO) 133 A7
BUTTERFLY CIR (PA) 135 F12
BUTTERFLY CT (HO) 128 I4
BUTTERFLY LN (HO) 128 I5
BUTTERGROVE DR (HO) 128 C3
BUTTERSTONE (HO) 132 B6
BUTTONHILL DR (MC) 133 J8
BUXLEY ST (HO) 133 H10
BUXTON ST (HO) 135 C8
BYLANE DR (BH) 129 J7
BYRNE ST (HO) 130 H2
BYRON ST (WU) 133 B11
BYWAY ST (HO) 129 I12
BYWOOD ST (HO) 130 E6
C E KING PKWY (HO) 131 A10, C9, E9
C ST (HO) 132 B4
CABILDO DR (HO) 132 C1
CABIN PL (FC) 132 K4
CABOT ST (HO) 130 C6
CABOTS LANDING DR/**1057** (HO) 128 B2
CABRERA LN (HO) 132 C3
CABRINA LN (HO) 132 C3
CACTUS FOREST DR (HO) 129 A9
CACTUS ST (HO) 130 H4
CACTUS ST (PA) 135 C9
CADAWAC RD (HO) 133 D8
CADDO LAKE LN (HO) 132 C3
CADDO RD (HO) 130 C6
CADENA RD (PA) 135 F10
CADILLAC ST (HO) 134 C2
CADMAN CT (HO) 133 D10
CADMUS ST (HO) 130 E1
CAESAR DR (HO) 132 F4
CAFFREY ST (HO) 135 I8
CAGE ST (HO) 130 J4
CAIRN VILLAGE (HO) 128 D1
CAIRNGALE (HO) 128 D1
CAIRNLADDIE (HO) 128 D1
CAIRNLASSIE (HO) 128 D1
CAIRNLEIGH DR (HO) 128 C1
CAIRNLOCH (HO) 128 D1
CAIRNLOMOND (HO) 128 D1
CAIRNSEAN (HO) 128 D1
CAIRNWAY (HO) 128 D2
CAIRNWAY CT (HO) 128 D1
CALADERO DR (HO) 132 C1
CALAIS RD (HO) 134 D3
CALDER ST (HO) 129 I12
CALDWELL (HO) 134 C5
CALENDAR ST (HO) 130 H2
CALGARY LN (HO) 130 C5
CALHOUN (HO) 134 D3
CALHOUN AV (HO) 130 K3
CALHOUN RD (HO) 134 B3
CALICO LN (PP) 129 I7
CALIFORNIA ST (HO) 130 K1
CALLAHAN DR (HO) 131 G10
CALLE LOZANO LN (HO) 128 B3
CALLERY CREEK DR (HO) 133 J10
CALLES ST (HO) 130 I5
CALLIE ST (HO) 134 A3
CALLOWAY ST (HO) 131 K7
CALUMET DR (HO) 134 B2
CALUMET DR (SL) 132 F3
CALVERTON DR (SL) 132 E2
CALVI CT (BA) 133 C10
CALVIN ST (HO) 129 C11
CALVIN ST (PA) 135 C9
CAM CT (SV) 129 H8
CAMARA LN (HO) 128 I4
CAMARGO ST (HO) 133 D7
CAMAY DR (HO) 130 D5
CAMBRIDGE (HO) 134 C1
CAMBRIDGE GLEN DR (HO) 133 F8
CAMBRIDGE LN (MC) 132 K6
CAMBRIDGE ST (HO) 134 D1
CAMDEN RD (PA) 135 E10
CAMELBACK CT (HO) 128 I3
CAMELIA ST (HO) 129 I12
CAMELLIA AV (PA) 135 F11
CAMELLIA ST (SL) 132 I2
CAMELOT LN (HC) 129 I8
CAMELOT LN (MC) 132 K6
CAMELOT PL (SL) 132 I4
CAMEO DR (HO) 129 F8
CAMERON ST (HO) 129 K12
CAMILLE ST (PA) 135 C11
CAMINO DEL SOL (HO) 132 C1
CAMINO RANCHO DR (HO) 132 C1
CAMPBELL (PA) 135 D9
CAMPBELL RD (HO) 129 E7
CAMPBELL ST (HO) 130 H3
CAMPDEN HILL RD (HO) 133 I10
CAMPEACHY LN (HO) 132 C3
CAMPHORWOOD DR (HO) 135 J9
CAMPOREE LN (HO) 132 C3
CAMPWOOD (SL) 132 I4
CAMWAY (HO) 130 E5
CAMWOOD ST (HO) 134 D6
CANAAN BRIDGE DR (HO) 128 C3
CANADA DR (PA) 135 G12
CANADA DRY (HO) 134 A4
CANADIAN ST (HO) 130 G2
CANAL (HO) 131 G11
CANAL ST (HO) 130 K5; 134 A6
CANARIDGE DR (HO) 133 J9
CANARY CIR (PA) 135 D9
CANARYWOOD DR (PA) 135 K9
CANASTA LN (HO) 132 C3
CANBERRA (HO) 134 G6
CANDA LN (HO) 132 C3
CANDACE ST (HO) 129 G8
CANDLE GREEN CT (HO) 133 G7
CANDLE GREEN LN (HO) 133 G7
CANDLE LN (HO) 133 F7
CANDLECREST DR (HO) 129 D12
CANDLEGLOW DR (HO) 129 E12

CANDLELEAF DR (HO) 129 E12
CANDLELIGHT LN (HO) 129 E11
CANDLEMIST DR (HO) 129 D12
CANDLER DR (HO) 130 B1
CANDLESHADE LN (HO) 133 H10
CANDLETREE DR (HO) 129 D12
CANDLEWICK ST (HO) 131 I10
CANDLEWOOD DR (HO) 128 J6; 129 J9
CANDY ST (HO) 131 I7
CANE FIELD DR (FC) 132 K3
CANEBRAKE LN/**1058** (HO) 132 C3
CANEBREAK CRSG (SL) 132 J3
CANEMONT ST (HO) 133 G8
CANERIDGE DR/**1059** (HO) 133 J9
CANFIELD (HO) 133 A7
CANFIELD ST (HO) 134 A3
CANINO RD (HO) 129 B12; 130 B1, B2
CANNA DR (CV) 131 H12
CANNIFF RD (HO) 135 F7
CANNOCK RD (HO) 133 C8
CANNON (HO) 134 E2
CANNON PASS CT (SL) 132 J4
CANNONADE DR (PA) 135 D12
CANOGA LN (HO) 129 G7
CANONERO DR (ST) 132 I6
CANONGATE DR (HO) 129 K10
CANTERBURY ST (HO) 134 C1
CANTERDALE (HO) 133 H12
CANTERLANE DR (HO) 134 I1
CANTERVIEW DR (HO) 134 I1
CANTERVILLE RD (HO) 134 I1
CANTERWAY DR (HO) 134 G3
CANTERWELL RD (HO) 133 I12
CANTON ST (HO) 134 A6
CANTRELL (HO) 133 D8
CANYON (HO) 134 E2
CANYON CT (MC) 132 K6
CANYON DR (MC) 135 K9
CANYON FOREST DR (MC) 129 A9
CANYON HILL ST (MC) 132 D2
CANYON MEADOWS/**1060** (MC) 132 K6
CAPE COD LN (HC) 129 I8
CAPE FORWARD DR (HC) 132 B3
CAPE HATTERAS DR (HO) 128 C3
CAPE HYANNIS DR (HO) 134 H3
CAPE PROVINCE DR (HO) 132 C3
CAPELLO DR (HO) 133 F9
CAPERTON ST (HO) 130 E3
CAPISTRANO ST (HO) 131 J9
CAPITAL ST (PA) 135 E11
CAPITOL AV (HO) 134 A6
CAPITOL ST (HO) 130 J2, K4, K5; 134 A5
CAPLIN ST (HO) 130 F5
CAPPAMORE ST/**1061** (HO) 131 I8
CAPRI (HW) 129 I8
CAPRI DR (JV) 128 A5
CAPRI ST (SL) 132 H2
CAPRICORN (ST) 132 G5
CAPRON ST (HO) 130 I4
CAPTAIN DR (HO) 132 C6
CAPTAINS WALK (HO) 128 H2
CARA CIR (PA) 135 F11
CARADINE (HO) 133 I9
CARAVAN DR (HO) 133 E7
CARAWAY CIR (HO) 132 C6
CARBONEAR DR (CV) 131 G12
CARBRIDGE DR (HO) 128 C1, E6
CARBY RD (HO) 130 B1, B2
CARDIFF RD (HO) 130 B2
CARDINAL AV (SL) 132 I3
CARDINAL CIR (PA) 135 D9
CARDINAL LN (HO) 128 I4
CARDONO LN (HO) 133 J9
CARDWELL DR (SV) 129 H8
CAREN CT (HO) 132 G6
CAREW ST (HO) 133 D7
CAREY ST (HO) 130 E5
CAREYWOOD DR (SL) 132 F3
CARGILL ST/**1062** (HO) 130 J6
CARIBBEAN LN (HO) 135 I8
CARIBE LN (HO) 134 J1
CARILLO DR (HO) 129 D10
CARINGORM DR (HO) 128 E1
CARINO DR (HO) 129 D10
CARIS (HO) 129 D10
CARL CT (ST) 132 I6
CARL LN (BH) 129 J7
CARL ST (HO) 130 H2
CARL ST (PA) 135 B9
CARLA ST (HO) 130 B2
CARLEEN RD (HO) 129 E10
CARLFORD CIR (HO) 129 F11
CARLINGFORD LN (HO) 128 H4
CARLINGTON DR (HO) 130 C3
CARLISLE ST (HO) 135 C7
CARLON ST (SP) 133 B11
CARLOS ST (HO) 130 G6
CARLOTA CT (HO) 133 E8
CARLSBAD CT (HO) 133 H8
CARLSBAD ST (HO) 133 H8
CARLSBAD ST (JV) 128 A5
CARLSON LN (HO) 134 H2
CARLTON DR (HO) 134 G2
CARMALEE (HO) 135 I8
CARMEL AV (HO) 129 C11
CARMELLA DR (PA) 135 B9
CARMEN ST (HO) 134 F3
CARMILENDA ST (AL) 130 A2
CARNARVON DR (HO) 129 I10
CARNATION (HO) 130 F1
CARNEGIE ST (WU) 133 B12
CARNELIAN DR (HO) 132 B4
CARNTOSH (HO) 128 D1
CAROL (BA) 133 C9
CAROL LN (HO) 134 C3
CAROL LYNN DR (MC) 133 I7
CAROLANE TR (BH) 129 I7
CAROLCHASE CIR (HO) 133 I8
CAROLCREST CIR (HO) 128 J4
CAROLCREST DR (HO) 128 I3
CAROLCREST ST (HO) 128 I3
CAROLINA WAY (WU) 133 B12
CAROLINE ST (HO) 130 K2; 134 A1
CAROLWOOD DR (HO) 130 E6
CAROTHERS ST (HO) 130 E5; 134 D5
CAROUSEL LN (HO) 129 F8
CARPENTER (PA) 135 E9
CARR ST (HO) 130 H3
CARRIAGE CT (HO) 131 C10
CARRIAGE HILL DR (HO) 128 J4
CARRIAGE LN (ST) 132 I6
CARRIAGE WAY (SL) 132 J3
CARRICK (HO) 130 D2
CARRIE ST (HO) 133 I12
CARRINGTON ST (HO) 130 H5
CARROLL DR (HO) 134 C1
CARROLTON (HO) 134 B4
CARROLTON ST (HO) 134 B4
CARRUTH LN (HO) 132 C3
CARSON RD (HO) 134 H5
CARSONDALE (HO) 135 E7
CART GATE DR (HO) 128 A3
CARTAGENA DR (HO) 133 F9
CARTER ST (HO) 130 G1
CARTER ST (PA) 135 B11
CARTERSVILLE ST (HO) 131 K7
CARTHAGE DR (HO) 135 I8
CARTWRIGHT RD (MC) 132 K5, K6; 133 K7
CARUSO FOREST DR (MC) 129 A9
CARUTHERS LN (HC) 129 I8
CARVED ROCK (HO) 133 H9
CARVEL CIR (HO) 132 C3
CARVEL LN (HO) 132 C5
CARVER RD (HO) 129 B11
CARY ST (HO) 130 J3

CASA LOMA DR (HO) 129 E7
CASABLANCA DR (HO) 129 A9
CASCADE POINT DR (HO) 128 D2
CASCADE ST (BA) 133 C10
CASCADE ST (PA) 135 D9
CASCADIA DR (BA) 132 B1
CASE ST (WU) 133 B11
CASETA DR (HO) 132 A1
CASH (ST) 132 H6
CASON ST (WU) 133 B12
CASPERSEN DR (JC) 131 J9
CAST CT (HO) 129 C7
CASTILIAN DR (CL) 131 G11
CASTLE CREEK DR (MC) 133 I7
CASTLE CT (HO) 134 A1
CASTLE FRASER (HO) 128 D1
CASTLE FRASER DR (HO) 128 D1
CASTLE GLEN DR (CV) 131 G12
CASTLE LN (CV) 132 H4
CASTLE PL (ST) 132 I6
CASTLE RIDGE DR (HO) 128 J4
CASTLE WAY LN (HO) 131 G10
CASTLEBAR CT (CL) 131 H11
CASTLEBAY DR (HO) 129 D9
CASTLECREEK LN (HO) 133 J10
CASTLEDALE DR (HO) 130 A4
CASTLEGORY RD (CL) 131 G11
CASTLEMONT (CL) 132 D2
CASTLEREAGH RD (HO) 133 I11
CASTLETON ST (HO) 130 C5
CASTLEVIEW LN (HO) 133 J8
CASTLEWOOD ST (HO) 133 D12
CASTOR DR (HO) 130 E1
CATALINA DR (PA) 135 D12
CATALINA LN (HO) 134 I6
CATALINA VILLAGE DR (HO) 132 C3
CATAMORE ST (HO) 130 C2
CATFORD (HO) 134 I6
CATHCART DR (HO) 129 C11
CATHEDRAL DR (HO) 134 G2
CATHER (HO) 130 D1
CATHERWOOD PL (HO) 131 H10
CATHEY LN (HO) 129 G8
CATINA LN (HO) 133 H10
CATTAILS LN (HO) 133 G8
CAUDLE DR (SV) 129 H8
CAUSEWAY DR (HO) 132 D3
CAVALCADE ST (HO) 130 G2, G4
CAVALIER AV (HO) 134 D4
CAVALIER LN (PA) 135 E9
CAVANAUGH ST (HO) 134 C4
CAVELL LN (SV) 129 H8
CAVERSHAM DR (HO) 133 D9
CAWDOR WAY (HW) 129 I7
CAXTON ST (HO) 130 C5
CAY SOL (HO) 131 C9
CAYLOR ST (HO) 130 K5
CAYTON AV (HO) 134 F6
CAYUGA (HO) 134 D1
CAYWOOD LN (HO) 129 G9
CEBRA RD (HO) 129 C11
CECIL ST (HO) 134 C1
CEDAR (HO) 133 I12
CEDAR CREEK DR (HO) 128 K6; 129 J10
CEDAR CREST BLVD (HO) 134 D4
CEDAR ELM LN (HO) 132 J1
CEDAR FORM LN (ME) 132 F4
CEDAR GAP LN (HO) 132 D4
CEDAR GARDENS DR (HO) 132 B1
CEDAR HILL CT (HO) 130 B4
CEDAR HILL LN (HO) 130 B4
CEDAR ISLE DR (HO) 128 C2
CEDAR OAKS LN (BA) 133 C10
CEDAR PASS CT/**1063** (HO) 128 J4
CEDAR PASS DR (HO) 128 K4
CEDAR POST LN (HO) 129 H7
CEDAR RIDGE DR (HO) 132 B1
CEDAR ST (BA) 133 B10
CEDAR TOP DR (HO) 129 B10
CEDARBRAKE DR (SV) 129 H8
CEDARBROOK DR/**1064** (SV) 129 G8
CEDARBURG DR (HO) 134 G4
CEDARCREST DR (PA) 135 C11
CEDARDALE DR (HO) 128 H6
CEDARHURST DR (HO) 133 F9
CEDARSPUR DR (SV) 129 H8
CEDARTOWNE LN (SL) 132 E2
CEDARVIEW LN (SL) 128 C5
CEDARWOOD CT (SL) 132 G2
CEDARWOOD ST (PA) 135 D9
CEDEL DR (HO) 129 F9
CELESTITE DR (HO) 132 B4
CELIA DR (HO) 131 J9
CELINA LN (HO) 129 D7
CELTIS ST (JC) 131 J9
CEMETARY RD (PL) 134 K6
CENTENARY (WU) 133 B12
CENTENNIAL DR (HO) 128 H6
CENTER (HO) 129 I12
CENTER CT (HO) 132 C4
CENTER DR (GP) 131 K8; 135 A8
CENTER POINT DR (HO) 133 E12
CENTER ST (HO) 129 I12; 130 I1
CENTER ST (PA) 135 C10
CENTER ST (ST) 132 I6
CENTERWOOD DR (HO) 131 I9
CENTRAL AV (PA) 135 D10
CENTRAL FALLS DR (PA) 128 C3
CENTRAL ST (HO) 135 C7
CENTRAL ST/**1065** (HO) 130 A4
CENTRALCREST ST (HO) 129 F9
CENTRE PKWY (HO) 132 E6
CENTURY DR (ST) 132 G5
CENTURY LN (HO) 131 J10
CENTURY SQUARE BLVD (SL) 132 H3
CEPHEUS (HO) 129 B10
CERRITOS DR (HO) 133 F9
CETTI ST (HO) 130 H3
CHADBOURNE CT (HO) 128 I3
CHADBOURNE DR (HO) 128 I3
CHADBROOK DR (HO) 132 F4
CHADWELL DR (HO) 132 F6
CHADWELL GLEN DR (HO) 132 B3
CHADWICK ST (JC) 131 J8
CHAFFIN ST (HO) 134 E5
CHAIN (HO) 134 F3
CHALCOS DR (HO) 135 D7
CHALFORD DR (HO) 132 E2
CHALMETTE ST (HO) 131 H9
CHAMBERLAIN DR (HO) 128 J3
CHAMBERLAIN RD (HO) 130 B3
CHAMBERS ST (HO) 135 G9
CHAMBOARD LN (HO) 129 E11
CHAMPION LN (HO) 129 C11
CHAMPLAIN BEND/**1066** (HO) 129 K10
CHANCERY RD (HO) 135 J10
CHANDLER ST (HO) 129 J12
CHANEY ALLEN (HO) 129 B11
CHANG-AN DR (MC) 133 H7
CHANNELSIDE (HO) 134 B6
CHANTILLY CIR (HO) 129 E12
CHANTILLY LN (HO) 129 E11
CHAPARRAL DR (HO) 128 G6
CHAPEL HILL DR/**1067** (HO) 132 E4
CHAPELLE CT (HO) 128 J4
CHAPELWOOD CT (PP) 129 I8

CHAPELWOOD LN (BH) 129 I7
CHAPIS ST (HO) 130 C3
CHAPMAN ST (HO) 130 F3, I3
CHARDONNAY DR/**1068** (HO) 128 J4
CHARIDGES DR (HO) 135 J11
CHARING CROSS DR (HO) 132 G6
CHARING WAY (HO) 133 G11
CHARIOT DR (HO) 132 F4
CHARLES (HO) 129 B11
CHARLES LN (TW) 132 F3
CHARLES RD (TW) 128 A4
CHARLES ST (HO) 130 C3
CHARLES ST (PA) 135 B9, C9
CHARLESMONT ST (HO) 130 C6
CHARLESTON (SL) 132 H4
CHARLESTON PARK DR (HO) 133 E11
CHARLESTON ST (HO) 134 C3
CHARLESTON/**1069** (SL) 132 H4
CHARLESTOWN COLONY DR (HO) 128 C2
CHARLIE LN (HO) 129 B9
CHARLIE ST (HO) 129 B11
CHARLIE VOIX ST (HO) 131 H10
CHARLINE (HO) 134 C2
CHARLMONT DR (HO) 132 D2
CHARLOTTE ST (WU) 133 B12
CHARLTON ST (GP) 135 A8
CHARNEY LN (GP) 129 A11
CHARNWOOD ST (HO) 130 E3
CHARPIOT (HO) 131 E9
CHARTER OAKS DR (HO) 130 B4
CHARTRES ST (HO) 130 J3; 134 A2
CHARTWELL CT (BH) 129 I7
CHARTWELL DR/**1070** (HO) 132 G6
CHARWON (HO) 130 A4
CHASE LAKE DR (HO) 128 J4
CHASE LN (HO) 129 D12
CHASE ST (HO) 130 E3, I3
CHASECREEK DR (HO) 133 I8
CHASEFIELD DR (HO) 133 I8
CHASEHILL DR (HO) 133 I8
CHASEMONT DR (HO) 133 I8
CHASERIDGE DR (HO) 133 I8
CHASEVIEW DR (HO) 133 I8
CHASEWIND DR (HO) 133 I8
CHASEWOOD DR (HO) 133 I8
CHASTON DR (HO) 128 A3
CHASWORTH DR (HO) 128 A3
CHATAM ST (BH) 128 J6
CHATEAU FOREST DR (HO) 129 C9
CHATEAU ST (HO) 130 F6
CHATFIELD ST (HO) 133 D11
CHATHAM ISLAND LN (HO) 133 G8
CHATHAM LN (HO) 129 K11
CHATSWORTH DR (HO) 129 H10
CHATTEN WAY (HW) 129 I7
CHATTERTON DR (HO) 128 G6
CHATWOOD DR (HO) 131 D7
CHAUCER DR (HO) 133 B12
CHAUMONT DR (HO) 135 K10
CHAZEN DR (JC) 131 J8
CHEAM CIR (HO) 131 H10
CHEATHAM LN/**1071** (HO) 131 J10
CHECKERBOARD ST (HO) 133 E9
CHEENA DR (HO) 133 E11
CHEER ST (HO) 133 A7
CHEEVES DR (HO) 130 B6
CHELSEA BLVD (HO) 134 A1
CHELSEA ST (BA) 133 C10
CHELSTON CT (SL) 132 F3
CHELSWORTH (HO) 132 D1
CHELTENHAM DR (HO) 133 D9
CHELTON ST (HO) 131 I10
CHENEVERT ST (HO) 134 A2
CHENEVERT ST/**1072** (HO) 130 J3
CHENEVERT ST/**1073** (HO) 130 J3
CHENNAULT RD (HO) 134 D4
CHER CT (HO) 129 A7
CHERBOURG RD (HO) 134 D4
CHEROKEE DR (PA) 135 D9
CHEROKEE ST (HO) 134 A1
CHERRY BEND DR (HO) 128 K4
CHERRY BROOK LN (PA) 135 E11
CHERRY CREEK DR (HO) 135 D8
CHERRY DAWN ST/**1074** (SL) 132 G3
CHERRY FOREST DR (HO) 129 B10
CHERRY HOLLOW LN (HO) 132 A2
CHERRY KNOLL DR (HO) 128 J4
CHERRY LN (PA) 135 D10
CHERRY MEADOW DR (PA) 130 A4
CHERRY MOUND RD (PA) 128 I2
CHERRY OAK CIR (HO) 129 C10
CHERRY OAK LN (HO) 129 C10
CHERRY PARK DR (HO) 128 A2
CHERRY RIDGE DR (HO) 128 J5
CHERRY SPRINGS DR (MC) 133 K7
CHERRY ST (HO) 130 G3
CHERRY TREE ST (HO) 129 D9
CHERRYBARK LN (HO) 128 I5
CHERRYDALE DR (HO) 134 E5
CHERRYHILL AV (HO) 134 D4
CHERRYHURST ST (HO) 130 K1
CHERRYWOOD ST (BA) 133 C10
CHERTSEY CIR (CV) 131 G12
CHERYL (HO) 133 H8
CHERYL LYNNE LN (HO) 133 G11
CHESAPEAKE WAY (HO) 129 K10
CHESHIRE LN (HO) 129 E11
CHESKA LN (PP) 129 J7
CHESNEY DOWNS/**1075** (HO) 132 D1
CHESS WOOD DR (HO) 132 B4
CHESSINGTON DR (HO) 132 G6
CHESSWOOD CIR (SL) 132 F3
CHESTERBROOK DR (HO) 132 G6
CHESTERFIELD DR (HO) 134 G2
CHESTERFIELD LN (ST) 132 H4
CHESTERSHIRE DR (PA) 135 C11
CHESTNUT FOREST DR (PA) 129 A9
CHESTNUT LN (PA) 135 D11
CHESTNUT ST (BA) 133 B10
CHESTNUT ST (HO) 130 I3
CHESTON DR (JC) 131 J8
CHESTWOOD DR/**1076** (HW) 129 I7
CHESWICK DR (JC) 130 B1
CHESWOOD (HO) 134 D4
CHETLAND PL DR (HO) 128 A2
CHETWOOD DR (HO) 133 C9
CHEVIOT CIR (HO) 132 D5
CHEVY CHASE CIR (SL) 132 I4
CHEVY CHASE DR (HO) 128 K2, K5
CHEVY CHASE DR (SL) 132 I4
CHEW ST (HO) 130 I5
CHEYENNE AV (PA) 135 F11
CHIA (HO) 135 D8
CHICAGO ST (HO) 134 C6
CHICHESTER ST (JV) 128 A6
CHICKADEE LN (HO) 134 G4

continue on next page

HOUSTON, *continued*

***Numbers** replace street names where map space is limited; municipality abbreviations appear in parentheses.*

AL	Aldine	GP	Galena Park	MC	Missouri City	SP	Southside Place
BA	Bellaire	HC	Hunters Creek Village	ME	Meadows	ST	Stafford
BH	Bunker Hill Village	HL	Hilshire Village	PA	Pasadena	SV	Spring Valley
BV	Brookside Village	HO	Houston	PL	Pearland	WU	West University Place
CV	Channelview	HW	Hedwig Village	PP	Piney Point Village		
FC	First Colony	JC	Jacinto City	SH	South Houston		
		JV	Jersey Village	SL	Sugar Land		

continue on next page

***Numbers** replace street names where map space is limited; municipality abbreviations appear in parentheses.*

AL	Aldine	GP	Galena Park	MC	Missouri City	SP	Southside Place
BA	Bellaire	HC	Hunters Creek Village	ME	Meadows	ST	Stafford
BH	Bunker Hill Village	HL	Hilshire Village	PA	Pasadena	SV	Spring Valley
BV	Brookside Village	HO	Houston	PL	Pearland	WU	West University Place
CV	Channelview	HW	Hedwig Village	PP	Piney Point Village		
FC	First Colony	JC	Jacinto City	SH	South Houston		
		JV	Jersey Village	SL	Sugar Land		

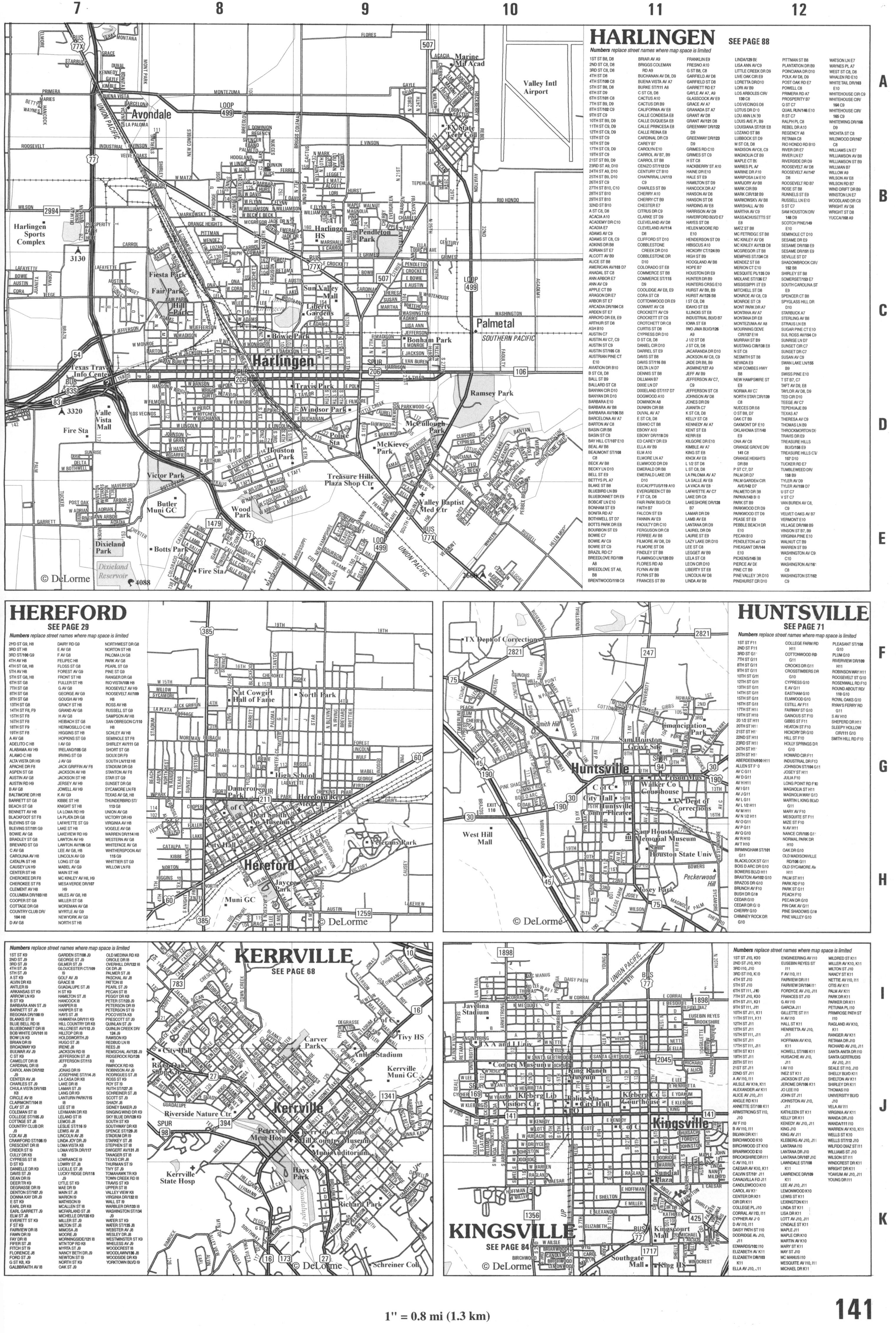
7
8
9
10
11
12
A
B
C
D
E
F
G
H
I
J
K
HARLINGEN
SEE PAGE 88
Numbers replace street names where map space is limited
Avondale
Harlingen Sports Complex
Valley Intl Airport
TX State Tech Coll
Harlingen HS
Pendleton Park
Fiesta Park
Fair Park
Hill Park
Sun Valley Mall
Liberty Gardens
Bowie Park
Bonham Park
Palmetal
SOUTHERN PACIFIC
Harlingen
Texas Travel Info Center
Valle Vista Mall
Fire Sta
Travis Park
Windsor Park
Ramsey Park
McCullough Park
Police Sta
McKievey Park
Houston Park
Treasure Hills Plaza Shop Ctr
Victor Park
Butler Muni GC
Wood Park
Valley Baptist Med Ctr
Dixieland Park
Dixieland Reservoir
Botts Park
Fire Sta
UNION PACIFIC
© DeLorme
HEREFORD
SEE PAGE 29
Numbers replace street names where map space is limited
Nat Cowgirl Hall of Fame
North Park
High School
Dameron Park
Hereford Reg Med Ctr
C of C
Deaf Smith Co Museum
City Hall
Veterans Park
Hereford
Jaycee Park
Muni GC
© DeLorme
HUNTSVILLE
SEE PAGE 71
Numbers replace street names where map space is limited
TX Dept of Corrections
Smith Hill
Emancipation Park
Sam Houston Grave Site
Huntsville
Prison Mus
Walker Co Courthouse
C of C
City Hall
TX Dept of Corrections
Huntsville Comm Theater
West Hill Mall
Sam Houston Memorial Museum
Sam Houston State Univ
Peckerwood Hill
Josey Park
© DeLorme
KERRVILLE
SEE PAGE 68
Numbers replace street names where map space is limited
City Hall
Carver Park
C of C
Tivy HS
Antler Stadium
River Oaks Shop Ctr
Kerrville Muni GC
Riverside Nature Ctr
Kerrville
Peterson Mem Hosp
Kerr Co Courthouse
Hill Country Museum
Muni Auditorium
Kerrville State Hosp
Hays Park
Guadalupe R.
Richard Park
Schreiner Coll
© DeLorme
Numbers replace street names where map space is limited
Javelina Stadium
TX A and I Univ
Conner Museum
King Ranch Museum
Kleberg Lib
Visitors Ctr
Police Sta
City Hall
Kleberg Co Courthouse
C of C
Kingsville
Sundial Plaza
Kingscourt Mall
KINGSVILLE
SEE PAGE 84
Southgate Mall
King HS
UNION PACIFIC
© DeLorme

1" = 0.8 mi (1.3 km)

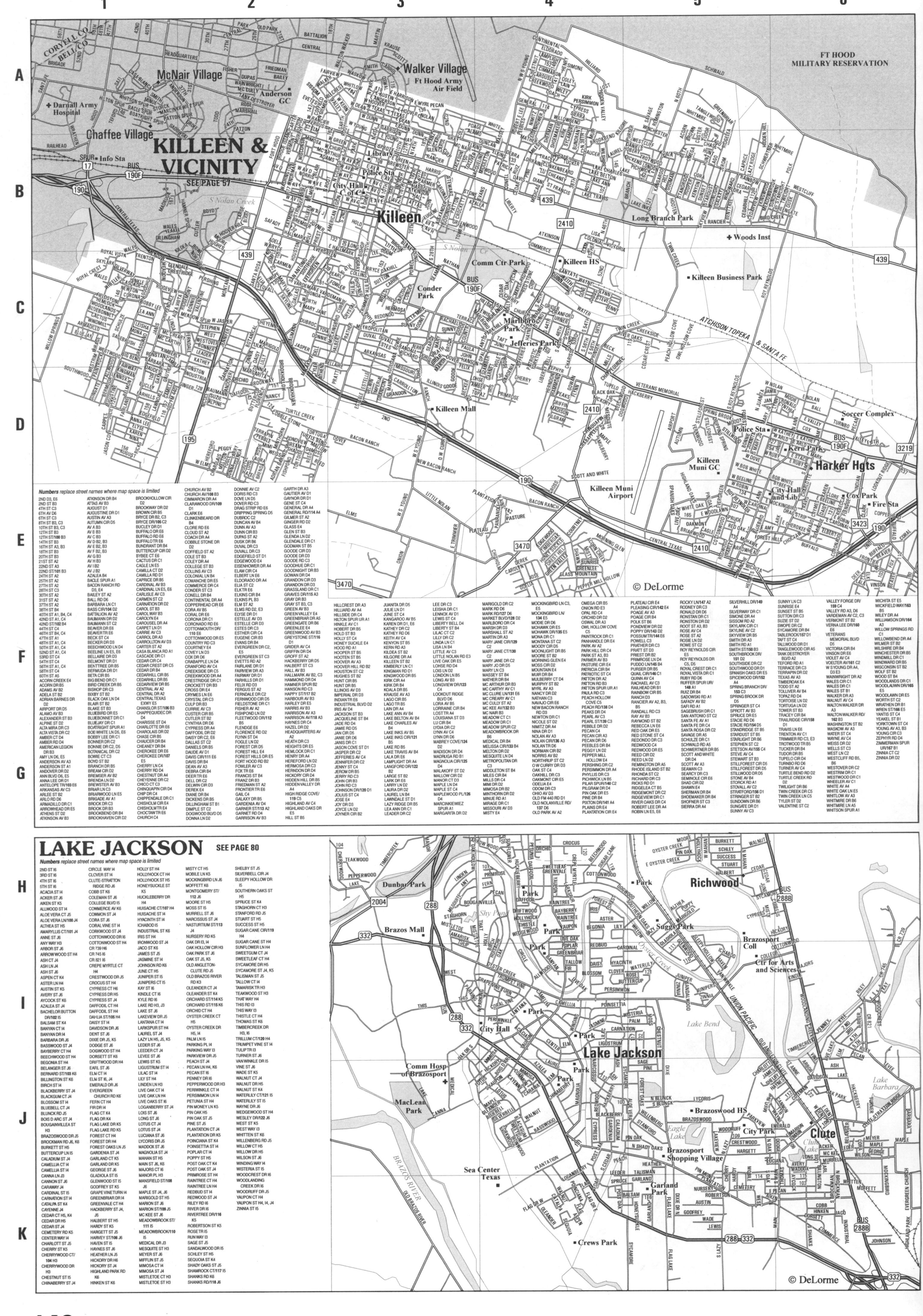

KILLEEN & VICINITY
SEE PAGE 57
McNair Village
Walker Village
Ft Hood Army Air Field
Darnall Army Hospital
Chaffee Village
Info Sta
FT HOOD MILITARY RESERVATION
Killeen
Library
Police Sta
City Hall
Long Branch Park
Woods Inst
Comm Ctr Park
Killeen HS
Killeen Business Park
Conder Park
Marlboro Park
Jefferies Park
Killeen Mall
Soccer Complex
Police Sta
Kern Park
Harker Hgts
Killeen Muni GC
Killeen Muni Airport
City Hall and Lib
Cox Park
Fire Sta
ATCHISON TOPEKA & SANTA FE
© DeLorme
Numbers replace street names where map space is limited
LAKE JACKSON
SEE PAGE 80
Numbers replace street names where map space is limited
Dunbar Park
Brazos Mall
Richwood
Suggs Park
Brazosport Coll
Ctr for Arts and Sciences
City Hall
Lake Jackson
Lake Bend
Comm Hosp of Brazosport
MacLean Park
Brazoswood HS
City Park
Clute
Brazosport Shopping Village
Sea Center Texas
Garland Park
Crews Park
Lake Barbara
UNION PACIFIC
BRAZOS RIVER
© DeLorme

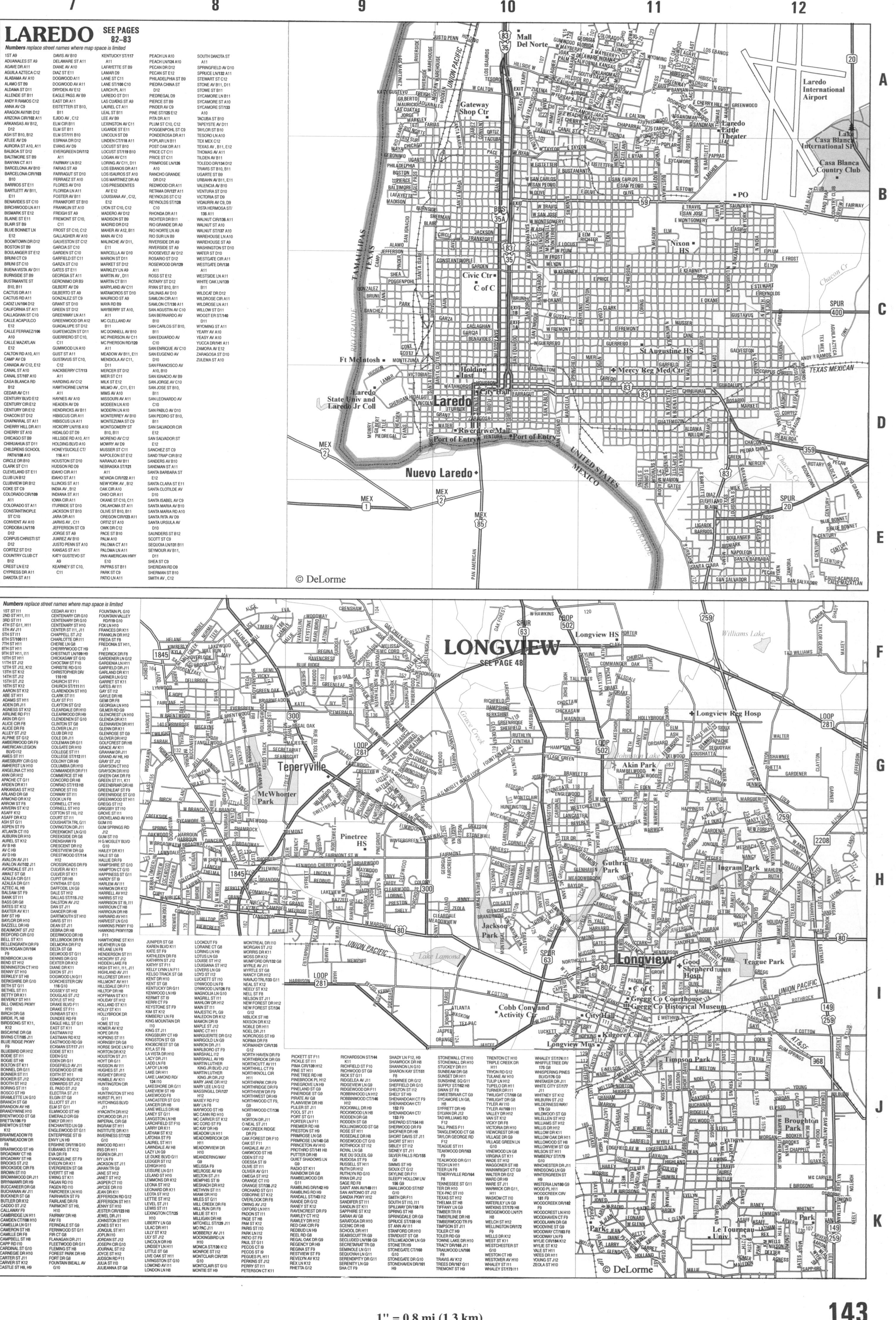

7
8
9
10
11
12
A
B
C
D
E
F
G
H
I
J
K
LAREDO
SEE PAGES 82–83
Numbers replace street names where map space is limited
Mall Del Norte
Laredo International Airport
Gateway Shop Ctr
Laredo Little Theater
Casa Blanca International SP
Casa Blanca Country Club
PO
Nixon HS
Civic Ctr
C of C
Ft McIntosh
St Augustine HS
Mercy Reg Med Ctr
Holding Inst
Laredo State Univ and Laredo Jr Coll
City Hall
Laredo
Rivertrive Mall
Port of Entry
Port of Entry
Nuevo Laredo
TAMAULIPAS
TEXAS
RIO GRANDE
UNITED STATES
MEXICO
UNION PACIFIC
TEXAS MEXICAN
Chacon Cr
© DeLorme
LONGVIEW
SEE PAGE 48
Numbers replace street names where map space is limited
Longview HS
Williams Lake
Longview Reg Hosp
Teneryville
McWhorter Park
Akin Park
Pinetree HS
Guthrie Park
Ingram Park
Jackson Park
Lake Lomond
Longview
Good Shepherd Hosp
Teague Park
C of C
Gregg Co Courthouse
Gregg Co Historical Museum
Cobb Conway and Activity Ctr
City Hall
Kilgore Coll
Longview Mus
Timpson Park
Broughton Park
Le Tourneau Univ
Park
Park
UNION PACIFIC
AT&SF
Grace Creek
© DeLorme

1" = 0.8 mi (1.3 km)

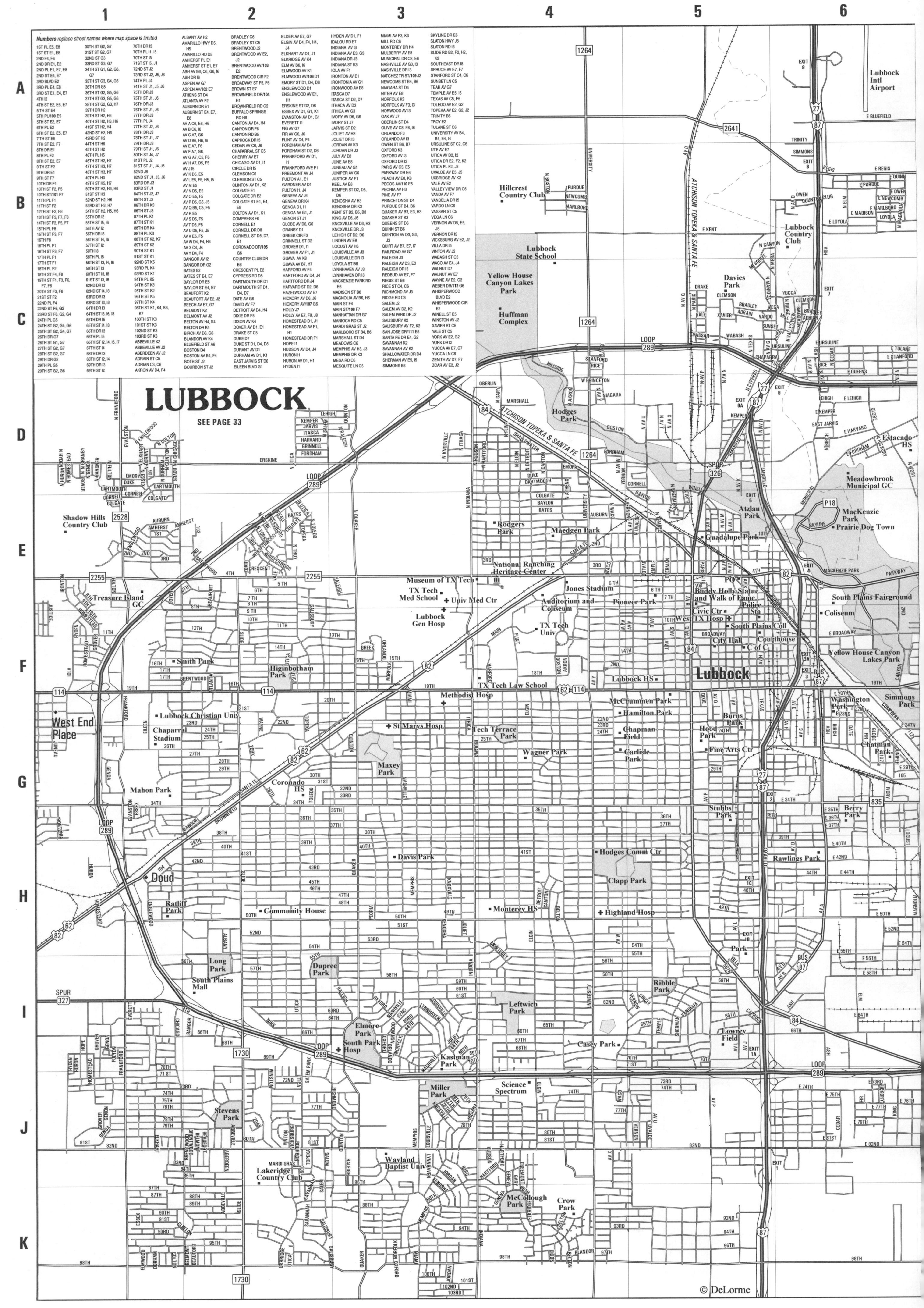
Numbers replace street names where map space is limited
LUBBOCK
SEE PAGE 33
Lubbock Intl Airport
Hillcrest Country Club
Lubbock State School
Yellow House Canyon Lakes Park
Huffman Complex
Lubbock Country Club
Davies Park
Hodges Park
Estacado HS
Meadowbrook Municipal GC
MacKenzie Park
Prairie Dog Town
Shadow Hills Country Club
Rodgers Park
Maedgen Park
Atzlan Park
Guadalupe Park
National Ranching Heritage Center
Museum of TX Tech
TX Tech Med School
Univ Med Ctr
Lubbock Gen Hosp
Jones Stadium
Auditorium and Coliseum
TX Tech Univ
Pioneer Park
Buddy Holly Statue and Walk of Fame
Civic Ctr
West TX Hosp
Police Sta
South Plains Coll
City Hall
Courthouse
South Plains Fairground
Coliseum
Yellow House Canyon Lakes Park
Treasure Island GC
Smith Park
Higinbotham Park
TX Tech Law School
Lubbock HS
Lubbock
Simmons Park
Methodist Hosp
McCrummen Park
Hamilton Park
Washington Park
West End Place
Lubbock Christian Univ
Chaparral Stadium
St Marys Hosp
Tech Terrace Park
Chapman Field
Burns Park
Hood Park
Chatman Park
Wagner Park
Carlisle Park
Fine Arts Ctr
Maxey Park
Mahon Park
Coronado HS
Stubbs Park
Berry Park
Davis Park
Hodges Comm Ctr
Rawlings Park
Doud
Clapp Park
Ratliff Park
Community House
Monterey HS
Highland Hosp
Long Park
Dupree Park
South Plains Mall
Ribble Park
Leftwich Park
Elmore Park
South Park Hosp
Kastman Park
Casey Park
Lowrey Field
Science Spectrum
Miller Park
Stevens Park
Wayland Baptist Univ
Lakeridge Country Club
McCollough Park
Crow Park
© DeLorme

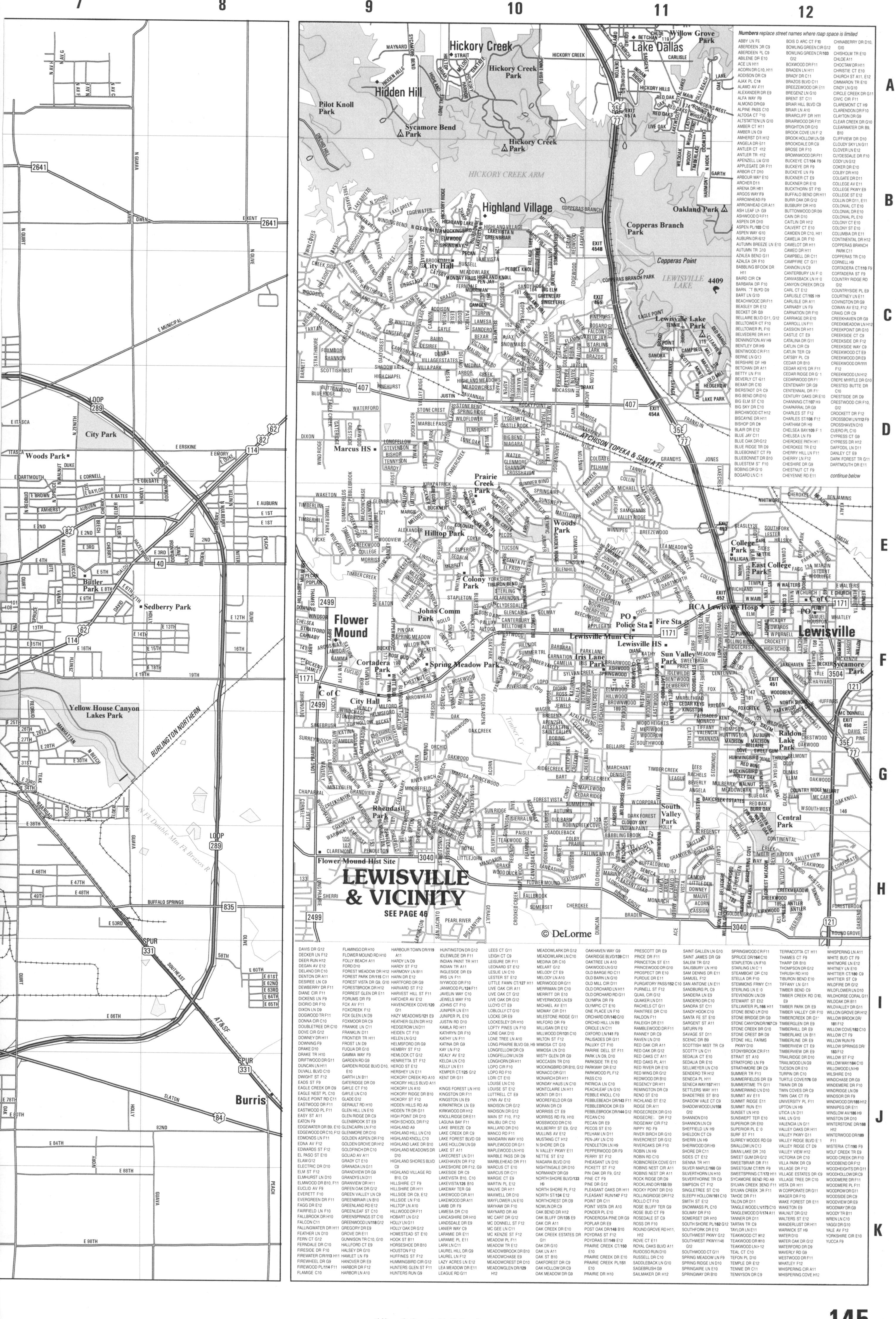
LEWISVILLE & VICINITY
SEE PAGE 46
© DeLorme
Numbers replace street names where map space is limited
continue below
Hickory Creek
Hidden Hill
Lake Dallas
Willow Grove Park
Pilot Knoll Park
Sycamore Bend Park
Hickory Creek Park
HICKORY CREEK ARM
Highland Village
Copperas Branch Park
Oakland Park
Copperas Point
LEWISVILLE LAKE
Lewisville Lake Park
City Hall
Marcus HS
Prairie Creek Park
Woods Park
Hilltop Park
Colony Park
College Park
East College Park
Flower Mound
Johns Comm Park
Spring Meadow Park
Cortadera Park
C of C
PO
Police Sta
Fire Sta
Lewisville Muni Ctr
Lewisville HS
HCA Lewisville Hosp
Lewisville
Sun Valley Park
Iris Lane Park
Sycamore Park
Radon Lake Park
South Valley Park
Central Park
Rheudasil Park
Flower Mound Hist Site
ATCHISON TOPEKA & SANTA FE
City Park
Woods Park
Butler Park
Sedberry Park
Yellow House Canyon Lakes Park
BURLINGTON NORTHERN
Burris
LOOP 289
SPUR 331
7
8
9
10
11
12
A
B
C
D
E
F
G
H
I
J
K

1" = 0.8 mi (1.3 km)

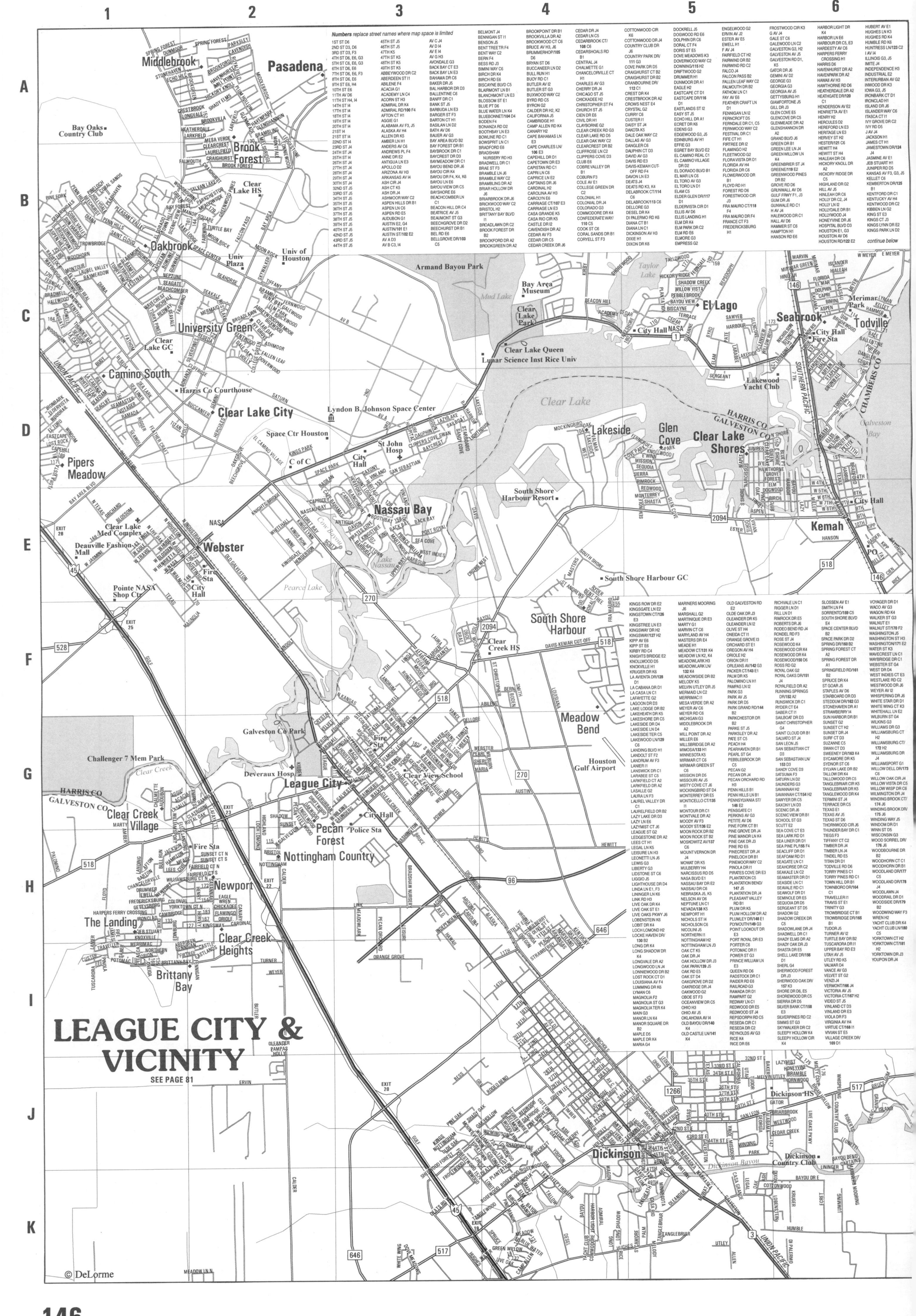

LEAGUE CITY & VICINITY
SEE PAGE 81
Numbers replace street names where map space is limited
continue below
Middlebrook
Pasadena
Bay Oaks Country Club
Brook Forest
Clear Lake HS
Oakbrook
Univ Plaza
Univ of Houston
University Green
Clear Lake GC
Camino South
Harris Co Courthouse
Clear Lake City
Lyndon B. Johnson Space Center
Space Ctr Houston
St John Hosp
City Hall
C of C
Pipers Meadow
Nassau Bay
Armand Bayou Park
Mud Lake
Bay Area Museum
Clear Lake Park
Clear Lake Queen
Lunar Science Inst Rice Univ
Taylor Lake
El Lago
City Hall
Seabrook
City Hall
Fire Sta
Todville
Merimar Park
Lakewood Yacht Club
Clear Lake
Lakeside
Glen Cove
Clear Lake Shores
Galveston Bay
South Shore Harbour Resort
Kemah
City Hall
PO
Clear Lake Med Complex
Deauville Fashion Mall
Webster
Fire Sta
City Hall
Pointe NASA Shop Ctr
Cow Bayou
Lake Nassau
Pearce Lake
South Shore Harbour GC
South Shore Harbour
Clear Creek HS
Meadow Bend
Houston Gulf Airport
Galveston Co Park
Challenger 7 Mem Park
Clear Creek
Deveraux Hosp
League City
Fire Sta
Clear View School
HARRIS CO
GALVESTON CO
Clear Creek Village
City Hall
Police Sta
Pecan Forest
Nottingham Country
Fire Sta
Newport
The Landing
Clear Creek Heights
Brittany Bay
Dickinson
Dickinson HS
Dickinson Bayou
Dickinson Country Club
UNION PACIFIC
SOUTHERN PACIFIC
CHAMBERS CO
HARRIS CO
GALVESTON CO
© DeLorme

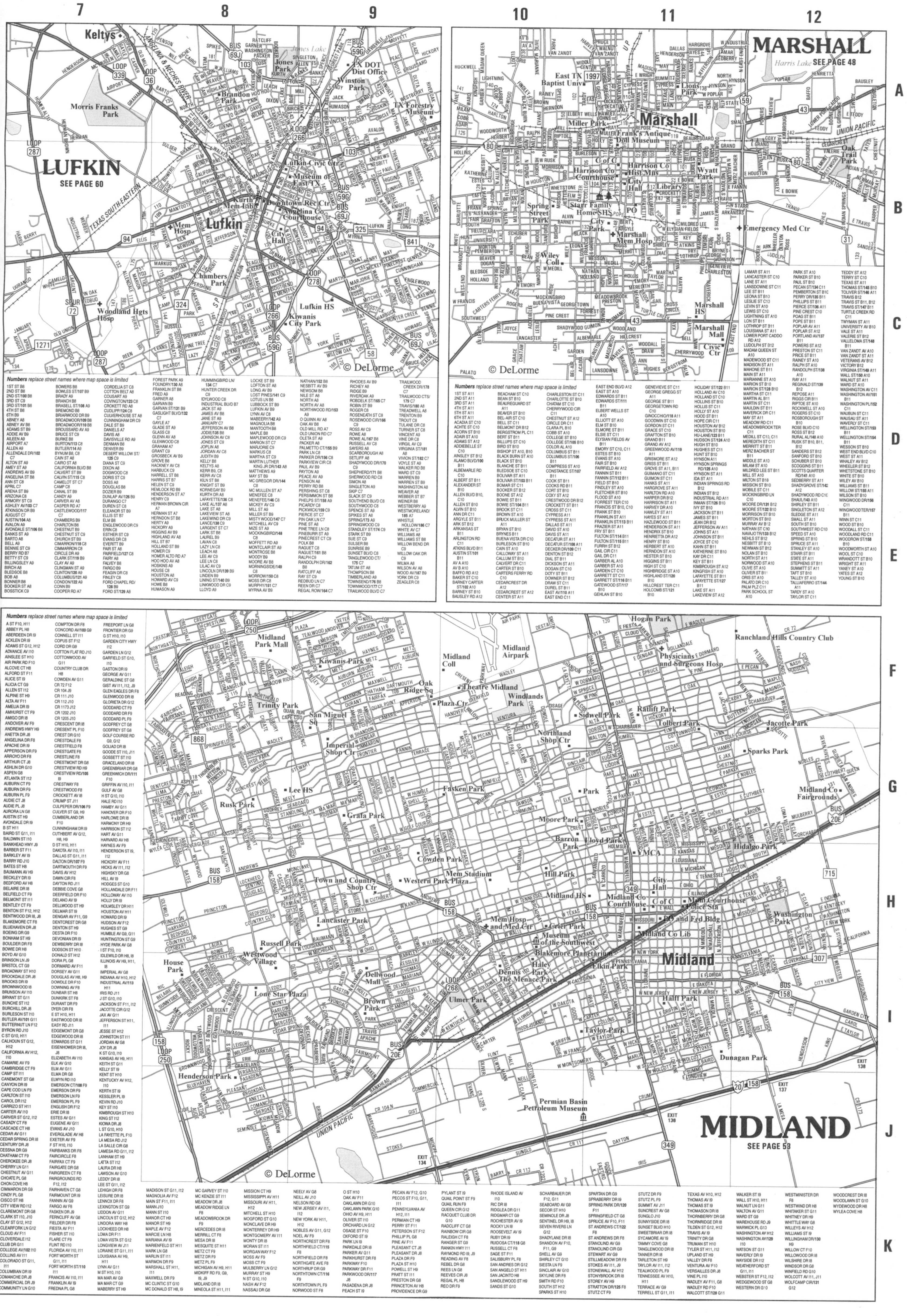

7
8
9
10
11
12
A
B
C
D
E
F
G
H
I
J
K
LUFKIN
SEE PAGE 60
Lufkin
Keltys
Morris Franks Park
Woodland Hgts Hosp
Lufkin HS
Kiwanis City Park
Chambers Park
Lufkin Civic Ctr
Museum of East TX
Downtown Rec Ctr
Angelina Co Courthouse
Kurth Mem Libr
Mem Hosp
City Hall
Brandon Park
Jones Park
TX DOT Dist Office
Winston Park
TX Forestry Museum
© DeLorme
MARSHALL
SEE PAGE 48
Marshall
Harris Lake
East TX Baptist Univ
Miller Park
Frank's Antique Doll Museum
Harrison Co Courthouse
Harrison Co Hist Mus
City Hall
Library
Wyatt Park
Spring Street Park
Starr Family Home SHS
City Park
Marshall Mem Hosp
Wiley Coll
Lions Park
Oak Trail Park
Emergency Med Ctr
Marshall HS
Marshall Mall
Civic Ctr
© DeLorme
MIDLAND
SEE PAGE 53
Midland
Midland Park Mall
Kiwanis Park
Midland Coll
Midland Airpark
Theatre Midland
Windlands Park
Oak Ridge Sq
Plaza Ctr
Trinity Park
San Miguel Sq
Imperial Shop Ctr
Northland Shop Ctr
Sidwell Park
Railift Park
Tolbert Park
Jacotte Park
Sparks Park
Ranchland Hills Country Club
Hogan Park
Physicians and Surgeons Hosp
Lee HS
Fasken Park
Park
Midland Co Fairgrounds
Rusk Park
Grafa Park
Moore Park
Barron Park
Lloyd Park
YMCA
Hidalgo Park
Cowden Park
Mem Stadium
Western Park Plaza
Town and Country Shop Ctr
Hill Park
City Hall
Midland HS
Midland Co Courthouse
C of C
Mem Courthouse
Police Sta
Washington Park
Lancaster Park
Mem Hosp and Med Ctr
Grier Park
PO and Fed Bldg
Midland Co Lib
Museum of the Southwest
Blakemore Planetarium
Russell Park
Westwood Village
House Park
Dellwood Mall
Haley Park
Dennis The Menace Park
Elkin Park
Lone Star Plaza
Brown Park
Ulmer Park
Halff Park
Taylor Park
Dunagan Park
Henderson Park
Permian Basin Petroleum Museum
© DeLorme

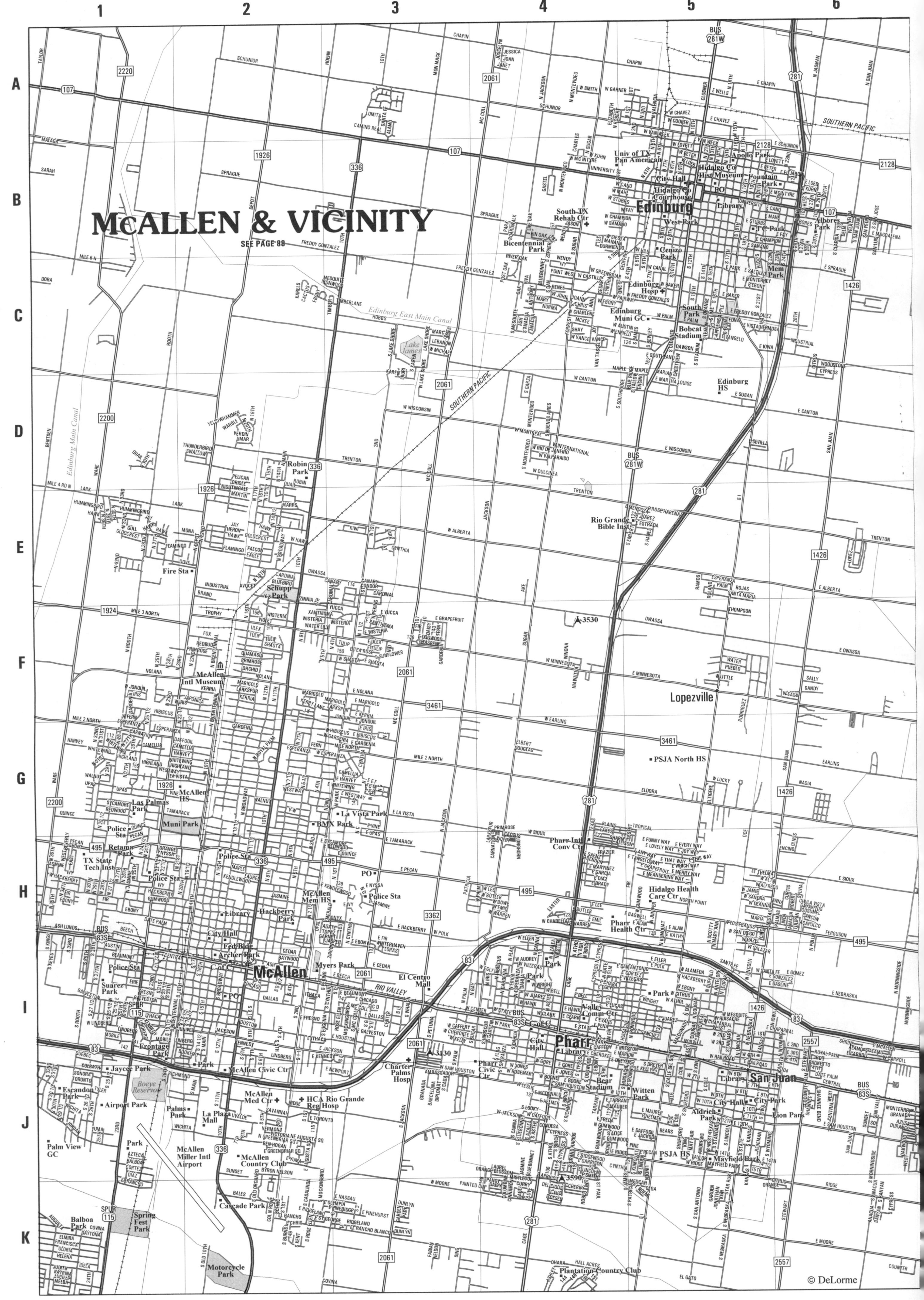
McALLEN & VICINITY
SEE PAGE 88
1
2
3
4
5
6
A
B
C
D
E
F
G
H
I
J
K
Edinburg
Univ of TX Pan American
City Hall
Hidalgo Co Hist Museum
Hidalgo Co Courthouse
Apollo Park
Fountain Park
PO
Library
West Park
South TX Rehab Ctr
Bicentennial Park
Cenizo Park
Albores Park
FC Park
Mem Park
Edinburg Hosp
Edinburg Muni GC
South Park
Bobcat Stadium
Edinburg HS
Edinburg East Main Canal
Lake James
SOUTHERN PACIFIC
Edinburg Main Canal
Robin Park
Rio Grande Bible Inst
Fire Sta
Schupp Park
McAllen Intl Museum
Lopezville
PSJA North HS
Las Palmas Park
McAllen HS
Muni Park
Police Sta
Retama Park
TX State Tech Inst
La Vista Park
BMX Park
Pharr Intl Conv Ctr
Hidalgo Health Care Ctr
McAllen Mem HS
Hackberry Park
Library
City Hall
Fed Bldg
Archer Park
C of C
McAllen
Myers Park
El Centro Mall
Pharr Health Ctr
Suarez Park
PO
Valley Comm Ctr
Pharr
Jaycee Park
Frontage Park
McAllen Civic Ctr
Charter Palms Hosp
Phar Civic Ctr
Bear Stadium
Witten Park
San Juan
Escandon Park
Airport Park
Boeye Reservoir
McAllen Med Ctr
HCA Rio Grande Reg Hosp
Palms Park
La Plaza Mall
Aldrich Park
City Park
Lion Park
Palm View GC
McAllen Miller Intl Airport
McAllen Country Club
PSJA HS
Mayfield Park
Cascade Park
Balboa Park
Spring Fest Park
Motorcycle Park
Plantation Country Club
© DeLorme

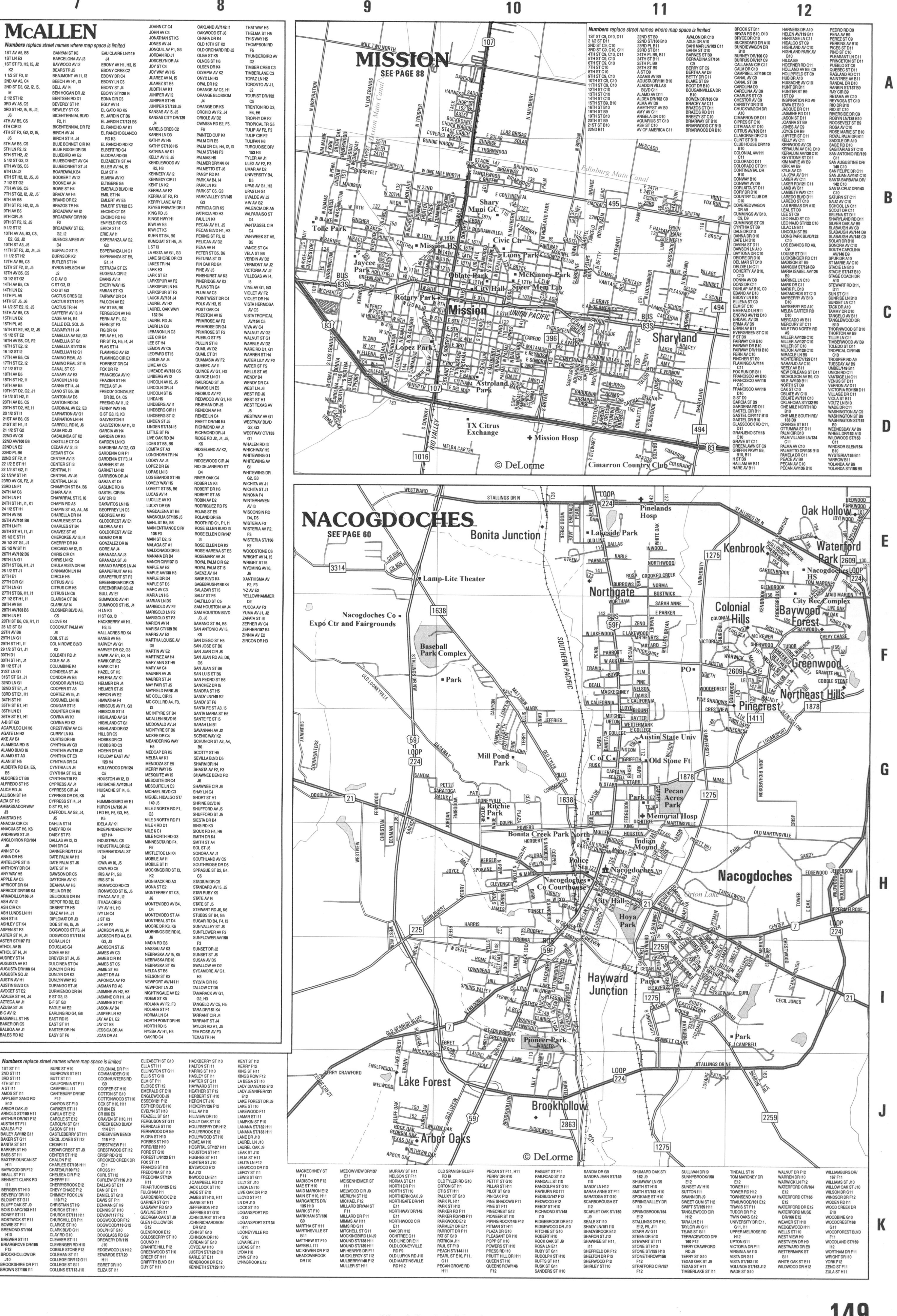
McALLEN
Numbers replace street names where map space is limited
MISSION
SEE PAGE 88
Tolle Park
Mission HS
Jaycee Park
Shary Muni GC
Civic Ctr
Lions Park
Oblate Park
City Hall
McKinney Park
Speer Mem Lib
Rotary Park
Mission
UNION PACIFIC
Lopez Park
Sharyland
Astroland Park
TX Citrus Exchange
Mission Hosp
Cimarron Country Club
© DeLorme
NACOGDOCHES
SEE PAGE 60
Bonita Junction
Pinelands Hosp
Lakeside Park
Oak Hollow
Kenbrook
Waterford Park
Lamp-Lite Theater
Northgate
Colonial Hills
Baywood Forest
City Rec Complex
Nacogdoches Co Expo Ctr and Fairgrounds
Baseball Park Complex
Greenwood
Northeast Hills
Pinecrest
Austin State Univ
Mill Pond Park
Old Stone Ft
Pecan Acres Park
Ritchie Park
Memorial Hosp
Bonita Creek Park North
Indian Mound
Nacogdoches
Nacogdoches Co Courthouse
City Hall
Hoya Park
Hayward Junction
Pioneer Park
Lake Forest
Brookhollow
Arbor Oaks
SOUTHERN PACIFIC
© DeLorme
Numbers replace street names where map space is limited
7
8
9
10
11
12
A
B
C
D
E
F
G
H
I
J
K
1" = 0.8 mi (1.3 km)

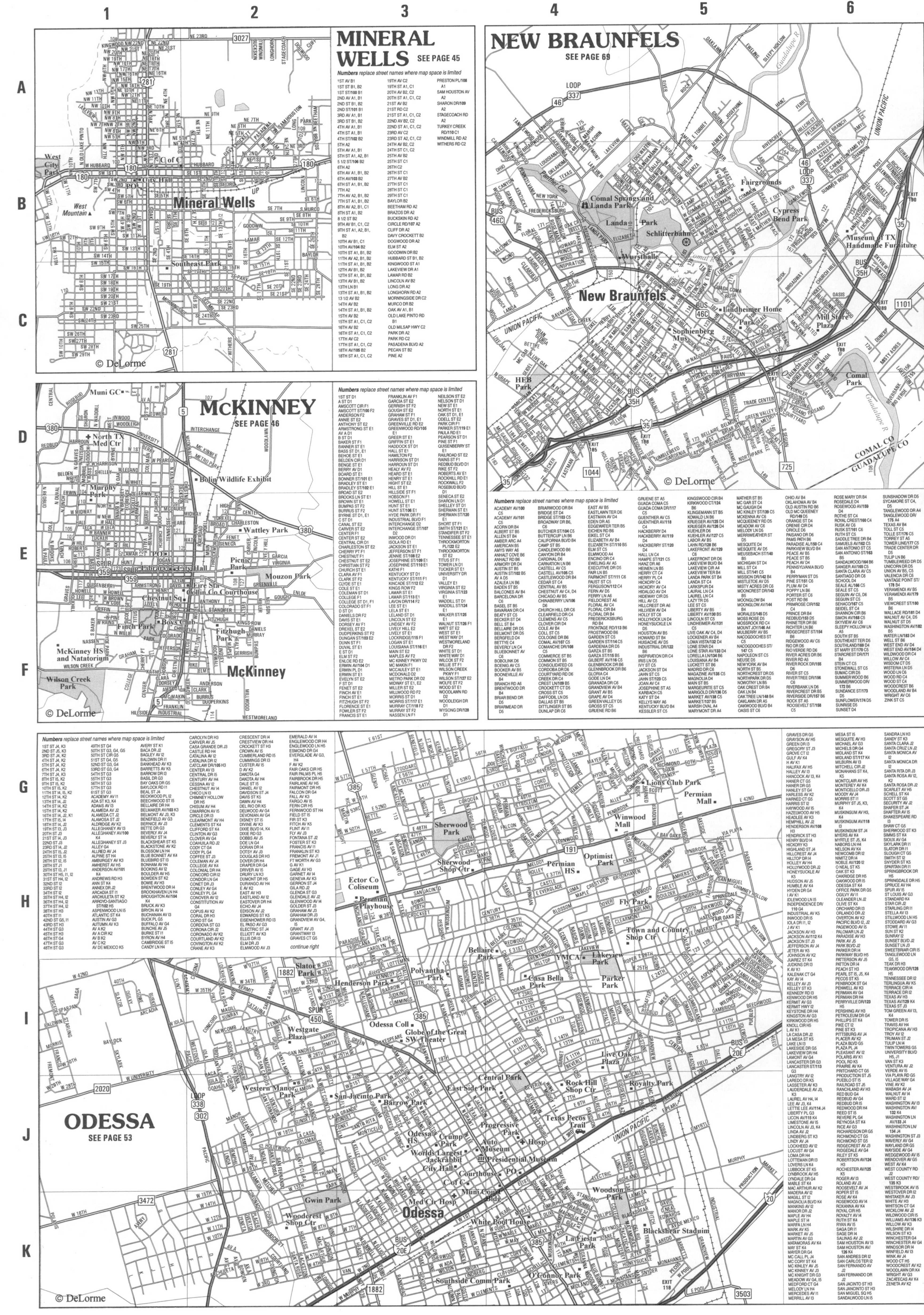
1
2
3
4
5
6
A
B
C
D
E
F
G
H
I
J
K
MINERAL WELLS
SEE PAGE 45
Numbers replace street names where map space is limited
Mineral Wells
West City Park
West Mountain
Southeast Park
City Hall
C of C
© DeLorme
NEW BRAUNFELS
SEE PAGE 69
Comal Springs and Landa Park
Landa Park
Schlitterbahn
Wursthalle
Fairgrounds
Cypress Bend Park
Museum of TX Handmade Furniture
New Braunfels
Lindheimer Home
Mill Store Plaza
Sophienberg Mus
HEB Park
Comal Park
UNION PACIFIC
COMAL CO
GUADALUPE CO
© DeLorme
McKINNEY
SEE PAGE 46
Numbers replace street names where map space is limited
Muni GC
North TX Med Ctr
Bolin Wildlife Exhibit
Murphy Park
Wattley Park
Picnic Park
Mouzon Park
City Hall
Fire Sta
Collin Co Courthouse
Chestnut Sq
Boys Club
Finch Park
Fitzhugh Park
McKinney HS and Natatorium
Wilson Creek Park
McKinney
© DeLorme
Numbers replace street names where map space is limited
ODESSA
SEE PAGE 53
Lions Club Park
Permian Mall
Sherwood Park
Winwood Mall
Sherwood Shop Ctr
Ector Co Coliseum
Permian Playhouse
Permian HS
Optimist Park
Fly Park
Town and Country Shop Ctr
Bellaire Park
YMCA
Lakeview Park
Parker Park
Slator Park
Henderson Park
Polyantha Park
Casa Bella Park
Odessa Coll
Globe of the Great SW Theater
Westgate Plaza
Live Oak Plaza
Western Manor Park
San Jacinto Park
Barrow Park
East Side Park
Central Park
Rock Hill Shop Ctr
Royalty Park
Progressive Park
Texas Pecos Trail
Odessa HS
Crump Park
Auto Museum
Worlds Largest Jackrabbit
Presidential Museum
City Hall
Courthouse
C of C
Muni Conv Bldg
Med Ctr Hosp
Gwin Park
Woodcrest Shop Ctr
Odessa
White Pool House
Woodson Park
La Fiesta Park
Blackshear Stadium
Southside Comm Park
O'Connor Park
UNION PACIFIC
© DeLorme

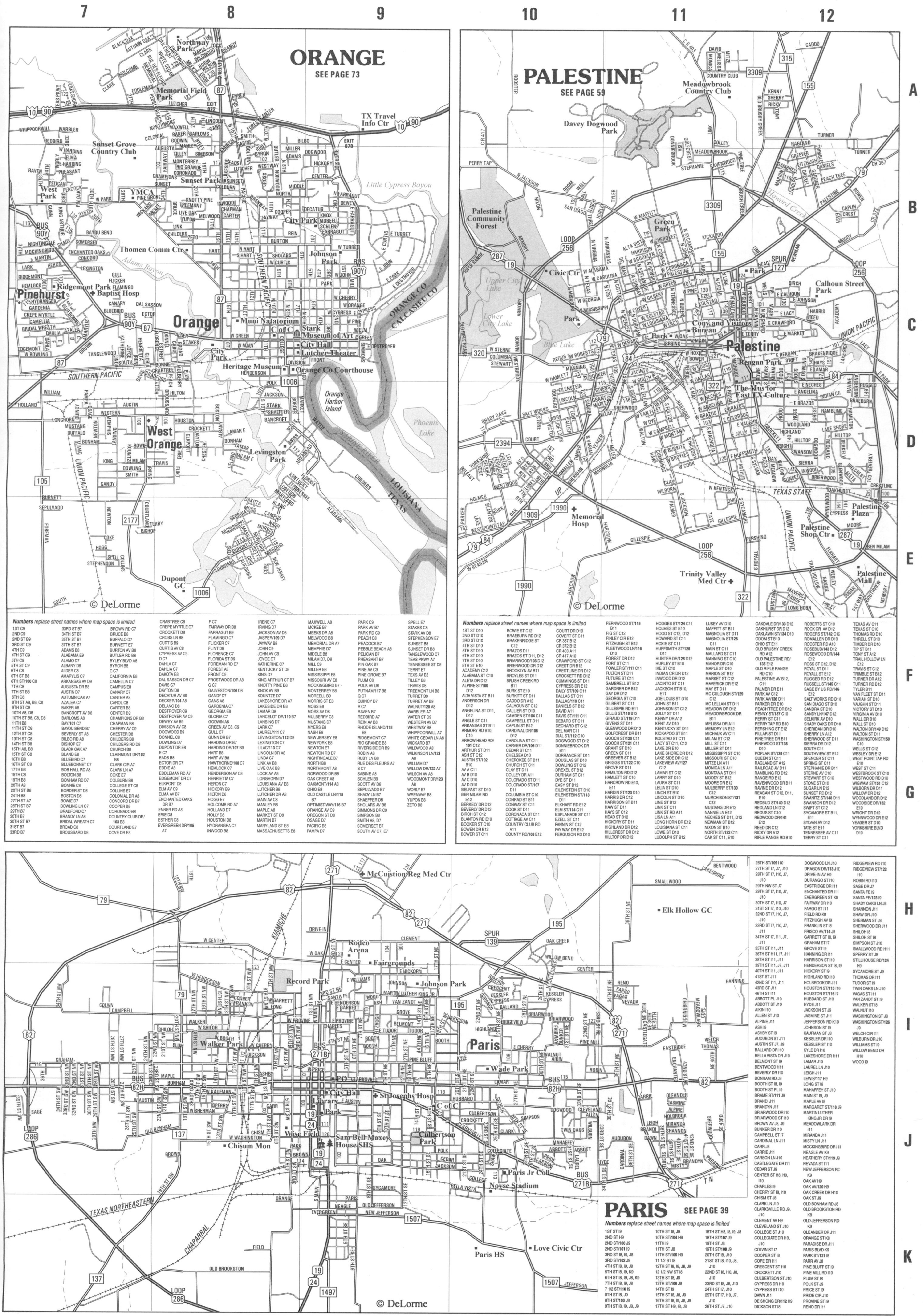

7
8
9
10
11
12
A
B
C
D
E
F
G
H
I
J
K
ORANGE
SEE PAGE 73
PALESTINE
SEE PAGE 59
PARIS
SEE PAGE 39
Orange
West Orange
Pinehurst
Palestine
Paris
Memorial Field Park
Sunset Grove Country Club
Sunset Park
YMCA
West Park
Thomen Comm Ctr
Ridgemont Park
Baptist Hosp
City Park
Johnson Park
Muni Natatorium
Stark Museum of Art
City Hall
Lutcher Theater
Heritage Museum
Orange Co Courthouse
Levingston Park
Orange Harbor Island
Phoenix Lake
Dupont GC
TX Travel Info Ctr
Little Cypress Bayou
Adams Bayou
SOUTHERN PACIFIC
UNION PACIFIC
LOUISIANA
TEXAS
ORANGE CO
CALCASIEU CO
Meadowbrook Country Club
Davey Dogwood Park
Palestine Community Forest
Green Park
Civic Ctr
Upper City Lake
Lower City Lake
Blue Lake
Conv and Visitors Bureau
Calhoun Street Park
Reagan Park
The Mus for East TX Culture
Memorial Hosp
Trinity Valley Med Ctr
Palestine Plaza
Palestine Shop Ctr
Palestine Mall
Howard Creek
TEXAS STATE
McCuistion Reg Med Ctr
Elk Hollow GC
Rodeo Arena
Fairgrounds
Record Park
Johnson Park
Walker Park
Wade Park
City Hall
Library
PO
St Josephs Hosp
C of C
Wise Field
Sam Bell Maxey House SHS
Culbertson Park
Chisum Mon
Paris Jr Coll
Noyse Stadium
Love Civic Ctr
Paris HS
TEXAS NORTHEASTERN
© DeLorme
Numbers replace street names where map space is limited

PLANO & VICINITY

SEE PAGE 46

Numbers replace street names where map space is limited

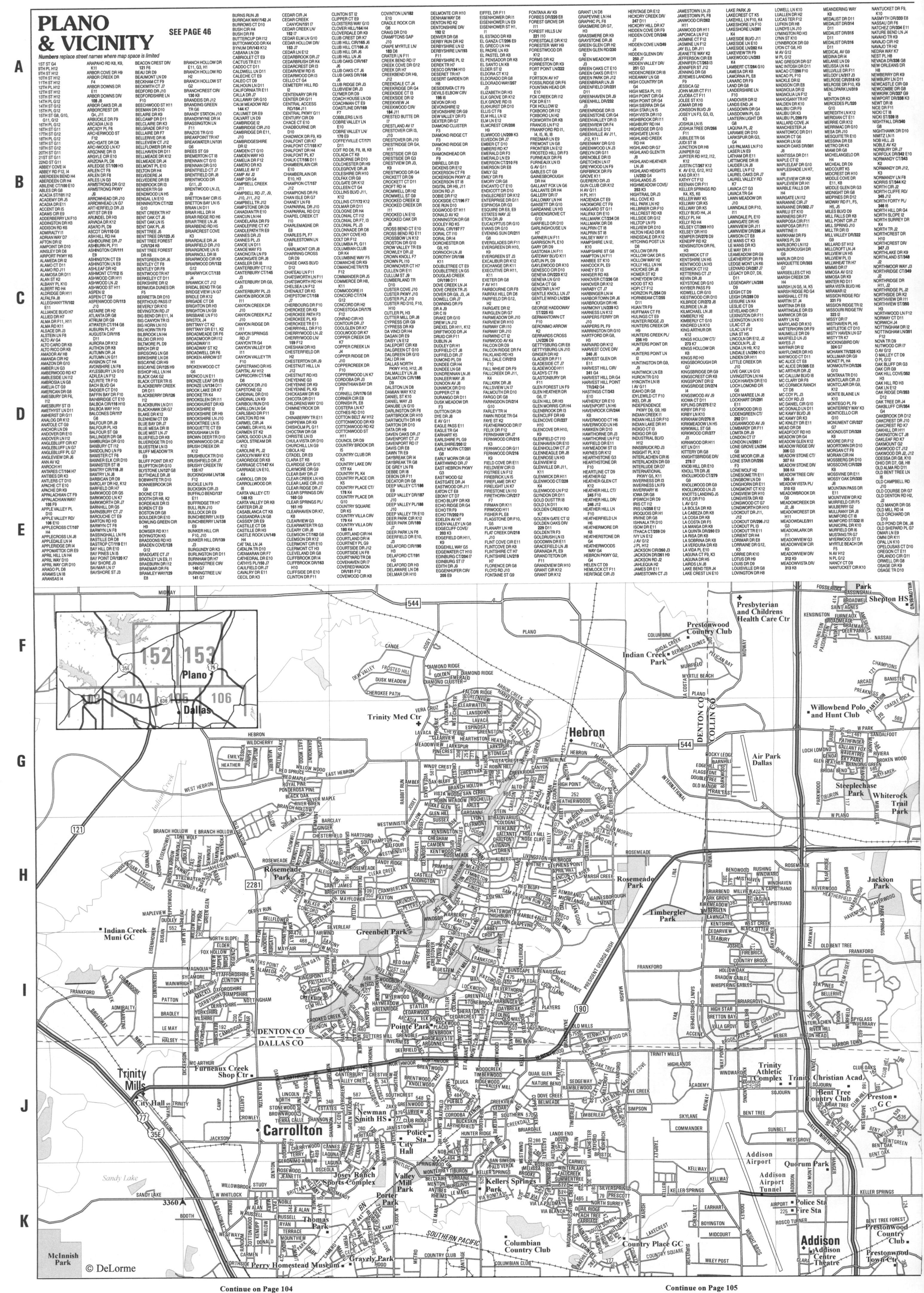

Continue on Page 104

Continue on Page 105

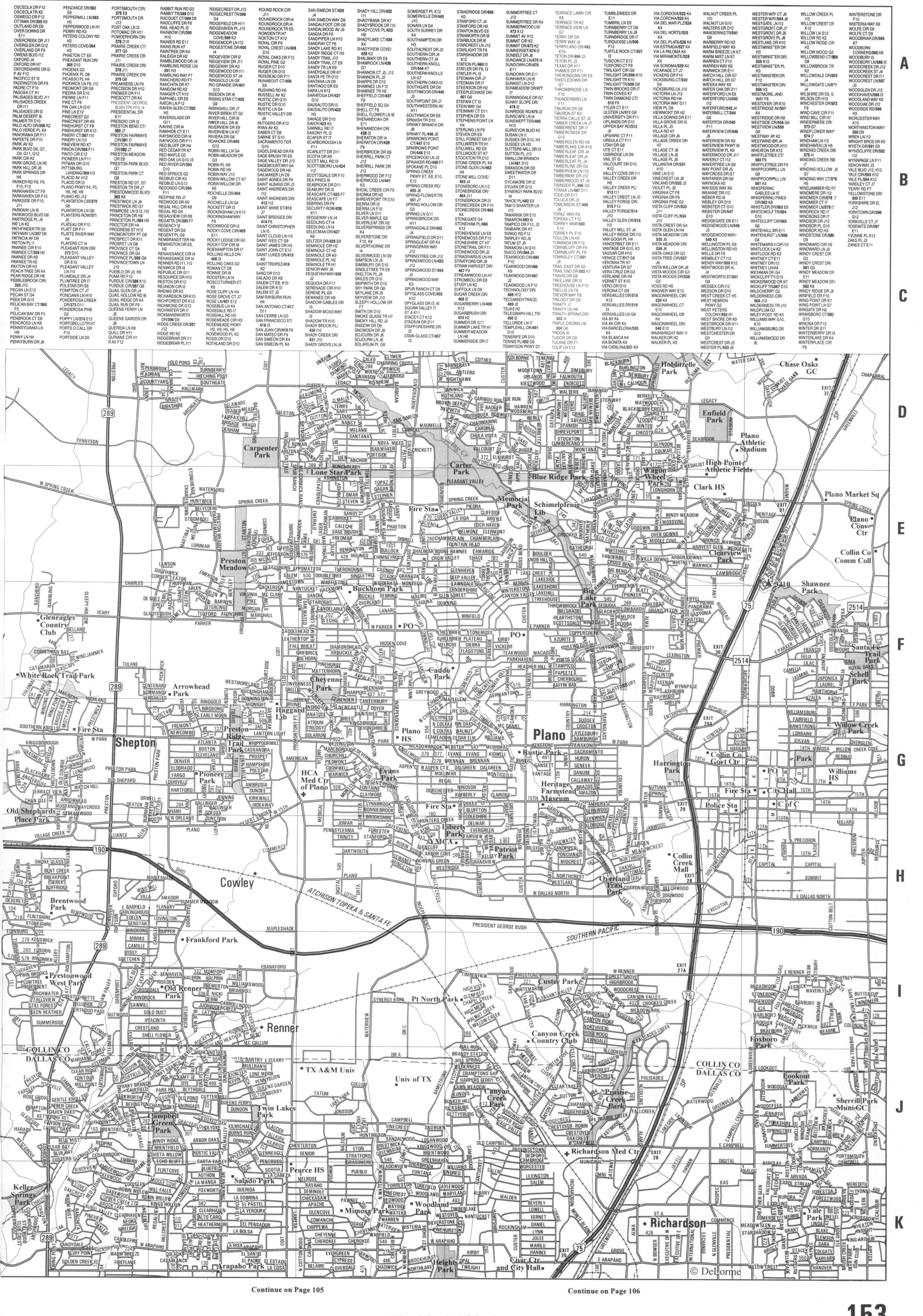

Continue on Page 105

Continue on Page 106

1" = 0.8 mi (1.3 km)

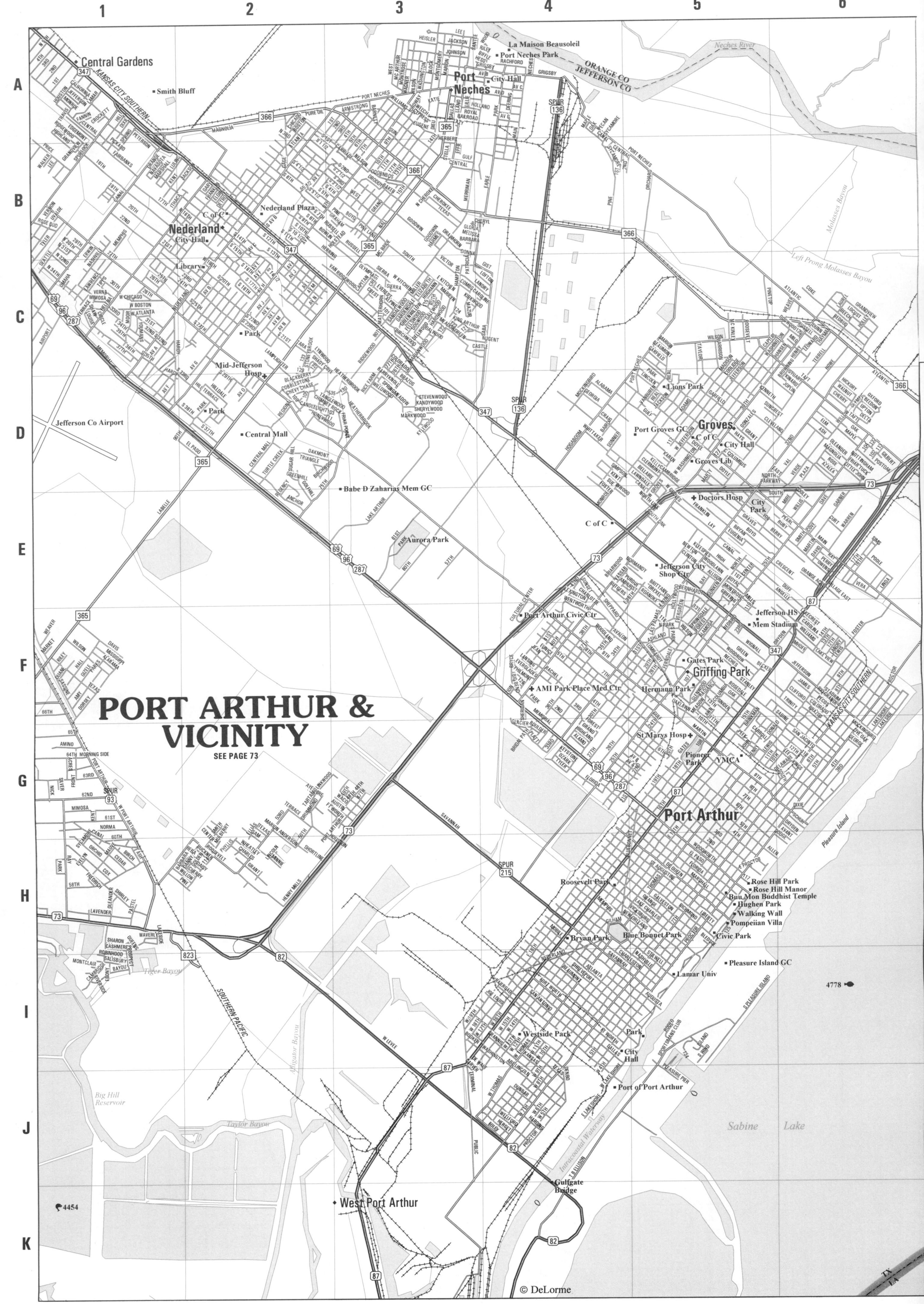

PORT ARTHUR & VICINITY
SEE PAGE 73
Central Gardens
Smith Bluff
La Maison Beausoleil
Port Neches Park
Port Neches
City Hall
Neches River
ORANGE CO
JEFFERSON CO
Molasses Bayou
Left Prong Molasses Bayou
Nederland
Nederland Plaza
C of C
City Hall
Library
Park
Mid-Jefferson Hosp
Jefferson Co Airport
Central Mall
Babe D Zaharias Mem GC
Aurora Park
Lions Park
Port Groves GC
Groves
C of C
City Hall
Groves Lib
Doctors Hosp
City Park
C of C
Jefferson City Shop Ctr
Port Arthur Civic Ctr
Jefferson HS
Mem Stadium
Gates Park
Griffing Park
Hermann Park
AMI Park Place Med Ctr
St Marys Hosp
Pioneer Park
YMCA
Port Arthur
Roosevelt Park
Bryan Park
Blue Bonnet Park
Rose Hill Park
Rose Hill Manor
Buu Mon Buddhist Temple
Hughen Park
Walking Wall
Pompeiian Villa
Civic Park
Pleasure Island GC
Lamar Univ
Pleasure Island
Westside Park
Park
City Hall
Port of Port Arthur
Tiger Bayou
Big Hill Reservoir
Taylor Bayou
Alligator Bayou
SOUTHERN PACIFIC
KANSAS CITY SOUTHERN
Intracoastal Waterway
Sabine Lake
Gulfgate Bridge
West Port Arthur
4778
4454
© DeLorme

PORT ARTHUR

***Numbers** replace street names where map space is limited*

1 1/2 ST B2
1ST AV A1, E5
1ST ST A2, A3, B4
2 1/2 ST B3
2ND A1
2ND AV F4, H5
2ND ST A3, B3, B5
3 1/2 ST B3
3RD A1
3RD AV F4, H5
3RD ST A2, A3, B3, G6
4 1/2 ST B2
4TH A1
4TH AV F4, H5
4TH ST A3, B3, G6, J4
5 1/2 ST B2
5TH AV A1, F4, G5
5TH ST A3, B2, G6, I4, J4
6TH AV G5
6TH ST B2, B3, G6, J4
7TH AV F4, G5
7TH ST B2, B3, H5, J4
8TH AV F4, G5
8TH ST B2, B3, F6, J4
9TH AV F4, G5
9TH ST B2, B3, F6, J4
10TH AV G5
10TH ST B2, B3, G5, I4
10 1/2 ST B2
11TH AV G5
11TH ST B2, B3, G5, I4
12TH AV G6
12TH ST B2, B3, F6, I4
13TH AV F5
13TH ST B2, B3, F6, H5, I4
14TH ST B2, B3, F6, I4
14 1/2 ST C2
15TH ST B2, B3, F5, I4
16TH ST B2, C2, E6, G5, I4
17TH ST B1, C2, E6, I4
18TH ST B1, C2, G5, I3, I4
19TH ST B1, C2, G5, I3
20TH ST B1, C2, G5
21ST ST B1, C2, G4
22ND ST B1, C2, G5
23RD ST C2, F5
24TH ST C2, G5
25TH ST C1, C2, E5, G4
26TH ST C1, G4
27TH ST B1, C2, G4
28TH ST C1, F5
29TH ST B1, D2, F5
30TH ST B1, C1, F4
31ST ST B1, C1, F5
32ND ST C1, D6, E5
33RD ST C1, D2, G4
34TH ST C1, F4
35TH ST C1, F4
36TH ST C1, D2, E5, F4
37TH ST C1, D2, F4
38TH ST F4
39TH ST D5
40TH ST F4
41ST ST F4
42ND ST E4
47TH ST G3
48TH G3
48TH ST G3
49TH ST G3
50TH ST G2
53RD ST G2
55 1/2 ST B2
57TH ST E3
58TH ST H1
60TH ST E3, G1
61ST ST E3, G1
62ND ST G1
63RD ST G1
64TH ST G1
65TH ST G1
66TH ST F1
73RD ST/**100** D6
75TH ST D2
76TH ST C3
77TH ST C3
80TH ST C3
90TH ST D1
ABE LINCOLN AV J4
ACRES AV G1
ADAMS BLVD D5
AIRPORT RD C1
ALABAMA AV D4, F1
ALAMO AV G4
ALAMOSA DR F5
ALLEN PL H5
ALLISON AV E5
ALPINE DR C3
AMHURST AV E4
AMINO ST G1
AMY ST F1
ANCHOR E2
ANDES DR/**101** C3
ANGELLE DR E6
ARMSTRONG AV A3
ASH AV D6, H1
ASHLAND DR F5
ATLANTA AV B2, I4
ATLANTA DR C1
ATLANTIC RD C6, D6
AUGUSTA AV I5
AUSTIN AV G3
AV A C1, G5
AV B A4, B2, G5
AV B AV C2
AV C A4, B2
AV D A4
AV E B2, C2
AV F C2, D1
AV G A4, C2
AV H B2, C2
AV I C2
AV J C2
AV K C2
AV L C2
AV M C2
AV N C2
AV O D2
AVALON AV F4
AVANT LN H6
AYESHIRE AV G2
AZALEA AV D6
BAIRD AV D4
BAKER AV B3
BARBARA CT B3
BARBARA LN H2
BARNETT PL A3
BARRYKNOLL D3
BAY ST E5
BAYOU DR I1
BEAUMONT AV I4
BEAUMONT ST C5
BECKER PL F5
BEECH AV C6
BELDON DR D6
BELLAIRE AV D5
BERNHARDT DR E5
BERRY AV E6
BETTY DR B4
BEXLEY/**102** D6
BIG BEND AV F4
BIRCH ST H1
BIRCHWOOD D2
BIRCHWOOD DR C3
BITTERNUT/**103** D2
BLACKBERRY LN D2
BLEDSOE PL H5
BLOCK ST A3
BLUEBONNET AV H5
BOOKER T WASHINGTON AV I3
BOSTON AV A2
BOSTON DR C1
BOULDER AV G4
BOWLIN AV B2
BOYD AV B3, E5
BRAZOS AV D3, F6
BRIARWOOD E4
BRIDAL PATH DR G4
BRINKMAN DR G5
BRITTANY AV E5
BROWNING D6
BRYAN AV E5
BRYCE ST F4
BUCKNER DR H2
C COLUMBUS D5
CALIFORNIA AV A1
CAMBRIDGE D5
CAMBRIDGE AV I1
CAMDEN LN/**104** D6
CANAL AV B1, E5
CANAL ST B4, G1
CANDLELIGHT CIR D2
CAPITAN DR C3
CAPITOL BLVD C5
CAROLINA AV F6
CAROLINE DR C4
CARRIAGE LN B3
CARROLL AV G5
CARVERTER I3
CASHMERE DR H1
CASTLE DR C4
CEDAR ST H1
CENTER ST E5, H2
CENTRAL AV B4
CENTRAL BLVD A1
CENTRAL DR B3
CENTRAL MALL DR D2
CHANDELLE LN/**105** D2
CHARLES AV H2
CHARLES AV/**106** E5
CHARLESTON AV I4
CHARLOTTE AV E4
CHEROKEE AV B3
CHERRY ST D6, H2
CHERYL CT B3
CHEVY CHASE LN D2
CHICAGO AV A2
CHICAGO DR C1
CHIMNEY ROCK CT D2
CIRCLE DR C1
CLERMONT ST D5
CLEVELAND AV D5
CLIFFORD AV F6
CLINTON E5
COBBLESTONE LN D2
COKE RD C6
COLORADO AV F6
COLORADO ST C3
COLUMBIA ST F5
COMBS DR C3
COOLEY AV E6
COOLIDGE BLVD C5
COVE DR E6
COX ST H1
CRAIG AV D4
CRESCENT DR E6
CREST CIR C3
CREST DR C3
CROCKETT ST A1
CULTURAL CENTER LN F4
CURT DR E6
CYPRESS ST A3
DAISY DR H2
DALLAS AV I4
DALLAS ST A3
DALWOOD C3
DANNY LN H2
DATE ST/**107** F5
DAVE ST E6
DAVID ST E6
DAVIS AV F1
DE QUEEN BLVD H5
DE WALT BLVD I3
DEERING ST A4
DELAWARE DR G6
DELLWOOD DR C3
DELTA DR D6
DENBO AV J4
DETROIT AV B2
DIEU ST A3
DIXIE BLVD A1
DIXIE DR G6
DODGE PL H6
DOGWOOD DR C6
DOGWOOD LN C3
DONALD ST G5
DONNA CT B3
DOORNBOS ST B3
DORSEY ST F1
DOYLE AV D5
DRAWHORN DR B3
DREXEL DR E5
DRODDY DR B3
DRUMMOND ST G2
DRYDEN EXT/**108** G5
DRYDEN PL G6
DRYDEN RD F6
DUANE ST F1
DUFF DR E6
DUNBAR AV J4
DUNN ST C6
EARLE ST B4
EAST DR D6
EBONY I1
EDGEMONT LN A1
EFFIE CIR B3
EL PASO AV D2, H5
ELGIN AV B2
ELIZABETH ST C3
ELLIAS ST G2
ELM AV D6
ERWIN ST B1
EUGENE AV A3
EUGENIA DR E5
EUNICE AV F4
EVELYN ST H1
EVEREST CIR C3
EVERGLADES AV F4
EVERGREEN DR F5
FAIRBANKS AV B1
FANNIN ST A1
FELLSWOOD DR C3
FERNDALE DR F5
FLORIDA AV G4, H5
FOLEY AV J4
FOREST AV G4
FOREST DR F5
FORT WORTH AV G3, I4
FOSTER AV E4
FRANKLIN AV B2, E5
FREDRICH ST H1
FRIAR POINT DR D3
FRIAR TUCK LN D6
FRONT AV G1
GAGE AV B2
GALEWOOD LN C3
GALVESTON AV H5
GARDENDALE RD C3
GARFIELD ST C5, D5
GARNER ST E6
GARY AV B2
GATES DR G5
GEORGE LN G6
GEORGIA AV D4
GILBERT AV D6
GILHAM CIR H4
GIST DR C4
GIZELE ST F1
GLACIER DR G4
GLENWOOD DR F5
GLORIA CT B3
GOLDEN LN H2
GOLFHILL E2
GONZALES LN D5
GOODWIN AV B3
GOODWIN CT B3
GRAHAM LN B3
GRAND AV G4
GRAND BLVD B3
GRANDVIEW AV C6
GRANDVIEW DR A1
GRANNIS AV I4
GRANT AV D5, H2
GRAVES AV E5
GREEN AV F5
GREENBRIAR LN/**109** D2
GREENHILL D2
GREENWILLOW DR C3
GRIFFING CT E5
GRIGSBY AV A4
GRIGSBY DR A4
GROVES CIR E5
GROVES CIR DR E5
GULF AV B3, F5
GULF ST D5
HALL ST F1
HAMPTON LN C3
HANSEN BLVD C6
HARDING AV J4
HARDWOOD DR C3
HARDY AV C1
HARDY CIR D1
HARMES CIR B3
HARRISON AV C5
HAYMAN C6
HAYS AV D5
HEATHERBROOK CT D3
HEATHERBROOK TR D3
HEISLER ST A3
HELENA AV C1
HENRY AV C6, G5
HENRY MILLS BLVD H2
HERBERT DR B3
HERGET AV J4
HERRING AV B3
HERRINGTER/**110** B3
HESS AV A4
HICKORY ST D6
HIGH AV E5
HIGHLAND AV G4
HIGHLAND BLVD A1
HILL ST A1
HILL TERRACE DR D2
HILLDALE DR D2
HOGABOOM RD D4
HOLLAND AV A4
HOLLEY AV C6
HOLLYWOOD DR E5
HOLSTEAD AV B3
HONEYWOOD TR D2
HOUSTON AV A1, G2
HOWE ST C6
HUGHANN ST C3
IMHOFF AV F6
INWOOD DR E4
ISLAND WAY I5
ITHACA AV B1
JACKSON AV A3, B2
JACKSON BLVD D5
JAMES AV F6
JEAN AV F4
JEFFERSON BLVD D5
JEFFERSON DR F6
JEFFERSON ST A1
JOE LOUIS AV I4
JOHN AV G5
JOHNSON AV A3
JOPLIN AV D6
KANDYWOOD D3
KANSAS AV I4
KAREN D5
KATIE AV A3
KELLY LN D5
KENNETH AV D5
KENT AV B1, D4, G1
KEYSTONE AV G4
KINARD AV D6
KING ARTHUR C4
KINGS CT G6
KIRKWOOD DR C3
KITCHEN DR C3
KLEESPIES E5
KYLEWOOD D3
LABELLE RD E1
LAKE ARTHUR DR E3
LAKE CHARLES AV H5
LAKE SHORE DR J4
LAKE VIEW AV F6
LAKECREST F6
LAKESHORE DR G6, J4
LAKESIDE DR G6
LAKESIDE PLZ H1
LAMAR AV A1
LAMPLIGHTER LN C2
LANDRY DR C4, F6
LANSING AV F4
LAS PALMAS DR F5
LAUREL ST C6
LAVENDER ST H1
LAWN ST F5
LAWNDALE AV D5
LAWRENCE AV C1
LAY AV E5
LAZY LN A3
LEE AV A3, G6
LEE ST B1
LEMONTREE/**111** D2
LEONARD AV C6
LEVEE RD I3
LEWIS DR G5
LEWIS FOSTER DR F6
LEWIS RD F6
LEXINGTON AV E4
LIBERTY AV H5
LILLIE ST A3
LINCOLN AV D5
LINCOLN LN H2
LINDA DR E6
LINKWOOD ST G2
LITTLE JOHN LN D6
LIVE OAK LN G6
LLANO ST A3
LOCUST AV C6
LOFTON DR C4
LOMBARDY DR F5
LOUISE DR C1
LULING AV B1
LYNWOOD LN C2
MADISON BLVD C5
MADISON BLVD/**112** D5
MAGNOLIA AV A2
MAGNOLIA LN D6
MAIN AV E6
MAIN ST A4
MANCHESTER LN/**113** D6
MAPLE D6
MAPLE ST A4
MAPLE ST/**114** H2
MARIANWOOD C3
MARILYN LN C3
MARION ANDERSON AV G2
MARION ST A3, C5
MARKET ST F1
MARKWOOD D3
MARSHALL AV B1, H5
MARTIN DR G5
MARTIN ST E6
MARTY ST D5
MARY LN/**115** C3
MATTERHORN DR C3
MAUVE AV H1
MAZUR DR C3
MC ARTHUR DR A3
MC BRIDE DR B3
MC KINLEY AV C5
MEADOW ST F5
MEADOWGREEN DR C3
MELISSA CT B3
MEMORIAL BLVD C1, F4
MEMPHIS AV B1, H4
MERRIMAN ST B3
MILLER ST C3
MILLS AV E5
MILO AV C6
MIMOSA DR C1
MIMOSA ST G1
MINNIE AV H2
MIRE ST E6
MISSISIPPI AV F1
MOBILE AV H4
MOCKINGBIRD LN D4, G6
MONROE BLVD E4
MONROE ST A1
MONTCLAIR DR I1
MONTGOMERY ST A3
MONTROSE AV E5
MONTROSE ST A3
MOOR DR C1
MORNING SIDE G1
MULBERRY ST H2
NALL ST B3
NASHVILLE AV B1, I5
NAVASOTA AV B1
NECHES AV F5
NECHES DR A4
NEDERLAND AV C2, I4
NELSON B3
NEW ORLEANS AV H5
NEWTON E5
NICK AV G1
NORMA ST G1
NORMANDY AV E5
NORTH DR D6
NORTH LINK E5
NORTH ST E5
NOTTINGHAM LN D6
NUGENT DR C4
OAK AV D6, F5
OAK ST A4
OAKLAWN AV F5
OAKMONT D2
OLEANDER LN D6
OLEANDER ST H1
OLYMPIA DR C3
OLYMPIC DR D6
OMAHA AV C1
ORANGE ACRE DR E6
ORANGE AV B1, H5
ORCHARD B5
ORCHID ST H1
ORDWAY ST A3
OWENS AV E6
OXFORD DR D6
OZARK AV G4
PARK AV D5
PARK DR D2, F5
PARK DR/**116** F5
PARK LN F4
PARK RD E3, H1
PARK RD/**117** H5
PARK ST A4
PARKS ST F1
PASTEL ST H1
PATRICIA LN B3
PEARL AV E6
PECAN ST A4
PECOS AV F6
PEEK AV G5
PERRY AV E6
PETERSON ST A1
PHILMONT AV F4
PHYLLIS ST H2
PICKARD AV B1
PINE LN B3
PINE LANE AV B3
PINE ST B4, H1
PINETOP RD C5
PARKWAY D5
PLATT AV G4
PLEASURE ISLAND RD I5
PLEASURE PIER DR J5
PLAZA ST D6
POOLE AV E6
PORT ARTHUR RD G1
PORT ARTHUR ST G3
PORT NECHES ATLANTIC RD B5
PORT NECHES AV A3
PORT NECHES RD D5
POSTOAK LN D6
PRICE ST B1
PROCTOR ST F6, H5, J4
PROSPECT AV I1
PUBLIC RD J3
PURDUE AV E5
PURE OIL RD A2
QUEENS CT/**118** G6
QUEENS DR H1
RACHEL AV F4
RACHFORD AV A4
RADIANCE AV F5
RAILROAD AV A3, I4
RAY AV E6, H1
REAL BLVD D5
REAL ST D5
REBA DR H2
RED BIRD ST/**119** F5
REDBIRD AV F5
REDBUD AV C6
REDWOOD DR/**120** C6
REGENCY DR D2
REGIONAL DR D2
REYNOLDS LN/**121** C3
RICE FARM RD D3
RICHMOND AV H5
RIDGEWOOD AV C3
RIDGEWOOD DR C3
RIDGEWOOD LN A1
RIFFLE AV A4
RILEY AV A4
RILEY ST F1
RIO GRANDE AV F6
RIVERSIDE I1
ROANOKE AV E5
ROBINHOOD DR I1
RODEO LN I5
RONSHIRE LN/**122** C3
ROOSEVELT AV C5, H2
ROSE AV D6
ROSE BUD ST B1
ROSEDALE DR F5
ROUNDTOWER LN/**123** C3
ROYAL AV A3, E5
RUBY DR E6
RUSSELL AV B3
RUSSELL CIR B3
RUSSELL ST C6
RUTGERS AV E4
RUTH LN C3
SABA LN C4
SABINE AV G6
SALISBURY DR I1
SAM AV G2
SAN ANTONIO AV I4
SAN JACINTO AV G6
SANDALWOOD DR C3
SANTEE ST A4
SASSER LN/**124** C3
SASSINE AV F1
SAVANNAH AV G3, I4
SCHUH PL G6
SEATTLE AV B1
SEAWALL DR/**125** H5
SEQUOIA AV/**126** F4
SHADY COVE C2
SHARON DR H1
SHAW DR C1
SHEPPARD AV F4
SHERIDAN LN F4
SHERYLWOOD D3
SHIRLEY ST H1
SHORT ST/**127** D5
SHORTLINE AV H2
SHREVEPORT AV I4
SIERRA CIR C3
SIERRA DR C3
SILVER AV G1
SIMPSON AV D4
SIMS AV E6
SLEEPY HOLLOW LN/**128** C2
SMITH ST E6, G2
SNIDER AV F5
SONNIER LN D4
SOUTH AV C3
SOUTH DR E6
SOUTH LINK E5
SOUTH ST G6
SPORTSMANS CLUB RD I5
SPRING ST A1
SPRINGDALE DR F5
SPRINGMEADOW D3
SPURLOCK RD B1
ST AUGUSTINE AV H5
STADIUM RD F6
STANLEY BLVD F5
STELLA CIR B3
STEVENWOOD D3
STILWELL BLVD I5
STONEGATE CT/**129** C2
STONEYBROOK LN C2
STUART DR D6
SUE AV D4
SUGAR HILL D2
SUN AV A3
SUNCREST DR D5
SUNKEN CT E5
SUNSET DR E4
SYCAMORE CT B4
SYCAMORE ST A4, H1
T B ELLISON PKWY J4
TAFT AV D6
TAFT ST D6
TANGLEWOOD D2
TARA LN C2
TARTAN ST G2
TAYLOR BLVD C5
TERRACE DR C1
TERMINAL RD J3
TERRACE AV G2
TERRELL ST C6
TEXAS AV B3, F1, J4
TEXAS ST G2
THOMAS J4
THOMAS BLVD H5, I4
TIMBERLEAF/**130** D3
TIPPS DR C1
TRAVIS ST A1
TRIANGLE D2
TRINITY AV F6
TURTLE CREEK DR D2
TYLER B1
TYLER AV G4
TYRRELL PKWY/**131** F5
UPTON DR D6
UVALDE B1
VAL ST D6
VAN AV C3
VANBUREN BLVD D5
VASSAR AV E4
VERA DR E6
VERDE ST D6
VERNA DR C1
VERNON B1
VICKSBURG AV H5
VICTOR DR C3
VILLAGE EAST BLVD E6
WACO AV G3
WAGNER ST A3
WALKER LN B1
WALNUT ST D6
WARREN ST E6
WASHINGTON A3
WASHINGTON BLVD C6, D5
WAVERLY CIR H1
WEAVER DR C6
WEAVER ST F1
WELCH AV A3
WELLFORD AV J4
WENTWORTH AV F4
WEST AV B3
WEST DR A3
WHEATLEY AV H2
WHITBY LN/**132** D6
WHITTAKER AV D4
WIGNALL AV F5
WILLIAMS AV A3, F6
WILLIS ST E6
WILLOW AV H2
WILLOW BEND LN/**133** C2
WILLOW ST D6
WILLOWOOD LN D3
WILSON AV C5, F1
WILSON DR F5
WILSON ST A3
WIND I5
WOOD ST A4
WOODFERN CT/**135** D3
WOODLAND AV F4
WOODLAWN DR E5
WOODROW DR F5
WOODWORTH BLVD H5
YOUMANS DR C1
ZION ST F4

PAMPA

SEE PAGE 30

***Numbers** replace street names where map space is limited*

14TH AV/**100** E8
15TH AV E8
16TH AV E8
17TH AV E7, E8
18TH AV E7, E8
19TH AV E7, E8
20TH AV E8
20TH AV/**101** E7
21ST AV E7
22ND AV E7, E8
23RD AV E7
24TH AV E8
25TH AV E8
25TH AV/**102** E7
26TH AV D8
27TH AV D8
28TH AV D8
29TH AV D8
29TH AV/**103** D7
30TH AV D8
30TH AV/**104** D7
31ST AV D8
32ND AV D8
AFT ST F7
ALBERT ST G8
ALLEN ST F8
ANNE ST F8
ASH ST G8
ASPEN DR E8
ATCHISON AV F8, G8
BALLARD ST F8, G8
BANKS ST E7, G7
BARNARD AV G8
BARNES ST/**105** G8
BARRETT ST/**106** G8
BEECH LN E8
BERYL ST G8
BOYD AV F7
BRADLEY DR F8
BROWN AV G8
BROWNING AV F8, G7
BRUNOW AV G8
BUCKLER AV G7
CAMPBELL AV/**108** G8
CANADIAN ST/**109** F8
CARR ST F8
CARTER AV G7
CARTER ST G7
CHARLES ST D7, F7
CHEROKEE DR E8
CHESTNUT DR D8
CHEYENNE RD E8
CHRISTINE ST F7
CHRISTY ST E7
CHRISTY ST/**110** G7
CINDERELLA DR/**111** D7
COFFEE ST E7
COMANCHE TR D8
COOK AV F7
CRANE RD E7
CRAVEN AV G8
CRESCENT DR E7
CREST AV/**112** F8
CREST RD E7
CROCKER ST G7
CULVER ST/**113** G8
CUYLER ST F8
DARBY AV F8
DAVIS ST G7
DEANE DR F8
DEER PL E8
DENVER AV G8
DOGWOOD LN D8
DOUCETTE ST F8
DOYLE ST F7, G7
DUNCAN ST E8
DWIGHT ST E7
ELM AV G8
EVERGREEN ST E8
FAULKNER ST E7
FIELDS ST G8
FIELDS ST/**114** G8
FINCH AV F7
FINLEY ST G8
FIR ST D8
FISHER ST F8
FLORIDA AV F7
FORD ST G8
FOSTER AV F8, G8
FRANCIS AV F8, G7
FRASER ST F8
FREDERIC ST G7
FROST ST F7
GARLAND ST F8
GILLESPIE ST G8
GILLESPIE ST/**115** F8
GORDON AV/**116** G8
GRAHAM ST/**117** G8
GRAPE E8
GRAPE LN E8
GRAY RD G8
GRAY ST F7, G7
GWENDOLEN ST F7
HAMILTON ST E7
HARLEM ST/**118** G8
HARVESTER AV F7, F8
HARVESTER RD F7
HAZEL ST F8
HENRY ST F8
HILL AV F8
HOBART ST G7
HOLLY LN E8
HOUSTON ST/**119** G8
HOUSTON ST/**120** F8
HUFF RD G7
HUGHES ST/**121** G8
JEAN ST F8
JORDEN ST F8
JUNIPER DR D7
JUPITER ST F8
KENTUCKY AV F7
KENTUCKY AV/**122** F8
KINGSMILL AV F8, G7
KIOWA PL D8
LAFFERTY ST G7
LAGUNA DR E8
LEA ST E7
LEFORS ST F8
LINCOLN AV F7
LINDA DR E7, E8
LLAND ST G7
LOCUST ST/**123** G8
LOUISIANA AV F7
LOVE ST G7
LOWRY ST F8
LYNN ST E7
MAGNOLIA ST F8
MALONE AV G8
MAPLE AV G8
MARIE ST F8
MARKET ST G7
MARY ELLEN ST E7
MEADOWLARK LN/**124** E8
MIAMI ST F8
MONTAGU AV F7
MORA AV F8
MURPHY AV G8
NAIDA ST F7, G7
NAVAJO RD D8
NELSON ST E7
NICKI AV E7
OCTAVUS ST G8
OKLAHOMA ST G7
OSBORN ST/**125** G8
PARK DR F8
PEMBROOK D7
PENNSYLVANIA AV F7, F8
PERRY ST G7
PITTS ST/**126** G8
POWELL ST F8
PRAIRIE DR G7
PRIMROSE LN E7
PURVIANCE ST G7
QUAIL PL E8
RANDY MATSON AV E8, F7
RED DEER ST F8
REID ST G8
RHAM ST G7
RIPLEY ST G7
ROBERTA ST F7
ROSE ST/**127** F8
ROSEWOOD LN D7
ROTH ST F8
RUSSELL ST F7, G8
SANDLEWOOD DR D7
SCHNEIDER ST/**128** G8
SCOTT AV G8
SEMINOLE DR D8
SENECA LN E7
SHORT ST F8
SIERRA DR D7
SIKES CIR F7
SIOUX PL E8
SIRROCO PL D7
SLOAN ST F8
SOMERVILLE ST F7, G8
SOMMERVILLE ST/**129** F7
STARKWEATHER ST F8
STARKWEATHER ST/**130** F8
SUMNER ST E7
TALLEY ST G8
TERRACE ST F8
TERRY RD D7
TEXAS AV F7
THUT ST G8
THUT ST/**131** G8
TIGNOR ST G8
TUKE ST G8
TURTLE CREEK LN E8
TWIFFORD ST F8
TYNG AV F8, G8
UN RD E7
VARNON DR/**132** G7
VIRGINIA AV F7
WALL ST G7
WARD ST F7, G7
WARREN ST F8
WASHITA DR E8
WELLS ST E7
WELLS ST/**133** G7
WEST ST G7, G8
WHEELER ST F8
WILKS ST G7
WILLISTON ST E7
WILLOW RD D7
WORREL AV E7
WORRELL AV E7
WYNNE ST F8
YEAGER ST F8
ZIMMERS ST E7

© DeLorme

ROUND ROCK

SEE PAGE 69

***Numbers** replace street names where map space is limited*

ABBEY RD G10
ABERDEEN DR D11
ALGARITA D12
AMANDA COVE G10
AMESWOOD DR D11
ANDERSON AV F11
ANDOVER DR E11
ASHWOOD CT F12
ASTER D12
AUSTIN AV F11
BAGDAD AV F11
BALSAM D12
BARRHALL DR D11
BASS RD E10
BAYLAND E12
BELAIRE DR G11
BELLMAR E12
BELLVIEW AV G11
BELLVIEW AV/**100** F11
BETH LN E12
BLACK JACK D10
BLACK ST E11
BLAIN ST F11
BLANCHARD DR G10
BLESSING AV G10
BLUE BONNET D12
BLUE JAY WAY G10
BLUFF DR G10
BLUFFTOP CIR G10
BONWOOD DR F10
BOWMAN D12
BOWMAN DR D11, E11
BOXWOOD F12
BRADDOCK LN D11
BRADMORE DR E11
BRAESGREEN DR D11
BRANDI LN E10
BREEZY CT G12
BRENTWOOD/**101** F10
BRIARWOOD F10
BROKEN BOW DR G11
BROWN ST/**102** F11
BRUSHY CREEK DR E11
BRUSHY CREEK RD E10
BUCKBOARD BLVD G11
BUCKSKIN DR G11
BUFFALO PASS/**103** G11
BURLESON COVE D11
BURLWOOD CT D11
BURNET ST F11
CACTUS DR G11
CAMBRIDGE DR G11
CAMEO DR/**104** D11
CASEY LN F12
CATHERINE CT G12
CEDAR BEND D10
CEDAR CREEK COVE G10
CEDAR FALLS ST F10
CHANDLER D12
CHAPARRAL D10
CHAPARRAL DR/**105** D10
CHERVIL D11
CHISHOLM RD D10, E10
CHISHOLM VALLEY DR G11
CHOWAN PL G10
CHOWAN WAY G10
CHRISTOPHER AV G11
CINCOTEAGUE WAY G10
CINDY CT G12
CIRCLE DR E12
CLARK ST E10
CLEAR WATER TR D11
CLEARVIEW COVE/**106** F12
COLLEGE ST F11
COMMERCE BLVD D11
COOKE ST/**107** E12
COTTONWOOD CT/**108** G12
COUNTRY AIRE DR D11
CR 125 E11
CR 170 G12
CR 172 G10
CREEK COVE E11
CREEK DR G12
CREEKMONT DR F10
CREEKVIEW DR G10
CRESTLINE CT E12
CRESTVIEW ST F10
CROSSWOOD DR/**109** G10
CUSHING DR G11
CUSHING PARK DR G11
CYPRESS LN D11
DALE COVE/**110** E11
DANA CT E12
DAVID CURRY DR D11
DEEPWOOD DR F10
DEER RUN F11
DEERFOOT CIR F11
DEERFOOT DR F11
DENFIELD DR/**111** D11
DENNIS DR E11
DIXIE LN G11
DOREEN CT E12
DOVE CREEK DR F11
DOVEHAVEN DR F11
DOVER LN G11
DRAGON DR F10
DRY CREEK COVE/**112** G11
DRY CREEK CT/**113** G11
DRY CREEK DR G11
EASTON DR/**114** D11
EDWARDS DR D11
EGGER AV E11
EGGER COVE/**115** D11
ELDER WAY F12
EMMANUEL E10
ENTERPRISE DR/**116** D11
FAIRLANE DR G11
FAIRLAWN COVE F12
FAIRWAY GREEN COVE/**117** F11
FANNIN AV E11
FARNSWOOD DR/**118** D11
FAWN RIDGE TR E10
FERNDALE DR F11
FIELDSTONE PL F11
FIRETHORN F12
FLINT ROCK DR G10
FLORENCE ST/**119** F11
FRONTIER TR/**120** G11
GALLOPING RD E10
GARDEN CT F11
GARDEN PATH F11
GARDEN PATH COVE/**121** F12
GARDENTER F12
GARDEN VALLEY COVE F11
GATTIS SCHOOL RD G11
GEORGE ST G11
GEORGETOWN ST E11
GLADVIEW DR F10
GLEN COVE E10
GLENDA DR F10
GLENMEADOWS DR E10
GLENWOOD F10
GLENWOOD COVE E10
GOODSON CT/**122** E12
GOODSON LN E12
GRAY OAK D10
GREEN MEADOW DR/**123** E11
GREEN MOUNTAIN COVE/**124** F12
GREEN VALLEY COVE/**125** F12
GREENBRIAR CT/**126** F12
GREENDOWNS DR F12
GREENHILL DR D11
GREENLAWN BLVD F12
GREENWICH PL G11
GREGORY LN/**127** D11
GREYSON DR/**128** E11
GROVE D10
HAMPTON WAY G12
HARRIS ST F11
HAWTHORNE F12
HEATHER DR E11
HEATWOOD CIR/**129** D11
HERMITAGE DR E10
HESTERS CROSSING RD G11
HIDDEN ACRES DR E12
HIDEAWAY LN/**130** F12
HIGHMEADOWS COVE/**131** E10
HOGAN E12
HOLLOW TREE E10
HONEY SUCKLE D12
HUNLAC COVE/**132** G10
HUNTER TR E10
HYRIDGE ST F11
INDUSTRIAL BLVD E10
INMAN LN E12
JEFFREY WAY D11
JINA LN E12
JOYCE LN G12
KAREN COVE/**133** E11
KAROLYN DR E11
KNOLLWOOD COVE/**134** G10
LAKE CREEK DR F10
LAKEVIEW COVE F10
LAKEWOOD LN F10
LAMAR DR D11
LAMPASAS ST/**135** F11
LANCASTER GATE DR/**136** G11
LANCE LN E12
LANTANA D12
LANTERN LIGHT E10
LARRY LN/**137** E11
LASSO DR G11
LATIGO TR E10
LAURA CT G10
LAUREL DR E11
LAUREL PATH D12
LAWNMONT DR F11
LEDBETTER E10
LESLIE CT G10
LEWIS ST F11
LIBERTY AV E12, F11
LILAC DR E11
LIME ROCK DR F10
LOGAN ST F11, F12
LONDON RD/**138** E12
LONG MEADOW DR D11
LYNDA SUE ST/**139** G10
MAGNOLIA DR G11
MAIN AV F12
MANDELL ST/**140** F11
MAPLE F12
MARTIN AV G10
MAYES ST D11, G11
MC NEIL RD F11, G10
MEADOWBROOK DR D12
MEADOWCREEK CIR F12
MEADOWCREEK COVE/**141** F12
MEADOWS DR E10
MELBOURNE E12
MESA PARK DR E11
MESSICK PL/**142** G10
MILAM AV F11
MILLS MEADOW DR E12
MIMOSA F12
MISTY MORNING WAY/**143** D11
MOBIL ST G11
MONTCLAIR DR G11
MORNING DEW COVE D11
MORNINGSIDE COVE G12
MOYE ST F12
NANCY DR E11
NASH F11
NELSON F11
NEW COVE E11
NICOLE CIR D11
NICOLE COVE/**144** E11
NORMEADOWS CIR E10
NORTHWEST DR E11
NOTTINGHAM HILL RD G12
OAK DR E11, F10
OAK MEADOW DR G10
OAK RIDGE DR G10
OAKMEADOWS COVE/**145** E10
OAKVIEW D10
OLD SETTLERS RD D11
OLD WEST DR G11
OLD WEST PL/**146** G11
ONION CREEK VILLAGE/**147** E11
OVERCUP D10
OXFORD BLVD G12
PACK SADDLE PASS G11
PALM VALLEY RD E11
PARK DALE CT G12
PARKFIELD CIR G12
PARKHILL COVE D11
PARKSIDE F10
PARKSIDE CIR G12
PARKSIDE COVE/**148** G12
PARKWAY E11
PECAN AV E11
PECAN LN E12
PENNY LN F10
PHLOX D12
PRAIRIE STAR D12
PROVIDENT LN E12
PURPLE SAGE DR G11
QUAIL CREEK CIR/**149** F11
QUAIL PARK DR/**150** F11
QUANAH DR/**151** G10
R R COVE/**152** F10
RABBIT RUN F12
RAINTREE F12
RAWHIDE DR G11
RAY BERGLUND BLVD F12
REMUDA CIR G11
RIDGECREST DR F11
RIDGELINE DR/**153** D11
RIDGEMONT ST F11
RIDGEROCK DR G10
RIDGETOP D11
RILEY COVE/**154** D11
RIVERLAWN ST F10
ROBB LN E11
ROCK COVE F12
ROCK CREEK DR G10
ROLLING GREEN/**155** D11
ROSEMARY F12
ROSEWOOD CT G12
ROUND ROCK AV F11
ROUND ROCK DR F10
ROUNDUP TR G11
RUSTLERS RD D10
RYE ST E11
SAGEBRUSH DR G11
SAINT WILLIAM AV G10
SAM BASS CIR E10
SARA DR E11
SAUNDERS DR D11
SHADOWBROOK CIR G10
SHADY PATH COVE/**156** F12
SHEPPARD ST F11
SHOTWELL D12
SIERRA COVE D11
SILVER SPUR DR G11
SILVERLEAF F12
SOUTHEASTERN TR G12
SOUTHWESTERN TR G12
SPRING BREEZE DR D12
SPRING HOLLOW E10
SPRING ST E11
SPRINGWATER/**157** E10
STAGECOACH TR E10
STIRRUP DR G11
STONE ST F11
STRATFORD COVE/**158** G12
STRATFORD CT G12
STRATFORD DR G12
SUMMIT ST E11
SUNBEAM COVE D12
SUNRISE RD E12
SUNSET DR E11
SYCAMORE F12
SYLVIA E10
TAMARA CT G10
TASSEY G11
TEJAS DR G10
TEXAS AV D11
TIMBERLINE DR E12
TIMBERWOOD DR E11
TOWER DR G11
TRAILWAY E11
TREY G11
TROY LN/**159** D12
VERBENA D12
VIRGINIA DR E11
VISTA AV E11
WAGON WHEEL DR/**160** G11
WAGONGAP DR G11
WALSH LN G10
WAYNE DR E11
WEST WIND G10
WESTCOTT DR E12
WESTMINSTER PL G11
WESTSIDE LN E10
WESTWOOD DR F10
WHIRLWIND TR G12
WHITE OAK D10
WHITE WING WAY F11
WILDWOOD DR G10
WILLIAM AV F10
WILLIAMS ST/**161** G11
WILLOW F12
WILLOWBEND COVE/**162** D11
WINDRIFT WAY G12
WINDSONG TR G12
WINDSOR RD G11
WINDY COVE G10
WINDY PARK CIR G12
WINDY PARK CT G12
WINDYPARK/**163** G12
WINSTED AV E11
WONDER E10
WOOD ROCK DR G10
WOODGREEN DR G10
WOODLIEF TR D12
WOODMILL DR G10
WOODS/**164** D10
WRIGHT CIR/**165** D11
WROXTON WAY/**166** E12
YAUPON TR F12
YORKSHIRE/**167** E12
YUCCA DR G11
ZPHYR LN G12

© DeLorme

PLAINVIEW

SEE PAGE 33

***Numbers** replace street names where map space is limited*

1ST ST J9
2ND ST J7, J9
3RD ST J9
4TH ST J7, J9
5TH ST J7, J9
6TH ST J9, K9
7TH ST J7, J9, K9
8TH ST J7, J9, K9
9TH ST I9, K9
10TH ST I7, I9, K9
11TH ST I9
12TH ST I8, I9
13TH ST I7, I9
14TH ST I8, I9
15TH ST I8
16TH ST I8
17TH ST I8
18TH ST I9
19TH ST I8
20TH ST I8, K8
21ST ST I7, I9
22ND ST I9
23RD ST H9
24TH ST H7, H9
25TH ST H8
26TH ST H8
27TH ST H8
28TH ST H8
29TH ST H8
30TH ST H8
31ST ST H8
32ND H9
32ND ST H8
AESTHETIC J8
AILEEN ST J8
ALPINE DR K9
AMARILLO ST I7
ASH ST I9, J9
AUSTIN ST I9, J9, K9
AYLESWORTH ST H9
BALTIMORE ST J9, K9
BEECH ST I9, J9
BLAKNEY BLVD K9
BORGER ST I7
BRAZIER ST I9
BROADWAY ST I9, J9
BRYAN ST K9
BULLOCK ST I9
BURLINGTON ST I8
CAMPBELL ST I9
CANYON ST J7
CARVER ST I9
CASTRO ST H7
CEDAR ST I9
COLLEGE AV H9
COLUMBIA ST J9
COMANCHE ST H8
CRESTWAY ST K9
CRESTWAY ST/**100** K9
DALLAS ST I7, J7
DATE RD H9
DATE ST I9, J9, K9
DENVER ST I9
EDGEMERE DR I7
EL PASO ST I9
ELM ST I9
ENNIS ST H7, I7
FAULKNER AV H9
FENCE OF TREES RD H9
FIR ST I9
FISHER AV H9
FLORAL J8
FLOYDADA J7
FLOYDADA ST I7
FORT WORTH AND DENVER RAILWAY/**101** I9
FRESNO ST H8, I9
GALVESTON ST H8, J8
GARLAND J7
GARLAND ST I7
GIVENS ST I9
GLADNEY AV H9
GRANDVIEW DR J7
GROVE ST I9
HENRY ST I9
HICKORY ST J9
HIGHLAND RD H7
HOLIDAY DR I7
HOLLIDAY H7, J7
HOUSTON ST I8
HOWARD ST H9
HOYLE AV H9
INDEPENDENCE ST H8
IRENE ST J8
ITASCA J7
ITASCA RD I7
IVY ST J9
JEFFERSON DR I7
JOLIET ST J8
JUANITA ST J8
JUNIPER ST J9
KERMIT DR H7
KIRCHWOOD DR J7
KIRCHWOOD PL J7
KIRCHWOOD RD J7
KOKOMO ST I8
LEXINGTON ST H8
LINDBERG ST K9
LOMETA H7
LOMETA DR J7
MAGAN H7
MANN ST H9
MESA DR H7
MILWAUKEE ST I8
NASSAU ST I8
NAUASOTA H7
NAVAJO TR H8
NORMA ST J8
NORTHWEST H7
NORTHWEST DR H7
OAK ST K9
OAKLAND ST I8
OWEN RD H7
PARKWAY DR J8
PECOS H7
PORTLAND ST I8
PURCELL DR K9
QUINCY ST H8, J8
RALEIGH ST I8
RED OAK LN H7
RIDGEWAY DR H7
ROCHELL ST H8
ROSELAWN ST K9
SABINE ST H8
SAINT LOUIS ST K9
SIDES DR H7
SIDES ST H7
SMITH ST H9
SMYTH ST I8
STEVENS ST H7
THOMAS BLVD J8
THUNDERBIRD DR/**102** H8
TRAVIS ST I8
TRINITY ST H8
UPCHURCH AV H9
UTICA ST I8
VERNON ST I8
VILLA DR H7
WAYLAND ST I8
WILSON ST H9
XENIA ST I8
YONKERS ST I7
ZEPHYR ST I7

© DeLorme

1" = 0.8 mi (1.3 km)

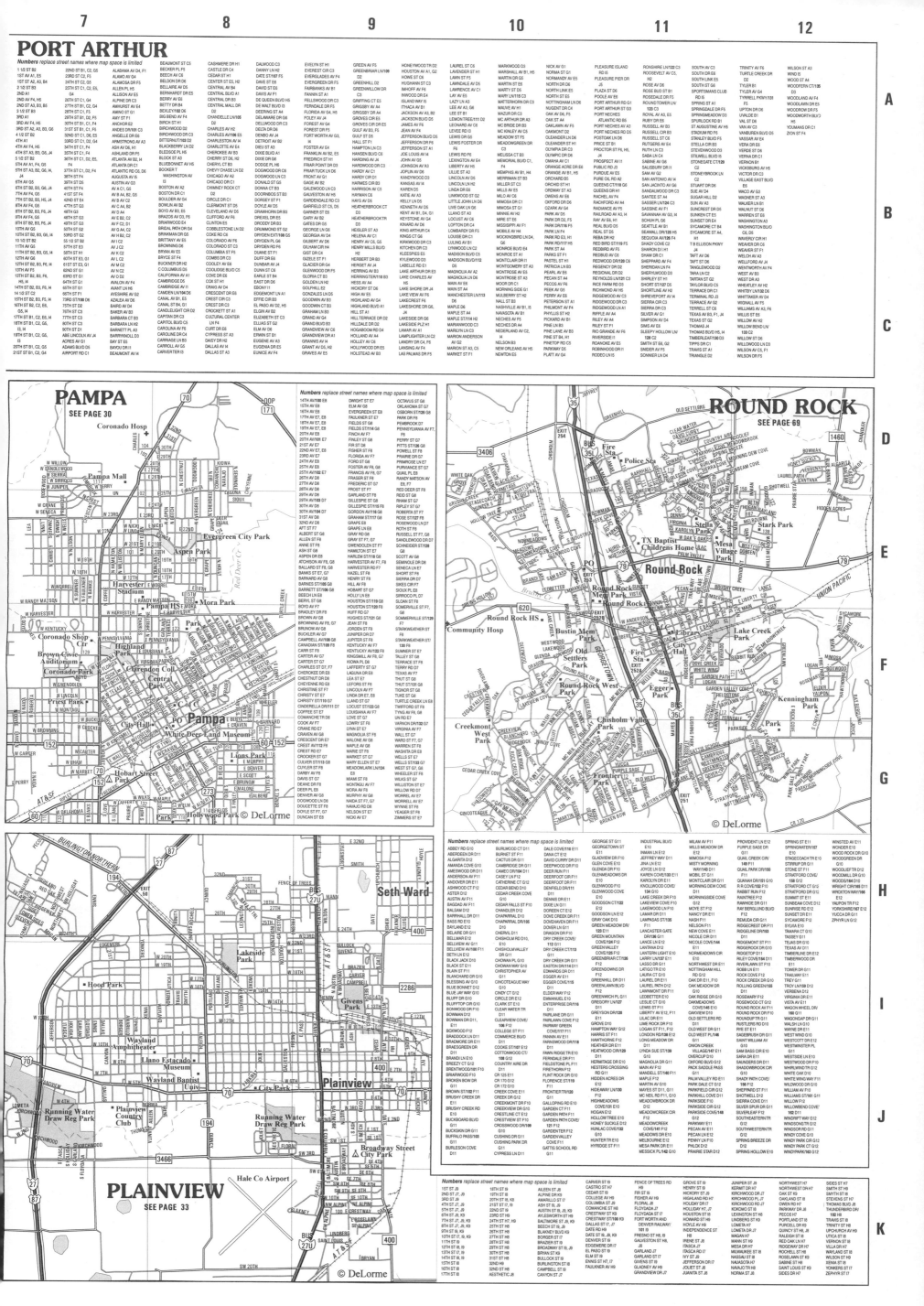

Continue on Page 158

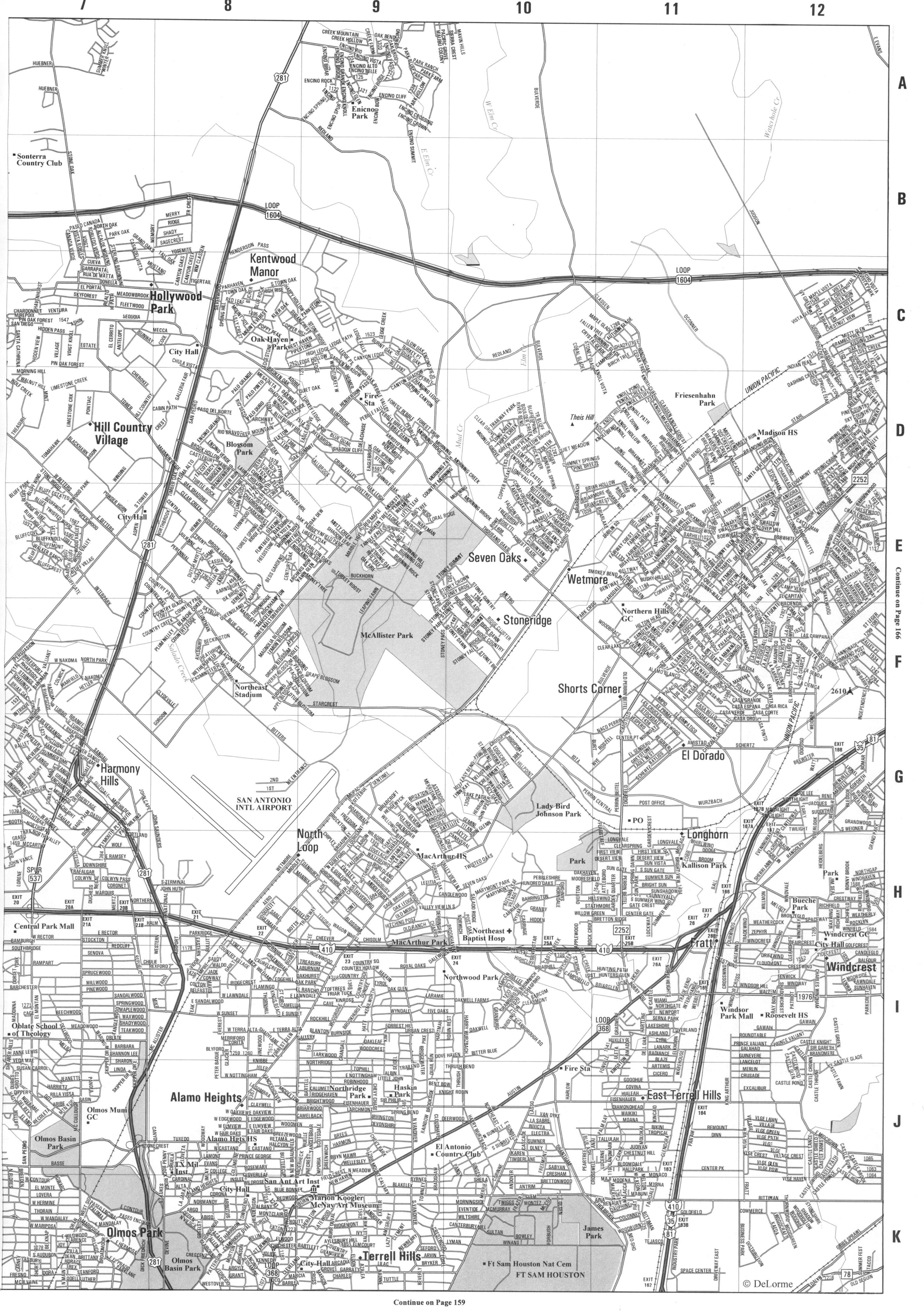

Continue on Page 166

Continue on Page 159

1" = 0.8 mi (1.3 km)

Continue on Page 156

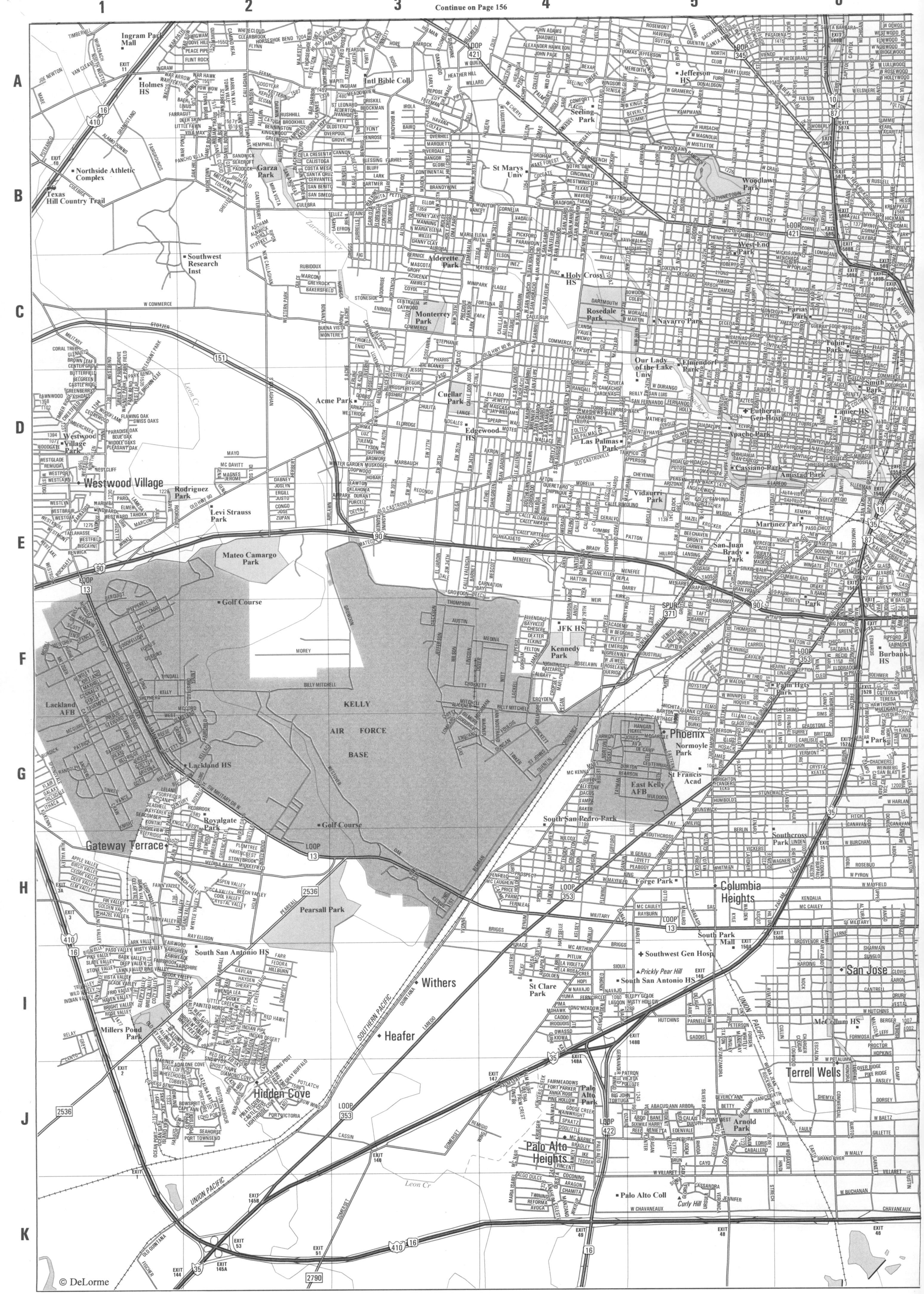

Continue on Page 157

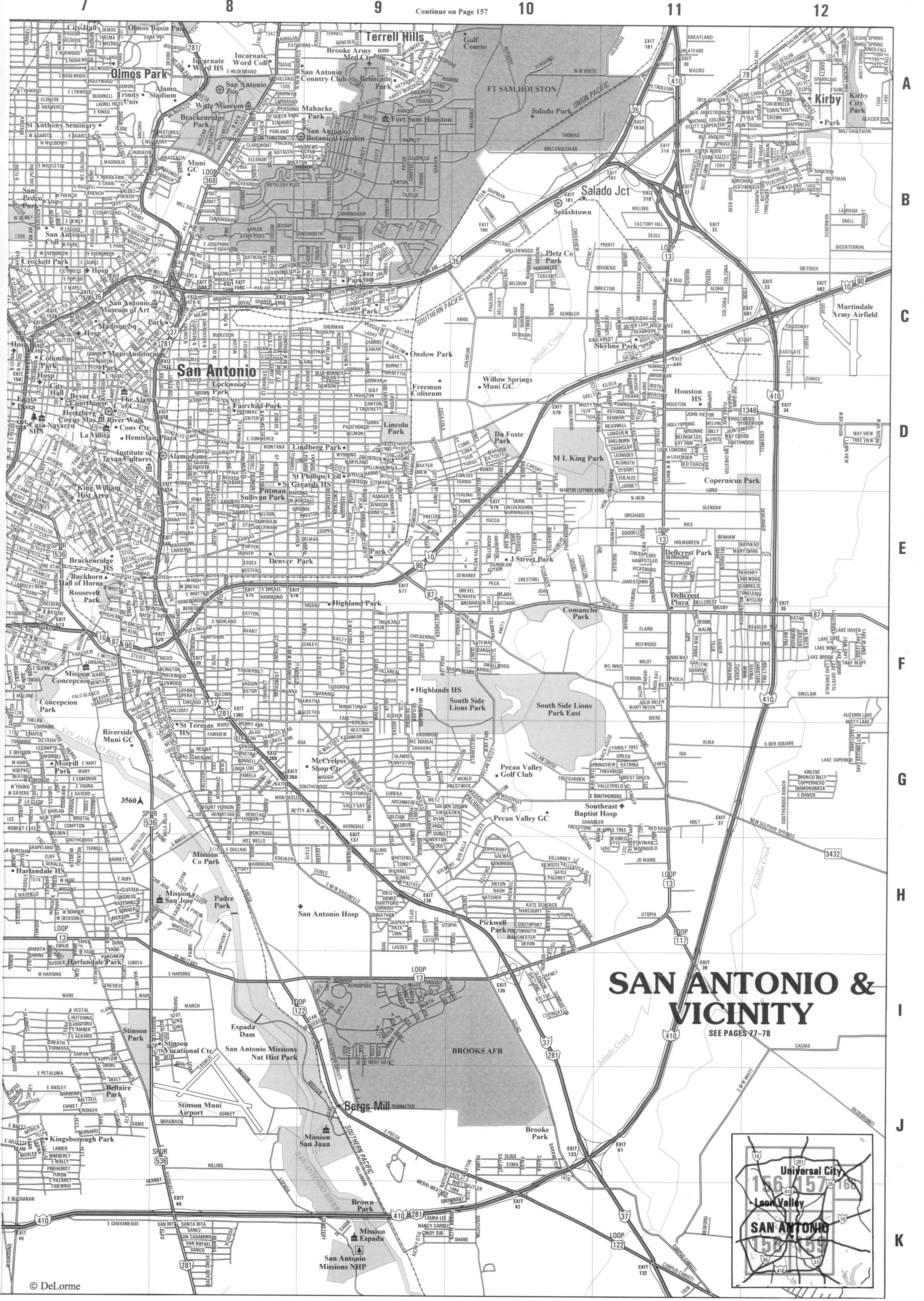

1" = 0.8 mi (1.3 km)

SAN ANTONIO & VICINITY INDEX

***Numbers** replace street names where map space is limited; municipality abbreviations appear in parentheses.*

AH	Alamo Heights	HC	Hill Country Village	KI	Kirby	OP	Olmos Park	TH	Terrell Hills
BH	Balcones Heights	HP	Hollywood Park	LA	Lackland Air Force Base	SA	San Antonio	WC	Windcrest
CH	Castle Hills			LV	Leon Valley	SP	Shavano Park		

1ST (SA) 158 H3; 159 I9
1ST AV (SA) 157 G8
2ND (SA) 158 H3
2ND AV (SA) 157 G8
3RD ST (SA) 159 D7
4TH ST (SA) 159 D7, I9
5TH (SA) 158 G5; 159 I9
6TH (SA) 158 G5; 159 I9
6TH ST/**1000** (SA) 159 C7
7TH (SA) 158 H3; 159 B9
8TH (SA) 158 H3; 159 I9, C7
9TH (SA) 159 B9, I9
9TH ST (SA) 159 C7
11TH (SA) 159 I9
12TH ST (SA) 159 C8, I9
13TH ST (SA) 159 B9, I9
14TH ST (SA) 159 I9
15TH ST (SA) 159 B9, I9
16TH ST (SA) 159 I9
17TH ST (SA) 159 B9, I9
18TH ST (SA) 158 D5, I9
19TH ST (SA) 158 C5, E5
20TH ST (SA) 158 C5
21ST ST (SA) 158 C5, F5
22ND ST (SA) 158 C5
23RD ST (SA) 158 C5
24TH ST (SA) 158 C5, D5
25TH ST (SA) 158 C5, D5

ANNAPOLIS ST (SA) 156 G4
ANNE LEWIS DR (SA) 157 I7
ANNIE AV (OP) 159 A7
ANSLEY BLVD (SA) 158 J6; 159 J7
ANTELOPE DR (HP) 157 C7
ANTIOCH DR (SA) 156 J5
ANTLER DR (CH) 156 I6
ANTOINETTE DR/**1008** (SA) 159 G8
ANTON DR (SA) 159 H10
ANTRIM DR (SA) 157 K10
ANZA DR (SA) 159 H9
APACHE ST (SA) 158 E6
APOLLO ST (SA) 159 I8
APPERSON ST (SA) 158 D5
APPLE BLOSSOM (SA) 157 F8
APPLE CREEK DR (SA) 159 G11
APPLE GREEN (SA) 156 I2
APPLE TREE DR (SA) 159 G11
APPLE TREE WOODS (SA) 156 D4
APPLE VALLEY DR (SA) 158 H1
APPLEGATE DR (SA) 156 G4

BARRETT AV (SA) 159 H7
BARRETT PL (SA) 158 F5
BARRINGTON PL (SA) 157 H10
BARRON DR (SA) 156 H1
BARRY HILL/**1022** (SA) 156 J1
BART STARR (SA) 156 H1
BARTELL DR (SA) 157 J9
BARTHOLOMEW ST (SA) 158 H4
BARTLETT COCKE (SA) 156 D1
BARTLETT PL (TH) 157 K9
BARTMER ST (SA) 158 B3
BARTON CT (SA) 158 G5
BASCUM BLVD (SA) 159 J7
BASILWOOD DR (SA) 156 J6
BASIN DR (SA) 157 J7
BASSE RD (SA) 156 J6; 157 J7
BASSETT (SA) 156 D5
BASSWOOD DR (SA) 156 I5
BASTROP ST (SA) 158 F6
BAUER ST (SA) 158 G6
BAUM RD (SA) 157 H12
BAUMAN (KI) 159 A12
BAXTER AV (SA) 159 D9

BLUE BONNET BLVD (AH) 157 K8
BLUE BONNET ST (SA) 159 D9
BLUE CREEK DR (SA) 156 D6
BLUE CREST LN (SA) 157 F8
BLUE HERON (SA) 157 E12
BLUE JAY DR (KI) 159 B12
BLUE MAX (SA) 156 D5
BLUE OAK (SA) 158 D1
BLUE QUAIL (SA) 157 D9
BLUE RIDGE ST (SA) 158 B4
BLUE ROCK DR (SA) 157 C8
BLUE SMOKE (SA) 156 E5
BLUE TOP LN (SA) 157 E12
BLUE WING RD/**1029** (SA) 159 K11
BLUEBERRY HILL (SA) 157 D9
BLUEBIRD LN (LV) 156 I1
BLUEFIELD DR (SA) 156 I5
BLUEGRASS LN/**1030** (WC) 157 I12
BLUEHILL RD (SA) 156 J4
BLUEMEL RD (SA) 156 H3
BLUET LN (CH) 156 I6
BLUEWOOD DR/**1031** (SA)

BRIARMEADOW (SA) 157 E11
BRIARMIST (SA) 157 D11
BRIARMONT/**1040** (SA) 157 D11
BRIARMORE (SA) 157 E10
BRIARPATH DR (SA) 156 F2
BRIARPINE (SA) 157 D11
BRIARPOINT (SA) 157 D11
BRIARSTONE (SA) 157 D11
BRIARWAY DR (SA) 157 G10
BRIARWICK DR/**1041** (SA) 157 E11
BRIARWOOD DR (SA) 157 J9
BRICE AV (SA) 159 E10
BRICK HOUSE DR (SA) 159 G11
BRIDEMAN ST (SA) 159 D11
BRIDGEWATER DR (SA) 157 I9
BRIDGEWOOD (SA) 157 E11
BRIDLE PATH (LV) 156 I1
BRIDLINGTON CT (SA) 157 I10
BRIGGS AV (SA) 158 H4
BRIGGS RD (SA) 158 I4
BRIGHT SUN LN (SA) 157 H11

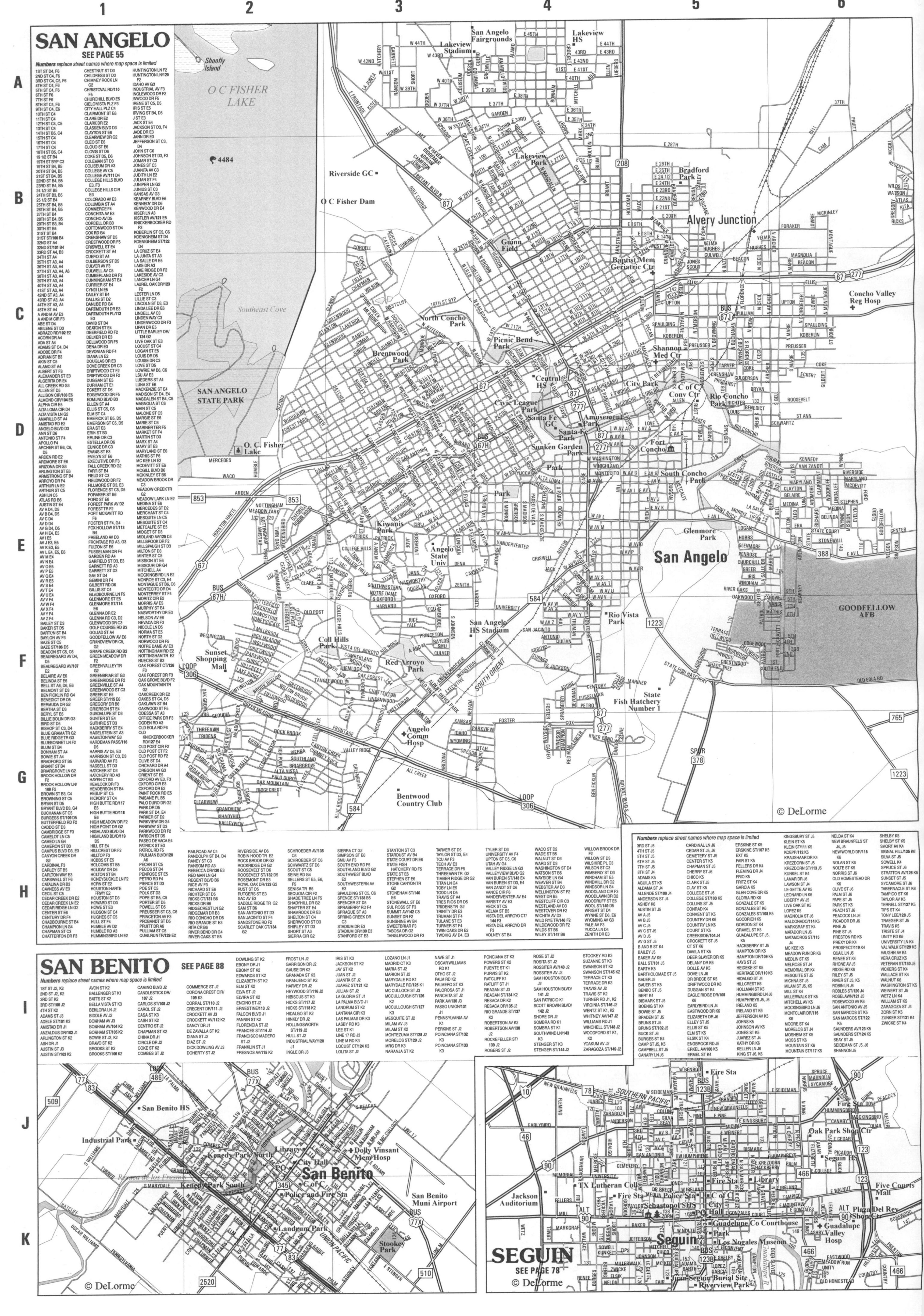

SAN ANGELO
SEE PAGE 55
Numbers replace street names where map space is limited
O C FISHER LAKE
Shoofly Island
Southeast Cove
SAN ANGELO STATE PARK
O. C. Fisher Lake
O C Fisher Dam
Riverside GC
San Angelo Fairgrounds
Lakeview Stadium
Lakeview HS
Lakeview Park
Bradford Park
Alvery Junction
Guinn Field
Baptist Mem Geriatric Ctr
Concho Valley Reg Hosp
North Concho Park
Picnic Bend Park
Brentwood Park
Shannon Med Ctr
Central HS
City Park
C of C Conv Ctr
Rio Concho Park
Civic League Park
Santa Fe GC
Santa Fe Park
Amusement Park
Sunken Garden Park
Fort Concho
South Concho Park
Kiwanis Park
Angelo State Univ
Glenmore Park
San Angelo
GOODFELLOW AFB
San Angelo HS Stadium
Rio Vista Park
Coll Hills Park
Sunset Shopping Mall
Red Arroyo Park
State Fish Hatchery Number 1
Angelo Comm Hosp
Bentwood Country Club
© DeLorme
SAN BENITO
SEE PAGE 88
Numbers replace street names where map space is limited
San Benito HS
Industrial Park
Kenedy Park North
Library
City Hall
PO
San Benito
Dolly Vinsant Mem Hosp
Kenedy Park South
C of C
Police and Fire Sta
San Benito Muni Airport
Landrum Park
Stookey Park
© DeLorme
SEGUIN
SEE PAGE 78
Fire Sta
Oak Park Shop Ctr
Seguin HS
TX Lutheran Coll
Library
Five Courts Mall
Jackson Auditorium
Sebastopol SHS
City Hall
Plaza Del Rey Shop Ctr
Guadalupe Co Courthouse
Guadalupe Valley Hosp
Seguin
Los Nogales Museum
Juan Seguin Burial Site
Riverview Park
© DeLorme

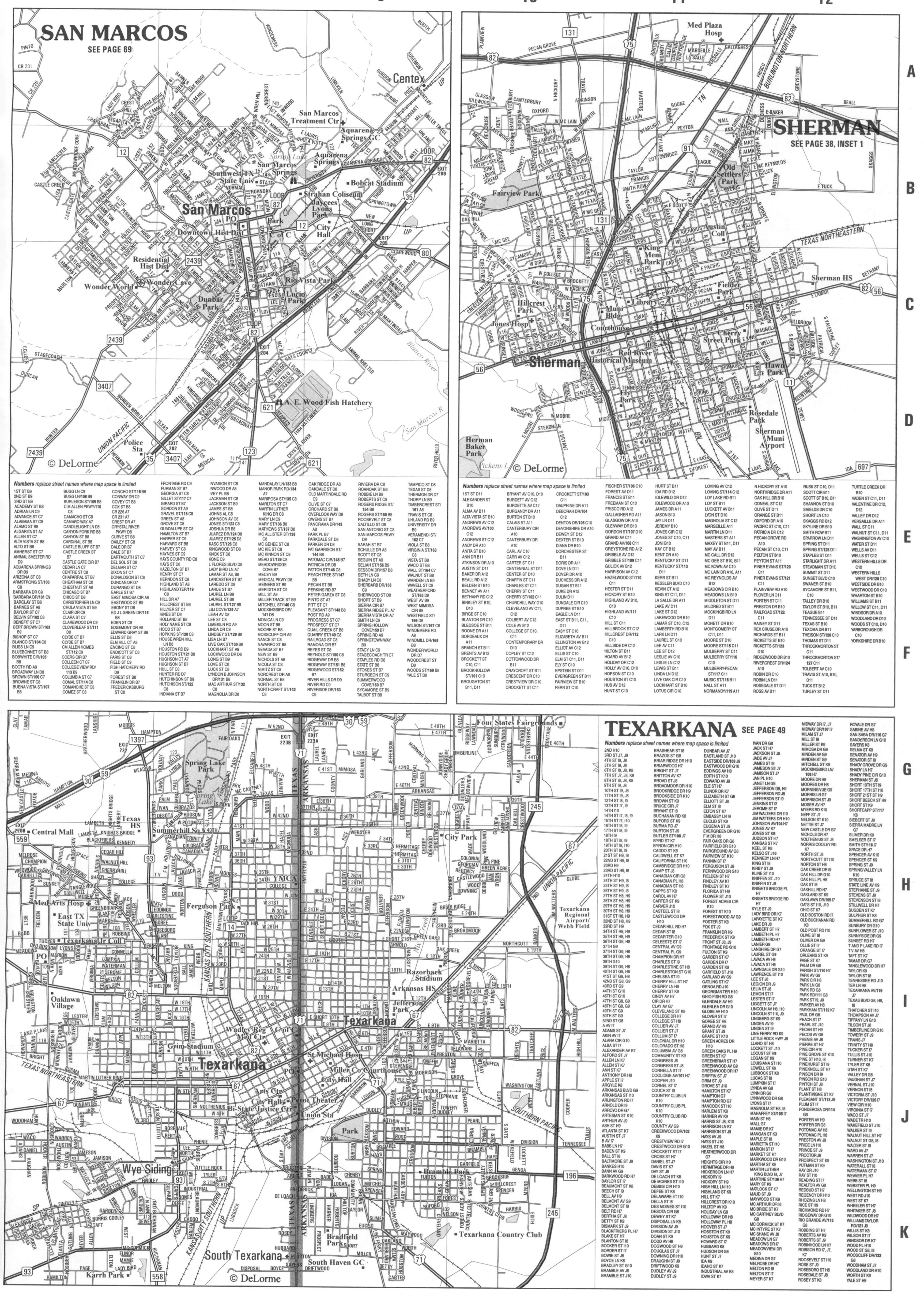

7
8
9
10
11
12
A
B
C
D
E
F
G
H
I
J
K
SAN MARCOS
SEE PAGE 69
San Marcos
Southwest TX State Univ
Aquarena Springs GC
Bobcat Stadium
Strahan Coliseum
Downtown Hist Dist
Residential Hist Dist
Wonder World
Wonder Cave
Dunbar Park
Rio Vista Park
Lucio Park
City Hall
A. E. Wood Fish Hatchery
Police Sta
Centex
San Marcos Treatment Ctr
© DeLorme
Numbers replace street names where map space is limited
SHERMAN
SEE PAGE 38, INSET 1
Sherman
Med Plaza Hosp
Old Settlers Park
Fairview Park
Austin Coll
King Mem Park
Sherman HS
Fielder Park
Hillcrest Park
Jones Hosp
Muni Bldg
Library
Courthouse
Cherry Street Park
Red River Historical Museum
Hawn Park
Ely Park
Rosedale Park
Sherman Muni Airport
Herman Baker Park
© DeLorme
Numbers replace street names where map space is limited
TEXARKANA
SEE PAGE 49
Numbers replace street names where map space is limited
Texarkana
Four States Fairgrounds
Spring Lake Park
Central Mall
Texas HS
Summerhill Sq
City Park
YMCA
Ferguson Park
Med Arts Hosp
East TX State Univ
Texarkana Jr Coll
Texarkana Regional Airport/ Webb Field
Razorback Stadium
Arkansas HS
Jefferson Park
Oaklawn Village
Wadley Reg Med Ctr
Grim Stadium
St Michael Hosp
Miller Co Courthouse
City Hall
Arts Ctr
Perot Theater
Bi-State Justice Ctr
Union Sta
Wye Siding
Bramble Park
Texarkana Country Club
Bradfield Park
South Texarkana
South Haven GC
Karrh Park
© DeLorme

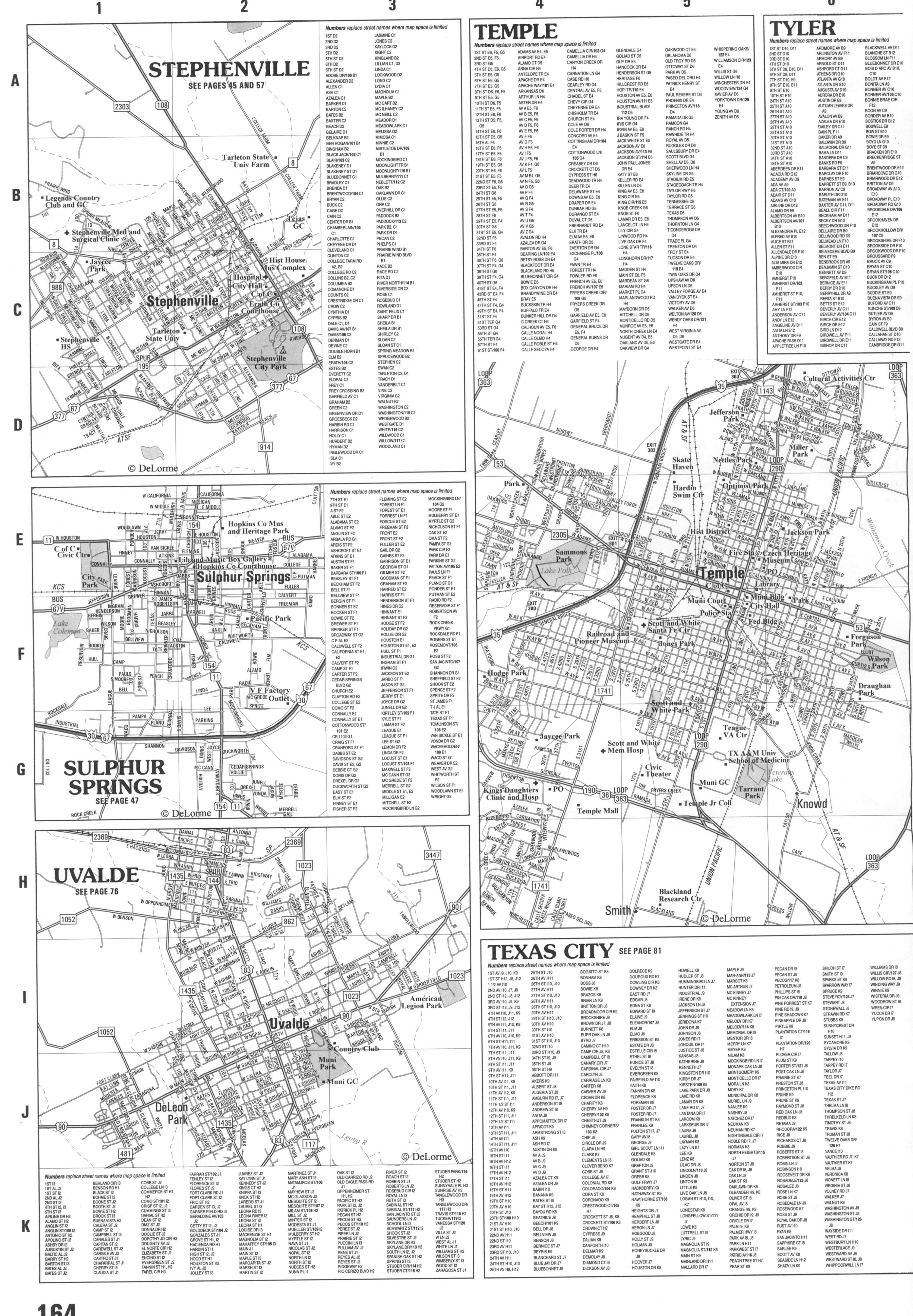
1
2
3
4
5
6
A
B
C
D
E
F
G
H
I
J
K
STEPHENVILLE
SEE PAGES 45 AND 57
Numbers replace street names where map space is limited
Stephenville
Tarleton State Univ Farm
Legends Country Club and GC
Stephenville Med and Surgical Clinic
Jaycee Park
Hist House/Mus Complex
Hospital
City Hall
Co Ct
Erath Co Courthouse
Tarleton State Univ
Stephenville HS
Stephenville City Park
Tejas GC
© DeLorme
TEMPLE
Numbers replace street names where map space is limited
TYLER
Numbers replace street names where map space is limited
SULPHUR SPRINGS
SEE PAGE 47
Sulphur Springs
Hopkins Co Mus and Heritage Park
C of C Civic Ctr
Lib and Music Box Gallery
Hopkins Co Courthouse
City Park
Lake Coleman
Pacific Park
V F Factory Outlet
© DeLorme
Numbers replace street names where map space is limited
Temple
Cultural Activities Ctr
Jefferson Park
Miller Park
Skate Haven
Nettles Park
Hardin Swim Ctr
Optimist Park
Jackson Park
Hist District
Sammons Park
Lake Polk
Fire Sta
Czech Heritage Museum
PO
Library
Muni Court
Police Sta
Muni Bldg
City Hall
Park
Fed Bldg
Scott and White Santa Fe Ctr
Railroad and Pioneer Museum
Jones Park
Ferguson Park
Wilson Park
Draughan Park
Hodge Park
Scott and White Park
Jaycee Park
Teague VA Ctr
Scott and White Mem Hosp
TX A&M Univ School of Medicine
Civic Theater
Kings Daughters Clinic and Hosp
PO
Muni GC
Tarrant Park
Temple Mall
Temple Jr Coll
Knowd
Blackland Research Ctr
Smith
© DeLorme
UVALDE
SEE PAGE 76
Uvalde
American Legion Park
Country Club
Muni Park
Muni GC
DeLeon Park
© DeLorme
Numbers replace street names where map space is limited
TEXAS CITY
SEE PAGE 81
Numbers replace street names where map space is limited

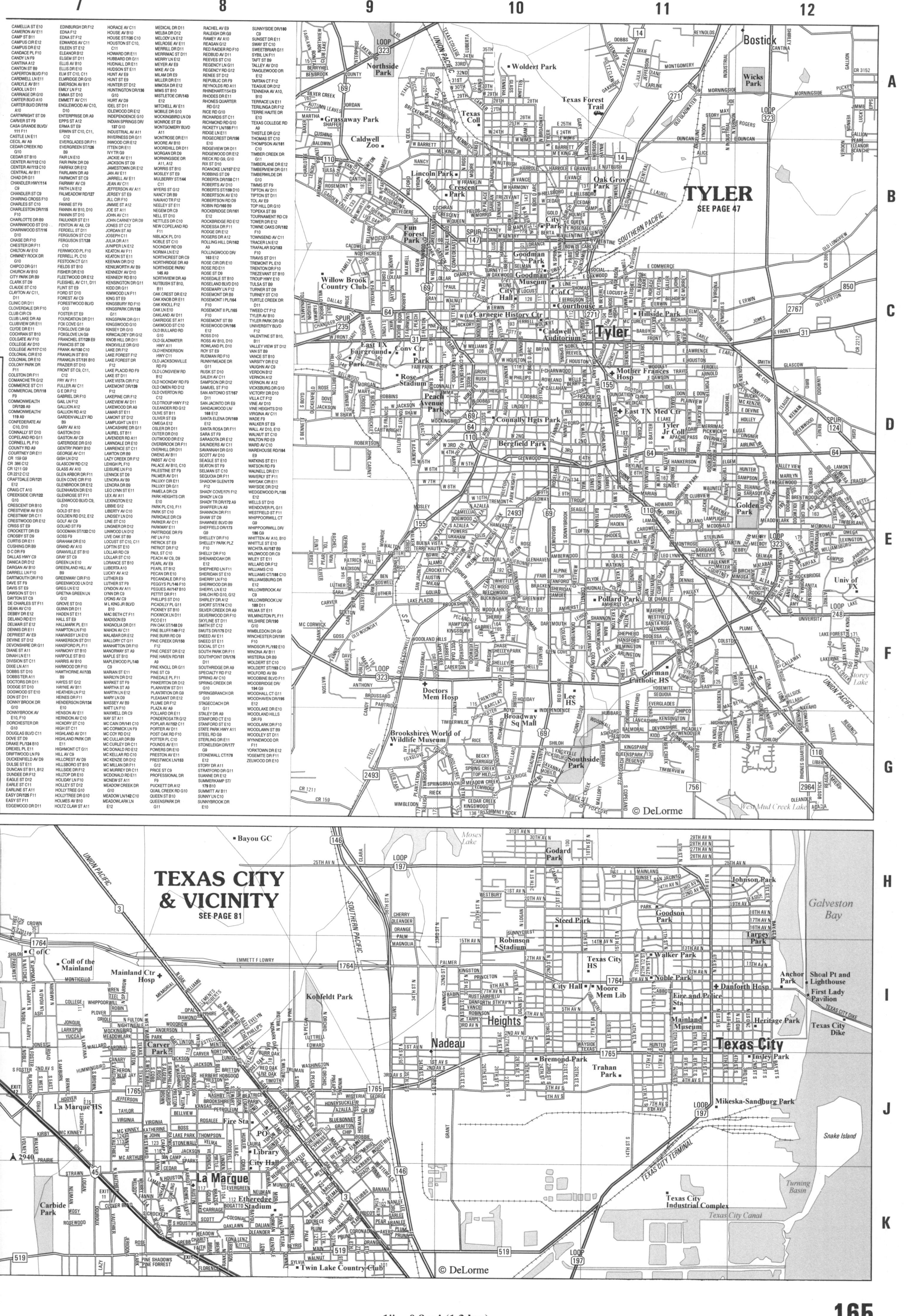
7
8
9
10
11
12
A
B
C
D
E
F
G
H
I
J
K
TYLER
SEE PAGE 47
Tyler
Bostick
Northside Park
Woldert Park
Wicks Park
Texas Forest Trail
Grassaway Park
Texas Coll
Caldwell Zoo
Lincoln Park
Crescent Park
Oak Grove Park
Fun Forest Park
Gold City Park
Goodman Park
Goodman Museum
Willow Brook Country Club
City Hall
CofC
Courthouse
Carnegie History Ctr
Caldwell Auditorium
Hillside Park
East TX Fairground
Conv Ctr
Park
Rose Stadium
Mother Frances Hosp
Peach Avenue Park
Connally Hgts Park
East TX Med Ctr
Tyler Jr Coll
Bergfield Park
Golden Park
Univ of TX
Pollard Park
Gorman Catholic HS
Doctors Mem Hosp
Lee HS
Broadway Sq Mall
Brookshires World of Wildlife Museum
Southside Park
Storey Lake
West Mud Creek Lake
UNION PACIFIC
SOUTHERN PACIFIC
© DeLorme
TEXAS CITY & VICINITY
SEE PAGE 81
Bayou GC
Moses Lake
Godard Park
Johnson Park
Galveston Bay
Goodson Park
Steed Park
Tarpey Park
Robinson Stadium
Texas City HS
Walker Park
C of C
Coll of the Mainland
Mainland Ctr Hosp
Noble Park
Danforth Hosp
Anchor Park
Shoal Pt and Lighthouse
First Lady Pavilion
Kohfeldt Park
City Hall
Moore Mem Lib
Fire and Police Sta
Heights
Mainland Museum
Heritage Park
Texas City Dike
Carver Park
Nadeau
Texas City
Insley Park
Bremond Park
Trahan Park
La Marque HS
Mikeska-Sandburg Park
Fire Sta
PO
Library
City Hall
Snake Island
La Marque
Etheredge Stadium
Carbide Park
Turning Basin
Texas City Industrial Complex
Texas City Canal
TEXAS CITY TERMINAL
Twin Lake Country Club
© DeLorme

1" = 0.8 mi (1.3 km)

UNIVERSAL CITY

SEE PAGE 78

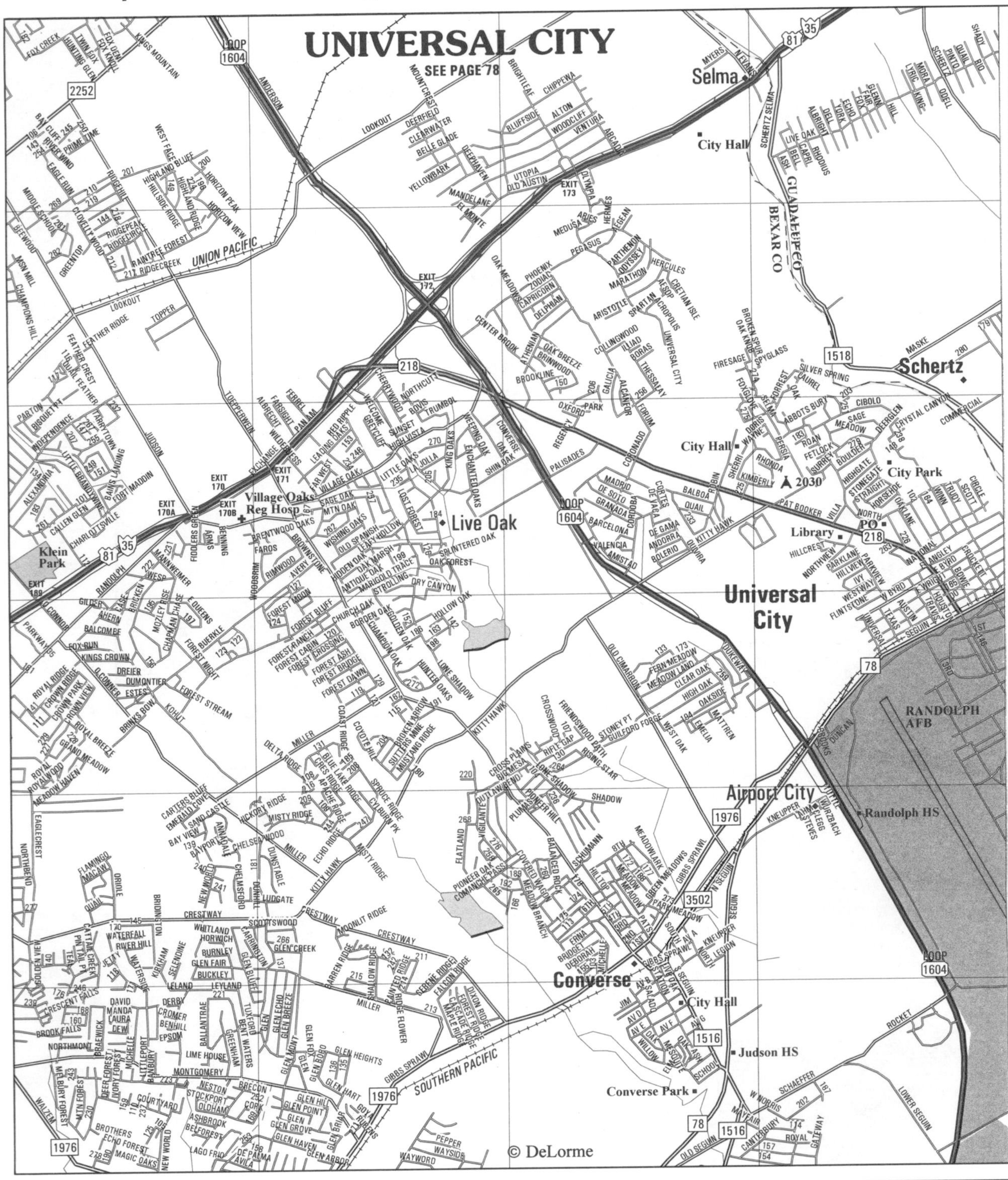

Continue on Page 157

© DeLorme

Numbers replace street names where map space is limited

1ST D4
1ST ST E3
2ND ST E3
3RD D4
3RD ST E3
4TH ST E3
5TH ST E3
6TH ST E3
8TH ST E3
ABBOTSBURY C4
ACROPOLIS DR B3
AEGEAN WAY B3
AESOP LN B3
AHERN DR D1
ALBRECHT LN C2
ALBRIGHT LN A4
ALCANFOR B3
ALEXANDRIA DR C1
ALTON BLVD A3
AMISTAD BLVD C3
ANDERSON ST A2
ANDORRA C3
ANNADALE E1
ANTIQUE OAK C2
APACHE RIDGE E2
ARCADIA DR A3
ARIES B3
ARISTOTLE B3
ARMS WAY C1
ASH DR F3
ASH LN A4
ASHBROOK F1
ATHENIAN B3
AUSTIN DR D4
AV A E3
AV B F3
AV D F3
AV F F3
AV G F3
AVERY C2
AVIATION BLVD/100 D4
AVILA F1
BAINS LANDING C1
BALANCED ROCK E3
BALBOA DR C3
BALCOMBE D1
BALLANTRAE F1
BANBURY F1
BARCELONA DR C3
BARREN RIDGE DR E2
BARTON MILL/101 C1
BAY CLIFF DR A1
BAY VIEW E1
BAYPORT E1
BEECHWOOD AV/102 C4
BEEWOOD DR B1
BELFOREST F1
BELL LN A4
BELLE GLADE BLVD A2
BENHILL F1
BENNING DR C1
BENT WATERS F1
BIG MESA D3
BISQUET PT C1
BLUE LAKE RIDGE RD D2
BLUFFSIDE BLVD A3
BOLERIO C3
BORAS B3
BORDEN OAK D2
BOULDER DR C4
BOVIS CT C2
BOWIE ST C4
BRAEWICK DR F1
BRECON F1
BRENDA DR/103 E3
BRENTWOOD OAKS C1
BRICKEN CIR C1
BRIDGET DR E3
BRIDINGTON E1
BRIGHTLEAF DR A3
BRINKS BOW D1
BRINWOOD B3
BROKEN ARROW RD D2
BROKEN SPUR DR B4
BROOK FALLS DR F1
BROOKLINE B3
BROOKS AV D4
BROTHERS LN F1
BROWNSTONE C2
BUCKLEY E1
BUERKLE RD D1
BURNLEY E1
BYRD BLVD C4, D4
CALLEN GLEN C1
CANTERBURY LN F3
CAPRI LN A4
CAPRICORN B3
CARRINGTON E1
CARTERS BLUFF E1
CASCADE RIDGE DR F2
CASE BLVD D1
CATTAIL CREEK E1
CATTLE BEND/104 D3
CENTER BROOK B3
CHAMPION OAK D2
CHAMPIONS HILL B1
CHAPEL FOREST/105 F1
CHAPMAN CHASE D1
CHARLOTTESVILLE C1
CHELMSFORD E1
CHELSEAWOOD E1
CHERRYWOOD LN C2
CHIMNEY NEST/106 A1
CHIPPEWA BLVD A3
CHURCH OAK D2
CHURCHWOOD/107 D3
CIBOLO TR C4
CIRCLE DR C4
CLEAR OAK D3
CLEARWATER BLVD A2
CLEGG ST E4
CLIPPER RIDGE RD/108 D2
CLOVELLY WOOD B1
COAST RIDGE RD D2
COLLINGWOOD B3
COMANCHE PASS TR E2
COMANCHE RIDGE/109 E2
COMMERCIAL PL C4
CONVERSE RD C3
COOL FOREST/110 F1
CORDOBA DR C3
CORK F1
CORONADO BLVD C3
CORTES C3
COURTYARD F1
COVERED WAGON E3
COYOTE HILL RD D2
CRESCENT FALLS F1
CRESCENT RIDGE RD D2
CRESTWAY E1
CRESTWAY DR E2
CRESTWAY RD E2
CRETIAN ISLE B3
CROCKETT DR C4
CROMER F1
CROSS PLAINS D3
CROSSWOOD D3
CROWN CT F4
CROWN PARK DR D1
CROWN RIDGE D1
CROWN VIEW D1
CROWN WAY DR/111 D1
CROWNPOINT DR/112 C1
CRYSTAL CANYON C4
CYLBURN PK E2
DANA DR/113 E3
DAVID F1
DE GAMA C3
DE PALMA F1
DE SOTO DR C3
DE VACA DR C3
DEBORAH DR E3
DEEPHAVEN DR A2
DEER FOREST F1
DEERFIELD BLVD A2
DEERGLEN C4
DELL LN A4
DELPHIAN B3
DELTA RIDGE DR D2
DERBY F1
DEW DR F1
DIXON RIDGE DR F2
DORIS DR C4
DOWNING ST/114 F4
DREIER D1
DRY CANYON TR C2
DUKEWAY ST D3
DUMONTIER D1
DUNCAN PL D4
DUNHILL E1
DUNSTABLE E2
EAGLE RUN DR A1
EAGLECREST BLVD E1
ECHO FOREST F1
ECHO LN A4
ECHO RIDGE E2
EL MONTE BLVD B2
ELM DR F3
EMELIA ST D3
EMERALD COVE E1
ENCHANTED OAKS C2
EPSOM F1
ERNA E3
ESTES DR D1
EVANS RD A3
EXCHANGE AV C2
FAIR LN A4
FALCON RIDGE DR E2
FALLEN PINE RD/115 D2
FAR WEST C2
FAROS CT C2
FARSIGHT LN C2
FEATHER CREST B1
FEATHER NEST/116 B1
FEATHER POINT RD/117 B1
FEATHER RIDGE DR B1
FERN MEADOW D3
FERREL B2
FETLOCK C4
FIDDLERS GREEN C1
FIRESAGE B3
FISHER COVE/118 E1
FLAMINGO E1
FLATLAND TR E2
FLINTSTONE DR D4
FOREST ASH RD D2
FOREST BLUFF RD D2
FOREST BOW RD/119 D2
FOREST BRIDGE RD D2
FOREST CABIN D2
FOREST CABIN RD/120 D2
FOREST CORNER RD/121 D2
FOREST CROSSING D2
FOREST DAWN RD D2
FOREST ECHO RD/122 D1
FOREST EDGE RD/123 D1
FOREST FERN RD/124 D2
FOREST FLAME/125 F1
FOREST MOON RD D2
FOREST NIGHT RD D1
FOREST NOOK/126 C2
FOREST RAIN DR/127 C2
FOREST RANCH D2
FOREST RANCH RD/128 D2
FOREST RIDGE DR F2
FOREST STREAM RD D1
FOREST SUMMIT RD/129 D2
FORREST TRAIL CIR C4
FORT MADDIN DR C1
FORT WAYNE/130 D3
FORTUNE RIDGE DR/131 D2
FORUM RD C3
FOX CREEK A1
FOX DEN A1
FOX KNOLL A1
FOX LN A4
FOX RUN D1
FOXGLOVE C4
FRIENDSWOOD PATH D3
GALICIA B3
GALLANT RIDGE DR/132 E2
GARDEN MEADOW/133 D3
GATEWAY DR F4
GEORGETOWN DR/134 C1
GIBBS SPRAWL RD E3, F2
GILDER BLVD D1
GLEN ARBOR DR F2
GLEN BLUFF E1
GLEN BORO F2
GLEN BREEZE F2
GLEN BRIAR DR F2
GLEN CREEK E2
GLEN CT F2
GLEN ECHO F2
GLEN FAIR E1
GLEN FOX F2
GLEN GROVE DR F2
GLEN HART F2
GLEN HAVEN ST F2
GLEN HEIGHTS F2
GLEN HILL DR F2
GLEN LARK/135 F2
GLEN MONT DR F2
GLEN POINT DR F2
GLEN POST/136 F2
GLEN SHADOW/137 E2
GLENTER F2
GLEN TRAIL DR F2
GLENN LN A4
GOLDEN GATE/139 E1
GOLDEN OAK TR D2
GOLDEN PT/140 E1
GOLDENVIEW E1
GOYA F2
GRANADA DR C3
GRAND MEADOW D1
GRAND POINT DR/141 D1
GRASS HOLLOW/142 D2
GRAY RIDGE DR/143 A1
GREEN CIR/144 B1
GREEN MEADOWS E3
GREENHAM F1
GREENTOP B1
GREYCLIFF C2
GUILFORD FORGE D3
GULF STREAM/145 E1
HARMON/146 D4
HENDERSON CAMP/147 C1
HERCULES B3
HERMES B3
HICKORY RIDGE RD E2
HIDDEN GROVE/148 C4
HIDDEN OAK TR C2
HIGH OAK D3
HIGH VISTA C2
HIGHGATE RD C4
HIGHLAND BLUFF DR A1
HIGHLAND PEAK DR/149 A1
HIGHLAND RIDGE DR A1
HIGHLANDVIEW/150 B3
HILL LN A4
HILLCREST DR C4
HILLSIDE RIDGE DR B1
HILLTOP AV E3
HILLVIEW DR C4
HOLLOW OAK D2
HOPES FERRY CROSSING/151 C1
HORIZON PEAK DR A1
HORIZON VIEW A1
HORSEHOE TR C4
HORWICH E1
HOUSTON ST D4
HUNTER OAKS D2
HUNTING GLEN A1
ILLIAD B3
INDEPENDENCE AV C1
IVORY FOREST DR F1
IVORY OAK/152 D2
IVY LN C4
JETTY E1
JIM WAY DR F3
JONQUILL/153 C2
JUDSON RD C1
KERRYBROOK DR/154 F4
KIMBERLY DR C3
KIMBERLY DR/155 E3
KING A4
KING OAKS DR C2
KINGS CROWN D1
KINGS CROWN/156 D1
KINGS MOUNTAIN A1
KINGSMAN/157 F4
KIRKHAM E1
KITTY HAWK RD C3, D2, E2
KNEUPPER RD E3, E4
KOHUT BLVD D1
LA JOLLA DR C2
LAGO FRIO F1
LAGUNA NORTE/158 F1
LAHM AV E4
LAKE FOREST DR/159 F1
LAKEWOOD PK/160 F1
LANDMARK 35/161 D1
LANGLEY BLVD C4
LAURA DR F1
LAUREL LN B4
LAUREL PINE RD/162 D2
LAZY FOREST/163 D2
LEADING OAKS C2
LEAFY HOLLOW C2
LEGION E3
LELAND DR F1
LEMONWOOD DR/164 C4
LEYLAND F1
LIME HOUSE F1
LINDBERGH BLVD/165 C4
LITTLE BRANDYWINE C1
LITTLE OAKS C2
LITTLEPORT F1
LIVE OAK BLVD A4
LIVE OAK ST E3
LONE SHADOW TR D2, D3
LONESOME VALLEY RD/166 E3
LOOKOUT RD A2, B1
LOST FOREST DR C2
LOWER SEGUIN RD F4
LUCKY OAKS/167 C2
LUDGATE E2
LYRIC A4
MACAW E1
MADRID DR C3
MAGIC OAKS F1
MALLARD PT/168 F1
MALLOW/169 F1
MANDA DR F1
MANDELANE DR A2
MANNWEIMER WAY C1
MAPLE RIDGE DR F2
MARATHON B3
MARBLEHEAD/170 E1
MARICOPA/171 F1
MARIGOLD TRACE C2
MASKE RD B4
MATTREN ST D3
MAYFAIR DR F3
MEADOW E3
MEADOW/172 E3
MEADOW ARBOR/173 D3
MEADOW BRANCH DR E3
MEADOW BURST DR/174 E3
MEADOW GATE DR/175 E3
MEADOW GROVE/176 F1
MEADOW HAVEN D1
MEADOW HILL/177 E3
MEADOW LAND D3
MEADOW SCARE RD/178 E3
MEADOW VIEW DR/179 B4
MEADOW WAY E3
MEADOW WAY DR C4
MEADOWLARK AV E3
MEDUSA B3
MELBURY FOREST DR F1
MESQUITE PASS RD/180 D2
MESQUITE ST F3
MICHELLE DR E3
MICHELLE WAY F1
MIDDLE SCHOOL A1
MILLER RD D2, E2, F2
MILLERS RIDGE/181 E2
MINERS GAP/182 A1
MISSION MILL B1
MISTY RIDGE RD E2
MONTGOMERY DR F1
MOONLIT RIDGE DR E2
MORA A4
MOSS RIDGE/183 C4
MOUNTAIN FOREST DR F1
MOUNTAIN OAK DR C2
MOUNTAIN SHADOW/184 C2
MOUNTCREST DR A2
MOZLEY RISE C1
MUSTANG RIDGE RD D2
MYERS AV A3
MYSTERY RIDGE DR/185 D2
NARROW PASS DR/186 D2
NATIONAL BLVD C4
NESTON F1
NEW WORLD E1, F1
NORRIS DR F4
NORRIS DR/187 F4
NORTH BLVD C4
NORTH MEADOW/188 E3
NORTH ST E3
NORTHBEND DR E1
NORTHCUTT B2
NORTHMONT DR F1
NORTHVIEW DR C4
NUGGET CREEK RD/189 E3
O CONNOR RD D1
OAK BREEZE B3
OAK CIR B4
OAK DR F3
OAK FOREST DR C2
OAK KNOB B3
OAK MARSH TR C2
OAK MEADOWS B3
OAK ST F3
OAK TER C2
OAKCHASE ST/190 F1
OAKLANE DR C4
OAKSIDE D3
ODELL A4
ODYSSEY DR B3
OLD AUSTIN RD A3
OLD CIMARRON TR D3
OLD SEGUIN RD F3
OLD SPANISH TR C2
OLD TOEPPERWEIN RD/191 D2
OLDHAM F1
OLYMPIA PKWY A3
ORIOLE E1
OUTLAW BEND E2
OXFORD DR C3
PAINTED RIDGE RD E2
PALIMINO CANYON RD/192 E2
PALISADES C3
PAN AM C2
PARK LN C3
PARK MEADOW E3
PARKLANE DR C4
PARKVIEW DR C4
PARKWAY 35 D1
PARTHENON B3
PARTON LN C1
PAT BOOKER RD C4
PATRICK HENRY DR/193 C1
PATSY DR E3
PEGASUS B3
PEPPER F2
PERSIA DR C4
PHOENIX B3
PIN TAIL PT E1
PINTO LN A4
PIONEER HILL E3
PIONEER OAK E2
PLAZA DR/194 D3
PLUMAS E3
POMEROY CIR/195 D1
PRIME TIME A1
PURPLE RIDGE DR/196 A1
QUAIL E1
QUAIL DR C3
QUAIL FEATHER B1
QUAIL LN A4
QUEENS CROWN/197 D1
QUEENS CT D1
QUIVIRA C3
RAINBOW FALLS/198 D2
RAINEY MEADOW LN/199 C2
RAINTREE FOREST B1
RAINTREE FOREST DR/200 A1
RAINTREE PATH/201 A1
RALSTON RD/202 F4
RANDOLPH BLVD C1
RED HORSE CIR/203 C4
RED RIPPLE C2
REDMANS PASS RD/204 D2
REGAL OAKS DR/205 C2
REGENCY CIR C3
REGENCY PL/206 B3
REVEILLE LN/207 C1
RHODIUS LN A4
RHONDA DR C4
RIDGE BEACH RD/208 D2
RIDGE COVE RD/209 E2
RIDGE FLOWER DR F2
RIDGE FOREST/210 A1
RIDGE GARDEN RD/211 E2
RIDGE MEADOW/212 B1
RIDGE MILE DR/213 F2
RIDGE MIST DR/214 E2
RIDGE MOON DR/215 E2
RIDGE PORT DR/216 D2
RIDGECIRCLE B1
RIDGECREEK B1
RIDGECREST/217 B1
RIDGEGLEN/218 B1
RIDGEHILL A1
RIDGEPASS/219 A1
RIDGEPEAK B1
RIFLE GAP D3
RIFLE ROCK/220 D2
RIMWOOD C2
RIO LN A4
RISING STAR D3
RIVER HILL E1
RIVER WIND DR A1
RIVULET/221 F1
ROAN CIR C4
ROBARDS ROW/222 C1
ROBIN DR C3
ROBIN FOREST DR/223 F1
ROCK BLUFF DR/224 A1
ROCKET LN F4
ROSE GARDEN DR/225 C3
ROSE WOOD DR/226 C4
ROYAL BLUFF/227 D1
ROYAL BREEZE D1
ROYAL CIR D1
ROYAL DR F4
ROYAL PASS/228 D1
ROYAL POINT DR/229 D1
ROYAL RIDGE DR D1
ROYALWOOD D1
RUBENS DR F2
RUSTIC FOREST/230 F1
SAGE DR C4
SAGE OAK DR C2
SAILING AWAY ST/231 C1
SALADO ST F3
SAMUEL PRESCOTT/232 C1
SAND CASTLE E1
SAND HILL/233 C3
SANDPIPER DR/234 C2
SANDY OAKS/235 C2
SCHAEFFER RD F4
SCHERTZ PKWY A4
SCHERTZ SELMA RD A4
SCHOOL ST F3
SCHUMANN E3
SCHUMANN RD/236 E3
SCOTT DR C4
SCOTTSWOOD E1
SEGUIN RD D4, E3
SEGUIN ST E3, F3
SELENDINE LN E1
SELMA RD C4
SERENE RIDGE DR E2
SHADOW E3
SHADOW FOREST/237 F1
SHADOWYCK/238 C4
SHADY CIR/239 F1
SHADY LN A4
SHALLOW RIDGE DR E2
SHERRI DR C3
SHIN OAK DR C2
SHINING STAR/240 E1
SILVER SHADOW/241 E1
SILVER SPRING B4
SKYLINE RIDGE DR/242 E2
SLEEPY FOREST DR/243 F1
SOUTH ST E3
SOUTHERN RIDGE/244 E2
SPANISH EARTH/245 A1
SPARTAN TER B3
SPINDRIFT/246 F1
SPLINTERED OAK TR C2
SPRUCE RIDGE DR D2
SPRUCE RIDGE/247 E2
SPYGLASS B4
STANDING OAKS/248 C2
STATION ST F3
STEVES ST E4
STOCKADE/249 C1
STOCKPORT F1
STONEGATE DR C4
STONEY PT D3
STRAIGHT LN C4
STROLLING LN C2
SUMMER SUSIE/250 A1
SUNCLIFF DR/251 C4
SUNSET TR C2
SURREY LN C4
SUTTERS MINE RD D2
SWINFORD/252 F1
TARRASA/253 F1
TARRYTOWN C1
TEAL WAY E1
TERLINGUA/254 A1
TEXAS DR D4
THESSALAY B3
THOMAS SUMTER/255 C1
TIGUEX/256 B3
TOEPPERWEIN RD C1
TOPPER PKWY B1
TRAILING OAKS WAY/257 C2
TRAPPERS RIDGE RD/258 E2
TRAVIS DR D4
TRUDY LN C4
TRUMBOL C2
TUMBLEBROOK/259 D3
TUTTLE E4
TUXFORD F1
TWIN FOX A1
TWIN SADDLES/260 E3
UNIVERSAL CITY BLVD B3
UNIVERSAL DR D4
UTOPIA BLVD A3
VALENCIA DR C3
VALLEY FORGE AV/261 C1
VALLEY OAK DR/262 C2
VENTURA BLVD A3
VIGILANTE TR E2
VILLA DR C4
VILLAGE OAK DR C2
VILLAGE GREEN DR/263 C4
WAGON CROSSIN/264 D3
WAGON TRAIN/265 E2
WALNUT TRACE/266 E2
WALZEM RD F1
WATERFALL E1
WATERSIDE E1
WAYNE C4
WAYNESBORO/267 C1
WAYSIDE F2
WAYWORD F2
WEEPING OAK C2
WELCOME DR C2
WELLS FARGO/268 E2
WENZEL RD/269 A1
WESP WAY C1
WEST FACE A1
WEST OAK D3
WESTWAY DR D4
WHISPERING OAKS/270 C2
WHISTLER/271 F2
WHITE SANDS TR/272 D2
WHITLAND E1
WILD MEADOW/273 E3
WILDERNESS TR C2
WILDRIDGE TR/274 B4
WILLOW DR F3
WILLOW WISP/275 C3
WIND BURN TR/276 E2
WINDBLUFF DR/277 E1
WINDSOR HOLLOW DR/278 F1
WINDY GAP/279 C4
WINDY MEADOWS DR/280 B4
WINN AV C4
WISHING OAKS WAY C2
WOODCLIFF BLVD A3
WOODS HOLE/281 B1
WOODSRIM C2
WORCHESTER WOOD/282 B1
WRIGHT BLVD C4
WURZBACH ST E4
YELLOWBARK BLVD A2
YORK LN A4
ZODIAC B3

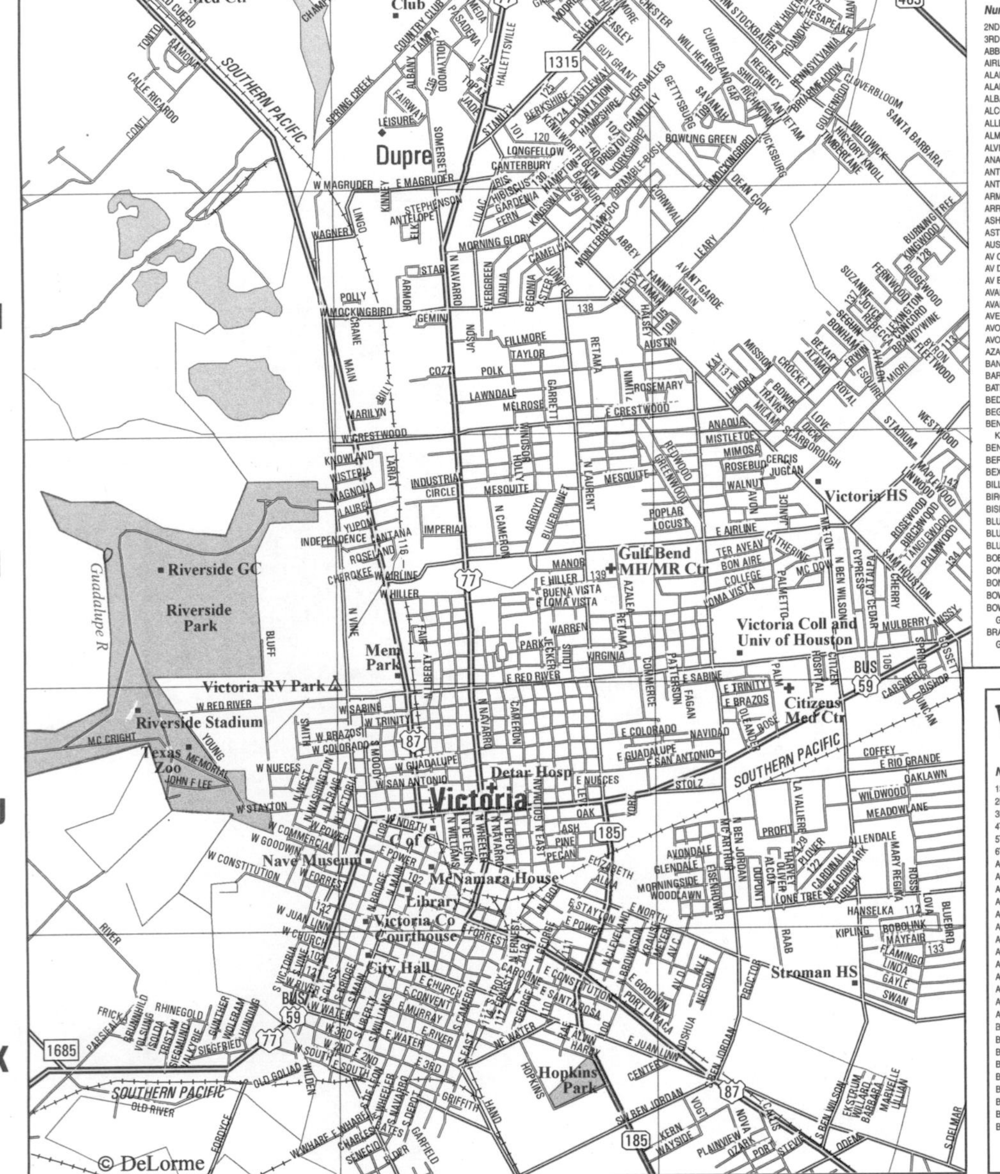

VICTORIA

SEE PAGE 79

Numbers replace street names where map space is limited

2ND ST K1, K2
3RD ST K1, K2
ABBEY DR H2
AIRLINE RD I2, I3
ALAMEDA CIR G2
ALAMO DR H3
ALBANY ST G2
ALCOA ST J3
ALLENDALE ST J3
ALMA ST J2
ALVIN ST K2
ANAQUA AV H3
ANTELOPE CIR H2
ANTIETAM DR G3
ARMORY DR H2
ARROYO DR I2
ASH ST J2
ASTER LN H2
AUSTIN AV H3
AV C K3
AV D K3
AV E K3
AVALON DR H3
AVANT GARDE DR H3
AVEAV TER I3
AVON DR I3
AVONDALE ST J3
AZALEA ST I2
BANBURY CT H2
BARBARA ST K3
BATES ST K2
BEDIVERE DR G2
BEGONIA LN H2
BEN JORDAN ST J3, K2, K3
BEN WILSON ST I3, K3
BERKSHIRE LN G2
BEXAR AV H3
BILLY DR H2
BIRCHWOOD DR I3
BISHOP ST J3
BLUEBIRD ST J3
BLUEBONNET DR I2
BLUFF ST I1
BOBOLINK LN K3
BON AIRE AV I3
BONHAM DR H3
BOWIE DR H3
BOWLING GREEN DR G3
BRAMBLE BUSH LN G3
BRANDYWINE LN H3
BRAZOS ST J1, J3
BRIARMEADOW LN G3
BRIDGE ST J2, K2
BRISTOL CT G2
BROWNSON ST K2
BROWNSON ST/100 K2
BRUNNHILD ST K1
BUENA VISTA ST I2
BURNINGTREE ST H3
BYRON DR H3
CALLE RICARDO LN G1
CALLIS ST K3
CAMELLIA LN H2
CAMERON ST I2, J2, K2
CANTERBURY LN G2
CARDINAL ST J3
CAROLINE ST K2
CARSNER ST I3
CASTLEWAY ST G2
CATALPA ST I3
CATHERINE CIR I3
CEDAR ST I3
CENTER ST K2
CERCIS DR I3
CHAMPIONS ROW G2
CHANTILLY ST G2
CHARLES ST K2
CHEROKEE LN I2
CHERRY ST I3
CHESAPEAKE AV G3
CHIPPENDALE LN/101 G2
CHURCH ST K1, K2
CIRCLE ST I2
CITIZEN DR I3
CLEVELAND ST K2
CLOVERBLOOM DR G3
COFFEY ST J3
COLLEGE DR I3
COLORADO ST J2
COMMERCE ST J2
COMMERCIAL ST J1
COMMERCIAL ST/102 J2
CONCORD LN H3
CONSTITUTION ST J1, K2
CONTI LN G1
CONVENT ST K2
CONVENT ST/103 K1
CORNWALL DR G2
COUNTRY CLUB DR G2
COZZI CIR H2
CRAIG ST J1
CRANE ST H2
CRESCENT DR/104 H3
CRESCENT DR/105 H3
CRESTWOOD DR H2, I2
CROCKETT AV H3
CUMBERLAND GAP G3
CURLEW ST J3
CYPRESS ST I3
DAHLIA LN H2
DE LEON ST J2, K2
DEAN COOK DR H3
DEL PAPA ST/106 I3
DELMAR DR K3
DEPOT ST J2, K2
DICK ST I3
DOVER DELL ST/107 G2
DUNCAN ST J3
DUPONT ST J3
EASLEY RD G2
EAST ST J2, K2
EISENHOWER ST J3
EKSTRUM ST K3
ELDER ST K2
ELIZABETH ST J2
ELK DR H2
ERNEST ST K2
ERWIN AV H3
ESQUIRE H3
EVERGREEN LN H2
FAGAN CIR J3
FAIR ST I2
FAIRWAY ST G2
FANNIN DR H3
FERN LN H2
FERNWOOD CIR H3
FILLMORE AV H2
FLAMINGO DR K3
FLEETWOOD DR H3
FORDYCE RD K1
FORREST ST J1, K2
FRICKA ST K1
GALAHAD ST G2
GARDENIA LN H2
GARFIELD AV K2
GARRETT ST H2
GAYLE DR K3
GEMINI CT H2
GEORGE ST K2
GETTYSBURG DR G3
GLASS ST K1
GLASS ST/108 J2
GLENDALE ST J3
GOLDENROD AV G3
GOLDMAN ST J2
GOODWIN AV J1, K2
GOSSETT ST I3
GREENWOOD DR I3
GRIFFITH DR K2
GUADALUPE ST J2
GUNTHER ST K1
GUY GRANT RD G2
HALLETTSVILLE HWY G2
HALSEY ST H2
HAMPSHIRE LN G2
HAMPTON CT G2
HAND RD K2
HANSELKA ST J3
HARPERS FERRY CROSSING/109 G3
HARRY ST K2
HARVEY LN J3
HIBISCUS LN H2
HICKORY KNOLL G3
HILLER ST I2
HOLLY ST I2
HOLLYWOOD BLVD G2
HOPKINS ST K2
HOSPITAL DR I3
HUMMEL ST/110 K2
HUMMEL ST/111 K2
HUMMINGBIRD LN/112 J3
HUNDING ST K1
IMPERIAL DR I2
INDEPENDENCE DR I1
INDUSTRIAL DR I2
IRIS LN G2
ISOLDA ST K1
IVANHOE DR/113 H3
JADE DR G2
JANICE ST I3
JASON ST H2
JECKER ST I2
JOHN F LEE DR J1
JOHN STOCKBAUER DR G3
JOSHUA ST K3
JOYCE LN H3
JUAN LINN ST J1, K2
JUGLAN DR I3
JUNIPER ST H2
KAY DR H3
KEMBLE DR G2
KENILWORTH GLEN G2
KERN DR K3
KING ARTHUR G2
KINGSWAY ST H2
KINGWOOD DR H3
KINNEY DR H2
KIPLING ST K3
KNOWLAND AV I2
KRAMER/114 K2
KRAUSE ST K2
LA VALLIERE ST J3
LAMAR DR H2
LANCELOT/115 G2
LANTANA AV I2
LARIAT LN I2
LARIMORE ST G2
LAUREL AV I2
LAURENT ST I2
LAWNDALE AV H2
LEARY LN H3
LEISURE LN G2
LENORA DR H3
LEVI ST J2
LEXINGTON LN H3
LIBERTY ST I2, K2
LILAC LN H2
LILLIAN ST K3
LINDA DR K3
LINGO LN H2
LINWOOD DR I3
LOCUST AV I3
LOMA VISTA ST I2, I3
LONE TREE RD J3
LONGFELLOW LN G2
LOUIS ST I2
LOVA DR J3
LOVE ST H3
LYNMOR DR/116 I2
MAGNOLIA AV I2
MAGRUDER DR G2
MAIN ST H2, J2, K2
MANOR DR I2
MANTZ ST/117 K2
MANTZ ST/118 K2
MAPLEWOOD DR I3
MARILYN DR H2
MARVELLE ST K3
MARY REGINA ST J3
MAYFAIR DR K3
MC ARTHUR ST J3
MC CRIGHT DR J1
MC DOW ST I3
MEADOWLANE ST J3
MEADOWLARK ST J3
MEDICAL DR/119 G1
MELROSE AV H2
MELROSE DR H3
MEMORIAL DR J1
MESQUITE LN I2
MEYER ST K3
MILAM DR H3
MILANN ST H3
MILTON ST I3
MIMOSA AV I3
MIORI LN H3
MISSION DR H3
MISSY LN I3
MISTLETOE AV I3
MOCKINGBIRD LN G3, H2
MODRED ST G2
MONTERREY ST H2
MOODY ST J2
MORNING GLORY DR H2
MORNINGSIDE ST J3
MOSSY OAKS LN/120 G2
MULBERRY ST I3
MURRAY ST K2
MURRAY ST/121 K1
NANTUCKET ST G3
NAVARRO ST H2, J2, K2
NAVIDAD ST J3
NEIL FOX DR H2
NELSON AV K3
NEW HAVEN ST G3
NIGHTINGALE ST/122 J3
NIMITZ ST H2
NORTH ST J2
NORTHSHIRE DR/123 G2
NORWICH GLEN/124 G2
NOTTINGHAM DR/125 G2
NOVA AV K3
NUECES ST J1, J2
OAK ST J2
OAKLAWN ST J3
ODEM ST K3
OLD CUERO HWY G1
OLD GOLIAD RD K1
OLD RIVER RD K1
OLEANDER DR J3
OLIVER ST J3
OZARK ST K3
PALM DR I3
PALMETTO DR I3
PALMWOOD DR I3
PARK AV I2
PARSIFAL ST K1
PASADENA DR G2
PATTERSON DR I3
PECAN ST J2
PENNSYLVANIA AV G3
PINE ST J2
PLAINVIEW ST K3
PLANTATION RD G2
PLOVER ST J3
POLK AV H2
POLLY ST H2
POPLAR AV I3
PORT LAVACA DR K2
PORT ST K3
PORTSMOUTH CIR/126 G3
POWER AV J1, J2
POWER ST K2
PROCTOR ST K3
PROFIT ST J3
PROVINCETOWN ST/127 G3
QUEENSWOOD TR/128 H3
RAAB AV K3
RAE ST K2
RAMONA LN G1
RAVEN ST/129 J3
REBECCA LN H3
RED RIVER ST I2, J1
REDWOOD DR I3
REGENCY AV G3
RETAMA CIR H2
RETAMA ST I2
RHINEGOLD ST K1
RICHMOND RD G3
RIDGEWOOD DR H3
RIO GRANDE ST J3
RIVER RD K1
RIVER ST K1, K2
ROANOKE DR G3
ROSE DR J3
ROSEBUD AV I3
ROSELAND AV I2
ROSEMARY DR H3
ROSEWOOD DR I3
ROSSI ST J3
ROYAL DR H3
SABINE ST I3, J2
SALEM RD G2
SALISBURY LN/130 G2
SAM HOUSTON DR I3
SAN ANTONIO ST J2, J3
SAN JACINTO AV/131 H3
SANTA BARBARA ST G3
SANTA ROSA ST K2
SANTA ROSA ST/132 J1
SAVANAH DR G3
SCARBOROUGH DR I3
SEAGULL DR/133 K3
SEGUIN AV H3
SENECIO ST K2
SHERWOOD DR/134 I3
SHILOH DR G3
SIEGFRIED ST K1
SIEGMUND ST K1
SMITH ST J1
SOMERSET PL G2
SOUTH ST K1, K2
SPOKANE ST/135 G2
SPRING CREEK RD G2
SPRING ST I3
STADIUM DR I3
STANLEY ST G2
STAR LN H2
STAYTON AV J1, J2
STEPHENSON ST H2
STEVIE AV K3
STOLZ ST J3
SUSSEX DELL/136 H2
SUZANNE LN H3
SWAN DR K3
TAMPA DR G2
TAMPICO CT H2
TANGLEWOOD DR I3
TAYLOR AV H2
TIMBERLANE DR G3
TONTO CIR G1
TOPAZ DR G2
TRAVIS AV H3
TRINITY ST J2, J3
TRISTAN ST K1
TROY ST J2, K2
VALKYRIE ST K1
VANESSA LN/137 H3
VERSAILLES ST G2
VICKSBURG DR G3
VICTORIA ST J2, K1
VICTORIA STATION RD/138 H2
VILLAGE DR/139 I2
VINE ST I2, K1
VIRGINIA AV I2
VOGT DR K3
VOLSUNG ST K1
WAGNER WAY H1
WALNUT AV I3
WARREN AV I2
WARWICK GLEN ST/140 G2
WASHINGTON ST J1
WATER ST K1, K2
WAYSIDE DR K3
WEST ST J1
WESTCHESTER ST G2
WESTWOOD DR I3
WHARF ST K1, K2
WHEELER ST J2, K2
WHISPERING CREEK DR/141 G2
WILDEN K1
WILDWOOD ST J3
WILL HEARD RD G3
WILLARD ST K3
WILLIAMS ST J2, K2
WILLIAMSBURG AV G3
WILLOWICK DR G3
WINDSOR ST H2
WISTERIA AV I2
WOLFRAM ST K1
WOOD DR/142 I3
WOODLAWN ST J3
YORK ST J2
YORKSHIRE LN G2
YOUNG DR J1
YUPON AV I2

WAXAHACHIE

SEE PAGE 46

Numbers replace street names where map space is limited

1ST ST J8
2ND ST J8
3RD ST J8
4TH ST J8
5TH ST J8
6TH ST J8
ADAM/100 K7
AIKEN ST K8
ALAMO CT I8
ALDRIDGE ST/101 J8
ALEXANDER DR I8
ALMOND ST I8
ANDERSON ST J8
ANNETTE LN I9
APACHE CT I9
ARDEN AV K7
AUBURN DR I8
AUORA AV I8
AV C K8
BARGER DR J8
BATEMAN/102 K8
BELL K7
BEN ST K8
BETHEL ST J8
BIRD LN I8
BOZE ST J8
BRACKENS ST/103 K9
BRADSHAW ST J8
BREEZWAY/104 J9
BRIAR J9
BRIGG J8
BROADHEAD RD J9
BROOKSIDE RD J7
BROWN ST I8
BRYNMAWR LN/105 J9
BRYSON ST J8
BUENA VISTA RD K7
BUFFALO CREEK DR I9
BURNET/106 K9
CAMPBELL ST I8
CANTRELL ST K7
CEDAR ST/107 I8
CENTER ST J8
CENTRAL ST/108 J7
CHAPMAN CIR/109 I8
CHARLOTTE AV/110 J8
CHEROKEE CT I9
CHEVY CHASE/111 J9
CHIEFTAIN I9
CHILES ST J8
CIRCLE ST J8
CIRCLE ST/112 J8
CLARK I8
CLEMSON CT I8
COATS ST K8
COLEMAN ST J9
COLLEGE ST J8, K8
COLUMBIA AV I8
COMPTON RD K7
COOK ST/113 K9
CORNELL LN I8
CRIDDLE ST J8
CUMBERLAND DR J9
CYNISCA ST J8
DARTMOUTH DR I8
DEWBERRY ST/114 K7
DILLON ST/115 K8
DRESDEN DR/116 K8
DREXAL K9
DRIFTWOOD LN I9
DUNAWAY ST K7
DUNLAP ST/117 K8
DUNN ST J8
EDGEFIELD ST/118 K8
ELDER ST J9
ELLIS ST K8
ELM K8
ENNIS ST J9
EQUALITY/119 K7
ETTA AV I8
EUBANK ST/120 K9
FAIRVIEW AV K8
FARLEY ST J8
FERRIS AV J8
FERRIS AV/121 J8
FINLEY ST/122 K8
FLAT ST J8
FLOYD ST J8
FRANKLIN ST/123 K8
FRIERSON ST K8
GETZENDANER AV K9
GIBSON ST J8
GIBSON ST/124 J8
GINGERBREAD LN I7
GIVENS ST K7
GRACE ST J8
GRAHAM ST K9
GRAND AV J7
GRAND AV/125 J7
GRAVEL ST K8
HACIENDA DR I9
HACKBERRY ST J9
HARBIN ST J8
HARDING ST/126 J7
HAWKINS ST J8
HENDERSON ST/127 K9
HENRIETTA ST/128 K8
HENRY/129 K8
HIGH SCHOOL DR I8
HIGHLAND AV I7
HILL LN I8
HILLTOP DR K7
HOWARD RD K8
HUTCHISON ST/130 K8
INDIAN DR I8
INDIAN TRACE I9
INDIANHILLS/131 I9
IROQUOIS I9
JACKSON ST J8
JARRETT/132 K8
JEFFERSON ST J7, K9
JOHN ARDEN DR I8
JOSEPH ST J8
JUSTICE RD K7
KAUFMAN ST J8
KINCHUM ST/133 K8
KIOWA I9
KIRKSEY ST I8
KIRVEN AV J8
LAKE PARK AV J9
LANCASTER ST J9
LAVISTA DR I8
LAWNDALE ST/134 I7
LEATHERWOOD ST/135 K9
LEGION ST/136 J8
LEWIS ST J9
LINCOLN RD/137 K7
LITTLE CREEK I8
LUCAS ST J7
LYNN AV I8
MADISON ST/138 K8
MAIN ST I7, J7, K9
MALE DON ST/139 J7
MARTHA ST J8
MARVIN AV J8
MARY LN I8
MATTEHWS ST K8
MC CUEN ST/140 K8
MC KENZIE J8
MC MILLAN ST J8
MEADOWVIEW/141 K7
MODENE AV/142 I8
MODENE ST I9
MONROE ST J8
MONTICELLO DR/143 J8
MORENE AV I9
MS CUEN ST/144 K8
MYERS ST/145 K8
MYRTLE AV I9
NIXON RD K7
NORTH GRAND AV I7
NORTHGATE DR I8
ODOM ST J7
OLIVE ST I8
ONEIDA ST K8
OPAL ST K7
OSCAR ST/146 J7
OVERHILL DR I8
PARK SCHOOL HOUSE RD K9
PARKS AV/147 J8
PASLEY ST/148 K7
PATRICK ST J7
PECAN ST J9
PENN J8
PENSACOLA/149 J8
PERRY ST K9
PETERS ST K9
PINSTON ST/150 K8
PUEBLO DR I9
PULASKI ST/151 J7
RAILROAD ST/152 K8
REDMAN/153 I9
RICHMOND DR/154 J8
RIVER OAKS BLVD J9
ROGERS ST J8, K7
ROSA ST J8
ROSS J9
ROSS AV J8
ROSS ST J8
ROUSSEAU ST/155 J8
ROYAL ST J8
RUTH ST K7
SADDLER ST/156 K8
SANTA FE CT I9
SAVANNAH/157 J8
SOLON RD I8
SPENCER ST/158 J7
STROUD/159 J7
SYCAMORE ST J8
TANGLEWOOD/160 J9
TEXTILE ST J8
THOMPSON ST K8
TRINITY LN I8
TUGGLE ST/161 K8
UNIVERSITY AV I8, J8
VANDERBILT LN I8
VASSAR CT I8
VILLANOVA CT I8
VIRGINIA AV J8
VILLAGE GATE DR/162 I7
VILLAGE GREEN CT I7
WATER ST J8
WEST K7
WILL ST K8
WILLIAMS ST J8
WILMINGTON ST/163 J8
WYATT ST J9
YOUNG ST/164 K8

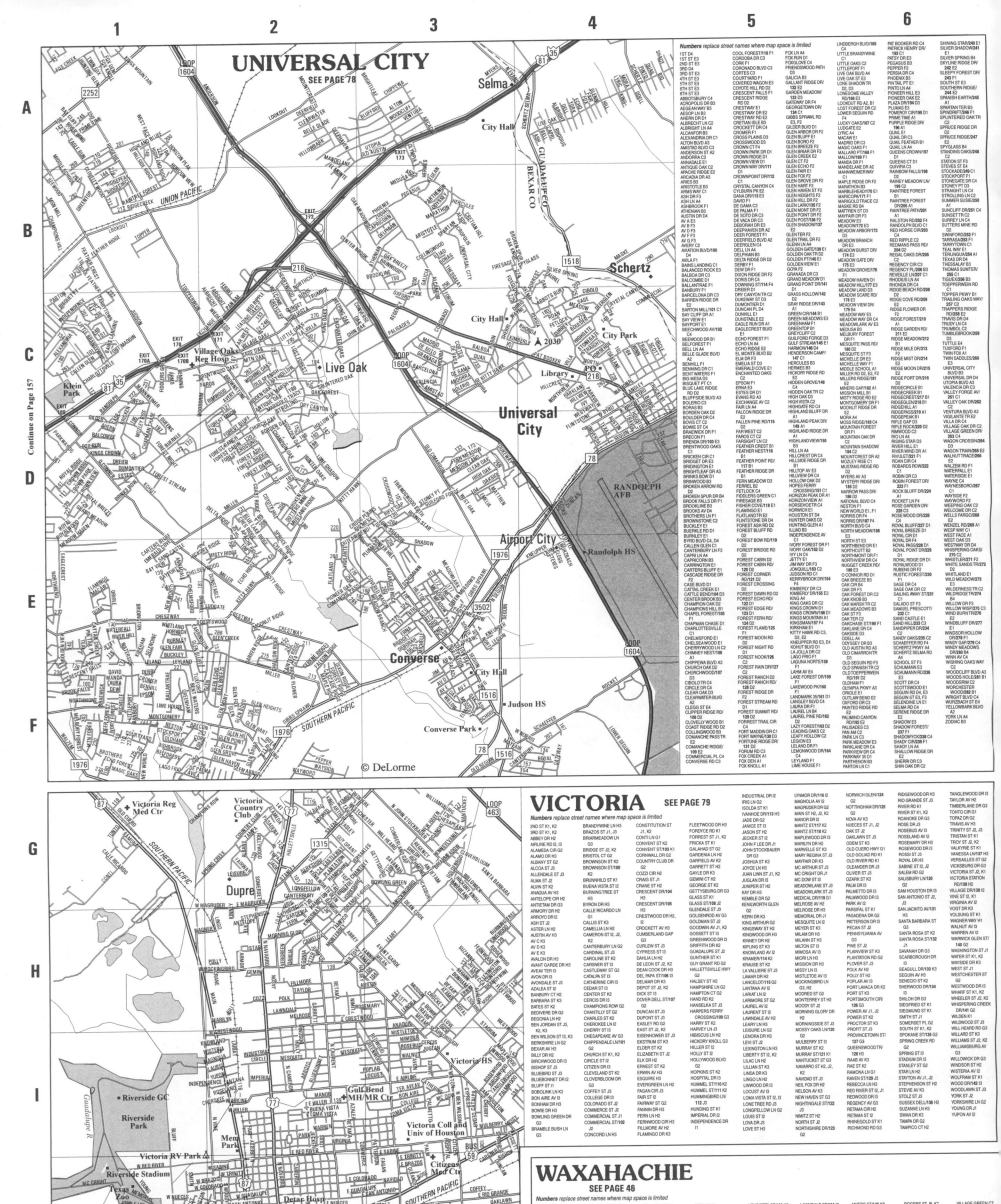

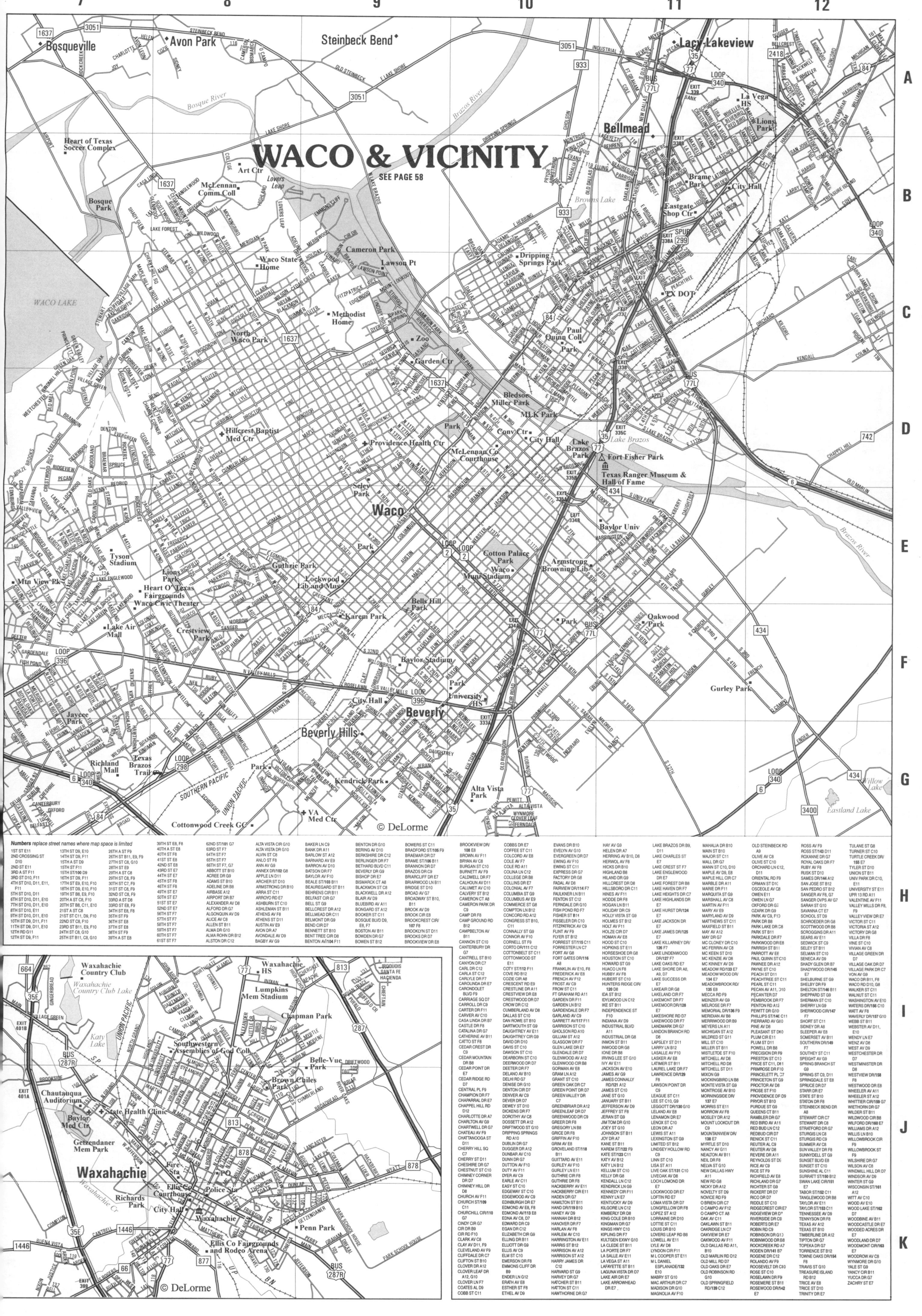

7
8
9
10
11
12
A
B
C
D
E
F
G
H
I
J
K
WACO & VICINITY
SEE PAGE 58
Bosqueville
Avon Park
Steinbeck Bend
Lacy-Lakeview
Bellmead
La Vega HS
Lions Park
Heart of Texas Soccer Complex
Art Ctr
McLennan Comm Coll
Bosque Park
WACO LAKE
Cameron Park
Lawson Pt
Waco State Home
Brame Park
City Hall
Eastgate Shop Ctr
Dripping Springs Park
TX DOT
Methodist Home
North Waco Park
Zoo
Garden Ctr
Paul Quinn Coll
Park
Bledsoe Miller Park
MLK Park
Hillcrest Baptist Med Ctr
Providence Health Ctr
McLennan Co Courthouse
Conv Ctr
City Hall
Lake Brazos Park
Fort Fisher Park
Texas Ranger Museum & Hall of Fame
Seley Park
Waco
Baylor Univ
Tyson Stadium
Guthrie Park
Lockwood Lib and Mus
Cotton Palace Park
Waco Muni Stadium
Armstrong Browning Lib
Lions Park
Heart O' Texas Fairgrounds
Waco Civic Theater
Mtn View Pk
Bells Hill Park
Karem Park
Oakwood Park
Lake Air Mall
Crestview Park
Baylor Stadium
Gurley Park
City Hall
Beverly
University HS
Jaycee Park
Beverly Hills
Richland Mall
Texas Brazos Trail
Kendrick Park
Alta Vista Park
Eastland Lake
Willow Lake
VA Med Ctr
Cottonwood Creek GC
© DeLorme
Waxahachie Country Club
Waxahachie Country Club Lake
Waxahachie HS
Lumpkins Mem Stadium
Chapman Park
Southwestern Assemblies of God Coll
Belle-Vue Park
Brown Chiles Park
Chautauqua Auditorium
State Health Clinic
Baylor Med Ctr
Getzendaner Mem Park
Waxahachie
Fire Sta
PO
Ellis Co Courthouse
Police Sta
Richards Park
City Hall
Waxahachie
Penn Park
Ellis Co Fairgrounds and Rodeo Arena
© DeLorme
Numbers replace street names where map space is limited

1" = 0.8 mi (1.3 km)

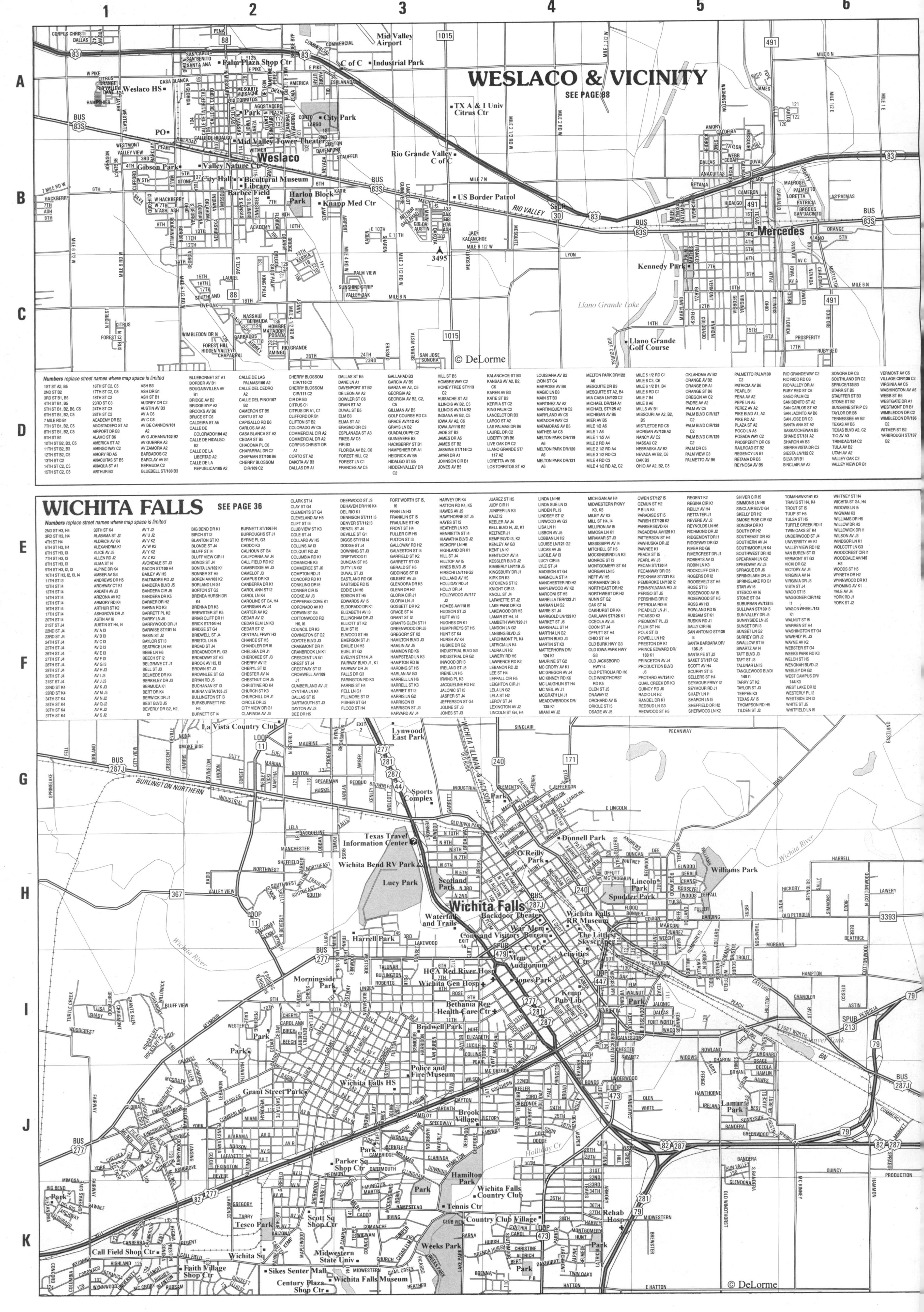
WESLACO & VICINITY
SEE PAGE 88
Weslaco
Mercedes
Numbers replace street names where map space is limited
WICHITA FALLS
SEE PAGE 36
Numbers replace street names where map space is limited
Wichita Falls
© DeLorme